Handbook of
American Popular
Culture

Handbook of

ADVERTISING
BEST SELLERS
CIRCUS AND OUTDOOR
  ENTERTAINMENT
DEATH IN POPULAR CULTURE
EDITORIAL CARTOONS
FOODWAYS
GAMES AND TOYS
HISTORICAL FICTION
OCCULT AND THE SUPERNATURAL
PHOTOGRAPHY AS POPULAR
  CULTURE
POPULAR ARCHITECTURE
POPULAR RELIGION AND THEORIES
  OF SELF-HELP
ROMANTIC FICTION
VERSE AND POPULAR POETRY
WOMEN IN POPULAR CULTURE

American Popular Culture

edited by
M. THOMAS INGE

VOLUME 2

GREENWOOD PRESS
WESTPORT, CONNECTICUT • LONDON, ENGLAND

Library of Congress Cataloging in Publication Data

Main entry under title:

Handbook of American popular culture.

   Includes index.
   1. United States—Popular culture. 2. United
States—Popular culture—Sources. 3. United States—
Popular culture—Bibliography. I. Inge, M. Thomas.
E169.1.H2643   301.2'1   77-95357

ISBN 0-313-21363-1   (vol. 2)

Library of Congress Catalog Card Number: 77-95357

ISBN: 0-313-21363-1

First published in 1980

Greenwood Press
A division of Congressional Information Service, Inc.
51 Riverside Avenue, Westport, Connecticut 06880

Printed in the United States of America

10 9 8 7 6 5 4 3 2

084997

For Russel B. Nye, again

Contents

Preface

The serious, scholarly study of mass or popular culture is a fairly recent phenomenon, although some early investigations were first initiated within the established disciplines. For example, sociologists have long found that the materials with which Americans amuse themselves are fascinating for what they reflect about the people and their attitudes, morals, and mores. Popular culture, in other words, is a mirror wherein society can see itself and better understand its character and needs. One unresolved circular problem this approach presents is the question of whether the mass media merely reflect what society wants or whether they influence it to want what the media provide. Is the violence commonly found on television there because we prefer to watch those shows that use it, or do we prefer to watch it because our baser instincts have been stimulated by its frequent use? Thus, the sociological study of popular culture has often been initiated in the name of other causes: to deal with social problems, to attempt to understand society and human nature, or to engage in moral reform.

Some of the early film studies took place in English departments, where literary critics realized that some of the same techniques applied to the appreciation of fiction, poetry, and drama could be applied with great profit to the appreciation of motion pictures. In order to justify offering a course in film, however, all too often it was necessary to make a literary attachment explicit in the description, thus the now almost obligatory "Fiction and Film" course found in most English curricula. Such courses usually examine adaptations of novels and stories into film. If the instructor reaches the simple conclusion that the novel is always better than the film version (and I know a few who do), little has been accomplished. If, on the other hand, the instructor uses the separate art forms to elucidate each other through an examination of the necessarily different artistic techniques and creative strategies as applied to similar subject matter, the result can be an increased respect for both forms of expression. Such an approach has encouraged the development of some perceptive film criticism.

It is no longer necessary to justify the study of the popular arts by an

ix

alliance with some other social or cultural purpose. We have come to recognize that each form or medium of expression has its own aesthetic principles, techniques, and ways of conveying ideas. Each has been subject to misuse and ineptitude, but each has also witnessed levels of artistic accomplishment remarkable by any standards, although finally each form must be evaluated within and by its own self-generated set of standards and objectives. There are hundreds of courses being taught in film, television, radio, science fiction, popular music, the detective novel, or comic art in American colleges and universities, sometimes with uneasy homes in departments of English, history, sociology, art history, mass communications, or American studies. The next decade will see the development of popular culture programs organized, as they should be, on an interdisciplinary basis. Already one degree-granting program has been established at Bowling Green State University in Ohio, which is also the seat of the Popular Culture Association and its publication, *Journal of Popular Culture*, established by Ray B. Browne in 1968. Scholars who have previously distinguished themselves in traditional fields are more frequently turning their attention to this new area of inquiry, as did Russel B. Nye in *The Unembarrassed Muse: The Popular Arts in America* (1970) and John Cawelti in *The Six-Gun Mystique* (1971).

This three-volume handbook is the first organized effort to assemble in one place the basic bibliographic data needed to begin the study of several of the major areas of popular culture. Each chapter, prepared by an authority on the subject, provides a brief chronological survey of the development of the medium; a critical guide in essay form to the standard or most useful bibliographies, reference works, histories, critical studies, and journals; a description of the existing research centers and collections of primary and secondary materials; and a checklist of works cited in the text. With this handbook, the student, scholar, librarian, or general reader can easily locate the kind of information needed to complete a research paper or project, answer a question, build a basic library, or read about a topic or personality as a matter of interest.

Undoubtedly the essays contain oversights in terms of research collections and published materials. In future editions, however, we hope to remedy oversights and make the essays more comprehensive and accurate. To that end, corrections and suggestions should be directed to the editor in care of the Department of English, Virginia Commonwealth University, Richmond, Virginia 23284.

I wish to thank Susan Woolford for her invaluable editorial assistance and for preparing the index.

M. Thomas Inge

Handbook of
American Popular
Culture

CHAPTER 1. Advertising
Elizabeth Williamson

Advertising has been described as an institution, a business, an industry, a discipline, a profession, a science, an art, and a talent. It has been defined as news, salesmanship in print, and mass communication. Some of the best minds in the business, outside the business, and on the fringes of the business have attempted to define and deal with this elusive subject. Scholars and advertising men themselves have examined the political, economic, social, ethical, historical, and religious aspects of advertising. Each of them has told us what advertising is, how it works, how it should work, and why it does not work; each has told us that advertising either deceives, informs, pleases, or frightens us.

Advertising has been attacked and defended by almost every segment of society. When it is advantageous, someone will admit to having used or even liked advertising. When it is not, the vindictiveness against advertising flies, even from public relations, marketing, and retailing specialists. Some popular culture books deal with advertising, but generally by including disparaging remarks. Examine a typical American history book and you will probably find little or no mention of advertising. Yet, to look at the advertisements of a nation is essentially to view most aspects of its existence. Advertising is the story of a nation's people. And, although advertising certainly did not originate in America, this country has probably done more than any other nation to use and foster advertising. It has been said that some foreign politicians have observed American advertisements as a gauge for measuring and understanding America's tastes and values. Advertising is probably the most pervasive form of popular culture and, surprisingly, has rarely been examined from this perspective.

To deal with that perspective is a task larger than the scope of this essay, which must necessarily be limited to a brief history of advertising and a survey of the most important books on the subject. Hopefully, by doing at least this much, this essay will convince the reader of the pervasiveness of advertising in American culture and will stimulate further research and investigation of advertising as a form of popular culture.

HISTORIC OUTLINE

Although the origins of advertising have been traced back to several very early sources, no one is exactly sure when the trade began. However, several evidences of written advertisements have been discovered and offered as the first recorded efforts in selling. The ones most often suggested are a Babylonian clay tablet announcing the services of an ointment dealer, scribe, and shoemaker, and a piece of papyrus from the ruins of Thebes offering a reward for the return of runaway slaves. The early history of advertising, replete with its accounts of Grecian town criers and Roman shop signs, is a fascinating one, and the reader is advised to consult the definitive histories listed elsewhere in this essay for a more thorough survey of early advertising history. Because of space limitations, we must necessarily begin with colonial America, which was beginning to implement already existing advertising methods, especially the shop sign and posted notices.

Advertising in America, which grew in conjunction with the expanding colonial economy, found its greatest impetus in newspapers, once the press had won its right to exist. As early as 1704 *The Boston Newsletter* carried advertisements for the return of some men's clothing and for the reward and capture of a thief. By the time of the Revolution, there were some thirty newspapers in America, each carrying substantial amounts of advertisements, mostly classified and local.

Although American advertising had reached a considerable sophistication and circulation, it was Benjamin Franklin who has earned—along with his many other credits—the title of father of American advertising, because he made important improvements in advertising methods. As a printer and a newspaperman, Franklin made major changes in the style and format of American advertisements. Most newspaper advertisements, which consisted of three- and four-line notices, were printed in various and uneven typefaces and were difficult to read. Franklin cleaned up the ads by separating individual notices with white spaces and then by adding bolder headings, thus making each ad distinctive from the rest. To make the advertisements even more distinctive, Franklin began using illustrations representative of the individual advertiser. He experimented with different symbols, such as ships, tools, horses, and books, which indicated the general contents of the advertisements. These symbols ranged in size from one and one-quarter inches to half columns and full columns and served as either borders or major graphics for the advertisements.

In addition to showing graphic expertise, Franklin was also the master of the written word. His knowledge of effective persuasive copy is obvious in the notice he wrote advertising his famous Franklin stove. He stressed not only the functional features of his invention but also the pleasures and comforts it would bring to the ladies. Advertising his brothers' super fine crown soap, he created this angle: "It cleanses fine Linens, Muslins, Laces, Chinces, Cambricks, etc. with Ease and Expedition, which often suffer more from the long and hard rubbing of the Washer, through the ill qualities of the soap than the wearing."

Although some men like Franklin led the way in improving advertising, the general state of advertising was a poor one. Most ads were simply notices for goods, services, land out west, slaves, or lost items. Advertisements were also used to attack competition and to announce the newest wonder drugs. Fraudulent medicine men and patent medicines, most often cited for giving advertising a disreputable image, would remain problems for advertisers for a long time.

Most of the advertisements of the shopkeepers of the late eighteenth century were directed toward the upper classes. Long notices informed the wealthy readers of the latest imported goods from England, Holland, and the Far East. Quality fabrics like chintzes and taffetas, and fragrant balms, spices, and perfumes were signs of wealth and prestige in the New World. The words "imported" and "just arrived" in an advertisement spoke of America's taste and the advertiser's audience, both of which changed after the revolutionary war. After the long struggle with England for independence, America felt drastic changes both socially and economically, and advertisements of that period reflected those changes. Once fashionable to own goods "just imported," it was now fashionable and more feasible to purchase "American-made" products, a tag that began to appear regularly in advertisements.

Newspaper growth matched the increasing American population and income, and, by 1820, some five hundred newspapers were serving more than nine million Americans. Although advertisements were still of uneven quality, they were almost certain to be read since advertisements, a little more than legal notices, flooded the newspapers. Newspapers prided themselves on the number, not the quality, of the ads that appeared in their pages. And the American reading public accepted the inundation of advertisements, along with the editorial policies of American newspapers, which remained highly partisan.

Technological advances in the early 1800s created many kinds of changes in the format and production of newspapers, especially in price reduction. The first penny newspaper, *The New York Sun*, was a 9 × 12 tabloid that rapidly reached a circulation of twenty thousand. Benjamin Day, its founder, soon met competition from a very shrewd editor, reporter, and founder of *The New York Herald*—James Gordon Bennett. Bennett charged two pennies for his paper and soon its circulation doubled that of the *Sun*. Both men experimented with advertisements. Day created a section called "Wants" and charged advertisers fifty cents per ad per day. Bennett immediately created the "Personals" column whose contents read much like those of today.

Bennett saw the power and profit in advertising and soon added restrictions to advertisers in his newspaper. At first he limited the time that a single advertisement could run to two weeks, but he later changed the limitation to one day. He also banned the use of illustrations. His idea was to give all advertisements equal importance and impact. Advertisers protested, but the *Herald's* circulation and the need for and effectiveness of advertising forced the advertisers to submit to Bennett's rules.

Bennett was successful in implementing his restrictions for a brief time until Robert Bonner of *The New York Ledger* matched wits with Bennett and won. Bonner, whose pulp magazine itself accepted no advertisements, did advertise for his magazine elsewhere. Deciding to break Bennett's boycott, Bonner bought whole pages in the *Herald* and simply repeated the announcement for his magazine in bold type over and over again. Sometimes he repeated a complete advertisement as many as ninety-three times in a single issue of the *Herald*.

Such competition and chaos demanded some sort of order, which soon arose in the form of a middle man, the advertising agent. Someone had to inform the advertiser about the various newspapers, rates, and options available to him, and someone had to help the newspaperman keep his pages filled with advertisements. The first advertising agent, Volney B. Palmer, who began as a newspaper advertising solicitor, decided to go "independent" and established several offices selling space for a few newspapers and charged a 25 percent commission for each advertisement. His first competitor was his own protégé, S. M. Pettingill, whom Palmer tried to run out of business by waging a slanderous war against him. Palmer was unsuccessful, however. In fact, Palmer ended up going insane, while Pettingill ended up as a very successful advertising agent and copywriter.

The creation of the advertising agent, which worked for a while, soon created its own competition and chaos. By the time of the Civil War, there were some twenty agents operating in ten cities. Although they claimed to follow the rates established by the newspapers, they often dickered to the point of cutting the editors' rates a healthy percentage, thus increasing their own commissions. The shrewd advertising agent became a wealthy man easily enough.

Out of the advertising agent struggle emerged a man who added stability and respectability to a floundering, but possibly good, system. George P. Rowell bought mass space in one hundred papers across the country and contracted to advertisers. Rowell also guaranteed payment to the newspapers for any ads for which he received a commission. He believed in truth in advertising and even wrote in an essay, "Honesty is by all odds the very strongest point which can be crowded in an ad." Rowell, in addition to his devotion to honesty, is known as the founder of *Printer's Ink* and as the publisher of the first American newspaper directory that gave estimates of the nation's newspaper rates and circulation.

Although Rowell stressed the need for honesty in advertising, he and many other agents made a great deal of money during the Civil War by advertising patent medicines. While it is easy for us today to point a finger at such men and such practices, it would be wise for us to reconsider the times. Even religious publications—the predecessors of magazines and the most influential medium in post-Civil War America—contained inordinate amounts of patent medicine advertisements. In fact, patent medicine advertising comprised 75 percent of all advertising in religious publications. Many temperance papers carried advertisements for medicines that were eighty-proof alcohol.

However, once the secret formulas of patent medicine began to be exposed, the public responded by showing disapproval of both the promoters of the products and of the advertising men. One result of the consumers' behavior was that certain advertising men again tried to clean up their unsavory reputation. F. Wayland Ayer, founder of N. W. Ayer and Son, became personally interested in the reputation of advertising after an associate made disparaging remarks about the nature of Ayer's business. Ayer responded by trying further to stabilize Rowell's efforts to establish rates between advertiser, publisher, and agent. Ayer initiated the open contract, which stipulated the amount of money that would be spent on advertising costs plus the agent's commission. The greatest impact of Ayer's system was that it became clear that the agent represented the advertiser. Ayer is also credited with being the man who first studied the market and produced the first marketing survey.

Most efforts to establish a greater rapport between agents and clients focused on newspaper activity since the few magazines that were successful in the mid-century refused to carry advertisements. J. Walter Thompson was the first advertising man to convince magazine publishers to accept advertisements. His success plus several events in the last three decades of the nineteenth century made magazines and magazine advertising the new American craze. Technological advances such as the Hoe high-speed rotary press and the halftone method of reproducing photographs, in addition to a reduction in second-class postal rates, and a 50 percent increase in the literacy rate, all contributed to the mass circulation of magazines. Mass magazines introduced Americans to the nationwide sale of products and to national advertising.

Today's readers, who complain about the number of advertisements in their favorite magazines, might be surprised to learn that *Harper's*, which initially shunned advertisements, by 1899 carried 135 pages of ads and

163 pages of editorials. J. Walter Thompson, who continued to control much of the advertising in existing magazines—mostly women's—was not the only man to recognize the profit in this area. Cyrus Curtis, magazine magnate, created magazines expressly for the purpose of advertising. Among his creations were *Ladies' Home Journal, Cosmopolitan,* and *McClure's.*

The twentieth century heralded in the age of American advertising. Outdoor advertising, the oldest form of the profession, received a new face when the first electric sign was erected in New York in 1891. Retailers actively engaged in advertising. Copywriter Claude Hopkins gave Americans a breakfast product "shot from guns," in addition to giving copy a new status in the advertising campaign. Americans were bombarded with advertising. Newspapers, magazines, transit ads, billboards, posters, and window displays echoed America's progress. The age of mass production, mass selling, and mass advertising had arrived. And Americans appeared to love it. Broadway, "The Great White Way," attracted thousands of tourists, as did the Hudson River steamboat excursions to Albany, during which passengers gazed at the lighted billboards that lined the riverbanks.

But many people began to worry about the moral, psychological, and physical effects that such mass production and mass selling would have on the American public. Outsiders (and insiders, too) wrote exposés attacking the new American way and fraudulent advertising; while on the other side, advertisers themselves grouped together to create organizations and clubs to regulate their own profession. Vigilance committees and campaigns to promote truth in advertising sprang up overnight. Agencies such as the Better Business Bureau, the Association of National Advertising Managers, and the American Association of Advertising Agencies developed policies to improve the effectiveness of advertising and to protect the consumer from fraudulent claims. *Printer's Ink*, the leading advertising trade paper, created a model statute for the regulation of advertising; it vowed to "punish untrue, deceptive, or misleading advertising." In 1916 advertising gained some crucial respectability when President Woodrow Wilson addressed the Associated Advertising Clubs of the World in Philadelphia.

The struggle between advertising groups and consumer groups continued, as did American prosperity, through the 1920s. Advertising benefited greatly from the prosperity and, at the same time, congratulated itself for its contributions to America's growth. The December 7, 1929 issue of *The Saturday Evening Post* carried 154 pages of advertising in a 268-page publication that sold for five cents. Another new medium of the 1920s—the radio—brought advertising billings to three and one-half billion dollars by the end of the decade.

In addition to the stockmarket crash of 1929 and the ensuing economic upheavals, advertisers had to struggle against other factors throughout the 1930s. Muckrakers launched new attacks; the Robinson-Patman Act of 1936 protected the little merchant from unfair competition by the big businessman; the Wheeler-Lea Act of 1938 gave the Federal Trade Commission more power over advertising; and the Federal Food, Drug, and Cosmetic Act of 1938 gave the administration authority over packaging and labeling.

But in spite of controls and criticism, advertising continued to survive and prosper. Radio remained the major advertising medium until the emergence of television, which quickly gave advertising a new source of expression, new challenges, and new problems. How successfully advertising will survive the electronic age, the problems of shortages, and an uncertain American economic future cannot be accurately predicted. But one thing is certain: advertising will face the new challenges just as it faced the ones presented to it throughout its early history in America.

REFERENCE WORKS

Although a massive amount of material has been written about advertising, very little has been done to organize this available body of material so that it is easily accessible and useful to the researcher. Some standard reference works do exist, but most are directed to the advertising man and serve as basic trade information sources. John M. Richard's *A Guide to Advertising Information Sources* is a fifty-nine-page pamphlet annotating 277 sources, mostly yearbooks, directories, and standard rate and data information. The material is divided into seventeen categories with such diverse and confusing titles as art, bibliographies, fairs and shows, legal, and general works. The *Guide*, compiled mostly for professionals, has a somewhat limited use as a general source book; it is also marred by typographical errors. Eleanor Blum's *Basic Books in the Mass Media* contains a chapter on "Advertising and Public Relations." Over sixty items in this section are annotated and listed alphabetically, but, much like Richard's *Guide*, Blum's checklist contains some highly specialized and widely diverse sources. While neither of these books contains material dated after 1971, together they provide an adequate resource for the standard advertising directories, handbooks, histories, and bibliographies. Both are indexed by subject, author, and title, with Blum's book containing a popular culture index.

A more practical basic bibliography for the layman, but somewhat dated and generally difficult to locate, is *One Hundred Books on Advertising*, compiled by Robert W. Haverfield. *Advertising: An Annotated Bibliography*, compiled by the J. Walter Thompson Company with an introduction by J. Treasure, is an equally obscure publication that has a British slant. However, the checklist is fairly recent and, although slight, contains a solid reading list of British and American interest. Treasure's introduction is lively, the organization of the checklist practical, and the annotations instructional. Of course, many books on advertising contain bibliographies that vary in quality, but a particularly good one can be found at the end of Roy Nelson's *The Design of Advertising*. Although it is not annotated, the checklist is thorough and divided into categories that follow the organization of the book. Nelson's bibliography provides a solid overview of the many areas within advertising; each section of the checklist also contains a list of related specialized periodicals.

Several marketing and public relations bibliographies are useful for locating materials on advertising. Scott Cutlip's *A Public Relations Bibliography* contains one section on advertising. Under the heading "Mass Media," Cutlip cites ninety-three items, mostly articles, in which advertising is treated as a public relations tool. Robert Bishop's continuation of Cutlip's bibliography provides a more thorough treatment of advertising. In *Public Relations: A Comprehensive Bibliography*, Bishop annotates some 160 items in a special section devoted to advertising. The items, both books and articles, are alphabetically arranged by author; no attempt has been made to categorize items within the section although there is cross-referencing and indexing. A few marketing bibliographies that treat advertising in various ways are: *A Basic Bibliography on Marketing Research* by Robert Ferber, et al.; Nevin W. Raber and Richard Coachys's *Marketing: A Selected List of Current Titles*; and David A. Revzan's *A Comprehensive Classified Marketing Bibliography*. Two specialized checklists covering articles on advertising are *Copy Testing: An Annotated Bibliography* and *Continuity in Advertising: A Selected Abstract Bibliography*.

No single index to advertising exists. After consulting the above bibliographies for articles on advertising, the researcher probably should consult the *Readers' Guide to Periodical Literature* and then, given his particular subject, examine any of the following indexes: *Accountants' Index*; *Applied Science and Technology Index*; *Art Index*; *Biological and Agricultural Index*; *Business Periodicals Index*; *Education Index*; *Index to Legal Periodicals*; *Public Affairs Information Index*; *Sociological Abstracts*; *Psychological Abstracts*; *and Women's Studies Abstracts*, to cite a few.

Numerous handbooks, texts, and how-to books on advertising exist, and it would be impossible and unnecessary to list them. The ones cited here and elsewhere in this essay are either representative of the kinds of books available or are considered particularly useful as primary and secondary sources of information.

One of the earliest encyclopedias of advertising was published in 1897. *Fowler's Publicity* is a one-thousand-page compendium of early advertising information and trivia. Although it is difficult to locate and certainly of not much practical use to the contemporary researcher, Nathaniel Fowler's encyclopedia is an important and interesting work to consult. *The Encyclopedia of Advertising* by Irvin Graham is a classic reference manual that lists over one thousand terms related to advertising and its many branches. Although divided into three sections, this encyclopedia is comprised mostly of section one, which defines alphabetically arranged advertising terms in great detail; section two groups terms according to subject matter; and section three is a directory of advertising associations, with addresses and statements of aim. More than a directory, this encyclopedia is a working manual meant to provide clear and instant access to the advertising vocabulary. Another massive work of similar format is S. Watson Dunn's *International Handbook of Advertising*.

Several other handbooks on advertising and related areas exist and, although directed to the businessman, they can serve as good basic reference works. Roger Barton's *Handbook of Advertising Management* contains thirty-two essays in nine parts that attempt to examine the principles, and not the details, of advertising. In the preface, Barton explains to advertisers that they cannot disregard the effects of their profession on the tastes and manner of their audiences. Barton's handbook contains a glossary of terms and is indexed. *The Dartnell Advertising Manager's Handbook* by Richard H. Stansfield and *The Dartnell Direct Mail and Mail Order Handbook* by Richard S. Hodgson should not be overlooked, if only because of their sheer size. Because it relates public relations and advertising, Howard Stephenson's *Handbook of Public Relations: The Standard Guide to Public Affairs and Communications* probably should be examined.

Printing and Promotion Handbook: How to Plan, Produce, and Use Printing, Advertising, and Direct Mail by Daniel Melcher and Nancy Larrick is an important work that covers many facets of advertising and production. Some other handbooks that deal with television production are Irving Settel and Norman Glenn's *Television Advertising and Production Handbook* and Martin Padley's *A Handbook to Television Advertising*. Settel and Glenn's *Handbook* is somewhat dated, while Padley's more recent publication defines terms and provides a discussion of issues in the television industry. Among the many books directed to the advertising artist, the following three are fairly representative sources of information: John Snyder's *Commercial Artist's Handbook*; John Quick's *Artists' and Illustrators' Encyclopedia*; and Johnny A. Gazurian's *The Advertising and Graphic Arts Glossary*. For handbooks on copywriting, see *Advertising Writing* by W. Keith Hafer and Gordon E. White and *The Compleat*

Copywriter: A Comprehensive Guide to All Phases of Advertising Communication by Hanley Norins.

Three good dictionaries to locate advertising terms are *Media/Scope's Dictionary of Terms*; *Ayer Glossary of Advertising and Related Terms*; and Laurence Urdang's *Dictionary of Advertising Terms*. Valerie Noble's *The Effective Echo: A Dictionary of Advertising Slogans* is an excellent book that treats the history of the advertising slogan; it also gives a lengthy definition of an effective slogan and a chronology of slogan lists published in *Printer's Ink*.

In a field such as advertising, textbooks often serve as good reference guides and handbooks. A few of the major texts are: *Advertising Theory and Practice* by Charles H. Sandage and Vernon Fryburger; *Advertising Procedure* by Otto Kleppner; *Advertising* by John S. Wright and Willis Winter; *Advertising: Its Role in Modern Marketing* by S. Watson Dunn and Arnold M. Barban; and *Advertising in America: An Introduction to Persuasive Communication* by Stanley M. Ulanoff.

One advertising directory is the *Madison Avenue Handbook*, which includes a guide to the city, a listing of addresses and telephone numbers of advertising agencies, and sources for media, talent, photography, illustration, television, film, and copy. *The Creative Black Book*, another directory of major services, includes indexing by regional subdivisions. However, the standard advertising directories are *The Standard Directory of Advertising Agencies* and *The Standard Directory of Advertisers*. Commonly called "The Red Books," these two directories contain the most updated list of agencies and advertisers available. The *Directory of Advertisers* lists some seventeen thousand companies and issues an annual geographical index. The *Directory of Advertising Agencies*, published three times a year, lists some four thousand United States and four hundred foreign agencies. Advertising Age's *Marketing Strategies of America's 125 Largest Advertisers* gives detailed accounts of the sales, expenses, and earnings of America's largest corporations. The book also offers a complete list of marketing, advertising, and sales personnel, along with the names of the advertising agencies that handle the accounts.

RESEARCH COLLECTIONS

Collections of advertisements are widely scattered among associations, advertising agencies, university libraries, public libraries, and historical societies. If one is interested in collections of advertisements of a particular product—for example, pharmaceuticals—one should consult the *Subject Directory of Special Libraries and Information Centers* by Margaret Labash Young et al. to locate pharmaceutical companies that keep collections of their products' advertisements. Although many companies maintain collections of their advertisements, rarely are these materials available for public inspection. The Advertising Research Foundation and the Association of National Advertisers are just two advertising associations that maintain research collections, which are mostly vertical files of clippings and speeches.

The J. Walter Thompson Company's Information Center in Chicago keeps files of clippings, reports, studies, and news releases, in addition to maintaining a collection of print advertisements now numbering over one hundred thousand items. The University of Wisconsin houses the Frank Thayer Collection on the Law of Mass Communications, and the University of Illinois Communication Library's collection focuses on communication theory and its effects. Political advertisements and posters are the emphasis of the collection at the University of Michigan Library. Yale University maintains a strong graphic arts collection, especially on nineteenth-century art, and catalogs, volumes, and scrapbooks on the history of eighteenth- and nineteenth-century trade cards. The Friendship Library at Fairleigh Dickinson University is the official depository for the outdoor advertising industry, and included among its twenty-five hundred items are fifteen original billboards.

The Ayer Collection of Business Americana at the Smithsonian Institution includes at least four hundred thousand advertisements from *The Saturday Evening Post*. The history of advertising and advertising periodicals is the emphasis of the collection at the New York Public Library, and the Cincinnati Art Museum Library is especially noted for its holdings of prints and engravings in advertising and the graphic arts. The Chicago Historical Society houses numerous advertising cards, theatre programs, and Chicago trade catalogs. A good collection of American advertising cards can also be found at the American Antiquarian Society.

HISTORY AND CRITICISM

The definitive history of advertising is Frank Presbrey's *The History and Development of Advertising*, which appeared in 1929. Presbrey's text surveys British and American advertising and, although dated, remains the soundest and most unbiased history of the profession. An earlier history appeared in 1874, *A History of Advertising from the Earliest Times* by Henry Sampson, but the book is slanted toward British advertising and is not very useful as a study of American advertising. In fact, chapter nineteen attacks colonial American advertisements on the grounds of naiveté, immorality, flippancy, and greed.

Thirty years after Presbrey's history, James Playsted Wood's *The Story of Advertising* appeared, which treats advertising as "a story of people" and as the primary expression of democracy. A sound, thorough, and complete history of advertising has not come out since 1958 when Wood's text was published. An historical exposé of advertising can be found in E. S. Turner's *The Shocking History of Advertising!*, whose premise suggests that advertising is a mirror of man. Turner admits to a pessimistic view of mankind; man is without grace, and advertising, unless it cleans its code of ethics, will continue to contribute to man's fallen state. On the lighter side is Frank Rowsome's *They Laughed When I Sat Down: An Informal History of Advertising in Words and Pictures*, which examines the history of magazine advertising between the Civil War and World War II. Rowsome, who titled his history after John Caples's famous advertisement, looks at the entertaining aspects of advertising as well as the informative and personal memoirs of early advertising men.

Most critical books on advertising are either exposés or defenses of the profession. However, there are a few which, for various reasons, have become important books in the study of advertising. Neil H. Borden's *The Economic Effects of Advertising* is a landmark study of the effects of advertising within a capitalistic society of free enterprise. In his 1954 study, *People of Plenty*, David Potter analyzes the role that advertising has played in America's history of economic abundance. In *Motivation in Advertising*, Pierre Martineau suggests that the primary function of advertising is to help people express their convictions and not to manipulate consumers. Rosser Reeves's *Reality in Advertising* formulates certain theories about advertising and argues that advertising men must begin to look objectively at their craft. In *Strategy in Advertising*, Leo Bogart deals with the generic characteristics of mass communications, focusing on media strategy. Bogart, in directing his media plans, suggests that advertising is the most visible aspect of modern society's values. Walter Taplin, in *Advertising: A New Approach*, attempts to overcome some of the negative judgments of advertising by looking at such issues as human wants and the role of information in persuasion tactics. Raymond A. Bauer and Stephen A. Greyser study the consumer judgment of advertising in their book *Advertising in America: The Consumer View*. In addition to providing an historical review of consumer attitudes toward advertising, Bauer and Greyser supply data analyzing Americans' reactions to advertisements and provide, as well, support and criticism of advertising in America. In *Madison Avenue, U.S.A.*, Martin Mayer offers a journalist's view of advertising agencies, examining them as both big businesses and professional services. Recently, Jib Fowler made an important contribution to the study of advertising and futures research with the publication of his book in 1976, *Mass Advertising as Social Forecast: A Method for Futures Research*.

A countless number of books attack advertising and propose consumer rights policies. And interestingly enough, many of these books are written by former advertising men. A 1934 exposé by James Rorty, *Our Master's Voice: Advertising*, attacks ad men as dull and hopeless demons and sadists. The book is also an excuse to attack Bruce Barton's bestseller *The Man Nobody Knows*, which argues that Jesus was the first ad man. Another early twentieth-century bestseller is Frederick Wakeman's *The Hucksters*. In *The Clowns of Commerce*, insider Walter Goodman explains that the extreme defensiveness of advertising men arises out of their own inner turmoils. Marshall McLuhan and Vance Packard probably produced some of the most popular treatises of the century against advertising. Among his many books, McLuhan's *The Mechanical Bride: Folklore of Industrial Man* and *Understanding Media: The Extensions of Man* deal most directly with advertising. In *Understanding Media*, McLuhan argues that advertising is the most faithful reflection of man's activities but that in its attempt to achieve universal programmed harmony, it will create its own demise. Vance Packard's *The Hidden Persuaders* offers the premise that we are being manipulated through psychological and social-scientific techniques.

Joseph J. Seldin's *The Golden Fleece* describes the postwar upheaval of American society and traces advertising's exploitation of the new middle class in their search for the good life. Another book that traces the roots of American industrialism and the relationship between capitalism and advertising is Stuart Ewen's *Captains of Consciousness: Advertising and the Social Roots of the Consumer Culture*. The exploitation of the consumer is again described and explained in *The Permissible Lie: The Inside Truth About Advertising*. Author Samm Sinclair Baker admits that in 1933 he decided to make his fortune in advertising and then later to expose its evils. Baker's book, first published in 1968, is an attempt to eliminate the evils of advertising and to enlarge its benefits for the whole nation. In 1972 Robin Wight argued that there exists an unseen but powerful consumer revolution against advertising and marketing. *The Day the Pigs Refused to Be Driven to Market* admits that the revolution has no marches, no manifestos, no leaders, and few formal followers, but that the movement is powerful. Three years later Jeffrey Schrank's *Deception Detection: An Educator's Guide to the Art of Insight* appeared, which reads as though it were the manifesto to the movement described by Wight. Schrank's book is a collection of ideas or survival skills that could be part of a consumer education course, among other things. Ivan L. Preston's *The Great American Blow-Up: Puffery in Advertising and Selling* argues that the consumer movement should stop nothing short of complete elimination of false, deceptive advertising. Ex-advertising man Giancarlo Buzzi assesses advertising in terms of its political, sociological, psychological, and moral aims and responsibilities. In *Advertising: Its Cultural and Political Effects*, Buzzi concludes that advertising itself is neither good nor evil, but is relative to its context.

Advertising has taken advantage of some particular American weaknesses, according to a few authors. Wilson Bryan Key's two books of the 1970s examine advertising's seductive techniques. *Subliminal Seduction* and *Media Sexploitation* conclude that through visual, auditory, and olfactory techniques the media program Americans into using cigarettes and alcohol and play on our sexual insecurity and obsessions. The health industry promoted by advertising is attacked in Ralph Lee Smith's *The Health Hucksters* and in Arthur Kallet and F. J. Schlink's *100 Million Guinea Pigs*. Thomas Whiteside exposes the tobacco industry and pleads for strong federal regulation of cigarette advertising in his 1971 book *Selling Death: Cigarette Advertising and Public Health*. America's susceptibility to politicians groomed by advertising is the subject of Joe McGinniss's *The Selling of the President 1968*.

Children, women, and minorities are also particular subjects of several books related to advertising. As early as 1938, an advertising-sponsored study of children and advertising appeared. E. Evalyn Grumbino's *Reaching Juvenile Markets: How to Advertise, Sell, and Merchandise Through Boys and Girls* was an attempt to study the changing interests of children and thus to "create better appeals to the juvenile market and so eliminate much of the exploitation of boys and girls, which is resented by all interested in the welfare of children." But the welfare of children has not been considered, argues Ron Goulart in *The Assault on Childhood*. Goulart exposes many of the assaults on children, including comics, television, the media, and advertising. In *Ladies of the Avenue*, Patricia E. Tierney bitterly discusses the sexism and prejudice within the advertising business world. A 1975 publication, *Advertising and Women*, sponsored by a consultive panel of the National Advertising Review Board, examines the portrayal of women in advertising. The panel discovered that there is a very real problem in the unfavorable image of women in commercials. Although it is a British publication, *Images of Women: Advertising in Women's Magazines* by Trevor Millum has much to offer in the study of that subject. Kathryn Weibel devotes one chapter to women and magazine advertising in her recent book, *Mirror Mirror: Images of Women Reflected in Popular Culture*. How to reach the black consumer is the subject of D. Parke Gibson's *The $30 Billion Negro*.

Advertising men love to write about themselves and each other, and there is no paucity of biographies and autobiographies of these men and women. Just a few of the most interesting and informative life stories follow. Chalmers Lowell Pancoast's *Trail Blazers of Advertising* is a collection of stories about advertising when it was a "game and an adventure," not a "science or profession." Pancoast writes in a lively, dramatic, and nostalgic style, and the book is filled with many personal anecdotes. Claude C. Hopkins, one of the giants of early advertising, wrote two important books, *My Life in Advertising* and *Scientific Advertising.* Estelle Hamburger's *It's a Woman's Business* is one of the first memoirs of advertising written by a woman. Earnest Elmo Calkins, author of several books on advertising, wrote his story as an ad man in *"And Hearing Not—".* John Gunther writes an engaging story of another early ad man in *Taken at the Flood: The Story of Albert D. Lasker.* James Webb Young's book *How to Become an Advertising Man* grew out of his lectures delivered at the University of Chicago to the trainees of the J. Walter Thompson Company. David G. Lyon's *Off Madison Avenue* and Jim Ellis's *Billboards to Buicks* offer both autobiographical insights to the advertising world and suggestions about starting an advertising agency. In *My First 65 Years in Advertising,* Maxwell Sackheim tells about his life in direct mail and offers hints about this lucrative aspect of advertising. *The Blue Streak: Some Observations Mostly About Advertising* contains a chronology of the personal memoirs of Fairfax M. Cone; Cone's own autobiography is *With All Its Faults: A Candid Account of Forty Years in Advertising.* Jerry Della-Femina's *From Those Wonderful Folks Who Gave You Pearl Harbor;* David Ogilvy's *Confessions of an Advertising Man* and *Blood, Brains, and Beer;* George Lois's *George, Be Careful;* Charlie Brower's *Me and Other Advertising Geniuses;* and Shirley Poly-koff's *Does She or Doesn't She? and How She Did It* all attest to the variety of backgrounds, experiences, philosophies, and personalities that exist in the world of advertising.

Since advertising pervades all areas of mass communications, it is possible here to discuss only the most basic books relating advertising to a particular branch of communications. The reader is therefore advised to consult the other chapters within this handbook if he is interested in the subject of advertising within a particular area of specialization. For example, see the chapter on television for material on the subject of advertising and television. *Outdoor Advertising: History and Regulation,* edited by John W. Houck, contains nine essays dealing with the oldest form of advertising. Although most of the essays deal with regulatory and aesthetic goals, one essay by Phillip Tucker, president of the Outdoor Advertising Association of America, provides a good survey of the history of outdoor advertising in America. Frank Luther Mott's *American Journalism* traces the historical development of newspapers in the United States, while *National Advertising in Newspapers* by Neil H. Borden et al., although published in 1946, offers some sound and still applicable newspaper advertising principles.

Histories of American magazines that also discuss magazine advertising are: Frank Mott's *A History of American Magazines*; James Playsted Wood's *Magazines in the United States*; Theodore Peterson's *Magazines in the Twentieth Century*; and James L. C. Ford's *Magazines for Millions: The Story of Specialized Publications*. In his history, Wood makes some statements about the state of the art of magazine advertisements, while Ford describes some of the serialized publications in the advertising profession.

In *A Decade of Radio Advertising*, Herman Hettinger gives a general survey of broadcast advertising in an attempt to define and evaluate its basic structure and its economic and social roles. *Television and Radio* by Giraud Chester et al. and *Advertising in the Broadcast Media* by Elizabeth J. Heighton and Don R. Cunningham are two good basic texts that provide broad overviews of the broadcasting industry in addition to exploring some of the finer details about the workings of the business. Although they are essentially how-to books, *Anatomy of Local Radio-TV Copy* by William A. Peck and *The Power Technique of Radio-TV Copywriting* by Neil Terrell contain some suggestions about the structure of commercials. Two histories of television are Martin Mayer's *About Television* and Erik Barnouw's *Tube of Plenty*. Lincoln Diamant's *Television's Classic Commercials: The Golden Years 1948-1958* gives an historical background of television commercials and also reprints sixty-nine television commercial classics. In *The Sponsored Film*, Walter J. Klein deals with the public relations and commercial aspects of the sponsored film industry. A pictorial history of motion picture, newspaper, and magazine advertising through the 1940s can be found in Russell C. Sweeney's *Coming Next Week: A Pictorial History of Film Advertising*.

Few critical studies of advertising copy and design exist. Manuel Rosenberg's *The Art of Advertising* is a 1930 version of a book of basic design for the advertising artist. Roy Paul Nelson's *The Design of Advertising*, first published in 1967, appeared in its second edition in 1973. Nelson's text, as mentioned earlier, contains an excellent bibliography in addition to being a solid sourcebook on typography and design. An overview of American advertising art is presented in a bicentennial edition, *200 Years of American Graphic Art: A Retrospective Survey of the Printing Arts and Advertising Since the Colonial Period* by Clarence Hornung and Fridolf Johnson, who admit that, although it would take years and ten volumes to do justice to such a topic, they have created a book that will "engage the reader and inspire him to further studies." Hornung and Johnson's scope is broad, whereas Theodore Menten's range is far more focused in his book *Advertising Art in the Art Deco Style*, a volume that contains some three hundred art deco ads and posters from nine countries originally produced between 1924 and 1940. Menten argues that advertising art really came into its own as never before in history during the art deco period. Stephen Baker, in *Visual Persuasion: The Effect of Pictures on the Subconscious*, contends that Americans have always demanded realism in their art and that advertising artists have yet to understand fully the effects of pictures on the subconscious. *Making Ads Pay* by John Caples, author of the famous ad, "They Laughed When I Sat Down," is a study of creativity and effective copywriting. Although it is a British publication, Geoffrey N. Leech's *English in Advertising: A Linguistic Study of Advertising in Great Britain* suggests the possibility of a similar study of American advertising.

Virtually nothing has been done to study speciality advertising, except for the work of George L. Herpel and Richard A. Collins, *Speciality Advertising in Marketing*. Herpel and Collins discuss the role, concept, and history of speciality advertising in addition to merchandising techniques. Very little has also been done with classified ads. A 1975 study, *Help Wanted: Case Studies of Classified Ads* by John Walsh, Miriam Johnson, and Marged Sugarman, tests the accuracy and effectiveness of classified ads listed in San Francisco and Salt Lake City newspapers. The findings show that in spite of the popularity of classified ads, they are inadequate, unscrupulous, and generally ineffective. Robert Glatzer studies the twenty most successful advertising campaigns in his book *The New Advertising: The Great Campaigns from Avis to Volkswagen*, while Frank Rowsome, Jr. retells the stories of two highly successful campaigns in *The Verse by the Side of the Road: The Story of the Burma-Shave Signs and Jingles* and *Think Small: The Story of Those Volkswagen Ads*. A compendium of ideas, along with reprints, commentaries, and anecdotes can be found in *Humor in Advertising . . . And How to Make It Pay* by Don Herold.

For collections of short, critical pieces about advertising, there is a wealth of material available to the reader. Books of advertising-related readings are widely used and are good resources for general information about the many areas of advertising. Just a sampling of some of these readers includes: *The Role of Advertising: A Book of Readings*, edited by Charles H. Sandage and Vernon Fryburger; *Advertising in America*, edited by Poyntz Tyler; *Speaking of Advertising*, edited by John S. Wright and Daniel S. Warner; *Exploring Advertising*, edited by Otto Kleppner and Irving Settel; *Advertising and Society*, edited by Yale Brozen; and *Advertising and the Public Interest*, edited by Salvatore F. Divita. Brozen's collection contains an excellent article by historian Daniel Boorstin, "Advertising and American Civilization," in which he discusses the concept of popular culture and advertising's role in American popular culture. Two editions compiled by *Advertising Age* are good general readers: *The New World of Advertising* is a collection of reprinted articles from *Advertising Age*, and *How It Was in Advertising*, a bicentennial edition, is an informative and entertaining selection of readings with an historical slant. Two anthologies on popular culture, coedited by Bernard Rosenberg and David Manning White, *Mass Culture: The Popular Arts in America* and *Mass Culture Revisited*, contain a total of three essays on advertising, all of which are disparaging.

There are an extraordinary number of advertising and related periodicals in existence. In scope and importance, *Advertising Age*, a weekly publication that includes news about all trade-related industries, dominates the others. In addition to news items, *Advertising Age* often includes critical articles and special bibliographies. In 1967, *Marketing/Communications* superseded *Printer's Ink*, which was the oldest advertising journal in America and remained an important publication until 1972 when it ceased publication. Special serialized publications abound for media, marketing, broadcasting, print, illustration, photography, graphics, and design. A brief list of just a few of these advertising periodicals appears at the end of this essay, and the reader is also advised to check section nine of Eleanor Blum's *Basic Books in the Mass Media* for annotations of a few other serialized publications.

REPRINTS

Reprint collections run the gamut from the whimsical to the scholarly to the professional. Julian Lewis Watkins's *The 100 Greatest Advertisements: Who Wrote Them and What They Did* includes a reproduction of each selected great advertisement along with extensive textual commentary by the author. Watkins's book, which first appeared in 1949, was followed in 1959 by a second edition with an additional thirteen advertisements. Edgar R. Jones takes a random look at some turn-of-the-century magazine advertisements in *Those Were the Good Old Days: A Happy Look at American Advertising, 1880-1930*. The book is a collection of nostalgia, and Jones admits to no sound rationale for including the ads; he intentionally refrains from editorial comments. Another reprint of early American advertisements is *Floyd Clymer's Scrapbook: Early Advertising Art*, an anthology that also contains Clymer's personal musings about advertising.

While these books represent the whimsical, nostalgic approach to the reprinting of advertisements, two more serious attempts to reprint collections are Bella Landauer's *Early American Trade Cards* and Mary Black's *American Advertising Posters of the Nineteenth Century*. Both of these books, which are results of the efforts to organize the massive collections of New York socialite Bella C. Landauer, contain useful annotations, critical notes, and indexes. *Early American Trade Cards* gives the definition and history of printed trade cards, while Mary Black, in her edition of posters from the Landauer collection, adds valuable notes and separate indexes of artists, engravers, and advertisers.

Collecting and reprinting advertisements devoted to one subject seems to be a favorite avocation of many people. Just a few examples of such books are: Arnold Fochs's *The Very Idea: A Collection of Retail Advertising Ideas*, containing what he considers the most effective local retail advertisements; Robert Karolevitz's *Old Time Agriculture in the Ads: Being a Compendium of Magazine and Newspaper Sales Literature Reminiscent of the Days When Farming Was the Way of Life and Horsepower Came in Horses!*, whose title reveals the nature of the book; and Lawrence Dietz's *Soda Pop: The History, Advertising, Art, and Memorabilia of Soft Drinks in America*, a textual and pictorial survey of the soda pop industry, with emphasis on Coke and its advertisements. Auto buffs seem to be particularly interested in examining advertisements as inducements to the consumer to participate in an already uniquely American cultural phenomenon—the automobile. Howard Garrett, in *The Poster Book of Antique Auto Ads, 1898-1920*, and Michael Frostick, in *Advertising and the Motor-Car*, reprint automobile ads more for their "artsy" and "quaint" qualities; Jane and Michael Stern and Peter Roberts go beyond merely reproducing advertisements in *Auto Ads* and *Any Color So Long as It's Black: The First Fifty Years of Automobile Advertising*. These authors all attempt to relate the advertisements to consumers' preferences and needs as well as to the product.

Many professional groups and organizations publish annuals that contain the advertisements considered the best of that year. *Art Directors Annual, Communication Arts Annual, Graphis Annual, Illustrators, Modern Publicity, The Penrose Annual*, and *The Print Casebooks* are just a few of the professional reprints produced yearly. Finally, advertising men themselves are beginning to reprint their individual work. George Lois's *The Art of Advertising* is a collection of his major ads and reflects not only the accomplishments of one man but also the tastes and culture of the American consumer. More books of this sort are beginning to appear and offer a legitimate cataloging of American popular culture.

BIBLIOGRAPHY

BOOKS AND ARTICLES

Advertising Age, ed. *How It Was in Advertising: 1776-1976*. Chicago: Crain Books, 1976.

———. *Marketing Strategies of America's 125 Largest Advertisers*. Chicago: Crain Communications, 1970.

Advertising and Women: A Report on Advertising Portraying or Directed to Women. New York: The National Advertising Review Board, March 1975.

Ash, Lee, ed. *Subject Collections: A Guide to Special Book Collections and Subject Emphases as Reported by University, College, Public, and Special Libraries, and Museums in the United States and Canada.* 4th ed. New York: R. R. Bowker, 1974.

Ayer Glossary of Advertising and Related Terms. 2d ed. Compiled and published by Ayer Press. Philadelphia: William J. Luedke, Publisher, 1977.

Baker, Samm Sinclair. *The Permissible Lie: The Inside Truth About Advertising.* Cleveland: World Publishing, 1968.

Baker, Stephen. *Visual Persuasion: The Effect of Pictures on the Subconscious.* New York: McGraw-Hill, 1961.

Barnouw, Erik. *Tube of Plenty: The Evolution of American Television.* New York: Oxford University Press, 1975.

Barton, Bruce. *The Man Nobody Knows: A Discovery of Jesus.* Indianapolis: Bobbs-Merrill, 1925.

————. *The Man and the Book Nobody Knows.* Rev. ed. Indianapolis: Bobbs-Merrill, 1956.

Barton, Roger, ed. *Handbook of Advertising Management.* New York: McGraw-Hill, 1970.

Bauer, Raymond A., and Stephen A. Greyser. *Advertising in America: The Consumer View.* Boston: Graduate School of Business Administration, Harvard University, 1968.

Bishop, Robert L., comp. *Public Relations: A Comprehensive Bibliography.* Ann Arbor, Mich.: A. G. Leigh-James, 1974.

Black, Mary. *American Advertising Posters of the Nineteenth Century.* New York: Dover Publications, 1976.

Blum, Eleanor. *Basic Books in the Mass Media.* Urbana: University of Illinois Press, 1972.

Bogart, Leo. *Strategy in Advertising.* New York: Harcourt, Brace & World, 1967.

Borden, Neil H. *The Economic Effects of Advertising.* Chicago: R. D. Irwin, 1942. Reprint. New York: Arno Press, 1976.

————, Malcolm D. Taylor, and Howard T. Hovde. *National Advertising in Newspapers.* Cambridge: Harvard University Press, 1946.

Brower, Charlie. *Me and Other Advertising Geniuses.* Garden City, N.Y.: Doubleday, 1974.

Brozen, Yale, ed. *Advertising and Society.* New York: New York University Press, 1974.

Buzzi, Giancarlo. *Advertising: Its Cultural and Political Effects.* Minneapolis: University of Minnesota Press, 1968.

Calkins, Earnest Elmo. *"And Hearing Not—." Annals of an Adman.* New York: Scribner's, 1946.

Caples, John. *Making Ads Pay.* New York: Harper & Brothers, 1957.

Chester, Giraud, Garnet R. Garrison, and Edgar E. Willis. *Television and Radio.* 4th ed. New York: Appleton-Century-Crofts Educational Division, 1971.

Clymer, Floyd. *Floyd Clymer's Scrapbook: Early Advertising Art.* New York: Bonanza Books, 1955.

Cone, Fairfax M. *With All Its Faults: A Candid Account of Forty Years in Advertising.* Boston: Little, Brown, 1969.
————. *The Blue Streak: Some Observations Mostly About Advertising.* Chicago: Crain Communications, 1973.
Continuity in Advertising: A Selected Abstract Bibliography. New York: McGraw-Hill, 1966.
Copy Testing: An Annotated Bibliography, 1960-1972. New York: Advertising Research Foundation, 1972.
The Creative Black Book. New York: Friendly Publications, 1970-.
Cutlip, Scott M., comp. *A Public Relations Bibliography.* 2d ed. Madison and Milwaukee: The University of Wisconsin Press, 1965.
Della-Femina, Jerry. *From Those Wonderful Folks Who Gave You Pearl Harbor.* Edited by Charles Sopkin. New York: Simon and Schuster, 1970.
Diamant, Lincoln. *Television's Classic Commercials: The Golden Years 1948-1958.* Communication Art Books. New York: Hastings House, 1971.
Dietz, Lawrence. *Soda Pop: The History, Advertising, Art, and Memorabilia of Soft Drinks in America.* New York: Simon and Schuster, 1973.
Divita, Salvatore F., ed. *Advertising and the Public Interest.* Chicago: The American Marketing Association, 1974.
Dunn, S. Watson, ed. *International Handbook of Advertising.* New York: McGraw-Hill, 1964.
Dunn, S. Watson, and Arnold M. Barban. *Advertising: Its Role in Modern Marketing.* 3d ed. Hinsdale, Ill.: The Dryden Press, 1974.
Ellis, Jim. *Billboards to Buicks: Advertising as I Lived It.* New York: Abelard-Schuman, 1968.
Ewen, Stuart. *Captains of Consciousness: Advertising and the Social Roots of the Consumer Culture.* New York: McGraw-Hill, 1976.
Ferber, Robert, Alain Cousineau, Millard Crask, and Hugh G. Wales, comps. *A Basic Bibliography on Marketing Research.* 3d ed. New York: American Marketing Association, 1974.
Fochs, Arnold, comp. and ed. *The Very Idea: A Collection of Retail Advertising Ideas.* Duluth, Minn.: A. J. Publishing, 1971.
Ford, James L. C. *Magazines for Millions: The Story of Specialized Publications.* Carbondale and Edwardsville: Southern Illinois University Press, 1969.
Fowler, Jib. *Mass Advertising as Social Forecast: A Method for Futures Research.* Westport, Conn.: Greenwood Press, 1976.
Fowler, Nathaniel Clark. *Fowler's Publicity: An Encyclopedia of Advertising and Printing, and All that Pertains to the Public-Seeking Side of Business.* New York: Publicity Publishing, 1897.
Frostick, Michael. *Advertising and the Motor-Car.* London: Lund Humphries, 1970.
Garrett, Howard, comp. *The Poster Book of Antique Auto Ads, 1898-1920.* Secaucus, N.J.: Citadel Press, 1974.
Gazurian, Johnny A. *The Advertising and Graphic Arts Glossary.* Los Angeles: Los Angeles Trade-Technical College, 1966.

Gibson, D. Parke. *The $30 Billion Negro*. New York: Macmillan, 1969.
Glatzer, Robert. *The New Advertising: The Great Campaigns from Avis to Volkswagen*. New York: Citadel Press, 1970.
Goodman, Walter. *The Clowns of Commerce*. New York: Sagamore Press, 1954, 1955, 1956.
Goulart, Ron. *The Assault on Childhood*. Los Angeles: Sherbourne Press, 1969.
Graham, Irvin. *The Encyclopedia of Advertising*. 2d ed. New York: Fairchild Publications, 1969.
Grumbino, E. Evalyn. *Reaching Juvenile Markets: How to Advertise, Sell and Merchandise Through Boys and Girls*. New York: McGraw-Hill, 1938.
Gunther, John. *Taken at the Flood: The Story of Albert D. Lasker*. New York: Harper & Brothers, 1960.
Hafer, W. Keith, and Gordon E. White. *Advertising Writing*. St. Paul, Minn.: West Publishing, 1977.
Hamburger, Estelle. *It's a Woman's Business*. New York: Vanguard Press, 1939.
Haverfield, Richard W., comp. *One Hundred Books on Advertising*. Bul. V66, No. 3, Journalism Series No. 162. University of Missouri, 1965.
Heighton, Elizabeth J., and Don R. Cunningham. *Advertising in the Broadcast Media*. Belmont, Calif.: Wadsworth Publishing, 1976.
Herold, Don. *Humor in Advertising. . .And How to Make It Pay*. New York: McGraw-Hill, 1963.
Herpel, George L., and Richard A. Collins. *Speciality Advertising in Marketing*. Homewood, Ill.: Dow-Jones-Irwin, 1972.
Hettinger, Herman S. *A Decade of Radio Advertising*. Chicago: University of Chicago Press, 1933. Reprint. New York: Arno Press, 1971.
Hodgson, Richard S. *The Dartnell Direct Mail and Mail Order Handbook*. 2d ed. Chicago: Dartnell Press, 1974.
Hopkins, Claude C. *My Life in Advertising*. Chicago: Advertising Publications, 1966.
———. *Scientific Advertising*. Chicago: Advertising Publications, 1966.
Hornung, Clarence P., and Fridolf Johnson. *200 Years of American Graphic Art: A Retrospective Survey of the Printing Arts and Advertising Since the Colonial Period*. New York: George Braziller, 1976.
Houck, John W., ed. *Outdoor Advertising: History and Regulation*. Notre Dame, Ind.: University of Notre Dame Press, 1969.
Jones, Edgar R. *Those Were the Good Old Days: A Happy Look at American Advertising, 1880-1930*. New York: Simon and Schuster, 1959.
Kallet, Arthur, and F. J. Schlink. *100 Million Guinea Pigs: Dangers in Everyday Foods, Drugs, and Cosmetics*. New York: Vanguard Press, 1933. Reprint. New York: Arno Press, 1976.
Karolevitz, Robert F. *Old Time Agriculture in the Ads: Being a Compendium of Magazine and Newspaper Sales Literature Reminiscent of the Days When Farming Was the Way of Life and Horsepower came in Horses!* Aberdeen, S. Dak.: North Plains Press, 1970.
Key, Wilson Bryan. *Subliminal Seduction: Ad Media's Manipulation of a Not So Innocent America*. New York: Signet, 1973.
———. *Media Sexploitation*. Englewood Cliffs, N.J.: Prentice-Hall, 1976.

Klein, Walter J. *The Sponsored Film.* New York: Hastings House, 1976.

Kleppner, Otto. *Advertising Procedure.* 6th ed. Englewood Cliffs, N.J.: Prentice-Hall, 1973.

———, and Irving Settel, eds. *Exploring Advertising.* Englewood Cliffs, N.J.: Prentice-Hall, 1970.

Landauer, Bella C. *Early American Trade Cards.* New York: William Edwin Rudge, 1927.

Leech, Geoffrey N. *English in Advertising: A Linguistic Study of Advertising in Great Britain.* London: Longmans, Green, 1966.

Lois, George. *The Art of Advertising: George Lois on Mass Communication.* New York: Harry N. Abrams, 1977.

———, with Bill Pitts. *George, Be Careful.* New York: Saturday Review Press, 1972.

Lyon, David G. *Off Madison Avenue.* New York: G. P. Putnam's, 1966.

McGinnis, Joe. *The Selling of the President 1968.* New York: Trident Press, 1969.

McLuhan, Marshall. *The Mechanical Bride: Folklore of Industrial Man.* New York: Vanguard Press, 1951.

———. *Understanding Media: The Extensions of Man.* New York: McGraw-Hill, 1964.

Madison Avenue Handbook. New York: Peter Glenn Publications, 1958-.

Martineau, Pierre. *Motivation in Advertising: Motives That Make People Buy.* New York: McGraw-Hill, 1957.

Mayer, Martin. *Madison Avenue, U.S.A.* New York: Harper & Row, 1958.

———. *About Television.* New York: Harper & Row, 1972.

Media/Scope. Dictionary of Terms Useful to Buyers of Advertising. Skokie, Ill.: Standard Rate and Data Service, 1966.

Melcher, Daniel, and Nancy Larrick. *Printing and Promotion Handbook: How to Plan, Produce, and Use Printing, Advertising, and Direct Mail.* 3d ed. New York: McGraw-Hill, 1966.

Menten, Theodore, comp. *Advertising Art in the Art Deco Style.* New York: Dover Publications, 1975.

Millum, Trevor. *Images of Woman: Advertising in Women's Magazines.* Totowa, N.J.: Rowman and Littlefield, 1975.

Mott, Frank Luther. *American Journalism: A History of Newspapers in the United States Through 260 Years: 1690 to 1950.* Rev. ed. New York: Macmillan, 1950.

———. *A History of American Magazines.* Cambridge: Harvard University Press, 1957.

Nelson, Roy Paul. *The Design of Advertising.* 2d ed. Dubuque, Iowa: William C. Brown, 1973.

The New World of Advertising. Chicago: Crain Books, 1975.

Noble, Valerie. *The Effective Echo: A Dictionary of Advertising Slogans.* New York: Special Libraries Association, 1970.

Norins, Hanley. *The Compleat Copywriter: A Comprehensive Guide to All Phases of Advertising Communication.* New York: McGraw-Hill, 1966.

Ogilvy, David. *Confessions of an Advertising Man.* New York: Atheneum, 1971.

————. *Blood, Brains & Beer: The Autobiography of David Ogilvy*. New York: Atheneum, 1978.

Packard, Vance. *The Hidden Persuaders*. New York: David McKay, 1957.

————. *The Status Seekers*. New York: David McKay, 1959.

————. *The Waste Makers*. New York: David McKay, 1960.

Padley, Martin, ed. *A Handbook to Television Advertising*. New York: National Retail Merchants Association, 1969.

Pancoast, Chalmers Lowell. *Trail Blazers of Advertising*. New York: The Grafton Press, 1926. Reprint. New York: Arno Press, 1976.

Peck, William A. *Anatomy of Local Radio-TV Copy*. 4th ed. Blue Ridge Summit, Pa.: Tab Books, 1976.

Peterson, Theodore. *Magazines in the Twentieth Century*. Urbana: University of Illinois Press, 1964.

Polykoff, Shirley. *Does She or Doesn't She? And How She Did It*. Garden City, N.Y.: Doubleday, 1975.

Potter, David Morris. *People of Plenty: Economic Abundance and the American Character*. Chicago: University of Chicago Press, 1954.

Presbrey, Frank. *The History and Development of Advertising*. Garden City, N.Y.: Doubleday, Doran, 1929.

Preston, Ivan L. *The Great American Blow-Up: Puffery in Advertising and Selling*. Madison: The University of Wisconsin Press, 1975.

Quick, John. *Artists' and Illustrators' Encyclopedia*. 2d ed. New York: McGraw-Hill, 1977.

Raber, Nevin W., and Richard Coachys, comps. *Marketing: A Selected List of Current Titles* by the Foundation for the School of Business, Indiana University, Bloomington. Published by Division of Research, Graduate School of Business (no date).

Reeves, Rosser. *Reality in Advertising*. New York: Alfred A. Knopf, 1960, 1961, 1973.

Revzan, David A. *A Comprehensive Classified Marketing Bibliography*. Berkeley: University of California Press, 1951.

Richard, John M. *A Guide to Advertising Information Sources*. Scottsdale, Ariz.: MacDougal Publishing House, 1969.

Roberts, Peter. *Any Color So Long as It's Black: The First Fifty Years of Automobile Advertising*. New York: William Morrow, 1976.

Rorty, James. *Our Master's Voice: Advertising*. New York: John Day, 1934. Reprint. New York: Arno Press, 1976.

Rosenberg, Bernard, and David Manning White, eds. *Mass Culture Revisited*. New York: Van Nostrand Reinhold, 1971.

————. *Mass Culture: The Popular Arts in America*. London: The Free Press, 1957.

Rosenberg, Manuel. *The Art of Advertising*. New York: Harper & Brothers, 1930.

Rowsome, Frank, Jr. *They Laughed When I Sat Down: An Informal History of Advertising in Words and Pictures*. New York: McGraw-Hill, 1959.

————. *Think Small: The Story of Those Volkswagen Ads*. Brattleboro, Vt.: Stephen Greene Press, 1970.

————. *The Verse by the Side of the Road: The Story of the Burma-Shave Signs and Jingles*. Brattleboro, Vt.: Stephen Greene Press, 1965.

Sackheim, Maxwell. *My First 65 Years in Advertising*. Blue Ridge Summit, Pa.: Tab Books, 1975.

Sampson, Henry. *A History of Advertising from the Earliest Times*. London: Chatto and Windus, Piccadilly, 1874. Reprint. Detroit: Gale Research Company, 1974.

Sandage, Charles H., and Vernon Fryburger. *Advertising Theory and Practice*. 9th ed. Homewood, Ill.: Richard D. Irwin, 1975. First ed., 1935.

————, eds. *The Role of Advertising: A Book of Readings*. Homewood, Ill.: Richard D. Irwin, 1960.

Schrank, Jeffrey. *Deception Detection: An Educator's Guide to the Art of Insight*. Boston: Beacon Press, 1975.

Seldin, Joseph J. *The Golden Fleece*. New York: Macmillan, 1963.

Settel, Irving, and Norman Glenn. *Television Advertising and Production Handbook*. New York: Thomas Y. Crowell, 1953.

Smith, Ralph Lee. *The Health Hucksters*. New York: Thomas Y. Crowell, 1960.

Snyder, John. *Commercial Artist's Handbook*. New York: Watson-Guptill, 1973.

Standard Directory of Advertisers: The Agency Red Book. New York: National Register Publication Company, 1964-.

Stansfield, Richard H. *The Dartnell Advertising Manager's Handbook*. Chicago: Dartnell, 1969.

Stephenson, Howard, ed. *Handbook of Public Relations: The Standard Guide to Public Affairs and Communications*. 2d ed. New York: McGraw-Hill, 1971.

Stern, Jane, and Michael Stern. *Auto Ads*. New York: David Obst Books, 1978.

Sweeney, Russell C. *Coming Next Week: A Pictorial History of Film Advertising*. Cranbury, N.J.: A. S. Barnes, 1973.

Taplin, Walter. *Advertising: A New Approach*. Boston: Little, Brown, 1960.

Terrell, Neil. *The Power Technique of Radio-TV Copywriting*. Blue Ridge Summit, Pa.: Tab Books, 1971.

Thompson, J. Walter Company. *Advertising: An Annotated Bibliography*. New York: National Book League, 1972.

Tierney, Patricia E. *Ladies of the Avenue*. London: Bartholomew House, 1971.

Turner, E. S. *The Shocking History of Advertising!* New York: E. P. Dutton, 1953.

Tyler, Poyntz, ed. *Advertising in America*. The Reference Shelf Vol. 31, No. 5. New York: H. W. Wilson, 1959.

Ulanoff, Stanley M. *Advertising in America: An Introduction to Persuasive Communication*. New York: Hastings House, 1977.

Urdang, Laurence, ed. *Dictionary of Advertising Terms*. Chicago: Tatham, Laird and Kudner, 1977.

Wakeman, Frederick. *The Hucksters*. New York: Rinehart, 1946.

Walsh, John, Miriam Johnson, and Marged Sugarman. *Help Wanted: Case Studies of Classified Ads*. Salt Lake City, Utah: Olympus Publishing, 1975.

Watkins, Julian Lewis. *The 100 Greatest Advertisements: Who Wrote Them and What They Did.* New York: Dover Publications, 1949, 1959.

Weibel, Kathryn. *Mirror Mirror: Images of Women Reflected in Popular Culture.* Garden City, N.Y.: Anchor Books, Doubleday, 1977.

Whiteside, Thomas. *Selling Death: Cigarette Advertising and Public Health.* New York: Liveright, 1971.

Wight, Robin. *The Day the Pigs Refused to Be Driven to Market: Advertising and the Consumer Revolution.* New York: Random House, 1972.

Wood, James Playsted. *The Story of Advertising.* New York: Ronald Press, 1958.

————. *Magazines in the United States.* 3d ed. New York: Ronald Press, 1971.

Wright, John S., and Daniel S. Warner. *Speaking of Advertising.* New York: McGraw-Hill, 1963.

Wright, John S., and Willis Winter. *Advertising.* 3d ed. New York: McGraw-Hill, 1971.

Young, James Webb. *How to Become an Advertising Man.* Chicago: Advertising Publications, 1963.

Young, Margaret Labash et al. *Subject Directory of Special Libraries and Information Centers.* 4th ed. Detroit: Gale Research, 1977.

ANNUALS

Art Directors Annual. (Also called *The Annual of Advertising Editorial & Television Art & Design*). New York: Watson-Guptill.

Communication Arts Annual. Palo Alto, Calif.: Coyne and Blanchard.

Graphis Annual. New York: Hastings House.

Illustrators. New York: Hastings House.

Modern Publicity. New York: Viking Press.

The Penrose Annual. New York: Hastings House.

The Print Casebooks. New York: Watson-Guptill.

PERIODICALS

Accountants' Index. New York, 1920-.

Advertising Age. Chicago, 1930-.

Applied Science and Tehnology Index. New York, 1958-.

Art Direction. New York, 1949-.

Art Index. New York, 1929-.

Biological and Agricultural Index. (Formerly *Agricultural Index*). New York, 1964-.

Broadcasting. Washington, D.C., 1931-.

Business Periodicals Index. New York: 1958-.

Communication Arts. Palo Alto, Calif., 1959-.

Education Index. New York, 1929-.

Gallagher Report. New York, 1951-.

Graphics: USA. New York, 1964-.

Illustrator. Minneapolis, 1916-.

Index to Legal Periodicals. Buffalo, N.Y., 1926-.

Madison Avenue. New York, 1958-.
Marketing/Communications. (Formerly *Printer's Ink*). New York, 1967-72.
Print. New York, 1939-.
Printer's Ink. See *Marketing/Communications.*
Psychological Abstracts. Washington, D.C., 1927-.
Public Affairs Information Index. New York, 1915-.
Readers' Guide to Periodical Literature. New York, 1900-.
Sociological Abstracts. New York, 1953-.
Television/Radio Age. New York, 1953-.
Women's Studies Abstracts. Rush, N.Y., 1972-.

CHAPTER 2. Best Sellers

Suzanne Ellery Greene

Books that became best sellers have received widely varying amounts of attention from literary critics and analysts, historians, and students of societal values and behavior. Those best sellers that scholars determined to be of intrinsic literary merit have been written about many times over and generally are still widely read. A few books, judged to typify the thought of a particular period or considered to have played some major role in influencing the course of history, are read and written about as historical documents. The vast majority of best-selling novels and non-fiction works have simply been forgotten until quite recently. Those books considered to be lacking in literary merit were relegated to a category of popular entertainment unworthy of serious study. Even with the growing interest in popular culture, comparatively few people have chosen to study these books either for their own content and style or as a tool for broad analysis.

Whenever an attempt is made to use a medium like popular books to study the attitudes and values or behavior of a given time period, or as these change over time, the question of cause and effect must be considered. Do best sellers receive wide acceptance because they reflect their times? Or do they influence their readers to espouse new values and undertake new modes of life? The best answer is both. If all the best sellers of a given period are surveyed, it will be apparent that they differ widely, both in their subject matter and concerns and in their value systems. Some will closely resemble those of a preceding era. Others will appear to be the product of a rebel, writing about a hoped-for future. It may be that the best sellers are most useful for tracing changes in dominant attitudes, beliefs, and behavior patterns as they take place over the decades. If popular books are to be used as a reflection of society, it is very important to determine the precise identity of the readers.

While many publishers have taken advantage of the nostalgia craze to issue studies and reminiscences of old films and radio shows, comic books, vaudeville, and other entertainment fields, very little has appeared about the best sellers sold to millions of Americans and read by twice or three times that many. Specific genres such as the mystery story or the western have received far more attention than best sellers generally. This essay will provide a brief account of the predominant groups of books that were popular in the United States from colonial times to the present and it will be a guide to the reference works and resources most useful to those who wish to study best sellers.

HISTORIC OUTLINE

Before an historic overview of American best sellers can be undertaken, several points must be established. The first is the nature of the best sellers to be considered. Although the Bible, several cookbooks, and a few other reference works have outsold most other books in the United States, these will be excluded from this study. All other fiction and nonfiction works will be considered. Second, in such a brief account, only the major trends can be noted. The best sellers of a given period are never homogeneous. Within every period, books more typical of an earlier era continue to appear and gain popularity. During this century, the number of popular books has grown so rapidly that broad categorizations are exceedingly difficult to establish. The function of this overview will be to provide a brief account of the major new developments and leading trends in best-selling literature from colonial times to the present.

The first press in America opened in 1638 in Cambridge, Massachusetts, in conjunction with Harvard College. Its early output consisted of almanacs, sermons, catechisms, and *The Whole Booke of Psalmes*, generally known as *The Bay Psalm Book* (1640). Most books were imported from England, and booksellers reported sales of romances, collections of poetry, school books, and religious books. By the 1660s, American presses had begun to publish books in large enough editions and of sufficiently general interest that their products began to gain a wide circulation. Religious books dominated the market, while books about peculiarities of the New World, especially tales of captivity among the Indians, also gained a large readership.

Traditionally, the first American best seller is said to be *The Day of Doom*, a versified account of the final judgment day written by Michael Wigglesworth in 1662 and printed by Samuel Green in Cambridge. Even a century later, some school children were required to memorize the seemingly endless stanzas about people doomed to an eternity in hell and about the lucky few who were chosen by God for heavenly bliss. In 1664, the first of four editions printed over thirty years of Richard Baxter's collection of sermons, *A Call to the Unconverted*, appeared. This was translated by John Eliot for circulation among the local Indian tribes. Books such as *The Pilgrim's Progress* by John Bunyan, reprinted in Cambridge in 1681, *Husbandry Spiritualized* (1709) by John Flavel, an anonymous *The History of the Holy Jesus* (1745), and James Hervey's *Meditations and Contemplations*, published in Philadelphia in 1750, mark a continuation of the wide appeal of religious subjects.

The *Captivity and Restoration of Mary Rowlandson* (1682) and John Williams's *The Redeemed Captive* (1707) exemplify the popular captivity tales. Adventure stories complete with massacres, survival through various sorts of cleverness, an eventual return home, all punctuated by Christian devotion, made lively reading for colonists who felt threatened by God's order and by the wilderness outside their small towns. These narratives provide a valuable indication of the English settlers' attitudes toward the Indians as well as their heavy reliance on God.

As the colonial period progressed, literary concerns grew wider, and the philosophical points of view of the authors became more varied. During the 1740s, American editions of Samuel Richardson's sentimental and didactic tale *Pamela* (1744) and Alexander Pope's *Essay on Man* (1747) were best sellers. The decade before the Revolution was marked by the appearance of political best sellers representing all points of view. John Dickinson's conservative *Letters from a Farmer in Pennsylvania* (1768), a treatise entitled *Conciliation with America* (1775) written by Edmund Burke, and Thomas Paine's provocative *Common Sense* (1776).

The titles of the best sellers that were published from the 1770s until the end of the eighteenth century sound like a reading list for an English literature course. Many of these works came to be considered classics, and, despite the Revolution, the majority were authored by Englishmen. This list includes such novels as *The Vicar of Wakefield* (1772) by Oliver Goldsmith, *Clarissa* (1786) by Samuel Richardson, *Tristram Shandy* (1774) by Laurence Sterne, and *Charlotte Temple* (1794) by Susanna Rowson. Poetry such as John Milton's *Paradise Lost* (1777), William Cowper's *The Task* (1787), and an edition of Robert Burns's *Poems* (1788) sold well. Thomas Paine's *Age of Reason* (1794) and Benjamin Franklin's *Autobiography* (1794) were both widely read. *The Federalist* (1788), arguing for the adoption of the new constitution, had a large audience. *Paradise Lost* and John Fox's *Book of Martyrs* (1793) indicate that religion had not been forgotten although it was relegated to a less central position than it had held a century earlier. It is quite evident that the readers of best sellers had a wide range of interests, were heavily influenced by British literary culture, but also read many American products.

History and heroism dominated the best sellers of the first three decades of the nineteenth century. Books written in America about American subjects predominated for the first time. Parson Mason Weems's *Life of Washington* (1800), in which the cherry tree story first appeared, was read avidly, even in rural areas where it was carried by itinerant book peddlers. Washington Irving's *History of New York* (1809) and his later *Sketch Book* (1819) enjoyed wide sales. Jane Porter's novels about patriotic heroes, *Thaddeus of Warsaw* (1804) and *Scottish Chiefs* (1810), helped prepare the way for the enormous success of the tales of adventure and nationalism by Sir Walter Scott, including *Guy Mannering* (1815), *Rob Roy* (1818), *Ivanhoe* (1820), and *Kenilworth* (1821). James Fenimore Cooper created a prototype American hero and his adventures as in *The Spy* (1821) and the Leatherstocking stories of *The Pioneers* (1823). *The Last of the Mohicans* (1826) and *The Deerslayer* (1841) were almost as widely read as Scott's novels. The popularity of Scott and Cooper continued through the century.

The 1830s and 1840s are marked by long lists of books that sold extremely well, in part because of the new practice of issuing cheap reprints of recent popular books. First in newspaper format, then in paperbound books, best sellers became available in twenty-five-cent editions. From this time on, cheap editions of popular books were always on sale for readers who could not afford the more expensive originals. Charles Dickens was an enormously popular author whose novels of sentiment and social reform were snatched up on issue. His sickly children, impoverished innocents, and evil rich men reduced thousands of American readers to tears and helped prepare the way for the American-produced, tear-jerking, sentimental novels that followed.

Dickens's works were not the only ones whose sales benefited from the inexpensive reprints. Readers who had not bought the earlier dollar editions of Scott and Cooper could now afford book purchases. Imitators of Scott, Cooper, and Dickens abounded. The best known was Joseph Holt Ingraham, who wrote thrillers such as *The Pirates of the Gulf* (1836), religious novels such as *The Prince of the House of David* (1855), and novels about life in the city such as *Jemmy Daly, or the Little News Vendor* (1843). Historical novels such as *The Last Days of Pompeii* (1834) by Edward Bulwer-Lytton and *The Three Musketeers* (1844) by Alexandre Dumas were popular, as were histories such as Jared Sparks's *Life of Washington* (1839), William Prescott's *Conquest of Mexico* (1843), and Thomas Macauley's *History of England* (1849). Maria Monk's *Awful Disclosures* (1836), an anti-Catholic tract purporting to reveal the scandals of life in a nunnery, added a bit of sensationalism to the best-seller lists.

Mid-nineteenth-century America supported the rise of the sentimental domestic novel, often written by and about women and problems such as poverty, prostitution, drunken and perfidious husbands and lovers—all presented from a woman's point of view. Nathaniel Hawthorne complained that "America is now wholly given over to a damned mob of scribbling women." Some examples of the more famous products of this group include *The Wide, Wide World* (1850) by Susan Warner and *The Lamplighter* (1854) by Maria S. Cummins. T. S. Arthur's *Ten Nights in a Bar-Room* (1854), written in a similar vein, was used as a temperance tract by various prohibition societies. Mrs. E. D. E. N. Southworth, the most prolific of the best-selling women authors, wrote over sixty novels, including *Ishmael* (1864) and *Self-Raised* (1864), which sold over two million copies each.

While the sentimental novels dealt with many of the problems that concerned the nation's reformers, the most divisive issue of all was largely ignored in the best sellers of the day. *Uncle Tom's Cabin*, written in 1852 by Harriet Beecher Stowe, was one of the few that directly attacked the slavery system and wielded an enormous impact in converting many disinterested readers into active opponents of slavery. Stowe's tear-jerking episodes and moralistic base closely resembled those of the other sentimental writers. *Uncle Tom's Cabin* stands as one of the few examples of a novel that clearly had a major impact on popular thought. Swinging many Northern readers to an antislavery position, the book gained acceptability by emphasizing the physical brutality and destruction of families inherent in slavery while omitting the questions of political rights and racial equality which, at that point, seemed an issue only to the most radical abolitionists.

The period of the late nineteenth and early twentieth century is marked primarily by the diversity of the popular forms, with no one innovation predominating. Sentimental and domestic novels, religious books, local color stories, historical fiction and nonfiction, adventures, some rather sensationalist exposés, and a few detective stories all gained wide readership throughout the period. Despite the fact that very few of these are read today, even by students of literary history, the period is important in that it marked out the broad categories of fictional best sellers as they have continued to the present day. Limitations of space permit only brief examples of these types to be given.

While Laura Jean Libbey produced sentimental domestic novels of the prewar sort, a new group of "glad-books" began to appear. Many centered on a child character and became children's classics. These include *Rebecca of Sunnybrook Farm* (1904) by Kate Douglas Wiggin and *Pollyanna* (1913) by Eleanor Porter. Grace Livingston Hill and Gene Stratton-Porter produced other glad-books, called "molasses fiction" by their critics, that remained best-selling types through World War I.

Religious novels like *St. Elmo* (1867) by Augusta J. Evans and *Barriers Burned Away* (1872) by Edward Payson Roe paved the way for some enormously popular writers like Lew Wallace, whose *Ben Hur* (1880) sold over a million copies through the Sears, Roebuck and Company mail-order catalog alone. Charles Sheldon's *In His Steps* (1897), in which he presented accounts of how contemporary people would change their lives if they really followed Christ's teachings, sold even more copies. Harold Bell Wright, in books like *The Shepherd of the Hills* (1907) and *The Eyes of the World* (1914), combined religious morality with the strenuous outdoor life and a love story, thus putting together a very successful formula that combined several of the most popular subjects of fiction. Lloyd Douglas, who later produced novels like *The Magnificent Obsession* (1929) and *The Robe* (1942), followed in this same tradition.

Not all historical novels were religious. Winston Churchill's historical stories such as *Richard Carvel* (1899) and *The Crisis* (1904) made him one of the most popular writers of the turn of the century. Owen Wister's *The Virginian* (1902) put before the American reading public a character who is sometimes described as the first cowboy hero. Westerns and other masculine adventure stories grew in popularity. Zane Grey, whose more than fifty novels were read by millions, remained on the best-seller lists from the appearance of *The Spirit of the Border* in 1906 through 1924 with *The Call of the Canyon*. Writers like H. Rider Haggard and Rudyard Kipling set their adventures in the more exotic settings of Africa and India. Jules Verne's fantasies about outer space and the world beneath the sea moved even further away from the familiar. Mystery stories like those of Arthur Conan Doyle in the late nineteenth century and Mary Roberts Rinehart in the early twentieth century marked the beginning of the rise to predominance of yet another sort of escapist adventure.

Two new kinds of literature caused an enormous sensation in the early twentieth century. The muckrakers' exposés about business, industry, and politics were read avidly. Books like Upton Sinclair's *The Jungle* (1906) about the Chicago meatpacking business shook the public. More sensationally, Elinor Glyn's *Three Weeks* (1907) drew both enthusiastic readers and official banning with its vivid account of a seduction scene and the following affair between an Englishman and a princess.

The questioning and criticism of society's traditional values and behavior patterns grew more pronounced and more popular during the 1920s. Readers turned away from political questions and emphasized a search for meaning in the life of the individual. Even Sinclair Lewis's social criticisms like *Main Street* (1920) and *Babbitt* (1922) showed the effect that forced conformity had on the individuals involved. More typical of the best-selling novels of the decade were *The Sheik* (1921) by Edith M. Hull and *The Private Life of Helen of Troy* (1925) by John Erskine, in which the characters simply took off and did their own thing. Nonfiction lists were dominated by histories, biographies, and fad books such as *Diet and Health* by Lulu Hunt Peters (1924), crossword puzzle books, and sagas of the South Seas.

The 1930s saw a swing back to historical novels. The leading characters almost invariably stood as successful examples of the old American rugged individualism. In books like *Drums Along the Mohawk* (1936) by W. D. Edmonds and *Northwest Passage* (1937) by Kenneth Roberts, the heroes prevailed against overwhelming odds by dint of their own hard work and intelligence. Two epics headed the best-seller lists for two consecutive years: *Anthony Adverse* by Hervey Allen in 1933 and 1934 and *Gone with the Wind* in 1936 and 1937. An obvious search for stable, moral values appeared in novels like Pearl Buck's *The Good Earth* (1931) and Lloyd Douglas's *The Magnificent Obsession* (1929) and *Green Light* (1935). Despite the severity of the Depression and the rising tide of nazism in Germany, neither fiction nor nonfiction best sellers dealt deeply with either problem until the very end of the decade.

Best sellers that appeared during the years from World War II to the present can be treated as one unit, despite some changes that have taken place. The major noticeable feature of all these books, both individual works of fiction and the aggregate yearly lists of both fiction and nonfiction, is the recognition of the complexity of the world. Politics, religion, sex, psychology, health, love, and many other topics are combined in one book and certainly over the lists of books. Social concerns, from poverty to minority rights to ecology, are reflected in the best sellers. Several major trends can be picked out of the enormous variety, which itself is the most outstanding feature of the period.

From the appearance of *Mein Kampf* on the best-seller list of 1939 through the middle 1950s, both fiction and nonfiction lists revealed a very wide interest in World War II and subjects related to it. Other than that, the best sellers reflected few political concerns until after 1955, when books like *On the Beach* (1957) by Neville Shute, *Dr. Zhivago* (1958) by Boris Pasternak, *Exodus* (1959) by Leon Uris, and *The Ugly American* (1959) by William Lederer and Eugene Burdick heralded increasing political awareness that was to continue, albeit unevenly, into the 1970s.

The historical romantic adventure story, a leading type of best seller for so long, declined in favor of novels like those mentioned above that treat contemporary problems and, a new favorite, suspense stories like two that came out in 1969—*Airport* by Arthur Hailey and *The Salzburg Connection* by Helen MacInnes. Many books, like Peter Benchley's sensational *Jaws* (1974), were made into films, which led to still higher book sales.

One other strong trend since World War II is the increasingly explicit descriptions of sex, both in the fictional characters' actions and in nonfiction best sellers like A. C. Kinsey's *Sexual Behavior in the Human Male* (1948) and the William H. Masters and Virginia E. Johnson study, *Human Sexual Response,* published in 1966. Popularized science, psychology, and health books, like Eric Berne's *Games People Play* (1965) and Jean Nidetch's *The Weight Watcher's Cook Book* (1968), received wide readership also.

From even a brief, oversimplified historical survey of American best sellers, it is clear that they do change drastically both in topics and in style, reflecting changes in the attitudes and the values of the readers. These are useful tools for looking at popular concerns in any given period and tracing their changes over a period of time.

REFERENCE WORKS

Surprisingly few reference works on best sellers are available to the researcher. Information on best sellers can be found in broader-based works on literature, intellectual history, and the publishing trade, but the researcher must dig a bit to find the specific information sought. Several exceptions to this generality provide the clear starting point for any study of American best sellers.

The classic study is Frank Luther Mott's analysis of best-selling books, *Golden Multitudes*, published in 1947. Although it treats books published only through 1945, it is clearly the most useful reference for the beginning researcher. Particularly valuable are the listings in appendixes A and B of the "overall best sellers in the United States" and the "better sellers." In Appendix A, Mott lists all books believed to have sold 1 percent or more of the total population at the beginning of the decade in which they appeared. Appendix B lists the runners-up. One possible drawback in working from Mott's list is that his use of cumulative sales figures leads to the inclusion of books that did not sell well when they first came out. In the main text of *Golden Multitudes*, Mott analyzes the major schools of popular literature and gives brief excerpts from many of the books he mentions.

James D. Hart's *The Popular Book* of 1950 is the other available survey that combines listings and historically organized analyses of best sellers. His list is selective and is not based on specific sales requirements. Hart's study provides an exhaustive bibliography for each chapter.

The other basic reference in the field is *80 Years of Best Sellers* by Alice Payne Hackett and James H. Burke. Hackett and Burke list the top ten best sellers for each year from 1895 to 1975, based on yearly sales figures. Separation of fiction and nonfiction lists begins in 1917. After each year's list, the authors present a very brief account of the connections between the books and annual events. Total sales figures for top best sellers and separate lists of novelty books, home reference books, cookbooks, juveniles, mysteries, religious novels, and westerns provide a good starting place for the topical researcher. Most of the figures here come from the trade journal *Publishers Weekly*.

For more detailed information, one can go straight to the source, *Publishers Weekly*, published by R. R. Bowker Company, or to *The Bowker Annual of Library and Book Trade Information. Publishers Weekly* began calculating best sellers in 1912. A literary magazine, *The Bookman*, contains lists from 1895, when it began publication. A listing of sources for comparisons with other nations can be found in another trade reference, *The Book Trade of the World*, edited by Sigfred Taubert. In two volumes, it provides basic information on the book business in most countries and a list of references for more detailed study.

A number of books exist that list books and/or authors and provide very brief information on each. These would provide a useful starting place for facts on a particular writer or best seller. Listing both books and authors are: James D. Hart's *The Oxford Companion to American Literature*, which has been updated several times, and *American Authors and Books, 1640-1940* by William J. Burke and Will D. Howe. Material on recent writers can be found in *Contemporary Authors: A Bio-Bibliographical Guide to Current Authors and Their Works*. Volume I came out in 1962, and a cumulative index appears regularly. One other possibly useful book in this category is *America in Fiction* by Otis W. Coan and Richard G. Lillard, which, by its own description, provides an annotated list of novels that interpret aspects of life in the United States.

Since there is not space in this chapter to list material on specific authors or books, it should be pointed out that the *Library of Congress Catalog* and the *National Union Catalog* would contain listings of most books under author, title, and subject headings. The *Readers' Guide to Periodical Literature* lists articles from selected periodicals by topic and author. Scholarly journal articles were indexed from 1907 to 1965 in the *International Index to Periodicals*. In 1966, it became the *Social Sciences and Humanities Index* and, in 1975, simply the *Social Sciences Index*. Journals of groups like the Modern Language Association are indexed separately, but do not contain much useful material on best sellers. A recently published index, entitled *Popular Abstracts*, contains brief summaries of articles from the *Journal of Popular Culture*, a number of which treat best sellers. The computerized data banks do not contain much useful material as of this writing.

RESEARCH COLLECTIONS

The most useful secondary material can be found in any large library. The best sellers themselves may be more difficult to locate. Recent best sellers are held in the collections of most large public libraries. Certainly, the nearest public library is the place to begin. When that source is exhausted, the easiest thing is to use the interlibrary loan facilities to locate and borrow specific books not available locally. Should you want to work in one place with a large collection of best sellers, the places to go are the New York Public Library and the Library of Congress in Washington. Their holdings are extensive; most books can be obtained through interlibrary loan facilities, however.

Several specialized collections merit mention. The New York Public Library owns a large collection of over thirteen thousand volumes of nineteenth-century fiction as well as the Beadle Dime Novel Collection of about fourteen hundred volumes. The Amelia Gayle Gorgas Library at the University of Alabama owns a complete set of the Armed Services editions of paperbacks issued during World War II. The Center for Research Libraries in Chicago, whose handbook and catalogs are available at member libraries throughout the nation, has several collections that might be useful in doing research on best sellers. The center's American Culture series consists of microfilm copies of fifty-two hundred works published by 1876. The titles are listed in the *Bibliography of American Culture, 1493-1875* compiled by David R. Weimer. A collection of *American Fiction* has on microfilm about twelve thousand titles listed in a bibliography of that name compiled by Lyle Wright. The center also owns a collection of early American imprints (1639-1800), nineteenth-century American literature, and forty thousand volumes of children's books. The Mugar Memorial Library at Boston University has a valuable research source in its Twentieth-Century Archives. This collection contains manuscripts, journals, diaries, reviews, and correspondence, as well as published works of a number of twentieth-century authors, including some who wrote best sellers. The archives are open to the public. A description of the holdings and a list of the individuals can be obtained from the Special Collections Department of the library.

HISTORY AND CRITICISM

Presenting a survey of the history and criticism of best sellers necessitates dividing the material into manageable categories; the most basic category consists of writings about the best sellers themselves, both overall surveys and period studies. The readership of the best sellers merits considerable attention, especially by the student who is looking for reflections and indications of changes in popular attitudes and values. For whom or to whom do these books speak? Studies in the history of publishing often provide information on the marketing and buying of the books and some interesting sidelights on the stories of individual best sellers. These as well as separate studies often provide information about book clubs and the appearance of various cheap editions, both of which have resulted in major changes in the makeup of the reading public. Published reviews provide an indication of the critical acclaim of a book and of what the potential reader thought he was getting. Excluded from this survey will be studies of specific types of books, such as mysteries and westerns, which are treated elsewhere in these volumes. Also omitted will be biographies of individual authors and works on individual best sellers; these can be easily located in any subject index. Almost no anthologies of excerpts from best sellers exist. The few books that do include reprinted material will be treated in this section since they all contain criticism as well.

Except for the lack of anthologies, enough general work on overall patterns of best sellers exists to give the beginning student or researcher a sound start. Russel B. Nye's widely used book on the popular arts in America, *The Unembarrassed Muse*, includes several chapters on popular literature, which form an excellent condensed survey. *Golden Multitudes* by Frank Luther Mott and *The Popular Book* by James D. Hart are the two major books that survey and analyze popular literature from the colonial period to the time of their writing (1947 and 1950, respectively). Both include inquiries into the readership, methods of circulation, and publishing trends, as well as commentary on the best sellers themselves. Nye and Hart assembled extensive bibliographies that are very useful.

The few books that do contain excerpts from best sellers do not deal with them exclusively. While they might be useful for classroom assignments, they would be of little value to the serious researcher who would have to read much more extensively. Three such collections do, however, deserve mention. *America Through the Looking Glass: A Historical Reader in Popular Culture*, edited by David Bruner et al., has selections from best sellers and other popular writing, both fiction and nonfiction. These are arranged chronologically and have been chosen as mirrors of the contemporary culture. While they are extremely well-chosen selections, the majority of the material does not come from best sellers. *Understanding American History Through Fiction*, edited by Warren A. Beck and Myles L. Clowers, also includes portions of a number of best sellers and other fictional works as well. These selections are arranged around such topics as manifest destiny, slavery, the growth of American capitalism, and World War II. These volumes would be a valuable addition to an American history course, but they do not contain enough material on best sellers to be useful for specialized research. One anthology, Donald McQuade and Robert Atwan's *Popular Writing in America*, contains an extensive section of excerpts from best sellers, both fiction and nonfiction. Selections include not only the standard ones like *Uncle Tom's Cabin* and *Poor Richard's Almanac*, but also portions of *Tarzan of the Apes*, *I, The Jury* by Mickey Spillane, *The Godfather, Love Story,* Emily Post's *Etiquette,* and Dale Carnegie's *How to Win Friends and Influence People.* This book would be the most useful to use for a classroom unit on best-selling literature but, once again, is far too limited for advanced work. All three of these books contain interpretive material relating chosen selections to the events and culture of their times.

Although the field is not overcrowded, a few other general interpretive efforts are available. Leo Gurko's *Heroes, Highbrows and the Popular Mind* touches on a lot of material germane to a study of best sellers. Gurko describes the most typical heroes of American popular literature and connects changes in these types to changing world conditions. His analysis is perceptive. Another analytical book containing many insightful comments is *The Half-World of American Culture* by Carl Bode. The author of both historical and literary studies, Bode here includes a number of best sellers in the material he uses to make cross-century comparisons. Q. D. Leavis's book, *Fiction and the Reading Public,* contains a section of analysis and comparison of old and recent best sellers, as well as the patterns, styles, and contents of "literary" and "popular" books. The author deals with books that were best sellers in Great Britain and in the United States and with the reading public of both countries. John G. Cawelti's *Adventure, Mystery and Romance* is a theoretical study of formulas seen in westerns, detective and crime fiction, and social melodrama. He develops a methodology that can be applied to other popular literary formulas. The title of James O'Donnell Bennett's book, *Much Loved Books: Best Sellers of the Ages,* tempts the reader in the field, but this series of articles from the Chicago *Tribune* is not particularly useful. Robert Bingham Downs's collection of essays, *Famous American Books,* consists of five- to ten-page studies of fifty books designed to illustrate and illuminate the impact of books on the course of history. He includes a number of best sellers, from the early *Day of Doom* down through Ralph Nader's *Unsafe at Any Speed.* His selections and analyses are quite good. Bernard Rosenberg and David Manning White edited *Mass Culture: The Popular Arts in America,* which contains a section on mass literature and includes chapters on the question of formula, who reads what books and why, and the role of paperback books. All these are applicable to any study of best sellers. A work that studies a rather technical aspect of the field is James Calvin Craig's *The Vocabulary Load of the Nation's Best Sellers, 1662-1945.* One final slim volume, a classic primarily because of its title, cannot go unmentioned. *Lincoln's Doctor's Dog* by George Stevens considers how a book becomes a best seller and concludes that, at least in 1938, word-of-mouth publicity led to the greatest sales. Stevens recounts stories about a number of best sellers, treating *Anthony Adverse* in the greatest detail.

A number of good period studies exist, some written specifically about popular literature, others more generally about the cultural life of a particular era. A work on colonial culture, *Literary Culture in Early New England, 1620-1730* by Thomas Goddard Wright, contains a remarkable listing of books held in public and in private collections, good material on the Boston booksellers, and provides interesting information on the reading elite. Although the emphasis lies in the area of high culture, the book's value is enhanced by providing the information necessary to make comparisons between elite and popular literature. Russel B. Nye's work, *The Cultural Life of the New Nation, 1776-1830*, contains a chapter entitled "The Quest for a National Literature," which concentrates more heavily on best sellers. The entire book provides a fine survey of the culture of the period. A more specialized study, Herbert Ross Brown's *The Sentimental Novel in America, 1789-1860*, includes many best sellers in its analysis. Other studies of early American novels include *The Rise of the American Novel* by Alexander Cowie and *The Early American Novel* by Lily D. Loshe.

Several books exist that treat best sellers of the mid-nineteenth century. A good starting place is Carl Bode's *The Anatomy of American Popular Culture, 1840-1861*, a thorough study that includes a section on "popular print" containing an analysis of fiction and nonfiction and comparing trends of that time with those of earlier periods. Bode considers both the works and their reception. Helen Papashvily's *All the Happy Endings* treats popular novels, as does a dissertation by Dorothy C. Hockey, "The Good and the Beautiful: A Study of Best-Selling Novels in America, 1865-1920." Quentin Reynolds's *The Fiction Factory*, a history of the publishing firm of Street and Smith, contains some interesting material on best sellers of the late nineteenth century. Grant C. Knight wrote a study on the final years of the nineteenth century, *The Critical Period in American Literature, 1890-1900*, which integrates the literary and social history of the time. No overall study exists connecting best sellers with the course of nineteenth-century history, and other than the books by Bode and Knight, most of the available material is literary criticism, not serious analysis of the popular culture.

More has been written about twentieth-century best sellers than about those of the preceding periods. Clearly the place to begin research is *80 Years of Best Sellers* by Hackett and Burke. In addition to the invaluable compilation of the yearly best sellers, the book contains a bibliography that includes most of the major articles written about best sellers during the century. Because that source is so complete, those articles will not be relisted here.

A number of volumes have been published on American literature of the twentieth century. The vast majority of those limit their concern to the critically acclaimed books rather than to the best sellers. A few best sellers, such as novels by Ernest Hemingway, William Faulkner, and Thomas Wolfe, are included in literary histories, but most are not. For points of comparison, it might be useful to look at standard works like Alfred Kazin's *On Native Grounds* and Malcolm Cowley's *The Literary Situation*; the latter treats a wider range of authors than does the former. Another useful volume, not specifically on best sellers, is John Hohenberg's work *The Pulitzer Prizes*. Hohenberg lists the prize winners, many of which were best sellers, and analyzes changing patterns in the selections, relating them to the course of world and national events.

A number of books study the best sellers of one decade or make comparisons over several decades. Grant C. Knight's integration of literature and social history, *The Strenuous Age in American Literature*, discusses many best sellers that appeared between 1900 and 1910. A Radcliffe College dissertation by Anna Lee Hopson entitled "Best Sellers: Media of Mass Expression" thoroughly compares the popular novels written from 1907 to 1916 with those written from 1940 to 1949. She concentrates on courtship and kinship relations. Suzanne Ellery Greene's *Books for Pleasure: Popular Fiction 1914-1945* uses best sellers as a reflection of changes in popular attitudes and values and treats such categories as political and religious involvement and beliefs, race and ethnicity, class relationships, family, and sex. The detailed methodology presented might prove useful to others working in this field. *Novelists' America: Fiction as History, 1910-1940* by Nelson Manfred Blake shows how a group of novels can be used to study social conditions and popular concerns. Although he concentrates on elite writers, best-selling authors like Sinclair Lewis and John Steinbeck are included. The book's bibliography lists general works about American fiction and biographical and critical studies of the individual authors.

Although much of the material on best sellers since World War II exists in the form of reviews, journal articles, or studies of individual writers, there are some books that make a useful introduction to the period. Among these are: *The Novel Now* by Anthony Burgess; *Recent American Fiction: Some Critical Views*, edited by Joseph Waldmeir; *Working for the Reader* by book reviewer Herbert Mitgang; *A Question of Quality*, edited by Louis Filler; and *Bright Book of Life* by Alfred Kazin. Most of these are collections of essays although Burgess's book provides a unified thematic study.

Book reviews provide an excellent source of information about contemporary opinions of best sellers by nationally recognized critics and by more popular writers. Although many newspapers, magazines, and journals review books, the listings here will be limited to those sources that yield the most material on the greatest number of best sellers.

Publishers Weekly, whose best seller listings began in 1912, has printed reviews of most major books since it first appeared in 1872. *The Library*

Journal prints some long reviews and many one-paragraph overviews designed primarily for librarians who are considering purchase. They are organized in topical sections. Since 1967, R. R. Bowker has published an annual volume of selections of reviews under the title, *The Library Journal Book Review*. Another early journal, *The Bookman*, calculated national best sellers from its first year in print and reviewed most major books that appeared from 1895 until it ceased publication in 1933. The *New York Times Book Review* became a separate section in 1896. Arno Press published a bound index to reviews from 1896 to 1970. In 1951, the *Times* published *A Century of Books*, a selection of one hundred reviews. Although the *New York Times* does not include every book published, its reviews, like those of *The Bookman*, provide much detail and a critical analysis. *The Booklist*, a publication of the American Library Association, tends to give very brief reviews of a large number of books. *The Saturday Review of Literature*, which became *The Saturday Review* in 1951, contains long reviews of all books that its editors have judged to merit discussion. One of the newest nationally circulated publications in this field is *The New York Review of Books*, which publishes detailed reviews and represents a comparatively elitist point of view. It should be noted that all these journals contain advertisements which are useful in understanding what the publisher wishes to convey to potential purchasers about his books.

Three indexes can aid significantly in a search for reviews of a particular book. The *Book Review Digest* prints indexes by subject and author and publishes a cumulative index every five years. It provides very brief excerpts that indicate the range of reviews. These can then be found in their entirety. Another good source for listings of reviews is provided by the *National Library Service Cumulative Book Review Index, 1905-1974*. In 1965, the Gale Research Company began publishing the *Book Review Index*, which provides simple listings of review by author and by year.

Numerous histories of the publishing industry and of the individual publishing houses contain some information on best sellers, especially as these are seen from the publisher's point of view. Some also consider the impact of factors like the first International Copyright Law of 1891, which gave a boost to American authors by cutting into the sale of cheap editions of pirated European works. Many books try to analyze the influence of developments like the growth of the paperback industry and the appearance of book clubs. Two excellent and thorough histories of the general field provide more than enough information for most readers. John William Tebbel's multivolume *A History of Book Publishing in the United States* contains a short section devoted to best sellers and numerous valuable charts. A briefer study, *Book Publishing in America* by Charles Allen Madison, includes a chronology of major events, information on the book clubs and inexpensive reprint editions, and a thorough bibliography that provides titles of many histories of individual publishing houses, memoirs, literary histories, criticism, and topical studies.

Several other sources deserve mention in this section. Charles Lee's history of the Book-of-the-Month Club, *The Hidden Public*, would be useful for someone interested in the relationship between best sellers and book clubs. It should be noted that most of the book clubs will provide the researcher or interested student with lists of their selections and perhaps other material on their operations. A number of studies of the paperback industry exist, including *Paperback Books: A Pocket History* by John Tebbel, *The Paperbound Book in America* by Frank L. Schick, and *Paper-Bound Books in America* by Freeman Lewis. Two anthologies that contain useful material on publishing history, book clubs, and cheap editions are the *Bowker Lectures on Book Publishing* published by the R. R. Bowker Company, and *Books and the Mass Market* by Harold Guinzburg, Robert W. Frase, and Theodore Waller.

Whenever best sellers are used as a tool to study the people who read them, it is essential to ascertain as precisely as possible the makeup of that reading public at the time under consideration. Most scientifically prepared studies have appeared since 1930 and treat only contemporary statistics. However, one excellent study, entitled *Literacy in Colonial New England* by Kenneth A. Lockridge, shows a method for analyzing such information from an earlier period. Three thorough studies treat reading during the Depression: Orion Howard Cheney in *Economic Survey of the Book Industry 1930-1931*, Douglas Waples in *Research Memorandum on Social Aspects of Reading in the Depression*, and Louis R. Wilson in *The Geography of Reading* consider book sales and library distribution and correlate them with geographic, cultural, and economic factors. Irving Harlow Hart noted in an article, "The One Hundred Leading Authors of Best-Selling Fiction from 1895 to 1944" in *Publishers Weekly*, that for the period 1919 to 1931 there was an 80-percent correlation between book store best sellers and books with the highest library circulation. Several articles reprinted in Rosenberg and White's *Mass Culture: The Popular Arts in America* deal with questions of reading habits and availability of books in the 1950s; the most useful are Bernard Berelson's article "Who Reads What Books and Why" and Alan Dutscher's account of "The Book Business in America." Roger H. Smith's *The American Reading Public: What It Reads* is a study from the 1960s.

Related to statistical information about the reading public are the more speculative studies about what makes a particular book sell well. In addition to comments on the subject in the various histories of the publishing industry, there are some surveys of buyers and studies of marketing techniques available. Useful insights can be found in *People and Books* by

Henry C. Link and Harry Arthur Hopf and in George Blagowidow's *Optimum Marketing of Trade Books: Based on Scientific Forecasting Methodology*. This latter work, while very technical, touches on many of the factors involved in choosing and marketing books. A less technical survey of why buyers choose certain books can be found in a *Publishers Weekly* article by Robert Banker, "What Makes a Book Sell?"

Clearly, much material related to best sellers is available. Much of this, however, comes from industry sources and does not provide the analytical structure needed by the serious student. No comprehensive work on best sellers has been published since Hart's *The Popular Book* came out in 1950. No good anthologies exist. In short, although they were read by more people than other books at a particular time, best sellers have been neglected as a tool for studying American culture.

BIBLIOGRAPHY

BOOKS AND ARTICLES

Banker, Robert. "What Makes a Book Sell?" *Publishers Weekly*, 166 (December 4, 1954), 2179-2182.

Beck, Warren A., and Myles L. Clowers. *Understanding American History Through Fiction*. New York: McGraw-Hill, 1975.

Bennett, James O'Donnell. *Much Loved Books: Best Sellers of the Ages*. New York: Liveright, 1927.

Blagowidow, George. *Optimum Marketing of Trade Books: Based on Scientific Forecasting Methodology*. New York: R. R. Bowker, 1965.

Blake, Nelson Manfred. *Novelists' America: Fiction as History, 1910-1940*. Syracuse: Syracuse University Press, 1969.

Bode, Carl. *The Anatomy of American Popular Culture 1840-1861*. Berkeley: University of California Press, 1959.

———. *The Half-World of American Culture*. Carbondale, Ill.: Southern Illinois University Press, 1965.

Bowker Annual of Library and Book Trade Information. New York: R. R. Bowker, 1955-.

Bowker Lectures on Book Publishing. New York: R. R. Bowker, 1957.

Brown, Herbert Ross. *The Sentimental Novel in America, 1789-1860*. Durham: Duke University Press, 1940.

Brown, Ray B., and Christopher Geist, eds. *Popular Abstracts*. Bowling Green, Ohio: Bowling Green University Popular Press, 1978.

Bruner, David, Robert D. Marcus, and Jorj Tilson, eds. *America Through the Looking Glass: A Historical Reader in Popular Culture*. Englewood Cliffs, N.J.: Prentice-Hall, 1974.

Burgess, Anthony. *The Novel Now*. New York: Norton, 1967.

Burke, William J., and Will D. Howe. *American Authors and Books, 1640-1940*. New York: Gramercy Publishing, 1943.

Cawelti, John G. *Adventure, Mystery and Romance.* Chicago: University of Chicago Press, 1976.

A Century of Books. New York: New York Times, 1951.

Cheney, Orion Howard. *Economic Survey of the Book Industry 1930-1931.* New York: R. R. Bowker, 1931.

Coan, Otis W., and Richard G. Lillard. *America in Fiction: An Annotated List of Novels That Interpret Aspects of Life in the United States.* Stanford: Stanford University Press, 1945.

Contemporary Authors: A Bio-Bibliographical Guide to Current Authors and Their Works. Detroit: Gale Research, yearly from 1962.

Cowie, Alexander. *The Rise of the American Novel.* New York: American Book, 1948.

Cowley, Malcolm. *The Literary Situation.* New York: Viking, 1954.

Craig, James Calvin. *The Vocabulary Load of the Nation's Best-Sellers, 1662-1945.* Ann Arbor: University Microfilms, 1954.

Downs, Robert Bingham. *Famous American Books.* New York: McGraw-Hill, 1971.

Filler, Louis. *A Question of Quality.* Bowling Green, Ohio: Bowling Green University Popular Press, 1976.

Greene, Suzanne Ellery. *Books for Pleasure: Popular Fiction 1914-1945.* Bowling Green, Ohio: Bowling Green University Popular Press, 1974.

Guinzburg, Harold K., Robert W. Frase, and Theodore Waller. *Books and the Mass Market.* Urbana: University of Illinois Press, 1953.

Gurko, Leo. *Heroes, Highbrows and the Popular Mind.* Indianapolis: Bobbs-Merrill, 1953.

Hackett, Alice Payne, and James H. Burke. *80 Years of Best-Sellers.* New York: R. R. Bowker, 1977.

Hart, Irving Harlow. "The One Hundred Leading Authors of Best Sellers in Fiction from 1895 to 1944." *Publishers Weekly,* 149 (January 19, 1946), 285-290.

Hart, James D. *The Popular Book: A History of America's Literary Taste.* New York: Oxford, 1950.

————. *The Oxford Companion to American Literature.* New York: Oxford, 1956.

Hockey, Dorothy C. "The Good and the Beautiful: A Study of Best Selling Novels in America, 1865-1920." Ph.D. dissertation, Western Reserve University, 1947.

Hohenberg, John. *The Pulitzer Prizes.* New York: Columbia University Press, 1974.

Hopson, Anna Lee. "Best Sellers: Media of Mass Expression." Ph.D. dissertation, Radcliffe College, 1951.

Kazin, Alfred. *On Native Grounds.* New York: Reynal and Hitchcock, 1942.

————. *Bright Book of Life.* Boston: Little, Brown, 1973.

Knight, Grant C. *The Critical Period in American Literature, 1890-1900.* Chapel Hill: University of North Carolina Press, 1951.

————. *The Strenuous Age in American Literature.* Chapel Hill: University of North Carolina Press, 1954.

Leavis, Q. D. *Fiction and the Reading Public.* London: Chatto and Windus, 1965.

Lee, Charles. *The Hidden Public.* New York: Doubleday, 1958.

Lewis, Freeman. *Paper-Bound Books in America.* New York: New York Public Library, 1952.

Library Journal Book Review. New York: R. R. Bowker, 1967-.

Library of Congress Catalogue. Ann Arbor: J. W. Edwards, 1943, 1948, 1953.

Link, Henry C., and Harry Arthur Hopf. *People and Books.* New York: Book Industry Committee, 1946.

Lockridge, Kenneth A. *Literacy in Colonial New England.* New York: Norton, 1974.

Loshe, Lily D. *The Early American Novel.* New York: Columbia University Press, 1907.

McQuade, Donald, and Robert Atwan. *Popular Writing in America.* New York: Oxford, 1974.

Madison, Charles Allen. *Book Publishing in America.* New York: McGraw-Hill, 1966.

Mitgang, Herbert. *Working for the Reader: A Chronicle of Culture, Literature, War and Politics in Books from the 1950s to the Present.* New York: Horizon Press, 1970.

Mott, Frank Luther. *Golden Multitudes: The Story of Best Sellers in the United States.* New York: Macmillan, 1947.

National Union Catalogue. Ann Arbor: J. W. Edwards, 1958-.

Nye, Russel B. *The Cultural Life of the New Nation, 1776-1830.* New York: Harper and Row, 1960.

————. *The Unembarrassed Muse: The Popular Arts in America.* New York: Dial Press, 1970.

Papashvily, Helen. *All the Happy Endings.* New York: Harper, 1956.

Reynolds, Quentin. *The Fiction Factory.* New York: Random House, 1955.

Rosenberg, Bernard, and David Manning White. *Mass Culture: The Popular Arts in America.* Glencoe, Ill.: Glencoe Free Press, 1957.

Schick, Frank L. *The Paperbound Book in America.* New York: R. R. Bowker, 1958.

Smith, Roger H. *The American Reading Public: What It Reads.* New York: R. R. Bowker, 1964.

Stevens, George. *Lincoln's Doctor's Dog.* Philadelphia: Lippincott, 1938.

Taubert, Sigfred, ed. *The Book Trade of the World.* New York: R. R. Bowker, 1972-1976. 2 vols.

Tebbel, John William. *Paperback Books: A Pocket History.* New York: Pocket Books, 1964.

————. *A History of Book Publishing in the United States.* New York: R. R. Bowker, 1972 (Vol. I) and 1975 (Vol. II).

Waldmeir, Joseph J., ed. *Recent American Fiction: Some Critical Views.* Boston: Houghton-Mifflin, 1963.

Waples, Douglas. *Research Memorandum on Social Aspects of Reading in the Depression.* New York: Social Science Research Council, 1937.

Weimer, David R. *Bibliography of American Culture 1493-1875.* Ann Arbor, Mich.: University Microfilms, 1957.

Wilson, Louis R. *The Geography of Reading.* Chicago: American Library Association and University of Chicago Press, 1938.

Wright, Lyle. *American Fiction: A Contribution Towards Bibliography.* San Marino, Calif.: Huntington Library, 1957-1969. 3 vols.

Wright, Thomas Goddard. *Literary Culture in Early New England, 1620-1730.* New Haven: Yale University Press, 1920.

INDEXES

Book Review Index. Detroit: Gale Research, 1965-.

International Index to Periodicals. New York: H. W. Wilson, 1907-1965.

National Library Service Cumulative Book Review Index, 1905-1974. Princeton: National Library Service Corporation, 1975.

New York Times Book Review Index. New York: Arno Press, 1973.

Readers' Guide to Periodical Literature. New York: H. W. Wilson, 1904-.

Social Sciences and Humanities Index. New York: H. W. Wilson, 1966-1974.

Social Sciences Index. New York: H. W. Wilson, 1975-.

PERIODICALS

Book Review Digest. New York, 1905-.

Booklist. Chicago, 1905-.

Bookman. New York, 1895-1933.

Library Journal. New York, 1876-.

New York Review of Books. New York, 1963-.

New York Times Book Review. New York, 1896-.

Publishers Weekly. New York, 1872-.

Saturday Review. New York, 1952-.

Saturday Review of Literature. New York, 1924-1951.

CHAPTER 3. Circus and Outdoor Entertainment

Don B. Wilmeth

HISTORIC OUTLINE

Of all forms of early American popular entertainment, excluding popular theatre, only the outdoor amusement industry and the circus have managed to survive changing times and tastes, despite noticeable alterations. The traveling tent circus has largely given way to presentation in permanent indoor arenas, and the traditional amusement park, despite the struggling survival of some, has evolved into the "theme" park, such as Disneyland or Six Flags Over Texas. To most observers, the differences between the various forms—be they circus, carnival, fair, or amusement park—are largely irrelevant. The memories evoked from each blur and meld into a single sensory recall. In reality, the various forms are quite different, and myriad examples can be isolated under the general heading of "outdoor entertainment" or, more correctly, "outdoor entertainment and environmental forms." In William F. Mangels's excellent but tentative survey, *The Outdoor Entertainment Business*, a long list of identifiable entertainments are enumerated: circuses, carnivals, amusement parks, carousels, roller coasters, dance halls, shooting galleries, penny arcades, world fairs, menageries, and so on. In this survey chapter, however, I have chosen to deal with only two major categories: (1) the circus and wild west exhibitions, and (2) outdoor amusements (fairs, exhibitions, pleasure gardens, amusement parks, carnivals, seaside resorts, and theme parks). Although the other public amusements indicated by Mangels are legitimate individual forms, the two areas of concern here represent the major forms of American outdoor entertainment past and present, incorporating a number of the other items mentioned by Mangels.

THE CIRCUS

In 1968 Marcello Truzzi, in "The Decline of the American Circus," defined the circus as "a traveling and organized display of animals and skilled performances within one or more circular stages known as 'rings' before an audience encircling these activities." This definition, which provides a workable framework for a study of the circus, includes the traditional circus and the wild west exhibition under the general category of a circus, but it excludes the carnival, which is socially a very distinct organization and depends, as does the amusement park, on its audience's active participation. The circus, on the other hand, demands a high degree of emotional empathy and passive involvement and thus is more closely related to traditional theatre, whereas the carnival and its kin have evolved from the medieval fair tradition. Despite Truzzi's identification of the wild west as a form of circus, its evolution and form are distinctive enough to be dealt with independently.

In its various forms, the circus is one of the oldest forms of popular entertainment. Historians have rather unsuccessfully attempted to trace the individual circus acts to antiquity, but the modern circus's connection with Rome's Circus Maximus or even earlier traditions is tenuous at best. The circus, as we know it today, more likely dates from the equestrian training circle of a much later period. Its clearest progenitor was Philip Astley who, in 1770, opened what amounted to a one-ring circus in London, featuring horsemanship acts and ultimately developing a form of theatre called "hippodrama." The European circuses stayed close to Astley's original form, often in fixed locations, although adding in time clowns, acrobats, jugglers, trapeze artists, trained animals, and other acts. In America the early trend was toward size and movement. In the course of the circus's history, there have been in America, Mexico, and Canada since 1771 over eleven hundred circuses and menageries (an even earlier tradition and one of the definite predecessors of the circus in England and America). The peak period of the American circus was in 1903, with approximately ninety-eight circuses and menageries in existence. The pattern since 1903 has been one of steady decline.

The early American circus, then, was virtually transported from England. Although elements of the circus existed prior to 1793 in the form of individual acts, the man who brought the previously disparate elements together in Philadelphia in 1793 was John Bill Ricketts, a Scotsman who arrived in America in 1792. In his permanent building in Philadelphia, Ricketts presented trick riding, a tightrope walker, and a clown. Ricketts had been a pupil of Charles Hughes, whose Royal Circus at Blackfriar's Bridge in London had been rival to Astley's since 1782. Subsequently,

Ricketts's circus made appearances in New York, Boston, and Albany, as well as other cities in the United States and Canada.

The opening of the Erie Canal in 1825 afforded the increasing number of American circuses greater freedom in travel; traveling animal menageries had continued to parallel the increasing number of circuses. By the end of the first quarter of the nineteenth century, efforts were made to merge the menagerie and the circus. The elephant, which was to have a key role in the American circus, was first exhibited in 1796; the second and the most famous early elephant in the new country, Old Bet, was shown by Hackaliah Bailey with great success until 1816. Old Bet has mistakenly been associated by historians with Nathan Howe's circus. Howe and his partner Aaron Turner also have been credited mistakenly with the introduction of the circus tent around 1824. Recent research indicates, however, that the tent was probably not introduced until 1826 by J. Purdy Brown.

During the first half of the nineteenth century, distinctive characteristics of the American circus began to evolve. The first circus parade dates from 1837, when a short-lived circus marched through the streets of Albany; in 1838, the circus first used rail travel as transportation (from Forsythe to Macon, Georgia); the first boat circus (under Gilbert Spalding and Charles Rogers), a forerunner of the show boat, dates from 1852. The 1890s and early years of this century saw many small railroad circuses traveling across the country, although wagon shows continued well into the twentieth century. Nevertheless, in time, motorized transportation and the railroad displaced mule power and horsepower. The circus of Tom Mix made the first transcontinental tour of the United States by a motorized circus in 1936.

Among the major changes in the pattern of the American circus, in addition to mobility, was the introduction of multiple rings, in contrast to the European one-ring format. Around 1873, William Cameron Coup added a second ring to the circus, utilizing the name of P. T. Barnum; in 1881, James A. Bailey negotiated the merger of several great circus operations, including Barnum's circus, and opened with a three-ring show. By 1885, virtually all American circuses had adopted the three rings. The circus now incorporated the menagerie, the concert, the side-show, and the street parade as integral ingredients.

The period between 1830 and 1870 saw the emergence of numerous prominent circuses in the history of the American circus, each with colorful and important histories: the George F. Bailey Circus; circuses utilizing the name of the "Lion King" (Isaac Van Amburgh); the several circuses of Seth B. Howes; the Mabie Brothers Circus; the Yankee (Fayette Ludovic) Robinson Circus; the John Robinson Circus; the Spalding and Rogers

Circus; the Dan Costello Circus; the Dan Rice Circus (capitalizing on the name of the early American clown); and the W. W. Cole Circus.

The so-called golden age of the American circus—which lasted until about 1917—began in 1871, when W. C. Coup persuaded P. T. Barnum, the showman and museum entrepreneur, to become a partner in a circus enterprise. Barnum lent his name to other shows in addition to Coup's, which ultimately caused a split with Coup in 1875. In 1880, Barnum joined James A. Bailey and James L. Hutchinson in a new operation. This lucrative partnership lasted until 1885 when Barnum refused to deal further with Bailey, and Bailey sold his interest to James Cooper and W. W. Cole. In 1887, after Barnum had experienced a number of setbacks, including the loss of a Madison Square Garden contract to the rival Adam Forepaugh Circus, Barnum gave Bailey full control of the circus and added his name to the new "Barnum & Bailey Greatest Show on Earth." During this golden age, a number of the older circuses continued to compete or operate in their own regional circuits; other new prominent circuses came into their own, including the Sells Brothers Circus, the Great Wallace Circus, and the Lemen Brothers Circus.

The Ringlings, the name most frequently associated with the circus today, were late arrivals on the circus scene. None of the five brothers was involved until 1882. After seeing a traveling circus in their hometown of Baraboo, Wisconsin, they began to do a variety show around Wisconsin. In 1895, after adding more circus acts and animals to their menagerie, they made their first tour outside the Midwest and entered Barnum and Bailey's territory in New England. A year after Bailey's death in 1907, the Ringlings bought the Barnum and Bailey Circus; they finally merged as one in 1918, becoming "Ringling Brothers and Barnum & Bailey Combined Shows."

Various competitors tried to shut out the Ringlings, but the circus had become big business, and their efforts were fruitless; after 1910, the circuses had declined in number and in extravagance. The street parade became obsolete; menageries virtually vanished; and even the big top would practically disappear. Mechanization deprived the circus of its uniqueness and flair; individual initiative became dampened as well. Today, only a dozen or so circuses travel in the United States and they are only a faint reminder of the glories of the traveling tent circus of the turn of the century. During the 1940s and 1950s, the larger circuses—the Clyde Beatty, the King Brothers, and the Ringling shows—experienced a series of disasters. In 1957, "The Greatest Show on Earth" was forced to put away its big top and perform only in permanent facilities, thus depriving the major circus in the United States of one of its great attractions. Ironically, despite the near disappearance of the circus, its total audience continues to grow (thanks in part to television and films) and its revenue to swell. As the modern circus adjusts to modern demands, its age-old appeal apparently continues unabated.

THE WILD WEST EXHIBITION

The so-called Wild West show is invariably associated with William Frederick "Buffalo Bill" Cody, who found the association of his enterprise with that of the circus or the use of the word "show" anathema. His billing was invariably "Buffalo Bill's Wild West," without the "show," and, if pressed, his general manager John M. Burke would insist that it was an exhibition. In its most ideal form, then, a wild west show may be defined as an exhibition illustrating scenes and events characteristic of the American Far West frontier.

The exact origin of the wild west show is difficult to pinpoint. The rodeo is related in part to the wild west exhibition, insofar as a traveling rodeo with hired contestants would fit a common definition; yet the rodeo is normally a competitive sport in which the contestants pay an entrance fee and receive no pay except prize money. Thus, the kinship between the rodeo and the wild west show should not be stressed, although, as mentioned below, they share a common beginning in terms of popularity. The wild west actually evolved in part from the "specs" (or spectacular pageants) of the circus, the old traveling menageries, early exhibitions of cowboy skills and Indians dating from the 1820s, and the numerous plays, novels, and cheap popular literature of the nineteenth century.

Most historians of the wild west show credit Cody with the consolidation and popularization of this form of entertainment. After ten seasons of performing in mediocre border melodramas built vaguely around his life and exploits as a scout, a buffalo hunter, and a frontiersman, Cody returned to his home of North Platte, Nebraska, in the summer of 1882. Upon his return, he was cajoled into planning the "Old Glory Blow-Out," a Fourth of July celebration of cowboy skill acts climaxed by a buffalo hunt in which Cody demonstrated with blank ammunition his methods of killing buffalo. This date in 1882, then, marks the upsurge of both the wild west show and the rodeo, although doubtless not the first examples of either. (The rodeo harks back to the byplay and showoffs of early cattle roundups; an early form of the wild west show was seen in New York by way of Boston in 1843; other elements of Cody's show existed prior to 1882.) What was new in Cody's wild west exhibition was the combination that spelled success. In its ultimate form, Cody's wild west became a dominant form of outdoor amusement, reaching its peak of popularity around 1893.

Cody's wild west was on the upswing in 1883. Initially, his operation was not very successful although it spawned a host of imitators. With the aid of Nate Salsbury, who joined Cody in 1884, and Dr. William F. Carver, whom he met in 1882-1883 (later, both Carver and Salsbury claimed to be the originator of the wild west concept), Cody, who was not a consummate showman, began to experience phenomenal success. With the puffed releases of his colorful press agent-manager, "Arizona" or "Major" John M. Burke, Cody's show became the epitome of the romanticized and glamour-ized American West, particularly in Europe, where Cody made several successful tours. At the beginning of its history, the wild west appeared to be a representation of the contemporary western scene but, as the old West vanished, it soon transcended the reality and created a legendary West based largely on illusion.

In its first decade, then, the wild west show had a contemporary interest that began to fade after the turn of the century. The format, which orig-inally had been new and unique, lacked variety, and showmen fell victim to the temptation to combine it with a circus or to add circus acts to its own pageantry. Gordon William Lillie, known as "Major Lillie," "Pawnee Bill," or "the White Chief of the Pawnees" (an early performer with Cody), thought the solution was to restyle his show as "Pawnee Bill's Historic Wild West and Great Far East." The latter included "every type of male and female inhabitant"—Hindu magicians, Singhalese dancers, Madagascar oxen cavalry, Australian bushmen, and so forth. Other shows featured notoriety. "Cummins's Wild West and Indian Congress" featured Red Cloud, Chief Joseph, Geronimo, and Calamity Jane. Despite the changing nature of the wild west show after the 1890s, the largest number of such entertainments flourished in the early years of the twentieth century. In the course of its history, according to Don Russell, the foremost historian of this phenomenon, there were over one hundred wild west shows. With the great proliferation of such organizations at the turn of the century, the shows became quite shabby. Cody's last European tour began in 1902 and by 1909 he had to merge his operation with that of Pawnee Bill. By 1908, the "101 Ranch Wild West Show," which began in 1892, became a perma-nent institution and major competition for the Cody-Pawnee Bill show. World War I marked the end of the golden era of outdoor show business, including the wild west show. By 1918, there were no major wild west shows, their popularity having been eclipsed by the increasing popularity of motion pictures and the growing appeal of the more "believable" por-trayal of the movie cowboy.

OUTDOOR ENTERTAINMENT

The American outdoor amusement industry evolved, as did the circus, from European traditions—the medieval fair and carnival and the seven-teenth-century pleasure garden. Indeed, it is possible to trace elements of the carnival, fair, and amusement park back to antiquity. Before the American Revolution, pleasure gardens, modeled on London's most famous gardens, Vauxhall and Ranelagh, appeared in major cities on the East

Coast. Like Vauxhall, which was the first internationally famous pleasure garden when it opened in 1661, the American version offered visitors food, drink, music, and free variety acts. As in England and France, the simple pleasure of strolling, eating, and drinking became tiresome, and amusements of a more thrilling and exciting nature were sought.

The end of the nineteenth century saw similar places of amusement develop, however, as a result of improved transportation and technology. With the invention of the trolley came the institution of so-called trolley parks. Dozens of such parks were established by street railways at the end of the line all over the country as an economical method of encouraging weekend riders to use the cars. Initially, these parks offered little that could not have been found at the earlier pleasure garden. During the nineteenth century, however, amusements offered at the gardens and at rural picnic groves and shore resorts began to increase in number and in sophistication. Also, by the 1880s, thanks to new technology, mechanical pleasure rides such as the carousel and a device called "the Ferris wheel" developed.

The most obvious stimulus for the outdoor amusement industry first began when the Vienna World's Fair was held at "The Prater" in Vienna in 1873. A new concept in outdoor entertainment was presented with its large array of amusement "machines" or rides, fun houses, games of chance, and other activities, which created a new and exciting kind of park. Although Jones's Woods, a grove of some one hundred fifty acres along the East River, offered New Yorkers in the early nineteenth century a large variety of amusements, it was not until 1893 and the World's Columbian Exposition in Chicago that American showmen sensed the lucrative potential of outdoor amusements.

The true emergence of the American carnival and the exploitation of amusement rides and concessions, then, is usually cited as 1893. Although an area outside the exposition fair proper, called the "Midway Plaisance," began slowly, when the concessionaires hyped its promotion and agreed that the assembled attractions should be moved to various cities, the idea of the street fair or modern carnival had been born. The traveling carnival was fully realized that same year when Frank C. Bostock presented a collection of attractions at Coney Island, the location later of the amusement park's great growth. Bostock's entertainment has been called the first modern carnival in that his efforts mark the first attempt to make portable a group of attractions. Initially these early carnivals were moved by horsedrawn wagons, but by 1914 the "Smith Greater Shows" was moved by truck.

As early as 1883 the more traditional state fairs were invaded by the amusement business and amusement zones were included at all the world fairs after Chicago in 1893. The trolley companies mentioned above followed suit and patterned a number of the trolley parks after such amusement areas. Today, the carnival business is a large industry. One of the largest of the traveling carnivals, the "Royal American Shows," travels on eighty double-length railroad cars loaded with 145 massive pieces of equipment. Their midway features more than fifty rides and attractions and seven under-canvas shows, illustrating vividly the three distinctive features of the carnival—riding devices, shows or exhibits, and concessions.

The modern concept of the amusement park developed at Coney Island, a beach resort in Brooklyn, New York, which contained a series of parks and independent entertainments. There, beginning in 1895, street railway companies and seaside entertainment entrepreneurs had witnessed the evolution of the ultimate model on which to base their operations. Coney Island's fame began when Billy Boynton built Sea Lion Park in 1895, followed by George C. Tilyou's Steeplechase Park in 1897, and then the purchase in 1903 of Boynton's park by Frederic W. Thompson and Elmer (Skip) Dundy. They rebuilt the Boynton park into a lavish version of the Midway Plaisance—Luna Park—at a cost of nearly $1 million. Luna offered, on a more or less permanent basis, a wildly eclectic environment of attractions, illuminated at night by more than two hundred fifty thousand incandescent lights. Across Surf Avenue from Luna, a real-estate speculator named William Reynolds quickly countered and spent $3.5 million to build Dreamland Park, where everything was on an even more exuberant scale, all lit by one million bulbs.

The great period of the traditional amusement park dates from Coney Island's spectacular growth at the turn of the century to about World War II, although its decline began, as did that of all outdoor entertainments, around World War I. However, while it lasted, the Coney Island model inspired countless other Luna Parks and Dreamlands all over America, until, by the early years of the new century, the amusement park had become a fixture of most large cities. From World War II to the present, the decline of the traditional amusement park has been slow but steady, with the announcement of the closing of major amusement parks a commonplace event. The lack of needed materials during the war, ultimate patrons' boredom with the aging attractions, natural disasters, and vandalism have all contributed to the traditional amusement park's demise.

According to a recent survey, there are, nonetheless, still more than one hundred major amusement parks in the United States. A large number of these parks, however, represent the latest phase of the outdoor amusement industry. As traditional parks declined in popularity, they were replaced by the "theme" parks, dating from the conception of Disneyland in Anaheim, California, which began in 1954. Apparently, the popularity of the amusement park is not waning. During the summer of 1976, over seventy-five million people attended such parks; more patrons rode roller coasters in

1977 than attended professional football and baseball games combined. Possibly, as Brooks McNamara has suggested, we are now approaching a kind of saturation point for this type of entertainment. If so, definite indications of such a development have yet to materialize fully. As I write this essay, there is in front of me a newspaper clipping announcing that a group of Hartford, Connecticut, developers have proposed building a $17.5 million amusement park to help the city's convention business. Early in 1978, it might be noted in closing, Crescent Park in Rhode Island, one of New England's oldest amusement parks, after a number of financially unsuccessful years, joined the list of defunct traditional amusement parks.

REFERENCE WORKS AND GENERAL SOURCES

This chapter is intended as a companion to my chapter "Stage Entertainments" in volume one of the *Handbook of American Popular Culture*. In that essay, the nature of popular entertainment and the study of the major staged forms (dime museum, medicine shows, minstrelsy, vaudeville, burlesque, popular theatre, early musical theatre and revue) were discussed and sources were provided. In order to conserve space and provide more coverage of those topics germane to this chapter, the overview from that essay and most of the general sources discussed there are excluded from this second essay. This present coverage, however, has been prepared as a separate and complete guide to sources on the circus and outdoor entertainments. It is suggested, nonetheless, that readers of volume two consult that initial chapter for a more thorough guide to American forms of popular entertainment.

To date, there are few detailed bibliographies or information guides to American popular entertainment. John H. Towsen's "Sources on Popular Entertainment" provides a reasonably good guide to general sources, including a list of basic research tools, libraries and museums, organizations, performer training, and a select bibliography. *American and English Popular Entertainment: An Information Guide* by Don B. Wilmeth should provide the most complete one-volume guide to major forms of popular entertainment thus far, with sections on organizations, periodicals and serials, and libraries and museums, along with over two thousand annotated sources. Wilmeth's select bibliographical guide entitled "American Popular Entertainment: A Historical Perspective" appeared in 1977.

Of the general sources on popular entertainment that put into perspective those forms discussed in this chapter, the most useful are Robert C. Toll's *On with the Show* and Samuel McKechnie's *Popular Entertainment Through the Ages*, the latter limited largely to English forms but nonetheless an excellent overview of entertainment forms. Brooks McNamara's brief essay, "The Scenography of Popular Entertainment," provides a good framework for studying the architecture and design of popular forms, including circuses and outdoor forms. Maurice Gorham's *Showmen and Suckers: An Excursion on the Crazy Fringe of the Entertainment World* explores the relationship between the showman and the sucker, a condition that prevails in all amusement forms discussed in this chapter. Heinrich Richard Falk's "Conventions of Popular Entertainment: Framework for a Methodology" and Brooks McNamara, in his introduction to a special issue of *The Drama Review* on "Popular Entertainments," provide useful approaches to the study of popular forms. The forthcoming publication of the *Proceedings of the Conference on the History of American Popular Entertainment,* edited by Myron Matlaw, will make available numerous insightful essays relevant to this chapter.

The most thorough reference incorporating fifteen thousand sources on most aspects of the circus and outdoor entertainment remains Raymond Toole-Stott's four-volume *Circus and Allied Arts, a World Bibliography.* Considering the large number of sources that appeared within the last half-dozen years, however, Toole-Stott must be considered more useful for older sources. The basic trade magazine for all forms of show business remains the weekly, *Variety.* This magazine and *Amusement Business* are major sources for studying the circus and outdoor entertainment.

THE CIRCUS

Of all forms of American popular entertainment, the circus has received the greatest attention, and information is the most plentiful. Still, a great deal of primary material remains in private collections, and many of the published sources are by amateur historians and devoted circus fans who, until recently, have avoided careful documentation. As a result, a comprehensive, reliably researched history of the American circus has yet to be written, although a number of efforts in that direction have recently appeared. In the meantime, students of the circus must refer to those published sources that are most reliable and search for information in circus collections and in the pages of various periodicals and serials. These will be discussed at the conclusion of this section.

The most comprehensive guide to the circus and an indispensable reference for anyone researching the circus is Raymond Toole-Stott's four-volume *Circus and Allied Arts, a World Bibliography* and his more selective list in *A Bibliography of the Books on the Circus in English.* Combined, Toole-Stott's major bibliographical volumes contain over fifteen thousand entries drawn from works in thirteen languages. It should be noted, however, that this guide is far more useful on foreign antecedents than it is on the American circus. Robert Sokan's *A Descriptive and Bibliographic Catalog of the Circus and Related Arts Collection at Illinois State University, Normal, Illinois* contains details on 1,373 items and is a useful guide as well. For the American circus, one would be well served to review Richard Flint's "A Selected Guide to Source Material on the American Circus" for his discussion of types of circusiana.

There are numerous general histories and surveys of the circus. George L. Chindahl's *History of the Circus in America* is especially good on the nineteenth century; John and Alice Durant's *Pictorial History of the American Circus* is sumptuously illustrated and contains a useful list of American circuses; and C. P. Fox and Tom Parkinson's *Circus in America* provides a decent coverage of the circus in its heyday. Isaac J. Greenwood's *The Circus: Its Origin and Growth Prior to 1835* remains a useful early history, as do R. W. G. Vail's "The Early Circus in America" and "This Way to the Big Top," and John J. Jennings's *Theatrical and Circus Life; or, Secrets of the Stage, Green-Room and Sawdust Arena*. Of all the available surveys, Earl Chapin May's *The Circus from Rome to Ringling* (not to be confused with the less definitive *Circus! From Rome to Ringling* by Marian Murray) is considered by many circus authorities the best single-volume history available. For the uninitiated, Mildred S. and Wolcott Fenner's *The Circus: Lure and Legend* covers the entire gamut of circus literature. Among the more recent world histories, Rupert Croft-Cooke's and Peter Cotes's *Circus: A World History* and Peter Verney's *Here Comes the Circus* offer generally reliable but undocumented accounts that place the American circus in international perspective. Also useful is Robert C. Toll's coverage of the circus in *On With the Show*. Although it is written in French, Henry Thetard's *La Marveilleuse Histoire du Cirque* is one of the more authoritative histories of world circus.

The English prototype of the early American circus is covered with scholarly exactitude in A. H. Saxon's *Enter Foot and Horse* and *The Life and Art of Andrew Ducrow & The Romantic Age of the English Circus*. Less reliable but still recommended are Thomas Frost's *Circus Life and Circus Celebrities*, a classic study of the early English circus, and M. Willson Disher's *Greatest Show on Earth*, which provides an informative and amusing history of Astley's. Recent unpublished scholarly studies include Paul Alexander Daum's "The Royal Circus 1782-1809: An Analysis of Equestrian Entertainments" and George Palliser Tuttle's "The History of the Royal Circus, Equestrian and Philarmonic Academy, 1782-1816, St. George's Fields, Surrey, England."

The early period of the American circus has recently received a careful and documented study by Stuart Thayer in *Annals of the American Circus 1793-1829*. Also useful are: James S. Moy's "Entertainments at John B. Ricketts's Circus, 1793-1800" and his doctoral dissertation, "John B. Ricketts's Circus 1793-1800"; William W. Clapp, Jr.'s *A Record of the Boston Stage*; Joseph Cowell's *Thirty Years Passed Among the Players in England and America*; John Durang's *The Memoirs of John Durang*, edited by Alan S. Downer; and Chang Reynolds's *Pioneer Circuses of the West.*

Of the plethora of sources on specific circuses or regions, the following offer informative and sometimes insightful accounts: Elbert R. Bowen's *Theatrical Entertainment in Rural Missouri Before the Civil War* and "The Circus in Early Rural Missouri"; Bob Barton's *Old Covered Wagon Show Days,* on the Cole Brothers wagon show in the 1890s; Fred Bradna and Hartzell Spence's *The Big Top: My 40 Years with the Greatest Show on Earth*; Bert J. Chipman's *Hey Rube,* which includes a roster of major circuses (1900-15); Herb Clement's *The Circus, Bigger and Better Than Ever?,* an account of smaller, contemporary circuses; Richard E. Conover's *The Affairs of James A. Bailey, The Great Forepaugh Show,* and *Give 'Em a John Robinson; This Way to the Big Top: The Life of Dexter Fellows,* the life story of the press agent for Ringling Brothers and Barnum & Bailey, by Dexter W. Fellows and Andrew A. Freeman; Henry Ringling North's *The Circus Kings,* on the Ringling family; the superior *Those Amazing Ringlings and Their Circus* by Gene Plowden; Fred Powledge's *Mud Show: A Circus Season,* a fascinating glimpse of a third-rate traveling circus during the 1974 season; and Gil Robinson's *Old Wagon Show Days,* an account of the John Robinson Circus.

Various general aspects of the circus, including the parade, circus life, and so forth have received considerable attention. Among these sources, the following are suggested: Courtney Ryley Cooper's *Circus Day,* impressions of circus life during the first half of this century; Antony D. Hippisley Coxe's *A Seat at the Circus,* a vivid description of a typical circus performance; the works of Charles Philip Fox, especially *Circus Parades, A Ticket to the Circus, A Pictorial History of Performing Horses,* and, with F. Beverly Kelley, the recent *The Great Circus Street Parade in Pictures*; Jill Freedman's *Circus Days,* a pictorial essay on the Beatty-Cole Circus; James A. Inciardi and David M. Petersen's "Gaff Joints and Shell Games: A Century of Circus Grift"; Jack Rennert's *100 Years of Circus Posters*; and Marcello Truzzi's "The American Circus as a Source of Folklore: An Introduction" and "Folksongs of the American Circus."

P. T. Barnum's ties to the circus are more tenuous than most people realize; his contributions to popular entertainment were covered more extensively in volume one of this handbook. The three most reliable biographies of Barnum, however, do include information on his associations with the circus: Neil Harris's *Humbug: The Art of P. T. Barnum* is the best-documented study of Barnum; Irving Wallace's *The Fabulous Showman* is a useful and generally reliable popular study; and M. R. Werner's *Barnum.* Additional sources on Barnum can be found in Nelle Neafie's *A P. T. Barnum Bibliography.* Because of Barnum's association with the museum, freaks and sideshows are closely related to his contributions to show business. Among the various works on this topic, the following are most comprehensive: Colin Clair's *Human Curiosities*; Frederick Drimmer's *Very Special People*; Leslie Fiedler's *Freaks: Myths & Images of the Secret Self*, the most stimulating and provocative study of the freak; Harry Lewiston, as told to Jerry Holtman, *Freak Show Man*; Daniel Mannix's *We Who Are Not as Others*; and Albert Parry's *Tattoo: Secrets of a Strange Art*.

The circus clown has recently received a superb treatment in John H. Towsen's *Clowns*, the only full survey of the clown in all its various forms. Among other surveys, the following are less comprehensive but useful: George Bishop's *The World of Clowns* is a well-illustrated but undistinguished work; and Lowell Swortzell's *Here Come the Clowns: A Cavalcade of Comedy from Antiquity to the Present* is not limited to the circus clown. Although written in French and not exclusively concerned with American clowns, any list of sources must include Tristan Remy's classic works *Les Clowns* and *Entrees Clownesque*.

Sources on performers and animal trainers are too extensive to list in any great number here. Most, however, are chatty autobiographies or biographies and include little that cannot be found in the more reliable general histories and surveys. A few, however, are worthy additions to the literature on the circus. Among these are the following: Bill Ballantine's *Wild Tigers and Tame Fleas*; Clyde Beatty's *The Big Cage*; Frank Bostock's *The Training of Wild Animals*, a good source on early methods of animal training; Courtney Ryley Cooper's *Lions 'N' Tigers 'N' Everything* and *With the Circus*; H. Hediger's *Studies of the Psychology and Behaviour of Captive Animals in Zoos and Circuses;* Lorenz Hagenbeck's *Animals Are My Life;* J. Y. Henderson's *Circus Doctor*, the career of the chief veterinarian of the Ringling Brothers, Barnum & Bailey Circus; Ernest Schlee Millette's *The Circus That Was*, the life of an acrobat; Edwin P. Norwood's *The Other Side of the Circus* and *The Circus Menagerie*; Roman Proske's *Lions, Tigers, and Me*; and Jake Posey's *Last of the Forty Horse Drivers*.

A few scholars outside of the immediate area of circus history have recently begun to show interest in the circus from the sociological point of view. Foremost among these is Marcello Truzzi, whose "The Decline of the American Circus" provides a perceptive and penetrating analysis of the circus. He has also edited a special issue of the *Journal of Popular Culture* on "Circuses, Carnivals and Fairs in America," which demonstrates new approaches to circus study. His studies of the carnival, discussed in the section on outdoor entertainment, are even more significant. Paul Bouissac, a linguist and semiotician, has provided a unique method for examining the circus in *Circus & Culture: A Semiotic Approach*; Walter M. Gerson looks at the circus as a social entity in "The Circus: A Mobile Total Institution"; Robert C. Sweet and Robert W. Habenstein examine significant changes in the circus since 1920 in "Some Perspective on the Circus in Transition."

The special language of the circus is included in Sherman Louis Sergel's *The Language of Show Biz* and is dealt with more explicitly in Bill Ballantine's "Circus Talk," George Milburn's "Circus Words," and David W. Maurer's "Carnival Cant: A Glossary of Circus and Carnival Slang."

Necessarily excluded from this bibliography, but of prime significance in the study and research of the circus, are articles from circus periodicals. The circus trade journals, the *New York Clipper* for the latter half of the nineteenth century and *Billboard* for this century, remain the best sources. Although quality and depth of contributions vary, essays in *Bandwagon*, the journal of the Circus Historical Society, provide useful glimpses at specific circuses and at limited time spans of circus history. Especially recommended are the contributions of Stuart Thayer, Fred D. Pfening, Jr., Richard Flint, Bob Parkinson, and Richard E. Conover. Of less value are essays in *White Tops*, the journal of the Circus Fans Association of America. A superb international journal is *Le Cirque Dans L'Univers*, published for the Club du Cirque in France.

The major circus collections are: the Circus World Museum Library in Baraboo, Wisconsin, which has a collection especially rich in advertising materials (a helpful brochure on its holdings is available upon request); the Hertzberg Circus Collection in San Antonio, Texas, with extensive holdings of late nineteenth-century material; the Joe E. Ward Collection of circus memorabilia in the Hoblitzelle Theatre Arts Library at the University of Texas in Austin; the Illinois State University Circus and Related Arts Collection in Normal, Illinois, possibly the best balanced collection in the United States; the McCaddon Collection in the Princeton University Library, which houses the working papers of the Barnum and Bailey Circus, ca. 1890 to 1910; the New York Historical Society, which holds the Westervelt Collection of Barnum material, plus some items on the circus; the Ringling Museum of the Circus in Sarasota, Florida, a relatively minor collection; and the Somers, New York, Historical Society, with materials on the early American circus from the area called the "cradle of the American circus."

THE WILD WEST EXHIBITION

Most general histories of the circus, as well as collections and periodicals listed in the previous section, contain some mention of wild west shows or house primary materials. There is, however, a growing literature devoted exclusively to this form of entertainment. The most definitive and comprehensive history to date is Don Russell's *The Wild West or, A History of the Wild West Shows*. Also useful are his essays "Cody, Kings, and Coronets," covering the first ten years of Buffalo Bill's wild west, and

"The Golden Age of Wild West Shows." Other studies of the form that provide varying points of view are: William Brasmer's "The Wild West Exhibition and the Drama of Civilization," a deprecating view of the phenomenon; Ellsworth Collings and Alma Miller England's *The 101 Ranch*, the definitive source on the Miller brothers; Fred Gipson's *Fabulous Empire, Colonel Zack Miller's Story*, a less reliable history of the 101 Wild West Show; Carolyn Thomas Foreman's *Indians Abroad*, a history of the foreign travel of Indians, including their associations with wild west shows; Milt Hinkle's "The Kit Carson Wild West Show" and "The Way a Wild West Show Operated"; Madelon B. Katigan's "The Fabulous 101," one of the better brief accounts of this important organization; Ruel McDaniel's "Requiem for the Wild West Shows," the career of Glenn Kischko, who witnessed the glory and death of the spectacles of the wild west show; Paul E. Mix's *The Life and Legend of Tom Mix*; Fred D. Pfening, Jr.'s *Col. Tim McCoy's Real Wild West and Rough Riders of the World*, the story of a late wild west enterprise; Joseph Schwartz's "The Wild West Show; 'Everything Genuine',", a good analysis of the show's appeal; Glenn Shirley's *Pawnee Bill: A Biography of Major Gordon W. Lillie*, which contains an informative history of the wild west show in general and valuable data on the association between the shows of Cody and Lillie; and Chauncey Yellow Rob's "The Menace of the Wild West Show," a strong attack on the effect of these shows on the American Indian.

As might be expected, most published material on the wild west concerns Buffalo Bill Cody and his exhibition. Among the dozens of biographies of Cody, a few deal not only with Cody's life before the wild west but also with the show itself and individuals associated with it (sources on Cody's acting career are included in volume one of this handbook). John Burke's *Buffalo Bill, The Noblest Whiteskin*, though not definitive, is readable and essentially correct; Rupert Croft-Cooke and W. S. Meadmore's *Buffalo Bill: The Legend, The Man of Action, The Showman* presents a sympathetic treatment of Cody; William E. Deahl, Jr., in "Nebraska's Unique Contribution to the Entertainment World," deals with the beginnings of the wild west show in 1883, and his "Buffalo Bill's Wild West Show in New Orleans" examines Cody's appearances at the 1884 World's Industrial and Cotton Exposition; Charles Eldridge Griffin's *Four Years in Europe with Buffalo Bill* reviews the 1903-07 seasons in Europe; Walter Havighurst presents a good popular account of "Little Sure Shot" in *Annie Oakley of the Wild West*; Albert Johannsen's *The House of Beadle and Adams* is the most complete reference source on the major publisher of dime novels and provides extensive coverage of Cody and stories about him; Jay Monaghan's *The Great Rascal: The Life and Adventures of Ned Buntline* is the best biography of Edward Zane Carroll Judson (Buntline) and provides adequate coverage of his associations with Cody; and Raymond W. Thorp's

Spirit Gun of the West, The Story of Doc W. F. Carver is the definitive biography of Cody's early associate.

In addition to Cody's numerous autobiographies—none very reliable—a number of biographies were written by Cody's relatives, including the fairly accurate picture of Cody in *Buffalo Bill, King of the Old West* by Elizabeth Jane Leonard and Cody's sister Julia Cody Goodman, and *Last of the Great Scouts* by Helen Cody Wetmore (also Cody's sister), but less reliable than the Goodman account. The two best biographical studies of Cody, however, are Don Russell's *The Lives and Legends of Buffalo Bill* and Henry Blackman Sell and Victor Weybright's *Buffalo Bill and the Wild West*, the latter combining biography with a knowledgeable analysis of the wild west presentation and the legend of Buffalo Bill. Richard J. Walsh's *The Making of Buffalo Bill*, written in collaboration with Milton S. Salsbury, is a fascinating study of the process by which Cody became a semi-legendary figure and how he was the subject of the deliberate and infinitely skillful use of publicity. A good visual sense of that exploitation can be seen in Jack Rennert's *100 Posters of Buffalo Bill's Wild West*.

Virtually all the circus collections and periodicals enumerated in the last section contain a great deal on the wild west show. From time to time, dozens of journals and magazines on the west include essays of interest on the subject of the wild west show. In addition to these collections already mentioned, the researcher should be familiar with the collections held in the Western History Department of the Denver Public Library, the Nebraska State Historical Society, and the Arizona Pioneers Historical Society. The best-known Buffalo Bill collection can be found at the Buffalo Bill Historical Center in Cody, Wyoming, which includes the Plains Indian Museum, the Buffalo Museum, and the Whitney Gallery of Western Art.

OUTDOOR ENTERTAINMENT

Fairs, pleasure gardens, expositions, carnivals, amusement parks, and other outdoor amusement forms are closely related to variety shows and the circus, but they have only recently been examined as entertainment vehicles with theatrical elements. Instead of conventional theatrical conventions, these forms depend more on entertainment environments and on a mobile audience. Only the major sources on outdoor entertainment can be mentioned in this article; it should be noted, however, that a number of these forms, in particular the American fair (other than world fairs) and the American pleasure garden, have received little serious attention. The special issue of the *Journal of Popular Culture* on "Circuses, Carnivals and Fairs in America," edited by Marcello Truzzi, makes an excellent beginning place for a study of these forms. Patrick C. Easto and Truzzi's "Towards an Ethnography of the Carnival Social System" includes a useful review and evaluation of much of the available literature.

In order to examine the American forms of outdoor entertainment, background sources are essential. The following items provide an adequate starting place: David Braithwaite's *Fairground Architecture: The World of Amusement Parks, Carnivals, and Fairs*; Thomas Frost's *The Old Showmen and the Old London Fairs* is a standard source; T. F. G. Dexter's *The Pagan Origin of Fairs*; Henry Morley's classic work, *Memoirs of Bartholomew Fair*; Ian Starsmore's *English Fairs*; and H. W. Waters's *History of Fairs and Expositions*. The pleasure garden is best covered in W. S. Scott's *Green Retreats, the Story of Vauxhall Gardens, 1661-1859*; James Southworth's *Vauxhall Gardens: A Chapter in the Social History of England*; and Warwick Wroth's *The London Pleasure Gardens in the Eighteenth Century* (with Edgar Arthur) and *Cremorne and the Later London Gardens*. The American equivalent has received little attention, although Joseph Jackson, in "Vauxhall Garden," discusses a Pennsylvania garden (1814-1824); David Ritchey, in "Columbia Garden: Baltimore's First Pleasure Garden," focuses on another early example; and Thomas M. Garrett's "A History of Pleasure Gardens in New York City, 1700-1865" surveys forty-eight such places of amusement. O. G. Sonneck, in *Early Concert Life in America (1731-1800)*, devotes much of this study to concerts performed at early pleasure gardens. Major world fairs are surveyed adequately in Edo McCullough's *World's Fair Midway: An Affectionate Account of American Amusement Areas from the Crystal Palace to the Crystal Ball*. David F. Burg's *Chicago White City of 1893* is the most recent and complete history of the World's Columbian Exposition, the major stimulant for the amusement business.

The best historical surveys of American outdoor entertainment are William F. Mangels's *The Outdoor Entertainment Business* and Joe McKennon's *A Pictorial History of the American Carnival*. Less comprehensive but still useful are Al Griffin's *"Step Right Up Folks!"* and Gary Kyriazi's *The Great American Amusement Parks*.

Specific sources on the carnival are quite uneven and vary from excellent to extremely mediocre, but they are still informative or revelatory. Among the better sources are: Marcello Truzzi and Patrick C. Easto's "The Carnival as a Marginally Legal Work Activity: The Typological Approach to Work Systems" and "Carnivals, Roadshows and Freaks"; William Lindsay Gresham's *Monster Midway*; Wittold Krassowski's "Social Structure and Professionalization in the Occupation of the Carnival Worker"; John Scarne's "Carnival, Fair, Bazaar, Arcade and Amusement Park Games"; Rollin Lynde Hartt's *The People at Play: Excursions in the Humor and Philosophy of Popular Amusements*; Theodore M. Dembroski's "Hanky Panks and Group Games Versus Alibis and Flats: The Legitimate and Illegitimate of the Carnival's Front End"; Don Boles's *The Midway Showman*; and John F. Cuber's "Patrons of Amusement Parks," a sociological study based on interviews with amusement park patrons in the Cleveland area in 1939.

The writing of Daniel Mannix, a former carnie, provides insights into carnival performers, especially *Step Right Up* and *We Who Are Not As Others*, discussed in the circus section (along with other sources on side-shows and freaks). A number of journalistic writers have captured carnival atmosphere, despite factual weaknesses: good examples are Arthur Lewis's *Carnival*, which makes entertaining reading, and Harry Crews's "Carny," which reveals more of the seamy side of carnival life, as does Susan Meiselas's *Carnival Strippers*. The slang of the carnival is explained in David W. Maurer's "Carnival Cant: A Glossary of Circus and Carnival Slang" and to a lesser degree in Sherman Louis Sergel's *The Language of Show Biz*.

In addition to the historical surveys of American outdoor entertainment mentioned above (Mangels, McKennon, Griffin, and Kyriazi), Brooks McNamara's "Come on Over: The Rise and Fall of the American Amusement Park" provides a succinct but useful summary of that development. Sylvester Baxter's "The Trolley in Rural Parks" and Day Allen Willey's "The Trolley-Park" provide an understanding of the recreation grounds run by street railway companies.

Coney Island and its amusement parks have been thoroughly studied by Peter Lyon, "The Master Showman of Coney Island" (George Tilyou); Edo McCullough, *Good Old Coney Island*; Robert E. Snow and David E. Wright, "Coney Island: A Case Study in Popular Culture and Technical Change"; and Oliver Pilat and Jo Ranson, *Sodom by the Sea: An Affectionate History of Coney Island*.

Seaside resorts and amusement areas are discussed in Charles F. Funnell's *By the Beautiful Sea: The Rise and High Times of That Great American Resort, Atlantic City*; Seon and Robert Manley's *Beaches: Their Lives, Legends, and Lore*; and in Richmond Barrett's *Good Old Summer Days*.

A well-researched and superbly illustrated book, *Pictorial History of the Carousel* by Frederick Fried, covers all aspects of this essential ingredient of all amusement parks. The latest phase of the outdoor amusement industry—the theme park—has received little detailed attention other than coverage in the survey sources listed above, although the special issue of *Theatre Crafts*, "Theme Parks," contains ten excellent essays on various aspects of the parks. The recent *Fun Land U.S.A.* by Tim Onosko provides a reliable guidebook to one hundred major amusement and theme parks plus a brief history, but it is intended more for the tourist trade than the serious student.

A study of any aspect of the amusement industry is incomplete without frequent use of *Amusement Business*, the "Bible" of the outdoor amusement business and a spin-off of *Billboard*, another major show business weekly paper. Of special interest is *Amusement Business*'s seventy-fifth anniversary issue (December 1969). There are no significant special collections that focus exclusively on forms of outdoor entertainment.

BIBLIOGRAPHY

BOOKS AND ARTICLES

General Sources

Falk, Heinrich Richard. "Conventions of Popular Entertainment: Framework for a Methodology." *Journal of Popular Culture*, 9 (Fall 1975), 480-81.

Gorham, Maurice [Anthony Coneys]. *Showmen and Suckers: An Excursion on the Crazy Fringe of the Entertainment World*. London: Percival Marshall, 1951.

McKechnie, Samuel. *Popular Entertainment Through the Ages*. 1931. Reprint. New York: Benjamin Blom, 1969.

McNamara, Brooks. [Introduction]. "Popular Entertainment Issue." *The Drama Review*, 18 (March 1974), 3-4.

———. "The Scenography of Popular Entertainment." *The Drama Review*, 18 (March 1974), 16-25.

Matlaw, Myron, ed. *American Popular Entertainment: Papers and Proceedings on the History of American Popular Entertainment*. Westport, Conn.: Greenwood Press, 1979.

Toll, Robert C. *On With the Show: The First Century of Show Business in America*. New York: Oxford University Press, 1976.

Toole-Stott, Raymond. *Circus and Allied Arts, a World Bibliography*. 4 vols. Derby, England: Harpur, 1958-1971.

Towsen, John H. "Sources on Popular Entertainment." *The Drama Review*, 18 (March 1974), 118-22.

Wilmeth, Don B. "American Popular Entertainment: A Historical Perspective." *Choice*, 14 (October 1977), 987-1004.

———. *American and English Popular Entertainment: An Information Guide*. Detroit: Gale Research, 1979.

———. "Stage Entertainment." In *Handbook of American Popular Culture*. Vol. 1. Edited by M. Thomas Inge. Westport, Conn.: Greenwood Press, 1979.

The American Circus

Ballantine, Bill. "Circus Talk." *American Mercury*, 76 (June 1953), 21-25.

———. *Wild Tigers and Tame Fleas*. New York: Rinehart, 1958.

Barton, Bob, as told to G. Ernest Thomas. *Old Covered Wagon Show Days*. New York: E. P. Dutton, 1939.

Beatty, Clyde, with Edward Anthony. *The Big Cage*. New York: Century, 1933.

Bishop, George. *The World of Clowns*. Los Angeles: Brooke House, 1976.

Bostock, Frank. *The Training of Wild Animals.* New York: Century, 1903.

Bouissac, Paul. *Circus & Culture: A Semiotic Approach.* Bloomington: Indiana University Press, 1976.

Bowen, Elbert R. "The Circus in Early Rural Missouri." *Missouri Historical Review,* 47 (October 1952), 1-17.

——. *Theatrical Entertainment in Rural Missouri Before the Civil War.* Columbia: University of Missouri Press, 1959.

Bradna, Fred, as told to Hartzell Spence. *The Big Top: My 40 Years with The Greatest Show on Earth.* New York: Simon and Schuster, 1952.

Chindahl, George L. *History of the Circus in America.* Caldwell, Idaho: Caxton Printers, 1959.

Chipman, Bert J. *Hey Rube.* Hollywood: Hollywood Print Shop, 1933.

Clair, Colin. *Human Curiosities.* New York: Abelard-Schuman, 1968.

Clapp, William W., Jr. *A Record of the Boston Stage.* 1853. Reprint. New York: Benjamin Blom, 1968.

Clement, Herb. *The Circus, Bigger and Better Than Ever?* New York: A. S. Barnes, 1974.

Conover, Richard E. *The Affairs of James A. Bailey.* Xenia, Ohio: The Author, 1957.

——. *The Great Forepaugh Show.* Xenia, Ohio: The Author, 1959.

——. *Give 'Em a John Robinson.* Xenia, Ohio: The Author, 1965.

Cooper, Courtney Ryley. *Lions 'N' Tigers 'N' Everything.* Boston: Little, Brown, 1924.

——. *With the Circus.* Boston: Little, Brown, 1930.

——. *Circus Day.* New York: Farrar & Rinehart, 1931.

Cowell, Joseph. *Thirty Years Passed Among the Players in England and America.* New York: Harper, 1844.

Coxe, Antony D. Hippisley. *A Seat at the Circus.* London: Evans Brothers, 1951.

Croft-Cooke, Rupert, and Peter Cotes. *Circus: A World History.* New York: Macmillan, 1976.

Daum, Paul Alexander. "The Royal Circus 1782-1809: An Analysis of Equestrian Entertainments." Ph.D. dissertation, Ohio State University, 1973.

Disher, M. Willson. *Greatest Show on Earth. Astley's—Afterwards Sanger's— Royal Amphitheatre of Arts, Westminster Bridge Road.* 1937. Reprint. New York: Benjamin Blom, 1969.

Drimer, Frederick. *Very Special People. The Struggles, Loves and Triumphs of Human Oddities.* New York: Amjon Publishers, 1973.

Durang, John. *The Memoirs of John Durang (American Actor, 1785-1816).* Edited by Alan S. Downer. Pittsburgh: University of Pittsburgh Press, 1966.

Durant, John, and Alice Durant. *Pictorial History of the American Circus.* New York: A. S. Barnes, 1957.

Fellows, Dexter W., and Andrew A. Freeman. *This Way to the Big Show: The Life of Dexter Fellows.* New York: The Viking Press (Halcyon House), 1936.

Fenner, Mildred S., and Wolcott Fenner, comps. and eds. *The Circus: Lure and Legend.* Englewood Cliffs, N.J.: Prentice-Hall, 1970.

Fiedler, Leslie. *Freaks: Myths & Images of the Secret Self.* New York: Simon and Schuster, 1978.

Flint, Richard W. "A Selected Guide to Source Material on the American Circus." *Journal of Popular Culture*, 6 (Winter 1972), 615-19.

Fox, Charles Philip. *Circus Parades: A Pictorial History of America's Pageant.* Watkins Glen, N.Y.: Century House, 1953.

————. *A Ticket to the Circus.* New York: Bramhall House, 1959.

————. *A Pictorial History of Performing Horses.* New York: Bramhall House, 1960.

————, and F. Beverly Kelley. *The Greatest Circus Street Parade in Pictures.* New York: Dover Publications, 1978.

————, and Tom Parkinson. *Circus in America.* Waukesha, Wis.: Country Beautiful, 1969.

Freedman, Jill. *Circus Days.* New York: Crown Publishers (Harmony Books), 1975.

Frost, Thomas. *Circus Life and Circus Celebrities.* 1875. Reprint. Detroit: Singing Tree Press, 1970.

Gerson, Walter M. "The Circus: A Mobile Total Institution." In his *Social Problems in a Changing World: A Comparative Reader.* New York: Thomas Y. Crowell, 1969.

Greenwood, Isaac J. *The Circus: Its Origin and Growth Prior to 1835.* 2d ed. New York: William Abbatt, 1909.

Hagenbeck, Lorenz. *Animals Are My Life.* Translated by Alec Brown. London: The Bodley Head, 1956.

Harris, Neil. *Humbug: The Art of P. T. Barnum.* Boston: Little, Brown, 1973.

Hediger, H[einrich]. *Studies of the Psychology and Behaviour of Captive Animals in Zoos and Circuses.* New York: Criterion Books, 1955.

Henderson, J. Y., as told to Richard Taplinger. *Circus Doctor.* Boston: Little, Brown, 1952.

Inciardi, James A., and David M. Petersen. "Gaff Joints and Shell Games: A Century of Circus Grift." *Journal of Popular Culture*, 6 (Winter 1972), 591-606.

Jennings, John J. *Theatrical and Circus Life; or, Secrets of the Stage, Green-Room and Sawdust Arena.* St. Louis: Herbert & Cole, 1882.

Lewiston, Harry, as told to Jerry Holtman. *Freak Show Man.* Los Angeles: Holloway House, 1968.

Mannix, Daniel. *We Who Are Not As Others.* New York: Pocket Books, 1976.

Maurer, David W. "Carnival Cant: A Glossary of Circus and Carnival Slang." *American Speech*, 6 (1931), 327-37.

May, Earl Chapin. *The Circus from Rome to Ringling.* 1932. Reprint. New York: Dover Publications, 1963.

Milburn, George. "Circus Words." *American Mercury*, 24 (November 1931), 351-54.

Millette, Ernest Schlee, as told to Robert Wyndham. *The Circus That Was.* Philadelphia: Dorrance, 1971.

Moy, James S. "John B. Ricketts's Circus 1793-1800." Ph.D. dissertation, University of Illinois, 1977.

————. "Entertainments at John B. Ricketts's Circus, 1793-1800." *Educational Theatre Journal*, 30 (May 1978), 186-202.

Murray, Marian. *Circus! From Rome to Ringling.* New York: Appleton-Century-Crofts, 1956.

Neafie, Nelle. *A P. T. Barnum Bibliography.* Lexington: University of Kentucky, 1965.

North, Henry Ringling, and Alden Hatch. *The Circus Kings.* Garden City, N.Y.: Doubleday, 1960.

Norwood, Edwin P. *The Other Side of the Circus.* Garden City, N.Y.: Doubleday & Page, 1926.

————. *The Circus Menagerie.* Garden City, N.Y.: Doubleday & Page, 1929.

Parry, Albert. *Tattoo: Secrets of a Strange Art.* 1933. Reprint. New York: Macmillan, 1971.

Plowden, Gene. *Those Amazing Ringlings and Their Circus.* New York: Bonanza Books, 1967.

Posey, Jake. *Last of the Forty Horse Drivers.* New York: Vantage Press, 1959.

Powledge, Fred. *Mud Show: A Circus Season.* New York: Harcourt Brace Jovanovich, 1975.

Proske, Roman. *Lions, Tigers, and Me.* New York: Henry Holt, 1956.

Remy, Tristan. *Les Clowns.* Paris: Bernard Grasset, 1945.

————. *Entrees Clownesque.* Paris: L'Arche, 1962.

Rennert, Jack. *100 Years of Circus Posters.* New York: Darien House, 1974.

Reynolds, Chang. *Pioneer Circuses of the West.* Los Angeles: Westernlore Press, 1966.

Robinson, Gil. *Old Wagon Show Days.* Cincinnati: Brockwell Publishers, 1925.

Saxon, A. H. *Enter Foot and Horse: A History of Hippodrama in England and France.* New Haven: Yale University Press, 1968.

————. *The Life and Art of Andrew Ducrow & The Romantic Age of the English Circus.* Hamden, Conn.: The Shoe String Press (Archon Books), 1978.

Sergel, Sherman Louis, ed. *The Language of Show Biz.* Chicago: Dramatic Publishing, 1973.

Sokan, Robert. *A Descriptive and Bibliographic Catalog of the Circus and Related Arts Collection at Illinois State University, Normal, Illinois.* Bloomington, Ill.: The Scarlet Ibis Press, 1975.

Sweet, Robert C., and Robert W. Habenstein. "Some Perspective on the Circus in Transition." *Journal of Popular Culture*, 6 (Winter 1972), 583-90.

Swortzell, Lowell. *Here Comes the Clowns: A Cavalcade of Comedy from Antiquity to the Present.* New York: The Viking Press, 1978.

Thayer, Stuart. *Annals of the American Circus 1793-1829.* Manchester, Mich.: Printed for the author by Rymack Printing Co., 1976.

Thetard, Henry. *La Merveilleuse Histoire du Cirque.* 2 vols. Paris: Prisma, 1947.

Toll, Robert C. *On With the Show: The First Century of Show Business in America.* New York: Oxford University Press, 1976.

Toole-Stott, Raymond. *Circus and Allied Arts, A World Bibliography.* 4 vols. Derby, England: Harpur, 1958-1971.
————. *A Bibliography of the Books on the Circus in English from 1773 to 1964.* Derby, England: Harpur, 1964.
Towsen, John H. *Clowns.* New York: Hawthorn Books, 1976.
Truzzi, Marcello. "The American Circus as a Source of Folklore: An Introduction." *Southern Folklore Quarterly,* 30 (December 1966), 289-300.
————. "Folksongs of the American Circus." *New York Folklore Quarterly,* 24 (September 1968), 163-75.
————. "The Decline of the American Circus: The Shrinkage of an Institution." In *Sociology and Everyday Life.* Edited by Marcello Truzzi. Englewood Cliffs, N.J.: Prentice-Hall, 1968.
————, ed. "Circuses, Carnivals and Fairs in America." *Journal of Popular Culture,* 6 (Winter 1972), 531-619.
Tuttle, George Palliser. "The History of the Royal Circus, Equestrian and Philharmonic Academy, 1782-1816, St. George's Fields, Surrey, England." Ph.D. dissertation, Tufts University, 1972.
Vail, R[obert] W[illiam] G[lenroie]. "The Early Circus in America." *Proceedings of the American Antiquarian Society,* N.S. 43 (April 1933), 116-85.
————. "This Way to the Big Top." *New York Historical Society Bulletin,* 29 (July 1945), 137-59.
Verney, Peter. *Here Comes the Circus.* New York & London: Paddington Press (Distributed in U.S. by Grosset & Dunlap), 1978.
Wallace, Irving. *The Fabulous Showman.* New York: Knopf, 1959.
Werner, M. R. *Barnum.* New York: Harcourt, Brace, 1923.

The Wild West Exhibition

Brasmer, William. "The Wild West Exhibition and the Drama of Civilization." In *Western Popular Theatre.* Edited by David Mayer and Kenneth Richards. London: Metheun, 1977.
Burke, John. *Buffalo Bill, The Noblest Whiteskin.* New York: G. P. Putnam, 1973.
Collings, Ellsworth, and Alma Miller England. *The 101 Ranch.* Norman: University of Oklahoma Press, 1937.
Croft-Cooke, Rupert, and W. S. Meadmore. *Buffalo Bill: The Legend, The Man of Action, The Showman.* London: Sidgwick and Jackson, 1952.
Deahl, William E., Jr. "Nebraska's Unique Contribution to the Entertainment World." *Nebraska History,* 49 (Autumn 1968), 283-97.
————. "Buffalo Bill's Wild West Show in New Orleans." *Louisiana History,* 16 (Summer 1975), 289-98.
Foreman, Carolyn Thomas. *Indians Abroad.* Norman: University of Oklahoma Press, 1943.
Gipson, Fred. *Fabulous Empire. Colonel Zack Miller's Story.* Boston: Houghton Mifflin, 1946.
Griffin, Charles Eldridge. *Four Years in Europe with Buffalo Bill.* Albia, Iowa: Stage Publishing, 1908.

Havighurst, Walter. *Annie Oakley of the Wild West*. New York: Macmillan, 1954.

Hinkle, Milt. "The Kit Carson Wild West Show." *Frontier Times*, 38 (May 1964), 6-11, 57-58.

―――. "The Way a Wild West Show Operated." *Frontier Times*, 43 (March 1969), 20-23, 50-52.

Johannsen, Albert. *The House of Beadle and Adams*. 3 vols. Norman: University of Oklahoma Press, 1950-1962.

Katigan, Madelon B. "The Fabulous 101." *True West*, 8 (September-October 1960), 6-12, 50-51.

Leonard, Elizabeth Jane, and Julia Cody Goodman. Edited by James William Hoffman. *Buffalo Bill, King of the Old West*. New York: Library Publishers, 1955.

McDaniel, Ruel. "Requiem for the Wild West Shows." *Frontier Times*, 36 (Winter 1961), 22-23, 40.

Mix, Paul E. *The Life and Legend of Tom Mix*. New York and South Brunswick: A. S. Barnes, 1972.

Monaghan, Jay. *The Great Rascal: The Life and Adventures of Ned Buntline*. New York: Bonanza Books, 1951.

Pfening, Fred D., Jr. *Col. Tim McCoy's Real Wild West and Rough Riders of the World*. Columbus: Pfening & Snyder, 1955.

Rennert, Jack. *100 Posters of Buffalo Bill's Wild West*. New York: Darien House, 1976.

Russell, Don. *The Lives and Legends of Buffalo Bill*. Norman: University of Oklahoma Press, 1960.

―――. *The Wild West or, A History of the Wild West Show*. Fort Worth: Amon Carter Museum of Western Art, 1970.

―――. "Cody, Kings, and Coronets." *The American West*, 7 (July 1970), 4-10, 62.

―――. "The Golden Age of Wild West Shows." *The Bandwagon*, 15 (September-October 1971), 21-27.

Schwartz, Joseph. "The Wild West Show; 'Everything Genuine'." *Journal of Popular Culture*, 3 (Spring 1970), 656-66.

Sell, Henry Blackman, and Victor Weybright. *Buffalo Bill and the Wild West*. New York: Oxford University Press, 1955.

Shirley, Glenn. *Pawnee Bill: A Biography of Major Gordon W. Lillie*. Lincoln: University of Nebraska Press, 1958.

Thorp, Raymond W. *Spirit Gun of the West, The Story of Doc W. F. Carver*. Glendale, Calif.: Arthur H. Clark, 1957.

Walsh, Richard J., in collaboration with Milton S. Salsbury. *The Making of Buffalo Bill*. Indianapolis: Bobbs-Merrill, 1928.

Wetmore, Helen Cody. *Last of the Great Scouts*. Duluth, Minn.: Duluth Press, 1899.

Yellow Rob, Chauncey. "The Menace of the Wild West Show." *Quarterly Journal of the Society of American Indians*, 2 (July-September 1914), 224-28.

Outdoor Amusements

Barrett, Richmond. *Good Old Summer Days.* Boston: Houghton Mifflin, 1952.

Baxter, Sylvester. "The Trolley in Rural Parks." *Harper's Monthly,* 97 (June 1898), 60-69.

Boles, Don. *The Midway Showman.* Atlanta: Pinchpenny Press, 1967.

Braithwaite, David. *Fairground Architecture: The World of Amusement Parks, Carnivals, and Fairs.* New York: Frederick A. Praeger, 1968.

Burg, David F. *Chicago's White City of 1893.* Lexington: The University Press of Kentucky, 1976.

Crews, Harry. "Carny." *Playboy,* 23 (September 1976), 96, 98, 195, 196.

Cuber, John F. "Patrons of Amusement Parks." *Sociology and Social Research,* 24 (September-October 1939), 63-68.

Dembroski, Theodore M. "Hanky Panks and Group Games Versus Alibis and Flats: The Legitimate and Illegitimate of the Carnival's Front End." *Journal of Popular Culture,* 6 (Winter 1972), 567-82.

Dexter, T. F. G. *The Pagan Origin of Fairs.* Perranporth, Cornwall, England: New Knowledge Press, 1930.

Easto, Patrick C., and Marcello Truzzi. "Carnivals, Roadshows, and Freaks." *Society,* 9 (March 1972), 26-34.

————. "Towards an Ethnography of the Carnival Social System." *Journal of Popular Culture,* 6 (Winter 1972), 550-66.

Fried, Frederick A. *Pictorial History of the Carousel.* New York: A. S. Barnes, 1964.

Frost, Thomas. *The Old Showmen and the Old London Fairs.* 1881. Reprint. Ann Arbor: Gryphon Books, 1971.

Funnell, Charles F. *By the Beautiful Sea: The Rise and High Times of That Great American Resort, Atlantic City.* New York: Alfred A. Knopf, 1975.

Garrett, Thomas M. "A History of Pleasure Gardens in New York City, 1700-1865." Ph.D. dissertation, New York University, 1978.

Gresham, William Lindsay. *Monster Midway.* New York: Rinehart, 1953.

Griffin, Al. *"Step Right Up Folks!"* Chicago: Henry Regnery, 1974.

Hartt, Rollin Lynde. *The People at Play: Excursions in the Humor and Philosophy of Popular Amusements.* Boston: Houghton Mifflin, 1909.

Jackson, Joseph. "Vauxhall Garden." *Pennsylvania Magazine of History and Biography,* 57 (1933), 289-98.

Krassowski, Wittold. "Social Structure and Professionalization in the Occupation of the Carnival Worker." Master's thesis, Purdue University, 1954.

Kyriazi, Gary. *The Great American Amusement Parks.* Secaucus, N.J.: Citadel Press, 1976.

Lewis, Arthur H. *Carnival.* New York: Trident Press, 1970.

Lyon, Peter. "The Master Showman of Coney Island." *American Heritage,* 9 (June 1958), 14-20, 92-95.

McCullough, Edo. *Good Old Coney Island.* New York: Charles Scribner, 1957.

————. *World's Fair Midway: An Affectionate Account of American Amuse-*

ment Areas from the Crystal Palace to the Crystal Ball. 1966. Reprint. New York: Arno Press, 1976.

McKennon, Joe. *A Pictorial History of the American Carnival.* Sarasota, Fla.: Carnival Publishers, 1972.

McNamara, Brooks. "Come on Over: The Rise and Fall of the American Amusement Park." *Theatre Crafts,* 11 (September 1977), 33, 84-86.

Mangels, William F. *The Outdoor Entertainment Business.* New York: Vantage Press, 1952.

Manley, Seon, and Robert Manley. *Beaches: Their Lives, Legends, and Lore.* Philadelphia: Chilton Book, 1968.

Mannix, Daniel. *Step Right Up.* New York: Harper and Bros., 1950.

————. *We Who Are Not as Others.* New York: Pocket Books, 1976.

Maurer, David W. "Carnival Cant: A Glossary of Circus and Carnival Slang." *American Speech,* 6 (June 1931), 327-37.

Meiselas, Susan. *Carnival Strippers.* New York: Farrar, Straus, and Giroux, 1976.

Morley, Henry. *Memories of Bartholomew Fair.* 3d ed. 1880. Reprint. Detroit: Singing Tree Press, 1969.

Onosko, Tim. *Fun Land U.S.A.* New York: Ballantine Books, 1978.

Pilat, Oliver, and Jo Ranson. *Sodom by the Sea: An Affectionate History of Coney Island.* Garden City, N.Y.: Doubleday, Doran, 1941.

Ritchey, David. "Columbia Garden: Baltimore's First Pleasure Garden." *Southern Speech Communication Journal,* 39 (Spring 1974), 241-47.

Scarne, John. "Carnival, Fair, Bazaar, Arcade and Amusement Park Games." In *Scarne's Complete Guide to Gambling.* Rev. ed. New York: Simon and Schuster, 1974.

Scott, W. S. *Green Retreats, the Story of Vauxhall Gardens, 1661-1859.* London: Odhams Press, 1955.

Sergel, Sherman Louis, ed. *The Language of Show Biz.* Chicago: Dramatic Publishing, 1973.

Snow, Robert E., and David E. Wright. "Coney Island: A Case Study in Popular Culture and Technical Change." *Journal of Popular Culture,* 9 (Spring 1976), 960-75.

Sonneck, O. G. *Early Concert Life in America (1731-1800).* Leipzig, Germany: Breitkopf and Hartel, 1907.

Southworth, James Granville. *Vauxhall Gardens: A Chapter in the Social History of England.* New York: Columbia University Press, 1944.

Starsmore, Ian. *English Fairs.* Levittown, N.Y.: Transatlantic Arts, 1976.

"Theme Parks." *Theatre Crafts,* 11 (September 1977), 112.

Truzzi, Marcello, ed. "Circuses, Carnivals and Fairs in America." *Journal of Popular Culture,* 6 (Winter 1972), 531-619.

Truzzi, Marcello, and Patrick C. Easto. "The Carnival as a Marginally Legal Work Activity: The Typological Approach to Work Systems." In *Deviant Behavior: Occupational and Organizational Bases.* Edited by Clifton D. Bryant. Chicago: Rand McNally, 1974.

Waters, H. W. *History of Fairs and Expositions.* London, Ontario: Reid Bros., 1939.

Willey, Day Allen. "The Trolley-Park." *The Cosmopolitan,* 33 (July 1902), 265-72.

Wroth, Warwick. *Cremorne and the Later London Gardens.* London: Elliot Stock, 1907.

————, and Arthur Edgar. *The London Pleasure Gardens in the Eighteenth Century.* London: Macmillan, 1896.

PERIODICALS

Amusement Business. Nashville, 1961-.
Bandwagon. Columbus, Ohio, 1951-.
Billboard. Los Angeles, 1894-.
Le Cirque Dans L'Univers. Vincennes, France, 1950-.
New York Clipper. New York, 1853-1924.
Variety. New York, 1905-
White Tops. Indianapolis, 1928-.

CHAPTER 4. Death in Popular Culture

Robert A. Armour and
J. Carol Williams

HISTORIC OUTLINE

Throughout American history, popular customs have reflected general American attitudes toward death. From the seventeenth-century folk art of tombstone carving, to the more elaborate nineteenth-century monuments, to this century's reproductions of Michelangelo's masterpieces in famous Forest Lawn Cemetery, the art that has adorned our cemeteries has made visible the values we have placed on death. Likewise, the rituals associated with death also represent popular values: hiring an *aanspreecker* in colonial Dutch American communities to visit the homes of friends of the deceased to announce the death; the quick burial in mass graves of the soldiers killed on Civil War battlefields; or the sight of an entire nation in mourning as it watches the riderless horse lead the body of a slain president to its resting place. The purpose of this introduction is to give an overview of popular attitudes toward death in America. Because of the many ethnic and religious variations that have existed side by side in this land, it is impossible to make generalizations about the attitudes toward death, which have varied with culture and time, but we can pinpoint some writers and events that were typical of their day.

One of the first books published in the Old World about America was an illustrated version of Thomas Hariot's *A Briefe and true report of the new found land of Virginia* (1590). This book, written by a fine scientist sent over by Sir Walter Raleigh to record the history of the new colony at Roanoke Island, was one of the earliest accounts of the customs of the people native to this land. Among the illustrations by John White is a drawing of an Indian burying ground, which consisted of a platform on high wooden columns inside a thatched hut of considerable size. The skin of a dead chief was stripped from the body, tanned, and then replaced over the skeleton so that the figure of the chief was preserved. Then, ac-

cording to the caption that accompanies the drawing, the body was placed
on the platform where one of the priests in charge of the dead murmured
prayers day and night. This, the earliest example of published writing
about death in North America, demonstrates that the Indians had concerns for their dead that are similiar to those still held by a large segment
of the population: interest in the preservation of the body, reverence for
the dead, and acceptance of the role of the clergy.

As the Europeans began to populate the eastern seaboard, they brought
with them, along with their political, economic, and artistic attitudes, ideas
about death. Those ideas found quick expression. During the first winter
in the new land, fifty-two of the original one hundred two settlers at the
Plymouth colony died before spring. And in Virginia, of the roughly 1,650
people who had come to the colony by 1625, approximately one thousand
had died; over three hundred had been killed in the Indian massacre of
1622. The deaths in Virginia were accepted as expected events; John Smith,
in his *History of Virginia* (1624), simply refers to the deaths and rails at
the leaders whose stupidity caused them. God is given credit for the good
things that happened at Jamestown, but He is not blamed for the suffering. This attitude established a pattern that was carried on in the southern
colonies throughout the colonial period. The writings of William Byrd II
discuss sicknesses and deaths, but there is only brief mention of the dying
process and no doubt of the afterlife. Even deists such as Thomas Jefferson
believed without much question in a future state of rewards and punishment, and the words of Philip Vickers Fithian, the tutor for the family of
Robert Carter of Virginia just before the Revolution, typify the concern
for the afterlife during the Enlightenment. When he thought he might be
dying during a serious illness, he resigned "myself body and soul and
Employment to god who has the hearts of all in his hand, and who I am
persuaded, if he has anything for me to do in Life, will preserve, and in a
measure fit me for it, if not, I am in his hand, let him do as seems good
in his eyes."

However, the attitude in the colonies controlled by the Puritans was by
no means so accepting or passive. These people began early in the education of their children to establish a healthy respect for death. Two of the
most popular books of Puritan New England were intended to instill in
children their parents' fears. James Janeway, in *A Token for Children*
(1676), taught them about the ever nearness of death, and *The New
England Primer* used thoughts about death to illustrate some of the
letters of the alphabet: "T—*Time* cuts down all/Both Great and Small"
and "X—Xerxes the great did die/So must you and I," among others.

Life was viewed by the Puritan as a pilgrimage, a difficult trip whose
ultimate goal is heaven. American Puritans were greatly influenced by
John Bunyan's *Pilgrim's Progress* (1678), and their expectations for life

and death followed closely Christian's pilgrimage through the temptations of life. The goal is the Celestial City, which can be reached only through death. This attitude led to a duality in the Puritan's ideas about death. One side of the Puritan said that death would bring relief from the travails of life and would bring the traveler into the presence of God. This side welcomed death, perhaps even longed for it. The other side of the Puritan realized that the dying person may not be among those chosen to be saved by God and therefore may well be damned to an eternity without the presence of God. In this manner the Puritan at once both glorified death and feared its consequences.

The words of the Puritan preacher Jonathan Edwards expressed this duality. In his *Personal Narrative* (ca. 1740) he wrote: "The heaven I desired was a heaven of holiness; to be with God, and to spend my eternity in divine love. . . . Heaven appeared exceedingly delightful, as a world of love; and that all happiness consisted in living in pure, humble, heavenly, divine love." Yet in his famous sermon, "Sinners in the Hands of an Angry God" (1741), he describes hell in such terms as to make death a frightening prospect: ". . . it is a great furnace of wrath, a wide and bottomless pit, full of the fire of wrath, that you are held over by in the hand of that God, whose wrath is provoked and incensed as much against you, as against many of the damned in hell. . . ."

The popular image of parsimonious and socially dull Puritans is put to the lie by a description of their funerals. Historical records demonstrate that substantial parts of estates were spent for the funeral of the deceased. In addition to the expected expenses for a coffin, winding sheet, and grave, large amounts of money were spent on gloves and rings for the invited guests at the funeral and for extensive amounts of spices, cider, and rum. The costs of the alcoholic beverages became one of the largest single expenses in a Puritan funeral. The practice, of course, was not restricted to the Puritan colonies, and people in other colonies also began to complain about the high cost of dying, especially the costs of providing gifts and drinks for the guests.

The importation of the romantic movement from Europe as the eighteenth century turned into the nineteenth led to a different attitude toward death in America. The romantics were fascinated with death, and thoughts of death dominated the "graveyard" writers who were central to the movement. Many writers in the early romantic period, such as Philip Freneau and William Cullen Bryant, meditated on the meaning of death; but perhaps the American writer best known for his compulsion about death was Edgar Allan Poe. Many of his poems and stories about death demonstrate a duality of horror and longing, but none illustrates the point better than some verses from "Annabel Lee" (1849), which describes the death of the narrator's girfriend:

And this was the reason that, long ago,
    In this kingdom by the sea,
A wind blew out of a cloud by night
    Chilling my Annabel Lee;
So that her highborn kinsmen came
    And bore her away from me,
To shut her up in a sepulchre
    In this kingdom by the sea.

The angels, not half so happy in Heaven,
    Went envying her and me—
Yes!—that was the reason (as all men know,
    In this kingdom by the sea)
That the wind came out of the cloud chilling
    And killing my Annabel Lee.

Some of the nineteenth-century theologians continued the Puritan concepts even though the Puritan movement itself had died out. John Owen, writing in Philadelphia in 1827, made an impassioned plea for the Calvinistic view of the afterlife. In *The Death of Death in the Death of Christ*, which was endorsed by thirteen other ministers from the city, Owen reinforced and restated the basic tenets of Calvinism: ". . . let these doctrines, of God's eternal *election*, the free grace of *conversion*, *perseverance*, and their *necessary* consequences, be asserted." In other words, salvation depended on God's determination to save a particular soul. This was not an uncommon view of death at the time, but one that was to be given less credence as the nineteenth century passed.

A few years later, another book, *The Tree and its Fruits or, The Last Hours of Infidels & Christians Contracted* (1839), coming out of the same city but written by the American Sunday-School Union, focused on the last hours of the dying. The effort was to show that the good died easily and the evil died with difficulty. "It is a fact," the Union writes, "which appears worthy of being more prominently held up to the view of all whose minds are in any degree interested in the great concerns of eternity, that nearly all those who have been conspicuous in the ranks of infidelity, have left this world in a tempest of horror and dismay, as though the anathema maranatha, pronounced against all who love not the Lord Jesus, had withered them before their time; whilst it is notoriously true, that those who meet death with the greatest composure, and who triumpht over all his terrors, are the men whose lives have adorned the gospel of God their Saviour."

A more moderate and eloquent view of death was presented in the dedication speech for Hollywood Cemetery in Richmond, Virginia, in June of 1849. Oliver Baldwin's view of death was no less traditional than those of Owen or the Union, but his ideas were more tempered with charity: "The Grave, the Grave, how simply but powerfully it speaks through the eye of the soul, and bids it meditate upon itself and its destiny. An ancient writer has said that man was taken from the dust of the earth to prompt him to humility. But a still stronger incentive to humility is the fact which he daily witnesses that to dust he must return." Dust, according to Baldwin, is the fate of all, not just those who are elected by God for salvation or those who have lived without sin and can expect an easy death. Baldwin went on to discuss at some length the value of a fine cemetery, both to those who expect to reside there shortly and to those who visit old friends and relatives there.

In 1859 Charles Darwin published *The Origin of Species*, which eventually changed the attitudes of many Americans toward death. Darwin, of course, challenged the historical accuracy of the Bible, but, in one way, his method was more of a challenge than his content. He had used science to arrive at conclusions that affected religion, and humankind was forced to decide between science and religion or to find a way to reconcile the two. Among the first to try the latter was William Rounseville Alger in *A Critical History of the Doctrine of Future Life* (1867). Alger was by no means a scientist, but he did view humankind as living in a scientific cycle in which all plants and animals have a place and a role: "The individual man dies . . . for the good of the species, and that he may furnish the conditions for the development of a higher life elsewhere. It is quite obvious that, if individuals did not die, new individuals could not live, because there would not be room. It is also equally evident that, if individuals did not die, they could never have any other life than the present." Alger claimed that this consideration made death a "necessity and benignity," rather than a horror; and he maintained that "the noble purpose of self-sacrifice enables us to smile upon the grave."

By the end of the century, writers were more consciously trying to reconcile Darwin with their own views of death. John Fiske, in *The Destiny of Man* (1892), attempted to show that his own Christian faith was not at odds with the theory of evolution. In his last chapter, he considered the afterlife, which is after all, he suggested, a religious matter not to be considered scientifically but accepted as a point of faith. Fiske put limits on the use of science and maintained that one must go beyond science to discover the truth about death. William James engaged himself in the same debate but used science to arrive at his conclusions in *Human Immortality* (1898). James wanted to show that the scientific assumption that life ends when the brain is dead is too limited. He argued that the brain has several functions: ". . . our soul's life, as we here know it, would none the less in literal strictness be the function of the brain. The brain would be the individual variable, the mind would vary dependently on it. But such dependence on the brain for this natural life would in no wise make immortal life impossible,—it might be quite compatible with super-natural life behind the veil hereafter."

While the intellectuals were trying to decide how to deal with the scientific problems raised during the century, others were finding different expressions of their ideas about death. Well-known writers, such as Henry Wadsworth Longfellow and Oliver Wendell Holmes, wrote poems that sought the solace of death; and writers less well known at the time, such as Walt Whitman and Emily Dickinson, adopted death as a major theme. Among the popular writers, however, death remained uncomplicated by theories of evolution and scientific methods. The elegiac and funeral verses of some sentimental poets received wide circulation and represented an altogether different attitude toward death than did the theories of ministers and psychologists or the poetry of Whitman and Dickinson. Julia A. Moore, the "Sweet Singer of Michigan," was renowned for her crude poetry inspired by the deaths of children:

LITTLE ANDREW

Andrew was a little infant,
And his life was two years old;
He was his parent's eldest boy,
And he was drowned, I was told.
His parents never more can see him
In this world of grief and pain,
And Oh! they will not forget him
While on earth they do remain.

One bright and pleasant morning
His uncle thought it would be nice
To take his dear little nephew
Down to play upon the raft,
Where he was to work upon it,
And this little child would company be—
The raft the water rushed around it,
Yet he the danger did not see.

This little child knew no danger—
Its little soul was free from sin—
He was looking in the water,
When, alas, the child fell in.
Beneath the raft the water took him,
For the current was so strong,
And before they could rescue him
He was drowned and was gone.

> Oh! how sad were his kind parents
> When they saw their drowned child,
> As they brought him from the water,
> It almost made their hearts grow wild.
> Oh! how mournful was the parting
> From that little infant son.
> Friends, I pray you, all take warning,
> Be careful of your little ones.

In the first decades of the twentieth century, the attitudes toward death did not change radically from those at the end of the previous one. Samuel McChord Crothers ended his *The Endless Life* (1905) with the allegory of Mr. Honest who dies peacefully: "Our doubts and fears vanish when we see Mr. Honest standing by the river's bank talking with happy earnestness with his friend Good-conscience. . . . Those who share that faith recognize, in all humility, their own limitations." And G. Lowes Dickinson in *Is Immortality Desirable?* decides, to no one's surprise, that it is: "To sum up, then, the immortality which I hold to be desirable, and which I suggest to you as desirable, is one in which a continuity of experience analogous to that which we are aware of here is carried on into a life after death, the essence of that life being continuous unfolding no doubt through stress and conflict, of those potentialities of Good of which we are aware here as the most significant part of ourselves."

Such attitudes remained typical through the middle part of the twentieth century; and indeed, it is possible to find some writers even in the seventh decade who claim to hold such traditional views. However, the growing importance of science, including the science of trying to understand the mind, and the diminishing importance of religion have changed attitudes. But some of the most significant changes in the attitudes toward death have resulted from other societal changes. The concept of the family has changed from one in which there were several generations of one family living under the same roof (as with the fictional Walton family on television) to one in which there are normally only two generations within a household—and then only until the children are old enough to move out on their own. This change, coupled with the growth of homes for the elderly and with increased mobility, means that children are less likely to see their grandparents die.

Another factor influencing that phenomenon is the growth of modern hospital facilities and the tendency for the aging to spend their last weeks in a hospital, both benefiting and suffering from life-prolonging treatment. The result is that very few people die at home now, as people did a century ago. If a person does not die accidentally on a highway, the likelihood is that he or she will die in the unfamiliar surroundings of a hospital room. The entire family probably will not be present, and surely the youngest children will be absent. One result of these changes is that children are likely to reach adulthood before they are in the presence of a dying person; the act of death becomes a mystery only to be described by older persons, or perhaps never even discussed at all.

Another change in our society that has influenced our attitudes concerns the growing dependence on the funeral home for its services. Early in this century, the undertaker would come to the home of the deceased and embalm the body there. It would be laid out in the parlor until time for the services and the body would then probably have been taken to a church for the religious service and from there to the grave site for burial. Many changes began to alter this procedure. First, the process of embalming was moved to the facilities of the undertaker, where the family was not bothered with the unpleasantness of it and where the risks of spreading contagious diseases were diminished. Then, many people found that rising building costs were forcing them to forego the luxury of a parlor, which formerly had been little used except for Sunday afternoon visits from the preacher and for funerals. Some houses were built without parlors, and, in others, the television set was moved in and the room became the family room or den, hardly places suitable for the display of a body. To complicate matters more, the size of the front door was reduced for architectural reasons, and the caskets would no longer fit through. The result was that the undertaker began to provide space in his building for the display of the body and for visitation by family and friends. The presence of death was taken from the home and moved to this other place, significantly called a "funeral home," and the room set aside for visitation was called the "parlor." The person who operated such an establishment no longer simply performed the basic services of an undertaker, but became a professional overseeing the entire process of the funeral. He, and even today he is almost always a man, gave himself a new title—"funeral director." He added a chapel to the building so that the body did not have to be taken to a church for services, and ultimately he relieved the family of much of the organizational responsibility for arranging for the disposition of a relative's body.

These changes mean that the presence of death is physically removed from the household and that some of the trauma of dealing with a death is passed from the hands of the family to those of a professional who is paid for his services. Those in the colonial period who complained about the high costs of funerals would be astounded by the bills presented today by hospitals, rest homes, and funeral directors for services rendered during a person's last days and the funeral that follows. But these professionals provide services that have become accepted by the large part of Americans at mid-twentieth century.

For many Americans, death has become an unfamiliar event, made mysterious and frightening by the fact that so few people experience its presence during their formative years. But there have been intellectual challenges to this system that have been influential. In 1963 Jessica Mitford wrote *The American Way of Death*, which was an exposé of the funeral industry. This book, and others like it, became the impetus for a more careful look at the funeral practices that had become so widely accepted. It challenged the necessity for embalming, expensive caskets, and elaborate cemetery plots; and some people began asking if the high expenses of a funeral were justified. The most pointed attack, however, was directed at the funeral directors themselves, who were accused of creating a myth about the value of their services. Mitford's book was sensational, and she used isolated cases, in some instances, to support her points; but the overall message of the book was accurate and led many people to question the methods of the American way of death.

Then, in 1969, Elizabeth Kubler-Ross wrote *On Death and Dying*, which became a major challenge to the way we have been treating our dying patients. Kubler-Ross, herself a medical doctor, demonstrated that often the dying patient is given good medical treatment but poor death counseling by medical professionals whose primary goal is the saving of life. Few physicians are trained to deal with the traumas of death and are not capable of assisting their patients with the problems of dying. Kubler-Ross has interviewed hundreds of dying patients and listened to their tales, and this book is in part a record of what they have told her and in part a plea for a better understanding and for more sensible treatment of the dying patient. It, like Mitford's book, has forced the American public to reconsider its attitude toward death.

These influences have led to mixed attitudes toward death in contemporary America. While the majority of Americans still insist on what they think of as a traditional view of death and funerals, there are signs that Mitford, Kubler-Ross, and others have had their impact. That attitudes have been changed somewhat is reflected in the general acceptance of college courses and church seminars on death, newspaper and magazine articles on the costs of funerals, memorial societies that discuss alternative means of disposing of the body, and television shows that even bring the presence of death into situation comedies. Suggestions for reform, however, meet with widespread resistance, and demonstrate that attitudes toward death are deep seated in our society. It is difficult to say whether the attitudes toward death in today's society lean toward tradition or openness; probably the former, but the tendency toward openness suggests that there may be continuing changes in attitudes.

REFERENCE WORKS

Death may be a personal concern, a philosophical issue, the subject of religious dogma, the source of emotional difficulties, a disruptive force in society, and the source of the demand for one's services. To claim that every academic discipline is interested in death from some perspective and that most everyday activities are touched by some aspect of death is not an exaggeration. Although the omnipresence of death and the varied interest in the topic have resulted in diverse materials on death, they have also complicated the task of the researcher. The researcher must locate within larger disciplines and areas of interests those works that apply rather specialized approaches to death.

Both general and specialized bibliographies on death and dying are now available to assist in researching the topic of death, but these rapidly become outdated as new books and articles appear. Robert Fulton, director of the Center for Death Education and Research at the University of Minnesota, has updated an earlier bibliography, *Death, Grief and Bereavement: A Bibliography 1845-1975*, which contains nearly four thousand entries that approach death primarily from an empirical perspective. Books dealing with suicide, literary works, and theological studies are excluded. The emphasis is on issues of contemporary concern such as terminal care, the definition of death, euthanasia, and sudden infant death syndrome. The bibliography is indexed by subject, and numbered entries are listed alphabetically by author.

A Bibliography of Books on Death, Bereavement, Loss, and Grief: 1935-1968 by Austin H. Kutscher, Jr. and Austin H. Kutscher, together with *Supplement 1, 1968-1972* by Austin H. Kutscher, Jr. and Martin Kutscher, is an uncritical bibliography, indexed by author, of approximately twenty-four hundred books published in the United States. These titles are grouped in forty categories, ranging from ancestor worship to undertaking and widows' allowances. In another general bibliography, *Death: A Bibliographic Guide*, Albert Jay Miller and Michael Acri classify nearly four thousand entries under seven headings, such as religion, theology, science, and nursing experiences. Citations are to professional journals, to books, and to articles in popular magazines. These entries are described briefly or not at all, but a very useful section on audiovisual media contains nearly two hundred references to films, filmstrips, microfilms, recordings and tapes, slides, transparencies, photographs and prints, and kits. Martin L. Kutscher has two recent helpful works, *A Comprehensive Bibliography of Thanatology Literature* and *A Cross-Index of Indices of Books on Thanatology*. A brief description of over two hundred of the leading fall and winter books on death from more than one hundred publishers can be found in *Publishers Weekly*, September 25, 1978.

Several specialized bibliographies are available. The National Institute of Mental Health published *Bibliography on Suicide and Suicide Prevention*, edited by Norman L. Farberow, which covered literature from 1897 to 1970. As yet, this bibliography has not been updated, but a partial survey of literature on suicide since 1975 can be found in *Bioethical Perspec-*

tives on Death and Dying: Summaries of the Literature, edited by Madeline M. Nevins. A special supplement is available of the *Bioethics Digest,* which contains over three hundred abstracts of articles published in the death and dying section of the first twelve issues of *Bioethics Digest* (May 1976 to April 1977). The abstracts are grouped in major topic sections and indexed by author.

A good specialized bibliography focusing on difficulties encountered by survivors of the deceased is *Adjustments to Widowhood and Some Related Problems: A Selective and Annotated Bibliography* by Cecile Strugnell. Approximately four hundred fifty entries are grouped in three major sections, the largest of which, "bereavement," is subdivided into bereavement of children, bereavement of the elderly widowed, and cross-cultural studies of bereavement. The entries are not indexed by either author or subject; however, the citations under each subheading are listed alphabetically by author, and each entry is carefully described.

Funeral Service: A Bibliography of Literature on Its Past, Present and Future, the Various Means of Disposition and Memorialization, edited by Barbara K. Harrah and David F. Harrah, contains approximately two thousand entries on aspects of the funeral industry. The entries are briefly described and are indexed by subject and author. The section of references to audiovisual materials and the section listing cemetery associations, memorial societies, and other funeral related organizations are most useful.

RESEARCH COLLECTIONS

The scarcity of special collections on death and the highly specialized nature of those that do exist is in part a function of the nature of the topic of death. Although the Columbia University Library is recognized as the repository for materials of the Foundation of Thanatology, the library reports that its works on death are dispersed through the main collection and cataloged under broader headings in its different libraries.

Existing special collections are specialized and limited in scope. The American Antiquarian Society in Worcester, Massachusetts, for instance, houses pamphlet and book collections containing the texts of approximately twelve hundred funeral sermons delivered between 1656 and 1830. Also housed there are three collections of photographs of New England gravestones. These collections, one by Harriette Marifield Forbes and the others by Daniel Farber, present photographs of entire stones, as well as details of sculptured aspects of stones, and are usually indexed by gravecutter and graveyard.

Several organizations interested in life after death have collections of literature on death, but these are usually limited to works dealing with communication with the dead and the survival of death. The Eileen J. Garrette Library of Parapsychology Foundation in New York City contains a reference collection of about ten thousand volumes, which includes such topics as survival of death, reincarnation, communication with the dead, and descriptions of deathbed out-of-body experiences. These materials are available for use only in the library. The Parapsychology Library at the Physical Research Foundation in Durham, North Carolina, houses six hundred books, three hundred bound periodical volumes, two hundred journals, and an annotated bibliography of "out-of-body experiences" sheets on file there. The materials are also available to the public for reference use only.

The Association for Research and Enlightenment, Virginia Beach, Virginia, has a collection of more than twenty-five thousand books that focus on psychic phenomena and spiritual growth. Among these are two hundred fifty titles on future life, three hundred fifty titles on reincarnation, and two hundred fifty titles on death and dying. Members of the association may borrow by mail, but nonmembers are permitted to use these resources at the center. The Theosophical Society in America, with its headquarters at Wheaton, Illinois, houses a fifteen-thousand-volume collection of works in occultism, mysticism, and theosophy. Books may be borrowed personally or by mail, and to assist study in certain areas, the society compiles a representative reading list on some subjects. The reading list on life after death, for example, contains over seventy entries briefly described, many of which are by Theosophical students.

Works on funeral customs and the funeral industry are collected at the San Francisco College of Mortuary Science and at the Beryl L. Boyen Library of the National Foundation of Funeral Service in Evanston, Illinois. Over five hundred books and bound periodical volumes on embalming, restorative art, funeral directing and management, and a special collection of color films on the burial customs of foreign countries are housed at the library of the San Francisco College of Mortuary Science. The holdings at the Boyen Library are considerably larger. Two hundred fifty thousand books, three hundred bound periodical volumes, and three hundred prints and pamphlets on bereavement, funeral and burial customs, and the funeral service are available for reference use only.

Other libraries that house specialized collections on death include the National Cancer Foundation Library of Cancer Cure, Inc. in New York City, which contains four hundred books, ninety bound periodical volumes, a number of archives items, articles, and documents on thanatology, gerontology, and counseling of advanced cancer patients. These materials are not available to the general public. The Gerontology Learning Resources Center of the Institute of Gerontology in Detroit, which is open to the public for reference use, has over six hundred fifty books and one hundred forty periodical volumes, approximately seven hundred fifty government documents, and clippings, pamphlets, bibliographies, and tapes on all aspects of gerontology, including death and aging.

Folk tales and superstitions transmitted orally from generation to generation that come close to the heart of the ordinary individual's concern with death are preserved at two universities. The Center of Intercultural and Folk Studies at Western Kentucky University at Bowling Green estimates that the Folklore and Folklife Archives there has at least two hundred tapes and perhaps two thousand manuscripts pertaining to death that have been gathered from various parts of Kentucky and adjoining states. Tapes and manuscripts of these collections are individually indexed, usually by area, informant, collector, and subject.

The William R. Perkins Library at Duke University contains the Frank Clyde Brown Papers. Between 1912 and 1948, Brown collected about thirty-eight thousand folktales and notes on folklore, fourteen hundred songs vocally recorded, and six hundred fifty musical scores from people in North Carolina and surrounding areas. Much of the folklore has been published in a seven-volume work entitled *The Frank C. Brown Collection of North Carolina Folklore*, edited by Newman Ivey White. Volume VI contains material on death, superstitions, and the afterlife.

JOURNALS

Although this is changing, journal materials available on death have reflected the same tendency toward specialization within existing fields that is found in special collections. Prior to 1970, a number of different magazines and professional journals had devoted single issues to the treatment of death, but no journals were available that dealt exclusively with the varied aspects of death and dying. The Fall 1968 issue of *Sociology Symposium* is primarily a collection of articles on various aspects of the funeral industry. The lead articles are followed by a bibliography of the sociology of death and six extensive book reviews. A publication of the American Psychotherapy Association, *Voices: The Art and Science of Psychotherapy* (Spring/Summer 1969), combines short articles with poems and cartoons to present a broad, readable, and personal perspective on the process of dying. Perhaps the most widely circulated of these magazines and journals that devoted a single issue for death and dying is *Psychology Today* (August 1969). That issue of *Psychology Today* (which describes itself as the magazine about psychology, society, and human behavior), contained six main articles on death in addition to the well-known "*Psychology Today* Questionnaire on You and Death" designed by Edwin Shneidman.

Other specialized journals have followed this pattern. *Prism*, a monthly magazine published by the American Medical Association for the discussion of nonclinical issues facing medicine, devoted its June 1975 issue to death. Most articles deal with the physician's confrontation with death in the medical profession, although several articles do discuss funeral practices and cemeteries. *Humanitas*, the journal of the Center for the Study of Human Development at the Institute of Man in Pittsburgh, covered death in its February 1975 issue. Articles are by authorities such as Elizabeth Kubler-Ross and sociologist Glenn M. Vernon, and the topics range from a discussion of the language of the dying patient to a discussion of death and the imagination. *Monist*, an international journal of general philosophical inquiry, explored philosophical problems of death in its April 1976 issue. Articles are written by professional philosophers on such topics as rationality and the fear of death and voluntary and nonvoluntary euthanasia. These articles are more limited in scope and are more academic than those previously mentioned.

As the first journal to deal exclusively with the many aspects of death, *Omega: An International Journal for the Psychological Study of Dying, Death, Bereavement, Suicide, and Other Lethal Behaviors* emphasizes the impact of death on the human being and on the human community. Although it is largely a psychological journal, the articles are nontechnical and are generally of popular appeal. Several books in death and dying literature are reviewed in each issue. The *Journal of Thanatology* began publication the following year and publishes short articles that are quite diverse in content, ranging from guides to interviewing the bereaved to a consideration of the Jewish view of organ transplants. *Death Education* is the newest of the journals focusing on death. The just completed first volume includes papers on the scope and history of death education, model death courses, and new counseling techniques. The journal is interdisciplinary and reports on programatic research and available resources, as well as on educationally related topics.

Two journals on suicide are available. *Suicide and Life-Threatening Behavior*, the official publication of the American Association of Suicidology, has a multidisciplinary approach to self-destructive and other destructive behaviors. Although the emphasis is on suicide, articles on topics such as sudden infant deaths and battered children appear. *Bulletin of Suicidology*, published by the Department of Health, Education, and Welfare, includes book reviews, brief reports, and articles, all focusing on suicide and suicide prevention.

HISTORY AND CRITICISM

Analyses of the past and present impact of death on American culture are found in most disciplines. Surveys of the history of the funeral industry, philosophical debates on death with dignity, and current psychological studies of bereavement in children all spotlight part of that impact. The materials available to the researcher are numerous and, to stress again, varied. Clearly, all such analyses cannot be covered in this short space, and, unfortunately, not even all the different approaches to the cultural impact of death can be covered. The discussion that follows centers on three main themes: American culture, the American funeral, and the American family; religion and the afterlife; and ethical and medical issues in death and dying. This will provide a general, but limited, survey of those works that explore the impact of death on American culture.

Perhaps the most neglected aspect of the American experience in the flood of death and dying literature is the historical backdrop for current beliefs and attitudes. A few recent essay collections begin to fill this gap. *Death in America*, edited by David E. Stannard, includes articles on the attitude toward death in pre-Civil War America, death in the American folk culture, and death and the Puritan child. Stannard expands his essay, which appears in this volume on death and the Puritan child, in *The Puritan Way of Death* and provides a detailed and exhaustive look at death and the Puritan way of life. *Death in the American Experience*, edited by Arien Mack, deals with death in the counter culture, in American poetry, and in the Christian and Judaic traditions. *Passing: The Vision of Death in America*, edited by Charles O. Jackson, represents the best of the volumes that treat death from a historical perspective. Jackson's aim is to explore the historical dimension of death and the responses to death. By organizing his material chronologically and by including essays that discuss attitudes in each century toward death, death rituals, and burial techniques, Jackson provides an excellent historical perspective on death in American culture.

Elizabeth Kubler-Ross's publication of *On Death and Dying* in 1969 was a turning point in death and dying literature and preceded an outpouring of works on death. Her now-famous volume described the highly technological situation in which we all must die and described five stages that dying patients often experience. The fear of death and dying surfaced, and talk began about what now was referred to as "the taboo topic"—the event we all deny will occur to us. Ernest Becker argues for the universality of this fear of death, not just for Americans, but for all human beings, in his Pulitzer Prize winner, *The Denial of Death*. The fear of death, the denial of death, and the taboo nature of death were echoed in a variety of works, especially in introductions to works on death and dying. Richard G. Dumont and Dennis C. Foss examine this aspect of America's view of death in *The American View of Death: Acceptance or Denial*. The authors see their primary contribution as providing a clear articulation of the acceptance-denial controversy and as providing a survey of the current social and scientific knowledge concerning Americans' attitudes toward death. Perhaps the most complete study available of the death attitudes of Americans in the late 1960s is Glenn M. Vernon's *Sociology of Death: An Analysis of Death Related Behavior*. From a sociological point of view, Vernon discusses the meaning of death in society, bereavement, fear of death, humor, and childhood experiences. *Death and Ethnicity: A Psychocultural Study* by Richard A. Kalish and David K. Reynolds provides a cross-ethnic comparison of death attitudes in America. Their study, which concentrates on black Americans, Japanese Americans, and Mexican Americans, is one of the very few cross-ethnic studies available.

The American funeral and the funeral industry have become an integral part of the American death. Robert W. Habenstein and William Lamers chart the development of the funeral industry from its earliest beginning to its present status as a nearly indispensable service to survivors of the deceased in *The History of American Funeral Directing*. But not everyone is comfortable with the role the industry now plays, and the industry has been the subject of intense criticism. Jessica Mitford's *The American Way of Death* is the best known of a series of sharp criticisms of American funeral customs and the commercial exploitation associated with those customs. Ruth Mulvey Harmer's *The High Cost of Dying* and Leroy Bowman's *The American Funeral: A Study in Guilt, Extravagance, and Sublimity* both sound the same notes as does Mitford's work. In each, the value of the costly funeral customs of Americans and the practices by the industry that reinforce these customs are viewed with a highly critical eye.

In the decade or so since the publication of these works, changes have occurred in the industry, motivated in part by these criticisms. But the criticism continues, as is evidenced by the 1978 final staff report to the Federal Trade Commission, *Funeral Industry Practices*. The most thorough examination of current funeral practices and customs, however, is *Funerals: Consumers Last Rights* by the editors of *Consumer Reports*. This objective examination presents an overview of the American funeral, details on arranging for a funeral and burial, alternatives to the American funeral, and suggestions of how to plan one's own funeral. An appendix provides extremely useful information regarding embalming and pre-need laws and gives full descriptions of embalming, restoration, and autopsy procedures. Another useful source is *A Manual of Death Education and Simple Burial* by Ernest Morgan, which has the advantage of being very compact yet comprehensive. This small booklet is distributed by most memorial societies and provides economical alternatives to the typical American funeral. The addresses are provided of donor clearing houses, eyebanks, tissue banks, and medical and dental schools that need body donations.

The manner in which a society buries its dead betrays much about its citizens' attitudes toward life and death. Cemeteries are extremely revealing. The gravestone carving of early cemeteries was probably the first, and certainly the most extensive, artistic expression of the view of death of early Americans. *Graven Images: New England Stonecarving and Its Symbols, 1650-1815* by Allan I. Ludwig and *Memorials For Children of Change: The Art of Early New England Stonecarving* by Dickran and Ann Tashjian combine fine photographs of grave carvings with commentary on the significance of and the development of the details of these carvings. Emily Wasserman's *Gravestone Designs: Rubbings and Photographs from Early New York and New Jersey* and Peter Benes's *The Masks of Orthodoxy: Folk Gravestone Carving in Plymouth County, Massachusetts, 1689-1805* provided similar analyses of more specific geographic areas. Not only the carvings, but also the epitaphs inscribed on the stones reveal attitudes toward death. *A Collection of American Epitaphs and Inscriptions with Occasional Notes* by Timothy Alden is a five-volume collection indexed by names mentioned, making access to this collection less cumbersome.

The physical layout of the cemetery is also telling. *Famous and Curious Cemeteries: A Pictorial, Historical, and Anecdotal View of American and European Cemeteries and the Famous and Infamous People Who Are Buried There* by John Francis Marion spotlights thirty-five cemeteries in the United States, including Forest Lawn Memorial Park in Glendale, California. Forest Lawn is the best known of the American cemeteries; and its promotional booklet, *Pictorial Forest Lawn*, through color photographs and narrative provides a tour of the architecture, the sculptural reproductions, and original art works on the grounds of Forest Lawn.

Many argue that the function of the funeral ceremony is to help the family through the period of grief over the deceased. *Acute Grief and the Funeral*, edited by Vanderlyn R. Pine, contains about thirty-five short essays by funeral directors, doctors, chaplains, and sociologists. Despite the title, the establishment of the role of the funeral industry in the grief process is the primary subject; and the articles reflect the position that the funeral is an invaluable ceremony for overcoming grief. Acute grief is given no extended analysis. Rabbinical Assembly published *The Bond of Life: A Guide Book for Mourners* by Rabbi Jules Harlow, which details the proper Jewish procedure for mourning. *The Bond of Life* is extremely valuable in helping one to understand the place of the funeral and death in the Jewish religion and in providing a framework within which one can grieve.

The funeral and the period of mourning are often the beginning rather than the end of the grief process. While studies of bereavement and grief most often focus on the bereavement in children, two works of general nature need mention. *Bereavement: Its Psychosocial Aspects*, edited by Bernard Schoenberg, is a good collection of sociological studies of bereavement as it relates to the family and to the health professional. The process of bereavement and the role of bereavement in human experience are also explored. Eric Bermann's *Scapegoat: The Impact of Death-Fear on An American Family* comes very near the core of the effects of death on

American families. A close-up of a single family involved in an extended death watch reveals the impact of death and the death-fear on the daily routines, social roles, and values. *Scapegoat* is an excellent mirror of American culture.

Two important works on bereavement deal with children. *A Child's Parent Dies: Studies in Childhood Bereavement* by Erna Furman and *The Child in His Family: The Impact of Disease and Death,* edited by James E. Anthony and Cyrille Koupernik, are both scholarly and well-written studies. The theoretical chapters on grief, mourning, and the effects of early parental death on child development in *A Child's Parent Dies* are balanced by case studies taken from a three-year project sponsored by the Cleveland Center for Research in Child Development. *The Child in His Family* is a collection of articles by recognized authorities and ties death to the cultural context in which it occurs. The problems we experience in coping with death are viewed as a result of our cultural values.

For those interested in how to talk with children about death, a small volume, *Talking About Death: A Dialogue Between Parent and Child* by Earl Grollman, is excellent. Grollman provides a context in which parents and children can discuss death as a real event in life. His presentation presumes that the parent is reluctant to discuss death and aims to break down that reluctance while focusing on the importance of the dialogue to the child. Very useful sections give descriptions and addresses of organizations that may be of help to the survivors, and describe and group by ages children's books, films, and cassettes that deal with death.

The most urgent religious and philosophical question raised by death is whether anything survives the death of the body and, if so, what the after death experience is like. Although the question seems universal and urgent, it has yet to be answered to everyone's satisfaction. Different major religious sects have each taken their stand on the place of death in their religions and on the possibility for future life. This belief in a future life is carefully and thoroughly examined in William Alger's *A Critical History of the Doctrine of Future Life*. This scholarly history covers, among other aspects, the rabbinical doctrine, the Hebrew doctrine, and the grounds for the belief itself. *Christian Beliefs About Life After Death* by Paul Badham is a more contemporary study that seeks to show the development of these beliefs and how they might be defended by an examination of first-century thought and the New Testament. *Death: Meaning and Mortality in Christian Thought and Contemporary Culture* by Milton Gatch not only details the history of the idea of death in the Judeo-Christian tradition, but it also studies religious and cultural attempts by Western societies to deal meaningfully with death.

The smaller sects that diverge from traditional paths usually have their own positions on death and the afterlife. Any information regarding the

positions of these groups is best sought directly from the national headquarters of these groups. Several do publish books or pamphlets that
specifically outline the sect's position on death and the afterlife. The
Watchtower Bible and Tract Society distributes *Is This Life All There Is?*,
which presents an interpretation of the Bible accounting for the presence
of death in the world and describing the resurrection of the dead. The
Church of Scientology published *Have You Lived Before This Life?* by
the church's founder, L. Ron Hubbard.

Oddly, several sects with a decidedly Eastern emphasis distribute publications on death and the afterlife. The Sanatana Dharma Foundation issues
a modern-day interpretation of the *Tibetan Book of the Dead* called *A
Manual for Guiding a Person Through the After Death Experience*, by
H. Charles Berner, while the Vedanta Society of California distributes
Life After Death by Swami Vivekananda, and the Ramakrishna-Viveda-
nanda Center offers *Man in Search of Immortality* by Swami Nikhilananda.

By far, the best evidence for life after death comes from spiritualism,
psychic phenomena, and deathbed experiences, but such evidence is neither
ample nor widely accepted. A good historical account of spiritualism and
its impact on American literature is Howard Kerr's *Mediums, and Spirit-
Rappers and Roaring Radicals: Spiritualism in American Literature 1850-
1900*. Kerr surveys alleged communications between the living and the
dead between 1845 and 1860 and analyzes the satiric and humorous literary
response to spiritualism and its impact on occult fiction. The history of the
movement and its impact is then extended to 1900. A good index makes
this a helpful source on spiritualism. Deathbed experiences of members of
the medical profession and people on their deathbeds are often cited as
evidence for life after death since the descriptions of these experiences
bear striking similarity to each other and to those experiences described in
The Tibetan Book of the Dead. The most well-known of the recent reports
of deathbed experiences, *Life After Life* by Ralph Moody, Jr., is primarily
a report of case studies of those who have come very close to dying. A
more empirical forerunner of Moody's work focusing on those attending
the dying is *Deathbed Observations by Physicians and Nurses* by Karlis
Osis. This survey of the observations of nine thousand nurses and doctors
reveals similarities in their observations of the dying and near dying that
are very similar to those reported by Moody.

Whether anything survives the death of the body is only one of the
crucial issues raised by death. Death in our world of increasing medical
knowledge and medical technology raises some extremely difficult medical
and ethical issues. We no longer agree, for example, on an issue so fundamental as what criteria should be used to determine when a person is dead.
Old issues such as euthanasia have again surfaced and have become the
subject of intense debate. Several general anthologies have recently

appeared that isolate some of these medical and ethical issues. Two good collections have exactly the same unimaginative, yet descriptive, title. *Ethical Issues in Death and Dying*, edited by Robert F. Weir, concentrates on the problems of determining when someone is dead, on whether we should allow someone to die, and on suicide. Verdicts of a number of recent court cases are included, and articles are written by lawyers, physicians, theologians, and psychologists. *Ethical Issues in Death and Dying*, edited by Tom L. Beauchamp and Seymor Perlin, covers similar issues, but it does so from a decidedly philosophical perspective. A section on the significance of life and death, containing excerpts from philosophical works, distinguishes this collection from Weir's in yet another way.

Euthanasia and death with dignity debates have immense personal and economic impact in our present society. Although the most celebrated patient in America in this regard is Karen Ann Quinlan (See, for example, *Karen Ann Quinlan: Dying in the Age of Eternal Life* by B. D. Colen and *Karen Ann: The Quinlans Tell Their Story* by Joseph and Julia Quinlan), the debate over euthanasia and death with dignity began many years earlier. *The Right to Die*, published by the Group for the Advancement of Psychiatry, contains fourteen articles resulting from a 1971 symposium on the question of when and under what circumstances a person may choose to terminate his or her life. *Death by Choice* by Daniel C. Maguire continues the debate by emphasizing changes in medical technology that make the issue crucial and by criticizing the tardiness of the body of law to deal with the issue. Jerry B. Wilson's *Death by Decision: The Medical, Moral, and Legal Dilemmas of Euthanasia* follows its historical account of euthanasia and its survey of religious views with a strong advocacy of mercy in caring for dying patients. One of the most useful single works on euthanasia is O. Ruth Russel's *Freedom to Die: Moral and Legal Aspects of Euthanasia*. The body of the text discusses changing attitudes toward death and dying and gives a historical review of both thought and action on euthanasia, as well as arguments and proposals for its legalization. The appendix contains petitions submitted to legislatures and to the United Nations, legislative proposals and bills, a list of societies promoting euthanasia, a discussion of the definition of death, living wills, and a list of articles, books, and relevant court cases.

Although aspects of death are usually discussed by a specialized discipline, general anthologies that cover a variety of topics are numerous. Some are extremely valuable; others are too superficial in their treatment of death and dying to be useful. *Man's Concern with Death* by Arnold Toynbee, one of the valuable collections, includes articles by Toynbee, Eric Rhocle, Niniam Smart, and others on attitudes toward death and dying. Another helpful anthology is *Death: Current Perspectives*, edited by Edwin Shneidman. His approach to death from societal, personal, cultural, and interpersonal perspectives is useful in getting a broad overview of death. The articles are generally well written and highly readable. *Death Inside Out*, edited by Peter Steinfels and Robert Veatch, centers on the possibility and concept of "a good death," while *A Book of Readings and Sources: Death and Society*, edited by James P. Carse and Arlene B. Dallery, uses articles on recent court cases, religious positions, and philosophical arguments to cover a variety of topics ranging from abortion to aging. Robert Fulton's *Death and Identity*, which was first published in 1965, has been revised and contains useful and interesting theoretical discussions of death as well as discussions of grief and of death in society. *The Meaning of Death* by Herman Feifel was one of the first general anthologies on death and, even though it has not been revised, it is still useful in providing an overview of death and dying. It also contains essays on several subjects—for example, death in modern art—that are neglected in more recent works.

Three projects that are under way to reprint, collect and distribute materials on death and dying should be mentioned. The Arno Press series, "Literature of Death and Dying," is a collection of approximately forty titles, including reprints of classical works on death and original anthologies. Although the project does not focus on American literature, it does include historical works that have been influential in America, as well as some American works. The Center for Death Education and Research in Minneapolis, Minnesota, has established a cassette library of lectures, interviews, discussions, and dialogues on death-related topics. Twenty-four titles are presently available. The center has compiled a fourth edition of Robert Fulton's *Death, Grief and Bereavement: A Bibliography, 1845-1975*, containing nearly four thousand references. In addition, a number of publications and films can be obtained through the center. Finally, Educational Perspectives Associates in DeKalb, Illinois, issues a multimedia catalog in their death and dying series, which is primarily designed for educational purposes. Filmstrips of cemeteries and funeral customs and cassettes on death in art, music, and literature are part of this series.

The books mentioned here have been selected from the vast amount of material available on death and should be considered no more than good places to begin one's own research on a specific aspect of death. The works cited here are also limited in being unrepresentive of the varied functions and manifestations of death in our culture. Death is a major theme in the visual and performing arts and its image is of major significance in popular culture. The lyrics of popular songs consistently reflect its darker side; the threat of death lurks behind the advertising of life insurance companies and the American Cancer Society. Death is a theme in literature, and more and more frequently it is being integrated as a theme into television programing. Very little has been written on the role death plays in these aspects of our culture. But, as discussion of death continues and as we continue to become increasingly aware of the presence of death in every part of our culture, analyses of these roles will no doubt contribute to the already large body of literature on the subject. We will then be much closer to an understanding of the popular cultural expression of and representation of death in America.

BIBLIOGRAPHY

BOOKS AND ARTICLES

Alden, Timothy. *A Collection of American Epitaphs and Inscriptions with Occasional Notes.* New York: Arno Press, 1977.

Alger, William Rounseville. *A Critical History of the Doctrine of Future Life.* New York: W. J. Widdleton, 1867.

American Sunday-School Union. *The Tree and Its Fruits or, the Last Hours of Infidels and Christians Contrasted.* Philadelphia: American Sunday School Union, 1839.

Anthony, James E., and Cyrille Koupernik, eds. *The Child in His Family: The Impact of Disease and Death.* Vol. 2. New York: John Wiley and Sons, 1973.

Badham, Paul. *Christian Beliefs About Life After Death.* New York: Barnes and Noble, 1976.

Baldwin, Oliver P. *Address Delivered at the Dedication of the Hollywood Cemetery.* Richmond: Macfarlane & Fergusson, 1849.

Beauchamp, Tom L., and Seymor Perlin. *Ethical Issues in Death and Dying.* Englewood Cliffs, N.J.: Prentice-Hall, 1978.

Becker, Ernest. *The Denial of Death.* New York: Macmillan, 1973.

Benes, Peter. *The Masks of Orthodoxy: Folk Gravestone Carving in Plymouth County, Massachusetts, 1689-1805.* Amherst: University of Massachusetts Press, 1977.

Bermann, Eric. *Scapegoat: The Impact of Death-Fear on an American Family.* Ann Arbor: University of Michigan Press, 1973.

Berner, H. Charles. *A Manual for Guiding a Person Through the After Death Experience: A Modern Day Interpretation Based upon "The Tibetan Book of the Dead."* Lucerne Valley, Calif.: Causation Press, 1967.

Bowman, Leroy. *The American Funeral: A Study in Guilt, Extravagance, and Sublimity.* Westport, Conn.: Greenwood Press, 1959.

Bunyan, John. *Pilgrim's Progress.* New York: New American Library, 1972.

Carse, James P., and Arlene B. Dallery. *A Book of Readings and Sources: Death and Society.* New York: Harcourt Brace Jovanovich, 1977.

Colen, B. D. *Karen Ann Quinlan: Dying in the Age of Eternal Life.* New York: Nash Publishing, 1976.

Crothers, Samuel McChord. *The Endless Life.* Boston: Houghton, Mifflin, 1905.

Darwin, Charles. *The Origin of Species.* New York: AMS Press, 1972.

"Death, Dying and Life After Life: A Lively Marketplace." *Publishers Weekly,* 214 (September 25, 1978), 92-98.

Dickinson, G. Lowes. *Is Immortality Desirable?* Boston: Houghton, Mifflin, 1909.

Dumont, Richard G., and Dennis C. Foss. *The American View of Death: Acceptance or Denial.* Cambridge, Mass.: Schenkman Publishing, 1972.

Edwards, Jonathan. *Representative Selections.* Edited by Clarence H. Faust and Thomas H. Johnson. New York: Hill & Wang, 1962.

Farberow, Norman L., ed. *Bibliography on Suicide and Suicide Prevention: 1897-1957 and 1958-1970.* Rockville, Md.: National Institute of Mental Health, 1972.

Feifel, Herman, ed. *The Meaning of Death.* New York: McGraw-Hill, 1965.

Fiske, John. *The Destiny of Man.* Boston: Houghton, Mifflin, 1892.

Fithian, Philip Vickers. *Journal and Letters of Philip Vickers Fithian.* Edited by Hunter Dickinson Farish. Charlottesville, Va.: Dominion Books, 1968.

Fulton, Robert, ed. *Death and Identity.* Bowie, Md.: The Charles Press, 1976.

―――. *Death, Grief and Bereavement: A Bibliography 1845-1975.* New York: Arno Press, 1977.

Funeral Industry Practices. Washington, D.C.: Bureau of Consumer Protection, Federal Trade Commission, 1978.

Funerals: Consumers Last Right. Mount Vernon, N.Y.: Consumers Union, 1977.

Furman, Erna. *A Child's Parent Dies: Studies in Childhood Bereavement.* New Haven: Yale University Press, 1974.

Gatch, Milton McC. *Death: Meaning and Mortality in Christian Thought and Contemporary Culture.* New York: Seabury Press, 1969.

Grollman, Earl A. *Talking About Death: A Dialogue Between Parent and Child.* Boston: Beacon Press, 1970.

Group for the Advancement of Psychiatry. *The Right to Die.* New York: Jason Aronson, 1974.

Habenstein, Robert W., and William Lamers. *The History of American Funeral Directing.* Milwaukee, Wis.: Bulfin Printers, 1962.

Hariot, Thomas. *A Briefe and True Report of the New Found Land of Virginia. . . , 1588,* as reprinted in *Virginia: Four Personal Narratives.* New York: Arno Press, 1972.

Harlow, Rabbi Jules, ed. *The Bond of Life: A Book for Mourners.* New York: The Rabbinical Assembly, 1975.

Harmer, Ruth Mulvey. *The High Cost of Dying.* New York: Collier Books, 1963.

Harrah, Barbara K., and David F. Harrah. *Funeral Service: A Bibliography of Literature on its Past, Present and Future, the Various Means of Disposition and Memorialization.* Metuchen, N.J.: Scarecrow Press, 1976.

Hubbard, L. Ron. *Have You Lived Before This Life?* Los Angeles: The Church of Scientology Publications Organization, 1959.

Is This Life All There Is? New York: Watchtower Bible and Tract Society of New York, 1974.

Jackson, Charles O. *Passing: The Vision of Death in America.* Westport, Conn.: Greenwood Press, 1977.

James, William. *Human Immortality.* Boston: Houghton, Mifflin, 1898.

Janeway, James. *A Token for Children.* New York: Garland Publishing, 1976.

Kalish, Richard A., and David K. Reynolds. *Death and Ethnicity: A Psycho-cultural Study.* Los Angeles: University of Southern California Press, 1976.

Kerr, Howard. *Mediums, and Spirit-Rappers and Roaring Radicals: Spiritualism in American Literature 1850-1900.* Chicago: University of Illinois Press, 1972.

Kubler-Ross, Elizabeth. *On Death and Dying.* New York: Macmillan, 1969.

Kutscher, Austin H., Jr., and Austin H. Kutscher, eds. *A Bibliography of Books on Death, Bereavement, Loss, and Grief: 1935-1968.* New York: Health Science Publishing, 1969.

Kutscher, Austin H., Jr., and Martin Kutscher. *A Bibliography of Books on Death, Bereavement, Loss, and Grief: Supplement 1, 1968-1972.* New York: Health Science Publishing, 1974.

Kutscher, M. L., et al., ed. *A Comprehensive Bibliography of Thanatology Literature.* New York: MSS Information, 1976.

————. *A Cross-Index of Indices of Books on Thanatology.* New York: MSS Information, 1976.

Ludwig, Allan I. *Graven Images: New England Stonecarving and Its Symbols, 1650-1815.* Middletown, Conn.: Wesleyan University Press, 1966.

Mack, Arien, ed. *Death in the American Experience.* New York: Schocken Books, 1974.

Maguire, Daniel C. *Death by Choice.* Garden City, N.Y.: Doubleday, 1974.

Marion, John Francis. *Famous and Curious Cemeteries: A Pictorial, Historical, and Anecdotal View of American and European Cemeteries and the Famous and Infamous People Who Are Buried There.* New York: Crown Publishers, 1977.

Miller, Albert Jay, and Michael James Acri. *Death: A Bibliographic Guide.* Metuchen, N.J.: Scarecrow Press, 1977.

Mitford, Jessica. *The American Way of Death.* New York: Simon and Schuster, 1963.

Moody, Ralph, Jr. *Life After Life.* New York: Bantam Books, 1975.

Moore, Julia A. "Little Andrew" as quoted in *Adventures of Huckleberry Finn.* Ed. by Sculley Bradley, Richmond Croom Beatty, and E. Hudson Long. New York: W. W. Norton, 1962.

Morgan, Ernest. *A Manual of Death Education and Simple Burial.* Burnsville, N.C.: Celo Press, 1977.

Nevins, Madeline M., ed. *Bioethical Perspectives on Death and Dying: Summaries of the Literature.* Rockville, Md.: Information Planning Associates, 1977.

The New England Primer. New York: Dodd, Mead, 1899.

Nikhilananda, Swami. *Man in Search of Immortality.* Kent, England: George Allen and Unwin, 1968.

Osis, Karlis. *Deathbed Observations by Physicians and Nurses.* New York: Parapsychology Foundation, 1961.

Owen, John. *The Death of Death in the Death of Christ. A Treatise of the Redemption and Reconcilliation That Is in the Blood of Christ.* Philadelphia: Green and M'Laughlin, 1827.

Pictorial Forest Lawn. Glendale, Calif.: Forest Lawn Memorial-Park Association, 1970.

Pine, Vanderlyn R., et al., eds. *Acute Grief and the Funeral*. Springfield, Ill.: Charles C. Thomas, 1976.

Poe, Edgar Allan. *Selected Prose and Poetry*. Edited by W. H. Auden. New York: Holt, Rinehart & Winston, 1950.

Quinlan, Joseph, and Julia Quinlan, with Phyliss Battelle. *Karen Ann: The Quinlans Tell Their Story*. Garden City, N.Y.: Doubleday, 1977.

Russell, O. Ruth. *Freedom to Die: Moral and Legal Aspects of Euthanasia*. New York: Human Sciences Press, 1975.

Schoenberg, Bernard, et al., eds. *Bereavement: Its Psychosocial Aspects*. New York: Columbia University Press, 1975.

Shneidman, Edwin, ed. *Death: Current Perspectives*. Palo Alto, Calif.: Mayfield Publishing, 1976.

Smith, John. *The General History of Virginia, New England, and the Summer Isles*. Cleveland: World Publishing, 1966.

Stannard, David E., ed. *Death in America*. Philadelphia: University of Pennsylvania Press, 1975.

———. *The Puritan Way of Death: A Study in Religion, Culture, and Social Change*. New York: Oxford University Press, 1977.

Steinfels, Peter, and Robert M. Veatch, eds. *Death Inside Out*. New York: Harper and Row, 1974.

Strugnell, Cecile. *Adjustment to Widowhood and Some Related Problems: A Selective and Annotated Bibliography*. New York: Health Sciences Publishing, 1974.

Tashjian, Dickran, and Ann Tashjian. *Memorials For Children of Change: The Art of Early New England Stonecarving*. Middletown, Conn.: Wesleyan University Press, 1974.

Toynbee, Arnold, et al. *Man's Concern with Death*. New York: McGraw-Hill, 1968.

Vernon, Glenn M. *Sociology of Death: An Analysis of Death Related Behavior*. New York: Ronald Press, 1970.

Vivekananda, Swami. *Life After Death*. Mayavati, Pithoragarh, Himalayas: Advaita Ashrama, 1975.

Wasserman, Emily. *Gravestone Designs: Rubbings and Photographs from Early New York and New Jersey*. New York: Dover Publications, 1972.

Weir, Robert F., ed. *Ethical Issues in Death and Dying*. New York: Columbia University Press, 1977.

White, Newman Ivey, ed. *The Frank C. Brown Collection of North Carolina Folklore*. Durham, N.C.: Duke University Press, 1964.

Wilson, Jerry B. *Death by Decision: The Medical, Moral, and Legal Dilemmas of Euthanasia*. Philadelphia: Westminster Press, 1975.

PERIODICALS

Bioethics Digest. Rockville, Md., 1976-.
Bulletin of Suicidology. Rockville, Md., 1967-.

Death Education. Washington, D.C., 1977-.
Humanities. Pittsburgh, Pa. 1965-.
Journal of Thanatology. New York, 1971-1975-.
Monist. La Salle, Ill., 1890-.
Omega: An International Journal for the Psychological Study of Dying, Death, Bereavement, Suicide, and Other Lethal Behaviors. Farmingdale, N.Y.: 1970-.
Prism. Chicago, 1973-1976.
Psychology Today. New York, 1967-.
Publishers Weekly. New York, 1872-.
Sociology Symposium. Bowling Green, Ky., 1968-.
Suicide and Life-Threatening Behavior. New York, 1971-.
Voices: The Art and Science of Psychotherapy. Orlando, Fla., 1965-.

CHAPTER 5. Editorial Cartoons

Nancy Pogel and
Paul Somers, Jr.

Although editorial cartooning has a long history in the United States, it originated in Europe. The key words—"cartoon" and "caricature"—derive from the Italian *cartone*, "a large sheet of paper," and *caricare*, "to exaggerate, change, or overload." The Englishman William Hogarth, whose moral indignation led him from fine art to satirical engravings denouncing the evils of his society, may be considered the first cartoonist. His successors, Thomas Rowlandson, George Cruikshank, and, especially, James Gillray, inspired emulation. Since that time, other Englishmen such as John Tenniel, David Low, and Ronald Searle, along with the Frenchmen Honoré Daumier and Jean Louis Forain, have influenced American artists. In recent years, the Australian Patrick Oliphant and the Canadian Paul Szep have become quite popular here. For the most part, however, the American editorial cartoonists have reflected the political and social moods of the nation, refining and simplifying their work to insure the maximum impact on a public with little time to ponder the complex drawings and lengthy captions of earlier times.

Herbert Block (Herblock) has defined the editorial cartoonist as "the kid who points out that the Emperor is without his clothes." From Ben Franklin to Jeff MacNelly, America has produced a long line of artists—left, right, and center—idealists and cynics whose work has tried to keep politics honest. Unfortunately, the political or editorial cartoonists who have not also been accepted by "high culture" enthusiasts as painters, printmakers, or major illustrators, have been relegated to secondary or backseat positions, as have so many artists in a variety of popular culture categories.

Thus, although early editorial cartoons or drawings by the most famous have been collected and celebrated, research into late nineteenth- and twentieth-century editorial cartooning has only begun to become a legitimate concern for scholars and collectors in the last few decades. Indexes are incomplete; independent bibliographical and biographical guides are virtually nonexistent; and serious critical analysis of editorial cartooning and cartoonists—stylistic, political, historical—remains in its infancy. The field is ripe for the energetic scholar who is patient and willing to break new ground.

HISTORIC OUTLINE

The editorial cartoon has been around much longer than the comic strip and it was taken seriously at an earlier date. No matter how poorly it was drawn or how tasteless it might have been, a widely distributed cartoon attacking a king or, in the United States, a president, could not be ignored.

American editorial cartooning probably began in 1747 with "Non Votis" or "The Wagoner and Hercules," the designing and/or drawing of which are attributed to Benjamin Franklin. Franklin is also associated with the second oldest extant political cartoon, "Join or Die," the representation of the colonies as a disjointed snake, which appeared in his *Pennsylvania Gazette* for May 9, 1754. The engraver was Paul Revere, whose 1770 engraving "The Boston Massacre" was widely circulated for its propaganda value. Revere had copied a drawing by Henry Pelham, stepbrother of John Singleton Copley.

Shortly before the Revolution, Franklin supposedly designed the cartoon "Magna Britannia: her Colonies Reduced" for distribution in England, hoping the symbolic representation of Britannia fallen from her place of eminence at the top of the globe, her limbs (each bearing the name of a North American colony) severed, would help sway England toward a more lenient colonial policy. Indeed, up to the point at which the French entered the war, mezzotints and engravings in London supported the colonists.

Few cartoons appeared during this period: Frank Weitenkampf has located a mere seventy-eight produced before 1828. An exception to the busy cartoons of the day—and one that seems almost modern in its simplicity—was drawn by Elkanah Tisdale in 1812. Gilbert Stuart has traditionally received the credit, but it was Tisdale who added a few pencil strokes to the map of Governor Elbridge Gerry's ingeniously contrived Essex County senatorial district, thus creating the dragonlike "gerrymander" and adding a word to our language.

Given the bitterness of partisan politics that characterized the early—not to mention the later—years of the Republic, it is surprising that there are so few cartoons of George Washington, who was scurrilously derided by his foes. William Murrell surmises that "too ardent" patriots have destroyed unflattering cartoons of the Father of Our Country. Thomas Jefferson was not so fortunate, and several cartoons survive that mock his Gallic and democratic proclivities. In fact, the first American cartoon designed for newspaper reproduction in the *New York Evening Post* (1814), dealt with Jefferson's highly unpopular Embargo Act.

Although Franklin, Tisdale, and others were well known, Edinburgh-born William Charles was the first to become famous here primarily as a political cartoonist. Charles drew heavily upon the works of English cartoonists Gillray and Rowlandson and left no disciples after his death in 1820, but he deserves to be remembered, nevertheless, for popularizing the political cartoon.

The next phase in the history of American editorial cartoons was initiated by the development of lithography, a process that was much faster than woodcuts and engravings. The first lithographed cartoon appeared in 1829; thereafter, lithographed cartoons flourished. Most of them were produced by the firms of Henry R. Robinson and Currier & Ives. Robinson's company produced many political lithographs between 1831 and 1849, and some were superior to those by Currier & Ives, a name that has become synonymous with lithography. The Currier & Ives firm produced over seven thousand different titles between 1840 and 1890 and sold some ten million copies, only eighty of which titles were political cartoons. They were realistic: faces were copied from photographs; and numerous balloons filled with finely printed dialogue floated over the stiff figures. As the Civil War approached, the firm often marketed cartoons, sometimes drawn to order, on both sides of a controversial issue. It is precisely the drawn-to-order nature of these cartoons that makes them seem so woodenly quaint today.

Although Currier & Ives documented the mid-century discord with their lithographs, especially those dealing with the campaigns of 1856 and 1860, the Civil War, and Abraham Lincoln, there were other media germinating that would soon leave the lithographers in the shade and would begin another phase in American editorial cartooning. Englishman Henry Carter arrived here in 1848, changed his name to Frank Leslie, and, by the mid-1850s, was embarked on a series of magazine ventures, the most successful of which was *Frank Leslie's Illustrated Newspaper* (later *Frank Leslie's Illustrated Weekly*). Other Leslie publications included *The Jolly Joker, The Cartoon, Chatterbox*, and *Phunny Phellow*. An impressive list of artists was employed by Leslie, as well as by *Vanity Fair, Harper's Weekly*, and the scores of other publications that appeared and disappeared abruptly: the Anglo-Irishman Frank Bellew, who was popular before the war and whose elongated caricature of Lincoln is still remembered, and many others, most notably the German Thomas Nast and the Viennese Joseph Keppler.

Born in Landau, Germany, in 1840, Thomas Nast came to New York

City at the age of six. He became deeply interested in art, especially in the great English cartoonists Leech, Tenniel, and Gilbert. Nast said that he was indebted to Tenniel for his striking use of animals as symbols. At fifteen, he won a job with *Frank Leslie's Illustrated Weekly*. During the Civil War, his illustrations for *Harper's Weekly* were extremely popular. He soon turned to a more emblematic, less reportorial style, which was sometimes allegorical, nearly always emotionally powerful. So effective a voice for the Union did he become that Lincoln called him "our best recruiting sergeant."

The South had its own German-born artist, Adalbert J. Volck, a Baltimore dentist who produced a few excellent caricatures, most notably twenty-nine "Confederate War Etchings" (1863). He scathingly portrayed Lincoln as a clown, a Negro, a woman, and an oriental dancer. Apparently, he gave up cartooning after the war.

Nast, however, continued to draw, and his style evolved into caricature. Eventually, it was through his battle against the Tweed Ring that he made his mark as one of America's most powerful editorial cartoonists. Incensed by the corruption of Boss Tweed, Nast began to fire his volleys from the pages of *Harper's Weekly*. He took Tammany Hall's own tiger and made it into a fearful symbol of marauding lawlessness, to be used against Tweed in the election of 1871. Tweed lost and went to jail in 1873. He escaped, only to be identified and arrested again in Spain because an official recognized him from one of Nast's cartoons. Unfortunately for Nast, right and wrong were never again so plainly distinguishable. His attacks remained formidable, but he was sometimes at a loss for a target, as his own Republican party proved itself susceptible to corruption. He quit *Harper's* in 1887 and lost much of his effectiveness. His investments failed, and by 1902 he had no choice but to accept the post of U.S. Consul to Guayaquil, Equador, where he died in December of the same year. But he left behind him such long-lasting symbols as the Tammany tiger and the Republican elephant, the less durable rag baby of inflation, and the Democratic donkey, which he did not create but did popularize. By his influence on public opinion, he demonstrated that a popular, forceful editorial cartoonist was someone to be reckoned with.

The passing of Nast did not leave a vacuum, however, for there arose the comic weeklies. Joseph Keppler, who came to St. Louis from Vienna in late 1867 or early 1868, started two German-language comic weeklies, both of which failed. In 1872, he went to New York and worked for Frank Leslie. He founded a German-language weekly, *Puck*, in 1876 and an English version in 1877. The magazine thrived and in less than ten years had a circulation of eighty thousand. An excellent cartoonist himself, Keppler employed many of the best artists of the time.

Puck's heyday partly overlapped Nast's decline. In 1884, Nast was disgruntled by the Republicans' nomination of the tainted James G. Blaine and expressed himself in a cartoon. The Democratic *Puck* joined in and revived an idea Keppler had used against Grant: the tattooed man. Bernard Gillam drew the scandalous series, depicting the husky Blaine in his undershorts, covered with tattoos representing his opponents' allegations of "corruption." The Republicans responded with Frank Beard's cartoon in *Judge*, dramatizing a rumor that Grover Cleveland was the father of an illegitimate child. Perhaps the most telling shot in the cartoon war was "The Royal Feast of Belshazaar Blaine and the Money Kings," drawn by Walt McDougall for the New York *World*. In the drawing, patterned after the *Last Supper*, Blaine, Jay Gould, and other New York financiers feast on such dishes as "patronage." Displayed on billboards around the state, the cartoon contributed to Blaine's defeat in New York and in the national election. According to Charles Press, this marked the real beginning of daily editorial cartooning as a profession.

One of *Puck*'s two great rivals, *Judge*, was founded in 1881 by a dissatisfied *Puck* cartoonist, James A. Wales. Perhaps *Judge*'s most famous symbol was the "Full Dinner Pail," cartoonist Grant Hamilton's embodiment of the prosperity of Republican William McKinley's first administration. As Stephen Becker points out, these "Full Dinner Pail" cartoons drawn by Hamilton and by Victor Gillam represented an advance in cartooning technique because of their greater simplicity and, therefore, immediacy, as compared to the crowded panel cartoons of the late nineteenth century. The third great comic weekly of the period was *Life*, founded in 1883 by *Harvard Lampoon* graduates led by J. A. Mitchell. Much, although not all, of its satire was social rather than political.

The development of newspaper cartooning was gradual; James Gordon Bennett had started the New York *Telegram* in 1867 and had used sensationalism to boost sales. In the first regular use of cartoons in a newspaper, he printed a front-page cartoon every Friday. Joseph Pulitzer, who bought the New York *World* in 1883, made an even bigger impression with editorial cartoons such as the devastating "Feast of Belshazaar." William Randolph Hearst took over the New York *Journal* in 1895 and began the great circulation war. He brought with him from San Francisco Homer Davenport, who is perhaps best remembered for his caricatures of Republican National Chairman Mark Hannah as smug and bloated, his suit decorated with dollar signs. Hearst snatched Frederick Burr Opper from *Puck* in 1899. Although critics have been condescending toward his technique, Opper was a cartoonist of great versatility and popularity, with a successful comic strip, "Happy Hooligan," and several telling series of political cartoons, such as "Alice in Plunderland" and "Willie and His Poppa." His career was unusual because of its variety and length and also because he was one of the few cartoonists able to make the changeover from the comic magazines, with their complicated, multifigured cartoons, to the daily newspapers, whose deadlines necessitated a more direct style and simpler designs.

The war with Spain provided cartoonists with inspiration for a while, but Theodore Roosevelt literally sustained them for years. His teeth, mustache, and glasses made him easy to draw. He was a favorite subject for two of the early twentieth century's best-known cartoonists: John T. McCutcheon and Jay N. (Ding) Darling. Charles Press has put them at the head of a group of cartoonists he labels "bucolic."

John Tinney McCutcheon was one of the most notable of a large group of outstanding midwestern cartoonists active around the turn of the century. He drew editorial cartoons and nostalgic panels, and illustrated books, such as his famous *Boys in Springtime*. Of his political cartoons for the Chicago *Tribune*, perhaps the best known are his 1932 Pulitzer Prize winner, "A Wise Economist Asks a Question," and "The Mysterious Stranger" (1904), which shows Missouri standing in line with states of the Republican column after it deserted the solid South to vote for Roosevelt.

Another durable midwesterner was Jay N. (Ding) Darling of Iowa. His "The Long, Long Trail," a 1919 tribute to Teddy Roosevelt, has often been reproduced. The duration of his career is shown by the dates of his Pulitzer Prizes—1924 and 1943; he received his last award when he was sixty-six. According to Stephen Becker, however, by that time he was "almost a throwback" to the less sophisticated days of the early part of the century.

In approximately the middle of these men's careers came the next major event in American History: World War I. During the three years of war before the American entry, major U.S. newspaper cartoonists, all but one of whom favored intervention on behalf of the French and English, were busy drawing German atrocities. The interventionist artists included W. A. Rogers and Nelson Harding of the Brooklyn *Eagle*. Dutch artist Louis Raemaekers, whose work appeared in the Hearst papers, is generally considered to be better than the Americans who drew for the Allied cause. The lone pen wielded in defense of neutrality belonged to Luther D. Bradley of the Chicago *Daily News*. He died early in 1917, before his anti-war convictions were tested. With the United States in the war, a Bureau of Cartoons, set up under the direction of George J. Hecht, successfully channeled cartoonists' work into the war effort by suggesting topics and otherwise maximizing the propaganda value of cartoons.

Luther Bradley was the only cartoonist for an important newspaper to oppose the war, but the radical cartoonists also opposed it and became prominent in the development of modern political cartooning. Much of their work appeared in *Masses* (1911-1917) and *Liberator* (1918-1924), because their uncompromising political views were unacceptable to the mainstream. They did not put their shoulders to the wheel of the Allied cause, but instead produced cartoons such as Robert Minor's in 1915, which presented the Army medical examiner's idea of the "perfect soldier": a muscular giant with no head.

Three of the radical cartoonists who were most important and most satisfied to be called cartoonists were Boardman Robinson, Art Young, and Robert Minor. Boardman Robinson was the most influential in terms of his effect on subsequent generations of political cartoonists, partly by virtue of his pioneering technique using crayon on grained paper, as Daumier and Forain did before him, and partly because of his position as an instructor at the Art Students League in New York from 1919 to 1930. Among those he influenced may be listed his fellow radical cartoonists Robert Minor and Clive Weed, as well as Oscar Cesare, Rollin Kirby, and Edmund Duffy.

Robert Minor gave up his successful career as a mainstream artist to draw cartoons that reflected his socialist and antiwar beliefs. He simplified his style to increase the impact of the intensely political cartoons he drew for *Masses*.

Art Young probably received the widest distribution of any of the radical cartoonists, partly because he came to socialism relatively late in life, after he had been on the staffs of several major newspapers. With *Masses* editor Max Eastman, Young was also sued unsuccessfully by the Associated Press for libel and was prosecuted in vain by the government under the Espionage Act for obstructing recruitment into the armed forces. In spite of government suppression, *Masses*, in its various forms, provided a forum for some of the best cartoonists of the period. Indeed, art editor John Sloan, along with George Bellows and George Luks, were acclaimed artists of the Ashcan school. It is precisely this exceptional degree of talent, coupled with a technique perfectly suited to the expression of moral outrage, that has made the names and influence of the radical cartoonists last longer than their more moderate contemporaries.

In 1922, the first Pulitzer Prize for editorial cartooning was awarded; it went to Roland Kirby of the New York *World*. If winning prizes is any indication, he was the dominant editorial cartoonist of the 1920s, winning again in 1925 and in 1929 (Nelson Harding won in 1927 and 1928). Kirby is considered to be a transitional figure between the early multifigure cartooning and the modern single-figure panels.

Many of the best comic artists of the 1930s drew social rather than political cartoons for magazines such as *The New Yorker*, *Vanity Fair*, and *Time*. The Depression, however, along with FDR and his NRA eagle, gave editorial cartoonists plenty of inspiration. As it happened, most cartoonists and most publishers were against Roosevelt. Notable exceptions were C. D. Batchelor, D. R. Fitzpatrick, and, at first, John T. McCutcheon.

Edmund Duffy, who has been called Kirby's heir, won three Pulitzer Prizes in the next decade: 1931, 1934, and 1940. Just as Rollin Kirby's famous "Mr. Dry" was not represented in any of his prize-winning cartoons, so Duffy's chinless little Ku Klux Klansman was also overlooked by the judges. Like Kirby, Duffy was influenced by Boardman Robinson and he is credited by Stephen Becker with continuing Kirby's move away from the crowded panels of the nineteenth century and toward the single-figure cartoon of those dominant figures of the mid-twentieth century, Herblock and Bill Mauldin.

The 1930s also gave cartoonists the slant-eyed figure of Japanese militarism and the easily caricatured Mussolini and Hitler. The St. Louis *Post-Dispatch*'s Daniel R. Fitzpatrick, in a style reminiscent of Boardman Robinson, made effective use of the swastika as a symbol of oppression. Fitzpatrick, who had won a Pulitzer Prize in 1926, would win another in 1955.

During World War II, Bill Mauldin's work in *The Stars and Stripes* provided a welcome relief from patriotic propaganda. He was a combat veteran himself, and his characters, Willie and Joe, were survivors, not heroes. The public took to them immediately. In 1945, Mauldin won the Pulitzer Prize. His popularity continued after the war, with some diminution: his style and the savagery behind it were too grating for a public that wanted amusement, not a crusade. When he returned to cartooning in 1958 with the St. Louis *Post-Dispatch*, he had switched to a lighter grease pencil and opened up his cartoons. And, as his Pulitzer Prize in 1959 for an anti-Russian cartoon showed, the targets were fatter. The civil-rights struggles of the 1960s provided him with the southern redneck to ridicule. Overall, Mauldin may be said to have moved in the same general direction as his liberal counterpart, Herbert Block.

Although Herbert L. Block, "Herblock," was an active cartoonist throughout the 1930s and was awarded the Pulitzer Prize in 1942, his preeminence generally begins after the war. He was one of the first cartoonists to oppose the anti-Communist hysteria, and he also assailed Senator Joseph McCarthy courageously. "Mr. Atom," his sinister personification of the bomb, ranks among the most effective cartoon symbols of the mid-twentieth century.

Among the younger men who have begun to challenge the dominance of Herblock and Mauldin is Patrick Oliphant, who came from Australia in 1964 to work for the Denver *Post*. As the story goes, he and his wife studied the past Pulitzer Prize-winning drawings, and he won one in 1966. Influenced by British cartoonist Ronald Searle, Oliphant has in turn influenced other artists with his fine, exuberant line and emphasis on sheer humor. A true satirist, he gets his laughs at the expense of the foolish, no matter what party or profession they belong to. He is presently with the Washington *Star*.

Another comparatively recent addition to the top echelon actually predates Pat Oliphant. An Iowa devotee of Ding Darling, Paul Conrad left the Denver *Post* in 1964 for the Los Angeles *Times*. Lawsuits filed by Mayor Sam Yorty and the Union Oil Company attest to Conrad's effectiveness there. Stephen Hess and Milton Kaplan's inclusion of Conrad in the "big four" with Herblock, Mauldin, and Oliphant is not universally accepted, but he is unarguably one of the very top cartoonists today. He may be accused of lack of subtlety, for he sometimes breaks bones in the process of drawing blood, but the sheer wildness of his concepts and his skill in executing them with fine and intricate lines make him deadly when he is on target. He won Pulitzer Prizes in 1964 and 1971.

The other important cartoonists drawing today are too numerous even to list here. Further, any attempt to classify them is bound to be unsatisfactory, for cartoonists resist being categorized just as adamantly as do writers. Keeping these caveats in mind, it is convenient to begin with the so-called new wave, a term used in the early 1960s to include Hugh Haynie of the Louisville *Courier-Journal*, Bill Sanders of the Milwaukee *Journal*, the resurgent Bill Mauldin, his Chicago contemporary John Fischetti, and other, generally liberal cartoonists such as Tony Auth of the Philadelphia *Enquirer*. Especially hard-hitting and somewhat younger, at least in terms of national prominence, are Tom Darcy of *Newsday*, Bill Shore of the Los Angeles *Herald Examiner*, and Paul Szep of the Boston *Globe*. A liberal, humanitarian cartoonist who often attains this high impact is Draper Hill of the Detroit *News*. Hill is also a leading American authority on the editorial cartoon. A "second beach head" was established by Don Wright of the Miami *News*, who has influenced Mike Peters of the Dayton *Daily News*, Doug Marlette of Charlotte *Observer*, Bob Englehart of the Dayton *Journal Herald*, and Duane Powell of the Raleigh *News Observer*.

Conservative cartoonists include Don Hesse of the St. Louis *Globe Democrat*, Charles Werner of the Indianapolis *Star*, Tom Curtis of the Milwaukee *Sentinel*, Wayne Stayskal of the Chicago *Tribune*, Jim Boardman of the Cincinnati *Enquirer*, and Karl Hubenthal of the Los Angeles *Herald-Examiner*. Jeff MacNelly of the Richmond *News Leader*, winner of two Pulitzer Prizes, comes closer than any of these to the free-swinging hilarity of Oliphant.

There is some disagreement as to whether or not Gary Trudeau and Jules Feiffer's use of the strip medium instead of the single panel disqualifies them as editorial cartoonists, although the awarding of the 1975 Pulitzer Prize to Trudeau is strong evidence on their behalf. At any rate, it is impossible to deny Trudeau's popularity among young people and liberals.

Feiffer has been effective since the late 1950s, not only in his merciless forays against the liberals' nemeses, but also in his equally merciless exposure of the self-deception and hypocrisy to which so many liberals fall prey.

Again, it must be emphasized that these groupings are approximate at best, for each cartoonist reacts according to his instincts, not according to some rigid party or liberal-conservative alignment. If there is a trend in editorial cartooning today, it is toward originality and spontaneity of style, with an increasing emphasis on humor for its own sake.

REFERENCE WORKS

Although general encyclopedias, art reference works, and journalism indexes and bibliographies lend some help with the best-known figures in the field—especially those who also have "high culture" reputations—few indexes, bibliographies, or biographical dictionaries deal exclusively or comprehensively with editorial cartooning or cartoonists.

The most comprehensive bibliographies that deal primarily with editorial cartooning appear in the major history and criticism books such as Stephen Hess and Milton Kaplan's *The Ungentlemanly Art*. Researchers should be sure to consult the second edition of Hess and Kaplan (1975), which has the longer bibliography. Even in this, the best bibliography, there are no page numbers in periodical entries, and the items are not annotated.

Another useful bibliography appears in Roy Nelson's *Cartooning*. Nelson deals with social and strip as well as editorial cartooning, and there is some annotation. The Fort Worth exhibition publication, *The Image of America in Caricature and Cartoons*, also contains an extensive bibliography, but it is of unannotated items. A number of these are American history references that have only indirect bearing on editorial cartooning.

Researchers may also wish to consult the bibliography at the end of Ralph E. Shikes's *The Indignant Eye*. The annotated list for the chapter on recent and American cartooning is especially valuable. More specialized history and criticism books about individual cartoonists, such as Morton Keller's *The Art and Politics of Thomas Nast*, deserve attention as well. The Keller book includes brief annotations for a number of significant Nast studies.

Among the standard references in journalism, *An Annotated Journalism Bibliography* should be consulted. Compiled by Warren C. Price and Calder M. Pickett, the bibliography lists forty-eight items under the "Cartoons, Cartooning" heading. J. Brander Matthews also wrote a bibliographical essay on comic periodicals in 1875 that is still of value today. Some other bibliographies look promising, but turn out to be disappointing. Wolfgang Kempkes's *The International Bibliography of Comics Literature* deals almost entirely with strips and contains only a few items on editorial cartooning.

It is also profitable to review reprints of the subject catalogs of major libraries with fine arts holdings such as the Harvard University's Fogg Library Catalog, the Metropolitan Museum of Art Library Catalog, and the Catalog of the Museum of Modern Art Library.

For periodical items, students may wish to go beyond the standard guides to look at the *Art Index*, which lists by subject as well as by artist. In addition, the Ryerson Library Index of the Art Institute of Chicago includes only periodical article references and thus serves a special function among art library catalogs. The search for books and articles about major figures in the field usually requires cartoonists' names since the subject indexes are not entirely trustworthy.

For annotated references to recent major book, festschriften, periodical articles, and exhibition catalogs, *RILA: Réportoire International de la Littérature de l'art (International Repertory of the Literature of Art)* is a good reference because *RILA* often includes items not listed elsewhere and because reviews are substantial. *RILA* indexes political cartooning under the Library of Congress heading, "Caricatures and Cartoons."

There are also only a few sources that provide shortcuts for researchers seeking biographical data on individual cartoonists, and none of these is both up to date and comprehensive. It is wise to use several to cross-check.

Over three hundred editorial cartoonists' photos and biographies (many prepared by the cartoonists themselves) appear in the latest edition of the *National Cartoonists' Society Album (1972-1977)*, edited by Mort Walker. The book's disadvantage is that editorial cartoonists are intermixed with magazine artists and strip cartoonists who are members of the society.

John Chase's *Today's Cartoon*, published in 1962, is a yearbook of 139 editorial cartoonists. It includes photos, biographical data, and informal commentary for each entry. Biographical sketches of some major cartoonists, together with photos of the artists, also appear in Lynne Deur's *Political Cartoonists*. Although this simple book can be categorized as history and criticism, the sketches are so brief that it is more helpful as a reference guide if depth is not a requirement.

Deur's book, as well as Walker's and Chase's, reprints representative cartoons for most of the cartoonists included. In addition, *The Image of America in Caricature and Cartoon* has a valuable appendix of 132 biographical sketches of figures involved in the Fort Worth exhibition. Although sketches are brief, this reference is more comprehensive than the others and contains historical as well as contemporary figures. A number of "how-to" books, such as Chuck Thorndike's *The Business of Cartoon-*

ing, also provide thumbnail sketches of a few political cartoonists of an earlier period. Thorndike includes C. D. Batchelor, "Ding" Darling, and John McCutcheon.

Some well-established editorial cartoonists are listed in *Who's Who in America* or *Who's Who in American Art.* To find out about a living editorial cartoonist currently working in the field, researchers may wish to consult the membership list of the Association of American Editorial Cartoonists, which is updated annually. The list is not available to the general public, but the association may respond to serious researchers. This list or a similar membership roster from the National Cartoonists' Society may omit several major figures who are not members.

Although there are no recently published indexes, Frank Weitenkampf's *Political Caricature in the United States, in Separately Published Cartoons . . . an Annotated List* indexes some of the most important editorial cartoons. The index is chronological, so that the book also serves as a history of editorial cartooning in the United States. Weitenkampf provides locations as well as descriptions for 1,158 cartoon entries.

RESEARCH COLLECTIONS

Until recently, research collections of editorial cartoons were hard to locate because such collections were not fully reported or cataloged. With the appearance of *The Image of America in Caricature and Cartoon,* there now exists a more complete list of cartoon collections in the United States, Canada, and Great Britain. It concentrates on U.S. collections; the Canadian and British references are included primarily where there are holdings directly related to U.S. history and culture. The list of private collectors is necessarily incomplete. The alphabetized inventory of collections, arranged by state, was compiled through the use of two thousand questionnaires and through personal contacts; in some cases, the library or personal collector has reported specifically what period or what cartoonists his collection covers and what has been cataloged. In other instances, however, and especially with regard to large collections, the information is too vague or too general and requires verification.

The largest collection of caricatures and cartoons is probably to be found in the Library of Congress. Bernard Reilly, of the Prints and Photographs Division, reports that the Library of Congress has four major collections of political cartoons. The most recently acquired is the extensive group that makes up the Swann Collection. These are nineteenth- and twentieth-century drawings that include approximately twenty-five hundred editorial cartoons, comic strips, and single caricatures. The collection has a checklist of artists and works. Use of the collection is presently restricted because of the delicate state of preservation of many of the items, but Reilly notes that cataloging and preservation measures are underway. The Cartoon Drawings Collection is a group of about twenty-two hundred early twentieth-century drawings by American artists primarily for political cartoons. A large portion of the collection was originally drawn for American newspapers and journals and was collected by George T. Maxwell and donated to the library. Reilly estimates that approximately one-quarter of the collection is cataloged and indexed and that there are catalog data sheets for another one-half of the works. About six hundred American cartoons from 1798 to 1900 are also collected in the library's Political Cartoon Print Collection, which is international in scope. In addition, the Cabinet of American Illustration, which is primarily a set of drawings for American magazine and book illustrations, contains approximately two hundred editorial and political cartoons, including work by Thomas Nast and Joseph Keppler. According to Reilly, a major preservation program is in progress to restore these drawings.

Other major editorial cartoon collections cited in *The Image of America in Caricature and Cartoon* or in Lee Ash's *Subject Collections* (4th ed., 1974) include the collections of the New York Public Library; the Smithsonian Institution; the Boston Public Library; the Lilly Library of the University of Indiana; the Hal Coffman Collection of the Fort Worth Texas Public Library; the New York Historical Society; the Syracuse University Library; the Chesler Collection of the Library of Fairleigh Dickinson University, Florham-Madison, New Jersey; the Free Library of Philadelphia; and the Philadelphia Museum of Art. Other noteworthy collections of American political or editorial cartoons can be found at the Fogg Art Museum of Harvard University; the John Carter Brown Library of Brown University; the Princeton University Library; the American Antiquarian Society Library, Worcester, Massachusetts; the Butler Institute of American Art; the Kenneth Spencer Research Library of the University of Kansas at Lawrence; and the University of Virginia's Alderman Library.

Specialized libraries, whose collections are limited to work concerned with a single public figure, often have political or editorial cartoons, but usually in relatively small numbers. Libraries and memorials such as Woodrow Wilson House, Washington, D.C.; the Herbert Hoover Presidential Library, West Branch, Texas; the Dwight D. Eisenhower Presidential Library, Abilene, Texas; the Calvin Coolidge Memorial Room, Northhampton, Massachusetts; the Franklin D. Roosevelt Presidential Library, Hyde Park, New York; the Theodore Roosevelt Birthplace National Historic Site, New York City; the Lyndon B. Johnson Presidential Library, Austin, Texas; and the Woodrow Wilson Birthplace Foundation, Staunton, Virginia, all have some collections of cartoons and caricatures relating to their special interests.

While the works of significant editorial cartoonists are frequently scattered among the major collections across the country, some libraries report substantial holdings of a particular cartoonist's works. The Bancroft Library of the University of California, Berkeley, has a collection of Rube Goldberg original drawings for editorial cartoons and comic strips. Pat Oliphant's cartoons for the Denver *Post* between 1965 and 1968 are in the library of the University of Colorado, Boulder; and some Paul Conrad original cartoons are held by the Syracuse University Library collection in New York. Clifford K. Berryman's cartoons may be seen at the Idaho State Historical Society in Boise, Idaho.

There is a collection of John T. McCutcheon cartoons in the Illinois Historical Society Library and at Northern Illinois University, DeKalb, Illinois; a larger number of several hundred McCutcheon works drawn from 1916-1945 are at the Northwestern University Library, Evanston, Illinois; and the largest group of McCutcheon drawings is at the Purdue University libraries in West Lafayette, Indiana. McCutcheon, a Purdue alumnus, is represented by eight hundred cartoons in his alma mater's collection.

Thomas Nast cartoons are held in a number of different collections, including the Library of Congress and the New York Public Library, which has a large group of mounted Nast drawings and checklists of his cartoons and the books that he illustrated. Other collections of Nast cartoons are reported by Columbia University Library, New York; the Art Institute of Chicago; Hopkins Center Art Galleries, Dartmouth College, Hanover, New Hampshire; the Cincinnati Art Museum; and the University of Rochester Library and Memorial Art Gallery. There are also smaller collections at Hamilton College, Clinton, New York, and at the Rutgers University Art Gallery, New Brunswick, New Jersey.

A major group of J. N. "Ding" Darling cartoons may be found at Drake University, Des Moines, Iowa, and in special collections at the University of Iowa Library, Iowa City. According to Lee Ash, the University of Iowa collection includes six hundred cartoons and four file drawers of manuscript material. There is an extensive subject index.

A major source for twentieth-century cartoons is the Albert Reid Collection at the University of Kansas in the Kenneth Spencer Research Library at Lawrence. To Reid's personal collection of cartoons were added the works of later cartoonists like Bill Mauldin, Rollin Kirby, and Daniel B. Dowling. That group also contains some of Nast's work.

Some Daniel J. Fitzpatrick cartoons are in general collections. One major reported collection of Fitzpatrick's work is held by the Missouri Historical Society, St. Louis. David Levine's caricatures and cartoons are collected by the Brooklyn Museum, New York, and Frederick Burr Opper cartoons are to be found in the Lake County Historical Society of Mentor, Ohio.

The Brooks Memorial Art Gallery, Memphis, Tennessee, has cartoons by J. P. Alley, and the Oregon Historical Society has a small collection of Homer Davenport's work. John Chase's cartoons are in the New Orleans Public Library and the Tulane University Library.

The social protest cartoons of Boardman Robinson are located in a number of major collections and also at the Munson-Williams Proctor Institute, Utica, New York, and at St. Bonaventure University, St. Bonaventure, New York. The Munson-Williams Proctor Institute also holds cartoons of Reginald Marsh and John Sloan, whose works are widely disseminated among important collections as well. The State Historical Society of Wisconsin has the H. T. Webster Collection, which contains cartoons from the progressive era through the 1950s.

Other cartoonists, such as Fred O. Seibel of the Richmond *Times-Dispatch*, are collected at the University of Virginia Library, Charlottesville, and the James Branch Cabell Library of Virginia Commonwealth University, Richmond. Tom Little of the Nashville *Tennesseean* has cartoons in the collections of the Joint University Libraries, Nashville, Tennessee. Adalbert J. Volck, the confederate Civil War cartoonist and illustrator, is collected in several libraries, notably in the Virginia Historical Society, Richmond; the Chicago Public Library; and the Peabody Institute, Baltimore.

In addition to the library collections, *The Image of America in Caricature and Cartoon* cites several private collectors, such as cartoonist-scholar Draper Hill of the Detroit *News*. Other nonlibrary collectors, such as the Museum of Cartoon Art and Hall of Fame in Rye Town, Port Chester, New York, report some political or editorial cartoons, but tend to specialize more in strip cartooning.

A rule of thumb for locating unrecorded or unreported collections, especially for cartoonists who did not acquire major or national reputations, is to consult the newspaper libraries where they worked and the libraries in the locales where they were best known.

HISTORY AND CRITICISM

The first real historian of the subject was Philadelphia-born James P. Malcolm, a fierce loyalist whose 1813 book, *An Historical Sketch of the Art of Caricaturing*, describes a very few caricatures dealing with the American war, while touching on Asian and European caricatures but emphasizing the British.

In 1862, Richard Grant White provided for *Harper's New Monthly Magazine* a survey of caricature from the time of the Egyptians up to the present in France and England, concluding with a plea for caricaturists to exercise restraint. In "The Limits of Caricature" in 1866, *The Nation* pointed out technical weaknesses in American caricature and concluded that "Upon the whole, we can hardly esteem caricature as an agreeable or particularly useful art; for fairness and good nature are almost impossible in the practice."

American scholarly consideration of editorial cartooning may be said to have begun in 1878, with James Parton's *Caricature and Other Comic Art*. Parton traced the history of caricature from Roman times to his own, devoting the final thirty-odd pages to early and later American caricature from Franklin to Nast. The study is still worthwhile and includes 203 illustrations.

A few years later, Arthur Penn noted "The Growth of Caricature" in *The Critic*, citing Parton as a source. He commented on the failure of American imitations of *Punch* and on the success of *Puck*, while criticizing it for weakness in pictorial social commentary. Writing in *The Century* in 1892, Joseph Bucklin Bishop dated political caricature in the United States from the first administration of Andrew Jackson. His scholarly interest in dating various cartoons is noteworthy.

Frederick Taylor Cooper and Arthur Bartlett Maurice's *The History of the Nineteenth Century in Caricature* is another valuable full-length early study. Over two hundred and fifty illustrations, many of them full-page, are a strong point of this book; it emphasizes French and British caricature but devotes considerable attention to the American forms, including Currier & Ives, Nast, *Puck*, and *Judge*, and to the rise of the daily newspaper cartoon at the close of the century.

Another scholarly milestone is Frank Weitenkampf's *American Graphic Art*, which appeared in 1912, was revised and enlarged in 1924, and reprinted in 1970. In a solid work that was a source for many subsequent researchers, Weitenkampf devoted some of the fifteen chapters to etching, lithography, and so on and examines caricature from Franklin up to the newspaper cartoonists of his own time, with extensive discussion of early comic periodicals, beginning with *Yankee Doodle* in 1856. Weitenkampf continued his consideration of editorial cartooning as a serious art form in 1913 with his illustrated article "American Cartoons of Today," which appeared in *Century*. Evaluating several contemporary cartoonists, he wrote that a review of the best of them "discloses an admirable average of elevated endeavor and intention."

Twenty years later came the first volume of William Murrell's indispensable *A History of American Graphic Humor*, which ranged from the earliest wood engravings through the Civil War. In addition to an extensive background, the book provides 237 illustrations, listing the source or location of each. Murrell's comments, necessarily brief, are nevertheless historically and aesthetically worthwhile. Published in 1938, volume 2 uses 242 illustrations in taking us up through the presidential campaign of 1936.

Between these two publication dates, Murrell's concise and useful "The Rise and Fall of Cartoon Symbols" appeared in *The American Scholar*. Thomas Craven's *Cartoon Cavalcade* presents strip and humorous cartoons as well as editorial ones, spanning from 1883 to 1943. Copiously illustrated, the book also included several essays by Craven relating the graphic humor of various periods to events and attitudes of the time. The next year, 1944, saw the publication of Allan Nevins and Frank Weitenkampf's *A Century of Political Cartoons*. In addition to an excellent nine-page introductory essay on caricature and cartoon, it provides generalizations on the artistic merits of the cartoons and their artists, as well as a history of American political cartooning until 1900. Many of the one hundred cartoons are accompanied by an explanatory one-page note, with sidelights on the artist.

Journalism professors have commented on editorial cartoons. Frank Luther Mott mentioned some historical highlights of the subject in *American Journalism*. Professor Henry Ladd Smith documented "The Rise and Fall of the Political Cartoon" in the *Saturday Review* in 1954, labeling the first quarter of this century the "golden age of the political cartoonists."

Stephen Becker's *Comic Art in America* is an important work, even though it devotes only one chapter (fifty-five pages) to editorial cartooning. Its strengths include the numerous illustrations and detailed coverage of the Pulitzer Prize years, 1922-1958. Becker's editorial comments are occasionally hyperbolic, but he provides an excellent overview and his judgments are sharper here than in some of the other chapters in this book, which critics have treated none too kindly.

The best book on American editorial cartooning is Stephen Hess and Milton Kaplan's *The Ungentlemanly Art* because of its comprehensiveness and its documentation of both print and graphic sources. Perhaps the authors lose some of the advantage of currency by devoting only fifty-four of the book's 173 pages to the chapter on "Newspapers, 1884-1975," even in the revised edition. After the introduction, subsequent chapters are arranged according to media: "Copper Engraving and Woodcut," "Lithography and Early Magazines," "Magazines," and "Newspapers." The thematic-topical organization of the newspaper chapter is quite effective. The revised edition of 1975 is only slightly revised, adding a dozen or so new bibliographical references and some current cartoons.

Other works, more restricted in subject matter, include Kenneth M. Johnson's *The Sting of the Wasp*, which has as its subject the San Francisco humor magazine *The Wasp*, which has unfortunately received far less attention than its contemporaries, *Puck* and *Judge*. Also specialized is Ralph E. Shikes's *The Indignant Eye*, subtitled "The Artist as Social Critic in Prints and Drawings from the Fifteenth Century to Picasso." In addition to providing an illustrated history of European protest art, Shikes devotes a seventy-page chapter to "The United States Since 1870," beginning with Nast, but doubling back to touch upon some early engravers and cartoonists. He deals with the major cartoonists from Keppler and Davenport up through the radical cartoonists, predictably ignoring more amiable artists such as Darling and McCutcheon. The remainder of the chapter is concerned primarily with printmakers, but he credits Herblock with doing much to keep dissent alive during the McCarthy years and reproduces two of his cartoons. In spite of its concentration on protest art, Shikes's work is helpful, not only for its consideration of some important cartoonists, but also because it provides artistic yardsticks for us to measure them by.

A book that is even more specialized than Shikes's is Richard Fitzgerald's *Art and Politics*, which tells the story of *Masses* and *Liberator* in the first chapter and devotes a chapter each to Art Young, Robert Minor, John Sloan, K. R. Chamberlain, and Maurice Becker. The thesis of this excellent study is, "While their [radical cartoonists'] greatest successes were in capturing the ferment of artistic and political dissent, their most significant failure was their continual inability to provide a deeper analysis of the role of art and politics in the culture." Fitzgerald includes an extensive bibliography of the art and politics of the period and sixty full-page illustrations.

Restricted chronologically is Mary and Gordon Campbell's *The Pen, Not the Sword*, which is an extensively illustrated anthology of the period of Nast, Keppler, Gillam, Opper, and other artists of the end of the nineteenth century, and is accompanied by some confusing background essays.

The Cartoon History of California Politics by Ed Salzman and Ann Leigh Brown grew out of a bicentennial exhibit at the University of California Museum of Art. Short essays provide background for the cartoons, which range from 1949 to 1977. Similarly, *The Image of America in Caricature and Cartoon* reproduces the exhibition presented at the Amon Carter Museum in Fort Worth, Texas. Ron Taylor, the Amon Carter Museum's curator of history, provides an introduction devoting two pages to an overview of American cartoons and caricatures, followed by thirty-seven pages of American history related to cartoons, especially some of those reprinted later in the book. Further, each of the 263 cartoons is accompanied by a brief paragraph that analyzes its background and point of view.

Syd Hoff, known for his *New Yorker* cartoons, is the author and editor of *Editorial and Political Cartooning*, which is divided into three sections: "the Old Masters," "the Moderns: U. S. and Canada," and "the Moderns: The World." Although it is unscholarly, the book is extensive and ecumenical in its inclusion of 700 cartoons by 165 cartoonists. Hoff provides informal background and sometimes makes instructive aesthetic judgments.

Especially valuable as a reference work and a source of illustrations is

Michael Wynn Jones's 1975 book, *The Cartoon History of the American Revolution*, although the reader is sometimes at a loss to determine on which side of the Atlantic a particular cartoon originated.

Charles Press's *The Political Cartoon* was published in 1979. Written from a political scientist's point of view, this extensively illustrated book emphasizes the role of editorial cartoonists in a democracy. Press devotes several chapters to an anecdotal history of American editorial cartooning. The chapter "Since World War II" is especially welcome for its coverage of today's cartoonists. The author is critical of some of the "new wave" cartoonists (Conrad, Darcy, Don Wright, Szep) and drops Conrad from Hess's "big four," leaving Herblock, Mauldin, and Oliphant. The chapter on politics in the strips is useful, as is the book overall, filling in background omitted by other studies. Roy Paul Nelson's history, *Comic Art and Caricature*, a valuable modern reference, appeared in 1978.

Another group of books deals primarily with world cartooning, but several merit our attention because they devote some space to Americans. Michael Wynn Jones's *The Cartoon History of Great Britain* provides good background on British cartoonists, as well as a chapter entitled "World War I—America to the Front." Draper Hill's three books, *Mr. Gillray, the Caricaturist*; *Fashionable Contrasts: 100 Caricatures by James Gillray*; and *The Satirical Etchings of James Gillray*, shed light on an English artist who had great influence on Americans.

Wider in scope but shorter in length, Clifford K. Berryman's booklet, *Development of the Cartoon*, is interesting primarily because its author was a well-known cartoonist. Most of its nineteen pages are concerned with an informal history of world cartooning and caricature, with some sketches of famous caricatures apparently drawn by Berryman himself. After a paragraph on Nast, he explains that lack of space prevents him from discussing modern cartoonists. H. R. Westwood's *Modern Caricaturists*, with an introduction by David Low, has a chapter on Rollin Kirby and one on D. R. Fitzpatrick. More recently, *Mightier Than the Sword* by W. G. Rogers surveys important European cartoonists and caricaturists. Its discussion of the relationship between British and early American cartoonists is helpful, and it treats Mauldin, Herblock, and Feiffer in the last chapter. The book has surprisingly few illustrations. While it provides more illustrations, Bevis Hillier's *Cartoons and Caricatures* touches only briefly on American cartoonists. *The Cartoon* by John Geipel, however, has fifteen pages on Americans, eclectically mixing editorial with social cartoonists as it goes from Revere to Herblock and Oliphant, touching on Charles Dana Gibson, Peter Arno, James Thurber, and others along the way. Other chapters deal with strip and animated cartoons.

There are several book-length studies of individual editorial cartoonists, including, from the early period: William A. Beardsley's *An Old New Haven Engraver and His Work: Amos Doolittle* and Harry B. Weiss's *William Charles, Early Caricaturist, Engraver and Publisher of Children's Books*. About Currier & Ives are the books: *Mr. Currier & Mr. Ives* by Russell Crouse, *Currier & Ives* by F. A. Conningham, and *Currier & Ives, Printmakers to the American People* by Harry T. Peters.

Not surprisingly, Thomas Nast is also well represented. The definitive biography is Albert Bigelow Paine's *Th. Nast: His Period and His Pictures*, warmly written with a wealth of personal details. Paine includes rare early drawings and sketches among the four hundred fifty illustrations he reproduces, and treats Nast, whom he had met, with contagious admiration and affection. An antidote to this subjectivity is Morton Keller's *The Art and Politics of Thomas Nast*, which sees bigotry as much as altruism behind Nast's campaign against the Irish-Catholic Tweed. The large-format book reproduces 241 cartoons and illustrations, mostly full-page. A third book on Nast—and the scholar would be wise to consult all three—is *Thomas Nast: Political Cartoonist* by J. Chal Vinson, which emphasizes in its forty-page text the events of Nast's life more than his personality and reproduces 154 drawings. Joseph Keppler is the subject of "Keppler and Political Cartooning" by Frank Weitenkampf in the *New York Public Library Bulletin* and of Draper Hill's excellent Harvard A.B. thesis, "What Fools These Mortals Be! A Study of the Work of Joseph Keppler, Founder of Puck."

In addition to Hill's, there are several unpublished theses and dissertations that contribute to the study of editorial cartooning: J. H. Bender, Jr.'s "Editorial Cartoonists: Development/Philosophy Today," Joseph Anthony Gahn's "The America of William Gropper, Radical Cartoonist," and Charles N. Faerber's "An Examination of the Career Patterns and Editorial Roles of a Number of Staff Editorial Cartoonists on Contemporary American English-Language Newspapers."

Of the books about single cartoonists, several deal with the radical cartoonists, two of which are titled *John Sloan*, one by Albert E. Gallatin and the other by Lloyd Goodrich. Albert Christ-Janer is the author of *Boardman Robinson*. Peter Marzio's *Rube Goldberg: His Life and Work* is at once biographical and critical.

Also, there are some autobiographies: *Art Young: His Life and Times*; John T. McCutcheon's *Drawn from Memory*; Walt McDougall's *This Is the Life!*; and Rube Goldberg's, which may be found in *Rube Goldberg vs. the Machine Age*, edited by Clark Kinnaird. Bill Mauldin's *A Sort of Saga* deals only with the artist's boyhood years.

Often overlooked, the "how-to" books sometime incorporate history, criticism, and illustrations in the course of their instruction. Worthwhile examples include: Grant Wright's *The Art of Caricature*, Dick Spencer

III's *Editorial Cartooning*, Roy Paul Nelson's *Cartooning*, and Rube Goldberg's "Lesson #19" in the *Famous Artists Cartoon Course*. Of these, Nelson's *Cartooning* is particularly important for its insights into the techniques and the aesthetics of the art of cartooning. Other worthwhile how-to books are Gene Byrnes's *The Complete Guide to Cartooning* and Clare Briggs's *How to Draw Cartoons*. Especially valuable is *Ye Madde Designer* by the influential British caricaturist David Low. Between March 1973, and March 1976, a series of instructive articles on cartoons and cartooning by Jack Markow also appeared in *Writer's Digest*.

PERIODICALS

There are a number of periodicals of historical importance for students of editorial cartooning (*Puck, Judge, Harper's Weekly, Caricature, Cartoons Magazine*, and so on), but only a few current periodicals deal with the subject. In some of these, editorial cartooning shares space with strip and social cartooning.

Cartoonist PROfiles, edited by cartoonist Jud Hurd, is a quarterly publication that interviews living artists and also contains features about important cartoonists of the past. Editorial cartoonists are frequently included, and each issue is regarded by collectors as a valuable item. *Cartoonist PROfiles* reproduces several cartoons by the featured artists as well as photographs of the cartoonists. Subscription correspondence should be addressed to: *Cartoonist PROfiles*, P.O. Box 325, Fairfield, Connecticut 06430. The Museum of Cartoon Art and Hall of Fame of Rye Town, Port Chester, New York, has published *Inklings* somewhat irregularly. *Inklings* reports on events and exhibits at the Museum and elsewhere; it also includes some special features about cartoonists and cartooning. In 1978, *Inklings* was merged with *Cartoon PROfiles* and will be distributed under its own name, but as an insert in the older periodical.

Cartoonews, published six times a year, is concerned with comic strips as well as editorial cartoons. Susbcriptions are available from the editor, Bill Sheridan, 330 Myrtle Street, Redwood, California 94062.

The National Cartoonists' Society, 9 Ebony Court, Brooklyn, New York 11229, produces the *American Cartoonist*, an annual, which recently began quarterly publication. Mail relating to the *American Cartoonist* should be sent to the editors, Box 2311, Bridgeport, Connecticut 06608. Similarly, the American Association of Editorial Cartoonists publishes the *AAEC Notebook* monthly. It includes reviews of new books and it is also a treasurehouse of interesting behind-the-scenes information. The association publications are generally distributed only to members, but special requests are usually honored. The AAEC's address is 475 School Street, S.W. Washington, D.C. 20024. Of additional help are the journalism periodicals, such as *Editor and Publisher* or Northwestern University's *Byline*, which are specialized sources for articles on political cartooning and its relationship to editorial policy and other phases of newspaper work.

ANTHOLOGIES

Anthologies of editorial cartoons fall roughly into three categories: those that are arranged by year or historical period; those that are concerned with a particular historical event, topic, or significant political figure; and those that collect a single political cartoonist's work.

In the first category, Charles Brooks's *Best Editorial Cartoons* of the year series deserves prominent mention. Published annually since 1973, it reprints cartoons by major editorial artists. Cartoons are arranged according to appropriate categories, which vary with each year. Although there is no text accompanying individual cartoons, recent forewords by "Blaine" in the 1976 edition and by Draper Hill in 1977 are interesting commentaries on the state of political cartooning as well as on the aesthetics of the art. The 1978 edition includes a special tribute to Cy Hungerford of the *Pittsburgh Post Gazette* in lieu of a foreword. In addition, Brooks lists winners of the Pulitzer Prize, the National Headliners' Club Awards, the National Newspaper Awards of Canada, and the Sigma Delta Chi Awards.

The International Salon of Cartoons publishes an anthology in conjunction with an international exhibition and judging held annually since 1964. Typical of these collections is *The Thirteenth International Salon of Cartoons*, a 690-page, 1976 version from the Montreal World's Fair exhibition. Cartoons are gathered by country of origin, and there are seventy pages of U.S. entries. Although a general introduction precedes them, no commentary accompanies specific cartoons.

Several other exhibitions have produced printed anthologies or exhibition catalogs. One of the most recent is Blaisdell and Selz's *The American Presidency in Political Cartoons: 1776-1976*, which reprints cartoons selected from the University of California (Berkeley) Art Museum's bicentennial exhibition. Professor Peter Selz, director of the museum, and Professor Emeritus Thomas Blaisdell of the political science department each contribute an introductory essay. The book collects 113 cartoons, and the accompanying text provides background to each cartoon. Earlier exhibitions such as the Syracuse University, Martin H. Bush Exhibition of June 1966, *American Political Cartoons* (1865-1965), gathered work by Thomas Nast, John T. McCutcheon, Homer Davenport, Clifford K. Berryman, Frederick Burr Opper, Jay (Ding) Darling, Carey C. Orr, Clarence D. Batchelor, Karl Hubenthal, Ray B. Justus, Don Wright, Richard Q. Yardley, and others.

Among the anthologists dealing with the early years in American history, Joan D. Dolmetsch has edited *Rebellion and Reconciliation*, which is a collection of satirical prints about the Revolution, including one hundred political satires from the Colonial Williamsburg collection. *A Cartoon History of U.S. Foreign Policy (1776-1976)* is a lively publication by the editors of the Foreign Policy Association and has an introduction by Daniel P. Moynihan. The book includes 196 prints, engravings, lithographs, and newspaper cartoons. An earlier book by the Foreign Policy Association published in 1968, *A Cartoon History of U.S. Foreign Policy Since World War I*, reprints the work of ninety editorial cartoonists and includes two hundred fifty reproductions. Special emphasis is on work by John Fischetti, Herblock, and Mauldin. Rollin Kirby's *Highlights: A Cartoon History of the Nineteen Twenties* is a chronologically arranged anthology of sixty full-page cartoons Kirby did for the New York *World*.

A number of anthologies specialize in war cartoons. *American Caricatures Pertaining to the Civil War* is one of several important Civil War collections. Published in 1918, it reproduces primarily Currier & Ives lithographs from the originals published between 1856 and 1872. Another significant collection is *The American War Cartoons* by Matt Morgan and others. Spanish-American War cartoons are found in Charles L. Bartholomew's *Cartoons of the Spanish-American War by Bart* and in Charles Nelan's *Cartoons of Our War with Spain*; World War I is the subject of George Hecht's *The War in Cartoons*, Louis Raemaekers's *America in the War* and Raemaekers' *Cartoon History of the War*, and Boardman Robinson's *Cartoons on the War*. The Chicago *Tribune* has published a *History of World War II in Cartoon*, which reprints war cartoons by McCutcheon and others.

Political campaigns have inspired a number of published cartoon collections as well. Pierce G. Fredericks edited *The People's Choice: The Issues of the 1956 Campaign as Seen by the Nation's Best Political Cartoonists*. The book contains 102 reproductions of works by many political cartoonists working in the late 1950s. Earlier anthologies of campaign cartoons include *The Political Campaign of 1912 in Cartoons* by Nelson Harding, and Bib Crockett and Jim Berryman's cartoons in the Washington *Evening Star* anthologies for the campaigns of 1948, 1952, and 1956. A more recent addition to this category of anthologies is Jeff MacNelly's *The Election That Was—MacNelly at His Best*, fifty-six pages of MacNelly cartoons from the 1976 campaign.

Still other anthologies collect reprints of cartoons pertaining to a particular political figure. "Ding" Darling's *As Ding Saw Hoover* and Clarence Batchelor's *Truman Scrapbook* fall into this category. One of the most important collections is *LBJ Lampooned*, edited by Charles Antin and Sig Rosenblum, which contains cartoon criticism of Lyndon B. Johnson by forty cartoonists including Mauldin, Feiffer, Oliphant, and Haynie. The book's six chapters are preceded by a classic commentary by Feiffer, which defines the position of many younger cartoonists on the war and LBJ. More recently, several books of individual cartoonist's work have been devoted to Watergate and the Nixon years. Jules Feiffer's *Feiffer on Nixon: The Cartoon Presidency*, Gary Trudeau's *Guilty, Guilty, Guilty!*, Paul Conrad's *The King and Us*, Paul Szep's *At This Point in Time*, Mike Peters's *The Nixon Chronicles*, Ranan Lurie's *Nixon Rated Cartoons*, Bill Sanders's *Run for the Oval Room . . . they can't corner us there!*, and Herbert Block's *Herblock's Special Report* are only a few among the best of these collections.

A much earlier anthology built around a single political figure was Albert Shaw's *A Cartoon History of [Teddy] Roosevelt's Career* published in 1910. Included are 630 cartoons and drawings, as well as other pictures to accompany a biographical text. Shaw also authored a two-volume cartoon history of Lincoln. Other Lincoln cartoons appear in Rufus Rockwell Wilson's *Lincoln in Caricature* and in an earlier collection that contains John Tenniel drawings, William S.Walsh's *Abraham Lincoln and the London Punch*.

Some other collections pertaining to particular figures or historical periods that are more difficult to categorize include *Red Cartoons from the Daily Worker*, edited by Walt Carmon and published in 1926 and 1928. The books are folio size, with fifty full-page cartoons in each folio. Those included read like a *Who's Who* among radical cartoonists.

Pulitzer Prize cartoonists are reprinted in several editions, most notably in John Hohenberg's *The Pulitzer Prize Story*. Hohenberg reproduces cartoons along with prize-winning features and editorials. An earlier edition, Dick Spencer III's *Pulitzer Prize Cartoons*, reproduces on full pages the Pulitzer winners from 1922 through 1950 and includes, not only capsule summaries of the year's events, but also informal biographical sketches and commentary to accompany each reproduction. Gerald W. Johnson's *The Lines Are Drawn*, like Hohenberg's book, is more current than Spencer's. It includes Pulitzer Prize-winning cartoons for the years 1922-1958, accompanied by essays based on the cartoons' historical contexts.

By far the largest category of anthologies is the one that includes collections of work by specific cartoonists. In the case of Mauldin or Herblock, who excel with a typewriter as well as a brush and pen, the accompanying commentary may also be by the cartoonist himself. Many of the best-known cartoonists from Nast to Oliphant have published several collections of their work. Darling, McCutcheon, Mauldin, Herblock, Feiffer, and Trudeau have been prolific. Hugh Haynie's *Hugh Haynie: Perspective*, Jeff MacNelly's *MacNelly: The Pulitzer Prize Winning Cartoonist*, Don Wright's *Wright On!*, David Levine's *No Known Survivors*, Doug Marlette's *The Emperor Has No Clothes,* and Pat Oliphant's *An Informal Gathering* are representatives of recent books that should not be missed.

BIBLIOGRAPHY

BOOKS AND ARTICLES

The "All American" Art—Cartooning. Brooklyn: Higgins Ink, 1944.
Allen, Edison. *Of Time and Chase.* New Orleans: Habersham, 1969.
American Caricatures Pertaining to the Civil War. New York: Brentano's, 1918.
American Political Cartoons (1865-1965). Syracuse University: Martin H. Bush Exhibition, June 1966.
Antin, Charles, and Sig Rosenblum, eds. *LBJ Lampooned: Cartoon Criticism of Lyndon B. Johnson.* New York: Cobble Hill Press, 1968.
The Art Index. New York: H. W. Wilson, 1933-.
Ash, Lee. *Subject Collections: A Guide to Special Book Collections and Subject Emphases as Reported by University, College, Public and Special Libraries, and Museums in the United States and Canada.* 4th ed. New York: R. R. Bowker, 1974.
Attwood, Francis G. *Attwood's Pictures: An Artist's History of the Last Ten Years of the Nineteenth Century.* New York: Life Publishing, 1900.
Auth, Tony. *Behind the Lines.* Boston: Houghton, Mifflin, 1977.
Bartholomew, Charles L. *Cartoons of the Spanish-American War by Bart.* Minneapolis: Journal Printing, 1899.
————. *Bart's Cartoons for 1902 from the Minneapolis Journal.* Minneapolis: Journal Printing, 1903.
Batchelor, Clarence. *Truman Scrapbook: Washington Story in Cartoons and Text.* Deep River, Conn.: Kelsey Hill Publishing, 1951.
Beard, Frank. *Fifty Great Cartoons.* Chicago: Ram's Horn, 1899.
Beardsley, William A. *An Old New Haven Engraver and His Work: Amos Doolittle.* Photostat in the Library of Congress, 1910.
Becker, Stephen. *Comic Art in America.* New York: Simon and Schuster, 1959.
Bender, J. H., Jr. "Editorial Cartoonists: Development/Philosophy Today." M.A. thesis, University of Missouri, 1962.
Berkowitz, Herb B. "Political Cartooning's Southern Revival." *Art Voices/South,* 1 (July/August 1978), 65-70.
Berryman, Clifford K. *Berryman Cartoons.* Washington, D.C.: Saks, 1900.
————. *Berryman's Cartoons of the 58th House.* Washington, D.C.: C. K. Berryman, 1903.
————. *The Bunk Book.* Washington, D.C.: Gridiron Club, Menu Committee, 1925.
————. "Development of the Cartoon." Columbia, Mo.: University of Missouri Bulletin, 1926.
Bishop, Joseph Bucklin. "Early Political Caricature in America." *The Century,* 44 (June 1892), 219-31.
Blaisdell, Thomas C., Jr., and Peter Selz. *The American Presidency in Political Cartoons: 1776-1976.* Santa Barbara: Peregrine Smith, 1976.

Blake, W. B. "The American Cartoon." *The Independent*, 74 (January 23, 1913), 214-17.

Block, Herbert. *The Herblock Book*. Boston: Beacon Press, 1952.

————. *Herblock's Here and Now*. New York: Simon and Schuster, 1955.

————. *Herblock's Special for Today*. New York: Simon and Schuster, 1958.

————. *Straight Herblock*. New York: Simon and Schuster, 1964.

————. *The Herblock Gallery*. New York: Simon and Schuster, 1968.

————. *Herblock's State of the Union*. New York: Simon and Schuster, 1972.

————. *Herblock's Special Report*. New York: Norton, 1974.

Bowman, Bowland Claude. *The Tribune Cartoon Book for 1901*. Minneapolis: Tribune Printing, 1901.

————. *The Tribune Cartoon Book for 1902*. Minneapolis: Tribune Printing, 1902.

Bradley, Luther. *Cartoons by Bradley*. Chicago: Rand McNally, 1971.

Briggs, Clare A. *How to Draw Cartoons*. New York: Harper and Brothers, 1926. 2d ed., Garden City, N.Y.: Garden City Publishing, 1937.

Brigham, Clarence S. *Paul Revere's Engravings*. Worcester, Mass.: American Antiquarian Society, 1954.

Brooks, Charles, ed. *Best Editorial Cartoons of 1972*. Gretna, La.: Pelican Publishing, 1973—annually.

Burck, Jacob. *Hunger and Revolt*. New York: *The Daily Worker*, 1935.

————. *Our 34th President*. Chicago: Chicago *Sun-Times*, 1953.

Byrnes, Gene. *The Complete Guide to Cartooning*. New York: Grossett & Dunlap, 1950.

The Campaign of '48 in Star Cartoons. Washington: *Evening Star*, 1948. Also by the same publisher: *The Campaign of '52* and *The Campaign of '56*.

Campbell, Mary, and Gordon Campbell. *The Pen, Not the Sword: A Collection of Great Political Cartoons from 1879 to 1898*. Nashville: Aurora Publishers, 1970.

Caricature and Its Role in Graphic Satire: An Exhibit by the Department of Art. Providence: Brown University, 1971.

"Caricature, Cartoon, and Comic Strip." *Encyclopaedia Britannica*. 15th ed., vol. III, 909-22.

Carl, Leroy Maurice. "Meanings Evoked in Population Groups by Editorial Cartoons." Ph.D. dissertation, Syracuse University, 1967.

Carmon, Walt, ed. *The Case of Sacco and Venzetti in Cartoons from the Daily Worker*. New York: *The Daily Worker*, 1927.

————. *Red Cartoons from the Daily Worker*. 2 vols. Chicago: *The Daily Worker* and *Workers Monthly*, 1927 and 1928.

"The Cartoon as a Means of Artistic Expression." *Current Literature*, 53 (October 1912), 461-64.

Cartoons of the War of 1898 with Spain. Chicago: Belford, Middlebrook, 1898.

Catalog of the Library of the Museum of Modern Art. Boston: G. K. Hall, 1976. 14 vols.

Catalogue of the Harvard University Fine Arts Library, The Fogg Art Museum.

Boston: G. K. Hall, 1971. 15 vols. *First Supplement.* Boston: G. K. Hall, 1976, 3 vols.

Cesare, Oscar. *One Hundred Cartoons.* Boston: Small, Maynard, 1916.

Chase, John, ed. *Today's Cartoon.* New Orleans: Hauser Press, 1962.

Christ-Janer, Albert. *Boardman Robinson.* Chicago: University of Chicago Press, 1946.

Cobb, Ron. *My Fellow Americans.* Los Angeles: Price, Stern, Sloan, 1970.

———. *Raw Sewage.* Los Angeles: Price, Stern, Sloan, 1970.

Conningham, F. A. *Currier & Ives.* Cleveland & New York: World Publishing, 1950.

Conrad, Paul. *The King and Us: Editorial Cartoons by Conrad.* Los Angeles: Clymer Publications, 1974.

———, and Malcolm Boyd. *When in the Course of Human Events.* New York: Sheed and Ward, 1973.

Contemporary Cartoons, An Exhibition of Original Drawings. San Marino, Calif.: Huntington Library, 1937.

Cooper, Frederick Taylor, and Arthur Bartlett Maurice. *The History of the Nineteenth Century in Caricature.* New York: Dodd Mead, 1904. Reissued, Detroit: Tower Books, 1971.

Craven, Thomas, ed. *Cartoon Cavalcade.* New York: Simon and Schuster, 1943.

Crawford, Charles, ed. *Cal Alley.* Memphis: Memphis State Press, 1973.

Crouse, Russell. *Mr. Currier and Mr. Ives.* Garden City, N.Y.: Doubleday, Doran, 1930.

Dahl, Francis. *What! More Dahl?* Boston: Hale, 1944.

———. *Dahl's Boston.* Boston: Little, Brown, 1946.

Darcy, Tom. *The Good Life.* New York: Avon, 1970.

Darling, Jay. *Cartoons from the Files of The Register & Leader.* Des Moines: *Register & Leader,* 1908.

———. *The Education of Alonzo Applegate and Other Cartoons.* Des Moines: *Register & Leader,* 1910.

———. *As Ding Saw Hoover.* Edited by John M. Henry. Ames: Iowa State College Press, 1954.

———. *Midwest Farming as Portrayed by a Selection from Ding's Cartoons.* Des Moines: Pioneer Hi-Bred Corn, 1960.

———. *Ding's Half Century.* Edited by John M. Henry. New York: Duell, Sloan and Pearce, 1962.

Davenport, Homer. *Cartoons.* New York: DeWitt, 1898.

———. *The Dollar or the Man? The Issue of Today.* Boston: Small, Maynard, 1900.

Deur, Lynne. *Political Cartoonists.* Minneapolis: Lerner Publications, 1972.

Diggs, R. *Great Diggs of '77.* San Francisco: Rip Off Press, 1977.

Dobbins, Jim. *Dobbins' History of the New Frontier.* Boston: Humphries, 1964.

Dolmetsch, Joan D. *Rebellion and Reconciliation.* Charlottesville: University Press of Virginia, 1976.

Donahey, James H. *Cartoons by Donahey.* Cleveland: Vinson and Korner, 1900.

Doyle, Jerry. *According to Doyle, A Cartoon History of World War II*. New York: G. P. Putnam's, 1943.

Drepperd, Carl. *Early American Prints*. New York: Century, 1930.

Eastman, Joel. *The Maine Thing, Some of My Best Friends Are Republicans*. Freeport, Me.: Bond Wheelright, 1964.

Faerber, Charles N. "An Examination of the Career Patterns and Editorial Roles of a Number of Staff Editorial Cartoonists on Contemporary American English-Language Newspapers." M.A. thesis, San Diego State University, 1977.

Feiffer, Jules. *Hold Me*. New York: Random House, 1962.

———. *Feiffer's Album*. New York: Random House, 1963.

———. *The Great Comic Book Heroes*. Random House, 1965.

———. *Feiffer on Civil Rights*. New York: Anti-Defamation League of B'nai B'rith, 1966.

———. *Feiffer on Nixon: The Cartoon Presidency*. New York: Random House, 1974.

Fischetti, John. *Zinga Zinga Za!* Chicago: Follett, 1973.

Fitzgerald, Richard. *Art and Politics*. Westport, Conn.: Greenwood Press, 1973.

Fitzpatrick, Daniel R. *Cartoons by Fitzpatrick*. St. Louis: *St. Louis Post Dispatch*, 1947.

———. *As I Saw It*. New York: Simon and Schuster, 1953.

Fleming, E. McClury. "Symbols of the United States from Indian Queen to Uncle Sam," in Ray Brown et al., eds. *Frontiers of American Culture*. West Lafayette, Ind.: Purdue University Press, 1968.

Foreign Policy Association. *A Cartoon History of U.S. Foreign Policy Since World War I*. New York: Vintage, 1968.

———. *A Cartoon History of U.S. Foreign Policy 1776-1976*. New York: Morrow, 1975.

Fredericks, Pierce, ed. *The People's Choice: The Issues of the 1956 Campaign as Seen by the Nation's Best Political Cartoonists*. New York: Dodd Mead, 1956.

Gahn, Joseph Anthony. "The America of William Gropper, Radical Cartoonist." Ph.D. dissertation, Syracuse University, 1966.

Gallatin, Albert E. *John Sloan*. New York: E. P. Dutton, 1925.

Geipel, John. *The Cartoon, a Short History of Graphic Comedy and Satire*. London: David & Charles, 1972. New York: A. S. Barnes, 1972.

Getlein, Frank. *The Bite of the Print*. New York: C. N. Potter, 1963.

Goldberg, Rube. "Lesson #19." *Famous Artists Cartoon Course*. Westport, Conn., 1956.

Goodrich, Lloyd. *John Sloan*. New York: Macmillan, 1952.

———. *Five Paintings from Thomas Nast's Grand Caricaturama*. New York: The Swann Collection of Caricature and Cartoon, 1970.

Graham, Bill. "*A Little Drum Roll Please. . . .*" Little Rock: *Arkansas Gazette*, 1974.

Gros, Raymond, ed. *T. R. in Cartoon*. New York: Saalfield Publishing, 1910.

Hancock, La Touche. "American Caricature and Comic Art." *The Bookman,* 16 (October 1902), 120-21; (November 1902), 263-74.

Harding, Nelson. *The Political Campaign of 1912 in Cartoons.* Brooklyn, N.Y.: *Daily Eagle,* 1912.

Haynie, Hugh. *Hugh Haynie: Perspective.* Louisville, Ky.: *The Courier Journal* and the *Louisville Times,* 1974.

Hecht, George, ed. *The War in Cartoons.* New York: Dutton, 1919.

Hess, Stephen, and Milton Kaplan. *The Ungentlemanly Art.* New York: Macmillan, 1968. Rev. ed., 1975.

Hill, Draper. "What Fools These Mortals Be! A Study of the Work of Joseph Keppler, Founder of Puck." A.B. thesis, Harvard College, 1957.

――――. *The Lively Art of J. P. Alley.* Memphis, Tenn.: Brooks Memorial Art Gallery, 1973.

――――. "Editorial Cartoons," in *Encyclopedia of Collectibles.* New York: Time-Life, 1978.

――――, ed. *Mr. Gillray, the Caricaturist.* London: Phaidon, 1965.

――――, ed. *Fashionable Contrasts, 100 Caricatures by James Gillray.* London: Phaidon, 1966.

――――, ed. "Illingworth on Target." An exhibition of the cartoons and drawings of Leslie Illingworth. Littleton, N.H.: *The Littleton Courier,* 1970.

――――, ed. *The Satirical Etchings of James Gillray.* New York: Dover Publications, 1976.

Hillier, Bevis. *Cartoons and Caricatures.* New York: E. P. Dutton, 1970.

Hoff, Syd. *Editorial and Political Cartooning.* New York: Stravon Educational Press, 1976.

Hohenberg, John, ed. *The Pulitzer Prize Story.* New York: Columbia University Press, 1959.

The Image of America in Caricature and Cartoon. Fort Worth, Tex.: Amon Carter Museum of Western Art, Swann Collection and Lincoln National Corp. of Fort Wayne, 1976.

Index to Art Periodicals. (Ryerson Library of Chicago Art Institute) Boston: G. K. Hall, 1962. 11 vols. *First Supplement,* Boston: G. K. Hall, 1975.

Johnson, Gerald W. *The Lines Are Drawn.* New York: J. B. Lippincott, 1958.

Johnson, Herbert. *Cartoons.* Philadelphia: J. B. Lippincott, 1936.

Johnson, Kenneth M. *The Sting of the Wasp.* San Francisco: Book Club of California, 1967.

Johnson, Malcolm, ed. *David Claypool Johnston.* Exhibition catalog of exhibition held by The American Antiquarian Society, Boston College, The Boston Public Library, and the Worcester Art Museum, Boston, March 1970.

Keller, Morton. *The Art and Politics of Thomas Nast.* New York: Oxford University Press, 1968.

Kempkes, Wolfgang. *The International Bibliography of Comics Literature.* Detroit: Gale Research, 1971. 2d rev. ed. New York: R. R. Bowker/Verlag Dokumentation, 1974.

Kenner, Hugh. "The Exploding Duck & Other Primal Tales." *National Review,* 30 (October 13, 1978), 1287-91.

American Popular Culture

Ketchum, Alton. *Uncle Sam, the Man in the Legend.* New York: Hill and Wang, 1959.

Kinnaird, Clark, ed. *Rube Goldberg vs. the Machine Age.* New York: Hastings House, 1968.

Kirby, Rollin. *Highlights: A Cartoon History of the Nineteen Twenties.* New York: William Farquhar Payson, 1931.

Krumbhaar, E. B. *Isaac Cruikshank.* Philadelphia: University of Pennsylvania Press, 1966.

Langsam, Walter C., and L. D. Warren. *The World & Warren's Cartoons.* Hicksville, N.Y.: Exposition Press, 1976.

Larkin, Oliver W. *Daumier, Man of his Time.* New York: McGraw-Hill, 1966.

Levine, David. *The Man from M.A.L.I.C.E.* New York: Dutton, 1966.

———. *Pens and Needles.* Boston: Gambit, 1969.

———. *No Known Survivors: David Levine's Political Plank.* Boston: Gambit, 1970.

———. *Artists, Authors, and Others: Drawings by David Levine.* Washington, D.C.: Smithsonian Institution, 1976.

Lewis, Ross. *Cartoons of R. A. Lewis.* Milwaukee: *The Milwaukee Journal,* 1968.

Library Catalog. (The Metropolitan Museum of Art) Boston: G. K. Hall, 1960. 25 vols.

"The Limits of Caricature." *The Nation,* 7 (July 19, 1866), 55.

Long, Scott. *Hey! Hey! LBJ! or He Went Away and Left the Faucet Running.* Minneapolis: Ken Sorenson Printing, 1969.

Low, David. *Ye Madde Designer.* London: The Studio, 1935.

———. *A Cartoon History of Our Times.* New York: Simon and Schuster, 1939.

Lurie, Ranan R. *Nixon Rated Cartoons.* New York: Quadrangle, New York Times Books, 1973.

———. *Pardon Me, Mr. President.* New York: Quadrangle, New York Times Books, 1975.

Lynch, John Gilbert Bohun. *A History of Caricature.* London: Faber and Gwyer, 1926.

MacNelly, Jeff. *MacNelly, the Pulitzer Prize Winning Cartoonist.* Richmond, Va.: Westover Publishing, 1972.

———. *The Election That Was—MacNelly at His Best.* New York: Newspaperbooks, 1976.

McCutcheon, John T. *Cartoons by McCutcheon.* Chicago: McClurg, 1903.

———. *The Cartoons That Made Prince Henry Famous.* Chicago: *Chicago Herald Record,* 1903.

———. *T. R. in Cartoons.* Chicago: McClurg, 1903.

———. *The Mysterious Stranger and Other Cartoons.* New York: McClure, Phillips, 1905.

———. *Congressman Pumphrey, the People's Friend.* Indianapolis: Bobbs-Merrill, 1907.

———. *John McCutcheon Book.* Selections by Franklin J. Meine and John Maryweather. New York: Caxton Club, 1948.

———. *Drawn from Memory.* Indianapolis: Bobbs-Merrill, 1950.

McCutcheon, John, et al. *History of World War II in Cartoon*. Chicago: *Chicago Tribune*, 1943.

McDougall, Walt. *This Is the Life!* New York: Alfred A. Knopf, 1926.

Malcolm, James P. *An Historical Sketch of the Art of Caricaturing*. London: Longman, Hurst, Rees, Orme, and Brown, 1813.

Manning, Reg. *Little Itchy Itchy and Other Cartoons*. New York: J. J. Augustin, 1944.

Markow, Jack. "Artists and Cartoonists Q's. Roads to Cartooning, Part I." *Writer's Digest*, March 1973, 36-39.

―――. "Artists and Cartoonists Q's. Roads to Cartooning, Part II." *Writer's Digest*, April 1973, 36-38.

―――. "Cartooning. Woman, Where Art Thou?" *Writer's Digest*, February 1974, 48.

―――. "Cartooning." *Writer's Digest*, October 1974, 50.

―――. "Cartooning." *Writer's Digest*, December 1974, 47.

―――. "Cartooning. Cartoon Schools." *Writer's Digest*, July 1975, 50-52.

―――. "Cartooning. Oliphant for President." *Writer's Digest*, March 1976, 48.

Marlette, Doug. *The Emperor Has No Clothes*. Washington, D.C.: Graphic Press, 1976.

Marzio, Peter C. *Do It the Hard Way, Rube Goldberg and Modern Times*. Washington, D.C.: Smithsonian Institution, 1970.

―――. *Rube Goldberg: His Life and Work*. New York: Harper & Row, 1973.

Matthews, Albert. *Brother Jonathan*. Cambridge, Mass.: Wilson, 1902.

―――. *Uncle Sam*. Worcester, Mass.: Davis Press, 1908.

Matthews, J. Brander. "The Comic Periodical Literature of the United States." *The American Biblioplast*, 7 (August 1875), 199-201.

Mauldin, William. *Up Front*. New York: World Publishing, 1945.

―――. *Back Home*. New York: William Sloane Associates, 1947.

―――. *What's Got Your Back Up?* New York: Harper and Row, 1961.

―――. *I've Decided I Want My Seat Back*. New York: Harper & Bros., 1965.

―――. *The Brass Ring*. New York: W. W. Norton, 1971.

―――. *A Sort of a Saga*. New York: Sloan, 1949. Reprinted, New York: Norton, 1973.

―――. *Mud & Guts*. A Look at the Common Soldier of the American Revolution. Published on the Occasion of the 200th Anniversary of the Encampment at Valley Forge. Division of Publications, National Park Service, U.S. Department of the Interior, 1978.

Morgan, Matt et al. *The American War Cartoons*. London: Chatto and Windus, 1874.

Morris, William C. *Spokesman—Review Cartoons*. Spokane: Review Publishing, 1908.

Mott, Frank Luther. *American Journalism*. New York: Macmillan, 1941. Rev. ed., 1950.

Murrell, William. "The Rise and Fall of Cartoon Symbols." *The American Scholar*, 4 (Summer 1935), 206-13.

―――. *A History of American Graphic Humor*. 2 vols. New York: Whitney

Museum, 1933, 1938. Reissued, New York: Cooper Square Publishers, 1967.

Nelan, Charles. *Cartoons of Our War with Spain.* New York: Stokes, 1898.

Nelson, Roy Paul. *Fell's Guide to the Art of Cartooning.* New York: Frederick Fell, 1962.

————. *Cartooning.* Chicago: Henry Regnery, 1975.

————. *Comic Art and Caricature.* Chicago: Contemporary Books, 1978.

Nevins, Allan, and Frank Weitenkampf. *A Century of Political Cartoons.* New York: Charles Scribner's, 1944. Reprinted, New York: Farrar, Straus & Giroux, 1975.

Oliphant, Pat. *The Oliphant Book.* New York: Simon and Schuster, 1969.

————. *Four More Years.* New York: Simon and Schuster, 1969.

————. *An Informal Gathering.* New York: Simon and Schuster, 1978.

Opper, Frederick Burr. *Willie and His Papa.* New York: Grosset & Dunlap, 1901.

————. *John, Jonathan, & Mr. Opper.* London: Grant Richards, 1903.

Osborn, R. *War Is No Damn Good.* Garden City, N.Y.: Doubleday, 1946.

Paine, Albert Bigelow. *Th. Nast: His Period and His Pictures.* New York: Pearson Publishing, 1904. Reissued, Gloucester, Mass.: Peter Smith, 1967. Reprinted, New York: B. Blom, 1971.

Parton, James. *Caricature and Other Comic Art.* New York: Harper and Bros., 1878. Reprinted, New York: Harper & Row, 1969.

Penn, Arthur. "The Growth of Caricature." *The Critic,* February 25, 1882, pp. 49-50.

Peters, Harry T. *Currier & Ives, Printmakers to the American People.* 2 vols. Garden City, N.Y.: Doubleday, Doran, 1929 and 1931.

Peters, Mike. *The Nixon Chronicles.* Dayton, Ohio: Lorentz Press, 1976.

Peterson, William J., ed. "A Treasury of Ding." *The Palimpsest,* monthly journal of the State Historical Society of Iowa, March 1972, pp. 81-177.

Press, Charles. "The Georgian Political Cartoon and Democratic Government." *Comparative Studies in Society and History,* 19 (April 1977), 216-38.

————. *The Political Cartoon.* Madison, N.J.: Fairleigh Dickinson Press, 1979.

Price, Warren C., and Calder M. Pickett. *An Annotated Journalism Bibliography, 1958-1968.* Minneapolis: University of Minnesota Press, 1970.

Punch. *Cartoons from Punch.* 4 vols. London: Bradbury and Agnew, 1906.

Raemaekers, Louis. *Raemaekers' Cartoons.* Garden City, N.Y.: Doubleday, Page, 1917.

————. *America in the War.* New York: Century, 1918.

————. *Raemaekers' Cartoon History of the War.* New York: Century, 1918-1919.

Rajski, Raymond B., ed., *A Nation Grieved, the Kennedy Assassination in Editorial Cartoons.* Rutland, Vt.: Charles E. Tuttle, 1967.

Reid, Albert Turner. *Albert T. Reid's Sketchbook.* Compiled by John W. Ripley and Robert W. Richmond. Topeka, Kans.: Shawnee County Historical Society, 1971.

RILA: Répertoire international de la littérature de l'art. (International Repertory of the Literature of Art). New York: College Art Association of America, 1975.

Robinson, Boardman. *Cartoons on the War.* New York: Dutton, 1915.

——. *93 Drawings.* Colorado Springs, Colo.: Colorado Springs Fine Art Center, 1937.

Rogers, William A. *Hits at Politics.* New York: R. H. Russell, 1896.

——. *America's Black and White Book.* New York: Cupples and Leon, 1917.

——. *A World Worth While.* New York: Harper, 1922.

Rogers, W. G. *Mightier Than the Sword.* New York: Harcourt, Brace and World, 1969.

Salzman, Ed, and Ann Leigh Brown. *The Cartoon History of California Politics.* Sacramento, Calif.: Journal Press, 1978.

Sanders, Bill. *Run for the Oval Room. . .they can't corner us there!* Milwaukee: Alpha Press, 1974.

Shaw, Albert. *A Cartoon History of Roosevelt's Career.* New York: Review of Reviews, 1910.

——. *Abraham Lincoln.* 2 vols. New York: Review of Reviews, 1929.

Shikes, Ralph E. *The Indignant Eye.* Boston: Beacon Press, 1969.

Shoemaker, Vaughn. *1938 A.D., 1939 A.D., 1940 A.D., '41 and '42 A.D., '43 and '44 A.D.,* and *'45 and '46 A.D.* Chicago: *Chicago Daily News,* 1939, 1940, 1941, 1943, 1945 and 1947. (A series of volumes.)

——. *Shoemaker.* Chicago: *Chicago American,* 1966.

Smith, Dorman H. *One Hundred and One Cartoons.* Chicago: Ring, 1936.

Smith, Henry Ladd. "The Rise and Fall of the Political Cartoon." *Saturday Review,* 37 (May 29, 1954), 708 ff.

Spencer, Dick III. *Editorial Cartooning.* Ames: Iowa State College Press, 1949.

——. *Pulitzer Prize Cartoons.* Ames: Iowa State College Press, 1951.

St. Hill, Thomas Nast. *Thomas Nast's Christmas Drawings for the Human Race.* New York: Harper and Row, 1971.

Swearington, Rodger. *What's So Funny Comrade?* New York: Praeger, 1961.

Szep, Paul. *In Search of Sacred Cows.* Boston: Boston *Globe,* 1968.

——. *Keep Your Left Hand High.* Boston: Boston *Globe,* 1969.

——. *At This Point in Time.* Boston: Boston *Globe,* 1974.

——. *The Harder They Fall.* Boston: Boston *Globe,* 1975.

——. *Them Damned Pictures.* Boston: Boston *Globe,* 1978.

The Thirteenth International Salon of Cartoons. Montreal: International Pavilion of Humour, 1976.

Thorndike, Chuck. *The Business of Cartooning.* New York: House of Little Books, 1939.

Trudeau, Gary B. *Guilty, Guilty, Guilty!* New York: Holt, Rinehart and Winston, 1973.

Vincent, Howard P. *Daumier and His World.* Evanston: Northwestern University Press, 1968.

Vinson, J. Chal. *Thomas Nast: Political Cartoonist.* Athens: University of Georgia Press, 1967.

Walker, Mort, ed. *National Cartoonists' Society Album, 1972-77.* New York: National Cartoonists' Society, 1977.

Walsh, William S. *Abraham Lincoln and the London Punch.* New York: Moffat, Yard, 1909.

Washington *Evening Star. The Campaign of '48.* Washington, D.C.: Washington *Star,* 1949. Also *The Campaign of '52* (1953), and *Campaigns of '56* (1957).

Webster, H. T. *The Best of H. T. Webster.* New York: Simon & Schuster, 1953.

Weiss, Harry B. *William Charles, Early Caricaturist, Engraver and Publisher of Children's Books.* New York: Public Library, 1932.

Weitenkampf, Frank. *American Graphic Art.* New York: Holt, 1912. Revised New York: Macmillan, 1924. Reprinted, New York: Johnson Reprint, 1970.

———. "Keppler and Political Cartooning." *Bulletin of the New York Public Library,* 42 (December 1938), 906-08.

———. *Political Caricature in the United States, in Separately Published Cartoons . . . an Annotated List.* New York: New York Public Library, 1953. Reissued, New York: Arno Press, 1971.

Westwood, H. R. *Modern Caricaturists.* London: Lovat Dickinson, 1932.

What America Thinks, Editorials and Cartoons. Chicago: What America Thinks Inc., 1941.

White, Richard Grant. "Caricature and Caricaturists." *Harpers Monthly Magazine,* 24 (April 1862), 586-607.

Whitman, Bert. *Here's How, About the Newspaper Cartoon, a Collection of Editorial Cartoons from the Past Decade.* Lodi, Calif.: Lodi Publishing, 1968.

Who's Who in America. 39th ed. 2 vols. Chicago: Marquis Who's Who, Inc., 1976.

Who's Who in American Art. New York: R. R. Bowker, 1935-.

Williams, R. E. "Humorous Cartoon." *Encyclopedia Americana,* V, 1976, 734-39.

Wilson, Rufus Rockwell. *Lincoln in Caricature.* New York: Horizon Press, 1953.

Wright, Don. *Wright On! A Collection of Political Cartoons.* New York: Simon and Schuster, 1971.

Wright, Grant. *The Art of Caricature.* New York: Baker Taylor, 1904.

Wynn Jones, Michael. *The Cartoon History of Great Britain.* New York: Macmillan, 1971.

———. *The Cartoon History of the American Revolution.* New York: G. P. Putnam's, 1975.

Young, Art. *On My Way.* New York: Liveright, 1928.

———. *The Best of Art Young.* New York: Vanguard, 1936.

———. *Thomas Rowlandson.* New York: Willey Book, 1938.

———. *Art Young: His Life and Times.* New York: Sheridan House, 1939.

Zimmerman, Eugene. *This & That About Caricature.* New York: Syndicate Press, 1905.

———. *Cartoons and Caricatures.* Scranton, Pa.: Correspondence Institute of America, 1910.

PERIODICALS

American Association of Editorial Cartoonists Notebook. Washington, D.C., 1973-.

American Cartoonist (formerly an annual *The Cartoonist*). Bridgeport, Conn., 1977-.

Byline. Evanston, Ill., 1975-.

Cartoonews. Orlando, Fla., 1975-.

Cartoonist PROfiles. Fairfield, Conn., 1969-.

Crimmer's: The Harvard Journal of Pictorial Fiction. Cambridge, Mass., 1974-76.

Editor and Publisher. New York, 1901-.

Inklings. Rye Town, Port Chester, N.Y., 1976-.

CHAPTER 6. Foodways
Charles Camp

Few subjects occupy a larger place in the American consciousness than food. In both a literal and a figurative sense, food serves to define individual and group identities; culturally acquired and nurtured matters of taste demark ethnic, regional, racial, and spiritual differences between Americans that otherwise might lack concrete expression. Indeed, within the maze of identities that characterizes contemporary American society, food offers one of the oldest and most evocative systems of cultural identification. While many characteristics of American ethnic groups, for example, have been obscured in our postindustrial society, we sense and know the difference between Italian and Greek pastries and between a Polish sausage and the common hotdog. We may lack very scientific procedures for describing the differences between these foods, but we regularly employ such distinctions as a way of defining (and celebrating) ethnic cultural diversity.

The past five years have seen an explosion of interest in food that apparently draws its energy from a variety of sources. The back-to-nature and whole-earth movements of the 1960s have contributed an increased public sensitivity to matters of diet and to the economic system that supplies most Americans with their daily bread. Interest in old-time ways of life, which led to something of a boom for American folklife studies, also sparked a more general curiosity about home cooking and other aspects of American domestic life. In the early 1970s, American industry began to catch up with European competitors in the manufacture of home cooking equipment that would permit the average American cook to produce virtually any dish desired. With the elevation of the Cuisinart food processor to the status of a mid-1970s icon, food became a general grid for plotting status and social position. *Time* and *Newsweek* covers heralded the "Cooking Boom," and, overnight, dozens of magazines, cookbooks, courses, and television programs sprang up to meet an ever-growing appetite for information.

The groundwork for the present food boom lies of course in the long-standing love affair that well-to-do Americans have had with French and other continental cuisine. As part of the social heritage that defined the elite, gourmet cooking (as it has been traditionally termed) places food within a European symbolic system that most Americans have found difficult to understand much less imitate. The food boom brought together grass-roots interest in American foodstuffs and domestic traditions and a system of defining social achievement and status that was previously restricted to the wealthier classes. The result is a curious mixture of Americana and gourmet styles, but also a refreshingly open consideration of the variety of American cookery.

As might be expected for an area of expression that has only recently found public acceptance, scholars have been reluctant to devote much energy to the study of food in American culture. Folklorists, anthropologists, and nutritionists have not often explored the behavioral aspects of food preparation and use, but some investigations of American foodways have yielded interesting information. To some extent, the multidisciplinary study of American foodways has been hindered by a lack of agreement on the basic unit of study. Nutritionists have been chiefly interested in foods and their nutritional properties. Anthropologists have focused on the role of food in the everyday life of primitive peoples and have occasionally studied the employment of food as a symbol in industrial cultures. Folklorists have studied the beliefs and customary practices related to food, but have recently begun to consider in a more consciously ethnographic fashion the relationship of food to other aspects of life in traditional communities.

In popular as well as anthropological works, the terminology of food research has never been adequate to the task of describing or analyzing food-related behavior. In common American speech, we use the same word—food—to describe the raw materials from which meals are prepared and the meals themselves. Nutritionists refer to patterns of food consumption and behavior as "food habits." Anthropologists commonly refer to the food culture of a self-defined group as the group's "ethnocuisine." And folklorists use the term "foodways" to describe the relationship between food and culture in the same way that "folkways" was formerly used to examine the traditions in traditional ways of life. The common denominator among these terms, and the unifying theme of this essay, is *culture*. Food *in* culture, food as a *symbol* of cultural identity, the preparation and consumption of food as a culture *unto itself*—these are some of the ways in which the relationship of food and culture can be explored.

There is much written about food that does not contribute to this field of study. Most cookbooks, which are simply collections of the author-editor's favorite recipes, have little to say about what people eat and why they do so. Books and articles about specific foods, their history, and their biological properties are most often stripped of the cultural "clothing" of the cooking and eating processes that reveal the cultural character of food-related behavior. Scientific monographs on the diet of primitive peoples offer lists of foods consumed by such peoples, but without the information about daily life that would permit reweaving the fabric of social life created by the interaction of food and culture.

What is useful to the study of food and American culture is the type of information that relates foods and/or techniques for their preparation and consumption to a specific locale, or group, or time of year. Occasionally, such information is found in unlikely places including restaurant guides, newspaper advertisements, and food industry trade association publications. But if the study of food in American culture is to focus on the connections between food and culture, we must be willing to search for new sources rather than simply rely on existing information.

HISTORIC OUTLINE

The history of American food mirrors the history of American society, with its periodic fluctuations between a longing admiration of European ways of life and an intense pride in things distinctively American. With the exception of native American contributions to American foodways, the development of a distinctively American food pattern has consisted of adapting a much larger range of native foodstuffs to immigrant cookery styles (and vice versa). Unlike European cookery, during the eighteenth and nineteenth century American food was noted for the quality of foodstuff (meat, fruits, and vegetables chiefly) and not for the quality of preparation. The domination of the food industry in nineteenth-century America by descendants of prominent English families did not advance the concept of a truly American way of eating, although, by mid-century, American oysters, shrimp, beef, and whiskey had begun to distinguish themselves.

Although European travelers in America often describe the crudity of American inns and other eateries, the simplicity of American foods and the bountiful supply of beef, seafood, and wild fowl impressed many visitors. What average Americans ate during that time is more difficult to determine; but it is clear that in the style of the log cabin, in which native materials are combined as simply as possible, the everyday diet of early Americans was based chiefly on local crops and meat and game supplies. This dependence on local foodstuffs defined the regional character of American cookery—a feature that is perhaps the most obvious distinction of American foodways.

The development of industrialized food technology and the use of railroads for shipping livestock and foodstuffs allowed for a wider choice of materials for the late nineteenth-century American cook. However, at the end of the century, most Americans had established a balance between the ethnic traditions in which their culture (and approach to food) was based and the regional food supplies. The result—a Texas German food style distinctively different from a mid-Atlantic German style, for example, —has not changed markedly in this century, despite the growing diversity of foodstuffs available to the average cook.

The goal of American agriculture and food technologists to supply the average cook with food supplies that defy season and locale was reached with the development of mechanized food preservation and transportation industries. With summer produce available year round, both frozen and fresh, the last physical limitation on American cookery was removed and the last regional boundaries were struck down. Restaurant systems that made use of standardized food technology quickly developed, and it was soon possible to follow a chain of franchised fast-food restaurants across the country in a string of virtually identical meals.

While critics at the time lamented the passing of cookery traditions that were grounded in time and space, it has become plain that Americans have developed a pluralistic approach to food much like the double vision with which they perceive popular entertainment, music, and other aspects of daily life. Frozen vegetables and syndicated fast-food have found their place in American life, but Americans still eat ten times as many tomatoes in the summer as in the winter, and the consumption of sausage, soups, and barbecue still varies widely from region to region.

REFERENCE WORKS AND HISTORY

The principal academic disciplines that have examined American foodways are anthropology, nutrition and health, sociology, geography, and folklore. By combining similar approaches and including some general publications, these fields can be reduced to three: nutrition and health, history and geography, and social sciences. Since most of the folkloristic study of foodways is of a social-scientific nature, I have included works in this area under social sciences. The books and articles discussed here and listed in the bibliography cross many academic battle lines, including the division between scholarly and popular works. The purpose of this outline is not only to discuss significant writings in each of the disciplines that has studied American foodways, but also to provide, through this discussion, a clearer notion of the different ways in which each academic field approaches the subject.

NUTRITION AND HEALTH

Although the fields of nutrition and health have contributed more information on American foodways than all other disciplines combined, relatively little of this information is accessible or useful to the student of American culture. As a whole, nutritionists deal with the description of culture only when it is necessary to deal with specific nutritional questions. Consequently, much of the literature cited here, while precise in the description of food habits, is thin on the correlation of food and culture. Among basic reference works in the field, the *Cumulated Index Medicus*, compiled by the U.S. Department of Health, Education, and Welfare, is the standard research index. Diet and nutrition studies from all major American and international journals are indexed quarterly. *Nutrition Abstracts and Reviews* is a monthly index and review of international nutrition research and includes topics related to food and culture. Joseph Dommers Vehling's *America's Table* is a dictionary of food terminology, useful primarily because it is the only work of its kind. The U.S. Department of Agriculture *Experimental Station Record* can be very difficult to use, but it offers the only widely available tool for sorting the annual flood of state circulars, bulletins, and special publications, many of which describe in fine detail the foodways of particular areas of the United States.

Of the score of food-related bibliographies published in the last ten years, two stand out. The best general review of scholarship in foodways within the fields of health and nutrition is Christine S. Wilson's *Food Habits: A Selected Annotated Bibliography*—a surprisingly thorough treatment of contemporary research. Marguerite Patten's *Books for Cooks* is primarily a listing of cookbooks and other general works on food, with no particular concern for culture. If nothing else, the Patten bibliography reveals the sharp increase in publications on American food during the past few years.

Waldo Lincoln's list of American cookery books published between 1742 and 1860 is a basic reference work much closer in approach and purpose to books listed in the history and geography section of this outline, but it is listed here with other bibliographies and guides to the literature for the sake of convenience. Lincoln's work was made current to 1960 by Bob Brown and Eleanor Parker, *Culinary Americana 1860-1960*, but unfortunately the coverage these authors bring to the post-Civil War era is much less complete than Lincoln's prewar coverage.

Much of the nutritionists' contribution to American foodways research lies in the development of quantitative data gathering methods. The publications of the National Research Council's Committee on Food Habits in this area represent the highest refinement of survey techniques, along with their inherent shortcomings. The quality of these surveys unfortunately derives in part from the narrowing of the research on food habits to the development of per capita consumption and diet profile statistics, neither of which is especially useful in the analysis of cultural aspects of food.

Among the approaches used by nutritionists, one of the most compatible with studies of American culture is the definition of culture patterns and the correlation of food habits with systems of social organization. Nutritionists view food patterns as the quantification of individual food behaviors and the expression of shared attitudes toward or consumption of particular foods. Patterns differ from food habits in the respect that the former are often based on extensive or repeated surveys, while the latter may be the expression of individualized or occasional eating habits. Clark F. Le Gros's hypothesis that food habits form the basis for more complex economic and social structures is not generally shared by fellow nutritionists. Edith M. Barber, E. N. Todhunter, and M. R. Trulson view contemporary food patterns as the result of historical processes—chiefly economic —which initially shape and gradually narrow the range of possible food habits. Faith Clark and Arthur H. Niehoff reject the inevitability of this historical model in favor of a more open-ended view of food patterns as the generalization of smaller-scale food-related behaviors which are themselves in constant flux.

In the nutritional literature, social and economic considerations are often combined, especially where the focus of analysis is the relationship between food and culture. Magnus Pyke and M. E. Lowenberg survey food-related behaviors that are affected or shaped by social patterns, while M. B. Loeb offers an often-assumed, but seldom-stated, alternative to more conventional social analyses. By pointing out that food habits tend to reinforce and extend the social systems of which they are a part, Loeb reverses the emphases of other studies, which ascribe a greater degree of social continuity to status systems and other cultural organizations than the food habit complex.

Among those few writers who span the fields of nutrition and culture, Magnus Pyke's books and articles come closest to drawing a substantial correlation between diet and behavior on a theoretical level. Pyke contends that American foods have found acceptance in Europe not because of their economic or nutritional advantages but because of cultural associations attached to them. In a 1975 essay, Pyke demonstrates how deeply issues of cultural meaning penetrate the study of food habits and the widespread association of foodways and other culturally based systems of meaning.

Nutritionists have written in considerable detail about the dietary habits and resultant problems of regional, ethnic, age, and sex groups. In retrospect, many of the older studies of this kind are most revealing as social documents rather than as foodways studies. Such is the case for a 1917 publication on Massachusetts's working women, which reveals growing public and government concern for this work force expressed through dietary reforms. Studies of minority religious groups, including Seventh-

Day Adventists (Doris E. Phillips, 1976), Muslims (A. H. Sakr, 1971), and Jews (B. Cassell, 1957), necessarily take cultural characteristics of group members into account when constructing dietary profiles since belief systems enter actively into matters of dietary choice and regulation.

Perhaps the most notable contribution of nutritionists to the study of American foodways and culture is ironically least known to contemporary scholars. In the 1930s and 1940s, the U.S. Department of Agriculture coordinated a special nutritional research effort in the southeastern states in response to reports of deteriorating public health. The health conditions were attributed to the combination of a depressed economy and a series of blights and droughts that reduced existing food supplies. The studies of diet-related diseases and general dietary practices in the Southeast comprise a unique social record, as well as the flowering of a method of regional nutritional analysis. Dorothy Dickins's work in Mississippi and Ada Moser's South Carolina research place nutritional concerns within cultural contexts that give them a social as well as a nutritional accuracy and importance. Although Dickins's work is limited to Mississippi, her techniques, which include yearly household inventories, in-depth personal interviews, photographs of houses and cooking areas, and detailed descriptions of everyday meals, established a high standard for regional studies in other areas.

Unfortunately, the bulletins and circulars in which Dickins's work and that of many other nutritionists who were part of the larger research project were published are often difficult to obtain. Like the general contribution of nutritionists to American foodways research, there is much concerning Dickins's work that may continue to remain beyond the reach of foodways scholars.

HISTORY AND GEOGRAPHY

The works discussed in this category are a mixed group of popular and scholarly writings about cookery, food in history, foodways and cultural geography, and other historical topics related to American food. Among these works, several are concerned with the description of cookery traditions defined by historical period, region, or ethnic group. Of these, only two—*James Beard's American Cookery* and *The American Heritage Cookbook*—are actual cookbooks. Special note is made of these books because they offer more to the reader than recipes and they share a concern for historical relationships between certain foods and aspects of American culture.

Prominent among other general works on American cookery are the books in the Time-Life American Cooking series. The two survey books in this series, written by James Patrick Shenton and Dale Brown, are especially useful, although the excellent photographs often take precedence over more detailed written descriptions of food patterns. The regional studies that comprise the remainder of the series (Dale Brown, Peter S. Feibleman, Jonathan Norton Leonard, Eugene Walter, and Jose Wilson) offer a good introduction to the cookery of an American region, including information on customs related to the preparation or eating of foods distinctive to a particular area. The books are lavishly illustrated, and, while the series does vary in quality by author (Brown and Wilson topping the list), it is a good source for general information. The format of the Time-Life publications (an oversize book of texts and photographs accompanied by a smaller, spiral-bound collection of recipes) is well suited to the material and recommends the series to library as well as to home use.

With the exception of the modified cookbooks discussed above, there are relatively few general works on American cookery that explore cultural matters. Waverly Root and Richard de Rochemont's *Eating in America* is the most recent and, with certain qualifications, the most thorough general history of American eating habits. The work that has long held this title, Richard Osborn Cummings's *The American and His Food* is more comprehensive in terms of social classes represented, but lacks the historical detail found in *Eating in America*. The shortcomings of Root and de Rochemont's work stem from the authors' fairly narrow definition of foodways and the restriction of their study to materials that describe the foodways of the elite class almost exclusively. Ironically, Waverly Root has written a book that avoids this very problem in *The Food of France*, a work whose subject has little to do with American cookery, but whose approach provides an interesting model for regional studies of American food.

More scholarly general treatments of food and culture include Rupert B. Vance's writings on the relationship of geography and health—diet providing the key to this relationship—and Max Sorre's excellent essay on food and cultural geography. G. L. Jordan, *Changing Food Habits in Relation to Land Utilization in the United States*, and Charlotte Elizabeth Biester, *Some Factors in the Development of American Cookbooks*, offer more focused studies, and they are the ones that are perhaps more difficult to acquire, but they point out important general considerations in the study of American foodways. Biester examines some of the historical issues that pertain to American cookbooks. In so doing, she raises significant questions regarding the value of such books as historical sources.

Calvin Trillin's books on American food, *American Fried* (1974) and *Alice, Let's Eat* (1978), are worthy of special note in this context simply because among those writers whose work reaches a general readership Trillin has the most to say about the relationship between American food and culture. Of his two books on food, *American Fried* is the better since more of its pages are devoted to the description of regional food specialties and to his search for what is genuinely American in American food. *Alice, Let's Eat* deals with much of the same material as the earlier work, but in less detail and with less emphasis on the foods themselves. Despite these qualifications, Trillin's books offer the freshest and most accessible approach to American food to emerge from the past decade, and *American Fried* may find a continuing usefulness as a text for American studies or foodways courses.

More specialized books that deal with American "popular" foods are just reaching the commercial market. Michael Lasky's *The Complete Junk Food Book* is similar to other works of its idiom (*The Complete Book of Running, The Robot Book, The Cat Book*, and so on) in the sense that much information has been gathered together on a particular subject, but the author has not taken great pains to make sense of it. Some interesting comments are made on the organization of the American fast-food industry, and there is something stimulating about seeing foods like Fritos, Sugar Babies, and Hi-C described in specific terms. But Lasky fails to explore in detail the matter that might have yielded a more interesting analysis—the cultural attachment Americans share for foods of this type. Paul Dickson's *Chow* is similarly a compendium of information on a type of food—in this case military—but the narrowness of the chosen subject provides for a better overall treatment. Dickson has also compiled an interesting collection of photographs and illustrations that depict scenes of food preparation and eating in military settings. Since the latter half of *Chow* consists of military versions of standard American recipes, the photographs do much to relieve the dreariness of the subject matter.

SOCIAL SCIENCES

As was the case with the previous group of works, the books and articles discussed in this category comprise a mixed body of writings that examines American foodways from a social-scientific perspective and offers analysis or theory pertaining to the social description of American food-related behavior. The works included here are a more select group than the nutritional studies, being limited to works chiefly concerned with the social-scientific study of food and culture rather than ethnographies that include information about foodways.

Prominent among the research conducted by social scientists in the area of American foodways is the work of the National Research Council's Committee on Food Habits. Although the committee actively functioned for only five years (1941-1945), the research and publications it sponsored are principally responsible for labelling the early 1940s as the "golden age" of American foodways research. Under the leadership of anthropologist Margaret Mead, the committee conducted wide-ranging research into the food habits of American ethnic minorities, refined field methods for the documentation of foodways, and served as a forum for the exchange of theories regarding the role of food-related behaviors within the American social system. The major publications of the Committee on Food Habits, *The Problem of Changing Food Habits* (1943) and the *Manual for the Study of Food Habits* (1945), brought to the attention of scholars and policymakers in various federal agencies the wealth of research that social scientists had to offer in the area of foodways and attempted to redefine the goals of food habit research in order to include behavioral as well as dietary considerations.

Much of the committee's work remained unfinished when the unit was dissolved in 1945, but Mead prepared a summary report and an updated bibliography on food habits, published by the National Research Council in 1964, entitled *Food Habits Research: Problems of the 1960s*. Outside her work with the committee, Mead wrote prolifically about the relationship between food and culture throughout the 1940s and 1950s. Although many of the articles listed in the bibliography are simply restatements of the Committee on Food Habits' goals, Mead also wrote on regional patterns in American diet and the concept of culture change as it pertains to food-related behaviors.

Other committee alumni who wrote on noncommittee topics include John Bennett, Margaret Cussler, and Mary Louise de Give. Bennett's 1964 article "An Interpretation of the Scope and Implications of Social Scientific Research in Human Subsistence" is perhaps the single most important article in the field, offering not only a careful analysis of then-current research, but also an insightful critique of social-scientific research strategies most often employed in foodways studies. Bennett's other writings, most of which detail his work in southern Illinois, provide a model for the analysis of field data, which goes beyond the statistical profiles of previous research. De Give and Cussler's *Twixt the Cup and the Lip* is an unusual mixture of anthropology and dietetics and is a landmark in the field of American foodways research. Although the authors' fieldwork was limited to the southeastern United States, the information they provide on the foodways of that region is extensive and thoughtfully analyzed.

Several anthropologists have been concerned with questions of cultural interpretation and symbolism inherent in food systems and behavior. Among general studies, Claude Levi-Strauss's "The Culinary Triangle" is perhaps most accessible and most widely applicable, but as Edmund Leach points out in *Culture and Communication*, it is not without its theoretical problems. Leach's concern with symbolic languages and the conscious manipulation of food behaviors for social ends is echoed in the writings of Octavio Paz and Roland Barthes. The latter's semiotic analysis of contemporary popular culture provides an approach to the study of food that is both object- and behavior-oriented.

Anthropologists Marvin Harris and Mary Douglas have explored the cultural basis of dietary avoidances and preferences from two different critical perspectives. Harris approaches ritual "treatments" of pork and potlatch ceremonies as cultural paradoxes, while Douglas uses Jewish dietary practices as a key to understanding not only nonfood-related group behaviors but also the cultural and historical premises upon which such behaviors are based.

I have chosen to discuss folklife studies of American foodways within the context of social-scientific inquiries as a body of research distinct from that of anthropology or sociology, not because folklorists have not been influenced in their work by social scientists, but because as a whole folklife foodways research has traditionally reflected the range of professional interests and methods that have typified food habits research in general. Among general works on traditional cookery, Jay Anderson's survey of American research, "Scholarship on Contemporary American Folk Foodways," and Don Yoder's chapter on folk cookery in Richard Dorson's *Folklore and Folklife* are most useful. Yoder has also outlined a method for the use of historical documents in his 1971 study of American foodways and has demonstrated the usefulness of this approach in the description of the history and social meanings of foods important to the folk culture of the Pennsylvania Germans.

Other studies of specific foods that emphasize the description of the cooking process and its cultural context include Thomas G. Burton and Ambrose N. Manning's study of folk preservation and canning techniques in rural Tennessee and R. Dodson's early account of tortilla making. John Gregory Bourke's more extensive description of folk foods of the Rio Grande Valley appeared in the *Journal of American Folklore* in 1895 and represents an original, if not entirely successful, attempt to define the importance of cultural continuities in the perpetuation of a cookery tradition. N. D. Humphrey and B. Chang offer accounts of food habits that reflect the values of the ethnic cultures in which they are followed. The difference between the nutritionist and the student of culture is made clear in a comparison of these accounts. Chang defines Chinese dietary beliefs in terms of their nutritional rather than ideational referrent, while, for Humphrey, the dietary practices of a group of northern Mexican-Americans are of folkloric interest by nature of their deviation from accepted public food habits and medical beliefs.

Among more theoretical writings on folklore and food, Marjorie Sackett outlines a method for using "folk recipes" as cultural characteristics by which the migration of new ideas and culture groups into a community can be measured. Unfortunately, the difference between folk and other recipes is not adequately spelled out, and the usefulness of this method is weakened. British folklorist Venetia Newall draws a less literal means of describing culture change and tradition that makes use of foods and cookery techniques as well as specific recipes. Although Newall's examples are drawn from Jamaican cultures in the Caribbean and in England, the broader basis of comparison and the attention to the social context of the cookery tradition make the conclusions regarding food and culture more widely applicable.

RESEARCH SOURCES

The previous section provided an overview of the scholarly and popular literature on American foodways within the framework of the major academic fields that have explored the relationship of food and culture. In this section, I shall offer some additional sources of information on foodways, ranging from popular publications, organizations, museums, films, and courses, to field trips and self-education projects suitable for scholastic or personal use. The materials I have included here represent my own view of what I find helpful in dealing with food and culture and the places where interests in specific aspects of this subject might be best explored.

GENERAL CIRCULATION PUBLICATIONS

Magazines and newspapers have long carried regular features and columns on food, although these articles have not generally dealt with cultural concerns until recently. Among the bright spots in magazine coverage of American foodways are Raymond Sokolov's monthly articles on specific foods in *National History* that began in 1974, and Calvin Trillin's "U.S. Journal" series in the *New Yorker*. Trillin's pieces tend to be longer than Sokolov's and explore a specific food event or locale in greater detail, but they are published on an occasional basis. Sokolov also publishes occasional articles in the *International Review of Food and Wine* and other food-oriented magazines.

The number of magazines that deal exclusively with food and wine is ever increasing, although few articles deal with *American* food, let alone cultural aspects of American food. The four major national food magazines, *Bon Appétit, Cuisine, International Review of Food and Wine*, and *Gourmet*, appeal to an audience that is apparently concerned with international, and especially continental, cookery. As a result, they have little to offer the student of American foodways. Often, local food magazines or restaurant guides supply the best information on local foods, although such magazines often cater to similarly gourmet tastes and sensibilities.

In the area of restaurants, there has been a mushrooming of book-length city restaurant guides in recent years. Although they do not always tell the whole story of an area's food culture (many people still eat at home these days), they do provide an interesting characterization of the ethnic groups, regional styles, and cultural self-image of specific cities. Many of the current guides are part of a new wave of restaurant criticism that has followed upon the success of the *Underground Gourmet* series begun by Simon and Schuster publishers in 1966. The *Underground Gourmet* books attempted to enlarge the pool of restaurants commonly reviewed and the criteria normally used to review them by applying a more democratic view of cookery and a more open view of what constitutes a good meal. Considering the series as a whole, some books are better than others; Richard Collin's *New Orleans Underground Gourmet* and Milton Glaser and Jerome Snyder's original New York guide head the list. While the chatty style of these guides is shared by the San Francisco and Washington, D.C., authors, these last two books lack the insight into food and culture that make Collin's book something more than a list of restaurants. If the *Underground Gourmet* series remains in print or in library collections long after the restaurant information is out of date, years from now we will have a unique record of the ethnic and regional character of some of the major American cities during the 1970s.

Richard Collin has written widely on food in addition to his work on the *New Orleans Underground Gourmet*. His recent *New Orleans Restaurant Guide* is not as interesting as the *Gourmet* and is poorly organized, but it charts the author's growing preoccupation with the cultural aspects of the eating experiences he records. Collin's two cookbooks are very much grounded in the New Orleans tradition and they are as educational as they are useful, but both are unfortunately often difficult to locate outside the New Orleans vicinity.

In New York City, the selection of places to eat and the guarding of "inside" information on excellent but unknown eateries are matters of urban folklore. But for outsiders, the wealth of literature on this single cookery scene can be stimulating. Gael Greene's book on New York restaurants, *Bite*, is not a guide per se, but rather an exploration of the economic and cultural intricacies of living in New York expressed in terms of food. Craig Claiborne's *Guide to Dining Out in New York* is a more conventional review of restaurants, but it is an interesting counterpart to Glaser and Snyder and Greene both in terms of what is reviewed and what is not. As was mentioned above, restaurant guides do not offer the kind of ethnographic information we might wish to have on American foodways, but as ephemeral publications that are part *of* as well as a commentary *on* popular cultural behavior, they have much to offer the student of American foodways.

ORGANIZATIONS AND TRADE PUBLICATIONS

Few fields of American industry are as well organized and publicized as food growers, processors, and merchandisers. Organizations range from the twenty-member Bee Industries Association and five-member Associated Pimiento Canners to the thirty-four-hundred-member Independent Grocers Alliance and the thirteen-thousand-member National Restaurant Association. Most trade organizations, even those with fairly small memberships, are in business to promote the distribution and use of their product or service. Consequently, they frequently distribute information on the history and uses of food crops and products or the function of a particular food-related service within the American diet and economy. A brief list of organizations and trade publications follows the bibliography, but readers are encouraged to follow individual interests by contacting organizations whose work or products are relevant to more general concerns.

LIBRARIES, MUSEUMS, AND SPECIAL COLLECTIONS

Many major national associations in the fields of nutrition and home economics maintain libraries for the use of their membership and, with special permission, the use of interested scholars and students. The American Home Economists Association, the National Association of Food Chains, and the National Canners Association all maintain libraries in the Washington, D.C., area. These libraries, along with the National Agriculture Library in Beltsville, Maryland, and the Library of Congress, are good sources for general works on American foodways and for special collections deposited by organization members or private scholars. In addition, many public and academic libraries have special collections in local culture that often include church-published local cookbooks and other ephemera unobtainable through other sources.

Most local museums acquire cooking equipment of historic importance or local significance, but some folk museums or museums of everyday life have explored the relationship of food and culture in greater detail. The Smithsonian Institution's Museum of History and Technology maintains a special collection of early American cooking equipment. Plymouth Plantation, Old Sturbridge Village, and Colonial Williamsburg, to name only a few, have conducted extensive research on the history of local foodways in addition to the preservation of artifacts. Williamsburg has also published monographs on the subject, including Jane Carson's excellent *Colonial Virginia Cookery*. In studying the development of a cooking technique or style, an examination of the equipment used in the preparation of food during an earlier period can be of considerable benefit.

FILMS

Many trade associations have produced promotional films on American foods and their history that may be of use to contemporary scholars and interested students. Such films often lack the sort of cultural information we might wish to have and some take liberties with the facts in order to make promotional points, but they can be integrated within courses and other educational programs for effective use. Only a few films have been made by folklorists or anthropologists that explore the relationship between food and culture. Prominent among these are Les Blank's films about Louisiana Cajun life, Texas-Mexican border culture, and New Orleans' Mardi Gras festivities. Although Blank's primary subject in each of these films is not food, but music, dance, or custom, the filmmaker has an ability to show the relationship between foodways and other expressive forms within a folk group. The films that deal with these three groups are *Spend It All, Chulas Fronteras*, and *Always for Pleasure*, respectively. Further information on them can be obtained from Flower Films, Box 9195, El Cerrito, California 94709. Another film recommended for classroom use in connection with foodways, folklore, and history is *Maple Sugar Farmer*, a portrait of a sugar-maker and the sugar-making process, distributed by The University of Michigan Audio-Visual Education Center, 416 4th Street, Ann Arbor, Michigan 48109.

COURSES, FIELD RESEARCH, AND SELF-EDUCATION

Teachers have long used field trips to factories of various kinds as educational experiences for their students, and many food-related industries are accustomed to dealing with requests by individuals or groups to view the inside of their operations. Even when the subject of study is an older nonindustrial food complex, there is often much to be learned by visiting dairies, mills, distilleries, and other food processing facilities. Tours and special information on specific topics must usually be arranged with the plant superintendent of the facility you wish to visit. Field research in American foodways is an activity that can be entered into by individuals or student groups with a minimum of experience in field techniques since every member of our society has a basic grasp of the subject matter. Unlike some culture areas that appear exotic or esoteric to the uninitiated, the study of foodways offers a shared and comparative experience upon which discussions of cultural variation and change may be based. Information about food is easily obtainable both from peers and from members of other social groups without encountering the resistance that frequently discourages the novice fieldworker. Students may, of course, use themselves as the first informants in a research project.

A newsletter on interdisciplinary research in foodways that keeps abreast of scholarly activity (publications, reviews, ongoing research, and courses being offered) and that publishes notices of research opportunities is issued triannually by the Foodways Section of the American Folklore Society. The newsletter, entitled *The Digest*, may be obtained by subscription from the Department of Folklore and Folklife, Logan Hall 415 CN, University of Pennsylvania, Philadelphia 19104.

BIBLIOGRAPHY

BOOKS AND ARTICLES

The American Heritage Cookbook and Illustrated History of American Eating and Drinking. New York: American Heritage Publishing, 1964.

Anderson, Jay Allan. "Scholarship on Contemporary American Folk Foodways." *Ethnologia Europaea,* 5 (1971), 56-63.

Barber, Edith M. "The Development of the American Food Pattern." *Journal of the American Dietetic Association,* 24 (July 1948), 586-91.

Barthes, Roland. "Ornamental Cookery." In his *Mythologies.* Paris: Editions du Seuil, 1957, pp. 78-80.

———. "Toward a Psychosociology of Contemporary Food Consumption." In Elborg Forster, and Robert Forster, eds., *European Diet from Pre-Industrial to Modern Times.* New York: Harper & Row, 1975, pp. 47-59.

Beard, James A. *James Beard's American Cookery.* Boston: Little, Brown, 1972.

Bennett, John. "Food and Culture in Southern Illinois." *American Sociological Review,* 7 (October 1942), 645-60.

———. "An Interpretation of the Scope and Implications of Social Scientific Research in Human Subsistence." *American Anthropologist,* 48 (October 1946), 553-73.

Biester, Charlotte Elizabeth. *Some Factors in the Development of American Cookbooks.* Field Study Number 2. Ann Arbor, Mich.: University Microfilms, 1950.

Bourke, John Gregory. "The Folk Foods of the Rio Grande Valley and of Northern Mexico." *Journal of American Folklore,* 8 (January-March 1895), 41-71.

Brown, Bob, and Eleanor Parker. *Culinary Americana: 1860-1960.* New York: Roving Eye Press, 1961.

Brown, Dale. *American Cooking.* New York: Time, Inc., 1968.

———. *American Cooking: The Northwest.* New York: Time, Inc., 1970.

Burton, Thomas G., and Ambrose N. Manning. "Folk Methods of Preserving and Processing Food." *East Tennessee University Monographic Series Number 3.* Johnson City, Tenn.: Institute of Regional Studies, 1966, pp. 27-31.

Carson, Jane. *Colonial Virginia Cookery.* Williamsburg, Va.: Colonial Williamsburg, Inc., 1968.

Cassell, B. "Jewish Dietary Laws and Food Customs." *Public Health Nursing,* 32 (November 1940), 685-87.

Chang, B. "Some Dietary Beliefs in Chinese Folk Culture." *Journal of the American Dietetic Association,* 65 (October 1974), 436-38.

Claiborne, Craig. *The New York Times Guide to Dining Out in New York.* Rev. ed. New York: Atheneum, 1968.

Clark, Faith, ed. *Symposium III: The Changing Patterns of Consumption of Food.* International Congress of Food Science and Technology. Proceedings of the Congress Symposia, 1962. Volume 5. New York: Gordon and Breach Science Publications, 1967, pp. 159-254.

Collin, Richard. *New Orleans Underground Gourmet.* New York: Simon and Schuster, 1973.

————. *New Orleans Restaurant Guide.* New Orleans: Strether and Swann, 1977.

————. *The Pleasures of Seafood.* New York: Holt, Rinehart, and Winston, 1977.

Committee on Food Habits, National Research Council. *The Problem of Changing Food Habits.* Bulletin of the National Research Council Number 108, October 1943. Washington, D.C.: National Research Council, 1943.

————. *Manual for the Study of Food Habits.* Bulletin of the National Research Council Number 111, January 1945. Washington, D.C.: National Research Council, 1945.

Cummings, Richard Osborn. *The American and His Food: A History of Food Habits in the United States.* Chicago: University of Chicago Press, 1940.

Cussler, Margaret, and Mary Louise de Give. *Twixt the Cup and the Lip: Psychological and Socio-Cultural Factors Affecting Food Habits.* New York: Twayne Publishers, 1952.

Dickins, Dorothy. "Food Preparation of Owner and Cropper Farm Families in the Shortleaf Pine Area of Mississippi." *Social Forces,* 22 (October 1943), 56-63.

————. "Changing Pattern of Food Preparation of Small Town Families in Mississippi." *Mississippi Agricultural Experimental Station Bulletin* 415 (1945), 1-56.

————, and R. N. Ford. "Geophagy Among Mississippi Negro School Children." *American Sociological Review,* 7 (February 1942), 59-65.

Dickson, Paul. *Chow: A Cook's Tour of Military Food.* New York: New American Library, 1978.

Dodson, R. "Tortilla Making." In *In the Shadow of History,* Texas Folklore Society Publications Number 15 (1939), 1-18.

Douglas, Mary. "The Abominations of Leviticus." In her *Purity and Danger.* New York: Praeger Books, 1966, pp. 41-57.

————. "Deciphering a Meal." In Clifford Geertz, ed., *Myth, Symbol and Culture.* New York: W. W. Norton, 1971, pp. 61-81.

Feibleman, Peter S., and the Editors of Time-Life Books. *American Cooking: Creole and Acadian.* New York: Time, Inc., 1971.

Glaser, Milton, and Jerome Snyder. *The Underground Gourmet.* Rev. ed. New York: Simon and Schuster, 1970.

Greene, Gael. *Bite.* New York: W. W. Norton, 1971.

Harris, Marvin. *Cows, Pigs, Wars, and Witches: The Riddles of Culture.* New York: Random House, 1974.

Humphrey, N. D. "Some Dietary and Health Practices of Detroit Mexicans." *Journal of American Folklore,* 58 (July 1945), 255-58.
Jordan, G. L. *Changing Food Habits in Relation to Land Utilization in the United States.* Carbondale: University of Illinois Press, 1933.
Kroc, Ray. *Grinding It Out: The Making of McDonald's.* Chicago: Henry Regnery, 1977.
Lasky, Michael S. *The Complete Junk Food Book.* New York: McGraw-Hill, 1977.
Leach, Edmund. "Cooking." In his *Culture and Communication.* New York: Cambridge University Press, 1976, pp. 60-61.
Le Gros, Clark F. "Human Food Habits as Determining the Basic Patterns of Economic and Social Life." *Nutrition,* 22 (January 1966), 134-45.
Leonard, Jonathan Norton, and the Editors of Time-Life Books. *American Cooking: New England.* New York: Time, Inc., 1970.
————. *American Cooking: The Great West.* New York: Time, Inc., 1971.
Levi-Strauss, Claude. "The Culinary Triangle." *Partisan Review,* 33 (Fall 1966), 586-95.
Lincoln, Waldo. *American Cookery Books, 1742-1860.* Worcester, Mass.: American Antiquarian Society, 1954.
Loeb, M. B. "The Social Functions of Food Habits." *Journal of Applied Nutrition,* 4 (1951), 227-29.
Lowenberg, M. E. "Socio-Cultural Basis of Food Habits." *Food Technology,* 24 (1970), 27-32.
Massachusetts State Department of Health. *The Food of Working Women in Boston.* Studies in Economic Relations of Women, vol. X. Boston: Women's Educational and Industrial Union, Department of Research, 1917.
Mead, Margaret. "Dietary Patterns and Food Habits." *Journal of the American Dietetic Association,* 19 (January 1943), 1-5.
————. "The Challenge of Cross-Cultural Research." *Journal of the American Dietetic Association,* 45 (December 1964), 413-14.
————. *Food Habits Research: Problems of the 1960s.* Washington, D.C.: National Research Council publication 1225, 1964.
Moser, Ada M. *Farm Family Diets in the Lower Coastal Plains of South Carolina.* South Carolina Agricultural Experimental Station *Bulletin* 319, 1939.
————. *Food Habits of South Carolina Farm Families.* South Carolina Agricultural Experimental Station *Bulletin* 343, 1942.
Newall, Venetia. "Selected Jamaican Foodways in the Homeland and in England." In Linda Degh, Henry Glassie, and Felix J. Oinas, eds., *Folklore Today.* Bloomington, Ind.: Indiana University Press, 1976, pp. 369-77.
Niehoff, Arthur H. "Food Habits and Cultural Patterns." In The Nutrition Foundation, Inc., *Food Science and Society.* New York: The Nutrition Foundation, 1969, pp. 45-52.
Patten, Marguerite. *Books for Cooks: Bibliography of Cookery.* N.p., 1975.
Paz, Octavio. "Eroticism and Gastronomy." *Daedalus,* 101 (Fall 1972), 67-85.
Phillips, Doris E., and Mary A. Bass. "Food Preservation Practices of Selected Homemakers in East Tennessee." *Ecology of Food and Nutrition,* 5 (Winter 1976), 29-36.

Pyke, Magnus. *Food and Society*. London: John Murray, 1968.

———. "The Influence of American Foods and Food Technology in Europe." In C. W. E. Bigsby, ed., *Superculture: American Popular Culture and Europe*. Bowling Green, Ohio: Bowling Green University Popular Press, 1975, pp. 83-95.

Read, R. B. *The San Francisco Underground Gourmet*. New York: Simon and Schuster, 1969.

Root, Waverly. *The Food of France*. New York: Alfred A. Knopf, 1958.

———, and Richard de Rochemont. *Eating in America: A History*. New York: William Morrow, 1976.

Sackett, Marjorie. "Folk Recipes as a Measure of Intercultural Penetration." *Journal of American Folklore*, 85 (January-March 1972), 77-81.

Sakr, A. H. "Dietary Regulations and Food Habits of Muslims." *Journal of the American Dietetic Association*, 58 (February 1971), 123-26.

Shenton, James Patrick et al. *American Cooking: The Melting Pot*. New York: Time, Inc., 1971.

Sorre, Max. "The Geography of Diet." In Phillip L. Wagner and Marvin W. Mikesell, eds., *Readings in Cultural Geography*. Chicago: University of Chicago Press, 1962, pp. 445-56.

Stern, Jane, and Michael Stern. *Roadfood*. New York: Random House, 1977.

Todhunter, E. N. "The History of Food Patterns in the U.S.A." In *Proceedings of the Third International Congress on Dietetics*. New York: The Nutrition Foundation, 1961.

Trillin, Calvin. *American Fried*. New York: Penguin Books, 1975.

———. *Alice, Let's Eat*. New York: Random House, 1978.

Trulson, M. R. "The American Diet: Past and Present." *American Journal of Clinical Nutrition*, 7 (January-February 1959), 91-97.

U.S. Department of Agriculture. *Experimental Station Record*. Washington, D.C.: U.S.D.A., 1889-.

U.S. Department of Health, Education, and Welfare. *Cumulated Index Medicus*. Washington, D.C.: National Institutes of Health, Public Health Service, 1959-.

Vance, Rupert B. "Climate, Diet, and Human Adequacy." In his *Human Geography of the South*. Chapel Hill: University of North Carolina Press, 1932, pp. 411-41.

Vehling, Joseph Dommers. *America's Table*. Chicago: Hostends, 1950.

Viorst, Judith, and Milton Viorst. *The Washington D.C. Underground Gourmet*. New York: Simon and Schuster, 1970.

Walter, Eugene. *American Cooking: Southern Style*. New York: Time, Inc., 1971.

Welsch, Roger. " 'We Are What We Eat': Omaha Food as Symbol." *Keystone Folklore Quarterly*, 16 (Winter 1971), 165-70.

Wilson, Christine S. "Food Habits: A Selected Annotated Bibliography." *Journal of Nutrition Education*, 5 (January-March 1973), supplement 1, 39-72.

Wilson, Jose. *American Cooking: The Eastern Heartland*. New York: Time, Inc., 1971.

Yoder, Don. "Sauerkraut in the Pennsylvania Folk Culture." *Pennsylvania Folklife*, 12 (Summer 1961), 56-59.
————. "Schnitz in the Pennsylvania Folk Culture." *Pennsylvania Folklife*, 12 (Fall 1961), 56-59.
————. "Historical Sources for American Foodways Research and Plans for an American Foodways Archive." *Pennsylvania Folklife*, 20 (Spring 1971), 16-29.
————. "Folk Cookery." In Richard M. Dorson, ed., *Folklore and Folklife: an Introduction*. Chicago: University of Chicago Press, 1972, pp. 325-50.

PERIODICALS

Bon Appétit. Los Angeles, Calif., 1955-.
Cuisine. Santa Barbara, Calif., 1970-.
The Digest. Philadelphia, Pa., 1977-.
Ecology of Food and Nutrition. London, 1971-.
Gourmet. New York, 1941-.
International Review of Food and Wine. New York, 1978-.
Journal of the American Dietetic Association. Chicago, 1925-.
Journal of Nutrition Education. Berkeley, Calif., 1969-.
Natural History. New York, 1900-.
New Yorker. New York, 1924-.
Nutrition Abstracts and Reviews. Boston, 1942-.

Sample List of Organizations and Trade Publications

Catfish Farmers of America P.O. Box 2451 Little Rock, Ark. 72203	*The Commercial Fish Farmer*
Shellfish Institute of North America 212 Washington Ave., Suite 9 Baltimore, Md. 21204	*Shellfish Soundings*
American Frozen Food Institute 919 18th St. N.W. Washington, D.C. 20006	*Frozen Food Report*
American Spice Trade Association Box 1267 Englewood Cliffs, N.J.07632	*Spiceletter*
American Sugar Cane League 416 Whitney Bldg. New Orleans, La. 70130	*The Sugar Bulletin*
Chocolate Manufacturers Assoc. of the U.S.A. 7900 Westpark Dr. Suite 514 McLean, Va. 22101	*The Story of Chocolate*

Independent Grocers Alliance Distributing Co.   *Grocergram*
5725 E. River Rd.
Chicago, Ill. 60631

International Federation of Beekeepers'
   Associations   *Apiatica*
Corso Vittorio Emanuele 101
00186 Rome, Italy

National Association of Chewing Gum
   Manufacturers   *The Story of Chewing Gum*
366 Madison Ave.
New York, N.Y. 10017

National Canners Association   *Canned Food Pack Statistics*
1133 20th St. N.W.
Washington, D.C. 20036

National Hot Dog & Sausage Council   *Hot Dog Fact Sheet*
400 W. Madison
Chicago, Ill. 60606

National Macaroni Manufacturers Association   *Macaroni Journal*
P.O. Box 336
Palatine, Ill. 60067

CHAPTER 7. Games and Toys

Bernard Mergen

Games and toys, as part of the larger topic of play, have been studied by anthropologists, folklorists, psychologists, and historians for a century, and there is general agreement that both are significant in shaping individual personality and cultures. While the use of games and toys is not limited to childhood, it is obvious that in our society these terms are usually reserved for children's activities, with the prefix "adult" attached to games and toys that are not primarily meant for minors. On the other hand, as Jac Remise has pointed out, most toys are made by adults to appeal and sell to other adults.[1] When is a painted replica of a soldier a toy, and when is it a miniature? When is throwing a ball a game, and when is it a sport? Purpose and context can help make some useful distinctions, but the study of games and toys quickly leads to related subjects such as leisure, child development, education, sport, and recreation. Indeed, it is difficult to abstract games and toys from the whole study of work and play.

Games must be subdivided into at least three categories: physical skill, strategy, and chance. Most games involve some combination of the three, and, more often than not, some kind of competition is involved between teams, players, or an individual with himself. Competition may be the key element in distinguishing between games and play since most recent definitions of play emphasize process rather than any specific activity. As Stephen Miller has written: "There are goals in play, but these are of less importance in themselves than as embodiments of the process involved in obtaining them. Process in play is not streamlined toward dealing with goals in the shortest possible way, but is voluntarily elaborated, complicated, in various patterned ways."[2] All games are played, but not all play is a game. Similarly, all toys are played with, but not all play involves toys. Toys may be thought of as props in activities that may involve competition, chance, learning, fantasy, entertainment, or even "doing nothing." Games and toys, especially those of children, provide us with material for understanding the development of the mind—of imagination and communication, of ritual and innovation.

HISTORIC OUTLINE

The games and toys of colonial children were those of their British, French, Dutch, and German ancestors. Paintings and engravings by Pieter Breughel, Jacob Cats, and other Dutch artists show children playing tag, blindman's bluff, jump rope, and leapfrog. They also depict a variety of stilts, hoops, tops, dolls, kites, and musical instruments. The sixteenth- and seventeenth-century child had a rich assortment of playthings, and there is no reason to suppose that the colonial child did not share in this abundance. Neither the rigors of frontier life nor the strictness of New England Puritanism could eliminate games and toys. Peter Wagner has recently noted that as early as 1649, Thomas Shepard castigated his congregation for spending the Sabbath "in rioting and wantonness, in sports and foolishness."[3]

Prosperity and changing values brought even greater variety to the toy market in the eighteenth century. Benjamin Franklin recalled buying imported toys in Boston in 1713, and English, German, and American potters made miniature dishes and tea sets in increasing quantities. The earliest surviving dolls' house, now in the collection of the Van Cortlandt Museum in New York City, is believed to date from 1774. If we extend the definition of toys, as Katharine McClinton does, to include "antiques of American childhood,"[4] we find interesting examples of silver whistles with coral and bells that were given as christening presents. These small noisemakers are often shown in eighteenth-century portraits of children, either held in a hand or worn on a silver chain around the child's neck. Silversmiths also made nursing bottles, porringers, and vessels with long spouts called "papboats" for the children of wealthy Americans. Pottery cradles made in England also found their way to the colonies, where they were sold for christening and birthday presents.

Older children and adults played with ivory or hardwood "cup and ball" toys, in which the object was to catch the ball in the cup or on the point of the handle that fitted into a small hole in the ball. Battledore and shuttlecock were popular outdoor games, as were marbles and ball games. Each game had its season; marbles came first, in the early spring, followed by kites, tops, and hoops. In New York, the sequence was slightly different, according to the adage: "Top-time's gone, kite-time's come, and April Fool's day will soon be here." Ball games—rudimentary forms of soccer and baseball—were played on holidays. According to William Wells Newell, "in Boston, *Fast-day* (the first Thursday of April) was particularly devoted to this sport. In England, the playing of ball at Easter-tide seems to have been a custom of the festival, inherited probably from pre-Christian ages. Foot-ball was a regular amusement on the afternoon of a New England Thanksgiving."[5] Bowling, hand ball, and hockey were other forms of ball games in seventeenth- and eighteenth-century America.

Indoor games of the same period included backgammon, chess, billiards, and various card games. As early as 1775, the *Pennsylvania Packet* advertised a card game to teach geography; but the heyday of educational card and board games was in the nineteenth century. The appearance of animals in many eighteenth-century family portraits suggests that pets were important elements in children's play. Dogs, cats, birds, squirrels, lambs, and even deer were part of the domestic scene. The legacy of Puritanism clouded the enjoyment of some of this kind of play, however, since the 1773 edition of *The New England Primer* illustrated the letter C with the rhyme: "The Cat doth play, And after slay." Samuel Goodrich described another indoor pastime of late eighteenth-century boys: "During my youthful days I found the penknife a source of great amusement, even instruction. Many a long winter evening, many a dull, drizzly day . . . have I spent in great ecstasy making candlerods or some other simple article of household goods, for my mother, or in perfecting toys for myself and my young friends. . . ."[6]

A generation later, Edward Everett Hale grew up with "an infinite variety of amusements—almost everything we wanted for purposes of manufacture or invention. Whalebone, spiral springs, pulleys and catgut, for perpetual motion or locomotive carriages, rollers and planks for floats . . . good blocks for building, carpenter's tools, a work-bench, and printing materials. . . . When we became chemists we might have sulphuric acid, nitric acid, litmus paper, or whatever we desired, so our allowance would stand it. I was not more than seven years old when I burned off my eyebrows by igniting gun-powder with my burning glass."[7] The 1830s and 1840s witnessed the birth of the American toy and game industry. William S. Tower, a carpenter in South Hingham, Massachusetts, organized a guild of toymakers in the late 1830s, and Franklin Peale exhibited a small steam locomotive made by Matthias Baldwin at the Peale family's Philadelphia museum. For the next forty years, wooden and metal toys were usually produced as a sideline by craftsmen engaged in cabinetmaking or tool manufacturing.

Paper toys and games were developed by stationers and lithographers. The titles of some board and card games echo the concerns of the period. In 1843, W. & B. Ives of Salem, Massachusetts, issued a highly moralistic board game, "The Mansion of Happiness," intended to teach young Americans to practice the virtues of industry, honesty, and sobriety. The following year introduced "The Game of Pope or Pagan or the Missionary Campaign or the Siege of the Stronghold of Satan by the Christian Army." By the 1860s, moralism began to be replaced by current events and an emphasis on material success. Milton Bradley's tremendously popular "The Checkered Game of Life," which appeared in 1860, alternated squares printed with "wealth," "happiness," "industry," and "ambition," with others labeled "gambling," "poverty," "jail," and "suicide."

"In 1868," according to McClinton, "four games of war and patriotism were packaged together under the title 'The Union Games.' "8 Anagrams, puzzles, Zoetropes (a slotted revolving drum that gives the viewer the sense of moving pictures), and conversation cards gained in popularity through the 1860s. Conversation cards, which printed questions such as "Have you ever been in love?" and "What is your favorite food?," were intended to enliven the "cold and ceremonious" social gatherings that European travelers often found in the United States. The McLoughlin Brothers' catalog of 1867 lists seven kinds of conversation cards, including "Loves and Likes," "Comical Conversation Cards," "Conversations on Marriage," and "Quizzical Questions and Quaint Replies." Another type of game involving dialogue is illustrated by "Japhet Jenkins and Sally Jones visit to Boston," copyrighted in 1867. In this game, cards with brief sentences are shuffled and dealt to the players who take turns reading them and filling in blanks in a book that tells the adventures of a pair of country bumpkins visiting the city.

In 1883, sixteen-year-old George S. Parker invented his first game, the "Game of Banking." Subsequent games also reflected the concerns of the Gilded Age. "The Game of Moneta: or Money Makes Money" appeared in the Montgomery Ward catalog of 1889, and a "Game of Business" came out in 1895. One of the most popular games of the period was marketed by the Crandalls in 1889 under the name "Pigs in Clover." This puzzle required the player to maneuver four marbles through a maze into a cardboard enclosure. Hundreds of thousands were sold, and the game seems to have been especially popular in Washington, D.C., where the symbolism of the spoils system was obvious. Political election games appeared regularly in the late nineteenth century, and an interesting study could be done by comparing the "Centennial Presidential Game" of 1876 with the "Presidential Election" game of 1892, "Politics" of the 1950s, and "Bigwig" in 1973.

Games and toys were inspired by every conceivable event. The Chicago Columbian Exposition of 1893 was commemorated in games, puzzles, and building blocks. "Sherlock Holmes" and "The Amusing Game of Innocence Abroad" profited from the popularity of the books that preceded them. "White Squadron Picture Puzzles" helped to make the names of the war ships *Baltimore*, *Chicago*, and *Monterey* familiar to American children. The 1886 catalog of sporting goods and games sold by the Peck &

Snyder Company lists chess, checkers, lotto, dominoes, Parcheesi, cards, bagatelle, cribbage, tetotums or spinning dice, and dice, as well as a board game called "The Monopolist." "On the board," the catalog reads, "the great struggle between Capital and Labor can be fought out to the satisfaction of all parties, and, if the players are successful, they can break the Monopolist, and become Monopolists themselves." Again, it would be instructive to compare this game with the well-known Parker Brothers game, "Monopoly," introduced in 1935. Robert H. Canary's essay on "Monopoly" and the 1950s "Game of Life" and James M. Hughes's comparison of "Monopoly" and "The Cities Game" are suggestive beginnings. The "Class Struggle" game, marketed in 1978 by political science professor Bertell Ollman, offers still another point of comparison.

The plethora of games in the twentieth century reveals much about American culture. Since most of these games involve elements of chance as well as strategy, they may reflect a growing uncertainty about the future and the desire to prepare individuals "to endure bad times in the hope of brighter futures." This is the hypothesis advanced by J. M. Roberts and Brian Sutton-Smith in their work on "Child Training and Game Involvement" in non-Western societies. Luck has always played a significant, if neglected, role in American thought, and a study of gambling games, especially among children, would be rewarding. The problem, of course, is that like other illegal activities, few records exist that describe gambling games. One of the few comes from Stewart Culin, an anthropologist and museum curator, who described "Street Games of Boys in Brooklyn, New York" in 1891. Culin found a game that the boys called "Pictures," which was played by shooting the cards found in cigarette packages toward a wall, the winner being the boy whose card landed nearest the wall. The winner then threw all the cards into the air and kept the ones that fell face up. Culin's ten-year-old informant claimed to be ignorant of the related game—penny pitching. "It was regarded among his associates as a vulgar game, and only practiced by bootblacks and boys of the lowest class, such as compose the 'gangs' that are a well-known feature of street life among the boys of our cities."[9]

There are many other kinds of toys that parallel adult activities. Toy models of steam engines, trains, telegraphs, telephones, washing machines, automobiles, and airplanes appeared soon after their introduction in the adult world. In some cases, an inventor seems to have no clear purpose and tries out his invention in toy form. Edison put one of his early phonograph cylinders in a "Talking Doll" in 1890. Dolls' houses and doll house furniture are obvious examples of toys that follow the fashion and changes in technology. Building materials are another example. In 1901, a British inventor, Frank Hornby, patented a set of construction materials made of thin strips of metal with perforations for nuts and bolts. His "Mechanics

Made Easy," or "Meccano," was soon copied in the United States as "Erector" sets, allowing American children to build skyscraper skeletons to mirror those outside their bedroom windows. Charles Pajeau's 1914 patent for "Tinkertoys" followed the same general idea of building in outline, but his colorful rods, knobs, and pulleys seem closer to the abstract forms of the Armory Show than to the cantilever of the Queensboro Bridge. Pajeau may also have borrowed his idea from Friedrich Froebel, whose rods, strings, and balls inspired the young Frank Lloyd Wright in 1876.

Occasionally, however, the power of toys to mold the habits and talents of children fails. During World War I, Edward Hurley, chairman of the United States Shipping Board, decided that Americans should learn the value of the merchant marine and persuaded the Ives Toy Manufacturing Company to make a copy of the standard merchant ship being constructed by the Emergency Fleet Corporation. In his letter to the company, Hurley wrote: "It is none too early to begin waking Americans to the importance of ships, putting ships and the sea into their daily thought and work, and making ships appeal to the imagination of everybody in the country. We want to reach the children as well as the grown-ups, and, in this connection knowing how closely toys follow popular interest and what an educative value they have, it has been in my mind to have this great new national interest before the men who invent and design your goods."[10] When the Ives catalog for 1919 appeared, the advertising copy echoed Hurley's patrotic note: A boy "can get thoroughly interested in the great game of commerce and the big Merchant marine of his country. He can talk it, play it and interest his chums in it. . . .Who knows but what it may lead them into the big business of transportation by sea that is going to play such a wonderful part in the future world trade of the United States?" The ironic end to this effort to build support for an American merchant marine was the bankruptcy of the Ives Company in 1929, a collapse that Ives's accountants attributed in part to poor sales of the toy merchant fleet.

Turning from toys to games played without equipment, the historical record is strongest for the years since 1883, when folklorists, psychologists, and anthropologists first began to study children's play systematically. In that year, William Wells Newell, linguist, poet, and folklorist, published *Games and Songs of American Children*. This collection of almost two hundred folksongs and counting-out rhymes, clapping and ring games, tag and guessing games gives us a sense of the complexity and formality of games in the 1870s. Few adults or children today would be willing to memorize the long poem, "Knights of Spain," that accompanied a popular kissing game. Some songs, such as the familiar "Barbara Allen," were used to circumvent the religious ban on dancing. As the ballad was sung, couples kept time with slow movements without changing place. Newell's research showed that most American games and songs had British and European origins. He was impressed by the conservatism of children in preserving these games, but he was also afraid that increased immigration, urbanization, and industrialization were destroying traditional games.

There is some evidence that cities made play difficult. In 1892, Washington, D.C., passed an ordinance that declared it unlawful "for any person or persons to play the game of football, or any other game with a ball, in any of the streets, avenues, or alleys in the cities of Washington and Georgetown; nor shall it be lawful for any person or persons to play the game of bandy, shindy, or any other game by which a ball, stone, or other substance is struck or propelled by any stick, cane, or other substance in any street, avenue, or alley. . . ."[11] In the same year, Helen and Robert Lynd tell us, Muncie, Indiana, made it illegal to pitch quoits or coins, to play cricket, bandy, cat, townball, or any other game of public amusement, or to discharge a gun, pistol, or firearm on Sunday. Both laws tell us a great deal about the play life of small cities and towns and about the kinds of games and where they were played. Whether the motive was a reformist hope that play could be regulated in school yards and playgrounds, or a conservative desire to maintain fundamental religious values, the 1890s and early twentieth century saw numerous efforts to redefine games and play.

Observers unanimously agreed that most children were "doing nothing" and wasting their time when they were not working. A survey in Milwaukee, Wisconsin, in 1911, put the percentages at 19 percent working, 31 percent playing, and 50 percent doing nothing on a typical November day.[12] A similar survey in Cleveland, Ohio, on June 23, 1913, found 10 percent working, 50 percent playing, and 40 percent of the city's children doing nothing.[13] Of those who were playing, 43 percent were described as "just fooling." Doing nothing and just fooling were categories that included: breaking windows, chalking suggestive words on buildings, standing around on corners, fighting, looking at pictures of women in tights on billboards, stealing, and gambling with dice, cards, buttons, marbles, and beer bottle tags. Joseph Lee, Luther Gulick, Henry Curtis, and others sought to improve opportunities for urban recreation under the supervision of professional playground directors. The founding of the Playground Association in 1906 and the publication the following year of the first issue of *The Playground* (now *Parks and Recreation*) mark the beginnings of highly organized children's games and play in the United States.

Typical of the way in which traditional games were appropriated by the recreation movement is a list published in the *Seventh Annual Report of the Department of Playgrounds* of Washington, D.C., in 1918. Games were divided into "Low Organized Games," "High Organized Games," "Quiet Games," "Races," "Relay," and "Memory and Sense Games." An example of each included: "Prisoners Base," "Basketball," "Boiler Burst," "Wheel-barrow," "All up Indian Club," and "Ghosts." Early surveys of games and play suggest that there have been important changes in game preferences among American children. For example, T. R. Croswell, who studied about two thousand schoolchildren in Worcester, Massachusetts, in 1896, found only four of one thousand boys playing cowboys and Indians and only two who mentioned playing with toy soldiers. Girls' game preferences seem to have changed more than boys' in the past century, with many more girls playing games that were played exclusively by boys in the past, such as leapfrog and red rover. Boys and girls now play few singing and dialogue games such as those recorded by Newell, and many of the rhymes that were recited with those games are now used in jump rope.

Brian Sutton-Smith argues that children's play has become more sophisticated and that fantasy play and games involving the manipulation of symbols have been encouraged by middle-class parents.[14] Playground planners in the United States are trying to introduce "Adventure Playgrounds," in which children are encouraged to organize and develop their own games and to build their own play structures. A new vocabulary has entered the playground movement: "loose parts," "ambiguity," "flexibility," "diversity," "change," and "open-endedness." The contemporary student of games is faced with a bewildering variety of theories and an equally confusing body of raw data. Games, toys, and play serve many functions, not the least of which is to help cope with a chaotic, violent, and even dangerous world. We should not be surprised to find much that is shocking in play, but we must try to understand what is actually going on, rather than imposed preconceived definitions of what is play and what it is not. We must try to discover what games and toys mean to the players. For that, we may well begin with ourselves.

REFERENCE WORKS

Since definitions of games, toys, and play vary widely, and because so little basic research has been done, this section will list several kinds of reference material. First, and most basic, are the handful of bibliographies that list primary and secondary works on games and play. For games in general, including those used in education and by the military, the most complete bibliography is in *The Study of Games*, edited by Elliott M. Avedon and Brian Sutton-Smith. Their book is also an anthology of articles on the historical, anthropological, and folkloristic aspects of games. A reference work that is similar in intent if not in scope is Jean Belch's *Contemporary Games*. Volume one is a directory listing about nine hundred decision-making or problem-solving games for educational purposes. Each entry is indexed by subject, age or grade, playing time, number of players, date originated, manufacturer, and designer. There is also a brief bibliography for each game. Volume two is a longer bibliography on games and game playing.

Child's Play, edited by R. E. Herron and Brian Sutton-Smith, is also an anthology with a bibliography of over seven hundred items on the theory of play and on psychological studies of children's play. It should be supplemented with Helen B. Schwartzman's "Research on Children's Play: An Overview and Some Predictions," and "Works on Play: A Bibliography," both of which may be found in *Studies in the Anthropology of Play: Papers in Memory of B. Allan Tindall*, edited by Phillips Stevens, Jr., Schwartzman's bibliography of over two hundred-fifty items combines both psychological and anthropological studies and includes publications through 1976. Barbara Kirshenblatt-Gimblett's *Speech Play* contains an excellent bibliographical essay on the linguistic and cultural aspects of play. Jean-Leo's *Jouets, jeux, livres d'enfant: repertoire bibliographique d'ouvrages utiles aux collectionneurs et aux chercheurs, augmente de nombreux articles inedits* is a useful starting place for foreign-language books and articles.

There is no bibliography on American toys, but Roland Renson and B. Van Reusel have published a brief list of works on European toys. Moreover, the distinction between reference works and general histories of toys and dolls is not clear. Among those books that are basically catalogs of different types of toys and games, *The Collector's Encyclopedia of Dolls* by Dorothy, Elizabeth, and Evelyn Coleman ranks high. Leslie Daiken's *Children's Toys Throughout the Ages* is typical of an older, collector's approach to the subject, but it is useful for its discussion of various definitions of toys. Daiken's *World of Toys: A Guide to the Principle Public and Private Collections in Great Britain* is also a useful starting place for the study of eighteenth- and nineteenth-century toys, especially since the United States imported a great many British and European toys.

For this country, the basic reference work is still Louis Hertz's 1947 guide, *The Handbook of Old American Toys*, which has a brief introduction to such topics as classification, identification, materials, and terminology. Hertz arranges his study by tin toys, cast iron, clockwork, wooden, steam, banks, cannon, cap pistols, musical toys, electric toys, trains, toy household equipment, games, wheel toys, and dolls. His more recent book, *The Toy Collector*, has useful chapters on research as well as a guide to manufacturers and to identification marks. Another excellent work is Katharine McClinton's *Antiques of American Childhood*, a guide that expands the definition of toy to include children's costumes, buttons, furniture, dishes, and needlework.

Specialized reference works include: Ann E. Grinham's *Japanese Games and Toys*; Ceil Chandler's *Toys and Dolls Made in Occupied Japan*; Kenny Harman's *Comic Strip Toys*; Gwen White's *Toys and Dolls: Marks and Labels*; Cecil Gibson's *A History of British Dinky Toys: Model Car and Vehicle Issues, 1934-1964*; and Linda Hannas's *The English Jigsaw Puzzle, 1760-1890; with a Descriptive Check-list of Puzzles in the Museums of Great Britain and the Author's Collection*. Fred Ferretti's *The Great American Marble Book* contains color illustrations of dozens of different kinds of marbles and the games played with them. Ferretti's *The Great American Book of Sidewalk, Stoop, Dirt, Curb, and Alley Games* is less successful because it only touches on each kind of game. A more satisfying collection is Alan Milberg's *Street Games*. Although they are not reference books in the usual sense, the Ferretti and Milberg books provide 1970s comparisons to the great collections of Douglas, Gomme, Newell, and the Opies.

Newell's classic *Games and Songs of American Children* has been cited above, but it is the British who provide the most comprehensive game surveys. *The Traditional Games of England, Scotland, and Ireland* by Alice Gomme, *London Street Games* by Norman Douglas, and *Children's Games in Street and Playground* by Iona and Peter Opie supply a detailed history of games of the past century. The Opies's more recent *The Lore and Language of School Children* adds still more to our knowledge of outdoor play. Roger D. Abrahams's *Jump-Rope Rhymes: A Dictionary*, Bess Lomax Hawes and Bessie Jones's *Step It Down: Games, Plays, Songs and Stories from the Afro-American Heritage*, and Paul G. Brewster's *American Non-singing Games* are the only American surveys since Newell that attempt a wide sample of selected types of play, although Mary and Herbert Knapp provide a useful beginning in *One Potato, Two Potato . . . The Secret Education of American Children*. For native Americans, Stewart Culin's *Games of North American Indians* remains unsurpassed. Brian Sutton-Smith's *The Games of New Zealand Children* and *A History of the Playground: A New Zealand Case Study, 1840-1950* offer an inventory of play from another transplanted English society.

Perhaps the most useful reference works for the student of games and toys are still the catalogs of the toy manufacturers and retailers and their trade publications. Some of the catalogs have been reprinted. Peck & Snyder's *Sporting Goods and Games 1886* has been published by the Pyne Press and contains an overwhelming assortment of uniforms, equipment, magic tricks, joke books and play scripts, microscopes and telescopes, steam toys, and magic lanterns. *The Wonderful World of Toys, Games and Dolls*, edited by Joseph J. Schroeder, Jr., contains reprints from the catalogs of F. A. O. Schwartz, Montgomery Ward, Marshall Field, and other stores from 1862 to 1930. By far the most important trade journal is *Playthings*, which has been published monthly since 1903. Each issue has articles on toy manufacturing and advertising from most of the large firms.

Other trade journals include: *Toy World*, which was published in San Francisco in the 1920s and which merged with *Toys and Novelties* (now *Toys*) in 1936; and the *Toy Manufacturer*, published in Atlanta. For the German toy industry, *Das Spielzeug*, published in Bamberg, provides trade information.

There are also several magazines and newspapers published by and for collectors: *Antique Toy World, Collectibles Monthly, Miniature Collector*, and *Toy Trains* are good examples. These publications are useful for discovering private collections and they often contain articles on toy and doll manufacturers. There are three published censuses of toy manufacturers—one in 1927, one in 1931, and another in 1940. The Department of Commerce also sponsored two studies of the international toy business—Jeannette M. Calvin's *International Trade in Toys* in 1926 and E. D. Schutrumpf's *World Trade in Toys* in 1939. Both volumes contain detailed statistics on exports and imports of toys in all industrialized countries. *Willson's Canadian Toy, Notion and Station Directory* provides a basic list of toy firms in that country, while *The Toy Trader and Exporter* and *Toy Trader Year Book* serve the British industry.

RESEARCH COLLECTIONS

Almost every museum and historical society has a collection of games, toys, and dolls that is used for an annual Christmas display. The student of games and toys should always begin research with a visit to the local museum. The next step would be to identify private collectors and collections. There are, however, a number of museums throughout the country with large and growing collections of toys. The following cannot claim to be a complete list of all the significant doll and toy collections, but it does represent a good sample of the museums that responded to the letter of inquiry I sent to about forty institutions in the summer of 1978. The museums are listed in alphabetical order, with the address and name of the appropriate curator when available. Researchers should always write in advance to the institution they wish to visit, so that the curator has time to assemble relevant materials.

The Atlanta Historical Society (P.O. Box 12423, Atlanta 30355) has a few items relating to nineteenth- and twentieth-century children's play. It has recently acquired a collection of twenty-six dolls. Lisa Reynolds, curator, has a special interest in the toy collection. There is also a new Toy Museum of Atlanta (2800 Peachtree Road, NW, Atlanta 30305). The Atwater Kent Museum (15 South Seventh Street, Philadelphia 19106) has a small collection of eighteenth-, nineteenth-, and twentieth-century dolls, as well as some iron toys and some blocks and board games. The Bucks County Historical Society and The Mercer Museum (Pine

Street, Doylestown, Pennsylvania 18901) have a small collection accessible by appointment with Laurie J. Rufe, curator. Among the animals, banks, blocks, dolls, dolls' houses, games, puppets, rocking horses, tops, and wagons, is a coffin made for a doll owned by Ella Good of Solebury, Pennsylvania, in about 1850.

A small, uncataloged collection of dolls, doll house furnishings, board games, trucks, and cars is available by appointment at the Chicago Historical Society (Clark Street at North Avenue, Chicago 60614). The Children's Museum (30th Street and Meridian, Indianapolis 46208) is one of the largest and most comprehensive children's museums. It has educational programs and exhibits of many kinds, and a permanent exhibit of toys is scheduled to open in December 1978. The museum owns a well-documented collection of over one thousand toy cars from the 1950s and has one of the largest toy train collections in the country. Mary Jane Teeters is curator of dolls and Judi Ryan is head of the Department of Collections. Colonial Williamsburg (P.O. Box C, Williamsburg, Virginia 23185) has a number of games and toys. There is no catalog, but there are files available to scholars for research by appointment.

The Colorado Historical Society (The Colorado Heritage Center, 1300 Broadway, Denver 80203) has a good collection of toys, including household items, board games, guns, ships, toy soldiers, cowboys, Indians, and badges. A collection of about two hundred dolls and a few toys may be examined in the Daughters of the American Revolution Museum (1776 D Street, NW, Washington, D.C. 20006). The Essex Institute (Salem, Massachusetts 01970) has dolls, dolls' houses, trains, and cast-iron wagons. An illustrated book, *Dolls and Toys at the Essex Institute*, by Madeline and Richard Merrill, describes the collection. Kenneth Wilson, director of collections, Greenfield Village and the Henry Ford Museum (Dearborn, Michigan 48121), describes the toys and games in his institution as "too numerous to mention." *Playthings of the Past: 19th and 20th Century Toys from the Collection of the Louisiana State Museum* in New Orleans describes the holdings of that museum. The Maryland Historical Society (201 West Monument Street, Baltimore 21201) has a large and varied toy collection, including some outstanding dolls' houses reflecting the architectural styles of the state.

A small collection of dolls, both homemade and commercial, a football game played with marbles, and a number of games taken from comic strips may be found at the Nevada Historical Society (1650 North Virginia Street, Reno 89503]. The Museum of International Folk Art, a division of the Museum of New Mexico (Box 2087, Santa Fe 87503) has a few contemporary toys, and its curators are negotiating for the purchase of the Girard Foundation Collection of 75,000 folk toys. This collection is partially described in Alexander H. Girard's *El Encanto de un Pueblo. The Magic of a People: Folk Art and Toys from the Collection of the Girard Foundation.* The Newport Historical Society (82 Touro Street, Newport, Rhode Island 02840) has a limited number of toys, but a large collection of dolls and furnished dolls' houses. One of the best exhibits of dolls' houses may be found in the Museum of the City of New York (1220 Fifth Avenue, New York 10029). John Noble, curator, has published widely on dolls, including an article in *19th Century*, "Big Apple's Little Houses." In the same city, the New-York Historical Society (170 Central Park West at 77th Street, New York 10024) has an extensive collection of nineteenth-century carved animals by Wilhelm Schimmel; a peddler's cart dated 1884 with miniature pots and pans; a walking doll patented in 1862 and sold under the name "Autoperipatetikos"; circus toys, including ball-jointed wooden animals, from Albert Schoenhut's 1902 "Humpty Dumpty Circus"; and tin toys from George W. Brown of Forestville, Connecticut, made in 1856.

Old Salem (Drawer F, Salem Station, Winston-Salem, North Carolina 27108) has late eighteenth- and nineteenth-century toys, games, dolls, and books that are going to be displayed in a Boys' School Museum. Old Sturbridge Village (Sturbridge, Massachusetts 01566) has four or five hundred toys, games, dolls, and dolls' tea sets exhibited in its buildings. *Child Life in New England* by Elizabeth George Speare draws on this collection. The Perelman Antique Toy Museum (270 South Second Street, Philadelphia 19106) has 225 of the 243 known types of mechanical banks made between 1867 and 1902. This private museum also contains many cap pistols and automatona. The Seattle Historical Society (2161 East Hamlin Street, McCurdy Park, Seattle, Washington 98112) has a collection of over two thousand dolls, several hundred toys and games, and several hundred books on marionettes and puppetry. A large collection of marionettes, as well as doll furniture, building blocks, mechanical toys, models, banks, stuffed toys, and games, is exhibited in the Toy Shop at the Shelburne Museum (Shelburne, Vermont 05482). Shelburne also has several hundred dolls in its variety unit and a small, but good, research library.

Both the National Museum of History and Technology and the National Museum of Natural History of the Smithsonian Instiution (Washington, D.C. 20560) have collections relating to games and toys. In the former, the Division of Domestic Life of the Department of Cultural History has the Sears Roebuck Collection of cast-iron toys. Some interesting material on nineteenth-century games and toys may be gleaned from the seventeen hundred lithographs in the Harry T. Peters's "America on Stone" Collection. The Division of Extractive Industries of the Department of Industries administers the millions of items in the Warshaw Collection of Business Americana, some of which relate to games and toys. The ethnographic collections of the Natural History Museum contain games and toys from around the world. The museum's library has the Human Relations Area

File, which facilitates cross-cultural comparisons of games and toys. Genre paintings often contain data on games and toys, and the collections of the National Gallery of Art, the Hirshhorn Museum and Sculpture Garden, the National Portrait Gallery, the Freer Gallery of Art, and the National Collection of Fine Arts should all be consulted. The library of the National Collection of Fine Arts houses the Inventory of American Painting executed before 1914, a computerized index of 175,000 paintings in public and private collections throughout the country. There are several entries under the subject classification "Sports and Games." The staff of the children's area of the Festival of American Folklife, especially Kate Rinzler, have gathered considerable material on games and children's lore. Tapes, video-tapes, and publications are available from the Office of American and Folklife Studies. The two newest Smithsonian museums—the National Air and Space Museum and the Museum of African Art—can provide information on toys and games in their respective areas of specialization.

Finally, also in Washington, four other institutions have valuable information on games and toys. The Library of Congress (Washington, D.C. 20540), through its rare book collections, folk music division, and in its vast holdings of prints and photographs, contains an unequalled store of material on games and toys. Within the Prints and Photographs Division, for example, the Farm Security Administration and Office of War Information photographs of America in the 1930s and 1940s, the Frances Benjamin Johnston and Theodor Horydczak collections and the George Grantham Bain Collection are especially rich on play, games, and toys in the period 1890 to 1945. The Copyright Division of the Library of Congress should also be consulted, as should the Patent Office (2021 Jefferson Davis Highway, Arlington, Virginia 20231). Another rich source for visual material is the Audio-Visual Division of the National Archives and Records Service. Here, for example, you can find the Helen Levitt photographs of children's chalk drawings in the streets of New York in the late 1930s and thousands of feet of motion picture film of children playing in the years 1914 to 1934, taken by cameramen for the Ford Motor Company. For color photographs of play and games in the 1970s, the files of Documerica at the Environmental Protection Agency (401 M Street, SW, Washington, D.C. 20460) contain some good examples.

The large collection of games and toys owned by the Society for the Preservation of New England Antiquities (Harrison Gray Otis House, 141 Cambridge Street, Boston 02114) is in storage and is inaccessible to scholars. Fortunately, this is not the case with the superb collections of the Margaret Woodbury Strong Museum (700 Allen Creek Road, Rochester, New York 14618). Here one can see many of the twenty-five thousand dolls, six hundred dolls' houses, and thousands of models, miniatures, toys, and playing cards that the museum owns. A new building is planned for

1979, which will provide more exhibit space. A knowledgeable staff, including H. J. Swinney, director; Lawrence L. Belles, chief curator; Mr. and Mrs. Blair Whitton, specialist curators; and Barbara Jendrick, curator of paper dolls, is also available. The Washington Dolls' House and Toy Museum (5236 44th Street, NW, Washington, D.C. 20015) is a small private museum founded by Flora Gill Jacobs, author of several books on dolls' houses and furniture. Mrs. Jacobs has a small, but excellent, collection of Schoenhut animals, including a circus, a Theodore Roosevelt safari, a Bliss village, and some games. A recent acquisition—an elaborate dolls' house made in Puebla, Mexico, in the early twentieth century—provides an interesting contrast to the houses made north of the Rio Grande.

Perhaps the finest collection of paper dolls and toys in the United States can be found in the library of the Winterthur Museum (Winterthur, Delaware 19735). The Maxine Waldron Collection of Children's Books and Paper Toys contains hundreds of items, mostly American, but with some English and European paper dolls, games, peep shows, panoramas, paper soldiers, valentines, and Christmas cards and decorations. Among the rare items are: the "Protean Figure of Metamorphic Costumes" published by S. and J. Fuller in 1811; "Flora, the Game of Flowers"; "Newton's New Game of Virtue Rewarded and Vice Punished"; and the paper dolls, "Lady of New York," "The Virtuous Girl," "Jenny Lind," "Little Henry," and "Ellen, or the Naughty Girl Reclaimed." Some of the other games, dolls, and toys in the Winterthur's collections may be seen in the rooms of the museum. Last, but not least, the State Historical Society of Wisconsin (816 State Street, Madison 53706) has a large collection of children's toys and games dating from the 1850s to the present. An annual Christmas exhibit, emphasizing playthings of Wisconsin children, displays some of the society's material. Carol T. Larsen, registrar of the museum, has a special interest in the subject of games and toys.

HISTORY AND CRITICISM

Games and toys have drawn attention from four winds of writers—hobbyists and collectors, who are usually interested in a fairly narrow aspect of the subject; moralists, who select examples from children's play to make points about the corruption of society; psychologists, who use games and toys to study human development; and a handful of historians, who have attempted to make the subject a respectable part of social history. Among the first of the serious collectors was Louis Hertz, whose numerous books have been cited throughout this essay. One of his best contributions to the history of toys is *Messrs. Ives of Bridgeport*, a study of the Ives Manufacturing Company's sixty years of toymaking. Another pioneer collector who has written well-researched books on dolls' houses is Flora

Gill Jacobs. Her *A History of Dolls' Houses*, which first appeared in 1953, is a fascinating account of these objects from the sixteenth century to the present. Her introduction contains one of the few discussions of what seems to be a universal human attraction for smallness and miniaturization. Her illustrations and text reveal a number of interesting details about the relation of dolls' houses to the "larger" world, including the fact that a California bungalow doll's house appeared in 1920, a doll's swimming pool in 1928, and a Frank Lloyd Wright-style house in 1936. Wooden furniture was rapidly replaced by metal after 1922, when Tootsietoy began to produce doll furniture for the mass market, and metal was challenged by plastic after 1946. Mrs. Jacobs's *Dolls' Houses in America: Historic Preservation in Miniature* continues her studies and develops the thesis that many regional architectural styles survive in unaltered form in these "toys."

Toys in America by Inez and Marshall McClintock falls between a collector's reference work and a historian's interpretative survey. Although they suspected "that toys might give some insight into our entire society: that the amount of play, the number and nature of toys might reveal a great deal about any stage of our history," they stick to descriptive narrative history and fail to prove "that toys and games were indeed accurate mirrors of the adult world." The same may be said of Jac Remise and Jean Fondin's *The Golden Age of Toys*, which was first published in Switzerland in 1967. The beautiful photographs, many in color, more than compensate for the lack of interpretation in the text, however. Patrick Murray's *Toys*, Charles Best's *Cast Iron Toy Pistols, 1870-1940: A Collector's Guide*, Betty Cadbury's *Playthings Past*, and David Pressland's *The Art of the Tin Toy* are all good examples of the excellent work done by curators and collectors in the past ten years.

Ever since 1882 when Herbert Spencer proclaimed the "gospel of relaxation," moralists and social critics have used games and play to argue that society is in desperate need of reform. Thus, in 1928, Stuart Chase attacked a hedonistic and mass-minded America in his essay on "Play" in Charles Beard's *Whither Mankind*. Twenty years later, David Riesman reversed Chase and found evidence for the development of "autonomous" man in the sphere of games and play. In *The Lonely Crowd*, Riesman went so far as to warn that "a conspiracy of silence about leisure and play is its best protection." The 1950s was a decade of great debate among sociologists and social critics about the proper uses of leisure. In France, both Roland Barthes and Roger Caillois published on the meaning of toys and games. Barthes, in *Mythologies*, saw toys as microcosms of the materialism of the adult world, while Caillois took a more detached stance in *Les Jeux et Les Hommes*, which was published in English as *Man, Play, and Games*. Nevertheless, Caillois moralizes about the loss of courtesy in competitive games and the corruption of masks into uniforms in contemporary society. This kind of criticism continued in the 1970s in an interesting variety of forms. Stanley Aronowitz has written of "The Egalitarian Promise of Children's Games," and Frank and Theresa Caplan, owners of Creative Playthings from 1944 to 1966, have expounded on *The Power of Play*. The Caplans drew on an impressive range of authorities from Cicero to Jean Piaget, but often overstated their case and frequently expressed a regrettable ethnocentrism: "We believe the Mexican, Asiatic, and Indian child for whom there is no lively play during early childhood loses the ability to create imaginary situations. An examination of the play materials of these cultures shows them to be made of clay, papier-mâché, and flimsy wood, none of which lend themselves to active use. . . . Introduce the rubber or vinyl doll, building blocks, and other unbreakable toys, and we maintain that the innate playfulness of these children would quickly be given active support." Two years earlier, in 1971, Edward M. Swartz had attacked the toy industry for unsafe toys and deceptive advertising. *Toys That Don't Care* follows Ralph Nader and other consumer advocates in finding considerable hazards in the marketplace. The industry lashed back with a moralist of its own. Marvin Kaye, former editor of *Toys*, wrote *A Toy Is Born* as a partial refutation of Swartz. Most of Kaye's book consists of brief chapters on well-known manufacturers—Lionel, Parker Brothers, Lesney, and others. Most readers will be touched by nostalgia for their childhoods when they read about the invention of Silly Putty at General Electric in 1945, Wham-O's first Frisbee in 1956, and Hasbro's G.I. Joe of 1963, but few will be convinced by Kaye's defense of the toy industry since the Child Protection and Toy Safety Act of 1969.

The third group of game and toy scholars is the psychologists, Beginning with G. Stanley Hall's studies in the 1880s, an impressive body of literature has developed. These are usefully summarized in Susanna Miller's *The Psychology of Play*. Among the major theorists in child development, Erik Erikson is the most readable. His *Childhood and Society* has influenced research in half a dozen fields in the past thirty years. Erikson's insistence on the opportunity for children to develop their imaginations through play has done much to make the study of play respectable. Recently, he has summarized these beliefs in a new book, *Toys and Reasons*, which takes its title from a line by William Blake: "The child's toys and the old man's reasons are the fruits of the two seasons." Jean Piaget has gone further than Erikson in arguing that play is essential for the development of adult intelligence. Throughout his work, but especially in *Play, Dreams and Imitation in Childhood*, Piaget reduces play to a function of thought and limits the role of play in creativity and innovation. This role is restored in Jerome Singer's *The Child's World of Make-Believe: Experi-*

mental Studies of Imaginative Play. The importance of fantasy is recognized by Jerome S. Bruner in several important studies and by Catherine Garvey in her book, Play.

A few studies are difficult to categorize, but remain important landmarks in the study of play. Roger G. Barker and Herbert F. Wright's One Boy's Day: A Specific Record of Behavior is the minute-by-minute record of a seven-year-old midwestern boy on April 26, 1949. The description, gathered by observers, parents, and teachers, illustrates the difficulty of labeling any particular activity as "play." Six Cultures: Studies of Child Rearing, edited by Beatrice B. Whiting, contains data on the Nyansongo of Kenya, the Rajputs of India, the Taira of Okinawa, the Mixtecans of Mexico, the Tarong of the Philippines, and "the New Englanders of Orchard Town"; but all the ethnographies are disappointingly sketchy on play. A much better description of American children at play appears in Sue Parrott's "Games Children Play: Ethnography of a Second-Grade Recess." Mexican children's games are well covered by Cecilia Gil de Partearroyo's Links into Past: A Folkloric Study of Mexican Children Relative to Their Singing Games and by Michael Maccoby's "Games and Social Character in a Mexican Village." Herbert Berry III and John Roberts provide a link between psychological and anthropological theories in their "Infant Socialization and Games of Chance," while Clifford Geertz offers an interpretation of a whole culture through its games in "Deep Play: Notes on the Balinese Cockfight." Another recent attempt to synthesize several theories of play is Mihaly Csikszentmihalyi's Beyond Boredom and Anxiety: The Experience of Play in Work and Games. Although his work is confined to adult behavior, Csikszentmihalyi's idea that play is a state between boredom and anxiety has applications to children's activities as well.

A note should be added on the application of psychological theories by playground planners and landscape architects. Beginning with Marjorie Allen's Planning for Play in 1969, a large number of books and articles have argued the necessity of including children in the planning process and making basic materials such as water, dirt, and wood available in playgrounds. Although playgrounds are still seen as a place where children should learn, the arrangement of equipment and the supervision tends to be much less didactic than in the past. This trend may be followed in M. Paul Friedberg's Play and Interplay: A Manifesto for New Design in Urban Recreational Environment, Paul Hogan's Playgrounds for Free, Richard Dattner's Design for Play, and Robin Moore's "Anarchy Zone: Encounters in a Schoolyard."

Historians, too, may trace their interest in games and toys back to the nineteenth century. E. B. Tylor, the British anthropologist, published "The History of Games" in The Fortnightly Review in 1879, and Alice Morse

Earle anticipated the revival of interest in the seventeenth and eighteenth centuries in 1899, with her *Child Life in Colonial Days*. The rediscovery of play in the 1880s left little time for stocktaking, however, and it is not until the 1920s and 1930s that historical studies began to appear. Clarence Rainwater published his history of playground reform, *The Play Movement in the United States: A Study of Community Recreation*, in 1922. The unwanted free time of the unemployed in the Depression forced a reassessment of *Americans at Play: Recent Trends in Recreation and Leisure Time Activities* by Jessie Steiner in 1933. At the end of that decade, Foster Rhea Dulles completed *America Learns to Play*, which is chiefly concerned with adult play, but which still provides the only comprehensive history of games and sports in this country.

Although it was not published in English until after his death, *Homo Ludens: A Study of the Play Element in Culture* by Johan Huizinga, first appeared in 1938. *Homo Ludens* remains today the one great study of play. Part history, part anthropology, part philosophy, *Homo Ludens* is, as Robert Anchor has pointed out, "neither a history of play, nor a history of the idea of play, nor a study of play as one among many other human activities. Rather it is a morphology of play, a study of play as a structure that manifests itself in all spheres of human culture."[15] Huizinga's chapter titles— "The Play-Concept as Expressed in Language," "Play and Contest as Civilizing Functions," "Play and Law," "Play and War," "Playing and Knowing" —suggest that he, too, thought that play was didactic. But his definition of play as "a voluntary activity or occupation executed within certain fixed limits of time and place, according to rules freely accepted but absolutely binding, having its aim in itself and accompanied by a feeling of tension, joy and the consciousness that it is 'different' from 'ordinary life,'" obviates any specific goal in play. Writing at a time when Hitler's uniformed Nazis were staging their pageants of conquest, Huizinga was critical of the corruption of play he observed in their rituals, yet he was convinced that civilization arose in play. *Homo Ludens* remains a rich and subtle cultural history from which all students of games, toys, and play can profit.

Since 1960, historians of childhood and children's play have been influenced by Philippe Aries's *Centuries of Childhood*. Aries's chapter on the games and toys of the French court in the seventeenth and eighteenth centuries is interesting, but his thesis that a period of childhood did not exist at that time has limited value for American historians. There is good evidence that our colonial ancestors did recognize several stages of childhood and youth, as Ross Beales shows in his essay, "In Search of the Historical Child: Miniature Adulthood and Youth in Colonial New England." J. H. Plumb is working on the history of childhood in England, while the sociologists Elizabeth and John Child have explored "Children and Leisure" in contemporary Britain. In the United States, the major work on games and play has been done by Brian Sutton-Smith, now at the University of Pennsylvania. Many of his pioneering articles have been reprinted in his *The Folkgames of Children*. From the historical standpoint, special attention should be given the essay he coauthored with B. G. Rosenberg, "Sixty Years of Historical Change in the Game Preferences of American Children." Sutton-Smith is also editor of the *Newsletter* of the Association for the Anthropological Study of Play, an organization of scholars interested in all aspects of games and play.

Beginning in 1975, a series of articles began to place the history of games and play in the larger context of social history. Bernard Mergen's "The Discovery of Children's Play" and "Children's Playgrounds in the District of Columbia" are attempts to describe the changing attitudes toward play held by American adults in the period 1880 to the present. These essays also point out the difference between adult expectations and children's actual behavior. Dom Cavallo's "Social Reform and the Movement to Organize Children's Play During the Progressive Era" is similar in intent, though narrower in focus. Mark A. Kadzielski's " 'As a Flower Needs Sunshine': The Origins of Organized Children's Recreation in Philadelphia, 1886-1911" is a good contribution to the history of play as well as to local history. Richard Knapp's unpublished doctoral dissertation, "Play for America: The National Recreation Association, 1906-1950," is essential for understanding the institutional structure of the park and recreation movement. The forthcoming book on the Boy Scouts by Jay Mechling should provide further understanding of the manipulation of play. Autobiographies can supply much needed information on the play life of the past. *Dorothy's World: Childhood in Sabine Bottom 1902-1910* by Dorothy Howard is an excellent example of an autobiography that focuses specifically on play and children's activities. Finally, the work of Robert Snow and David Wright in attempting to link technological change and leisure has implications for the study of games and toys. Their "Coney Island: A Case Study in Popular Culture and Technical Change" is a model for future research.

For further comparisons with the history of games and toys in other countries, a half-dozen studies are available. Karl Ewald Fritzsch's *An Illustrated History of Toys* is especially good on German toy production. A *History of Toys* by Lady Antonia Fraser presents a popular survey. Closer to home, Musée de Quebec's *Le jouet dans l'univers de l'enfant, 1800-1925*, Robert Lionel Séguin's *Les jouets anciens du Quebec*, and Harry Symons's *Playthings of Yesterday: Harry Symons Introduces the Percy Band Collection* offer some basic information on the history of Canadian toys. Séguin's book suggests that toys in Quebec and the northeastern United States are basically similar, but that the Quebecois had some unusual folk toys such as the *pite* or *tapecul*—a narrow sled with a vertical post in the middle and a handle for sledding or skiing standing up. South of the border, *Los Juegos Infantiles en las Escuelas Rurales* by Ramón Garcia Ruiz is an older study that still has much merit, while Francisco Javier Hernández's *El Juguete Popular en México: estudio de interpretacion* is a scholarly monograph on toys from the pre-Hispanic period to the present.

ANTHOLOGIES

The anthologies by Elliott Avedon and Brian Sutton-Smith and by R. E. Herron and Sutton-Smith have already been mentioned as has Phillips Stevens's *Studies in the Anthropology of Play*, which is made up of papers presented at the second annual meeting of the Association for the Anthropological Study of Play. The proceedings of the first meeting of TAASP were published as *The Anthropological Study of Play: Problems and Prospects*, edited by David F. Lancy and B. Allan Tindall. The proceedings of the third meeting, edited by Michael Salter, is titled *Play: Anthropological Perspectives*. A fourth volume will be edited by Helen B. Schwartzman. A useful reprinting of early articles is *A Children's Games Anthology: Studies in Folklore and Anthropology*. For recent scholarship in psychology, see Jerome Bruner and associates, *Play—Its Role in Development and Evolution*. Curiously, Robert H. Bremner's three-volume anthology, *Children and Youth in America: A Documentary History*, has nothing on games and toys. Jerome Bruner's *Play—Its Role in Development and Education* contains a wide range of articles by psychologists, as does Sutton-Smith's *The Psychology of Play*, which is part of a twenty-one volume reprint series on play and games.

NOTES

1. Jac Remise, *The Golden Age of Toys* (Greenwich, Conn.: New York Graphic Society, 1967), p. 11.
2. Stephen Miller, "Ends, Means, and Galumphing: Some Leitmotifs of Play," *American Anthropologist*, 75 (February 1973), 97.
3. Peter Wagner, "Literary Evidence of Sport in Colonial New England: The American Puritan Jeremiad," *Stadion*, 2 (1976), 235.
4. Katharine McClinton, *Antiques of American Childhood* (New York: Bramhall House, 1970).
5. William Wells Newell, *Games and Songs of American Children* (New York: Harper & Brothers, 1883), p. 176.
6. Elizabeth George Speare, *Child Life in New England 1790-1840* (Sturbridge, Mass.: Old Sturbridge Booklet Series, 1961), p. 18.
7. Speare, p. 19
8. McClinton, p. 227.

9. Stewart Culin, "Street Games of Boys in Brooklyn, New York," *Journal of American Folklore*, 4 (July-September 1891), 234-35.

10. *Emergency Fleet News*, January 1, 1919, p. 9.

11. U.S. Department of Labor, Children's Bureau, *Facilities for Children's Play in the District of Columbia* (Washington, D.C.: Government Printing Office, 1917), p. 68.

12. *The Playground*, 6 (May 1912), 51.

13. George Johnson, *Education Through Recreation* (Cleveland: The Survey Committee of the Cleveland Foundation, 1916), p. 49.

14. Brian Sutton-Smith, "The Two Cultures of Games," in *The Folkgames of Children* (Austin, Tex.: Published for the American Folklore Society by the University of Texas, 1972), pp. 295-311.

15. Robert Anchor, "History and Play: Johan Huizinga and His Critics," *History and Theory*, 17 (February 1978), 77-78.

BIBLIOGRAPHY

BOOKS AND ARTICLES

Abrahams, Roger D. *Jump-Rope Rhymes: A Dictionary*. Austin: University of Texas Press, 1969.

Allen, Marjorie. *Planning for Play*. Cambridge: MIT Press, 1969.

Anchor, Robert. "History and Play: Johan Huizinga and His Critics." *History and Theory*, 17 (February 1978), 63-93.

Andrews, Peter. "Games People Played." *American Heritage*, 23 (June 1972), 64-79, 104-05.

Aries, Philippe. *Centuries of Childhood*. New York: Alfred A. Knopf, 1962.

Aronowitz, Stanley. "Together and Equal: The Egalitarian Promise of Children's Games." *Social Policies*, 4 (November/December 1973), 78-84.

Avedon, Elliott M., and Brian Sutton-Smith, eds. *The Study of Games*. New York: John Wiley, 1971.

Babcock, William Henry. "Games of Washington Children." *American Anthropologist*, 1 (July 1888), 243-84.

Barker, Roger G., and Herbert F. Wright. *One Boy's Day: A Specific Record of Behavior*. New York: Harper, 1951.

Barthes, Roland. *Mythologies*. New York: Hill and Wang, 1972.

Beales, Ross W. "In Search of the Historical Child: Miniature Adulthood and Youth in Colonial New England." *American Quarterly*, 27 (October 1975), 379-98.

Belch, Jean. *Contemporary Games*. 2 vols. Detroit: Gale Research, 1973.

Berry, Herbert III, and John Roberts. "Infant Socialization and Games of Chance." *Ethnology*, 11 (July 1972), 296-308.

Best, Charles W. *Cast Iron Toy Pistols, 1870-1940: A Collector's Guide*. Englewood, Colo.: Rocky Mountain Arms and Antiques, 1973.

Bremner, Robert H. et al., eds. *Children and Youth in America: A Documentary History*. 3 vols. Cambridge: Harvard University Press, 1970.

Brewster, Paul G. *Children's Games and Rhymes*. Chapel Hill: University of North Carolina Press, 1952.

————. *American Nonsinging Games*. Norman: University of Oklahoma Press, 1953.

Bruner, Jerome S., Alosin Jolly, and Kathy Sylva, eds. *Play—Its Role in Development and Evolution*. New York: Basic Books, 1976.

Burns, Thomas A. "*The Game of Life*: Idealism, Reality, and Fantasy in the Nineteenth- and Twentieth-Century Versions of a Milton Bradley Game." *The Canadian Review of American Studies*, 9 (Spring 1978), 50-83.

Cadbury, Betty. *Playthings Past*. Newton Abbot, England: David and Charles, 1976.

Caillois, Roger. *Man, Play, and Games*. London: Thames and Hudson, 1962.

Calvin, Jeannette M., comp. *International Trade in Toys*. Washington, D.C.: Government Printing Office, 1926.

Canary, Robert H. "Playing the Game of *Life*." *Journal of Popular Culture*, 1 (Spring 1968), 427-32.

Caplan, Frank, and Theresa Caplan. *The Power of Play*. Garden City, N.Y.: Anchor Press/Doubleday, 1973.

Cavallo, Dom. "Social Reform and the Movement to Organize Children's Play During the Progressive Era." *History of Childhood Quarterly*, 3 (Spring 1976), 509-22.

Champlin, John D., and Arthur E. Bostwick. *The Young Folks' Cyclopaedia of Games and Sports*. New York: H. Holt, 1890.

Chandler, Ceil. *Toys and Dolls Made in Occupied Japan*. Houston, Tex.: Chandler's Discriminating Junk, 1973.

Chase, Stuart. "Play." In *Whither Mankind*. Edited by Charles Beard. New York: Longmans Green, 1928.

Child, Elizabeth, and John Child. "Children and Leisure." In *Leisure and Society in Britain*. Edited by M. Smith, S. Parker, and C. Smith. London: Allen Lane, 1973, pp. 135-47.

A Children's Game Anthology: Studies in Folklore and Anthropology. New York: Arno Press, 1976.

Coleman, Dorothy S., Elizabeth A. Coleman, and Evelyn J. Coleman. *The Collector's Encyclopedia of Dolls*. New York: Crown, 1968.

Croswell, T. R. "Amusements of Worcester School Children." *Pedagogical Seminary*, 6 (September 1899), 314-71.

Csikszentmihalyi, Mihaly. *Beyond Boredom and Anxiety: The Experience of Play in Work and Games*. San Francisco: Jossey-Bass Publishers, 1975.

Csikszentmihalyi, Mihaly, and Stith Bennett. "An Exploratory Model of Play." *American Anthropologist*, 73 (1971), 45-58.

Culin, Stewart. *Games of North American Indians*. Twenty-fourth Annual Report to the Bureau of Ethnology. Washington, D.C.: Government Printing Office, 1907.

————. "Street Games of Boys in Brooklyn, New York." *Journal of American Folklore*, 4 (July-September 1891), 221-37.

Daiken, Leslie. *Children's Toys Throughout the Ages*. New York: Praeger, 1953.

————. *World of Toys: A Guide to the Principal Public and Private Collections in Great Britain.* Kent: Lambarde Press, 1963.

Dattner, Richard. *Design for Play.* Cambridge: MIT Press, 1974.

Douglas, Norman. *London Street Games.* London: St. Catherine Press, 1916.

Dulles, Foster Rhea. *America Learns to Play.* New York: Appleton-Century, 1940.

Earle, Alice Morse. *Child Life in Colonial Days.* New York: Macmillan, 1899.

Erikson, Erik. *Childhood and Society.* New York: Norton, 1950.

————. *Toys and Reasons.* New York: Norton, 1977.

Ferretti, Fred. *The Great American Marble Book.* New York: Workman, 1973.

————. *The Great American Book of Sidewalk, Stoop, Dirt, Curb, and Alley Games.* New York: Workman, 1975.

Fraser, Lady Antonia. *A History of Toys.* New York: Spring Books, 1972.

Friedberg, M. Paul. *Play and Interplay: A Manifesto for New Design in Urban Recreational Environment.* New York: Macmillan, 1970.

Fritzsch, Karl Ewald. *An Illustrated History of Toys.* Leipzig: Edition Leipzig, 1968.

Garvey, Catherine. *Play.* Cambridge: Harvard University Press, 1977.

Geertz, Clifford. "Deep Play: Notes on the Balinese Cockfight." *Daedalus,* 101 (Winter 1972), 1-37.

Gibson, Cecil. *A History of British Dinky Toys: Model Car and Vehicle Issues, 1934-1964.* Hemel Hempstead: Model Aeronautical Press, 1966.

Gil de Partearroyo, Cecilia. *Links into Past: A Folkloric Study of Mexican Children Relative to Their Singing Games.* Mexico: Editorial Jus, 1953.

Girard, Alexander H. *El Encanto de un pueblo. The Magic of a People: Folk Art and Toys from the Collection of the Girard Foundation.* New York: Viking, 1968.

Gomme, Alice. *The Traditional Games of England, Scotland and Ireland.* 2 vols. London: D. Nutt, 1894-1898.

Grinham, Ann E. *Japanese Games and Toys.* Tokyo: Hitachi, 1973.

Hall, G. Stanley. "The Contents of Children's Minds." *Princeton Review,* 11 (May 1883), 249-72.

Hannas, Linda. *The English Jigsaw Puzzle, 1760-1890, with a Descriptive Check-list of Puzzles in the Museums of Great Britain and the Author's Collection.* London: Wayland, 1972.

Harman, Kenny. *Comic Strip Toys.* Des Moines, Iowa: Wallace-Homestead Books, 1975.

Hawes, Bess Lomax, and Bessie Jones. *Step It Down: Games, Plays, Songs and Stories from the Afro-American Heritage.* New York: Harper & Row, 1972.

Hernández, Francisco Javier. *El Juguete Popular en México: estudio de interpretacion.* Mexico: Ediciones Mexicanas, 1950.

Herron, R. E., and Brian Sutton-Smith, eds. *Child's Play.* New York: John Wiley, 1971.

Hertz, Louis. *The Handbook of Old American Toys.* Wethersfield, Conn.: Mark Haber, 1947.

————. *Messrs. Ives of Bridgeport.* Wethersfield, Conn.: Mark Haber, 1950.

————. *The Toy Collector.* New York: Funk and Wagnalls, 1969.

Hogan, Paul. *Playgrounds for Free.* Cambridge: MIT Press, 1974.

Howard, Dorothy. *Dorothy's World: Childhood in Sabine Bottom 1902-1910.* New York: Prentice-Hall, 1977.

Hughes, James M. "A Tale of Two Games: An Image of the City." *Journal of Popular Culture,* 6 (Fall 1972), 357-62.

Huizinga, Johan. *Homo Ludens: A Study of the Play Element in Culture.* London: Routledge and Kegan Paul, 1949.

Jacobs, Flora Gill. *A History of Dolls' Houses.* New York: Scribner's, 1953, 1964.

————. *Dolls' Houses in America: Historic Preservation in Miniature.* New York: Scribner's, 1974.

Jean-Leo. *Jouets, jeux, livres d'enfant: repertoire bibliographique d'ouvrages utiles aux collectionneurs et aux chercheurs, augmente de nombreux articles inedits.* Bruxelles: Le Grenier du collecionneur, 1974.

Kadzielski, Mark A. " 'As a Flower Needs Sunshine': The Origins of Organized Children's Recreation in Philadelphia, 1886-1911." *The Journal of Sport History,* 4 (Summer 1977), 169-88.

Kaye, Marvin. *A Toy Is Born.* New York: Stein and Day, 1973.

Kirshenblatt-Gimblett, Barbara, ed. *Speech Play.* Philadelphia: University of Pennsylvania Press, 1976.

Knapp, Mary, and Herbert Knapp. *One Potato, Two Potato. . .The Secret Education of American Children.* New York: Norton, 1976.

Knapp, Richard. "Play for America: The National Recreation Association, 1906-1950." Ph.D. diss., Duke University, 1971.

Lancy, David F., and B. Allan Tindall, eds. *The Anthropological Study of Play: Problems and Prospects.* Cornwall, N.Y.: Leisure Press, 1976.

Louisiana State Museum, New Orleans. *Playthings of the Past: 19th and 20th Century Toys from the Collection of the Louisiana State Museum.* New Orleans: Louisiana State Museum, 1969.

McClintock, Inez, and Marshall McClintock. *Toys in America.* Washington, D.C.: Public Affairs Press, 1961.

McClinton, Katharine. *Antiques of American Childhood.* New York: Bramhall House, 1970.

McGhee, Zach. "A Study of the Play Life of Some South Carolina Children." *Pedagogical Seminary,* 7 (December 1900), 459-78.

Maccoby, Michael et al. "Games and Social Character in a Mexican Village." *Psychiatry,* 2 (May 1964), 150-62.

Mechling, Jay. "Sacred and Profane Play in the Boy Scouts of America." Paper for the Association for the Anthropological Study of Play, 4th Annual Meeting, March 23, 1978, South Bend, Ind.

Mergen, Bernard. "The Discovery of Children's Play." *American Quarterly,* 27 (October 1975), 399-420.

————. "Children's Playgrounds in the District of Columbia, 1902-1942." In *Records of the Columbia Historical Society of Washington, D.C., 1975-1976.* Charlottesville, Va.: University Press of Virginia, in press.

Merrill, Madeline O., and Richard Merrill. *Dolls and Toys at the Essex Institute.* Salem, Mass.: Essex Institute, 1976.

Milberg, Alan. *Street Games.* New York: McGraw-Hill, 1976.

Miller, Stephen. "Ends, Means, and Galumphing: Some Leitmotifs of Play." *American Anthropologist*, 75 (February 1973), 87-98.

Miller, Susanna. *The Psychology of Play*. New York: Pelican Books, 1968.

Moore, Robin. "Anarchy Zone: Encounters in a Schoolyard." *Landscape Architecture*, 69 (October 1974), 364-71.

Murray, Patrick. *Toys*. New York: Dutton, 1968.

Musée de Quebec. *Le jouet dans l'univers de l'enfant, 1800-1925*. Quebec: Musée de Quebec, 1977.

Newell, William Wells. *Games and Songs of American Children*. New York: Harper & Brothers, 1883.

Noble, John. "Big Apple's Little Houses." *19th Century*, 4 (Spring 1978), 98-101.

Opie, Iona, and Peter Opie. *The Lore and Language of School Children*. Oxford: Clarendon Press, 1960.

————. *Children's Games in Street and Playground*. Oxford: Clarendon Press, 1969.

Page, Hilary Fisher. *Toys in Wartime*. London: G. Allen & Unwin, 1942.

Parrott, Sue. "Games Children Play: Ethnography of a Second-Grade Recess." In *The Cultural Experience: Ethnography in Complex Society*. Edited by James Spradley and David McCurdy. Chicago: Science Research Associates, 1976, pp. 207-19.

Piaget, Jean. *Play, Dreams and Imitation in Childhood*. New York: Norton, 1962.

Plumb, J. H. "The New World of Children in Eighteenth-Century England." *Past and Present*, 67 (May 1975), 64-93.

Pressland, David. *The Art of the Tin Toy*. New York: Crown, 1976.

Rainwater, Clarence. *The Play Movement in the United States: A Study of Community Recreation*. Chicago: University of Chicago Press, 1922.

Remise, Jac, and Jean Fondin. *The Golden Age of Toys*. Greenwich, Conn.: New York Graphic Society, 1967.

Renson, Roland, and B. Van Reusel. "Toy Bibliography." In The Association for the Anthropological Study of Play *Newsletter*, 4 (Spring 1978), 17-18.

Riesman, David. *The Lonely Crowd*. New Haven: Yale University Press, 1950.

Roberts, J. M., M. J. Arth, and R. R. Bush. "Games in Culture." *American Anthropologist*, 61 (1959), 597-605.

Roberts, J. M., and Brian Sutton-Smith. "Child Training and Game Involvement." *Ethnology*, 1 (1962), 166-85.

Rosenberg, B. G., and Brian Sutton-Smith. "Sixty Years of Historical Change in the Game Preferences of American Children." *Journal of American Folklore*, 74 (January-March 1961), 17-46.

Ruiz, Ramón Garcia. *Los Juegos Infantiles en las Escuelas Rurales*. Mexico City: El Nacional, 1938.

Salter, Michael. *Play: Anthropological Perspectives*. West Point, N.Y.: Association for the Anthropological Study of Play, 1978.

Scheffler, Lilian. "The Study of Traditional Games in Mexico: Bibliographical Analysis and Current Research." In *The Anthropological Study of Play:*

Problems and Prospects. Edited by David Lancy and B. Allan Tindall. Cornwall, N.Y.: Leisure Press, 1976, pp. 58-66.

Schroeder, Joseph J., Jr., ed. *The Wonderful World of Toys, Games and Dolls.* Northfield, Ill.: Digest Books, 1971.

Schutrumpf, E. D. *World Trade in Toys.* Washington, D.C.: Government Printing Office, 1939.

Schwartzman, Helen B. "Research on Children's Play: An Overview and Predictions." In *Studies in the Anthropology of Play: Papers in Memory of B. Allan Tindall.* Edited by Phillips Stevens, Jr. West Point, N.Y.: Leisure Press, 1977, pp. 105-15.

Séguin, Robert-Lionel. *Les jouets anciens du Quebec.* Montreal: Lemeac, 1969.

Seventh Annual Report of the Department of Playgrounds. Washington, D.C.: Government Printing Office, 1918.

Singer, Jerome L. *The Child's World of Make-Believe: Experimental Studies of Imaginative Play.* New York: Academic Press, 1973.

Snow, Robert E., and David E. Wright. "Coney Island: A Case Study in Popular Culture and Technical Change." *Journal of Popular Culture,* 9 (Spring 1976), 960-75.

Speare, Elizabeth George. *Child Life in New England 1790-1840.* Sturbridge Village: Old Sturbridge Village Booklet Series, 1961.

Sporting Goods and Games 1886: Peck & Snyder. Princeton, N.J.: The Pyne Press, 1971.

Steiner, Jesse Frederick. *Americans at Play: Recent Trends in Recreation and Leisure Time Activities.* New York: McGraw-Hill, 1933.

Stevens, Phillips, Jr., ed. *Studies in the Anthropology of Play: Papers in Memory of B. Allan Tindall.* West Point, N.Y.: Leisure Press, 1977.

Sutton-Smith, Brian. *The Games of New Zealand Children.* Berkeley: University of California Press, 1959.

————. *The Folkgames of Children.* Austin: Published for the American Folklore Society by the University of Texas, 1972.

————. *A History of the Playground: A New Zealand Case Study, 1840-1950.* Wellington: The New Zealand Council of Educational Research, in press.

Swartz, Edward M. *Toys That Don't Care.* Boston: Gambit, 1971.

Symons, Harry. *Playthings of Yesterday: Harry Symons Introduces the Percy Band Collection.* Toronto: Ryerson Press, 1963.

Tylor, E. B. "The History of Games." *The Fortnightly Review,* 31 (n.s. 25), (1879), 735-47.

U.S. Bureau of Census. *Census of Manufacturers: 1927. Carriages and sleds, children's toys, games, and playground equipment, sporting and athletic goods, not including firearms or ammunition.* Washington, D.C.: Government Printing Office, 1929.

————. *Census of Manufacturers: 1931.* Washington, D.C.: Government Printing Office, 1931.

————. *16th Census of the United States 1940. Manufacturers: 1939. Toys and Sporting and Athletic Goods.* Washington, D.C.: Government Printing Office, 1941.

Wagner, Peter. "Literary Evidence of Sport in Colonial New England: The American Puritan Jeremiad." *Stadion* (1976), 233-49.
White, Gwen. *Toys and Dolls: Marks and Labels.* Newton, Mass.: C. T. Branford, 1975.
Whiting, Beatrice B., ed. *Six Cultures: Studies of Child Rearing.* New York: John Wiley, 1963.
Willson's Canadian Toy, Notion and Stationery Directory. Toronto: Willson's Directories, 1956.
Yoffie, Lea Rachel Clara. "Three Generations of Children's Singing Games in St. Louis." *Journal of American Folklore,* 60 (January-March 1947), 1-151.

PERIODICALS

Antique Toy World. Chicago.
The Association for the Anthropological Study of Play: *Newsletter.* Philadelphia, Penn., 1974-.
Collectibles Monthly. York, Penn., 1977-.
The Doll Reader. Riverdale, Md., 1973-.
Miniature Collector. New York.
The Playground. New York, 1907-1915; Cooperstown, N.Y., 1916-1923; Greenwich, Conn., 1923-1924; New York, 1924-1929; *Playground and Recreation,* New York, 1929-1930; *Recreation,* New York, 1931-1965; *Parks and Recreation,* Arlington, Va., 1966-.
Playthings. New York, 1903-.
Das Spielzeug. Bamberg, Germany, 1909-.
Toy and Hobby World. New York, 1963-.
Toy Manufacturer. Atlanta, Ga., 1957-.
Toy Retailer (title varies). Atlanta, Ga., 1953-1962.
The Toy Trader and Exporter. London, England, 1908-.
Toy Trader Year Book. Watford, England, 1969-.
Toy Trains. Silver Spring, Md., 1951-.
Toy Wholesaler. Atlanta, Ga., 1959-.
Toy World. San Francisco, Calif., 1927-1936.
Toys. New York, 1972-.
Toys and Games. Montreal, Canada, 1973-.
Toys and Novelties. Chicago, 1909-1972.
Toys and Playthings. Montreal, Canada, 1957-.
Toys International. London, England, 1962-.

CHAPTER 8. Historical Fiction

R. Gordon Kelly

Any consideration of historical fiction begins with the troublesome matter of definition. What is an historical novel? Sir Walter Scott, whose Waverly novels effectively established a model adhered to by writers for nearly a century afterward, was less dogmatic on the subject than some of his successors. In giving to *Waverly* the subtitle "It Is Sixty Years Past," he implied a setting at least two generations in the past; while in his preface to *Ivanhoe*, he offered few prescriptions, concentrating rather on defending his practice against the anticipated charge of "polluting the well of history with modern inventions." Ernest Leisy, author of the principal study of American historical fiction, adopted the broadest of definitions— "A historical novel is a novel the action of which is laid in an earlier time" —and reduced Scott's half century in the past to a generation, "so rapid are changes [in the United States]." And Avrom Fleishman, with Georg Lukács, the most theoretically oriented commentator on the historical novel, accepts essentially the same definition, adding only the specification that "real" historical persons be present in the story: "When life is seen in the context of history, we have a novel; when the novel's characters live in the same world with historical persons, we have a historical novel."[1] For the purposes of this essay, however, the broader definition is preferable in order to avoid excluding those costume historical romances that might not qualify under Fleishman's slightly more restrictive definition. Because it is with the *popular* historical novel that we shall be concerned in this essay, little attention is given to those classic works of American fiction—*The Scarlet Letter* or *The Red Badge of Courage*, for example—which a broad definition of historical fiction would otherwise warrant including.

HISTORIC OUTLINE

The historical novel has been a staple of American publishing since the first quarter of the nineteenth century, when, following the War of 1812, the call for a national literature and an American Scott was as explicit as Rufus Choate's oration "The Importance of Illustrating New England History by a Series of Romances like the Waverly Novels" (1810). The form was especially popular with readers in the 1820s and 1830s, again at the turn of the century, and in the 1930s and 1940s. With *The Spy* (1821), James Fenimore Cooper successfully demonstrated that Scott's methods could be applied to American materials. Dramatizing the fratricidal nature of the Revolution in his depiction of the Warren family's divided loyalties, Cooper laid the foundations for an international reputation and encouraged a host of imitators. So well-received were *The Spy* and *The Pilot* (1823) that Cooper projected a series of thirteen historical novels, one for each of the Revolutionary colonies, although he completed only one, *Lionel Lincoln* (1825). His subsequent historical fiction included *The Wept of Wishton-wish* (1829), set during King Philip's War; *Wyandotte* (1843), set in western New York State during the Revolution; and *The Oak Openings* (1848), set in frontier Michigan during the War of 1812. He also wrote three novels with European settings in which he deliberately set out to show the differences between his and Scott's perceptions of the same things: eighteenth-century Venice (*The Bravo*, 1831); Germany on the eve of the Reformation (*The Heidenmauer*, 1832); and Switzerland in the early eighteenth century (*The Headsman*, 1883). Cooper's Leatherstocking novels are too well known to require description.

By the mid-1820s, "with Waverly galloping over hill and dale; the 'Spy' lurking in every closet; the mind everywhere supplied with 'Pioneers' on the land and soon to be with 'Pilots' on the deep," American writers were rushing to imitate Cooper.[2] Faced with the number of historical novels coming to market as early as 1824, a critic for *The North American Review* began a review of *The Wilderness, or Braddock's Time* on a note of asperity: "It has been a question seriously agitated among our cisatlantic literati, even at so late a period as since the publication of this journal [begun in 1815] whether America did or did not afford sufficient materials for a new and peculiar historical romance; yet now, so prolific are we in this species of production that the reader who keeps pace with the outpourings of the press . . . must have some industry and a great deal of patriotism."[3] Among the most successful with the reading public were southern romancers like William H. Caruthers in *The Cavaliers of Virginia* (1834) and John Pendleton Kennedy, who found in the Virginia planter an American analogue to Scott's English noble or Scottish laird in *Swallow Barn* (1832) and *Horse Shoe Robinson* (1835). The most prolific of southern historical novelists was William Gilmore Simms, who drew judiciously on Scott and Cooper for structural elements and on his own early experience, as well as on research, for convincing detail in describing early colonial South Carolina in *The Yemassee* (1835), for example, a novel of Indian warfare that still repays reading for its treatment of the Yemassee Indians and their allies. In Simms's wake, John Esten Cooke continued to romanticize southern life until well past mid-century, by which time the historical romance, increasingly out of fashion because of the rise of literary realism, became ever more hackneyed and conventionalized.

The three most popular historical novels published before the Civil War are instructive of the principal ways in which American writers made use of the past. Two of the novels exploited the nation's constitutive conflicts—warfare with the Indian and separation from the British. Robert Montgomery Bird dramatized the former in his bloody, widely read account of frontier revenge, *Nick of the Woods* (1837), while Judge Daniel P. Thompson's *The Green Mountain Boys* (1839) celebrated his forebears' struggle to defend their homes, first against land jobbers and then against Burgoyne and his soldiers. The third best-selling historical romance of the antebellum period, Joseph Holt Ingraham's *The Prince of the House of David* (1855), depicted the chief episodes in the life of Jesus as seen by a young Jewess and demonstrated the profits to be made from tapping the populace's religious idealism, as romances of the Revolution had already amply demonstrated with regard to nationalism and patriotism.

The mid-1850s to the mid-1880s was a period of lessened popularity for historical fiction as a genre. The historical romance continued to attract readers, but the decades were without conspicuous best-selling historical novels. A number of works from the 1870s and 1880s were informed by realism and the increasing preoccupation with local color: for example, Edward Eggleston's *The Circuit Rider* (1874); Mary Hartwell Catherwood's novels of France's New World colonies such as *The Romance of Dollard* (1888); George Washington Cable's *Old Creole Days* (1879) and *The Grandissimes* (1880); and Harold Frederic's *In the Valley* (1890), a tale of the Mohawk Valley in the French and Indian War. By the mid-1890s, however, the historical romance was once more the reigning form of popular fiction. Frank Luther Mott, the principal historian of best sellers, claims that fully half of the best-selling fiction of the period 1894-1902 consisted of historical romances. The revival of the genre's popularity began quietly enough in 1880 with the publication of a religious novel set in Rome at the time of Christ, which was dismissed initially by reviewers as anachronistic. By 1896, however, a nationwide survey revealed that *Ben-Hur: A Tale of the Christ*, by the Civil War general Lew Wallace, was circulated more than any other book in eight out of ten libraries. Widely imitated (for example, Marie Corelli's *Barrabbas*, 1894; and Florence Kingsley's *Titus, A Comrade of the Cross*, 1894), *Ben-Hur* eventually appeared in editions that were authorized by the Holy See as well as retailed by Sears Roebuck—an achievement probably without precedent in American publishing. Combining the historical values of Scott and the moral values of the genteel tradition, it has been credited with battering down the last vestiges of prejudice against fiction.[4] With this last resistance overcome, with Stevenson and Kipling reviving the romance in England, and with patriotism in this country aroused by our adventuring in Cuba and the Philippines, the historical romance flourished and dominated popular fiction until the 1920s.

The stream of historical fiction flowed in several channels at the turn of the century. The commercial success of Anthony Hope Hawkins's *The Prisoner of Zenda* (1894), set in the mythical Balkan kingdom of Ruritania, established a vogue for costume romance that lasted a decade and encouraged a number of American imitators, among the more successful of whom were Richard Harding Davis in *The Princess Aline* (1899) and Harold MacGrath in *Arms and the Woman* (1899) and *The Puppet Crown* (1901). However, the Ruritanian formula was most successfully exploited by George Barr McCutcheon, an obscure Indiana journalist, in *Graustark* (1901), a tale that combined love and adventure with the unabashed celebration of the American virtues of its clean-cut hero. The inordinate popularity of the pseudohistorical romance waned as sales of *Graustark* tailed off—McCutcheon's sequel *Beverly of Graustark* (1904) failed to surpass *Graustark*'s sales. The publication in 1907 of George Ade's parody of the Ruritanian romance, *The Slim Princess*, put an end to the popularity of that formula. In the same year, however, the publication of Elinor Glyn's *Three Weeks* presaged the form's survival in the "bosom and bravado" historical novels of the 1930s, by adding sex—three weeks of lovemaking in a Graustarkian setting—to the Hope-McCutcheon formula.

Romances with historical European settings, as opposed to the misty midregions of Ruritania, were also popular with American readers at the turn of the century. F. Marion Crawford wrote more than forty novels with European settings, for example, *Via Crucis* (1898) and *In the Palace of the King* (1900); S. Weir Mitchell's *The Adventures of Francois* (1898) was set during the French Revolution; Robert Chambers's *Ashes of Empire* (1898) was based on the Franco-Prussian War; and Charles Major's *When Knighthood Was in Flower* (1898) told in archaic language of Mary Tudor's love for a man who was her social inferior. All were best sellers and were more credible historical fiction than the Ruritanian romances.

American settings predominated, however, and among the writers who both rode the crest of the historical romance's popularity and distinguished themselves somewhat from the mass of journeymen writers on the basis of their narrative skill and historical knowledge were S. Weir Mitchell, Paul Leicester Ford, Winston Churchill, Mary Johnston, and Maurice Thompson, author of the very popular tale of the Revolution in the Old Northwest, *Alice of Old Vincennes* (1900). Mitchell's revolutionary war tale of a free or fighting Quaker, *Hugh Wynne* (1898), was not only a commercial success, but also an influential model for writers seeking psychological realism. Paul Leicester Ford brought the knowledge and research skills of a trained historian to his writing of *Janice Meridith* (1899), a tale of the Revolution set in New Jersey.

Winston Churchill won acclaim for three novels especially: *Richard Carvel* (1899), a story of the Revolution, in which the Annapolis-trained Churchill presented a virtuoso description of the battle between John Paul Jones's *Bonhomme Richard* and the British man-of-war *Serapis*; *The Crisis* (1901), in which Churchill portrayed the bitter division of feeling in Missouri, particularly in St. Louis, before and during the Civil War; and *The Crossing* (1904), a story of George Rogers Clark's campaign in the Northwest Territory during the Revolution.

Mary Johnston, the daughter of a Confederate officer, wrote more than twenty historical novels, mostly set in the South during the Revolution or the Civil War. Beginning her career with *The Prisoners of Hope* (1898), she hit her stride in *To Have and to Hold*, a best seller in 1900. In *The Long Roll* (1911) and in *Cease Firing* (1912), she traced the course of the Civil War with meticulously researched detail and evident Southern sympathies.

So great was the popularity of historical fiction that a number of writers, whose earlier works were in a different vein, temporarily joined the ranks of historical novelists. Mary E. Wilkins Freeman's *The Heart's Highway* appeared in 1900, the year that saw the publication, too, of Edward Bellamy's *The Duke of Stockbridge*, a story of Shays's Rebellion that had appeared as a magazine serial in 1879. The following year saw the publication of Sarah Orne Jewett's *The Tory Lover*. Frank Stockton's *Kate Bonnet* was published in 1902.

By 1905, the extraordinary popular appeal of the historical novel was waning and did not really revive until the 1930s, when enthusiasm for Hervey Allen's sprawling tale of the Napoleonic era, *Anthony Adverse*

(1933), proved to be a prelude to the unprecedented popularity of Margaret Mitchell's *Gone with the Wind* (1936). Nevertheless, interest in the historical novel had increased in the wake of World War I, and the 1920s saw the publication of a number of notable historical novels: James Boyd's *Drums* (1925) and *Marching On* (1928), which dealt with the Revolution and Civil War respectively and were informed by a soldier's knowledge of military tactics; Walter D. Edmond's *Rome Haul* (1929), a painstakingly accurate portrayal of life along the Erie Canal in its heyday; and Edna Ferber's *Cimarron* (1930). The Revolution and the Civil War, pioneer life, and the opening of the West would continue to furnish historical novelists with their staple subjects.

A new note in the historical fiction of the 1930s was the blend of scrupulous historical research and unconventional interpretation of men and events, exemplified in the work of Kenneth Roberts, who produced a half-dozen well-crafted, exciting novels during the decade. In *Arundel* (1930), Roberts's hero is none other than tradition's archtraitor Benedict Arnold; and in *Oliver Wiswell* (1940), Roberts presented the Revolution from the loyalist point of view. Even more revisionist in orientation was the work of Howard Fast, whose *The Last Frontier* (1941) was an indictment of the Indian Wars of the 1870s, and whose *The American* presented a defense of John Peter Altgeld, the Illinois governor maligned for his pardon of the convicted Haymarket anarchists. Fast's special interest, however, was the Revolution, which he explored in five novels: *Two Valleys* (1933), *Conceived in Liberty* (1939), *The Unvanquished* (1942), *Citizen Tom Paine* (1943), and *The Proud and the Free* (1950).

Fiction of the flashing rapier and heaving bosom school also enjoyed a considerable measure of popularity during the 1940s, paced by such commercial successes as Kathleen Winsor's *Forever Amber* (1944), a lineal descendant of Elinor Glyn's pioneering *Three Weeks*; by Thomas Costain's costume pieces such as *The Black Rose* (1945) and *The Silver Chalice* (1952); and by the indefatigable Frank Yerby, whose *The Foxes of Harrow* (1946) was followed by twenty-two more novels, which have sold some twenty million copies to date.

Although the popularity of *Gone with the Wind* has not been matched by any subsequent historical novel, that fact should not obscure the considerable popularity of the form down to the present day. According to Russel B. Nye, at least one historical novel has reached the best-seller lists every year since 1931, and he estimates that 10 percent of all books published in paperback today may be considered historical fiction.[5] The extraordinary popularity of John Jakes's multivolume saga of an American family, beginning with *The Bastard* (1976), offers convincing proof that *mutatis mutandis* the spirit of nationalism that Cooper and his contemporaries so successfully exploited is alive and well.

REFERENCE WORKS

BIBLIOGRAPHIES AND GUIDES

Arguably the most useful reference work for studying the historical novel in the United States would be a comprehensive list based on a clearly formulated concept of historical fiction, organized chronologically by date of publication, and supplemented by both an author-title index and a well-constructed subject index. However, no such comprehensive bibliography or checklist of historical fiction by American authors is currently available. *American Historical Fiction* by A. T. Dickinson, Jr., now in its third edition, lists and briefly annotates over twenty-four hundred titles, but it includes only historical novels set in the United States and published since 1917. Agreeing with Ernest Leisy that "the historical novel is one which the action is laid in some identifiable past time," Dickinson organizes his list chronologically (for example, colonial America to 1775) and geographically (for example, the Middle West, 1783-1893). An extensive subject index as well as an author-title index makes *American Historical Fiction* a useful reference guide within the limitations noted earlier. Dickinson's work is best supplemented by reference to Leisy's standard study discussed below, *The American Historical Novel*, to which is appended a selective list of historical novels not treated in his text, and by reference to Otis Coan and Richard Lillard's *America in Fiction*, now in its fifth edition, an annotated list, primarily of novels, organized under regional and topical headings: the frontier, farm and village, politics, and so on. Like many other compilers, Coan and Lillard invoke minimum standards of literary excellence and so exclude popular but "unenduring" writers (F. Marion Crawford, Frank Yerby, and others) who are, of course, of particular interest to cultural historians and students of popular culture.

A Guide to Historical Fiction, in its tenth edition, compiled now by Leonard B. Irwin following the death of its originator, Hannah Logasa, has the virtue of including historical novels set abroad, but the list is designed primarily to identify relatively "good" books, published in the main since 1940, "for the use of schools, libraries, and the general reader." *World Historical Fiction Guide* by Daniel D. McGarry and Sarah Harriman White is a selective guide to historical novels by American and European authors published before 1900. It is organized broadly by period and geographical area, with alphabetical listing by author within each subdivision. Inclusion in the *Guide* is based on literary criteria that discriminate against popular fiction generally. A disappointing effort is Jack Warner Van Derhoof's *A Bibliography of Novels Related to American Frontier and Colonial History*, which is an alphabetical listing by author, with cursory annotations, of over sixty-four hundred titles. Van Derhoof's confused discussion of his principles of selection does not inspire confidence in his list: "In many instances inclusion or exclusion of a title depended on the moment of decision. A title might be excluded on first notice then inserted or included than [*sic*] removed. This does not obviate personal error and ignorance." The absence of a subject index greatly reduces the usefulness of Van Derhoof's labors.

Brief but helpful checklists of historical fiction can be found in Howard Mumford Jones and Richard M. Ludwig's well-known *Guide to American Literature and Its Backgrounds Since 1890* and in the original edition of the *Harvard Guide to American History* by Oscar Handlin and others, which also includes a compressed but thoughtful discussion on the scholarly uses of historical fiction. Older bibliographies that may still be profitably consulted on occasion are: Jonathan Nield's *A Guide to the Best Historical Novels and Tales*, 5th edition, which is heavily weighted toward British historical fiction but which includes the most extensive bibliography in print of commentary on historical fiction for the period 1890-1929; Reverend James R. Kaye's *Historical Fiction Chronologically and Historically Related*; Ernest A. Baker's *A Guide to Historical Fiction*, which like Nield's is heavily British but which lists some juvenile historical fiction that more recent compilers ignore; and William M. Griswold's *A Descriptive List of Novels and Tales Dealing with the History of North America* (1895).

Specialized bibliographies of historical fiction include: the list of over five hundred Civil War novels published before 1950 appended to Robert Lively's excellent study, *Fiction Fights the Civil War*; Rebecca W. Smith's "Catalogue of the Chief Novels and Short Stories . . . Dealing with the Civil War and Its Effects, 1861-1899"; H. U. Ribalow's selective bibliography "Historical Fiction on Jewish Themes"; and checklists of writings by and about Kenneth Roberts by George Albert and Ruth Stemple.

RESEARCH COLLECTIONS

Despite the popularity of historical fiction and its long history as a staple of the American publishing industry, libraries appear to have made little effort to establish extensive, broadly based research collections of historical novels. In addition, few private collectors appear to have interested themselves in the form, in contrast to the intense interest shown in, and the significance of private collections of, such other popular forms as the detective novel, the comic book, and literature for children. The Wilmer Collection of Civil War novels at the University of North Carolina, the basis for Lively's *Fiction Fights the Civil War*, testifies to the idiosyncratic enthusiasm of one collector, Richard H. Wilmer, Jr. Consisting of over five hundred titles when it was given to the library in 1946, the Wilmer Collection has been systematically augmented over the years. A more broadly based collection, emphasizing American historical fiction, is the University of Pittsburgh's Hervey Allen Collection, numbering some two thousand volumes. A number of more specialized collections devoted to particular authors are relevant to the study of popular historical fiction. Among these are collections of materials relating to: James Lane Allen in the Margaret I. King Library, University of Kentucky; Winston Churchill in the Dartmouth University Library; Mary Johnston in the University of Virginia Library; John Pendleton Kennedy at the Peabody Institute of the City of Baltimore, a collection described by Lloyd Griffin in "The John Pendleton Kennedy Manuscripts"; George Barr McCutcheon and Charles Major, both of whose literary manuscripts are in the Purdue University Library, the latter collection described by W. M. Hepburn in "The Charles Major Manuscripts in the Purdue University Libraries"; F. Van Wyck Mason in the Houghton Library, Harvard University; S. Weir Mitchell in the University of Pennsylvania Library; Kenneth Roberts in the Library of Congress as well as in the library of Phillips Exeter Academy; and William Gilmore Simms at the University of South Carolina, a collection described by John R. Welsh in "The Charles Carroll Simms Collection."

HISTORY AND CRITICISM

There are few major studies of the historical novel as a form, and the best of these—combining theoretical sophistication, substantial scholarship, and critical acumen—are European or British. Still a readable essay, though by now rather commonplace in its views, is Herbert Butterfield's *The Historical Novel* (1924). Although Butterfield treats the British historical novel, and primarily the great Victorian romancers, his discussion of the relationship between history as a scholarly endeavor and history in and through fiction, as well as his efforts to formulate an appropriate critical approach to the historical novel, deserve thoughtful consideration. The most formidable history and criticism of the genre is George Lukács's *The Historical Novel*; written in 1936, it was translated into Russian and published in Moscow the following year, but was not available in an English translation in the United States until 1963. Lukács has had no discernible influence on American students of the historical novel, and Cooper, the only American novelist that he considers, receives only two pages of discussion; but Lukács's erudition and theoretical framework make *The Historical Novel* an indispensable work. A more recent study, one designed in part to correct Lukács's picture of English historical fiction, is Avrom Fleishman's *The English Historical Novel: Walter Scott to Virginia Woolf.* Fleishman prefaces the substantive chapters of his study with a challenging discussion of the problems inherent in formulating a critical theory of historical fiction. In comparison with the work of Lukács and Fleishman, *The House of Desdemona, or the Laurels and Limitations of Historical Fiction* by Lion Feuchtwanger is disappointing. Feuchtwanger, who was both a trained historian (Ph.D., Munich) and a prolific writer of historical novels, offers little of theoretical interest, but he devotes a long chapter to the American historical novel, on which his views are decidedly idiosyncratic.

The principal study of American historical fiction, Ernest E. Leisy's *The American Historical Novel,* was preceded by several highly selective discussions. Arthur Hobson Quinn, in *American Fiction,* devoted the better part of a chapter to the "romance of history" in the last two decades of the nineteenth century and also considered the historical novels of F. Marion Crawford and S. Weir Mitchell in his chapters on those popular authors. In *Cavalcade of the American Novel,* Edward Wagenknecht described the revival of historical fiction in the 1930s; Alexander Cowie devoted a chapter in *The Rise of the American Novel* to a discussion of Cooper and the historical romance; and Carl Van Doren discussed the development of the historical romance in two chapters of *The American Novel.* Nevertheless, Leisy is substantially correct when he claimed in 1950 that *The American Historical Novel* was the first comprehensive treatment of that popular, but greatly neglected, form of American fiction. Leisy organized his work by historical period—colonial American, the Revolution, the westward movement—arguing that that arrangement would best serve his readership, which he took to be "the intelligent lay reader who is interested in the nation's past and who wants a rather full account of the materials and methods of American historical fiction." Brief chapter introductions are followed by descriptions and evaluations of historical novels grouped under topical headings and discussed usually, but not invariably, in the order of publication. Leisy typically provides between a one-half-page and one-page plot summary and commentary on any given novel, a practice that leads inevitably to superficial description and dogmatic-seeming judgments: for example, "The novel [John Esten Cooke's *Henry St. John*] . . . blends history and romance better than its predecessor, but is too attenuated for the modern reader." A short introductory chapter, "History Vivified," and a cursory conclusion state Leisy's generalizations about the development and cultural function of the form. As an extensively annotated catalog, *The American Historical Novel* retains its indispensability. No one in the thirty years since its publication has sought to bring it up to date or to build upon it. However, *Versions of the Past: The Historical Imagination in American Fiction* by Harry B. Henderson was conceived as a corrective to Leisy's view that historical novels present merely "fictionalized" history and so are best categorized in terms of the events they portray. Henderson concentrates his attention instead on classic American novels, proposing "to treat *Satanstoe, The Scarlet Letter, Billy Budd, A Connecticut Yankee in King Arthur's Court, The Red Badge of Courage* and *Absalom! Absalom!* as though they belonged in significant respects to the same literary category," namely historical fiction, in order "to create an appreciation of the self-awareness and complexity of the historical imagination of American writers." Adopting a strategy reminiscent of such critics as Vernon L. Parrington, Philip Rahv, and others, Henderson posits two structures of the historical imagination in the nineteenth century—two "theories of social representation" implicit in the work—on the one hand, of the "progressive" historians George Bancroft and John L. Motley and, on the other, the "holistic" historians William H. Prescott and Francis Parkman. By "progressive" Henderson means to designate "the historian's ruling belief that the historical treatment of a subject should be constantly informed by the notion of historical progress and improvement in human affairs." "Holistic" historians, by contrast, "were less interested in selecting those social institutions which might most clearly illustrate the theme of Progress than they were in creating an illusion of a whole civilization or culture, in which each institution or characteristic of a society might be seen as integral to the total culture." Henderson's close reading of classic American texts is richer and more exciting than these two ideal types might suggest, however, and his views on the relationship between fiction and history can be usefully contrasted to those of David Levin (*In Defense of Historical Literature*); but *Versions of the Past* is concerned, not with historical fiction as a popular genre, but with the historical imagination of canonical authors.

The history of the popular historical novel remains to be written, but Frank Luther Mott, in *Golden Multitudes*, identifies and describes best-selling historical novels in the chapters "History for the Millions, 1830-1870" and "The Romantic Parade." Scattered references to popular historical fiction can be found in James Hart's standard work *The Popular Book*, and Russel Nye touches briefly on the genre in *The Unembarrassed Muse*.

The Civil War has been the inspiration—if that is the most appropriate term—for more historical novelists than any other event in the nation's history, with the possible exception of the Revolution; and the Civil War novel and the effect of the war on American letters have been the subject of excellent studies. A good place to begin considering the sub-genre of

Civil War fiction is Bernard DeVoto's compressed but intelligent essay "Fiction Fights the Civil War," which is the same title as Robert Lively's absolutely first-rate examination of 512 Civil War novels. Lively, a trained historian who taught at Vanderbilt and Wisconsin before moving to Princeton, writes incisively and provocatively on the social function of Civil War fiction and attempts to answer what he calls "the simplest questions": who wrote Civil War fiction and from what perspectives; what shifts of interest and interpretation have occurred; and what historical methods were employed by the novelists. A brief final chapter, "The Uses of Fictional History," is a concise, informed discussion of the value of historical novels. Three subsequent articles are useful footnotes to Lively's study: Samuel Pickering, "A Boy's Own War," which considers the juvenile fiction of Horatio Alger, "Harry Castelmon" (Charles A. Fosdick), and "Oliver Optic" (William Taylor Adams); Robert L. Bloom, "The Battle of Gettysburg in Fiction," which assesses the historical accuracy of novelists' account of that battle; and R. B. Harwell, "Gone with Miss Ravenel's Courage; or Bugles Blow So Red: A Note on the Civil War Novel."

Daniel Aaron's *The Unwritten War: American Writers and the Civil War* contains only limited reference to the Civil War novels analyzed by Lively; Aaron's study being an effort to reveal how the war "more than casually touched and engaged a number of writers" although, paradoxically, with a few notable exceptions, writers have said little that was revealing about the meaning of the conflict, in Aaron's view.

Although the Revolution has long been the subject of historical novels, no study analogous to Lively's has been written until now. Michael Kammen's *A Season of Youth: The American Revolution and the Historical Imagination*, which was published as this essay was going to press, rests to a considerable extent on an analysis of the ways in which historical novelists since Cooper have conceptualized the nation's rite of passage and the degree to which historical novelists anticipated professional historians in their emphasis on various aspects and interpretations of the war. An acute, but sharply limited, discussion of fiction on the Revolution is Donald A. Ringe's "The American Revolution in American Romance," which is narrower in focus than its title might suggest, but which compares the work of Cooper, Kennedy, and Simms with that of their now less well-known contemporary John Neal. A number of other articles that analyze the Revolution as depicted in the writings of individual authors are cited below, in the section that discusses scholarship on selected popular historical novelists. Southern authors' approaches to their region's past is discussed by S. Van Auken in "Southern Historical Fiction in the Early Twentieth Century." "The Dream Life of the New Woman as Mirrored in Current Historical Heroines" is an analysis of popular historical romances in the *Forever Amber* mold by David T. Bazelon, who generalizes boldly from a sample of three novels about the hopes and aspirations of twentieth-century American women.

Surprisingly little attention has been given to historical novels set in Puritan New England. Adelheid Staehelin-Wagernagel's *The Puritan Settler in the American Novel Before the Civil War* traces changing attitudes toward the Puritans; describes the treatment of various character types such as the magistrate, the minister, the merchant, and women; and concludes with a discussion of Puritan "features"—piety and resignation, fanaticism and bigotry, intolerance and persecution, and so on. On the major figures, Cooper and Hawthorne especially, the author is derivative and pedestrian, but there is useful material on minor novelists.

STUDIES OF SELECTED AUTHORS

Given the lack of both scholarly and critical interest in popular historical fiction, it is not surprising that relatively little substantial work has been done on individual practitioners of the form, particularly those noted primarily for the popularity of their work with the reading public rather than for their literary skill: a devalued product does not inspire interest in the producer. With a few notable exceptions, commentary on authors of historical novels runs in well-worn, conventional channels: assessments of the historical accuracy of a work, analyses of an author's use of sources or his interpretation of the events or era that form the setting for a work. Following is a representative cross-section of commentary on authors of popular historical fiction, most of it in the form of essays in professional literary and historical periodicals. Hervey Allen's *Anthony Adverse* provoked charges of plagiarism in 1933 from some critics, charges that Allen himself answered in an article cited elsewhere in this essay. A more responsible approach to aspects of Allen's technique is taken by H. K. Siebenek in "Hervey Allen and Arthur St. Clair," an article buried, unfortunately, in one of the more inaccessible regional historical journals. "George Washington Cable and the Historical Romance" by R. B. Eaton argues that the difficulties many critics have had in coming to terms with *The Grandissimes* stem from Cable's efforts to assimilate two distinct genres in the work. Cable's work as an "historical romancer" is surveyed in a chapter of Louis D. Rubin's authoritative study, *George Washington Cable: The Life and Times of a Southern Heretic.*

Winston Churchill, the most popular American novelist in the first fifteen years of this century, is treated by Robert Schneider in *Novelist to a Generation: The Life and Thought of Winston Churchill.* "Winston Churchill: A Study in the Popular Novel" is an incisive essay by two noted historians, Richard and Beatrice Hofstadter, who see Churchill absorbed with the split between business values and human values at the turn of the century, though the full weight of this concern is felt more in his political novels, for example, *Coniston* (1906), than in the historical fiction for which he is better known. Commentary on James Fenimore Cooper, who was acclaimed the American Scott by his admiring contemporaries, is, of course, extensive; and there is no need here to reproduce citations that are readily accessible elsewhere—for example, in James F. Beard's comprehensive and judicious bibliographical essay on Cooper in *Fifteen American Authors Before 1900*. Two recent articles of particular relevance, owing to the renewed interest in the depiction of the Revolution by historical novelists, are James F. Beard's "Cooper and the Revolutionary Mythos" and H. D. Peck's "Repossession of America: The Revolution in Cooper's Trilogy of Nautical Romances" (*The Pilot, The Red Rover,* and *The Water Witch*). Peck argues that the novels reveal, not only the psychological basis out of which Cooper's later conservatism grew, but they also show his successful solution to the problem that history posed for his art.

The work of Walter D. Edmonds, best known for *Rome Haul* and *Drums Along the Mohawk*, both are carefully researched romances set in his native New York State, is briefly and approvingly surveyed by Dayton Kohler in "Walter D. Edmonds: Regional Historian." Edmonds's description of his own working habits and preparation for writing historical fiction is cited below. The historical fiction of Mary Johnston is sensitively discussed by Edward Wagenknecht in "The World and Mary Johnston" as well as in *Cavalcade of the American Novel*. In " 'As Much History as . . . Invention'," C. H. Bohner assesses John Pendleton Kennedy's use of surviving historical documents in writing *Rob of the Bowl*. William S. Osborne takes up the same issue in another Kennedy novel, "John Pendleton Kennedy's *Horse Shoe Robinson:* A Novel with 'the Utmost Historical Accuracy'."

As might be expected, *Gone with the Wind* has received more attention than most popular historical novels because of its extraordinary visibility, due in part to the success of the movie version. In "Tara Twenty Years After," Robert Y. Drake tried valiantly to encourage critics to take a second, more careful, look at the novel as "an epic treatment of the fall of a traditional society." The general critical estimate of the novel, however, is more nearly exemplified in Floyd C. Watkins's "*Gone with the Wind* as Vulgar Literature," which condemns Mitchell's novel for, among other things, its oversimplified regionalism, its prudery, and its false picture of the South and of human nature. J. W. Mathews's "The Civil War of 1936: *Gone with the Wind* and *Absalom! Absalom!*" makes some primarily mechanical comparisons of sales figures and reviews but without coming to any very interesting conclusions. Dawson Gaillard's "*Gone with the Wind* as Bildungsroman, or Why Did Rhett Butler Really Leave Scarlet

O'Hara?" discusses the heroine as a "new woman" at odds with the older social type of the Southern lady. Finis Farr's *Margaret Mitchell of Atlanta* does not probe sufficiently into the novel's popularity or into Mitchell's relationship with her publisher, among other aspects. Mitchell's correspondence concerning the novel, from its publication in 1936 to her death in 1949, has recently been published: *Margaret Mitchell's "Gone with the Wind" Letters*, edited by Richard Harwell.

Commentary on the physician-novelist S. Weir Mitchell has generally ignored his historical fiction to concentrate on his use of psychological themes, but in "Weir Mitchell and the Genteel Romance," Kelly Griffith, Jr. provides a useful account of the tradition of historical romance at the turn of the century and assesses Mitchell's contribution to it.

Conrad Richter has received disproportionately more attention than other twentieth-century historical novelists. In addition to the Twayne series study, *Conrad Richter* by Edwin W. Gaston, Jr., there is *Conrad Richter's America* by Marvin LaHood, which groups Richter's novels in terms of their geographical setting, and *Conrad Richter's Ohio Trilogy: Its Ideas, Themes, and Relationship to Literary Tradition* by Clifford D. Edwards.

A useful introduction to the work of Kenneth Roberts is the collection of essays, "For the Quinquennial of Kenneth Roberts," by A. H. Gibbs and others. A brief, but judicious, assessment of Roberts's efforts to blend historical "fact" and entertaining "fiction" is Grace L. Nute's review of *Northwest Passage*.

One of the more interesting essays in the field of historical fiction is M. D. Bell's "History and Romance Convention in Catherine Sedgwick's *Hope Leslie*," an essay that moves away from a simplistic concern with the author's fidelity to historical "fact" to considerations of how Sedgwick shaped her material to the existing conventions of romance and what she sought to communicate in and through those conventions.

A good deal of attention has been focused on William Gilmore Simms in the last fifteen years, as scholars have sought to legitimate his canonical status. C. Hugh Holman, whose unpublished dissertation deals with Simms's theory and practice of historical fiction, provides a starting point for a consideration of Simms's revolutionary war fiction in "William Gilmore Simms's Picture of the Revolution as a Civil Conflict." Holman's essay can be supplemented by R. J. Bresnahan's "William Gilmore Simms's Revolutionary War: A Romantic View of Southern History," which contains some interesting material on changes in Simms's ideas about his region's past, to the interpretation of which Simms contributed extensively both in fiction and in historical writing. Scholarship on Simms is comprehensively described and evaluated by Charles S. Watson in "William Gilmore Simms: An Essay in Bibliography."

Despite the influence of *Ben-Hur* in the late nineteenth century, interest in the novel and in Wallace has been minimal. Brief references in Hart and Mott aside, the best source of information is Irving McKee's biography *Ben-Hur Wallace: The Life of General Lew Wallace.*

The work of William Ware, a Unitarian minister and the author of three widely read antebellum historical novels, is analyzed by Curtis Dahl in "New England Unitarianism in Fictional Antiquity: The Romances of William Ware." Like M. D. Bell's essay on *Hope Leslie* cited above, Dahl's is a stimulating exploration of the ideological uses to which historical fiction has been put, in this case in the service of liberal religious opinion.

The novels of Frank Yerby, one of the most consistently successful of contemporary popular historical romancers since the publication of *The Foxes of Harrow*, were generally ignored. Recently, however, critics became interested in how Yerby, an expatriate black American, was depicting race relations in his fiction, the audience for which was largely white. Jack B. Moore's "The Guilt of the Victim: Racial Themes in Some Frank Yerby Novels" challenges earlier critics, contending that Yerby "in no way turned his back upon his race" after his first popular success. Another view of Yerby's work is provided by Darwin Turner in "Frank Yerby as Debunker," where he discusses Yerby's efforts to undermine historical myths, the persistence of which can be traced in large measure to uncritical historical novelists.

Authors of historical fiction have often felt obliged to explain or defend the significance and value of their work, especially during the last seventy-five years, which has generally been a period of unremitting critical contempt for the genre. Scott's preface to *Ivanhoe*, setting out in some detail a view of historical fiction that was to be influential for a century, is still a valuable place to begin and invites comparison with Simms's preface to the revised version of *The Yemassee*. F. Marion Crawford's lengthier discussion of historical fiction in *The Novel—What Is It?* also deserves mention. In *A Certain Measure: An Interpretation of Prose Fiction*, Ellen Glasgow describes her intentions and methods in writing *The Battle-Ground* (1902), the first in a series of novels designed to compose a social history of Virginia from 1850. A particularly thoughtful and reflective piece on the writing of historical fiction is G. P. Garretts's "Dreaming with Adam: Notes on Imaginary History," in which he discusses the development of his ideas for *Death of the Fox: An Imaginary Version of the Last Days of Sir Walter Raleigh* (1971). Garrett concludes: "I came to cling to the notion that the proper subject and theme of historical fiction is what it is—the human imagination in action, itself dramatized as it struggles with surfaces, builds structures with facts, deals out and plays a hand of ideas, and most of all, by conceiving of the imagination of others, wrestles with the angel . . .of the imagination."

A more conventional point of view, emphasizing the historical novelist's dependence on extensive research, is expressed by Hervey Allen in "The Sources of *Anthony Adverse*," a spirited reply to the benighted critics who accused him of plagiarism; by Walter D. Edmonds in "How You Begin a Novel," a concise account of his research for *Drums Along the Mohawk*, his widely read tale of the Mohawk Valley of New York during the Revolution; in Mackinley Kantor's dogmatic and defensive lecture "The Historical Novel," delivered at the Library of Congress; and by one of the masters of the swashbuckling romance, Raphael Sabatini, in "Historical Fiction," in which he discusses his writing as embodying three distinct approaches to the historical novel. Esther Forbes, who wrote widely acclaimed historical fiction both for adults and children, discusses her decision to write historical fiction in "Why the Past?" A. B. Guthrie addresses the same question in his essay "The Historical Novel." In "The Novel of Contemporary History," John R. Hersey discusses the clarifying function of fiction in modern life; he lists and briefly describes the "valid motives" that presumably inform his own work. Two superficial essays that offer tips to the novice writer deserve the skepticism reserved for racetrack touts: Frank G. Slaughter's "History and Fiction" and John Brick's "Writing the Historical Novel."

Much of the discussion of historical fiction implies, when it does not overtly turn on, familiar distinctions that are rooted in common usage: fact and fiction, observation and imagination, real and unreal, truth and—what? falsehood is perhaps too strong, but it comes near enough the mark, even today, reminding us of a residual common-sense skepticism concerning the truth claims of "fiction." Historical fiction invites the historian's scorn for playing fast and loose with the facts, even while literary critics abuse it for its slavish subservience to the documentary record—"mere" fact. And both historian and critic have nothing but contempt for the costume romances—*Forever Amber* in a thousand guises—devoid of both historical accuracy and literary value that bulk so large in the history of the genre. In "The Views of the Great Critics on the Historical Novel," Ernest Bernbaum traces the Victorian critics' scorn for historical fiction to a naive empiricism, but his judicious essay and implicit warning failed to have any appreciable impact on the terms in which the genre tended to be discussed during the 1930s and 1940s, as the following citations make clear. Bernard DeVoto, for example, emphasized the novelist's obligation to historical fact in offering qualified approval to the changes that he perceived taking place in the best historical novels of the 1930s in "Fiction and the Everlasting *If*." Edmund Fuller, himself an historical novelist, made much the same point in distinguishing "interpretive" novels (good) from "romantic" novels (bad) in "History and the Novelists." Orville Prescott, in the essays "Popularity" and "The Art of Historical Fiction" included in *In My Opinion*, is only slightly more complex, developing a fivefold categorization, the largest—and worst—group made up of novels based on superficial research and cheaply sensational plots, the smallest group composed of works that combine exhaustive research and a high order of literary skill. In essentially the same terms, Jay Williams claims that the good historical novelist deserves to be recognized and valued as a synthesizer and illuminator of the past in "History and Historical Novels."

The problematical nature of historical fiction has seldom been so clearly defined as in the debate occasioned by the publication in 1968 of William Styron's "meditation" on history, *The Confessions of Nat Turner*. Styron was widely criticized for tampering with the historical record. ". . . the Nat Turner created by William Styron has little resemblance to the Virginia slave insurrectionist who is a hero to his people," wrote John H. Clarke, in his introduction to *William Styron's Nat Turner: Ten Black Writers Respond*, challenging Styron's claim that, in the absence of extensive documentary evidence, he had merely exercised the novelist's license to fill in the record from his imaginative resources. A critical counterweight to *Ten Black Writers Respond* and to Mike Thelwell's "Mr. Styron and The Reverend Turner" is George Core's "*The Confessions of Nat Turner* and the Burden of the Past."

NOTES

1. Avrom Fleishman, *The English Historical Novel* (Baltimore: Johns Hopkins University Press, 1971), p. 4.
2. Lydia M. Child, *Hobomok, a Tale of Early Times*, quoted in Ernest Leisy, *The American Historical Novel* (Norman: University of Oklahoma Press, 1950).
3. *North American Review*, 19 (July 1824), 209.
4. James D. Hart, *The Popular Book* (New York: Oxford University Press, 1950), p. 164.
5. *The Unembarrassed Muse* (New York: Dial Press, 1970), p. 46.

BIBLIOGRAPHY

BOOKS AND ARTICLES

Aaron, Daniel. *The Unwritten War: American Writers and the Civil War*. New York: Alfred A. Knopf, 1973.

Albert, George. "Bibliography of Kenneth Roberts." *Bulletin of Bibliography*, 17 (September and October 1942), 191-92, 218-19; 18 (January and February 1943), 13-15, 34-36.

Allen, Hervey. "The Sources of *Anthony Adverse*." *Saturday Review of Literature*, 10 (January 13, 1934), 401.

Baker, Ernest A. *A Guide to Historical Fiction*. London: George Routledge & Sons, 1914.

Bazelon, David T. "The Dream Life of the New Woman as Mirrored in Current Historical Heroines." *Commentary*, 8 (September 1949), 252-57.

Beard, James F. "James Fenimore Cooper." In *Fifteen American Authors Before*

1900. Edited by Robert A. Rees and Earl B. Harbert. Madison: University of Wisconsin Press, 1971.

———. "Cooper and the Revolutionary Mythos." *Early American Literature*, 11 (Spring 1976), 84-104.

Bell, M. D. "History and Romance Convention in Catherine Sedgwick's *Hope Leslie*." *American Quarterly*, 22 (Summer 1970), 213-21.

Bernbaum, Ernest. "The Views of the Great Critics on the Historical Novel." *PMLA*, 41 (June 1926), 424-41.

Bloom, Robert L. "The Battle of Gettysburg in Fiction." *Pennsylvania History*, 43 (October 1976), 309-27.

Bohner, C. H. "'As Much History as . . . Invention': John P. Kennedy's *Rob of the Bowl*." *William and Mary Quarterly*, 17 (July 1960), 327-40.

Bresnahan, R. J. "William Gilmore Simms's Revolutionary War: A Romantic View of Southern History." *Studies in Romanticism*, 15 (Fall 1976), 573-87.

Brick, John. "Writing the Historical Novel." In *Writer's Roundtable*. Edited by Helen Hull and Michael Drury. New York: Harper & Bros., 1959.

Butterfield, Herbert. *The Historical Novel: An Essay*. Cambridge: Cambridge University Press, 1924.

Clarke, John H., ed. *William Styron's Nat Turner: Ten Black Writers Respond*. Boston: Beacon, 1968.

Coan, O. W., and R. G. Lillard, eds. *America in Fiction*. 5th ed. Palo Alto, Calif.: Pacific Books, 1967.

Core, George. "*The Confessions of Nat Turner* and the Burden of the Past." *Southern Literary Journal*, 2 (Spring 1970), 117-34.

Cowie, Alexander. *The Rise of the American Novel*. New York: American Book, 1951.

Crawford, F. Marion. *The Novel—What Is It?* New York: Macmillan, 1893.

Dahl, Curtis. "New England Unitarianism in Fictional Antiquity: The Romances of William Ware." *New England Quarterly*, 48 (March 1975), 104-15.

DeVoto, Bernard. "Fiction Fights the Civil War." *Saturday Review of Literature*, 17 (December 18, 1937), 3-4.

———. "Fiction and the Everlasting *If*: Notes on the Contemporary Historical Novel." *Harpers*, 177 (June 1938), 42-49.

Dickinson, A. T., Jr. *American Historical Fiction*. 3d ed. Metuchen, N.J.: Scarecrow Press, 1971.

Drake, Robert Y., Jr. "Tara Twenty Years After." *Georgia Review*, 12 (Summer 1958), 142-50.

Eaton, R. B. "George Washington Cable and the Historical Romance." *Southern Literary Journal*, 8 (Fall 1975), 82-94.

Edmonds, Walter D. "How You Begin a Novel." *Atlantic Monthly*, 158 (August 1936), 189.

Edwards, Clifford D. *Conrad Richter's Ohio Trilogy: Its Ideas, Themes, and Relationship to Literary Tradition*. The Hague: Mouton, 1970.

Farr, Finis. *Margaret Mitchell of Atlanta: The Author of Gone With the Wind*. New York: William Morrow, 1965.

Feuchtwanger, Lion. *The House of Desdemona, or the Laurels and Limitations of Historical Fiction.* Trans. Harold A. Bisilius. Detroit: Wayne State University Press, 1963.

Fleishman, Avrom. *The English Historical Novel.* Baltimore: Johns Hopkins University Press, 1971.

Forbes, Esther. "Why the Past?" In *What is a Book?* Edited by Dale Warren. Boston: Houghton Mifflin, 1935.

Fuller, Edmund. "History and the Novelists." *American Scholar,* 16 (Winter 1946-1947), 113-24.

Gaillard, Dawson. "*Gone with the Wind* as Bildungsroman, or Why Did Rhett Butler Really Leave Scarlet O'Hara?" *Georgia Review,* 28 (Spring 1974), 9-18.

Garrett, G. P. "Dreaming with Adam: Notes on Imaginary History." In *New Directions in Literary History.* Edited by Ralph Cohen. Baltimore: Johns Hopkins University Press, 1974.

Gaston, Edwin W., Jr. *Conrad Richter.* New York: Twayne, 1965.

Gibbs, A. H. et al. "For the Quinquennial of Kenneth Roberts." *Colby Library Quarterly,* 6 (Summer 1962), 83-132.

Glasgow, Ellen. *A Certain Measure: An Interpretation of Prose Fiction.* New York: Harcourt, Brace, 1943.

Griffin, Lloyd W. "The John Pendleton Kennedy Manuscripts." *Maryland Historical Magazine,* 28 (December 1953), 327-36.

Griffith, Kelly, Jr. "Weir Mitchell and the Genteel Romance." *American Literature,* 44 (May 1972), 247-61.

Griswold, William M. *A Descriptive List of Novels and Tales Dealing with the History of North America.* Cambridge, Mass.: Griswold, 1895.

Guthrie, A. B. "The Historical Novel." In *Western Writing.* Edited by G. W. Haslam. Albuquerque: University of New Mexico Press, 1974.

Handlin, Oscar et al., eds. *Harvard Guide to American History.* Cambridge: Harvard University Press, 1954.

Hart, James D. *The Popular Book.* New York: Oxford University Press, 1950.

Harwell, Richard. "Gone with Miss Ravenel's Courage; or Bugles Blow So Red: A Note on the Civil War Novel." *New England Quarterly,* 35 (June 1962), 253-61.

————, ed. *Margaret Mitchell's "Gone With the Wind" Letters, 1936-1949.* New York: Macmillan, 1976.

Henderson, Harry B. *Versions of the Past: The Historical Imagination in American Fiction.* New York: Oxford University Press, 1974.

Hepburn, W. M. "The Charles Major Manuscripts in the Purdue University Libraries." *Indiana Quarterly for Bookmen,* 2 (July 1946), 71-81.

Hersey, John R. "The Novel of Contemporary History." In *The Writer's Book.* Edited by H. R. Hull. New York: Harper's, 1950.

Hofstadter, Richard, and Beatrice Hofstadter. "Winston Churchill: A Study in the Popular Novel." *American Quarterly,* 2 (Spring 1950), 12-28.

Holman, C. Hugh. "William Gilmore Simms's Picture of the Revolution as a Civil Conflict." *Journal of Southern History,* 15 (November 1949), 441-62.

————. "William Gilmore Simms's Theory and Practice of Historical Fiction." Ph.D. dissertation, Unversity of North Carolina, 1949.

Irwin, Leonard B., comp. *A Guide to Historical Fiction.* 10th ed. Brooklawn, N.J.: McKinley Publishing, 1971.

Jones, Howard M., and Richard M. Ludwig. *Guide to American Literature and Its Backgrounds Since 1890.* 4th ed. Cambridge: Harvard University Press, 1972.

Kammen, Michael. *A Season of Youth: The American Revolution and the Historical Imagination.* New York: Alfred A. Knopf, 1978.

Kantor, McKinley. *The Historical Novelist's Obligation to History.* Macon, Ga.: Wesleyan College, 1967.

————. "The Historical Novel." In *Literary Lectures Presented at the Library of Congress.* Washington, D.C.: Library of Congress, 1973.

Kaye, James R. *Historical Fiction Chronologically and Historically Related.* Chicago: Snowdon Publishing, 1920.

Kohler, Dayton. "Walter D. Edmonds: Regional Historian." *English Journal,* 27 (January 1938), 1-11.

LaHood, Marvin J. *Conrad Richter's America.* The Hague: Mouton, 1975.

Leisy, Ernest E. *The American Historical Novel.* Norman: University of Oklahoma Press, 1950, 1952.

Levin, David. *In Defense of Historical Literature.* New York: Hill and Wang, 1967.

Lively, Robert A. *Fiction Fights the Civil War.* Chapel Hill, N.C.: University of North Carolina Press, 1957.

Lukács, Georg. *The Historical Novel.* Trans. Hannah and Stanley Mitchell. Boston: Beacon, 1963.

McGarry, Daniel D., and Sarah Harriman White. *World Historical Fiction Guide.* 2d ed. Metuchen, N.J.: Scarecrow Press, 1973.

McKee, Irving. *Ben-Hur Wallace: The Life of General Lew Wallace.* Berkeley: University of California Press, 1947.

Major, Charles. *When Knighthood Was in Flower.* Indianapolis: Bobbs-Merrill, 1898.

Mathews, J. W. "The Civil War of 1936: *Gone with the Wind* and *Absalom! Absalom!*" *Georgia Review,* 21 (Winter 1967), 462-69.

Moore, Jack B. "The Guilt of the Victim: Racial Themes in Some Frank Yerby Novels." *Journal of Popular Culture,* 8 (Spring 1975), 746-56.

Mott, Frank Luther. *Golden Multitudes.* New York: Macmillan, 1947.

Nield, Jonathan. *A Guide to the Best Historical Novels and Tales.* 5th ed. New York: Macmillan, 1929.

Nute, Grace L. "Northwest Passage." *Minnesota History,* 19 (March 1938), 76-78.

Nye, Russel. *The Unembarrassed Muse.* New York: Dial Press, 1970.

Osborne, William S. "John Pendleton Kennedy's *Horse Shoe Robinson:* A Novel with 'the Utmost Historical Accuracy'." *Maryland Historical Magazine,* 59 (September 1964), 286-96.

Peck, H. D. "Repossession of America: The Revolution in Cooper's Trilogy of Nautical Romances." *Studies in Romanticism,* 15 (Fall 1976), 589-605.

Pickering, Samuel. "A Boy's Own War." *New England Quarterly,* 48 (September 1975), 362-77.

Prescott, Orville. *In My Opinion*. Indianapolis: Bobbs-Merrill, 1952.

Quinn, Arthur Hobson. *American Fiction*. New York: Appleton-Century, 1936.

Ribalow, H. U. "Historical Fiction on Jewish Themes: A Selected Bibliography." In *Jewish Book Annual*, 23 (1965-1966), 63-69.

Ringe, Donald A. "The American Revolution in American Romance." *American Literature*, 49 (November 1977), 352-65.

Rubin, Louis D. *George Washington Cable: The Life and Times of a Southern Heretic*. New York: Pegasus, 1969.

Sabatini, Raphael. "Historical Fiction." In *What is a Book?* Edited by Dale Warren. Boston: Houghton Mifflin, 1935.

Schneider, Robert. *Novelist to a Generation: The Life and Thought of Winston Churchill*. Bowling Green, Ohio: Popular Press, 1976.

Scott, Walter. "Preface" to *Ivanhoe*. Philadelphia: M. Carey & Son, 1820.

Siebenek, H. K. "Hervey Allen and Arthur St. Clair." *Western Pennsylvania History Magazine*, 30 (September 1947), 73-94.

Simms, William Gilmore. "Preface" to *The Yemassee*. Rev. ed. New York: Redfield, 1853.

Slaughter, F. G. "History and Fiction." In *The Writer's Handbook*. Edited by A. S. Burack. Boston: The Writer, 1958.

Smith, Rebecca W. "Catalogue of the Chief Novels and Short Stories by American Authors Dealing with the Civil War and Its Effects, 1861-1899." *Bulletin of Bibliography*, 16 (October 1939), 193-94; 17 (January-April 1940), 10-12, 33-35, 53-55, 73-75.

Staehelin-Wagernagel, Adelheid. *The Puritan Settler in the American Novel Before the Civil War*. Bern, Switzerland: Francke, 1961.

Stemple, Ruth. "Kenneth Roberts: A Supplementary Checklist." *Bulletin of Bibliography*, 22 (October 1959), 228-30.

Thelwell, Mike. "Mr. Styron and the Reverend Turner." *Massachusetts Review*, 9 (Winter 1968), 7-29.

Turner, Darwin. "Frank Yerby as Debunker." *Massachusetts Review*, 9 (Summer 1968), 569-77.

Van Auken, S. "Southern Historical Fiction in the Early Twentieth Century." *Journal of Southern History*, 14 (May 1949), 157-91.

Van Derhoof, Jack Warner. *A Bibliography of Novels Related to American Frontier and Colonial History*. Troy, N.Y.: Whitston, 1971.

Van Doren, Carl. *The American Novel*. Rev. ed. New York: Macmillan, 1940.

Wagenknecht, Edward. "The World and Mary Johnston." *Sewanee Review* (April 1936), 188-206.

———. *Calvalcade of the American Novel*. New York: Holt, 1952.

Watkins, Floyd C. "*Gone with the Wind* as Vulgar Literature." *Southern Literary Journal*, 2 (Spring 1970), 80-103.

Watson, Charles S. "William Gilmore Simms: An Essay in Bibliography." *Resources for American Literary Study*, 3 (Spring 1973), 3-26.

Welsh, John R. "The Charles Carroll Simms Collection." *South Atlantic Bulletin*, 31 (November 1966), 1-3.

Williams, Jay. "History and Historical Novels." *American Scholar*, 26 (Winter 1956-1957), 67-74.

CHAPTER 9. Occult and the Supernatural

Robert Galbreath

Throughout American history, often during periods of social tension and rapid change associated with secularization, the occult has been conspicuous in popular culture. This was true of late seventeenth-century New England, the Second Great Awakening and social ferment of the early nineteenth century, industrialization during the Gilded Age, the interwar years, and the recent countercultural rejection of technocratic society. But popular occultism is by no means confined to social crisis or to a search for alternative values. During the seventeenth and much of the eighteenth centuries, the occult was part of the dominant value structure of society. In more recent times, popular occultism has partaken of and contributed to the American preoccupation with optimism, self-development, community, and reform. The study of American popular occultism may thus contribute to understanding the persistence and displacement of beliefs and the processes of social change.

As a concept, the occult is unwieldly. By extension from its Latin root, *occulēre* (to cover over, hide, conceal), "occult" now signifies anything hidden or secret, in the sense of being mysterious to ordinary understanding and scientific reason. In some cases, the phenomena are believed to be occult in only a superficial or extrinsic sense. Although they are mysterious now, they may be eventually confirmed or disproven by science. Other phenomena are said to be intrinsically occult, inherently unknowable by scientific reason, but still accessible to occult modes of cognition latent in everyone. The occult therefore encompasses the study and interpretation of unusual phenomena and experiences, together with techniques and disciplines for awakening occult modes of cognition and for utilizing occult energies for various ends.

At least six broad categories of beliefs, phenomena, and practices are covered by contemporary popular usage of "occult" and similar terms ("psychic," "esoteric," "paranormal," "mystical," "supernatural"): (1)

Anomalies of human and natural history—disputed phenomena and theories, such as UFOs, the Loch Ness monster, the Bermuda Triangle, lost continents, and the chariots of the gods, which do not fit into or contradict prevailing scientific and historical knowledge; (2) *Psi phenomena*—the field studied by scientific parapsychology, comprising extrasensory perception, psychokinesis, and so-called survival phenomena (presumed evidence for postmortem existence), which are all thought to be extrasensorimotor in nature, that is, outside the person's normal sensory and muscular processes; (3) *Transpersonal experiences*—experiences in which the ordinary personality is transcended, erased, or replaced, as in trance mediumship, spirit or demonic possession, inspiration or enthusiasm, revelation, meditation, and mysticism (oneness with the ultimate); (4) *Occult sciences, arts, or technologies*—disciplines based on the deliberate cultivation of natural or acquired psychic abilities to satisfy specific needs, as in magic (control of natural or occult forces), prediction and divination (including astrology, Tarot cards, the I Ching), characterology (character analysis by means of astrology, phrenology, numerology, and so on), and health and healing (including faith healing, mind cure, psychic surgery); (5) *Occult religions*—organized practices for the primary purpose of worshipping, celebrating, or serving natural forces and pagan or mythological deities, as in both traditional and modern witchcraft, voodoo, Satanism, neopaganism; and (6) *Metaphysical occultism*—systems of teachings and practices that lead the individual, by means of occult modes of cognition, to personal empirical knowledge of metaphysical truths and principles, as in Theosophy, Anthroposophy, Rosicrucianism, or Gnosticism.

Needless to say, these categories overlap. Numerous occult organizations combine elements from two or more categories. Nor are all six categories equally significant for American popular culture. It is also difficult always to differentiate clearly between the occult and such closely related areas as religious cults and sects, Asian religions in America, positive thinking and self-help, psychotherapy, psychedelics, millennialism, utopianism, and youth culture.

Because the occult is so broad, academic study of it has lacked focus. Although there are numerous parapsychological organizations for the scientific study of occult phenomena, there is no scholarly association for the historical, religious, and social-scientific study of the occult in general. In the present situation, one must seek scholarly articles on the occult in journals devoted to American studies, folklore, history, history of science, literature, parapsychology, philosophy, popular culture, psychology, religion, and sociology. In this essay, the discussion must be strictly limited to materials pertinent to American popular culture. Folklore and most high culture are omitted. Many aspects of the occult cannot be considered, but

the bibliographies and reference works listed below will guide the reader
to the necessary materials.

REFERENCE WORKS

BIBLIOGRAPHIES

Robert Galbreath's "The History of Modern Occultism: A Bibliographical Survey" discusses approximately three hundred bibliographies, reference works, and scholarly studies on nearly all aspects of American and
European occultism (except witchcraft), with primary emphasis on the
nineteenth and twentieth centuries. Although some items in that essay
must unavoidably be repeated here, the two essays are different in scope,
and readers of the present discussion should consult the earlier one for
additional bibliographies, general histories of the occult, studies of specific occult practices and themes, literature and the occult, and European
occultism. It is worth noting that in the eight years between essays, a
significant number of substantial new works on the occult have been
published.

Oliver J. Delaney's "The Occult: Diabolica to Alchemists" lists and
annotates approximately one hundred bibliographies and reference works
in all areas of the occult. Although marred by inaccuracies and omissions,
it is still useful. J. Gordon Melton's paper, "Sources and Resources for
Teaching the Occult," guides the user through general works, bibliographies, catalogs, libraries, encyclopedias, dictionaries, and a selected list
of specialized studies. Cris Popenoe's *Books for Inner Development: The
Yes! Guide* classifies and annotates over eight thousand in-print publications, both popular and scholarly, including writings by occultists and
mystics, but excluding magic, Satanism, and witchcraft. K. M. Hyre and
Eli Goodman's *Price Guide to the Occult and Related Subjects* lists alphabetically by author 8,243 used books and their market prices as listed by
thirty-nine dealers, but the lack of annotations and classification and the
restriction to used books seriously limit the volume's usefulness as a
reference tool.

The more specialized bibliographies tend to be of greater value. Nelson
R. Burr's two-volume *A Critical Bibliography of Religion in America* and
the shorter, but more recent, *Religion in American Life* are helpful on
sects, cults, and Oriental religious groups. The *Critical Bibliography of the
History of Science and Its Cultural Influences*, published as the fifth issue
of each of the annual volumes of the journal *Isis*, regularly surveys scholarship on "pseudo-sciences." David E. Smith's "Millenarian Scholarship in
America" and Weston La Barre's "Materials for a History of Studies of
Crisis Cults: A Bibliographic Essay" are invaluable guides to topics that

bear strongly on the occult in America. *Zetetic Scholar,* "an independent scientific review of claims of anomalies and the paranormal," edited by Marcello Truzzi, and its predecessors *Explorations* and *The Zetetic,* have afforded some measure of bibliographic control over the diffuse areas of the occult by publishing reviews, checklists, and bibliographies. Umesh Sharma and John Arndt have compiled *Mysticism: A Select Bibliography,* a listing without classification or annotation of "the best works that have appeared in English or in English translation since 1900." The index is inadequate. J. Gordon Melton's *A Reader's Guide to the Church's Ministry of Healing* provides an extensive, well-organized list of books concerning spiritual healing in the nineteenth and twentieth centuries, as it appeared both in "mainline" churches and in such movements as New Thought, Christian Science, Spiritualism, and Pentecostalism. Lynn E. Catoe's thorough *UFOs and Related Subjects: An Annotated Bibliography* admirably classifies, annotates, and indexes more than sixteen hundred items up to 1969.

For parapsychology, the authoritative guide is now *Parapsychology: Sources of Information,* compiled under the auspices of the American Society for Psychical Research by Rhea A. White and Laura A. Dale, which is a rigorously selective bibliography of the most reliable materials on all aspects of parapsychology. Each entry is thoroughly annotated, with references provided to the more significant book reviews. Encyclopedias, journals, and organizations are also treated, as well as earlier bibliographies and the published catalogs of various psychical research and Spiritualist libraries. Robert H. Ashby's *The Guide Book for the Study of Psychical Research* also provides useful information on English and American libraries, organizations, and publications, with lengthy bibliographies divided into beginning and advanced levels and selectively annotated. For witchcraft, the most recent guide is Donald Nugent's "Witchcraft Studies, 1959-1971: A Bibliographical Survey," a comprehensive review of materials on witchcraft from antiquity to the present. For the so-called classic period of witchcraft (late medieval to early modern times), there is H. C. Erik Midelfort's "Recent Witch Hunting Research, or Where Do We Go from Here?," an analysis of 509 items, most published since 1940. More or less in response, E. William Monter's "The Historiography of European Witchcraft: Progress and Prospects" indicates the still considerable gaps in our knowledge.

DIRECTORIES

Among the more worthwhile directories arising from the current occult revival are: Hans Holzner's *The Directory of the Occult,* which gives data, addresses, and evaluations of parapsychological, metaphysical, witch, and pagan groups, individual practitioners, and much else; June and Nicholas

Regush's *PSI: The Other World Catalogue*, a guide to books, periodicals, organizations, and equipment pertaining to parapsychology, life energies (including pyramid power), methods of psychic and spiritual development, healing, and "mysteries of time and space"; and *Spiritual Community Guide*, compiled by the Spiritual Community of San Rafael, California, now in its fourth edition (1979), which surveys New Age centers, communities, bookstores, and natural food stores and restaurants. The latest edition of the *Guide* notes that it includes only about 10 percent of the names in its computerized files. Many other national and regional directories exist; most that I have seen are woefully incomplete and amateurish. For the 1920s and 1930s, see the various directories compiled by William C. Hartmann: *Hartmann's Who's Who in Occult, Psychic and Spiritual Realms* (retitled for the second edition *Who's Who in Occultism, New Thought, Psychism and Spiritualism*) contains extremely detailed lists of officials, authors, organizations, and books; *Hartmann's International Directory of Psychic Science and Spiritualism* provides the same type of data for the Spiritualist field alone. Any thought that occultism is simply a recent fad will be quickly dispelled by referring to Hartmann's invaluable compilations.

Two brief directories of scholars working in the occult should also be mentioned. Marcello Truzzi's "The *Zetetic's* Researcher Directory" (January 1976) lists names, addresses, and interests of scholars and social scientists. The "Interim Directory of Scholars Interested in the New Religious Movements in America" (1978), prepared by the Program for the Study of New Religious Movements in America of the Graduate Theological Union, Berkeley, is broader in scope. An older work that is still of value is *Biographical Dictionary of Parapsychology*, edited by Helene Pleasants.

ENCYCLOPEDIAS AND DICTIONARIES

A large number of encyclopedias of questionable worth exist in the occult field. There are two reputable multivolume works, one being the distinguished and indispensable *Encyclopaedia of Religion and Ethics* (13 volumes), edited by James Hastings. Now more than fifty years old, it remains the standard in its field and is well worth consulting on all aspects of the occult. G. R. S. Mead's article on "Occultism," for example, is a classic statement of metaphysical occultism. The nearest occult equivalent to Hastings is the ambitious *Man, Myth & Magic* (24 volumes), edited by Richard Cavendish. Lavishly illustrated, comprehensive, and with a distinguished editorial board (C. A. Burland, Glyn Daniel, E. R. Dodds, Mircea Eliade, William Sargant, John Symonds, R. J. Zwi Werblowsky, and R. C. Zaehner), it is, nonetheless, somewhat uneven in execution. Some articles are outstanding: Ellic Howe on astrology and on German racist groups; E. R. Dodds on theurgy; R. J. Zwi Werblowsky on Cabala; Rosa-

lind Heywood, M. R. Barrington, and R. G. Medhurst on mediums; and
Richard H. Robinson on Buddhism. But others are trivial or not up to date,
and some lack bibliographies. Overall, the general level is good.

Only a few single-volume encyclopedias require notice. Lewis Spence's
An Encyclopaedia of Occultism is of the same vintage as Hastings. Compiled by a prolific English occult author, it is an intelligent and reasonably
comprehensive work that is still in print. Nandor Fodor's *Encyclopaedia
of Psychic Sciences* is limited to Spiritualism and psychical research; it is
particularly helpful on journals and organizations. Leslie A. Shepard has
combined, revised, and augmented Spence's and Fodor's works in his two-
volume *Encyclopedia of Occultism and Parapsychology*. Some three thousand entries from the older works are included, often in revised form, and
approximately one thousand new entries have been added, with extensive
bibliographical information. In the aftermath of *Man, Myth & Magic*,
Richard Cavendish has gone on also to edit the *Encyclopedia of the Unexplained: Magic, Occultism and Parapsychology*. Some of the same contributors appear in both encyclopedias, but the more recent work emphasizes the period of the nineteenth and twentieth centuries and the fields
of psychical research, magic, metaphysical occultism, and divination.
Although the viewpoint is said to be one of "sympathetic neutrality," some
contributors do not hesitate to judge their subjects, often negatively. But
in his excellent introduction, J. B. Rhine, who is the consultant on parapsychology, stresses the need for caution and for comparative studies.
Among specialized encyclopedias, see: E. Cobham Brewer's *A Dictionary
of Miracles*; Gustav Davidson's *A Dictionary of Angels*; John Ferguson's
An Illustrated Encyclopaedia of Mysticism and the Mystery Religions;
Rossell Hope Robbins's *The Encyclopedia of Witchcraft and Demonology*;
and Arthur Edward Waite's *A New Encyclopaedia of Freemasonry*.

RESEARCH COLLECTIONS

Library holdings and manuscript collections in the various categories of
the occult have not yet been adequately identified. Lee Ash's *Subject Collections* lists a number of library holdings under such headings as "Mysticism," "Occult Sciences," "Psychical Research," "Spiritualism," "Theosophy," and "Witchcraft." Four private organizations have libraries of
exceptional interest that are open to the public. The Eileen J. Garrett
Library of the Parapsychology Foundation, Inc. (29 West 57th Street,
New York, New York 10019) houses seven thousand volumes, complete
runs of many journals, and more than one hundred current periodicals in
all areas of the occult. The primary emphasis is, of course, on parapsychology. The library of the American Society for Psychical Research (5 West
73rd Street, New York, New York 10023) is slightly smaller (six thousand

volumes) and is more strictly limited to parapsychology. The Olcott Library and Research Center of The Theosophical Society in America (P.O. Box 270, Wheaton, Illinois 60187) contains approximately twenty thousand volumes on Theosophy, Eastern religions, philosophy, and science. The Association for Research and Enlightenment, Inc. (67th Street at Atlantic Avenue, P.O. Box 595, Virginia Beach, Virginia 23451) also possesses some twenty thousand volumes in all fields of the occult, plus fully indexed transcripts of Edgar Cayce's more than fourteen thousand psychic "readings." All four libraries are most receptive to inquiries and helpful in all matters.

The Houdini Collection of Magic and Spiritism at the Library of Congress consists of Houdini's collection of scrapbooks, posters, catalogs, and some five thousand books, including a particularly fine collection of Spiritualist works. The Yale University library houses some Andrew Jackson Davis letters, the Mellon Collection of Alchemy and the Occult (cataloged by Ian Macphail in 1969), and large holdings on witchcraft. The University of Pennsylvania library contains the Seybert Collection of Books on Spiritualism, Mesmerism, and Animal Magnetism and the Henry Charles Lea Collection on Witchcraft. What is said to be the largest collection of witchcraft—the Andrew D. White Collection (cataloged by Martha J. Crowe in 1977)—may be found at Cornell University library, together with the Loewy Collection of Materials on Freemasonry and Secret Societies. Brown University has the John William Graham Collection of Literature of Psychic Science, which formed the basis for S. R. Morgan's *Index to Psychic Science*. The John G. White Folklore Collection of the Cleveland Public Library and the Mandeville Collection in Parapsychology and Occult Sciences at the University of Illinois Education and Social Science Library are also notable. The State Historical Society of Wisconsin's holdings are exceptionally rich on Spiritualism, including books, pamphlets, proceedings, journals, and manuscripts.

HISTORIC OUTLINE / HISTORY AND CRITICISM

In the absence of substantial research, it can only be hypothesized that occult beliefs were present among the earliest European settlers in the New World. The subsequent history of the occult in America, to the extent that it has been documented, suggests a complex of native American and African traditions; European folklore and customs; European intellectual traditions since late antiquity of a homocentric universe, the relationship of microcosm and macrocosm, the great chain of being, and the efficacy of magic, witchcraft, and astrology; imported European and (later) Asian systems; and movements either indigenous to America or distinctively shaped by their experiences here. J. Gordon Melton's article, "Toward a

History of Magical Religion in the United States," stands virtually alone as an analysis of a single occult strand across the centuries; it ranges across folk magic, Salem witchcraft, voodoo, ritual magic, and contemporary neopaganism.

The rediscovery of the occult by the recent youth culture has misled some overly enthusiastic writers to assert that the occult per se constitutes an "alternative reality tradition," an "underground stream," or a "counter-culture" that periodically reappears in Western history as a challenge to mainstream culture. Thus Robert S. Ellwood's otherwise valuable account of *Religious and Spiritual Groups in Modern America* is seriously weakened by attempting to place the groups within "the history of an alternative reality in the West" (the title of his second chapter). Ellwood and other exponents of the "underground" approach, among whom should be counted Theodore Roszak, *The Making of a Counter Culture*, and James Webb, *The Occult Underground*, generally overlook the fact that until the late seventeenth and eighteenth centuries the occult functioned integrally both as part of mainstream culture (for example, the occult beliefs enumerated above) and in the ideologies, often millenarian, of radically dissenting groups during the late Middle Ages, the Reformation, and the English Civil War. In his effort to transform dominant beliefs into an alternative tradition, Ellwood ignores the existence of the radically dissenting groups that might with more justice be described as "alternative." (See Galbreath's "Cults and the Occult in Modern America" for a detailed assessment of Ellwood.) It is precisely on such groups that Nathan Adler focuses his book *The Underground Stream*, a psychohistorical study of the "antinomian personality" as it has been manifested among the Gnostics (the "hippies of religion"), heretics, witches, romantics, and (his main concern) hippies. As a study of a particular personality type today, the book is not without interest; but its historical scholarship is far too slight and spotty to make a significant contribution.

As these books demonstrate, it is often necessary to approach commentaries on recent occultism with some skepticism and in the light of the considerable scholarship on the history of the occult in the pre-modern West. Among the more notable contributions are: Lynn Thorndike's *A History of Magic and Experimental Science* (8 volumes); Norman Cohn's *The Pursuit of the Millennium*; Frances A. Yates's *Giordano Bruno and the Hermetic Tradition* and *The Rosicrucian Enlightenment*; Christopher Hill's *The World Turned Upside Down*; Keith Thomas's *Religion and the Decline of Magic*; and Robert Darnton's *Mesmerism and the End of the Enlightenment in France*. But, as the remainder of this essay will show, even in modern times when the occult has demonstrably been displaced from the world view of mainstream secularized society, the periodic manifestations of popular occultism speak to many kinds of needs that must be differentiated, not conflated into "countercultural" rebelliousness.

The occult in seventeenth-century America is, with the notable exception of Salem witchcraft in 1692, virtually unexplored territory. Even earlier witchcraft has attracted relatively little attention. Frederick C. Drake's article, "Witchcraft in the American Colonies, 1647-1662," now provides a detailed overview and chart of witch cases for the period that saw the most indictments and executions. Drake concludes that Salem was in fact an "aberration" from the pattern of earlier cases. Salem also needs to be seen in the context of European witchcraft, a subject that can be explored readily through Julio Caro Baroja's synthesis *The World of the Witches* and Jeffrey Burton Russell's *Witchcraft in the Middle Ages*, the latter linking the development of belief in organized witchcraft to the rise of heresy. Salem, of course, has been studied intensively for more than a century. The literature is too vast to be surveyed here, but guidance can be secured from the previously mentioned bibliographical articles and from the books mentioned here. The most recent comprehensive treatment is Chadwick Hansen's *Witchcraft at Salem*, a well-written consideration from the perspective of American studies that continues the usual practice of dwelling on the trials themselves, but differs in concluding that three of the accused were in all probability guilty as charged. He shows clearly the extent to which New England society was permeated by belief in witchcraft, but the evidence he adduces from the trial records to document the practice of black magic has been criticized.

When Hansen's volume was published in 1969, a remarkable renaissance of scholarship on European witchcraft was already in progress. Monter's essay on "The Historiography of European Witchcraft" describes not only the more sophisticated versions of familiar approaches but also the development of new perspectives and methodologies derived from the social sciences, especially anthropology. Here the prime examples are Keith Thomas's *Religion and the Decline of Magic* and especially Alan D. J. Macfarlane's *Witchcraft in Tudor and Stuart England*. Macfarlane's microcosmic analysis of Essex villages points to the hidden tensions and pressures of village life, rather than to external factors such as war, economic recession, or the arrival of a witch-hunter, as the basic stimulus for witchcraft accusations. This approach has been applied to Salem by John Demos in "Underlying Themes in the Witchcraft of Seventeenth-Century New England" and by Paul Boyer and Stephen Nissenbaum in *Salem Possessed: The Social Origins of Witchcraft*. Demos's study uncovers evidence of generational conflict, deviant personalities of the accused, tensions between neighbors, severe aggressive impulses underlying the "fits" of the accusers, and prominent oral themes of psychoanalytic significance in the historical record. Boyer and Nissenbaum, who earlier edited *Salem-Village Witchcraft: A Documentary Record of Local Conflict in Colonial New England*, provide the fullest portrait of the factionalism and social tensions that divided Salem Village and shaped the way in which the accusations were handled. The book is a subtle, illuminating, well-written reconstruction of a small community at war with itself. The psychological processes by which worry about economic matters was transformed into accusations of witchcraft are, however, rather tentative and elusive.

Witchcraft is only one subject treated in Herbert Leventhal's heavily documented *In the Shadow of the Enlightenment: Occultism and Renaissance Science in Eighteenth-Century America*. Focusing on the period 1714-1776, Leventhal explores the hitherto largely unsuspected survivals of occult beliefs and Renaissance science (the Elizabethan world picture) in enlightenment America. Drawing extensively from folklore, almanacs, periodicals, correspondence, and books of the period, he documents the continuity of astrology (though in decline), witch beliefs (but not executions), alchemy, geocentrism, the great chain of being, the doctrines of qualities, spirits, and humors, and the curious indigenous belief in the supernatural power of rattlesnakes. Leventhal demonstrates, somewhat surprisingly, that occult beliefs fared rather better in eighteenth-century America than did Renaissance science, but his analysis of the factors influencing both the persistence and displacement of beliefs is sketchy.

By the 1780s, with both revolution and romanticism in the air, European occultism experienced a rebirth at all levels of culture. Popular culture is explored with considerable acumen in Darnton's *Mesmerism and the End of the Enlightenment in France*. Occultism continued as a constant of European cultural life throughout most of the nineteenth and twentieth centuries, with peaks of popularity at mid-century, the fin de siècle, between the world wars, and again in recent years. These developments, together with their American counterparts, are surveyed in James Webb's two volumes, *The Occult Underground* (nineteenth century) and *The Occult Establishment* (twentieth century). Although they are awkwardly organized and unsophisticated in historical methodology, the books offer a wealth of detail, based on extensive reading in English, French, and German sources.

Popular interest in the occult seems not to have revived until the late 1820s and 1830s in America, with the introduction of animal magnetism and phrenology from Europe. By the later 1830s and 1840s, a kaleidoscopic whirl of occultisms, revelations, new religions, and reform movements were sweeping across the country. *The Rise of Adventism*, edited by Edwin S. Gaustad, contains authoritative surveys of revivalism, health reform, communitarianism, millennialism, Spiritualism, and Adventism during this period. Alice Felt Tyler's classic *Freedom's Ferment* treats these and other such developments as transcendentalism, Mormonism, the Shakers, and political and humanitarian reform movements. Specialized studies of phrenology include: John D. Davies's *Phrenology: Fad and Science: A 19th-Century American Crusade*, which presents the history of phrenology and its impact on education, medicine, penology, religion, and other areas; and Madeleine B. Stern's biography, *Heads and Headlines: The Phrenological Fowlers*. The development of mesmerism into mind cure, Christian Science, and New Thought is traced in Frank Podmore's still valuable *From Mesmer to Christian Science*, first published in 1909 as *Mesmerism and Christian Science*. The visionary teachings of Emanuel Swedenborg were another European influence on American developments at this time; see Marguerite Beck Block's *The New Church in the New World: A Study of Swedenborgianism in America*. J. Stillson Judah has written the most suggestive general interpretation of nineteenth-century American occultism in *The History and Philosophy of the Metaphysical Movements in America*. Judah traces the emergence—from origins in Swedenborgianism, mesmerism, and transcendentalism—of a viewpoint that he calls "metaphysics," a practical philosophy, both religious and scientific, that concerned itself with the application to daily life of the absolute truths and deeper realities that are said to exist beyond the dimension of daily sense-experience. Judah describes this outlook as highly pragmatic, experiential, and optimistic, one that rejects both creedal orthodoxies and blind faith in the name of self-realization through identification with the divine principle within every individual. He classifies the metaphysical movements into three broad categories: Spiritualism, Theosophy (and its allies), and mind cure (New Thought, Christian Science, Divine Science, Religious Science, Unity). These categories are not equally metaphysical, and more specialized literature must be consulted for comprehensive treatments of individual movements.

Spiritualism began in the United States as a means of contacting spirits of the dead through human mediums. The motives there, besides sensationalism, were the consolation afforded to the bereaved and the supposedly scientific or empirical evidence of life after death. The latter motive —evidence of life after death—subsequently influenced the establishment of psychical research to examine scientifically the claims made by and for mediums. Spiritualist metaphysics was developed from various sources, among them the Swedenborgian-like works of the "Poughkeepsie seer," Andrew Jackson Davis, who is the subject of Robert W. Delp's article, "Andrew Jackson Davis: Prophet of American Spiritualism." A thoughtful popular history of American Spiritualism, which pays full attention to the background in animal magnetism, Swedenborgianism, and Shaker spiritualism, is provided by Slater Brown's *The Heyday of Spiritualism*. The background of the first incident in popular Spiritualism—the "spirit-rappings" associated with the Fox sisters in 1848 near Rochester—is exhaustively examined by Whitney R. Cross in *The Burned-Over District: The Social and Intellectual History of Enthusiastic Religion in Western New York, 1800-1850*; but Earl Wesley Fornell's biography of *The Unhappy Medium: Spiritualism and the Life of Margaret Fox* is inadequate. Howard Kerr combines popular culture, history, and literary criticism in *Mediums and Spirit-Rappers and Roaring Radicals: Spiritualism in American Literature, 1850-1900*. Easily the best work on its subject, Kerr's study considers humorous and satirical writings, occult fiction, and major works by Howells, Twain, and James; it is also strong on post-Civil War Spiritualist history. Robert Dale Owen, a leading Spiritualist, is the subject of a fine biography by Richard W. Leopold. A superior regional study is available in Mary Farrell Bednarowski's article, "Spiritualism in Wisconsin in the Nineteenth Century," which clearly sets forth the Spiritualist opposition to the institutional churches of the day, while seeking to reconcile the competing claims of science and religion.

American Spiritualism is placed in an international context in Frank Podmore's thorough and critical *Mediums of the 19th Century*, first published in 1902 as *Modern Spiritualism: A History and a Criticism*. George Lawton's *The Drama of Life After Death: A Study of the Spiritualist Religion* was an early attempt at sociological and psychological analysis. A more recent comparative sociological examination of British and American Spiritualism is Geoffrey K. Nelson's *Spiritualism and Society*, a work that is more useful on Britain than on America.

The most recent scholarly consideration of Spiritualism is R. Laurence Moore's *In Search of White Crows: Spiritualism, Parapsychology, and American Culture*. Although it is broadly conceived, the book does not claim to be a full history of either Spiritualism or psychical research. Part I treats nineteenth-century Spiritualism, the factors underlying its appeal and subsequent decline, its relationship with orthodox Christianity, and —especially interesting—mediumship as an instance of female professionalism. Rather than following Spiritualism into the twentieth century, Moore turns to the rise of psychical research in response to Spiritualistic claims and traces its transformation into twentieth-century scientific parapsychology. A major theme of the book, expressed in its title (from one of William James's essays on psychical research), is the ongoing concern of Spiritualists, parapsychologists, and their critics with finding credible instances of psychical phenomena.

Besides Moore's book, there is little else to report on the history of American psychical research. D. Scott Rogo's *Parapsychology: A Century of Inquiry* is useful, as are the popular biographies of famous mediums investigated by psychical researchers, Mrs. Margery Crandon (*Margery* by Thomas R. Tietze) and Mrs. John H. Curran, the famous Patience

Worth case (Irving Litvag's *Singer in the Shadows*). Mention should also be made of Michael McVaugh and Seymour Mauskopf's "J. B. Rhine's *Extra-Sensory Perception* and Its Background in Psychical Research," a history of science study of Rhine's pioneering book. Little has been done to analyze the impact of parapsychology on popular culture.

The second of Judah's metaphysical movements began in New York in 1875 with the establishment of the Theosophical Society. One of the most influential of all modern occult movements, its impact has been greatest on England. Scholarly non-Theosophical literature on Theosophy is sparse and largely concerned with its international history. There is no satisfactory biography of H. P. Blavatsky, the guiding personality of Theosophy; the best is probably Gertrude Marvin Williams's *Priestess of the Occult*. Arthur H. Nethercot's two volumes, *The First Five Lives of Annie Besant* and *The Last Four Lives of Annie Besant*, are solid chronologies but are weak on analysis of the second most decisive figure in the history of Theosophy. Mary Lutyens's biography, *Krishnamurti: The Years of Awakening*, depicts the life of the young Indian who was trained by Annie Besant and Charles Leadbeater to be the "vehicle" for the impending incarnation of the Lord Maitreya, until his famous renunciation of all messianic claims in 1929 and his subsequent break with Theosophy. There is a useful, detailed chapter on Theosophy in Charles S. Braden's study of American cults and sects, *These Also Believe*. Alvin Boyd Kuhn's *Theosophy: A Modern Revival of Ancient Wisdom* is extremely useful on the early history; it also links Theosophy to the American religious experience. In this connection, see chapter 61 of Sydney E. Ahlstrom's *A Religious History of the American People* and Carl T. Jackson's excellent survey with bibliography of "Oriental Ideas in American Thought" in the *Dictionary of the History of Ideas*.

The third type of metaphysical movement—mind cure—is discussed in Podmore's *From Mesmer to Christian Science* and in several chapters of Braden's *These Also Believe* (New Thought, Christian Science, Unity). Braden has also written a history of New Thought, *Spirits in Rebellion*. The literature on Christian Science is mostly beyond the scope of the present essay. See, however, Robert Peel's two-volume biography, *Mary Baker Eddy: The Years of Discovery* and *Mary Baker Eddy: The Years of Trial*, written by a Christian Scientist. Stephen Gottschalk's *The Emergence of Christian Science in American Religious Life* focuses on the period 1885-1910, when Christian Science became institutionalized. The development of mind cure into self-help and positive thinking is traced in Donald Meyer's *The Positive Thinkers*.

From the days of Johannes Kelpius in the late seventeenth century and the Ephrata community in 1732, occult and mystical ideas have often formed the basis of intentional communities. Two introductions to further reading on this topic are Mark Holloway's *Heavens on Earth: Utopian Communities in America, 1680-1880* and Robert S. Fogarty's bibliographical survey, "Communal History in America." The utopian experiments of the charismatic occult leader Thomas Lake Harris and of the Theosophists are described in word and photograph in Paul Kagan's *New World Utopias.* (Harris's extraordinary career, and that of his English associate Laurence Oliphant, are recounted in Herbert W. Schneider and George Lawton's *A Prophet and a Pilgrim.*) On the Theosophists there is also the monograph by Emmett A. Greenwalt, *The Point Loma Community in California, 1897-1942: A Theosophical Experiment.* Laurence Veysey's *The Communal Experience: Anarchist and Mystical Counter-Cultures in America* is a richly documented historical study of considerable interest. As examples of "mystical" communes, Veysey examines Vedanta monasteries that were founded in the wake of Swami Vivekananda's introduction of the ideas of Swami Ramakrishna at the 1893 World Parliament of Religions in Chicago, and a contemporary commune in New Mexico based on the teachings of Gurdjieff and Sufism. Another Vedanta community in Nevada, which follows the teachings of Paramhansa Yogananda, is analyzed by the sociologist Ted A. Nordquist in *Ananda Cooperative Village.*

During the nineteenth century, America had been hospitable to an extraordinary range of occult movements that emphasized character analysis, health, metaphysical self-development, communal experiments, and efforts to heal the rift between science and religion. American-style Spiritualism had an international impact, as did New Thought. America also became one of the pioneers in psychical research, and it was in New York that Theosophy was officially launched.

But the United States did not participate to any noteworthy extent in the European revival of ritual magic associated with the names of Eliphas Lévi in France and the Hermetic Order of the Golden Dawn in England. (For these developments see: Webb's two volumes; Francis King's *Ritual Magic in England: 1887 to the Present Day*—misleadingly retitled for the American edition *The Rites of Modern Occult Magic*; and Christopher MacIntosh's *Eliphas Lévi and the French Occult Revival.*) Nor does America seem to have experienced the "rising tide" of interest in prophecy, astrology, and alchemy that G. R. S. Mead described in England in 1912. But it may simply be that no one has bothered to investigate these areas and that much of interest awaits discovery. There can be little doubt that mysticism was strong at certain levels of society during the nineteenth century—Quakerism, transcendentalism, Vedanta come to mind—but it has not been systematically studied. Hal Bridges, however, has investigated twentieth-century mysticism in *American Mysticism: From William James to Zen,* an intelligent although somewhat spotty survey, with excellent bibliography, of William James, Rufus Jones, Thomas Merton, D. T. Suzuki, Aldous Huxley, Alan Watts, and others.

In the aftermath of World War I, interest was high in psychical phenomena, mediumship, Vedanta philosophy, and Krishnamurti. An influential popular account, first published in 1935, was Rom Landau's *God Is My Adventure: A Book on Modern Mystics, Masters and Teachers.* Among Landau's subjects were J. Krishnamurti, Count Hermann Keyserling, Rudolf Steiner, Meher Baba, G. I. Gurdjieff, P. D. Ouspensky, and Dr. Frank Bushman of Moral Rearmament. None was American, but many had American followings. Intelligent, insightful accounts of many of the cults of the period are contained in Braden's *These Also Believe* (for example, Psychiana, the I Am movement, the Oxford Group movement) and in H. T. Dohrman's *California Cult: The Story of "Mankind United."* On Gurdjieff, the major work is now J. G. Bennett's *Gurdjieff: Making a New World.*

The American prophet and psychic diagnostician Edgar Cayce attracted much attention until his death in 1945, but arguably not as much as he does now. Of the many books that have appeared about him, none is satisfactory; but it is worth noting that Jess Stearn's *Edgar Cayce—The Sleeping Prophet* was a best seller upon publication in 1967. That indefatigable collector of anomalies, Charles Fort, is the subject of Damon Knight's biography, *Charles Fort: Prophet of the Unexplained.* An unfriendly, but informative, review of eccentric beliefs and pseudoscience of the interwar years and on into the 1950s is Martin Gardner's *Fads and Fallacies in the Name of Science.* Gardner discusses hollow and flat earthers, dianetics, general semantics, health and food fads, Atlantis, pyramidology, flying saucers, Immanuel Velikovsky, Bridey Murphy, and Charles Fort himself.

Interest in the occult continued steadily through World War II and the postwar period, with flurries of enthusiasm over flying saucers, hypnotic regression to past lives (Bridey Murphy), and Zen Buddhism, until 1966-1968, when the occult captured, or was captured by, youth culture and the mass media. Indeed, the best popular survey of the current occult scene, Nat Freedland's *The Occult Explosion,* argues that this revival is historically unique in its convergence with advanced technology, not least of all in the areas of media hype and commercial exploitation. Marcello Truzzi's important article, "The Occult Revival as Popular Culture," contends that today's mass version of occultism constitutes a "pop religion," displaying a "playful contempt" for the supernatural. But neither author denies that there is also an audience for serious occult ideas, an audience that Freedland believes is growing. Mircea Eliade ("Cultural Fashions and the History of Religions" in his *Occultism, Witchcraft, and Cultural Fashions*) concludes, from a study of recent French vogues for Claude Lévi-Strauss's structuralism, for Pierre Teilhard de Chardin, and for Louis Pauwels and Jacques Bergier's occult synthesis *The Morning of the Magicians*, that they represent a rejection of pessimism and nihilism, an exaltation of physical nature, and "a nostalgia for what might be called a macrohistory" (planetary and cosmic history). In a second essay in the same volume, "The Occult and the Modern World," Eliade states that it is the "attraction of a *personal* initiation" that explains the occult revival, which must therefore be seen as constituting an optimistic view of human potential. Much the same sort of conclusion emerges from what is undoubtedly the finest analysis of the appeal to contemporary Americans of Asian systems of religion and meditation (Zen Buddhism, Meher Baba, Subud, transcendental meditation, Krishnamurti, Tibetan Buddhism), in Jacob Needleman's *The New Religions*: the rejection of existentialism, the need for the cosmic, the emphasis upon mind, transformation, and discipline.

Freedland's *The Occult Explosion* and John Godwin's less satisfactory *Occult America* together survey the entire occult revival—popular, commercial, and intellectual. The most useful and comprehensive account of organizations is found in Ellwood's *Religious and Spiritual Groups in Modern America*, a work that is enlivened by the author's firsthand reports on his experiences with each group and by the inclusion of brief texts and doctrinal statements, some written especially for the volume. Christopher Evans's *Cults of Unreason* emphasizes Scientology, but also considers UFO cults, radionics, and Eastern meditation groups. *On the Margin of the Visible: Sociology, the Esoteric, and the Occult*, edited by Edward A. Tiryakian, is an uneven collection of social science papers, many on recent movements. By contrast, *Religious Movements in Contemporary America*, edited by Irving I. Zaretsky and Mark P. Leone, shows social science methodology at its best, with numerous, often illuminating, contributions on Spiritualism, Satanism, Scientology, and other "marginal" movements. Scientology is also analyzed sociologically by Roy Wallis in *The Road to Total Freedom*, while J. Stillson Judah considers *Hare Krishna and the Counterculture* in the light of the history of religions. On modern witchcraft and Satanism, see: Truzzi's "The Occult Revival as Popular Culture" and his contribution to Zaretsky and Leone's volume; Arthur Lyons's *The Second Coming: Satanism in America*; and Susan Roberts's *Witches, U.S.A.*, one of the better popular surveys. The mysterious Carlos Castaneda and his equally mysterious shaman don Juan are subjected to a searching inquiry in *Castaneda's Journey: The Power and the Allegory*, by Richard de Mille.

The cosmic dimension of modern occultism can be approached through Ellic Howe's *Astrology: A Recent History Including the Untold Story of*

Its Role in World War II (the English edition is more simply called *Urania's Children*), which traces modern astrology from its emergence in the 1880s in the Theosophical Society to the development of newspaper astrology in the 1930s and its role in World War II. "Astrology as Popular Culture" is treated by Marcello Truzzi, who clearly distinguishes different levels of interest and belief. Astrology and the many other forms of modern prophecy and prediction are discussed in Martin Ebon's popular account, *Prophecy in Our Time.* What happens in a flying-saucer cult predicting the imminent end of the world is analyzed by Leon Festinger and colleagues in *When Prophecy Fails,* in terms of cognitive dissonance. The historian David Michael Jacobs traces the development of *The UFO Controversy in America,* while John A. Keel analyzes "The Flying Saucer Subculture" (with extensive bibliography). Finally, Erich von Däniken's "chariots of the gods" theme has been challenged by Ronald Story's *The Space-Gods Revealed* and in a scholarly examination of archaeoastronomy, *In Search of Ancient Astronomies,* edited by E. C. Krupp.

ANTHOLOGIES AND REPRINTS

There are no anthologies of primary sources on American occultism, except readers on Salem, of which the most important is Boyer and Nissenbaum's *Salem-Village Witchcraft.* The numerous brief readings in Ellwood's *Religious and Spiritual Groups in Modern America* are the nearest thing to a general anthology. Nearly half of Tiryakian's *On the Margin of the Visible* reprints documents, some of considerable value, but none is American in origin. Both *The Flying Saucer Reader,* edited by Jay David, and *The ESP Reader,* edited by David C. Knight, reprint many cases, documents, and excerpts that pertain to American developments. Of the many anthologies of mysticism, *The Protestant Mystics,* edited by Anne Freemantle, gives extensive space to Americans, from the German Rosicrucian immigrant Johannes Kelpius in the seventeenth century, to the Quaker Thomas R. Kelly and, surprisingly, to e. e. cummings.

Many publishers have taken advantage of the present enthusiasm for the occult to reprint scarce titles. Dover Publications, University Books, Inc., and Samuel Weiser have been particularly active. Arno Press has published two reprint collections, The Occult (1976), edited by James Webb, and Perspectives in Psychical Research (1975), edited by Robert L. Morris. The sixty-seven volumes reprinted in the two series include American, English, French, and German items, among then several early works on American Spiritualism and an 1857 volume on alchemy by General Ethan Allen Hitchcock, an American occult author who is beginning to attract attention.

BIBLIOGRAPHY

BOOKS AND ARTICLES

Adler, Nathan. *The Underground Stream: New Life Styles and the Antinomian Personality.* New York: Harper & Row, 1972.

Ahlstrom, Sydney E. *A Religious History of the American People.* New Haven: Yale University Press, 1972.

Ash, Lee. *Subject Collections: A Guide to Special Book Collections and Subject Emphases as Reported by University, College, Public and Special Libraries, and Museums in the United States and Canada.* 4th ed. New York: R. R. Bowker, 1974.

Ashby, Robert H. *The Guide Book for the Study of Psychical Research.* New York: Samuel Weiser, 1972.

Baroja, Julio Caro. *The World of the Witches.* Trans. O. N. V. Glendinning. Chicago: University of Chicago Press, 1965.

Bednarowski, Mary Farrell. "Spiritualism in Wisconsin in the Nineteenth Century." *Wisconsin Magazine of History,* 59 (Autumn 1975), 3-19.

Bennett, J. G. *Gurdjieff: Making a New World.* New York: Harper & Row, ca. 1973 (1974).

Block, Marguerite Beck. *The New Church in the New World: A Study of Swedenborgianism in America.* New York: Holt, 1932.

Boyer, Paul, and Stephen Nissenbaum, eds. *Salem-Village Witchcraft: A Documentary Record of Local Conflict in Colonial New England.* Belmont, Cailf.: Wadsworth, 1972.

————. *Salem Possessed: The Social Origins of Witchcraft.* Cambridge: Harvard University Press, 1974.

Braden, Charles S. *These Also Believe: A Study of Modern American Cults & Minority Religious Movements.* New York: Macmillan, 1949.

————. *Spirits in Rebellion: The Rise and Development of New Thought.* Dallas: Southern Methodist University Press, 1963.

Brewer, E. Cobham. *A Dictionary of Miracles, Imitative, Realistic, and Dogmatic.* Philadelphia, 1884. Reprint. Detroit: Gale, 1966.

Bridges, Hal. *American Mysticism: From William James to Zen.* New York: Harper & Row, 1970.

Brown, Slater. *The Heyday of Spiritualism.* New York: Hawthorn, 1970.

Burr, Nelson R. *A Critical Bibliography of Religion in America.* (*Religion in American Life.* Edited by James Ward Smith and A. Leland Jamison. Vol. IV, Parts 1 and 2.) Princeton: Princeton University Press, 1961.

————. *Religion in American Life.* (Goldentree Bibliographies in American History. Edited by Arthur S. Link.) New York: Appleton-Century-Crofts, 1971.

Catoe, Lynn E. *UFOs and Related Subjects: An Annotated Bibliography.* Washington, D.C.: Government Printing Office, 1969.

Cavendish, Richard, ed. *Man, Myth & Magic: An Illustrated Encyclopedia of the Supernatural.* 24 vols. New York: Marshall Cavendish, 1970.

————, ed. *Encyclopedia of the Unexplained: Magic, Occultism and Parapsychology.* New York: McGraw-Hill, 1974.

Cohn, Norman. *The Pursuit of the Millennium: Revolutionary Millenarians and Mystical Anarchists of the Middle Ages.* Rev. ed. New York: Oxford University Press, 1970.

Critical Bibliography of the History of Science and Its Cultural Influences. Edited by John Neu. Published as Part 5 of each annual volume of *Isis.*

Cross, Whitney R. *The Burned-Over District: The Social and Intellectual History of Enthusiastic Religion in Western New York, 1800-1850.* Ithaca, N.Y.: Cornell University Press, 1950.

Crowe, Martha J. *Witchcraft: Catalogue of the Witchcraft Collection in Cornell University Library.* Ithaca, N.Y.: Cornell University Library, 1977.

Darnton, Robert. *Mesmerism and the End of the Enlightenment in France.* Cambridge: Harvard University Press, 1968.

David, Jay, ed. *The Flying Saucer Reader.* New York: New American Library, 1967.

Davidson, Gustav. *A Dictionary of Angels.* New York: Free Press, 1967.

Davies, John D. *Phrenology: Fad and Science: A 19th-Century American Crusade.* New Haven: Yale University Press, 1955.

Delaney, Oliver J. "The Occult: Diabolica to Alchemists." *Reference Quarterly,* 11 (Fall 1971), 7-14.

Delp, Robert W. "Andrew Jackson Davis: Prophet of American Spiritualism." *Journal of American History,* 54 (June 1967), 43-56.

de Mille, Richard. *Castaneda's Journey: The Power and the Allegory.* Santa Barbara, Calif.: Capra Press, 1976.

Demos, John. "Underlying Themes in the Witchcraft of Seventeenth-Century New England." *American Historical Review,* 75 (June 1970), 1311-26.

Dohrman, H. T. *California Cult: The Story of "Mankind United."* Boston: Beacon Press, 1958.

Drake, Frederick C. "Witchcraft in the American Colonies, 1647-1662." *American Quarterly,* 20 (Winter 1968), 694-725.

Ebon, Martin. *Prophecy in Our Time.* New York: New American Library, 1968.

Eliade, Mircea. *Occultism, Witchcraft, and Cultural Fashions.* Chicago: University of Chicago Press, 1976.

Ellwood, Robert S., Jr. *Religious and Spiritual Groups in Modern America.* Englewood Cliffs, N.J.: Prentice-Hall, 1973.

Evans, Christopher. *Cults of Unreason.* New York: Farrar, Straus & Giroux, 1974.

Ferguson, John. *An Illustrated Encyclopaedia of Mysticism and the Mystery Religions.* London: Thames & Hudson, 1976.

Festinger, Leon, Henry W. Riecken, and Stanley Schachter. *When Prophecy Fails.* Minneapolis: University of Minnesota Press, 1956.

Fodor, Nandor. *Encyclopaedia of Psychic Sciences.* London, 1934. Reprint. New Hyde Park, N. Y.: University Books, 1966.

Fogarty, Robert S. "Communal History in America." *Choice,* 10 (June 1973), 578-90.

Fornell, Earl Wesley. *The Unhappy Medium: Spiritualism and the Life of Margaret Fox.* Austin: University of Texas Press, 1964.

Freedland, Nat. *The Occult Explosion.* New York: Putnam's, 1972.

Fremantle, Anne, ed. *The Protestant Mystics*. Boston: Little, Brown, 1964.

Galbreath, Robert. "The History of Modern Occultism: A Bibliographical Survey." *Journal of Popular Culture*, 5 (Winter 1971), 726-54. Reprinted in *The Occult: Studies and Evaluations*. Edited by Robert Galbreath. Bowling Green, Ohio: Bowling Green University Popular Press, 1972.

————. "Cults and the Occult in Modern America." *History of Religions*, 13 (May 1974), 323-31.

Gardner, Martin. *Fads and Fallacies in the Name of Science*. Rev. ed. New York: Dover, 1957.

Gaustad, Edwin S., ed. *The Rise of Adventism: Religion and Society in Mid-Nineteenth-Century America*. New York: Harper & Row, 1974.

Godwin, John. *Occult America*. Garden City, N.Y.: Doubleday, 1972.

Gottschalk, Stephen. *The Emergence of Christian Science in American Religious Life*. Berkeley: University of California Press, 1973.

Greenwalt, Emmett A. *The Point Loma Community in California, 1897-1942: A Theosophical Experiment*. Berkeley: University of California Press, 1955.

Hansen, Chadwick. *Witchcraft at Salem*. New York: Braziller, 1969.

Hartmann, William C., ed. *Hartmann's Who's Who in Occult, Psychic and Spiritual Realms*. Jamaica, N.Y.: Occult Press, 1925.

————, ed. *Who's Who in Occultism, New Thought, Psychism and Spiritualism*. 2d ed. Jamaica, N.Y.: Occult Press, 1927.

————, ed. *Hartmann's International Directory of Psychic Science and Spiritualism*. Jamaica, N.Y.: Occult Press, 1930.

Hastings, James, ed. *Encyclopaedia of Religion and Ethics*. 13 vols. Edinburgh: T. & T. Clark; New York: Scribner's, 1908-1927.

Hill, Christopher. *The World Turned Upside Down: Radical Ideas During the English Revolution*. London: Temple Smith, 1972.

Holloway, Mark. *Heavens on Earth: Utopian Communities in America, 1680-1880*. 2d ed. New York: Dover, 1966.

Holzer, Hans. *The Directory of the Occult*. Chicago: Regnery, 1974.

Howe, Ellic. *Astrology: A Recent History Including the Untold Story of Its Role in World War II*. New York: Walker, 1968.

Hyre, K. M., and Eli Goodman, comps. *Price Guide to the Occult and Related Subjects*. Los Angeles: Price Guides, 1967.

Jackson, Carl T. "Oriental Ideas in American Thought." *Dictionary of the History of Ideas*, 3 (1973), 427-40.

Jacobs, David Michael. *The UFO Controversy in America*. Bloomington: Indiana University Press, 1975.

Judah, J. Stillson. *The History and Philosophy of the Metaphysical Movements in America*. Philadelphia: Westminster Press, 1967.

————. *Hare Krishna and the Counterculture*. New York: Wiley-Interscience, 1974.

Kagan, Paul. *New World Utopias: A Photographic History of the Search for Community*. New York: Penguin Books, 1975.

Keel, John A. "The Flying Saucer Subculture." *Journal of Popular Culture*, 8 (Spring 1975), 871-96.

Kerr, Howard. *Mediums and Spirit-Rappers and Roaring Radicals: Spiritualism* in *American Literature, 1850-1900.* Urbana: University of Illinois Press, 1972.

King, Francis. *Ritual Magic in England: 1887 to the Present Day.* London: Neville Spearman, 1970. U.S. ed.: *The Rites of Modern Occult Magic.* New York: Macmillan, 1971.

Knight, Damon. *Charles Fort: Prophet of the Unexplained.* Garden City, N.Y.: Doubleday, 1970.

Knight, David C., ed. *The ESP Reader.* New York: Grosset & Dunlap, 1969.

Krupp, E. C., ed. *In Search of Ancient Astronomies.* Garden City, N.Y.: Doubleday, 1977.

Kuhn, Alvin Boyd. *Theosophy: A Modern Revival of Ancient Wisdom.* New York: Holt, 1930.

La Barre, Weston. "Materials for a History of Studies of Crisis Cults: A Bibliographic Essay." *Current Anthropology,* 12 (February 1971), 3-44.

Landau, Rom. *God Is My Adventure: A Book on Modern Mystics, Masters and Teachers.* London: Ivor Nicholson and Watson, 1935; Faber, 1941; Allen & Unwin, 1964.

Lawton, George. *The Drama of Life After Death: A Study of the Spiritualist Religion.* New York: Holt, 1932.

Leopold, Richard W. *Robert Dale Owen: A Biography.* Cambridge: Harvard University Press, 1940.

Leventhal, Herbert. *In the Shadow of the Enlightenment: Occultism and Renaissance Science in Eighteenth-Century America.* New York: New York University Press, 1976.

Litvag, Irving. *Singer in the Shadows: The Strange Story of Patience Worth.* New York: Macmillan, 1972.

Lutyens, Mary. *Krishnamurti: The Years of Awakening.* New York: Farrar, Straus & Giroux, 1975.

Lyons, Arthur. *The Second Coming: Satanism in America.* New York: Dodd, Mead, 1970.

Macfarlane, Alan D. J. *Witchcraft in Tudor and Stuart England.* London: Routledge & Kegan Paul, 1970.

McIntosh, Christopher. *Eliphas Lévi and the French Occult Revival.* New York: Samuel Weiser, 1974.

Macphail, Ian, ed. *Alchemy and the Occult: A Catalogue of Books and Manuscripts from the Paul and Mary Mellon Collection.* 2 vols. New Haven: Yale University Press, 1969.

McVaugh, Michael, and Seymour Mauskopf. "J. B. Rhine's *Extra-Sensory Perception* and Its Background in Psychical Research." *Isis,* 67 (June 1976), 161-89.

Mead, G. R. S. "The Rising Psychic Tide" (1912). In his *Quests Old and New.* London: G. Bell, 1913, pp. 226-47.

Melton, J. Gordon. *A Reader's Guide to the Church's Ministry of Healing.* Evanston, Ill.: Academy of Religion and Psychical Research, 1973.

———. "Sources and Resources for Teaching the Occult." Reproduced paper available from the author, Institute for the Study of American Religion, Box 1311, Evanston, Ill. 60201.

————. "Toward a History of Magical Religion in the United States." *Listening,* 9 (Autumn 1974), 112-33.

Meyer, Donald. *The Positive Thinkers.* Garden City, N.Y.: Doubleday, 1965.

Midelfort, H. C. Erik. "Recent Witch Hunting Research, or Where Do We Go from here?" *Papers of the Bibliographical Society of America,* 62 (1968), 373-420.

Monter, E. William. "The Historiography of European Witchcraft: Progress and Prospects." *Journal of Interdisciplinary History,* 2 (Spring 1972), 435-51.

Moore, R. Laurence. *In Search of White Crows: Spiritualism, Parapsychology, and American Culture.* New York: Oxford University Press, 1977.

Morgan, S. R., comp. *Index to Psychic Science.* Swarthmore, Pa.: n.p., 1950.

Needleman, Jacob. *The New Religions.* Garden City, N.Y.: Doubleday, 1970. Rev. ed. New York: Pocket Books, 1972.

Nelson, Geoffrey K. *Spiritualism and Society.* New York: Schocken, 1969.

Nethercot, Arthur H. *The First Five Lives of Annie Besant.* Chicago: University of Chicago Press, 1960.

————. *The Last Four Lives of Annie Besant.* Chicago: University of Chicago Press, 1963.

Nordquist, Ted A. *Ananda Cooperative Village: A Study in the Beliefs, Values, and Attitudes of a New Age Religious Community.* Uppsala, Sweden: Borgströms Tryckeri, 1978.

Nugent, Donald. "Witchcraft Studies, 1959-1971: A Bibliographical Survey." *Journal of Popular Culture,* 5 (Winter 1971), 710-25. Reprinted in *The Occult: Studies and Evaluations.* Edited by Robert Galbreath. Bowling Green, Ohio: Bowling Green University Popular Press, 1972.

Peel, Robert. *Mary Baker Eddy: The Years of Discovery.* New York: Holt, Rinehart and Winston, 1966.

————. *Mary Baker Eddy: The Years of Trial.* New York: Holt, Rinehart and Winston, 1971.

Pleasants, Helene, ed. *Biographical Dictionary of Parapsychology.* New York: Garrett Publications/Helix Press, 1964.

Podmore, Frank. *From Mesmer to Christian Science: A Short History of Mental Healing.* 1909. Reprint. New Hyde Park, N.Y.: University Books, 1963.

————. *Mediums of the 19th Century.* 2 vols. 1902. Reprint. New Hyde Park, N.Y.: University Books, 1963.

Popenoe, Cris. *Books for Inner Development: The Yes! Guide.* New York: Random House, 1976.

Program for the Study of New Religious Movements in America. "Interim Directory of Scholars Interested in the New Religious Movements in America." Available from the Program, 2465 LeConte Ave., Berkeley, Calif. 94709.

Regush, June, and Nicholas Regush. *PSI: The Other World Catalogue.* New York: Putnam's, 1974.

Robbins, Rossell Hope. *The Encyclopedia of Witchcraft and Demonology.* New York: Crown, 1959.

Roberts, Susan. *Witches, U.S.A.* New York: Dell, 1971.

Rogo, D. Scott. *Parapsychology: A Century of Inquiry.* New York: Taplinger, 1975.

Roszak, Theodore. *The Making of a Counter Culture.* Garden City, N.Y.: Doubleday, 1969.

Russell, Jeffrey Burton. *Witchcraft in the Middle Ages.* Ithaca, N.Y.: Cornell University Press, 1972.

Schneider, Herbert W., and George Lawton. *A Prophet and a Pilgrim.* New York: Columbia University Press, 1942.

Sharma, Umesh, and John Arndt, comps. *Mysticism: A Select Bibliography.* Waterloo, Ontario: Waterloo Lutheran University, 1973.

Shepard, Leslie A., ed. *Encyclopedia of Occultism and Parapsychology.* 2 vols. Detroit: Gale, 1977.

Smith, David E. "Millenarian Scholarship in America." *American Quarterly,* 17 (Fall 1965), 535-49.

Spence, Lewis. *An Encyclopaedia of Occultism.* 1920. Reprint. New Hyde Park, N.Y.: University Books, 1960.

Spiritual Community. *Spiritual Community Guide.* San Rafael, Calif.: Spiritual Community, 1972.

———. *Spiritual Community Guide #4 1979.* San Rafael, Calif.: Spiritual Community, 1978.

Stearn, Jess. *Edgar Cayce—The Sleeping Prophet.* Garden City, N.Y.: Doubleday, 1967.

Stern, Madeleine B. *Heads and Headlines: The Phrenological Fowlers.* Norman: University of Oklahoma Press, 1971.

Story, Ronald. *The Space-Gods Revealed: A Close Look at the Theories of Erich von Däniken.* New York: Harper & Row, 1976.

Thomas, Keith. *Religion and the Decline of Magic.* New York: Scribner's, 1971.

Thorndike, Lynn. *A History of Magic and Experimental Science.* 8 vols. New York: Columbia University Press, 1923-1958.

Tietze, Thomas R. *Margery.* New York: Harper & Row, 1973.

Tiryakian, Edward A., ed. *On the Margin of the Visible: Sociology, the Esoteric, and the Occult.* New York: Wiley-Interscience, 1974.

Truzzi, Marcello. "The Occult Revival as Popular Culture: Some Random Observations on the Old and the Nouveau Witch." *Sociological Quarterly,* 13 (Winter 1972), 16-36.

———. "Astrology as Popular Culture." *Journal of Popular Culture,* 8 (Spring 1975), 906-11.

———. "The *Zetetic's* Researcher Directory." January 1976. Available from the author, Dept. of Sociology, Eastern Michigan Univ., Ypsilanti, Mich. 48197.

Tyler, Alice Felt. *Freedom's Ferment.* Minneapolis: University of Minnesota Press, 1944.

Veysey, Laurence. *The Communal Experience: Anarchist and Mystical Counter-Cultures in America.* New York: Harper & Row, 1973.

Waite, Arthur Edward. *A New Encyclopaedia of Freemasonry.* Rev. ed. 2 vols. N.d. Reprint. New Hyde Park, N.Y.: University Books, 1970.

Wallis, Roy. *The Road to Total Freedom: A Sociological Analysis of Scientology.* New York: Columbia University Press, 1977.

Webb, James. *The Occult Underground.* La Salle, Ill.: Open Court, 1974.

———. *The Occult Establishment.* La Salle, Ill.: Open Court, 1976.

White, Rhea A., and Laura A. Dale, comps. *Parapsychology: Sources of Information.* Metuchen, N.J.: Scarecrow Press, 1973.

Williams, Gertrude Marvin. *Priestess of the Occult.* New York: Alfred A. Knopf, 1946.

Yates, Frances A. *Giordano Bruno and the Hermetic Tradition.* Chicago: University of Chicago Press, 1964.

———. *The Rosicrucian Enlightenment.* London: Routledge and Kegan Paul, 1972.

Zaretsky, Irving I., and Mark P. Leone, eds. *Religious Movements in Contemporary America.* Princeton: Princeton University Press, 1974.

PERIODICAL

Zetetic Scholar. Ypsilanti, Mich. 1978-. The latest version of a periodical that has appeared successively as *Explorations* (newsletter; 4 issues, 1972-1973); *The Zetetic* (newsletter; 3 issues, 1974-1975); and *The Zetetic: Journal of the Committee for the Scientific Investigation of Claims of the Paranormal* (journal; 2 issues under Marcello Truzzi's editorship, 1976-1977).

CHAPTER 10. Photography as Popular Culture

Richard N. Masteller

Photography has enjoyed popularity in America since 1839, when news of its first widely successful form, the daguerreotype, reached American shores from France. Since these early days, a multitude of photographic formats have entered and passed from the scene, recording it for posterity, shrinking the world while expanding its horizons, and feeding contradictory human desires for scientific information, romantic escapism, and comfortable home truths. Contemporary considerations of the photographic image stress its status as a surrogate reality; the image, could we but learn to read it, might reveal the social construction of reality inherent in the mind of its maker, in the minds of its depicted subjects, perhaps even in the minds of its viewers.

Nevertheless, the riches and significance afforded the researcher in photography have only recently begun to be harvested. While the field of "fine art" or "creative" photography has profited most from this critical attention, the intractable billions of images produced by less accomplished photographers have proved difficult to reduce to patterns of order or significance, and "popular" photography has thus suffered from comparative neglect. This essay is designed to survey such information as exists and to suggest a framework for approaching photography as an artifact of popular culture.

To be considered in the province of popular culture, photography must at least involve a large number of people. It may be useful to divide popular photography into three categories: photography of the people, by the people, and for the people. In its earliest years, the making of photographs by large numbers of people was impossible. Most were without the necessary technical knowledge and financial resources, and the medium itself was experimental and unpredictable. Yet beginning with the daguerreotype and continuing in subsequent forms such as the tintype and the *carte-de-visite*, the photograph drew thousands of people to portrait studios, whether elaborate establishments on Fifth Avenue in New York City in the 1850s or temporary quarters set up by itinerant photographers in hotel rooms across America. The legacy is still alive today—in the portable landscapes and floodlights of the nearby K-Mart. One category of popular photography is, therefore, practiced by commercial photographers: it is photography of the people.

The second category—photography by the people—designates those who take their own photographs but who are relatively untrained photographers. These are the snapshooters, the holiday or vacation practitioners, those who are interested primarily in recording an event or perhaps in capturing a "pretty" picture. Although the outer limits of this group include more serious amateur photographers who join camera clubs and perhaps develop their own films and photographs, the largest number of people in this category are likely to have somebody else (or the camera itself in contemporary "instant" photography) complete the photograph they have taken. In essence, photography by the people designates the work of largely untutored recordmakers.

Photography for the people is the third category of popular photography. It designates the realm of photomechanically reproduced imagery for advertising and information transmission of all kinds, whether in books, magazines, and newspapers, on handbills, bubble gum cards, or political campaign literature. This is clearly an enormous area for research, but it is one that must concern us least here, in part because it borders on areas explored by other analysts of popular culture, and in part because large numbers of people, although exposed to it, do not have the same direct involvement in the production of the imagery as they do in the other two categories of popular photography.

Photography as an artifact of popular culture, then, is most directly photography of the people or by the people: large numbers are exposed to it or engage in it. But unlike photography for the people, such as that taken by photojournalists, photography of or by the people is not translated into another visual medium; and unlike creative photography (photography despite the people?), popular photographers have less artistic and technical training and less desire to produce images for isolated aesthetic contemplation.

HISTORIC OUTLINE

Although the world's first photograph, which was the result of an eight-hour exposure, has been dated to 1826, the first technique to receive worldwide acclaim was named by and for its inventor, Louis J. M. Daguerre. As early as 1837, Daguerre produced a permanent image on a daguerreotype, a thin, copper plate which he silvered, sensitized to light, exposed in a *camera obscura,* and developed in mercury vapor. The technical details of his process were made public at a joint meeting of the French Academy of Sciences and the Academy of Fine Arts on August 19, 1839; within five months, over thirty editions of Daguerre's manual had spread the details throughout Europe, to Russia, and to the United States.

Memoirs, letters, newspaper accounts, and cartoons reveal that the public at large was enamored of the "mirror with a memory," especially as refinements in the early 1840s shortened the exposure time and improved the image quality. Although landscapes and cityscapes were common subjects, portraiture was the most prevalent subject matter of daugerreotypes. In 1849, *Godey's Lady's Book* suggested that daguerreotypists were "limning faces at a rate that promises soon to make every man's house a Daguerreian Gallery." Such galleries, often quite elaborate, were opened in major American cities, while itinerant daguerreotypists found eager sitters in smaller towns and villages. To protect the delicate images from tarnish and abrasion, daguerreotypes were most often covered with a brass mat and glass and inserted in elaborately tooled leather cases, padded with silk or velvet. But they were also placed in brooches, medallions, and watch cases. Depending on size and competition, daguerreotype portraits ranged from twenty-five cents to fifty dollars; the average price usually fluctuated from two dollars to seven or eight dollars. In 1853, the *New York Herald Tribune* estimated that approximately three million American daguerreotypes were being produced annually.

Photography of the people soon benefited from additional inventions. Every daguerreotype was unique; although daguerreotype copies of daguerreotypes were made, the mass production of photographic images had to await not only a negative-positive system of picture making, but also a sufficiently detailed image to rival the precision of the daguerreotype. In France in 1850, L. D. Blanquart-Evrard announced his process of printing photographs on a thin paper coated with albumen. In England in 1851, Frederick Scott Archer made negatives composed of light-sensitive collodion on glass, obtaining a more precise image more quickly than had previous negative processes. Ambrotypes on glass, dating from about 1854, and melainotypes or ferrotypes (later called tintypes), dating from 1856, were based on Archer's collodion process. Until near the end of the century, however, the albumen paper print made from a collodion negative was the dominant process in photography.

Predicated on the replicability and mass production inherent in the negative-positive process, the *carte-de-visite* rose in popularity as the daguerreotype waned. *Cartes-de-visite,* patented in France by Disdéri in 1854, were small albumen portraits about 4 by 2½ inches, pasted on cards about 1/16 inch thick. They were made with a camera fitted with multiple lenses which enabled eight exposures to be made on the same negative.

At the beginning of the 1860s, "cardomania" skyrocketed. In England, seventy thousand portraits of the Prince Consort were sold during the week following his death. In America during January 1861, the E. and H. T. Anthony Company, the largest photographic company in the nineteenth century, made one thousand portraits a day of Major Robert Anderson, who was a central figure in the attack on Fort Sumter. Images of other soldiers, and of poets, musicians, and entertainers were supplied to meet an insatiable demand. After Lincoln's assassination, photomontage *cartes* appeared of George Washington welcoming Lincoln into Heaven. One's ordinary, earthly neighbors also appeared in *cartes*. An advertisement in *Leslie's* on January 7, 1860, offered "Your Photograph On a Visiting Card: 25 Copies for One Dollar." Although they may not often have been left as calling cards, they were traded with friends and mailed to distant relatives, especially during the Civil War. Although Disdéri died a pauper, he became a millionaire on the strength of his patent. School children today continue the same ritual he first popularized.

The birth of the family album can be dated to 1860, when the photographic industry began to produce albums with specially cut-out pages for the insertion of *cartes*. At first they were only slightly larger than the *cartes*, but albums became more elaborate as picture formats changed. By 1870, the E. and H. T. Anthony Company listed nearly five hundred album styles. Some were simple, but many were lavish: they were several inches thick, leather-bound, gilt-edged, sometimes inlaid with mother-of-pearl, and usually fitted with heavy, engraved metal clasps. Such designs reflect the preciousness attached to photographs of the people.

The albumen print made at a photographer's studio remained the dominant form of photography of the people throughout the last four decades of the nineteenth century, but a variety of merchandising tactics gave the appearance of innovation. Although artificial, painted backdrops were used in England prior to 1851, they were relatively scarce in America during the 1840s and 1850s. Throughout the 1860s they became more common. In the comfort of the studio one could sit in front of a Greek temple or stand before a sylvan scene. Elaborate accessories proliferated—artificial rocks, rustic fences, plaster Grecian urns. In 1870, the studio of José Mora, one of the more flamboyant and successful New York City photographers, was equipped with fifty painted backgrounds—soon to grow to one hundred fifty. His clientele of socialites and celebrities could choose among "plains and mountains, tropic luxuriance and polar wastes," Egypt or Siberia. Matching the proliferation of backgrounds was a proliferation of image sizes. The "cabinet" size, about 4 by 6 inches, became popular in America about 1867. It brought new considerations about retouching negatives and posing sitters because poor technique and less "photogenic" subjects were more apparent in its larger size. "Boudoir" prints, "promenade" prints, and "imperial" prints followed in the 1870s—all were enterprising tactics to foster photography of the people.

Photography by the people can be dated, with some plausibility, to the rise of amateur exchange clubs in the 1850s in England and America. These small groups of people had sufficient funds and sufficient technical training to make their own images of their friends and surroundings. But the flowering of photography as practiced by the masses of people is more logically dated to 1888, when George Eastman announced his Kodak camera with the slogan, "You Push the Button, We Do the Rest." The Kodak was easily portable; it could be held in the hand and weighed only 1½ pounds. It was bought already loaded with a roll of film that would take one hundred circular photographs 2½ inches in diameter. When the roll was fully exposed, the camera was returned to the factory where it was unloaded, reloaded with fresh film, and returned to the owner along with the prints that had been developed from the first film. As Eastman wrote in the owner's manual, "Photography is thus brought within the reach of every human being who desires to preserve a record of what he sees. Such a photographic note book. . .enables the fortunate possessor to go back by the light of his own fireside to scenes which would otherwise fade from the memory and be lost."

The cost of the Kodak camera, together with its first roll of film, was twenty-five dollars; processing the exposed film and loading new film cost another ten dollars. By October 1889, the company was receiving sixty to seventy-five Kodaks and processing six to seven thousand negatives a day. By early 1900, thirty-five different Kodak cameras had been marketed. One of them, the "Brownie," was introduced especially for use by children; it cost one dollar and took six pictures on a roll of film that cost fifty cents to buy and develop. Over one hundred thousand were sold within a year in England and America. Numerous variations of its basic design kept it the most popular roll-film box camera, and it survived in one form or another essentially until the advent of the Instamatic camera in 1963.

In the twentieth century, photography of the people has continued despite the enormous increase in photography by the people, and despite the attack by fine-art photographers on studio portraiture at the turn of the century. The Photo-Secession Exhibition in 1902 and the opening of the Little Galleries of the Photo-Secession in 1905 were the culmination of a decade of increasing antagonism between those who desired to establish photography as an art form, those who practiced photography less seriously as a hobby in the Kodak manner, and those whose commercial aims were paramount. There is not sufficient space here to detail their various battles. But the assumptions behind commercial photography early in the century continued unchanged. Although softly focused imagery replaced the more excessive artificial backdrops of the late 1800s, studio portraiture continued to aim for revelation of "character," and studios continued to produce the formal family portrait, which reasserted solidarity and continuity in the face of social change. At the same time, studios cultivated their role in recording rites of passage: birthdays of children, graduations, weddings, and anniversaries. While the creative photographers whom Alfred Stieglitz chose to welcome to the Photo-Secession evolved into a small circle of confidantes, photographers of the people continued to hold to commercially successful conventions of portraiture. Meanwhile, hobbyists continued to look to burgeoning periodicals of amateur photography, such as *American Photography, Photo Era,* and *Photo-Beacon,* for advice on taking pictures. As snapshooters, they continued to indulge in an entertaining, relatively untaxing hobby.

The diverse innovations of twentieth-century photographic technology have attempted to cater to these contradictory aims. We shall note only the most important of these innovations.

The Leica camera was first marketed in 1925 and fully refined by 1932. Offered as a camera for professional photojournalists and serious amateurs, its innovative, compact design provided freedom of movement, while its thirty-five millimeter negative and excellent lens produced detailed images. As a relatively expensive camera, it created a market somewhere between the largest number of casual snapshooters and the professional photographers. While the inexpensive box camera evolved over the years into the Instamatic, the efficient design of the Leica spurred other manufacturers to produce the Contax, the Exakta, the Nikon, and other thirty-five millimeter cameras, and photography by the people spread further across the spectrum of economic and social classes.

Color photography had its first widely celebrated success in 1907, when the Lumière brothers (Auguste Marie, Louis Nicolas, and Louis Jean) marketed their Autochrome process, which produced a unique positive transparency, as did the Kodachrome film first marketed in 1935. In 1941, Kodacolor film was introduced; this negative film allowed any number of positives to be made. Today, the large majority of amateur photographs are in color, in either transparency or positive print form.

The industry's desire to increase photography by the people has not only spurred the invention of various color processes, but it has also led to increasingly simplified, automatic cameras. Photoelectric exposure meters were marketed in the early 1930s and incorporated into some cameras in 1938. Today, a wide range of fully automatic cameras has given new significance to the original Kodak slogan, "You Push the Button, We Do the Rest."

One of the most startling innovations in popular photography occurred despite Kodak's dominance in the marketplace. In 1947, Dr. Edwin Land announced the invention of his instant-picture process, and a year later the first Polaroid-Land camera went on sale. In 1956, the one millionth Polaroid camera was sold. Polaroid's series of innovations, such as shorter development times, more sensitive black-and-white film, instant color film (1963), and development outside the camera (1972), have all helped to make photography by the people easier and, some would say, as dramatic as the original daguerreotype process.

Photography of and by the people will continue to occupy a central position in American popular culture. The average number of photographs taken per household annually has increased from fifty-two in 1965, to seventy-five in 1970, to ninety-four in 1975. Almost thirty-four hundred drive-in photofinishing kiosks were operating in 1976; their yearly growth rate averages 20 percent. Magazines that cater to amateur photographers are thriving. Both *Modern Photography* and *Popular Photography*, begun in 1937, have current circulations of over five hundred thousand, and each month they treat their readers to an endless variety of product news, equipment testing, and picture-making tips. Studio photography—photography of the people—remains largely formal, but it has learned to adopt the candid styles and informal poses that some of these innovations have fostered. Photography by the people today reflects the same fascination with technical innovations and the same desire for effortless records and revelations that accompanied the rise of popular photography in the nineteenth century.*

REFERENCE WORKS

The reference tools available in other disciplines are only now being developed for photography. The few that exist either attempt incomplete surveys of the whole realm of photography or focus on creative photographers. The student of popular photography must thus begin with three histories that might better be listed under the section "History and Criticism" in this essay; I shall discuss them here because they are well-illustrated, fundamental introductions to some of the evidence that subsequent analysis must shape into culturally illuminating studies of the medium's popularity.

Helmut and Alison Gernsheim's *The History of Photography from the Camera Obscura to the Beginning of the Modern Era* is currently out of print, but larger libraries should have copies, and a revision is being contemplated. Written by the eminent collectors who assembled the Gernsheim Collection at the University of Texas, the text is organized by

*Many of the details in this brief outline have been derived from Beaumont Newhall's *The History of Photography from 1839 to the Present Day*, and from Robert Taft's *Photography and the American Scene: A Social History, 1839-1889*, both of which are discussed in the following section.

chronology and by technical advances in the history of the medium. The major divisions of the text treat photography's prehistory, its invention, the early years, the collodion period, and the gelatin period. A section on aerial, criminal, underwater, and medical photography precedes sections on the evolution of color photography and on photography and the printed page. The text has a British orientation, and coverage ends about 1914. But, of the three core histories, it is the most complete in its coverage of the science and mechanics of photography, and it supplies some helpful data that allow one to begin to theorize about the subsequent popular influence of the medium. It also has a wealth of esoteric names and details not readily available elsewhere.

Beaumont Newhall's *The History of Photography from 1839 to the Present Day* is the only inexpensive general history currently available. Sometimes referred to as the dean of photohistorians, Newhall began his career as an art historian. The seeds of his *History* were sown in the first exhibition of photography to be held at the Museum of Modern Art in New York, an exhibition Newhall organized in 1937. The revised edition covers the prehistory of photography to about the mid-1950s. For studying photography as a popular phenomenon, the greatest limitation of the text is its predominant focus on "creative" photography; perhaps less obvious is a preference for a purist, unmanipulated photography that was seen as "modern" in the 1930s and 1940s. Nevertheless, the book is essential. Individual chapters consider the popular daguerreotype; "portraits for the million" (ambrotypes, tintypes); and documentary photography during and after the Civil War, at the turn of the century, and in the 1930s. The facts surrounding the rise of photojournalism and brief discussions of *Life*, *Look*, and the advent of the photo essay are also included. The book thus provides a stage from which to begin a consideration of the influence of photography on popular culture.

The third indispensable (and also inexpensive) history is Robert Taft's *Photography and the American Scene: A Social History, 1839-1889*. Like the Gernsheim and Newhall texts, Taft's chapters are organized by chronology and by process. Unlike the Gernsheims and Newhall, however, Taft's focus is exclusively American, and he is less concerned with "artistic" images. Although his fictional scenarios of social interaction are sometimes quaint ("How many a bashful beau has had his pangs of embarrassment eased by the relieving words, 'Let's look at the pictures in the album!'"), they are grounded in almost five hundred footnotes gathered from a wide range of primary sources, including American photographic and nonphotographic periodicals. He has good discussions of the rise of amateur photographic exchange clubs, of family albums, of western expeditionary photography before and after the Civil War, and of the entrance of photography via the halftone screen into newspapers and cultural organs such as *Harper's Monthly* and *The Century*. Completed in 1938, his text is dated in some respects, but it remains an indispensable resource and guide to original material. Of the three histories, Taft's comes closest to "a social history."

One other recent history is best discussed in this section. William Welling's *Photography in America: The Formative Years 1839-1900* repeats some of the material in Newhall and Taft and has little analysis of photography's social or cultural ramifications. But the book is distinguished by the extensive number of carefully documented facsimile reprints of excerpts and illustrations from early journals, guides, and newspaper notices demonstrating the appeal of photography in America. It is thus a convenient compendium for the person without access to original nineteenth-century materials.

There are few bibliographies concerned with photography, and none that focus on popular photography. The two-volume *Photographic Literature: An International Bibliographic Guide to General and Specialized Literature on Photographic Processes, Techniques, Theory. . .*, compiled by Albert Boni, cites essays from the nineteenth century to 1970, but it is slanted toward technical aspects of the medium. An *Index to Articles on Photography 1977*, edited by William Johnson, surveys over eighty American and foreign periodicals and cites some three thousand eight hundred references from 1977, covering a range of photographic concerns from broad historical questions to studies of individual, contemporary creative photographers. The creative aspects of the medium are emphasized, and the bulk of the entries are organized by photographer's name. Portions of the index first appeared bimonthly, beginning in November 1978, in *Afterimage*, the periodical of the Visual Studies Workshop.

Some broader, obvious reference tools—the *Art Index*, the *Reader's Guide to Periodical Literature*, the *Social Science Index*, and the *Humanities Index*—should be consulted under particular subject headings, such as "photography clubs and societies." The larger number of citations in the *Reader's Guide* compared to the *Social Science Index* or *Humanities Index* reflects both the popularity of photography and the dearth of scholarly articles devoted to it. An index that attempts to cover the spectrum of modern art including photography is *Artbibliographies Modern*. It began in 1971 with the title *LOMA 1969* (*Literature of Modern Art 1969*) and assumed its present title with volume two. With volume four it began abstracting some of the articles and books it cites. *Art Design Photo*, begun in 1974 and edited by Alexander Davis, continues the format of unabstracted citations begun in *LOMA 1969;* its typography and layout make it difficult to use, but it surveys a wider range of periodicals than does *Artbibliographies Modern*.

A useful survey of primary sources and secondary aids is Marsha Peters and Bernard Mergen's " 'Doing The Rest': The Uses of Photographs in American Studies." Directing their essay toward historians and American studies scholars, Peters and Mergen raise initial questions and suggest ways of approaching the rich photographic evidence pervading our past and present society.

Other reference tools aid more particular concerns. Arnold Gassan's *A Chronology of Photography* tends to be idiosyncratic; in two-thirds of the text, he discusses primarily creative photographers and the ostensible social and cultural influences surrounding their work. But the final one-third of the book is a useful, although occasionally inaccurate, chronology that juxtaposes events and milestones in the development of photography with events in other arts, in literature, and in world history. William Welling's *Collector's Guide to Nineteenth-Century Photographs* not only illustrates kinds of photographs, but also lists nineteenth-century photographic journals and late nineteenth-century photographic societies and their officers. He also briefly discusses major present-day repositories. William Culp Darrah's two books, *Stereo Views: A History of Stereographs in America and Their Collection* and *The World of Stereographs*, are essential starting points for any study of the immensely popular stereograph, the double photograph that appeared three-dimensional in a stereoscope. The first book includes: a history of the invention, development, and merchandising of the format; lists of stereographers; information for identifying and classifying the myriad number of views; and brief discussions of popular views. His second book expands the first; it contains three hundred illustrations, lists of thirty-five hundred stereographers in North America and forty-two hundred in other parts of the world, and brief discussions of eighty subjects that appeared frequently in stereograph cards. Critical analysis is minimal, but, as reference guides, Darrah's books help chart the vast domain of stereographs.

Several texts directed toward collectors who are interested in cameras and other photographica can serve as useful reference tools and provide clues to the rich sociological and cultural implications of popular photography. One of the better guides is George Gilbert's *Collecting Photographica: The Images and Equipment of the First Hundred Years of Photography*. Gilbert includes photographs of early equipment, original prices, and a selection of ads from the popular press. He also reproduces examples of other photographica spawned by the rise of amateur photography; the Montgomery Ward Catalog of 1900, for example, contained an ad for photo belt buckles, photo watch charms, and photo garter belts ("It is now quite a fad for the ladies to wear the picture of a favored one on her garter"). Adding to the book's utility are appendixes of important dates, guides to dating equipment, and a detailed chart outlining "A Brief History of Most Eastman and Kodak Cameras, 1887-1939." Restricting itself to camera equipment, *A Century of Cameras from the Collection of the International Museum of Photography at George Eastman House,* written by Eaton S. Lothrop, Jr., includes photographs of such items as the book camera, the watch camera, and the concealed vest camera. The book features 130 items ranging from the 1839 Giroux Daguerreotype camera to the 1940 Minox, a brief technical description for each, and a citation to an original advertisement appearing in amateur photographic or popular magazines.

Finally, three disparate sources may be useful for scholars researching particular areas of photography. Turn-of-the-century information may be garnered from *Cassell's Cyclopaedia of Photography,* edited by Bernard E. Jones. Published in 1911 and reprinted in 1973, the volume is useful for period descriptions of techniques, processes, and formulas, as well as for biographical entries and historical sketches of photographic societies. Scholars interested in present-day business statistics should consult the *Wolfman Report on the Photographic Industry in the United States,* compiled annually since 1952 by Augustus Wolfman. In it, one can learn, for example, that disposable personal income rose 184 percent from 1950 to 1968, while public spending for picture-making rose 641 percent; and that approximately 6.7 billion photographs were taken by amateurs in 1975. *The Photography Catalog,* compiled by Norman Snyder, Carole Kismaric, and Don Myrus, is modeled on *The Whole Earth Catalog.* Of some relevance to contemporary popular photography are sections listing current books, magazines, and picture sources, while the pervasiveness of photography in our culture is reflected in sections devoted to the spectrum of equipment currently available, to schools and workshops, to galleries, and to issues of collecting photographs.

RESEARCH COLLECTIONS

Guides exist or are in preparation for locating significant "fine art" photographs, but the much broader range of photographs of interest to students of popular culture has not been given similar attention. What follows is a brief discussion of major national resources and some general suggestions for tapping the photographic materials probably available wherever scholars may be located.

Ann Novotny's *Picture Sources 3: Collections of Prints and Photographs in the United States and Canada* is an invaluable guide to 1,084 collections. Although it is not restricted to photographs, it has useful summaries of holdings in major collections, a note on access and costs, and indexes arranged by geographical location and by subject matter. Novotny cites some sixty-five locations of potential interest to researchers in photojournalism or the history and art of photography, ranging from the Library of

Congress to the files of *Parade Magazine*. *Photography: Source and Resource*, compiled by Steven Lewis, James McQuaid, and David Tait, is primarily a book of essays intended as a "sourcebook for creative photography," but an "index to collections" in various (usually art) museums includes some more general historical collections. The index is arranged by state, and each institution lists its number of holdings alphabetically by name of photographer. An updated version is being released in the fall of 1979.

Washington, D.C., houses major repositories of photography, many of which are noted in Shirley Green's *Pictorial Resources in the Washington, D.C. Area*. The two most comprehensive are the Smithsonian Institution's Division of Photographic History in the National Museum of History and Technology, and the Prints and Photographs Division of the Library of Congress. The former houses a History of Photography Collection consisting of some five hundred thousand pictorial items ranging from daguerreotypes to modern color prints. Catalogs to these holdings are in preparation. The latter is one of the most comprehensive resources in the country. Here are such collections as the Civil War photographs of Mathew Brady and his associates; the one hundred twenty thousand glass-plate negatives of the George Bain Collection, which constitutes the major portion of the first important newspicture agency in the United States; and the two hundred seventy thousand negatives and one hundred fifty thousand photographs gathered by the Historical Section of the Farm Security Administration from 1935 to 1943. Paul Vanderbilt's *Guide to the Special Collections of Prints and Photographs in the Library of Congress* is an out-of-print guide to these holdings, arranged alphabetically by collection and including brief descriptions of their contents.

New York City is another major repository. The New York Public Library has extensive collections, as does the Museum of the City of New York. At the other end of the state in Rochester, the International Museum of Photography at George Eastman House is the only museum in the United States devoted exclusively to photography. It maintains an international collection of about one million images and about fifty thousand historical and contemporary books and periodicals. That portion of the collection presently cataloged is arranged by photographer, but the museum is engaged in a long-term project of computer cataloging that will allow a researcher to retrieve images by process, subject matter, nationality, and other categories. The museum has extensive collections of daguerreotypes, *cartes-de-visite*, stereographs, and studio photographs, and its collection of rare nineteenth-century photographic periodicals is among the best in the country.

The Gernsheim Collection of about one hundred fifty thousand images and six thousand books and periodicals is housed in the Humanities

Research Center at the University of Texas in Austin. Like the collection at the International Museum of Photography at George Eastman House, this is an international collection spanning the history of the medium, and is especially rich in nineteenth-century items.

Other important materials lie scattered throughout the United States in state and local historical societies and in university archives, which one can begin to approach by consulting the *Directory of Historical Societies and Agencies in the United States*. Michael Lesy's innovative *Wisconsin Death Trip* was based on the Charles Van Schaick Collection in the State Historical Society of Wisconsin; his *Real Life: Louisville in the Twenties* drew on the commercial photographs taken by the firm of Caulfield and Shook in the 1920s, which are now available in the Photographic Archives of the University of Louisville. The New York State Historical Association in Cooperstown houses some fifty-five thousand images. The University of Washington in Seattle has about two hundred thousand images covering the period from 1860 to 1930 in Washington Territory, Alaska, and Canada. The Bancroft Library of the University of California in Berkeley contains over one million picture items. These examples point to the fact that state and local historical societies and university archives are a treasure trove of neglected resources because large numbers of photographs and family photograph albums eventually find their way to such repositories.

The scholar who hopes to study photography as an artifact of popular culture might best start at home, but not just in the local historical society. Arangements can sometimes be made with local camera stores to survey long-unclaimed photographs, and members of local camera clubs are usually happy to share their hobby with whoever will listen and look. Finally, scholars should not overlook the homes of their friends or their own dens and attics.

HISTORY AND CRITICISM

Many of the texts that follow give information—and repeat information—essential to any serious student of photography as an artifact of popular culture. But to systematize that information remains, for the most part, the task of scholars whose work is yet to be completed because the texts are frequently as intractable to the systematic concerns of cultural analysts as the imagery itself.

Included in the ensuing discussion, then, are older works that treat aspects of photographic history; these works provide a sense of the medium as it was becoming popular. There follows a discussion of texts that focus on particular photographic formats or processes. Popular appeal and dissemination were, after all, tied to these technical aspects of the medium.

The flaw in the texts organized around processes or formats is that larger social and cultural implications are frequently subordinated or ignored. This section will conclude with recent, more theoretical works that provide models for addressing these larger implications.

Besides the standard historical references—Gernsheim, Newhall, and Taft, and the recent text by Welling—older histories can provide evidence and clues to an investigator attempting an analysis of photography as a popular phenomenon. Erich Stenger's *The History of Photography: Its Relation to Civilization and Practice*, translated by Edward Epstean, is primarily technical and oriented toward European, particularly German, photography. But Stenger includes anecdotal sections on amateur photography, the role of the *carte-de-visite*, the advent of identification and criminal photography, and a compendium of photographic references appearing in popular, nonphotographic literature. John Werge's *The Evolution of Photography* is more a primary than a secondary source. It is a meandering reminiscence of Werge's impressions and reactions to the enterprise of photography in the nineteenth century and of his visits to exhibitions, salons, and studios in England and in America. The second part of the book reprints some of his eclectic articles that first appeared in photographic journals of his day. W. Jerome Harrison's *A History of Photography Written as a Practical Guide and an Introduction to Its Latest Developments* and Gaston Tissandier's *A History and Handbook of Photography* are each oriented more toward technical and scientific discussions than toward photography as a popular phenomenon. But they are useful as evidence of the widespread fascination with scientific experimentation and technique that inextricably accompanied the advent and progress of photography. The third part of Tissandier's text, moreover, "The Applications of Photography," examines various social uses. He anticipates telegraphic communication of photographs and suggests that photographs of criminals be displayed in public places: "it would thus be possible to make the arrest of malefactors, upon whom the police are unable to lay their hands, more easy. It would be the same with dead bodies which had not been claimed by anyone."

Other useful, older works should be consulted to get a flavor for the growth of the medium in the nineteenth century. The printing history of John Towler's *The Silver Sunbeam* recommends it to students of popular culture. There were four editions of one thousand copies each from January through November 1864, plus other editions in 1866, 1869, 1870, 1873, and, finally, the ninth edition in 1879. It was sold in England and America, and Spanish translations appeared in 1876, 1884, and 1890. Rather than revisions each edition included supplements on the latest techniques; the first edition of 351 pages had grown to 599 pages by the ninth edition. The 1969 reprint of the first edition includes advertisements and is worth perusal by scholars who are seeking insights into the scientific methods that had to be mastered to practice photography before the advent of dry plates and the Kodak camera.

Besides such scientifically oriented manuals, books were published to help the commercial photographer succeed. Marcus Aurelius Root's *The Camera and the Pencil Or the Heliographic Art* was written by a successful Philadelphia daguerreotypist. The book attempts to establish his profession as a fine art, mixing chapters of advice on putting clients at ease and on coloring photographs with chapters invoking Plato, Cicero, Joshua Reynolds, Edmund Burke, and John Ruskin on the varieties of the beautiful. As such, it is evidence of the early pretensions of this popular art to a fine-art status. H. J. Rodgers's *Twenty-Three Years Under a Skylight, or Life and Experiences of a Photographer* is a rather lightweight manual designed primarily to aid portrait photographers in solving the problems of posing and costume, but Rodgers's text is also interesting for its simplistic, popular considerations of physiognomy and phrenology as it relates to portraiture. James F. Ryder's *Voigtlander and I: In Pursuit of Shadow Catching. A Story of Fifty-Two Years' Companionship with a Camera* is a rambling reminiscence by a successful photographer in New York State and later in Cleveland, whose career began in the daguerreotype era and lasted until the turn of the century.

General histories and reminiscences have diminished as critics recognize the problematic diversity of the medium. Yet two recent works continue in a style resembling the historical survey, with the virtue of beginning to address the social implications of popular photography. Concentrating on French society, Michel F. Braive's *The Era of the Photograph: A Social History* lacks full documentation, but it is useful both because it cites contemporary accounts of how, for example, family albums or *cartes-de-visite* fostered group entertainment and because it attempts to relate the varieties of photographs to their social contexts. It also includes black and white reproductions of numerous lithographs demonstrating the popularity of the invention. Alan Thomas's *Time in a Frame: Photography and the Nineteenth-Century Mind* has a British orientation. The value of the book lies in its cogent speculations about the effect of photographic imagery on the people viewing it and in Thomas's attempts to "read" images in socially meaningful ways. With studio photography, he carefully traces the importance of "fashionable display" among the upper classes and its echo among the lower classes. Discussing family albums, he stresses the importance of both the image sequence and the images themselves. The occasional tension between "actuality" (the real elements depicted in the portrait) and "arrangement" (of costume and pose, for example) is for Thomas a rich source of visual information leading to social and psychological insights about the persons portrayed. Such insights must be offered cautiously, but

Thomas's arguments are more convincing than some proposed by other writers and are worth consideration as an attempt to go beyond the mere reiteration of photography's popularity to some cultural observations based on that popularity.

Having examined these surveys and reminiscences, one should turn to studies of particular processes. Daguerreotypes can initially be approached through four studies. Helmut and Alison Gernsheim's L. J. M. Daguerre: The History of the Diorama and the Daguerreotype is a well-documented introduction to its subjects, tracing developments in France, America, Britain, and Germany. Beaumont Newhall's The Daguerreotype in America follows the method of his History: he establishes origins, traces technical developments, and identifies practitioners. Separate chapters consider the thirty-seven daguerreotype galleries operating on Broadway in 1853 and the itinerant daguerreotypists traveling by wagon through small towns and rural regions. Good reproductions of daguerreotypes and brief biographical sketches of daguerreotypists are included. Richard Rudisill's Mirror Image: The Influence of the Daguerreotype on American Society adds an important dimension to Gernsheim and Newhall by relating the popularity of the daguerreotype to its social and cultural function. Rudisill suggests that the daguerreotype affected life in the United States in three ways: it encouraged cultural nationalism, promulgating affective images that reinforced notions of an American character; it furthered the transition from an agrarian to a technological society, in that the image was produced with a fascinating mechanical and scientific instrument; and it reinforced faith in the truth and spiritual insight one gained from carefully perceiving the works of God in nature. Rudisill's book includes excellent reproductions, numerous quotations from a wide range of original sources, and a useful annotated bibliography. The fourth source concerning daguerreotypes is more specialized. Floyd and Marion Rinhart's American Miniature Case Art illustrates and identifies the variety of often elaborate cases made to hold daguerreotypes.

Cartes-de-visite have not received extensive treatment in any one source, but Gernsheim, Newhall, and Taft devote pages to the subject. Max Kozloff, in "Nadar and the Republic of Mind," an article primarily about the portraitist, speculates on the appropriateness of the carte-de-visite in a growing mass society: "Like the Gatling gun of 1862, its aim was [to] decrease the ratio of effort to output by mechanizing the product. Poses could be standardized, droves of assistants could be hired, and sales volume could be increased. . . . Whether directly or not, most portraits registered the bonding of people to their community, if only because innumerable clues were given to show their place within its hierarchies. . . . (This state of affairs did not hamper individualism, but it certainly categorized it.)"

Kozloff's wide-ranging essays on photography, collected in *Photography and Fascination*, should be consulted.

Scholars interested in stereography might begin with Oliver Wendell Holmes's three articles in the *Atlantic Monthly*: "The Stereoscope and the Stereograph," "Sun-Painting and Sun-Sculpture; With a Stereoscopic Trip Across The Atlantic," and "Doings of the Sunbeam." The third article makes incidental reference to the stereograph, but the first two helped popularize the format, as did Holmes's contribution toward designing a convenient hand-held viewer. As mentioned in the section on "Reference Works," William Culp Darrah's *Stereo Views* and *The World of Stereographs* are essential guides. *Points of View: The Stereograph in America: A Cultural History*, edited by Nathan Lyons and Edward Earle, raises the kinds of social and cultural questions that most discussions of photography ignore. The illustrated anthology includes essays on ethnic portrayals in stereographs, on the stereograph as a commodity, and on the use of stereographs in visual education in the schools. A chronology of stereography is incorporated in a chronology of other socially and culturally significant events.

The burgeoning of amateur photography that occurred with the invention of the Kodak cameras provides rich material for sociological and cultural studies. One should first consult the Gernsheim, Newhall, and Taft histories and George Gilbert's *Collecting Photographica*. Beaumont Newhall's "How George Eastman Invented the Kodak Camera" is an informative essay. But the most detailed analysis of the development of the popular photographic industry is Reese Jenkins's *Images and Enterprise: Technology and the American Photographic Industry, 1839-1925*. Using Eastman Kodak Company as a case study, Jenkins is concerned with the industrialization that made photography popular. His is the only book—among the many dealing with technical advances in photography—that relates such advances to theoretical models of industrial and technological change familiar to economic historians. The merchandising that Jenkins examines is treated more humorously by Eaton Lothrop in "Personality Cameras." He discusses and illustrates cameras that tied into children's storybook or cartoon heroes, beginning with the Brownie and followed by such variations as the Donald Duck camera, the Hopalong Cassidy camera, and the Brenda Starr Cub Reporter camera, down to the more recent Charlie-Tuna camera (available in 1972 for $4.95 and three labels from a can of Star-Kist tuna) and the Mick-a-matic camera, which came in the shape of Mickey Mouse's head and was large enough to cover one's face when it was held up to take a photograph. A somewhat useful summary of recent trends in the art and business of photography is Charles Reynolds's "Forty Years of Evolution and Revolution."

Some of the wide-ranging theoretical works to be discussed at the conclusion of this section analyze the imagery spawned by this spread of photography as a popular hobby. But some recent, more focused studies of family albums and snapshots have begun to raise important questions and provide models both to emulate and to avoid.

A well-illustrated introduction to the topic is Ellen Maas's *Das Photoalbum 1858-1918: Eine Dokumentation zur Kultur- und Sozialgeschichte.* Less successful is Jeffrey Simpson's *The American Family: A History in Photographs.* Simpson's book is organized into important categories, including the public image of the family, the roles of courting and of the home, families as economic units, and families as social units. But an unacknowledged tension exists between the specifics of the imagery and the more suspicious generalizations of his prose. By selecting his images from a variety of public and private repositories, which themselves had removed the images from their original spatial and temporal contexts, he offers us a construction about *the* American family that is finally unsatisfying. His book demonstrates, by omission, the importance of context, the need to understand the motivations and satisfactions that originally surrounded the making of particular images.

A catalog that accompanied an exhibition of artifacts and photographs at the State Historical Society of Wisconsin, George Talbott's *At Home: Domestic Life in the Post-Centennial Era, 1876-1920,* recognizes the importance of this context. Talbott draws distinctions among, for example, a midwestern merchant prince who could afford elaborate studio portraits and a handsome commissioned album, a struggling homesteader who could afford only a view of his family taken in front of his home by a traveling photographer, and a poor urban laborer who could afford only a cheap tintype taken by a street photographer. Talbott suggests that such photographs, whatever their class origin, functioned as family keepsakes, demonstrating what people were proud of, what they thought interesting, and what they wanted to show others.

Karin Becker Ohrn's "Making Belief: Contexts for Family Photographs" is another model of a contextual approach to family albums and their social significance. Ohrn postulates the existence of a folk aesthetic in amateur photography, discusses in detail three amateur albums, and speculates on the psychological significance they held for their makers. She emphasizes the centrality of the home and family, the recurrent images of the hearth and dining-room table, and suggests that such photographs buttressed a belief in familial continuity and solidarity across space and time.

In "The Family Photo Album as a Form of Folklore," Amy Kotkin reports some results of her work with the Smithsonian Institution's Family Folklore Program. She underscores the importance of interviewing the people who are most closely connected with the images and suggests that family photographs function on three levels: viewed over time, they serve as the basis for family legends and thus family continuity; as part of material culture, their similarities in pose and setting suggest widely shared familial values; finally, they show evidence of becoming part of the rituals they record and in that sense help to create the very family life they depict. Kotkin concludes with a list of questions important for analyzing family albums: who takes the photographs, who arranges the album, where is it kept, and how often and under what circumstances is it viewed?

Studio portraiture first filled the pages of family albums, and it needs more exploration than it has received. Bevis Hillier's *Victorian Studio Photographs* is a book of images and biographical sketches of famous people drawn from the files of a British studio. It has brief introductions describing the typical Victorian studio and discussing portrait photographers as descendents of portrait painters. Of greater use is Estelle Jussim's "From the Studio to the Snapshot: An Immigrant Photographer of the 1920s," an important study because she pays attention to the social context of a Russian immigrant photographer and because she attempts to relate photographic format and style to cultural changes. Drawing on Erving Goffman's work, Jussim suggests that the studio portrait creates an idealized self as a stay against flux and chaos; the photographer's task is "the establishment of a suitable stage upon which the self [can] act out its delusional systems, its ideal." The snapshot portrait, however, reflects a loss of faith in this ideal: it captures only "a shard of the whole personality . . . an accidental recording of a gesture. . . ." *Wedding*, compiled by Barbara P. Norfleet, selects seven professional studios across the country, ranging from the late nineteenth-century to the mid-1960s, and reproduces candid and formal wedding photographs, along with unfortunately brief excerpts from interviews with photographers. Norfleet's images and interviews support Jussim's argument about idealized portraiture. Said one photographer: "I also know what to avoid and what to bring out in the work—what they like and what they don't like. I'll get a divorced mother and dad in the same group for a picture when the couple said I could never do it." Norfleet's book avoids intensive analysis, but provides raw material and hints at the analysis that might be pursued.

If professional portraiture filled the first albums and often fills wedding albums, present-day albums are filled with snapshots taken by amateurs. Unfortunately, contemporary snapshots have not been studied extensively, although Michael Lesy is currently engaged in interviews and the gathering of images. Examples of his method have appeared in *Afterimage* as "Snapshots: Psychological Documents, Frozen Dreams" and "Fame and Fortune: A Snapshot Chronicle." His book, *Men, Women, and Children*, will include nearly five hundred snapshots, oral histories, and an interpretive essay; it is scheduled for publication in early 1980. In *American Snapshots*, Ken Graves and Mitchell Payne reproduce a little over one hundred images from "hundreds of thousands" of snapshots they viewed. Unfortunately, their selection was primarily idiosyncratic: "We picked images which were extraordinary for us, relying on our photographic intuition and sensitivity." The book is filled with mostly comic and ironic images, removed from all context of the albums they may have been in or the tales they may have evoked from their owners. Another disappointing anthology, *The Snapshot*, compiled by Jonathan Green, consists of brief headnotes written by creative photographers, followed by a selection of their images demonstrating that they can master, or at least mimic, the snapshot style. Only the essay by Steven Halpern, "Souvenirs of Experience: The Victorian Studio Portrait and the Twentieth-Century Snapshot," redeems the book—again because of his sensitive evocation of the contexts and implications surrounding formal, materialistic Victorian portraiture and informal, experiential snapshots.

The Snapshot Photograph: The Rise of Popular Photography, 1888-1939 by Brian Coe and Paul Gates concerns the Kodak camera in Britain. The initial chapters discuss, too briefly, the social background of popular photography, distinguish it from professional photography and advanced amateur photography, and plausibly date the beginning of popular photography to the invention of the Kodak camera in 1888. The assertion that naive, untutored snapshooters captured more truthful depictions of the "character" of their subjects than did other kinds of photographers is unexplored. Subsequent chapters give a detailed history of Kodak cameras popular in England. The book does not deliver the social analysis its title implies, but its selection of snapshots gathered under such categories as "Leisure," "The Seaside," and "Interiors" may be useful.

There remain a few works, grounded in fields such as information theory, cultural anthropology, intellectual history, or American studies, that suggest ways of approaching larger cultural critiques centering on the prevalence and import of popular photography.

In *Prints and Visual Communication*, William M. Ivins, Jr., asserted that photographs provided an important new way of reporting on reality because they were without the syntax of mediation that had characterized previous information transferral systems. Important as his study was, this view was a misconception about the transparency of the photographic medium, and much subsequent work has been devoted to correcting his assumptions and extending the implications of the corrections. See Joel Snyder and Neil Allen's "Photography, Vision and Representation," and especially Estelle Jussim's *Visual Communication and the Graphic Arts: Photographic Technologies in the Nineteenth Century*, which is an extensive examination of the effect of photomechanical processes on the transmission of graphic images. Jussim's focus on other graphic arts concerns photography *for* the people. But for studying photography as popular culture, the import of works using information theory is their insistence that no photograph or its reproduction is an unmediated "window" on the world: to presume so is to be a victim of the medium, rather than an analyst of it.

An anthropological approach occurs in several important works. John Collier's *Visual Anthropology: Photography as a Research Method* provides a technical, practical, and theoretical guide to using the camera in field study. His suggestions for approaching photographic evidence apply equally well to the analysis of popular photography. *Studies in the Anthropology of Visual Communication* is a recent journal with continuing interest in film, video, and photography as research tools and as cultural artifacts. A recent issue featured Joanna Cohan Scherer's "You Can't Believe Your Eyes: Inaccuracies in Photographs of North American Indians." She underscores the fact that popular stereographs of Indians must be assessed as artifacts of a dominant culture, not as ethnographically accurate depictions of North American tribes. Also in the journal, Richard Chalfen's "Cinéma Naïveté: A Study of Home Moviemaking as Visual Communication" is methodologically relevant to the study of popular photography. Chalfen divides the process of film communication into four kinds of events for systematic investigation—planning events, filming events, editing events, and exhibition events. He examines the components of each event— the participants, topics, settings, message forms, and codes—in order to understand the photographic artifact as an expressive medium, as visual communication, and as a social activity. See also his "Introduction to the Study of Non-Professional Photography as Visual Communication."

In the area of American studies, Alan Trachtenberg's "Image and Ideology: An Approach to the Cultural Study of Photographs" analyzes the work of Alfred Stieglitz, Jacob Riis, and Lewis Hine to underscore the point that photographs are "a second-hand view—not only a picture, but someone's picture." "Western Views in Eastern Parlors: The Contribution of the Stereograph Photographer to the Conquest of the West" by Richard N. Masteller pursues a similar thesis in studying the work of E. O. Beaman, an eastern photographer who participated in John Wesley Powell's survey of the Colorado River in 1871-1872. Allan Sekula's "On the Invention of Photographic Meaning" also focuses on the importance of context. The value of William Stott's *Documentary Expression and Thirties America* includes its ability to relate Farm Security Administration photography to other modes of expression and analysis prevalent in the 1930s. All these works are models of research and analysis based on the assumption that photographs are embedded in a social and cultural matrix: the matrix is as much the subject of study as the photographs themselves.

Some of the most provocative recent writings about photography, directly concerned with its role in popular culture, are Susan Sontag's essays, collected in her recent book, *On Photography*. An earlier manifestation of some of her ideas can be found in Walter Benjamin's "The Work of Art in the Age of Mechanical Reproduction" and in Marshall McLuhan's "The Photograph: The Brothel-without-Walls" in his book, *Understanding Media: The Extensions of Man*. Benjamin worried that the capacity for unlimited photographic reproduction would destroy the "aura" surrounding the unique work of art, an "aura" he defined as "the unique phenomenon of a distance, however close at hand." Further, the mass-produced photograph had political as well as aesthetic consequences, such mass reproduction helping to create a mass society. Decades later McLuhan agreed, suggesting not only that the photograph created a sense of accelerated transience in the world, abolishing both space and time, but that it also wiped out national frontiers and cultural barriers. Sontag's analyses take these ideas much further than can be summarized here. Aphoristic, meditative, paradoxical, she is deeply troubled by the acquisitive, aggressive act of photography and argues that we are both victims and victimizers in a cave of shadows we have ourselves created: "A way of certifying experience, taking photographs is also a way of refusing it—by limiting experience to a search for the photogenic, by converting experience into an image and souvenir." Although her book has outraged some creative photographers, its popularity is another indication of how deeply photography has penetrated our cultural habits. Focusing on photography not only as an artifact of popular culture but also as an artifact of Western culture, her analyses are disturbing perhaps because she has come so close to penetrating our surrogate selves.

ANTHOLOGIES AND REPRINTS

There are few reprints of work pertinent to photography as a popular culture phenomenon. Beaumont Newhall's *On Photography: A Source Book of Photo History in Facsimile* contains twenty-eight articles. Although most are written by creative photographers and pertain to photography as a fine art, a few more popular accounts are included. *Photographers on Photography*, edited by Nathan Lyons, draws its thirty-nine essays from the ranks of twenty-three professional and creative photographers. Although it does not treat photography as a phenomenon of popular culture, it is a useful compendium of issues thoughtfully addressed.

In 1973, Arno Press issued The Literature of Photography series, sixty-two out-of-print nineteenth- and twentieth-century books, manuals, and treatises covering the spectrum of scientific, technical, and artistic aspects of photography both in America and abroad. While many of the works are technically oriented, this emphasis reflects the mixture of scientific experimentation, ingenuity, and fascination that accompanied the development of photography in the nineteenth century; in addition, a few titles (cited in the section "History and Criticism") are important for tracing photography's professionalization and popularization. In 1979, Arno issued Sources of Modern Photography, a companion series of fifty-one titles.

Finally, Research Publications, Inc., 12 Lunar Drive, Woodbridge, Connecticut 06525, is preparing a History of Photography microfilm series of two thousand one hundred monographs and pamphlet titles and approximately one hundred twenty-five periodicals covering the history, technology, and aesthetics of photography both in America and abroad. Currently scheduled for completion in the fall of 1979, the series will utilize a refined microfilm image capable of conveying the nuances of the original photographs that were often tipped into nineteenth-century periodicals. Although the series is relatively expensive, it will be a major resource, making available to larger libraries important items that exist in only a few national and international collections.

BIBLIOGRAPHY

BOOKS AND ARTICLES

Artbibliographies Modern. Santa Barbara, Calif.: American Bibliographical Center and Clio Press, 1973-.

Benjamin, Walter. "The Work of Art in the Age of Mechanical Reproduction." In *Illuminations.* New York: Harcourt, Brace, and World, 1968, pp. 219-53.

Boni, Albert, ed. *Photographic Literature: An International Bibliographic Guide to General and Specialized Literature on Photographic Processes, Techniques, Theory.* . . . 2 vols. New York: Morgan and Morgan, 1962, 1972.

Braive, Michel F. *The Era of the Photograph: A Social History.* Translated by David Britt. London: Thames and Hudson, 1966.

Chalfen, Richard. "Cinéma Naïveté: A Study of Home Moviemaking as Visual Communication." *Studies in the Anthropology of Visual Communication,* 2 (Fall 1975), 87-103.

————. "Introduction to the Study of Non-Professional Photography as Visual Communication." In *Saying Cheese: Studies in Folklore and Visual Communication.* Edited by Steven Ohrn and Michael Bell. Folklore Forum, Bibliographic and Special Series, No. 13 (1975), 19-25.

Coe, Brian, and Paul Gates. *The Snapshot Photograph: The Rise of Popular Photography, 1888-1939.* London: Ash and Grant, 1977.

Collier, John. *Visual Anthropology: Photograph as a Research Method.* New York: Holt, Rinehart, and Winston, 1967.

Darrah, William Culp. *Stereo Views: A History of Stereographs in America and Their Collection.* Gettysburg, Pa.: Times and News Publishing, 1964.

————. *The World of Stereographs.* Gettysburg, Pa.: William C. Darrah, 1977.

Davis, Alexander, ed. Art Design Photo. London: Idea Books, 1974-.

Directory of Historical Societies and Agencies in the United States and Canada. 10th ed. Nashville, Tenn.: American Association for State and Local History, 1975.

Gassan, Arnold. A Chronology of Photography. Athens, Ohio: Handbook Company, 1972. Distributed by Light Impressions, Inc., Rochester, N.Y.

Gernsheim, Helmut, and Alison Gernsheim. L. J. M. Daguerre: The History of the Diorama and the Daguerreotype. 2d rev. ed. New York: Dover, 1968.

————. The History of Photography from the Camera Obscura to the Beginning of the Modern Era. 2d ed. New York: McGraw-Hill, 1969.

Gilbert, George. Collecting Photographica: The Images and Equipment of the First Hundred Years of Photography. New York: Hawthorne Books, 1976.

Graves, Ken, and Mitchell Payne. American Snapshots. Oakland, Calif.: Scrimshaw Press, 1977.

Green, Jonathan, ed. The Snapshot. Aperture, 19, No. 1 (1974). Also issued in book form at Millerton, N.Y.: Aperture, 1974.

Green, Shirley. Pictorial Resources in the Washington, D.C. Area. Washington, D.C.: Government Printing Office, 1976.

Halpern, Steven. "Souvenirs of Experience: The Victorian Studio Portrait and the Twentieth-Century Snapshot." In The Snapshot. Edited by Jonathan Green. Millerton, N.Y.: Aperture, 1974, pp. 64-67.

Harrison, W. Jerome. A History of Photography Written as a Practical Guide and an Introduction to Its Latest Developments. 1887. Reprint. New York: Arno Press, 1973.

Hillier, Bevis. Victorian Studio Photographs. Boston: David Godine, 1975.

Holmes, Oliver Wendell. "The Stereoscope and the Stereograph." Atlantic Monthly, 3 (June 1859), 738-48.

————. "Sun-Painting and Sun-Sculpture; With a Stereoscopic Trip Across The Atlantic." Atlantic Monthly, 8 (July 1861), 13-29.

————. "Doings of the Sunbeam." Atlantic Monthly, 12 (July 1863), 1-15.

Ivins, William M., Jr. Prints and Visual Communication. 1953. Reprint. New York: Da Capo, 1969.

Jenkins, Reese. Images and Enterprise: Technology and the American Photographic Industry, 1839-1925. Baltimore: Johns Hopkins University Press, 1976.

Johnson, William, ed. An Index to Articles on Photography 1977. Rochester, N.Y.: Visual Studies Workshop Press, 1978.

Jones, Bernard E., ed. Cassell's Cyclopaedia of Photography. 1911. Reprint. New York: Arno Press, 1973.

Jussim, Estelle. Visual Communication and the Graphic Arts: Photographic Technologies in the Nineteenth Century. New York: R. R. Bowker, 1974.

————. "From the Studio to the Snapshot: An Immigrant Photographer of the 1920s." History of Photography, 1 (July 1977), 183-99.

Kotkin, Amy. "The Family Photo Album as a Form of Folklore." Exposure, 16 (March 1978), 4-8.

Kozloff, Max. "Nadar and the Republic of Mind." Artforum, 15 (September 1976), 28-39.

————. *Photography and Fascination*. Danbury, N.H.: Addison House, 1978.

Lesy, Michael. *Wisconsin Death Trip*. New York: Pantheon-Random House, 1973.

————. *Real Time: Louisville in the Twenties*. New York: Pantheon-Random House, 1976.

————. "Snapshots: Psychological Documents, Frozen Dreams." *Afterimage*, 4 (October 1976), 12-13.

————. "Fame and Fortune: A Snapshot Chronicle." *Afterimage*, 5 (October 1977), 8-13.

————. *Men, Women, and Children*. New York: Pantheon-Random House, 1980.

Lewis, Steven, James McQuaid, and David Tait, comps. *Photography: Source and Resource*. State College, Pa.: Turnip Press, 1973. Distributed by Light Impressions, Inc., Rochester, N.Y.

Lothrop, Eaton S., Jr. *A Century of Cameras from the Collection of the International Museum of Photography at George Eastman House*. Dobbs Ferry, N.Y.: Morgan and Morgan, 1973.

————. "Personality Cameras." *Image*, 20 (March 1977), 22-27.

Lyons, Nathan, ed. *Photographers on Photography*. Englewood Cliffs, N.J.: Prentice-Hall, 1966.

Lyons, Nathan, and Edward Earle, eds. *Points of View: The Stereograph in America: A Cultural History*. Rochester, N.Y.: Visual Studies Workshop Press, 1979.

Maas, Ellen. *Das Photoalbum 1858-1918: Eine Dokumentation zur Kultur- und Sozialgeschichte*. Munich: Karl M. Lipp, 1975.

McLuhan, H. Marshall. "The Photograph: The Brothel-without-Walls." In *Understanding Media: The Extensions of Man*. New York: McGraw-Hill, 1964, pp. 188-202.

Masteller, Richard N. "Western Views in Eastern Parlors: The Contribution of the Stereograph Photographer to the Conquest of the West." *Prospects: An Annual Journal of American Cultural Studies*, 6 (1980).

Newhall, Beaumont. *On Photography: A Source Book of Photo History in Facsimile*. Watkins Glen, N.Y.: Century House, 1956.

————. "How George Eastman Invented the Kodak Camera." *Image*, 7 (March 1958), 59-64.

————. *The History of Photography from 1839 to the Present Day*. Rev. and enl. ed. New York: Museum of Modern Art, 1964.

————. *The Daguerreotype in America*. 3d rev. ed. New York: Dover, 1976.

Norfleet, Barbara P. *Wedding*. Cambridge: The Carpenter Center for the Visual Arts, Harvard University Press, 1976.

Novotny, Ann, ed. *Picture Sources 3: Collections of Prints and Photographs in the United States and Canada*. New York: Special Libraries Association, 1975.

Ohrn, Karin Becker. "Making Belief: Contexts for Family Photography." Unpublished paper presented at the Biennial Convention, American Studies Association, Boston, October 1977.

Peters, Marsha, and Bernard Mergen. " 'Doing the Rest': The Uses of Photographs in American Studies." *American Quarterly*, 29 (1977), 280-303.

Reynolds, Charles. "Forty Years of Evolution and Revolution." *Popular Photography*, 80 (May 1977), 97, 144-45, 222.

Rinhart, Floyd, and Marion Rinhart. *American Miniature Case Art*. New York: A. S. Barnes, 1969.

Rodgers, H. J. *Twenty-Three Years Under a Skylight, or Life and Experiences of a Photographer*. 1872. Reprint. New York: Arno Press, 1973.

Root, Marcus Aurelius. *The Camera and the Pencil Or the Heliographic Art*. 1864. Reprint. Pawlet, Vt.: Helios, 1971.

Rudisill, Richard. *Mirror Image: The Influence of the Daguerreotype on American Society*. Albuquerque: University of New Mexico Press, 1971.

Ryder, James F. *Voigtlander and I: In Pursuit of Shadow Catching. A Story of Fifty-Two Years' Companionship with a Camera*. 1902. Reprint. New York: Arno Press, 1973.

Scherer, Joanna Cohan. "You Can't Believe Your Eyes: Inaccuracies in Photographs of North American Indians." *Studies in the Anthropology of Visual Communication*, 2 (Fall 1975), 67-78.

Sekula, Allan. "On the Invention of Photographic Meaning." *Artforum*, 13 (January 1975), 36-45.

Simpson, Jeffrey. *The American Family: A History in Photographs*. New York: Viking, 1976.

Snyder, Joel, and Neil Allen. "Photography, Vision and Representation." *Critical Inquiry*, 2 (1975), 143-69.

Snyder, Norman, Carole Kismaric, and Don Myrus. *The Photography Catalog*. New York: Harper and Row, 1976.

Sontag, Susan. *On Photography*. New York: Farrar, Straus and Giroux, 1977.

Stenger, Erich. *The History of Photography: Its Relation to Civilization and Practice*. Translated by Edward Epstean. Easton, Pa.: Mack Printing, 1939.

Stott, William. *Documentary Expression and Thirties America*. New York: Oxford University Press, 1973.

Taft, Robert. *Photography and the American Scene: A Social History, 1839-1889*. 1938. Reprint. New York: Dover, 1964.

Talbott, George. *At Home: Domestic Life in the Post-Centennial Era, 1876-1920*. Madison: State Historical Society of Wisconsin, 1976.

Thomas, Alan. *Time in a Frame: Photography and the Nineteenth-Century Mind*. New York: Schocken, 1977.

Tissandier, Gaston. *A History and Handbook of Photography*. 2d ed. 1878. Reprint. New York: Arno Press, 1973.

Towler, John. *The Silver Sunbeam*. 1864. Reprint. New York: Morgan and Morgan, 1969.

Trachtenberg, Alan. "Image and Ideology: An Approach to the Cultural Study of Photographs." Unpublished paper presented at the American Studies symposium, University of Iowa, January 1977.

Vanderbilt, Paul. *Guide to the Special Collections of Prints and Photographs in the Library of Congress*. Washington, D.C.: Government Printing Office, 1955.

Welling, William. *Collector's Guide to Nineteenth-Century Photographs.* New York: Collier-Macmillan, 1976.

————. *Photography in America: The Formative Years 1839-1900.* New York: Thomas Y. Crowell, 1978.

Werge, John. *The Evolution of Photography.* 1890. Reprint. New York: Arno Press, 1973.

Wolfman, Augustus, comp. *Wolfman Report on the Photographic Industry in the United States.* New York: Modern Photography Magazine, 1952 (and subsequent annual editions).

PERIODICALS

(This checklist of periodicals is divided into three categories. Listed first are nineteenth- and early twentieth-century photographic periodicals for primary research. The second category of primary materials consists of contemporary mass-market periodicals aimed at amateur photographers. The third category consists of journals that analyze photography and photographic aesthetics and occasionally contain articles of relevance to photography as an artifact of popular culture.)

Nineteenth- and Early Twentieth-Century Periodicals

American Amateur Photographer. Brunswick, Me. and New York, 1889-1907.
The American Annual of Photography. Boston and New York, 1887-1953.
American Journal of Photography. Philadelphia, 1879-1900.
American Journal of Photography and the Allied Arts and Sciences. New York, 1852-1867.
American Photography. Boston, 1907-1953.
Anthony's Photographic Bulletin. New York, 1870-1902.
Camera Craft. San Francisco, 1900-1942.
Camera Notes. New York, 1897-1903.
Camera Work. New York, 1903-1917.
The Daguerreian Journal. New York, 1850-1851.
Humphrey's Journal of Photography and the Allied Arts and Sciences. New York, 1852-1870.
The Philadelphia Photographer. Philadelphia, 1864-1888.
Photo-Beacon. Chicago, 1889-1907.
Photo Era Magazine. Boston, 1898-1932.
Photograms of the Year. London, 1895-1925.
The Photographic and Fine Art Journal. New York, 1854-1860.
The Photographic Art Journal. New York, 1851-1853.
Photographic Journal. London, 1853-.
Photographic Journal of America. Philadelphia, 1915-1923.
Photographic Mosaics. Philadelphia and New York, 1866-1901.
Photographic Times. New York, 1871-1915.
Photo-Miniature. New York and London, 1899-1936.
Wilson's Photographic Magazine. Philadelphia, 1889-1914.

Contemporary Mass-Market Periodicals
Camera. Lucerne, Switzerland, 1922-.
Camera Thirty-Five. New York, 1957-.
Modern Photography. New York, 1937-.
Popular Photography. Chicago, 1937-.
U.S. Camera Magazine. New York, 1938-.

Contemporary Analytical Periodicals
Afterimage: A Publication of the Visual Studies Workshop. Rochester, N.Y.: 1972-.
Creative Camera. London, 1963-.
Exposure: Journal of the Society for Photographic Education. New York, 1963-.
History of Photography. London, 1976-.
Image: Journal of Photography and Motion Pictures of the International Museum of Photography at George Eastman House. Rochester, N.Y., 1952-.
Studies in the Anthropology of Visual Communication. Temple University, Philadelphia, 1973-.

CHAPTER 11. Popular Architecture

Richard Guy Wilson

Of all the elements that make up popular culture, architecture is surely the most omnipresent. One can turn off the Rolling Stones, refuse to watch "Charlie's Angels," ignore Harold Robbins, be revolted by Big Macs, and reject the message of Mr. Clean; yet, unless one becomes a hermit and retires to the mythical cave, the man-made environment intrudes. The buildings one lives in, works in, and plays in, reveal personal and cultural values; they are records of growth, progress, decay, and decline and, if properly understood, they can serve as an environmental diary. While to some eyes architecture is only the very rarefied "high art" or the top 5 percent of the built environment, if properly construed, architecture is concerned with all forms of design—from skyscrapers and homes of the wealthy to highways, McDonald's restaurants, suburban ranches, mobile homes, plastic pink flamingos in the yard, and Ethan Allen settees.

The vast array of the mass enviornment, whether it is called popular architecture or modern vernacular, constitutes at least 95 percent of our surroundings. There is a need to understand this environment in all its aspects, not just the currently popular subjects of fast-food palaces and the strip, but other aspects as well, such as urban sprawl, shopping centers, ranch-styled homes, and the symbolic meanings people ascribe to or invest in their buildings. Since the late eighteenth century and the development of a modern consciousness, most historians have felt that buildings are concrete expressions of a culture and a world view. While this idea is perhaps more easily acceptable in terms of such public or semipublic monuments as the East Wing of the National Gallery of Art in Washington, D.C., or the Chartres Cathedral in France—to take two extremes—recently there have been other views. Richard Oliver and Nancy Ferguson, in writing about fast-food restaurants, diners, gas stations, and historical villages, claim that "by their very familiarity, they can and do act as mirrors of our culture." The profound shifts created by the industrial revolution have affected the built environment in many ways, most of which have been ignored. A radical discrepancy exists between the tastes, needs, and preferences of professionals—historians, critics, architects, urban designers and planners, and the decision makers whose policies they inform—and the people whose lives they influence.

Popular architecture, as does all architecture, generally fulfills two functions: first, it encloses or houses some type of activity, and second, it communicates. The methods of communication through different signs and symbol systems are at the core of the study of popular architecture. The physical elements of coach lanterns and shutters on a house, the twisting nudes in front of Caesar's Palace in Las Vegas, and the blinking lights of "OVER A BILLION SOLD" convey messages of social status, association with the past, and information. To understand popular architecture, we must look at it not simply as an art of building, but as a tangible expression of a way of life.

HISTORIC OUTLINE

In the West before the late eighteenth century, nearly all architecture was of two basic types, either folk (or vernacular or traditional) or academic high art. By folk architecture we mean buildings of a preindustrial society—whether houses, shops, or barns—that are based on one or a very few types that admit of only a few individual variations. The architect or designer, as such, does not exist; the building type is carried in the collective consciousness of the culture. Construction is either by the final consumer or a tradesman not far removed from the consumer, and local materials are used. Academic high-art architecture refers to specialized buildings, each one an original or unique creation (though self-consciously in a "style"), and the designer is a professional or an amateur who specializes in or has aspirations to the creation of significant monuments.

Popular architecture emerged with the industrial revolution. With popular architecture, production is changed; building materials and even entire buildings are mass-produced by a team or teams of specialists who are generally far removed from the ultimate consumer. Instead of one building type prevailing, there are many, with innumerable variations within each type. The forms, plans, and images of the buildings are products of fashion and are acquired through popular magazines, trade journals, books, governmental agencies, travel, and the media. The images refer to history, high art, technology, status, patriotism, and individual fantasies. Semiotically, popular architecture is fashion- or style-consciousness, and the symbols are generally chosen for their immediate impact.

Academic high-art architecture has continued, of course, in the modern world. Modern architecture strives for subtle symbols, abstractions of

ideas and emotions that are available only to the initiated. High-art architecture lacks the directness and immediacy of most popular architecture.

Who designs popular architecture? The answer is anybody and everybody, although some are more responsible than others. Buildings by aca-
demically trained architects are not necessarily examples of high art; in
fact, architects have been responsible for the mass-produced Mobil service
station, ranch-styled homes, and Miami Beach hotels. There is hardly a
building activity of the modern age that architects have not participated
in, and they serve on the design staffs of Holiday Inns, Disney World, the
Rouse Corporation, and the Winnebago Company. But there are others,
such as industrial designers, who have also designed mass-produced commercial buildings. The profession of the industrial designer did not emerge
until the 1930s, but he quickly became the hero of the new technological
mass-production age. Walter Dorwin Teague, one of the first, designed
the enamel-paneled, machinelike Texaco service station. Another source
for the designs of popular architecture is the builder or contractor. Building is an old and honored tradition, but its increasing technological nature
precludes much design by actual workers today. And, of course, there is
finally the consumer, who decides to add a clip-on mansard roof to his
storefront or put a French Provincial door on his ranch house and a plastic
deer in the front yard.

The relationship between popular architecture and high-art architecture
has never been stable; and, in spite of the elitist "trickle down" theory
that high art always informs low art or that popular architecture "rips
off" high-art architecture, the reverse is often true. Taste, which used to
be a sign of class and wealth, is no longer an operable guide; the nouveaux
riches have taken care of that. Who actually informs the taste of architecture and the processes by which it trickles down, or up, or sideways
needs considerable study. But it is evident that plans, forms, and images
constantly shift from one level to another. Recently, there has been a great
spurt of interest by academic high-art architects in the archetypal image
of the 1930s—the sleek, shiny streamlined diner. Now, as they are passing
out of existence to be replaced by colonial- and Mediterranean-styled
diners, they are discovered and appropriated. Or one can look at materials
such as shingles, which have moved over the years from a vernacular
exterior covering-up into the range of high art, back into the hands of the
builder and Levittown, and once again back to becoming the chic material.

Communication of the styles and motifs of popular architecture is generally transmitted by one of two methods: experientially, through observation and travel; or secondhand, through books, magazines, and trade
journals. The first method, of course, is nebulous and depends on studying
specific individuals; the second method—the media—has, however, left a
more tangible record. Early in the nineteenth century in the United States

books that spread knowledge of stylistic details began to appear, intended for mass circulation. The earliest were builders' guides such as Asher Benjamin's *The American Builder's Companion* and Minard Lafever's *The Modern Builder's Guide*. Their contents were plates illustrating details or ornament and construction, with possibly a few elevations and plans of complete buildings. They helped spread the fashion for styles such as federal, then Greek revival, and finally gothic revival to builders, carpenters, and of course consumers. Their continuation in print, in some cases nearly thirty years after first publication, accounts for the *retardare* appearance of some buildings in more provincial areas.

About mid-century, a new type of publication appeared, the house pattern book, which was filled with plans and designs of complete buildings. The most popular of these were Andrew Jackson Downing's *Cottage Residences* and *The Architecture of Country Houses*, Gervase Wheeler's *Rural Homes*, and Samuel Sloan's *The Model Architect*. While many designs of large pretentious homes were illustrated in these books, there were also "working men's cottages," "laborers' cottages," and other small houses shown, along with details that would allow anyone with either skills or some funds to update their homes. This type of publication continued throughout the nineteenth century in a virtual flood of titles and editions, such as George Woodward's *Woodward's National Architect*, E. C. Gardner's *Homes and how to make them*, and the Palliser Company's *New Cottage Homes and Details*. These books served as dream manuals for the masses. House details could be adapted from them by a local builder or architect, and, in many cases, such as that of the Palliser Company, complete sets of plans could be purchased at a nominal cost. The men responsible for these books were a varied lot: a few had some architectural background, but many were simply glorified carpenters who adopted high-art styles for mass consumption.

Another method of communication was through magazines. Between 1846 and 1892, *Godey's Lady's Book* published four hundred fifty house designs. In the 1860s, several magazines that were directed specifically at the builder and carpenter, such as *The American Builder* and the *Architectural Review and American Builder's Journal*, came into being. The first professional architectural magazine in the United States, *The American Architect and Building News*, was not founded until 1876.

With small modifications, these same patterns have remained into the 1970s. Certainly one of the greatest influences on home design has been the mass-circulation homemaker magazines. Although they advocated different approaches to architectural style, interior furnishings, and gardens, a study of these magazines is essential to any understanding of the popular culture of the home. Some of these advocated strong points of view at different times. In its early years, *The House Beautiful* supported the arts

and crafts movement and bungalow design. More famous was the *Ladies'*
Home Journal, which, at the turn of the century, sponsored home design
by architects such as Frank Lloyd Wright. It was through Wright's designs in the *Journal* that many builders and homeowners learned to imitate
his work. Other *Journal* architects were more conservative and advocated
styles ranging from colonial to Mediterranean. Other magazines, such as
The American Home, have been almost single minded in their sponsorship
of "early American" as the fit style for Americans. Today, the strong direction in homemaker magazines such as *Better Homes and Gardens* is
twofold: first, a natural trend, and second, a rich eclecticism.

Tangential to the homemaker magazines are how-to-do-it magazines
such as *Early American Life,* which is filled with nostalgia of the "good
old" days. The advertisement states: "Your Dream Home—there's at least
one house in every issue of *Early American Life,* complete with floor
plans." These can be in any number of styles, but most frequently in the
stockade and Cape Cod styles. *Popular Mechanics,* the best known of the
how-to-do-it magazines, has always exercised a strong influence on taste
in home and furniture design.

Specialized trade journals are probably the major new contribution of
the twentieth century. Professional architectural magazines such as *Pro-*
gressive Architecture and *The Architectural Record* have affected popular
taste minimally, but they are important for tracing ideas. Far more important are magazines such as *House & Home: The Magazine of Housing,*
Qualified Remodeler, and *Professional Builder,* which are directed at the
construction industry. They deal with products and styles in articles such
as "Bathroom Design: The Opulant Look" and "How to Facelift Old Buildings Without Losing Their Charm." Then there are specialized trade journals of other industries such as service stations and restaurants. The impact
of fast-food can be felt in many of the magazines, for example, *Restaurant*
Business and *Nation's Restaurant News.* Many of them feature articles
on designs and images of the fast-food industry.

Books or specialized issues of magazines devoted to home design have
had a long history in the twentieth century. Most have been on the order
of the house pattern books and present images and ideas that can be
adapted or copied at will. Collections of designs by architects, such as
The Architectural Record Book of Vacation Houses or *A Treasury of*
Contemporary Houses, are important since a vast range of styles from
radical to conservative are shown. *The Building Guide* of *House & Garden*
magazine for 1963-1964 offered forty houses and plans ranging from the
contemporary to the traditional and included designs entitled "A Combination of Ranch and Colonial" and "The Plantation House in Miniature."
Some books convey conventional wisdom. *The Book of Houses* advised
in a chapter entitled "What Price Style?" that "Style, of course, is a sub-

jective factor and if a family is emotionally drawn toward a 'Cape Cod' or a 'Georgian,' serious consideration should be given to a home of that type." Images of other building types are communicated in much the same manner. Books on office design, shopping centers, and factories abound, although they are of course directed at the professional in the field rather than toward the public. But books such as *Motels, Hotels and Restaurants* by Architectural Record have influenced buildings around the world.

While popular architecture began to emerge in the eighteenth century with the Industrial Revolution, it and the associated components in the man-made environment have not been the subject of serious study until very recently. Among architects and historians, the reasons are fairly obvious: popular architecture was not serious and lacked the imprint of *Kultur*. The study of architecture, whether historical or contemporary, has been usually confined to monuments: churches, temples, memorials, theaters, forums, palaces, homes of the elite, and buildings designed by architects who aspire to greatness. A result of Germanic pedantic scholarship and English dilettantism, architecture is usually studied chronologically, and concentration is on a critical and evaluative analysis of the styles, forms, plans, ornament, and details. While the culture and the purpose of a building are sometimes noted, the building is generally seen as existing independently in space and time. From the 1930s onwards, the preoccupation in both the United States and Europe with "modern architecture" led to a further separation from the field of popular architecture. Concerned with totally abstract designing in modern materials and techniques and completely removed from the area of historical recall, nostalgia, or recognizable motifs, modern architecture developed its own language. While the historians of modern architecture have paid some attention to issues of prefabrication and industrial warehouses and factories, they have focused largely on a history of designs by major architects. In these studies, as in the more traditional historical studies, the mention of a Howard Johnson restaurant, a cozy Cape Cod cottage from Mount Vernon estates, or an entryway to Forest Lawn Cemetery in southern California, would be only in the most negative terms.

Variations from the study of certifiable monuments can be seen in the interest in early American and vernacular architecture. Early American architecture is basically preindustrial vernacular, and the study of this type and regular vernacular have been more concerned with the details and recording of buildings than with any investigation into meanings of the buildings and their culture. One exception has been the work of Henry Glassie in his two major books, *Patterns in the Material Folk Culture of the Eastern United States* and *Folk Housing in Middle Virginia*. In the latter book, Glassie applies the structuralism of Claude Lévi-Strauss and Noam Chomsky to vernacular houses; while his results are dense and open to question, he offers some suggestions for studying popular architecture.

Along with the other revolutions of the 1960s, a sense of crisis in the architectural and design world has led, in the 1970s, to a greater recognition of popular architecture and the necessity for understanding the entire man-made environment. One significant change was the sense of failure of modern architecture; the brave new world envisioned in the 1930s, where "total design" could improve man's life, was a hoax. Most consumers disliked, if not downright hated, modern buildings, not only for their sterile quality and uncomfortable feeling, but also because they simply did not work well. Urban renewal, a product of modern architectural city planning, proved to be worse than the illness it was supposed to correct. When it was published in 1961, Jane Jacobs's *The Death and Life of Great American Cities* was viewed as heretical for her celebration of the messy vitality of the street. Today, it is the received orthodoxy. While there are still many architects and critics who profess an admiration for modern architecture, the continual bombardment of questions and alarming failures has opened the doors for some recognition of popular architecture.

The Museum of Modern Art in New York—the citadel of avant-garde modern chic—provided several new directions in the mid-1960s. In 1964, the exhibit *Architecture Without Architects* by Bernard Rudofsky (and his book of the same name) presented the thesis that centuries-old buildings executed by common men without the aid of designers could present eternal themes of architecture. The exhibit showed not only homes and temples of primitive peoples but also granneries and fertilizer bins. Rudofsky has gone on to exploit this unself-conscious theme in *The Prodigious Builders*. In 1966, the Museum of Modern Art published Robert Venturi's *Complexity and Contradiction in Architecture*, the first openly critical look at the theories of modern architecture.

Robert Venturi and Charles Moore have been among the leaders of architects who argue that popular architecture is worthy of study. Venturi's *Complexity and Contradiction* was concerned more with a rather dense design philosophy and, except for the notorious phrase, "Main Street is almost alright," was not really concerned with popular architecture. But, *Learning from Las Vegas* by Venturi, Denise Scott Brown, and Steven Izenour was concerned with popular architecture and argued that architects should look at the strip; for in spirit, if not style, it approached the grandeur of the Roman Forum, or "Las Vegas is to the Strip what Rome is to the Piazza." Charles Moore's writings have been felicitous with significant comments on suburban and motel culture. Another harbinger of the change has been the example of Peter Blake. In 1964, he published *God's Own Junkyard*, a great diatribe against popular architecture. But within ten years, he was writing admiring articles on the virtues of Disney World and the strip. *Progressive Architecture* magazine, the high priest of modern architecture, devoted its June 1978 issue to "Taste in America" and contained articles on McDonald's design evolution and on suburbia.

The other critical shift that began in the 1960s and still continues is the burgeoning historic preservation movement. As a movement, historic preservation can be traced back to the mid-nineteenth century in the United States and abroad. Until the 1960s, it was generally viewed as elitist and concerned with historic houses and recreations of olden times in Williamsburg and other museum villages. But in the 1960s, historic preservation became more populist in outlook and less concerned with the individual high-art building and more concerned with entire neighborhoods. Nods of approval have been given to lesser classes of structures such as service stations, billboards, and even outhouses. Preservation studies have been carried out in working-class neighborhoods such as the Old West Side in Ann Arbor, Michigan, which is a blue-collar, German enclave.

In the last few years, other writers, such as architectural and art historians, sociologists, planners, and anthropologists, have spluttered forth a variety of papers, articles, and books that have contributed to knowledge in the area. However, the field is still virtually wide open, and, while some research progresses on diverse topics such as gas stations, fast-food restaurants, and amusement parks, there is plenty for everybody to do. Basic research needs to be done in every area, and methodological approaches need to be discussed. Several societies dealing with different aspects of popular architecture have been founded recently, but they have delivered little and seem more interested in collecting dues.

REFERENCE WORKS

There are no major reference works devoted specifically to popular architecture, and, here as elsewhere, one has to make piecemeal use of other sources. For dictionaries, the *Dictionary of Architecture and Construction*, edited by Cyril M. Harris, is undoubtedly the best and most complete. It is directed at the professional and is well illustrated with abundant references.

To be able to understand properly the illusions and references popular architecture makes, it is important to identify the style or styles of a building. There is no general guidebook to architectural style. For the United States, Marcus Whiffen's *American Architecture Since 1780* is the best. It is arranged somewhat like a field guide to birds or wildflowers and has abundant illustrations, brief historical descriptions, and a bibliography on most of the major styles. Fairly good coverage is provided on architecture until about 1915, but is uneven thereafter. Unfortunately, his major concern is high-style architecture. The student should certainly be aware of major European styles, and, in the absence of a guidebook, J. C. Palme's edition of *Sir Banister Fletcher's A History of Architecture* probably provides the most illustrations.

Biographical information on American architects can be found in Withey's *Biographical Dictionary of American Architects (Deceased)*. All levels of architects are included, but it is by no means complete. Columbia University's *Avery Obituary Index of Architects and Artists*, which includes even more obscure figures, is also useful.

For access to periodicals, the major work is the *Avery Index to Architectural Periodicals*, produced by the staff at the Avery Architectural Library at Columbia University. This is a retrospective index to most English-language architectural periodicals and selected foreign and other periodicals. It is updated with supplements every few years. While it is primarily concerned with architectural periodicals, the *Avery Index* contains a vast gold mine of information that is conveniently indexed not only under author of article, architects, and location, but also under subject headings such as "Moving Picture Theaters" and "Restaurants." Unfortunately, there is no heading for "Diners" or "Fast-Food."

There is no comprehensive bibliography of American architectural books. Although it is limited in scope, Henry-Russell Hitchcock's *American Architectural Books, a List of Books, Portfolios, and Pamphlets on Architecture and Related Subjects Published in America Before 1895* is the best for the period. It contains a comprehensive listing of builder's guides and pattern books, which are a major source for studying the dissemination of popular architectural idioms.

RESEARCH COLLECTIONS

Architecture, by its very nature, is generally a static entity and, while one can point to mobile homes and the ephemeral creations of the strip, architecture is hardly collectable. Most research on architecture can be divided into two aspects: actual field work and collection of data; and library or archival work, where drawings, plans, photographs, magazines, books devoted to buildings, and materials devoted to their creators can be found. While the collecting of architectural records and drawings (both presentation and working drawings) has grown in recent years, there is no collection specifically devoted to popular architecture. Many university libraries are avidly pursuing collections for their local areas, but storage and study space for the bulky materials is always a problem. The Committee for the Preservation of Architectural Records, Inc. at 15 Gramercy Park South, New York 10003 acts as a clearing house for information and publishes a free newsletter that contains information and research queries. They have recently published a two-part guide, *Architectural Research Materials in New York City*, that will be a model for other areas.

Most collections of architectural records tend to emphasize the unique architect, and the depositing of materials relating to popular creations is not common. The major collections are in the Avery Architectural Library at Columbia University; the Smithsonian Institution's Museum of History and Technology in Washington, D.C.; the Cooper-Hewitt Museum in New York; the Library of Environmental Design at the University of California, Berkeley; the library at the University of California, Santa Barbara; and the Northwest Architectural Archive at the University of Minneapolis. These collections may have materials that would be related to popular architecture.

Much of the original documentation on popular architecture remains in the hands of the original owners or patrons. Large corporations such as Mobil Oil, Sunoco, Austin, McDonald's, and White Tower have opened their files to qualified researchers. No published work has been done on popular housing, but the Levit Corporation, Jim Walker Corporation, and local builders could be contacted.

For extensive collections of books and periodicals that relate to popular architecture, the Avery Architectural Library at Columbia University is easily the best in the United States, if not in the world. Other extensive collections are the architectural or design libraries at the University of California, Berkeley, the University of Michigan, and the University of Virginia.

Photographs are, of course, one of the primary records of architecture and the sometimes transient creations of popular architecture. Local collections in libraries, newspapers, and museums should always be consulted. Undoubtedly, the major national collection is at the Library of Congress, Prints and Photographs Division. Photographs of all types, from amateur to professional, including the Farm Security Administration's records of the 1930s, are deposited there. A wealth of material on the popular landscape awaits use.

Also housed in this same division at the Library of Congress are the deposited records of the Historic American Buildings Survey (HABS). As a division of the National Park Service, HABS was founded during the Depression as an attempt to record many of the fast-disappearing creations of the built environment through field research, photographs, and scale drawings. After a period of hiatus, HABS was refounded in 1957 and continues today to send out field teams throughout the United States and its territories to record architecture. While much of the focus of HABS has been on high-art architecture, attention in recent years has been paid to movie theaters, service stations, and middle-class housing. As the projects are completed, the records along with drawings, photographs, and negatives are deposited in the Library of Congress. Unfortunately, no complete index exists to HABS; the first catalog published in 1941 is long out of date. In recent years, catalogs for individual states, cities, and special subjects, such as Robert Vogel's compilation, *The New England Textile Mill Survey,* have been issued. In 1969, the Historic American Engineering Record (HAER) was established; it performs essentially the same function as HABS, but is more concerned with bridges, locks, railroad stations, piers, and factories. A catalog of the materials deposited in the Library of Congress through 1975 is available.

Finally, one might note the National Register of Historic Places, which is also in the National Park Service, and the various state preservation agencies. While these are not official research collections, they frequently contain significant amounts of information and materials on both common and extravagant structures. The 1966 Historic Preservation Act mandated that every state must have a historic preservation office and the methods of accomplishing a statewide survey of notable structures. The products of the survey will prove to be invaluable.

HISTORY AND CRITICISM

Because so little research has been done on popular architecture, there are really no books devoted specifically to the topic as a whole. To gain a perspective on popular architecture, one must refer to a wide range of books and articles.

Writings on the theory and methodology of the study of popular architecture are few and far between. Smatterings of ideas can be found in essays by J. Meredith Neil, Marshall Fishwick, and Dennis Alan Mann, and one can turn back to the standard works on popular culture such as that by Herbert J. Gans, *Popular Culture and High Culture.* Probably the most important search for a methodology has been done by Alan Gowans: first, in *The Unchanging Arts,* which was devoted largely to the other arts, but which did have some comments on architecture and importantly defined "high art" and "low art"; and then in his rather ponderously titled *On Parallels in Universal History Discoverable in Arts and Artifacts.* This work, last subtitled "An Outline Statement," is a theory that: what is art has changed over time; the arts must be interpreted in their historic terms; and "Taste Is Determined by Ideology." The implications for popular architecture are manifest, and, while much needs to be fleshed out, it is an important beginning. George Kubler's *The Shape of Time* has a somewhat different emphasis and argues that all man-made things can be viewed as art existing in a linked succession. As indicated earlier, the works by Henry Glassie offer several possibilities, and one should also look at Amos Rapoport's *House Form and Culture*, which, although devoted to the buildings of primitive peoples, offers many suggestions.

In architecture proper, the most current methodology is semantics and the application of the linguistic theory of signs of Saussure and Pierce. Most of the writing has been jargon-ridden and obscure, but the main intent has been to demonstrate that all buildings and their furnishings carry meanings, whether intended or not. The most understandable introduction is Geoffrey Broadbent's article, "A Plain Man's Guide to the Theory of Signs in Architecture." One should also look at Charles Jencks and George Baird's collection of essays, *Meaning in Architecture*, and a very recent three-part essay by Jencks in *Architecture & Urbanism*.

Another area for the student to be aware of is the actual impact on humans of the intangibles of space and form. This is also an undeveloped field with surprisingly little research done on perception and the cultural usages of space. Beginnings have been made in a readable form by anthropologists such as Edward T. Hall in *The Hidden Dimension* and psychologists such as Robert Sommer in *Personal Space* and in *Design Awareness*. Kent Bloomer and Charles Moore's *Body, Memory and Architecture* is written from an architect's point of view and while brief, offers some important insights. There are numerous other technical articles and research reports the student can pursue if needed.

The book that comes closest to a general history of American architecture and that pays some attention to popular culture is Alan Gowans's *Images of American Living: Four Centuries of Architecture and Furniture as Cultural Expression*. While Gowans's concentration is on high-art architecture, he does attempt to note some of the popular permeations. It was published in 1964 and needs to be updated. Vincent Scully's *American Architecture and Urbanism* indicates an important concern, but is marred in this case by a personal Ruskinian prose that has little substance. James Marston Fitch's *American Building: The Historical Forces That Shaped It*, while a general history, focuses more on the physical and technological factors. His presentation is very good for the period prior to the twentieth century, but it is dissipated after that point. Again, the focus is almost completely on high art. John Kouwenhoven's *The Arts in Modern American Civilization*, while published in 1948, is the only book that has seriously attempted to give a fresh look at American material artifacts and study their uniqueness as typically American. His comments on the vernacular tradition are worth reading.

Technological or construction history is a separate category from architecture because of its specialized nature. The best overall study of the American contribution is Carl Condit's two-volume work, *American Building Art*, which has been condensed and revised into one volume, *American*

Building: Materials and Techniques. These are pioneer attempts, with a strong virtue in that Condit understands technical language but can write literate English as well. James Marston Fitch has made a contribution here with his second volume, *American Building: The Environmental Forces That Shape It.* His book is a physiological study of the different sensory elements that make up buildings and is an important work. The title of Sigfried Giedion's *Mechanization Takes Command: A Contribution to Anonymous History* is self-explanatory; it is the first serious attempt to trace many of the contributions to modern life such as bathtubs, kitchen ranges, and heating. Reyner Banham's *The Architecture of the Well-Tempered Environment* is more narrowly focused and deals with the period from the late nineteenth century to the 1960s and with the usages high-art architects have made of air conditioning, dropped ceilings, fluorescent lighting, and forced-air heating. Banham is critical and prescriptive in nature, and, if he had a hero, it would be Willis Carrier. However, Banham's perceptions are astute and his thinking as always is original; the book is a must.

Books on furniture, interiors, and the decorative arts proliferate and encompass everything from how to collect Victoriana to serious studies of specific furniture types. All are of some value, but for the purposes of the student looking for a broad overview, there is little of value. Russell Lynes's *The Tastemakers,* published in 1954, is dated, but it is a popular history of American interior design that pays considerable attention to mass taste. The recent revival of interest in art deco or moderne of the 1920s and 1930s has resulted in several books that deal with the decorative arts from a popular point of view. Bevis Hillier's *Art Deco* and his essay in the Minneapolis Institute of Art's *The World of Art Deco* deals with the entire range of objects from furniture to architecture. Specifically American is Martin Grief's *Depression Modern: The Thirties Style in America*; although it is superficial, it makes a beginning and contains a wealth of photographs. Hillier's later book, *The Decorative Arts of the Forties and Fifties, Austerity/Binge* is devoted mainly to England, but the parallels with the United States are close enough for it to be of value. It is the first known attempt to deal with what is jokingly known in the trade as "art yucko." Studies that attempt to interpret individual tastes in interior decoration are far too rare. M. H. Harmon's *Psycho-Decorating: What Homes Reveal About People* is based on interviews with one hundred middle-income women who have decorated their own homes. The book is extremely limited and filled with unsupportable interpretative generalizations, but it indicates a direction that should be investigated.

The history of the American landscape—urban, suburban, and rural—and how to analyze it has a significant number of books of some importance. John Reps's *The Making of Urban America: A History of City*

Planning in the United States, while focusing on the more formal or designed creations, includes everything from garden cities to railroad speculator towns. It is well done and has many illustrations. For a wider view of the landscape in all its guises, John Brinckerhoff Jackson is clearly superior. His magnum opus on the history of the American landscape is not completed, and we must be content with a collection of his essays entitled *Landscapes*, with his one book, *American Space: The Centennial Years, 1865-1876*, and with old copies of *Landscape* magazine, which he edited. There are, of course, many many picture books on American cities; however, one is far superior and should be the model—Harold M. Mayer and Richard C. Wade's *Chicago: Growth of a Metropolis*. Adequate attention is paid to the everyday realities of popular architecture. For freeways, there is one good book—Lawrence Halprin's *Freeways*—that teaches some of the possible aesthetics of freeway design. Another class of books is the critical-analytical study that generally contains some history along with a methodology of how to look at the landscape. Most of these prejudicially call the popular environment "goop" and "crap" and contain prescriptive remedies; however, used with care, they are important. Examples are: Kevin Lynch's *The Image of the City*; Donald Appleyard, Kevin Lynch, and John R. Meyer's *The View from the Road*; Ian Nairn's *The American Landscape: A Critical View*; Richard Saul Wurman's *Making the City Observable*; and Grady Clay's *Closeup: How to Read the American City*, which contains an extensive analysis of the strip.

Turning to specific studies on popular architecture, quite clearly the entry point should be Tom Wolfe's seminal essay, "Las Vegas (What?) Las Vegas (Can't hear you! Too Noisy) Las Vegas!!!" on the Versailles of Las Vegas. Next is the previously mentioned Venturi, Brown, and Izenour's *Learning from Las Vegas*. This is written from an architect's and urban planner's point of view and provides an insightful look at all the elements of the American strip—gas stations, signs, parking lots, and "ugly and ordinary architecture." The actual history is slim, but the interpretation is challenging.

If Las Vegas is the Versailles of popular architecture, then Los Angeles is the Holy City. Reyner Banham's *Los Angeles: The Architecture of Four Ecologies* is every bit as important as the Venturi et al. book and probably offers a more profound interpretation. Banham's book is a mix between high art and popular architecture and he identifies the four ecologies: the ocean front, the foothills, the plains of Id, and, finally, freeway world, or autotopia. He appreciates the American scene as only an outsider can, for he is an Englishman. Another book about Los Angeles is David Gebhard and Harriette Von Brenton's *L.A. in the 30's*. It contains many examples of high-art architecture, but it also looks at the early drive-ins, freeways, and movie lots.

Several exhibits have led to some rather ephemeral but important studies on popular architecture. *Signs of Life: Symbols in the American City* is a slim catalog of an important exhibit organized by Venturi, Brown, and others at the Renwick Gallery of the Smithsonian Institution in 1976. The exhibit documented popular taste in the American home, the strip, and the street; hopefully a fuller publication will be forthcoming. An earlier catalog for the Institute of Contemporary Art in Philadelphia—*The Highway*—contains essays by Venturi and Brown. In 1978, the Cooper-Hewitt branch of the Smithsonian Institution held an exhibit on architectural packaging and looked at four popular American building types: fast-food restaurants, diners, gasoline stations, and museum-village restorations. An article by the curators of the exhibit appeared in *Architectural Record* for February 1978, and also as a reprint catalog. Finally, a planned exhibit on Catskill resort hotels has resulted in an article in *Progressive Architecture* by John Margolies and Elizabeth Cromley.

For the most part, studies of specific popular architect building types are still in the embryo stage. Richard Gutman's important article on diners in *Yale Perspecta* is supposed to lead to a book sometime in 1979. John Baeder, a painter, has recently produced a book titled *Diners* that contains reproductions of his work and offers some insights. An article by Paul Hirshorn and Steven Izenour on White Tower hamburger stands is also supposed to result in a book. McDonald's, the roadside shrine of the fast-food industry, has been the subject of a master's thesis by James M. Abbott and John K. Grosvenor, an article in *Progressive Architecture*, and the entire summer 1978 issues of the *Journal of American Culture*. McDonald's offers the clearest case of design responsiveness to changing tastes, from the early flamboyant tin sheds to the sophisticated clip-on mansards and English Tudor trim of today. Several studies are supposedly underway on service stations; one can find numerous articles on them in architectural journals, along with the usual master's theses, but there has been little of substantial content. One should look at Jim Morgan's "Mobil," which discusses the attempt to "tone up" Pegasus's image. A master's thesis by Gary Wolf on the Sunoco gas station is one example of a complete study. Movie theaters have probably received the most attention, and there are two books on them, neither of very high quality: Ben M. Hall's *The Best Remaining Seats* and Dennis Sharp's *The Picture Palace*. Hall's is a nostalgic romp through the past, with an excellent collection of pictures, while Sharp's is English-oriented and treats generally the high-art architect's productions. It is almost unbelievable that mass housing, from an architectural point of view, still has no adequate study; the only ones attempted are from foreign points of view. Maurice W. Barley covers nine hundred years of the English house in *The House and Home*, and it is of limited use. Martin Pawley's *Architecture Versus Housing* has some history of the large housing block, but, as suggested by the title, it is polemical in outlook. Foreign students are actually far ahead of Americans, and one should check for methodological insights in Robin Boyd's *Australia's Home*. In the same line, Alan Crawford and Robert Thorne's pamphlet *Birmingham Pubs, 1890-1939* makes pregnant suggestions for the study of American bars and saloons. The architecture of amusement parks and recreation has also received little attention in the United States. Critical articles abound on Disneyland, Disney World, and others; they can be located through the periodical indexes. There is one picture book: Gary Kyriazi's *The Great American Amusement Parks*.

The role of the industrial designer has started to be assessed in such books as Donald Bush's *The Streamlined Decade*, a particularly insightful treatment of the 1930s. Contemporary accounts by the designers themselves, such as Walter Dorwin Teague's *Design This Day* and Harold Van Doren's *Industrial Design*, can be read.

The historic preservation movement is also beginning to produce some literature that is of importance to the study of popular architecture. The National Trust for Historic Preservation in Washington, D.C., produces a quarterly journal—*Historic Preservation*—that frequently contains articles dealing with the mass environment. *America's Forgotten Architecture* by the National Trust, Tony Wrenn, and Elizabeth Mulloy is the best general introduction to preservation, with a substantial text and numerous illustrations. Finally, there are many preservation plans and reports that have at least a passing interest, such as Richard Guy Wilson and Jeff Vaughn's *The Old West Side*, which deals with a middle-class inner-city housing area.

ANTHOLOGIES AND REPRINTS

There have been few anthologies of literature on popular architecture, except for those issued from the Popular Culture Press at Bowling Green University. *Popular Architecture*, edited by Marshall Fishwick and J. Meredith Neil, collects articles dealing with a variety of subjects; some are appropriate and others are far afield from the subject. Other essays on popular architecture subjects have appeared in *The Arts in a Democratic Society*, edited by Dennis Alan Mann, and in *Icons of America*, edited by Ray B. Browne and Marshall Fishwick.

Reprints have proven to be the major source of builders' guides and house pattern books. The major publishers in this line have been Dover Press, Da Capo Press, and the American Life Foundation and Study Institute. The list would be very long if the hundred or so reprinted titles were noted here. The bibliography at the end of this essay lists those that have been referred to earlier.

BIBLIOGRAPHY

BOOKS AND ARTICLES

Abbott, James M., and John R. Grosvenor. "Corporate Architecture and Design Theory: A Case Study of McDonald's." Master's thesis, Miami University, 1976.

Appleyard, Donald, Kevin Lynch, and John R. Meyer. *The View from the Road.* Cambridge: MIT Press, 1964.

Architectural Record. *A Treasury of Contemporary Houses.* New York: F. W. Dodge, 1954.

————. *Motels, Hotels and Restaurants.* 2d ed. New York: F. W. Dodge, 1960.

————. *The Architectural Record Book of Vacation Houses.* New York: McGraw-Hill, 1977.

Baeder, John. *Diners.* New York: Harry N. Abrams, 1978.

Banham, Reyner. *The Architecture of the Well-Tempered Environment.* Chicago: University of Chicago Press, 1969.

————. *Los Angeles: The Architecture of Four Ecologies.* New York: Harper & Row, 1971.

Barley, Maurice W. *The House and Home: A Review of 900 Years of House Planning and Furnishing in Britain.* Greenwich, Conn.: New York Graphic Society, 1971 [1963].

Benjamin, Asher. *The American Builder's Companion.* 6th ed. New York: Dover, 1969 [1827].

Blake, Peter. *God's Own Junkyard: The Planned Deterioration of America's Landscape.* New York: Holt, Rinehart and Winston, 1964.

Bloomer, Kent C., and Charles W. Moore. *Body, Memory and Architecture.* New Haven: Yale University Press, 1977.

Boyd, Robin. *Australia's Home: Its Origins, Builders and Occupiers.* Ringwood, Victoria: Penguin Books, 1968 [1952].

Broadbent, Geoffrey. "A Plain Man's Guide to the Theory of Signs in Architecture." *Architectural Design,* 47 (July-August 1977), 474-82.

Browne, Ray B., and Marshall Fishwick, eds. *Icons of America.* Bowling Green, Ohio: Bowling Green Popular Press, 1978.

Bush, Donald J. *The Streamlined Decade.* New York: George Braziller, 1975.

Clay, Grady. *Close-up: How to Read the American City.* New York: Praeger, 1973.

Columbia University. *Avery Obituary Index of Architects and Artists.* Boston: G. K. Hall, 1963.

————. *Avery Index to Architectural Periodicals.* 2d ed. Boston: G. K. Hall, 1973. 15 vols. plus supplements.

Committee for the Preservation of Architectural Records. *Architectural Research Materials in New York City: A Guide to Resources in All Five Boroughs.* New York: Committee for the Preservation of Architectural Records, 1977. 2 vols.

Condit, Carl W. *American Building Art.* New York: Oxford University Press, 1960, 1961. 2 vols.

————. *American Building: Materials and Techniques*. Chicago: University of Chicago Press, 1968.

Crawford, Alan, and Robert Thorne. *Birmingham Pubs, 1890-1930*. Birmingham: Center for Urban and Regional Studies, University of Birmingham and the Victorian Society, Birmingham Group, 1975.

Dean, John P., and Simon Breines. *The Book of Houses*. New York: Crown, 1946.

Downing, Andrew Jackson. *Cottage Residences*. Watkins Glen, N.Y.: Library of Victorian Culture, 1967 [1842].

————. *The Architecture of Country Houses*. New York: Dover, 1969 [1850].

Fishwick, Marshall, and J. Meredith Neil, eds. *Popular Architecture*. Bowling Green, Ohio: Bowling Green Popular Press, n.d. [1975].

Fitch, James M. *American Building: The Historical Forces That Shaped It*. Boston: Houghton Mifflin, 1966.

————. *American Building: The Environmental Forces That Shape It*. Boston: Houghton Mifflin, 1972.

Gans, Herbert J. *Popular Culture and High Culture*. New York: Basic Books, 1975.

Gardner, Eugene C. *Homes and how to make them*. Boston: J. R. Osgood, 1885.

Gebhard, David, and Harriette Von Brenton. *L. A. in the 30's*. Santa Barbara, Calif.: Peregrine Smith, 1975.

Giedion, Sigfried. *Mechanization Takes Command: A Contribution to Anonymous History*. New York: Oxford Unversity Press, 1948.

Glassie, Henry. *Pattern in the Material Folk Culture of the Eastern United States*. Philadelphia: University of Philadelphia Press, 1968.

————. *Folk Housing in Middle Virginia: A Structural Analysis of Historic Artifacts*. Knoxville: University of Tennessee Press, 1975.

Gowans, Alan. *Images of American Living: Four Centuries of Architecture and Furniture as Cultural Expression*. Philadelphia and New York: J. B. Lippincott, 1964.

————. *The Unchanging Arts: New Forms for the Traditional Functions of Art in Society*. Philadelphia and New York: J. B. Lippincott, 1971.

————. *On Parallels in Universal History Discoverable in Arts and Artifacts*. Watkins Glen, N.Y.: Institute for the Study of Universal History, 1974.

Grief, Martin. *Depression Modern: The Thirties Style in America*. New York: Universe Books, 1975.

Gutman, Richard. "Diner Design, Overlooked Sophistication." *Yale Perspecta*, 15 (1975), 41-55.

Hall, Ben M. *The Best Remaining Seats*. New York: C. N. Potter, 1961.

Hall, Edward T. *The Hidden Dimension*. New York: Doubleday, 1966.

Halprin, Lawrence. *Freeways*. New York: Reinhold, 1966.

Harmon, M. H. *Psycho-Decorating: What Homes Reveal About People*. New York: Wyden Books, 1977.

Harris, Cyril M., ed. *Dictionary of Architecture and Construction*. New York: McGraw-Hill, 1975.

Hillier, Bevis. *Art Deco*. London: Studio Vista, 1965.

————. *The Decorative Arts of the Forties and Fifties, Austerity/Binge.* New York: Clarkson N. Potter, 1975.

Hirshorn, Paul, and Steven Izenour. "Learning from Hamburgers." *Architecture Plus,* 1 (June 1973), 46-55.

Historic American Building Survey, National Park Service. *Historic American Building Survey.* Washington, D.C.: Department of the Interior, 1941.

Hitchcock, Henry-Russell. *American Architectural Books, a List of Books, Portfolios, and Pamphlets on Architecture and Related Subjects Published in America Before 1895.* New York: Da Capo Press, 1975.

House & Garden. *The Building Guide. Fall-Winter, 1963-1964.* New York: Conde Nast, 1963.

Institute for Contemporary Art. *The Highway.* Philadelphia: Institute for Contemporary Art, 1970.

Jackson, John Brinckerhoff. *Landscapes, Selected Essays.* Edited by Ervin H. Zobe. Amherst: University of Massachusetts, 1970.

————. *American Space: The Centennial Years, 1865-1876.* New York: W. W. Norton, 1972.

Jacobs, Jane. *The Death and Life of Great American Cities.* New York: Random House, 1961.

Jencks, Charles. "The Architectural Sign." *Architecture & Urbanism,* 78 (April, May, June 1978), 3-10, 70-78, 115-28.

Jencks, Charles, and George Baird, eds. *Meaning in Architecture.* New York: George Braziller, 1970.

Kouwenhoven, John. *The Arts in Modern American Civilization.* New York: Norton, 1948.

Kubler, George. *The Shape of Time: Remarks on the History of Things.* New Haven: Yale University Press, 1962.

Kyriazi, Gary. *The Great American Amusement Parks.* Secaucus, N.J.: Citadel Press, 1976.

Lafever, Minard. *The Modern Builder's Guide.* New York: Sleigh, 1833.

Lynch, Kevin. *The Image of the City.* Cambridge: The Technology Press and Harvard University Press, 1960.

Lynes, Russell. *The Tastemakers.* New York: Harper, 1954.

Mann, Dennis Alan, ed. *The Arts in a Democratic Society.* Bowling Green, Ohio: Bowling Green Popular Press, 1977.

Margolies, John, and Elizabeth Cromley. "Upward and Inward with Time." *Progressive Architecture,* 59 (February 1978), 46-51.

Mayer, Harold M., and Richard C. Wade. *Chicago: Growth of a Metropolis.* Chicago: University of Chicago Press, 1969.

Minneapolis Institute of Art. *The World of Art Deco.* New York: Dutton, 1971.

Moore, Charles, Gerald Allen, and Donlyn Lyndon. *The Place of Houses.* New York: Holt, Rinehart and Winston, 1974.

Morgan, Jim. "Mobil." *Architecture Plus,* 1 (June 1973), 56-64.

Nairn, Ian. *The American Landscape: A Critical View.* New York: Random House, 1965.

National Trust for Historic Preservation, Tony P. Wrenn, and Elizabeth D. Mulloy. *America's Forgotten Architecture*. New York: Pantheon, 1976.

Neil, J. Meredith. "What About Architecture?" *Journal of Popular Culture*, 5 (Fall 1971), 280-88.

Oliver, Richard, and Nancy Ferguson. "Place, Product, Packaging." *Architectural Record*, 163 (February 1978), 116-20.

Palliser, Palliser & Company. *New Cottage Homes and Details*. New York: Da Capo Press, 1975 [1887].

Palmes, J. C. *Sir Banister Fletcher's A History of Architecture*. London: University of London, The Athlone Press, 1975.

Pawley, Martin. *Architecture Versus Housing*. New York: Praeger, 1971.

Rapoport, Amos. *House Form and Culture*. Englewood Cliffs, N.J.: Prentice-Hall, 1969.

Renwick Gallery, National Collection of Fine Arts, Smithsonian Institution. *Signs of Life: Symbols in the American City*. New York: Aperture, 1976.

Reps, John W. *The Making of Urban America: A History of City Planning in the United States*. Princeton: Princeton University Press, 1965.

Rudofsky, Bernard. *Architecture Without Architects*. Garden City, N.Y.: Doubleday, 1964.

———. *The Prodigious Builders*. New York: Harcourt, Brace, Jovanovich, 1977.

Scully, Vincent J. *American Architecture and Urbanism*. New York: Praeger, 1969.

Sharp, Dennis. *The Picture Palace*. New York: Praeger, 1969.

Sloan, Samuel. *The Model Architect*. Philadelphia: E. S. Jones, 1852.

Sommer, Robert. *Personel Space*. Englewood Cliffs, N.J.: Prentice-Hall, 1969.

———. *Design Awareness*. San Francisco: Rinehart, 1972.

Teague, Walter Dorwin. *Design This Day*. New York: Harcourt, Brace, 1940.

Van Doren, Harold. *Industrial Design: A Practical Guide*. New York: McGraw-Hill, 1940.

Venturi, Robert. *Complexity and Contradiction in Architecture*. New York: Museum of Modern Art, 1966.

Venturi, Robert, Denise Scott Brown, and Steven Izenour. *Learning from Las Vegas*. Cambridge: MIT Press, 1972. Rev. ed., 1977.

Vogel, Robert. *The New England Textile Mill Survey*. Washington, D.C.: Historic American Building Survey, National Park Service, 1971.

Wheeler, Gervase. *Rural Homes, or sketches of houses suited to American country life, with original plans, designs, etc.* New York: Charles Scribner, 1851.

Whiffen, Marcus. *American Architecture Since 1780: A Guide to the Styles*. Cambridge: Massachusetts Institute of Technology Press, 1969.

White, Charles E. *The Bungalow Book*. New York: Macmillan, 1923.

Wilson, Richard Guy, and Jeff Vaughn. *The Old West Side*. Ann Arbor: The Old West Side Association, 1971.

Withey, Henry F., and Elsie R. Withey. *Biographical Dictionary of American Architects (Deceased)*. Los Angeles: New Age Publishing, 1956.

Wolf, Gary Herbert. "The Gas Station: The Evolution of a Building Type as

Illustrated Through a History of the Sun Oil Company Gasoline Station."
Unpublished Master's thesis, University of Virginia, 1974.

Wolfe, Tom. *The Kandy*Kolored Tangerine*Flake Streamline Baby.* New York: Farrar, Straus & Giroux, 1965.

Woodward, George. *Woodward's National Architect.* Watkins Glen, N.Y.: American Life Foundation and Study Institute, 1977 [1868].

Wurman, Richard Saul. *Making the City Observable.* Minneapolis: Walker Art Center, and Cambridge: Massachusetts Institute of Technology Press, 1971.

PERIODICALS

The American Architect and Building News. Boston and New York, 1876-1938.

The American Builder. Chicago and New York, 1865-1895.

The American Home. New York, 1928-.

The Architectural Record. New York, 1891-.

Architectural Review and American Builder's Journal. Philadelphia, 1868-1870.

Better Homes and Gardens. Des Moines, Iowa, 1922-.

Early American Life. Harrisburg, Pa., 1970-.

Godey's Lady's Book and Lady's Magazine. Philadelphia, 1830-1898.

Historic Preservation. Washington, D.C., 1949-.

House & Garden. New York, 1901-.

House & Home: The Magazine of Housing. New York, 1952-.

The House Beautiful. Chicago and New York, 1896-.

Ladies' Home Journal. New York, 1883-.

Landscape. Santa Fe, N. Mex., and Berkeley, Calif., 1951-.

Nation's Restaurant News. New York, 1967-.

Popular Mechanics. New York, 1902-.

Professional Builder and Apartment Business. Chicago, 1936-.

Progressive Architecture. Stamford, Conn., 1926-.

Qualified Remodeler. Chicago, 1975-.

Restaurant Business. New York, 1902-.

CHAPTER 12. Popular Religion and Theories of Self~Help

Roy M. Anker

The notion of self-help has a long, energetic, and prolific life in American culture. Put plainly, past and present self-help ideologies have no common seminal idea or generative figure but vary in emphasis in different historical periods. As this essay title suggests, the numerous mutations of the self-help theme in the flux of American experience stem from diverse and often contradictory strains of popular and elite, religious and secular, and esoteric and conventional influence. As such, the development and the persistence of the self-help ethos are not easy phenomena to delineate. In this tangled knot of influence and expression are found such contrasting spirits as Benjamin Franklin and Ralph Waldo Trine, Andrew Carnegie and Mary Baker Eddy, and William James and Norman Vincent Peale. For better or worse, the self-help heritage perhaps offers one of those unifying modes of thought and feeling that knits together the religious, social, and ethnic pluralism of a change-ridden national history.

The aspiration toward self-betterment does not, of course, arrive new and full-blown in America with the landing of the Pilgrims or the popularity of Horatio Alger's Ragged Dick juvenile novels. As is the case with any human propensity that attains prominence for a while in a given culture, the seeming universality of human nature dictates that other societies in other times and places exhibit, to a lesser degree, similar traits and longings. In all communities, from antiquity to the present, can be found histories and tales of celebrated individuals who, by their own efforts or with divine aid, counter adverse circumstance to better their material and psychic well-being.

By definition, all literature, whether oral or written, has implicit didactic or inspirational elements that bid the listener-reader to emulate the superior qualities of the hero. Those modern books that proclaim their how-to intentions only make this didactic function in literary history fully explicit. The Mesopotamian *Epic of Gilgamesh* (2000 B.C.), for example, heralds the strength, courage, and fortitude of its hero in overcoming vindictive passion to slay monsters and to build city walls that insured the safety of his native people. So, too, the adulation of the wit and guile of Odysseus played a formative role in creating respect for rational control in what came to be classical culture, with its Platonic and Aristotelian confidence that truth and inner tranquility might be attained through the exercise of reason. This central Greek emphasis later formed the basis for a vigorous minority tradition in Christianity. As early as the fourth century A.D.—a theological watershed for historic Christendom—Pelagius, a classically learned English scholar, stressed the potential of each individual to arrive at truth through rational discernment and to achieve salvation through good works, thereby disputing Augustine's insistence on faith and right-eousness as the exclusive and irresistible gifts of divine grace. Similarly, the Reformation has Calvinists, heirs of Augustine, confronting heretic Jacob Arminius, who was another proponent of the individual's rational and ethical resolution as sufficient paths to God and Heaven.

HISTORIC OUTLINE

Whatever lively currency and effect the notion of self-help has had in American culture, it is clear that this ideal of individual effort and improvement does not first originate in America. The Puritan culture that was to dominate the first century of American life had its roots in England and before that in the European Reformation. Its visions of religion and culture had imbibed the Calvinistic spiritual dialectic between man's radical fallenness and God's gift of grace and salvation. The result was an acute consciousness of the moral insufficiency of natural man. This sense of unworthiness led to a rigoristic ethic in pursuit of sanctification—the acquisition of godliness, which was the long process of righting the self in fulfilling the promise and reality of grace, of making oneself Christlike or fit for God. This religious disposition no doubt found its fruition in John Bunyan's *A Pilgrim's Progress* (1678), an immensely popular tale of worldly temptation, spiritual struggle, and redemption—a fictional how-to rendering of the earthly sojourner's path to salvation. The same impulse for offering practical help and inspiration appeared in Englishman Lewis Bayly's *The Practice of Piety* (1612), which, in its twenty editions, offered advice on the route to godliness, and in Englishman Joseph Alleine's *The Sure Guide to Heaven* (1672), which sold fifty thousand copies in the colonies.

The most influential American expression of the tension between worldly activity and the piety of salvation came in Puritan divine Cotton Mather's

The Christian at His Calling (1701), in which the author stressed a two-faceted vocation for the believer. The first, or general, calling entailed conversion and allegiance to Jesus Christ. The second stressed worldly vocation, wherein the Christian engaged in practical employment for the benefit of society. Whatever task the Christian undertook was not primarily for personal gain but for the good of his fellows. The importance of Mather's formulation was that it not only emphasized the obligation of gainful activity but it served also as a justification for secular pursuits. The duty of an energetic vocation in the business of supplying others and oneself with necessities and goods repudiated any lingering traditions of quietism or monastic withdrawal. For the Christian, work was founded in gratitude and looked to stewardship.

Some erosion of the Puritan's concept of the meanings and uses of wealth and work came with the Enlightenment and with self-help's most famous poularizer, Benjamin Franklin. For this entrepreneur-inventor-philosopher, who was himself a poor boy made good, wealth itself was a sign of virtues that were the fruit of willed and stalwart action—industry, frugality, and perseverance. In the widely popular collection of Poor Richard's sayings, *The Way to Wealth* (1758), Franklin provided ready advice on the practical values and attitudes necessary to get ahead. Largely missing from this work or from the *Autobiography* (1788), in which Franklin becomes his own hero, is any kind of religious sanction for economic activity. Rather than seeing the accumulation of wealth as beneficial to God or fellow man, it exists largely for the individual and is the product of individual effort. Whereas wealth results from concerted personal initiative and is independent of luck, it reflects on the achiever's character. In the manner of Enlightenment's optimistic rationalism, the requisite traits and virtues are apparent to all and do not flow from and are not directed toward any special notion of Grace. Besides the status enjoyed from amassing wealth, its particular fruit lies in the improved and disciplined character that the individual must forge for himself in order to obtain the wealth.

While Franklin gave his blessing to economic acquisition, other assorted figures in eighteenth-century and early nineteenth-century America wished to sound a note of caution. For one, a less prominent Enlightenment influence from America's patrician sector hoped for a different understanding of the nature of opportunity in an expanding nation. A part of Thomas Jefferson's democratic ideal rested on a broad faith in the potential of small sociopolitical bodies to inspire and to improve their membership. Self-help was here fostered to encourage the development of the whole person, intellectual and moral, and not just his money- or status-making skills. It is safe to say that Jefferson, while insisting on the formal separation of church and state, nonetheless wished to invest the state with functions of inculcating virtue in a manner comparable to a surrogate church. The expanded and learned notion of self-help Jefferson wished to instill effected no constraint on the populace as it and its self-help advocates rushed head-long to embrace the seemingly limitless range of economic possibility.

From a lingering Puritan ambivalence toward wealth through the first half of the nineteenth century came a far greater dissent from a host of popular culture expressions. The famous "ecclectic readers" (1836-1857) of William Holmes McGuffey brought the self-help ethos to more than one hundred million juvenile readers, urging at once the values of assertiveness and diligence and the charity of Christian love. In *Lectures to Young Men* (1844), the famous pulpiteer Henry Ward Beecher coun-seled that the honest effort leading to wealth was a gift and glory of God that was too easily subverted by greed and uncharitableness. Popular novelist and essayist T. S. Arthur advised in numerous books that the way to success was through hard work that always carries service to others as a primary goal. And far from the image of Horatio Alger as a sponsor of an up-by-the-bootstraps mythos, Alger's many heroes are most always lost orphans with good blood, a lot of luck, modest ambitions, and kindly intentions. In approximately one hundred Alger novels, the greedy, exploi-tative, and selfishly wealthy or ambitious persons often come upon bad fortune for their unkindness.

During the latter part of the century, which was the height of the Indus-trial Revolution, the prominent churchman Lyman Abbott, in *How to Succeed* (1882), echoed the attitudes of most Protestant clergy in urging economic success within a proper view of the obligations of stewardship and warnings about greed. It was good to get ahead and use one's full potential, but avarice threatened always to obliterate the import of what-ever virtues were exercised in the process of wealth-getting. Success was for an end beyond itself.

The late nineteenth-century caution expressed by Alger, Abbott, and others was partly countered, however, in the enormously successful lecture-pamphlet "Acres of Diamonds" by Baptist minister Russell Con-well, the founder of Temple University. Conwell argued that it was the Christian's duty to acquire wealth, for its accumulation developed char-acter and its possession brought the power to do good. The printed version of the lecture had wide circulation, in addition to the fact that Conwell delivered it some six thousand times throughout his meteoric career.

The self-help tradition initiated in America by Mather and repeated in substance by Beecher, Abbott, and others until the beginning of the twen-tieth century stressed the primacy of certain virtues of hard work and responsibility as the way toward the improvement of one's character and the acquisition of success. The resources for achievement lay in the makeup of every man, and the attainment of prestige or wealth, seen as a Christian duty in glorifying God and helping neighbor, depended on the individual's fortitude and resolution. Such an ethic is understandable and perhaps appropriate in the open mercantile society of early nationhood on a rich and undeveloped continent.

While the average man, church member or not, was encouraged by manifold religious and secular sources in his culture to pursue economically and socially gainful purposes, he was almost as often cautioned against the invidious and subtle temptation of greed wherein the vision of God and social concern was displaced at enormous cost to the individual and society. Thus, there exists an almost constant attitude of ambivalence toward the improvement of the individual's material circumstance, and seldom did any self-made man justify his wealth in terms of selfish economic gain or the fair spoils of the victor in a competitive marketplace. Andrew Carnegie's famous Social Darwinist essay, "Gospel of Wealth," in the *North American Review* (1889) stands out as an atypical expression of the business and self-help mentality up to and including Carnegie's own time. Because of greatly changing social and economic conditions, Carnegie's tract sounds the death knell in America for an energetic individualism based on the aspirant's potential for diligence, prudence, and perseverance.

The history of self-help and religion assumes a different character and perhaps even a more significant role in American history from several sources: the life of an innovative and inquisitive New England clockmaker named Phineas P. Quimby, the fathering genius of the New Thought movement; its numerous latter-day offshoots that variously partake of its spirit; and possibly, depending upon the way one reads a shadowy historical record, Mary Baker Eddy's Christian Science. Quimby published only a few articles during his life that in no way account for the seminal and decisive role he plays in the history of American religious life. Rather, his import is felt through the writing and institutional development done by those he treated in his many years of healing practice, notably Mary Baker Eddy. Without Quimby—this modest and comparatively obscure physician of the mind from Maine—the texture of much popular modern self-understanding would be notably different. His influence is readily and daily observable in a myriad of present-day, quasi-Christian, intention-shaping and attitude-inspiring books and assorted electronic media spots. In a thoroughly secular realm, his influence is no less prominent in preparing a receptive ground for the theories and methods of modern psychotherapeutic practice.

An adequate appreciation of Quimby and his curious and mostly unrecognized influence is necessary to understand fully most modern self-help philosophies. Quimby's career and thought began with an accidental self-cure. Apparently doomed by tuberculosis in his early thirties, Quimby attempted to repeat the experience of a friend for whom horseback riding had been curative. Unable to ride because of his weak state, Quimby opted instead for carriage trips. On one such excursion, Quimby's horse balked, and the invalid was forced to run it up a long hill. Soon invigorated by this effort, he drove the beast furiously homeward, arriving there in possession of his old health. The incident planted an intellectual seed in Quimby that was to begin blossoming some years later when he attended a lecture and demonstration by a traveling mesmerist (hordes of whom were then roaming the countryside cashing in on the national curiosity about hypnosis, which was first introduced to America in 1836). Quimby read all he could on the topic and started testing its capability with volunteers. One willing subject, Lucius Burkmar, exhibited unusual clairvoyant powers in the diagnosis of disease and the prescription of remedies.

Eventually, Quimby put together the import of the carriage ride years before and the apparent healing successes obtained through the use of Burkmar. While he still accepted the trance-induced clairvoyant diagnosis of Burkmar, Quimby soon realized that many of Burkmar's patently ridiculous prescriptions could have no causal connection with the cures produced. They were, in effect, placebos in which the patients nonetheless had trusted. Healing was accomplished by the patient's faith in the medicine, not by the medicine itself. From this recognition, it was but a step to the conclusion that the operative and efficacious principles herein were the suggestion of healing at a subconscious level and the confidence of the patient in the remedy prescribed. The disease, then, could be judged to be purely mental or psychological—the product of the patient's mistaken perception of self and reality. Supposing this to be the case, the route to cure was simply a matter of changing the disturbed mental condition or wrong beliefs of the patient, of reshaping the attitudes and the faith of the ill.

Those ideas would always form the base of Quimby's healing theory and practice, although he came to redirect two of its important elements. First, after some years of practice, Quimby became sufficiently knowledgeable and confident about the psychological bases underlying his treatment procedure to discard his previous use of hypnotism as a diagnostic and therapeutic tool. The same diagnostic and therapeutic fruit could be gained, he concluded, through the conscious mind's clairvoyant receptivity to the patient's mood and malady and by explanation and mental suggestion through conversation; these are principles which, in diluted form, constitute important elements in modern psychotherapy.

A second alteration in Quimby's thinking would have great consequence for the history of New Thought and Christian Science as well as for American religious life. Quimby's early experiments with hypnosis and healing arose from a wholly practical and personal incentive—specifically, the matter of getting well. As in the reigning medical practice of the day, Quimby was justly concerned with mundane matters of cause and effect. To an uncertain extent and for obscure reasons—mysteries that plague historians to this day—Quimby gradually moved to spiritualize his previously purely mundane mental cure. He came to believe that he had discovered the healing principle in the miracles of Jesus in the New Testament. This insight involved a re-envisioning of the makeup of the human person, especially in recognizing the existence in each individual of an unconscious, which was deemed by Quimby to be a divine element partaking of the very substance of God. It was this agent or portion of the self—the repository of divine wisdom that was much cultivated by Quimby —that allowed Quimby to penetrate other minds to treat and diagnose wrong belief that denies the primacy of spirit in the attainment of health. That this radically new method treating bodily ills was effective there was little doubt in either Quimby's mind or the minds of many of his contemporaries. It has been estimated that from his Portland office Quimby treated twelve thousand patients in seven years. Two of his most devoted followers were the daughters of the respected United States Supreme Court Justice Ashur Ware.

Surely the most controversial, if not also the most famous, of all self-help figures who have kinship with Phineas P. Quimby was Mary Baker Eddy, the founder and still-ruling spirit of the Church of Christ, Scientist (or as it is better known, Christian Science), which joins Mormonism as one of the two purely indigenous American religions. Of the multitude of new sects and cults that flourished in the Gilded Age, only Christian Science went on to become a formal churchly body possessed of a governing ecclesiastical structure, a well-defined doctrinal core, and a devotional system of weekly services and evangelical outreach. The Church prohibits publication of membership figures, but recent scholars have estimated that its worldwide membership, mostly located in the United States, has grown since its beginnings in 1879 to one-third of a million members in over three thousand local congregations.

As in the case of its Christian parent religion, of which it is a heretical offshoot, Christian Science can also be said to have started with a fall. On February 1, 1866, the occasional semi-invalid, would-be poetess, and dabbler in occult healing, the then Mrs. Mary Baker Patterson was injured when she slipped and fell on the ice in Lynn, Massachusetts. In her later recollections, she declared that she was miraculously healed from paralysis and probable death while reading the Bible three days after the accident. The notes of her attending physician mention neither the supposed seriousness of the injury nor an immediate restoration of health. Furthermore, in a letter in mid-February to Julius Dresser, later a founder of New Thought, Mrs. Patterson makes no reference to a sudden cure and acknowledges the persistence of her back affliction and asks for physical healing from the man who was a likely successor to Quimby. Without new historical evidence, the controversy over Mrs. Eddy's illness and healing is not likely to dissipate.

Unfortunately, this same historical ambiguity surrounds Mrs. Eddy's personality and several crucial events in her life, including the origin and partial authorship of some of her seminal ideas and writings. On the question of literary origins, debate has raged for decades over whether Eddy stole from Quimby or Quimby from Eddy, and again no resolution of the dispute seems likely on the basis of present evidence. Mrs. Eddy first had contact with Quimby, then well known as a mesmeric healer, in 1862, four years before her famous fall, when she sought his aid for a chronic spinal disorder and nervous exhaustion. She experienced immediate relief and subsequently became a friend of Quimby and his advocate in the press, although she was later to discount his influence on the fully developed system of Christian Science. During her friendship with Quimby, she did have access to numerous unpublished writings of Quimby, now known as the "Quimby Manuscripts." Since the present copies are imprecisely dated, in various handwritings, and possibly the work of some of Quimby's patients, it is difficult to tell when and from whom the sometimes contradictory and fragmentary thoughts actually originated.

Apart from the seemingly irresolvable questions of intellectual indebtedness, it is important to note what Quimby did do for Mrs. Mary Baker Eddy. For some years before encountering Quimby, the frequently bedridden Mrs. Eddy had pursued relief and dabbled in Spiritualism, mesmerism, and various healing theories. During the Gilded Age, these theories were part of a national craze and offered frequent and lively topics of conversation in both taverns and drawing rooms. Her experience with Quimby convinced Mrs. Eddy of the reality of mental healing, and forever after she devoted herself to the genesis and strategies of healing. Quimby also gave Mrs. Eddy an initial step-by-step method by which to go about treating patients, although she was later to discard and indict certain of Quimby's methods, such as the use of manipulation of the head, which is reminiscent of the laying-on of hands.

Defenders of Christian Science have contended that the founder's teachings, which are to this day the exclusive theological core and rule for the Scientist, go far beyond Quimby's thought. Christian Science bears no resemblance to New Thought and was the happy result of the healing method and reality encountered by Mrs. Eddy in the aftermath of her fall in Lynn in 1866. Christian Science's supposed dependence on Quimby, it is argued, results from subsequent interpreters of Quimby, largely Warren Felt Evans and Julius and Annetta Dresser, who unjustly read back into Quimby many of the concepts discovered by Mary Baker Eddy. For the

Scientist, Quimby was a mesmeric mind curist who was entirely devoid of any religious framework for his theory and practice. His work was only subsequently spiritualized and "scientized" by disciples who concealed his fundamental reliance on the suggestion techniques of hypnotism. Again, the confusion of dating and authorship surrounding Phineas Quimby's manuscripts affords little help in clarifying the matter.

The best-selling book that provoked this welter of long and intense debate is Mrs. Eddy's *Science and Health* (1875). The work underwent numerous revisions—sixteen editions in all during her lifetime—each further clarifying and changing certain emphases. With regard to the book's real impact, sales figures of *Science and Health,* which are said to be in the millions, are deceptive because Christian Scientists were required to purchase each new edition, which averaged one every two years between the first edition in 1875 and Mrs. Eddy's death in 1910. From the beginning, however, despite these incidental alterations, the unique religious vision of *Science and Health* remained the same. Its most famous and controversial theological statement, on which its practice of healing rests, ventures a step beyond the idealism of transcendentalism and denies altogether the reality of matter. The physical world and the ills of mortality seen in sin, disease, and death are errors or illusions of humankind's mortal mind. Mrs. Eddy reasons to this conclusion from the premise that an all-good and wholly spiritual God could not create entities of matter and evil that contradict its essential nature.

Human consciousness, then, is only the manifestation of an entirely benign and spiritual Divine Mind. The more the individual apprehends the purely spiritual nature of his own being and his likeness to God, the more he is able to vitiate the effects of false belief in materiality and its woe-ridden by-products. Insofar as this goal is attained, the devotee becomes less susceptible to the sin and illness that result from belief in materiality. Healing occurs when the mind turns from its acceptance of the sway of material belief and is released to the pure contemplation of the love of God. Probably the largest intellectual problem with Christian Science—one often pointed out by its orthodox Christian critics—pertains to how the mortal mind, whose product is evil, however illusory, ever comes into existence if all reality is the spiritual manifestation of a good and completely spiritual deity. Defenders readily acknowledge the problem and let it rest as an enigma, suggesting that the truth of Christian Science can only be grasped from within its belief system, wherein exists a beautiful logic to its assertions.

The importance of Christian Science for an understanding of self-help and religion lies in its notion that adversity proceeds from wrong belief and attitudinal disorientation. Christian Scientists avow that their emphasis on spiritual struggle in discarding illusion and material trust distinguish it from the facile optimism of New Thought and positive thinking. There is a prominent strain, however, that regards first health and then economic success or "supply," as it is called by Scientists, to be reliable evidence of proper belief and God's favor. Indeed, Mrs. Eddy and her followers have stressed that the proof of their belief lies in the empirically observable effect of healing and improved health, which is but a step from economic reassurance. In any case, later disciples of both Quimby and Eddy were less cautious in ascribing wealth as well as health to new found trust in the power of mind and attitude to enhance spiritual, physical, and material well-being.

For a multitude of reasons involving cultural susceptability and readiness, Mrs. Eddy's Christian Science made a tremendous impact on late nineteenth-century American society. The woman, who at age fifty was penniless and working on a book no one would wish to publish, would retire three decades later as the spiritual and political head of a sizeable, well-established, and accepted, if not quite respected, church body. But there, in the transition from controversial sect to respectable denomination, Mrs. Eddy's influence in American culture ceases to grow, although it does not end altogether. The history of an energetic, radical, religious movement pioneered by a magnetic leader begins to assume the characteristics of institutional denominationalism. The authoritarian character of Mrs. Eddy's writing and self-understanding explicitly held that her particular interpretation of scripture and statement of doctrines were handed down by God and were therefore definitive and final. Any attempt by a Christian Scientist to rephrase or add to the substance of belief delineated in *Science and Health* was to be prohibited. This ultra-conservative theological rigidity led, during Eddy's life, to the expulsion of prominent Christian Scientists and, after the founder's death, to the absolute central control of the Church and the writings of all members by an executive board.

This same tenor is still evidenced today in the fact that while Christian Science worship services have largely copied mainline Protestant liturgy, they have supplanted the sermon with readings from *Science and Health*. Any further words of interpretation on matters of which Mrs. Eddy once spoke could only prove superfluous and risk inadvertent distortion. Christian Science initially produced a major ideological formulation on the dominance of spirit in man and provided strategies for self-cure. Given its prohibition against any re-expression by anyone of Mrs. Eddy's theology, and given orthodoxy's traditional suspicion of Christian Science's off-beat metaphysics, its persisting influence is open to question. This conclusion is supported by the failure of the denomination to sustain its dramatic early growth. Since the death of Mrs. Eddy, membership increases have paralleled population growth. The observer must look to the movement known as the New Thought—the other offspring of Phineas Quimby —to detect the route by which American culture became beguiled by the notion of self-help through religion.

To be sure, Mary Baker Eddy was not the only person healed by Phineas Quimby in his Portland housefront office. In 1863, the year after Quimby healed the founder of Christian Science, he successfully treated for nervous collapse Warren Felt Evans, who had just left the Methodist ministry for the Swedenborgian Church of the New Jerusalem. Six years later, and six years before Eddy's *Science and Health*, Evans published *The Mental Cure: Illustrating the Influence of the Mind on the Body, Both in Health and Disease, and the Psychological Method of Treatment* (1869). While it was not a best-seller, *The Mental Cure* enjoyed steady attention, going through seven editions in sixteen years. Evans's second book, *Mental Medicine* (1873), is known to have gone through fifteen editions in its first twelve years, indicating persistent interest in Evans's thought.

Evans was religious throughout his life, and when he met Quimby, he was enamored with the esoteric Swedish physicist-philosopher Emmanuel Swedenborg. Evans recognized in Quimby the use of the same principles by which Jesus healed and—still further—the logical and practical extension of philosophic idealism. Evans's fourth book, *The Divine Law of Cure*, is devoted to demonstrating the extent to which some of the best philosophic minds of Europe and America—for example, Hegel, Berkeley, Fichte, Coleridge, and Edwards—prepared a theoretical base for mental healing. By his fifth book, *The Primitive Mind Cure: The Nature and Power of Faith, or Elementary Lessons in Christian Philosophy and Transcendental Medicine* (1885), which went through five editions in one year, Evans had expanded his range of intellectual support to include Oriental thought, in which there was beginning to be considerable American curiosity. And in his last book, *Esoteric Christianity and Mental Therapeutics* (1886), Evans was even more characteristically like New Thought in his trust in a kind of philosophic universalism wherein ancient and modern creeds bear significant portions of fundamental truth. Like Evans, many subsequent and less prominent New Thought writers would seek intellectual support for their thinking. In America, they would most often find support in transcendentalism and Ralph Waldo Emerson, who chose to ignore both Christian Science and New Thought.

Throughout his six books, Evans reiterates basic conclusions from Quimby and shares many views with Mary Baker Eddy. There is always the insistence on the dominance of spirit or mind over matter. Unlike Eddy, Evans does not see matter as necessarily illusory, allowing rather that it does exist independently of human consciousness. Disease is the failure to recognize the ultimacy of spirit and the presence of Christ or God in every person, a potentiality made manifest through Jesus of Nazareth. The route to health is through dispelling the idea or conviction of the sway of disease, which results from partial recognition of a kindly and loving God that forms the true self, residing primarily in the subconscious portions of the mind. The sufferer is in need of affirmation and hopeful thinking, which is the medium of all cures and a method to be used by later New Thoughtists and Norman Vincent Peale. Wrong or pessimistic thinking brings bodily ills.

New Thought gradually gathered momentum from the enthusiasm of other Quimby followers and of dissidents and exiles from Christian Science. Among the other famous patients of Quimby was Julius Dresser, who first visited Quimby in 1860 and was healed. While there, he met fellow-patient Annetta Seabury, whom he married in 1863. Dresser decided to discard his ambition to become a Baptist minister; he entered journalism, moved west, and returned to Boston in 1883, where he and his wife set up mental practice according to Quimby. While they published little of their own, they did attract attention by accusing Mary Baker Eddy of pirating from the manuscripts of Phineas Quimby, a controversy that has yet to be successfully resolved. The son of Annetta and Julius Dresser, Horatio, became the chief and most respected chronicler of New Thought, having studied with William James at Harvard, where he won the Ph.D. in philosophy.

The middle-aged Ursula Gestefeld cured herself after reading *Science and Health*. A zealous supporter thereafter of Mrs. Eddy, she went so far as to write an adulatory book on Mrs. Eddy and Christian Science entitled *Ursula N. Gestefeld's Statement of Christian Science* (1888). For her efforts, she was driven out of the Church by Mrs. Eddy. She subsequently started her own periodical called *The Exodus*, which soon had a club of devoted followers.

Emma Curtis Hopkins similarly became a devoted follower of New Thought after being driven from Christian Science in a series of disputes with Mrs. Eddy. A powerful speaker, she soon attracted a large following, an organization bearing her name, and a theological seminary in Chicago. Such people as the Dressers, Ursula Gestefeld, Emma Hopkins, and numerous others, often with their own following, books, and periodicals, joined together in 1914 to form the International New Thought Alliance, which did much to spur the notions of New Thought. One such member of the New Thought movement was the prestigious Boston Metaphysical Club, which met for the first time in 1895. All these diverse people, whose exact number is impossible to gauge, shared in the general hopes and tenets of mental healing as spelled out by Quimby and Evans. The sole point of division was perhaps how much they individually wished to "theologize" notions of incarnation, sin, and the existence of matter. In any case, differences were not sufficiently acute to cause acrimony or schism.

New Thought received a new level of public attention and a controversial new theme in 1897, with its first authentic best-seller, *In Tune with the Infinite: Fullness of Peace, Power, and Plenty*, by Ralph Waldo Trine. The book contained straightforward explanations of the main precepts of New Thought. Its acceptance by a largely orthodox reading public resulted in part from the fact that Trine, a skilled stylist and expositor, tended to blur some of the key differences between conservative Christianity and New Thought, and when choices in phraseology came, Trine tended to use the language of tradition. As a whole, *In Tune with the Infinite* sought to emphasize the closeness of conventional Christian thinking and New Thought. Most readers saw in it the noble inspiration of established wisdom rather than the influence of esoteric philosophy or any particular healing cult. What readers encountered in Trine's book was an explicit presentation of a latent strain in New Thought and Christian Science—that is, the promise of prosperity and economic plenty as the inevitable result of being in tune with the Infinite.

Whether this new conspicuous element accounted for Trine's success is impossible to tell. Spiritual tranquility and physical well-being had been a part of Quimby's pioneering views and were expounded by his disciples. Here, the hope of wealth and personal power began to equal, if not surpass, the expectations of health and psychic repose. A little over a decade before, Warren Felt Evans had expounded on "the power of faith" to heal in *The Primitive Mind Cure*. But until Trine's book, the emphasis on "supply," as Mary Baker Eddy called it, had been largely subordinated to the individual's ability to influence his own person—the mind and the body. Trine's work extended control of the self outward to suggest a causal connection between spiritual attitude and financial reward and success.

If most readers were not aware of the New Thought they were getting in Trine's book, the same can be said for the wisdom and service offered by New Thought's only enduring and widely recognized organization, the Unity School of Christianity, founded in Kansas City by Emma Hopkins's disciples Charles and Myrtle Fillmore. In 1887, the Fillmores had been in ill health when they heard Dr. E. B. Weeks lecture on Hopkins's doctrines. For the first time, Myrtle Fillmore saw herself as a child of God over whom sickness had no power. So began a healing that took some two years, but healed she was. Impressed friends, as well as her initially skeptical husband Charles, began to inquire into the causes of Myrtle's healing. Eventually convinced, Charles began publication of a magazine called *Modern Thought* in 1889. In 1890, the Society of Silent Help was announced in its pages. This organization grew out of weekly prayer meetings by the Fillmores and their friends, wherein they would specifically pray for the suffering, troubled, and needy, using the New Thought healing concept known as "absent treatment" or thought transference. The group grew quickly, becoming known simply as Silent Unity, and requests for prayers flooded the magazine's offices. Today, this service is offered around the clock, and one hundred fifty people are employed to handle over half a million requests annually. So successful have been its methods that they are now imitated by evangelist Oral Roberts and possibility-thinking television preacher Robert Schuller.

Eschewing the opportunity to become a church, Silent Unity became the Unity School of Christianity, devoted to the soft-sell promulgation of its New Thought Christianity through books, pamphlets, and media advertising, and to the daily practice of healing and aid first initiated by Silent Unity. Today, Unity continues to publish *Wee Wisdom*, begun in 1893, the oldest children's magazine in America, with a circulation of around a quarter of a million readers. Begun in 1924, *Daily Word*, a monthly inspirational booklet for adults, has a circulation of one hundred eighty thousand. In addition, there are *Weekly Unity* (1909), a mixture of newsletter and magazine; *Progress* (1924), which is oriented toward adolescents; and *Good Business* (1924), advocating the proposition that Christian ethics is good business practice. The message of Unity finds its way into even more homes through television and radio advertising that features inspirational talks by prominent Hollywood celebrities.

While it is not a formal church, Unity has found it necessary to authorize leaders and ministers for the local Unity centers that have sprung up across the country. Unity's publishing enterprise and its extensive headquarters-campus in suburban Kansas City is supported mostly by small contributions from donors. The organization is run by the children and grandchildren of the founders. While its rhetoric sounds like orthodox Christianity, it remains very much a descendent of New Thought in its emphasis on the partial divinity or Christliness of each person, the possibility of healing through the recognition of that Christly potential, and the ready supply of material blessing.

One of the best known of all avowed New Thought figures in the twentieth century, amounting to national celebrity status, was Emmet Fox, a best-selling author and a noted preacher who regularly preached to thousands in New York's Hippodrome and in Carnegie Hall. In 1930, in order to carry on the work started in his native England, Fox came to America where he found an enthusiastic following. The titles of his popular books amply illustrate his connection to New Thought, of which he was an ordained minister in the Church of Divine Science. *Power Through Constructive Thinking* (1932), *Make Your Life Worthwhile* (1942), and *Find and Use Your Inner Power* (1940) announce the unlimited and divine potentiality of each individual, which is unleashed through affirmative prayer that eliminates pessimism and fear, the sources of psychic stress, illness, and failure. Realizing God and the reality of divine love and assuming a new mentality yielded tangible evidences of its truth and efficacy in increased health and prosperity.

Fox's prominence was soon upstaged from an unexpected and surprising source. From dour Dutch Calvinism and America's oldest denomination—the small Reformed Church in America—came the message of ex-Methodist Norman Vincent Peale, whose best-selling books and frequent radio and television appearances have made his name and his "positive-thinking" credo household words. Peale admits to having been influenced deeply by New Thought during a crisis of relevance early in his ministry. The insights learned then proved useful when Peale assumed his present pastorate in the 1940s at New York City's prestigious Marble Collegiate Church, where he encountered much psychic dis-ease among the well-to-do.

Along with psychiatrist Smiley Blanton, a future coauthor, Peale established an extensive psychological counseling service in his new parish. His main work, though, has been his books, whose titles once again show obvious connections with New Thought. *A Guide to Confident Living* (1948) was on the best-seller list for two years, selling over six hundred thousand copies, and *The Power of Positive Thinking* (1952) sold two and one-half million copies in four straight years near the very top of best-seller lists. Now in its thirty-third volume, the magazine *Guideposts: A Practical Guide to Successful Living*, edited and published by Peale, has a circulation of over one million readers. It is estimated that in 1957 Peale reached a weekly audience of thirty million people through an extensively syndicated newspaper column, a radio program reaching one million homes, a television show on more than one hundred stations, a column in *Look*, and the monthly *Guideposts*.

Peale, in effect, borrows many of his major ideas and methods from New Thought, although he is careful to de-emphasize theologically questionable matters, such as the presence of Christ in each person and the stature of Jesus. Nonetheless, Peale has retained emphasis on the impact of attitude or confidence on self-perception, social acceptance, and worldly success. Peale has further stressed the tangible evidences of fruits of changed thinking as witnesses to the efficacy of his theories. His literary method is largely comprised of strategies to accomplish these ideological ends. While previous New Thought writers have largely written straight and sometimes detailed exposition of their ideas, Peale's books are aphoristic and anecdotal, with patterns of statement and exemplum, ad infinitum.

The decades of Peale's success saw a popular ecumenical consensus about his goals of inner confidence and hope, if not his exact methods and inspiration. Boston Rabbi Joshua Loth Liebman's *Peace of Mind* (1964) stayed near the top of the best-seller list for three years, eventually selling well over one million copies. Liebman combined modern depth psychology with Judaism in a guide to overcoming self-hatred, disabling guilt, and social maladjustment. The liberal Protestant preacher of Riverside Church in New York City, Henry Emerson Fosdick, in *On Being a Real Person* (1943) and other books, again melded psychology with religion. A positive faith was necessary to overcome pessimism, lethargy, and loneliness. By cultivating one's inner resources, the person could engage in, as the title of another of Fosdick's popular books puts it, *Adventurous Religion* (1926).

In contrast to Liebman's and Fosdick's trust in the new psychology, Roman Catholic Fulton Sheen counseled a return to orthodox and mildly ascetic Christianity in his best-selling *Peace of Soul* (1949) and *Life Is Worth Living* (1953). Self-control and repose proceeded from bringing one's anxiety and self-seeking to God. Conservative evangelical Protestantism found a spokesman in revivalist preacher Billy Graham with his *Peace of God* (1953). Like Sheen, Graham's solutions to psychic distress ignored the new psychologies and partook of the well-established Protestant tradition of pietism. Graham repeated the same counsel more than two decades later in his best-selling manual *How to Be Born Again* (1977).

The fundamentalism in which Graham had his roots had long featured its own tradition of religion as a path to the solution of one's ethical, spiritual, and physical ills. Revivalist pleas have always manifested, at least implicitly, an appeal to self-interest insofar as the sinner was urged to accept God's grace and avoid the fires of hell. The more extreme healing sects have emphasized in addition faith as the route to emotional and physical well-being. A former revivalist and now a television personality and president of Oral Roberts University in Tulsa, Oklahoma, Oral Roberts began his ministry on such a platform. The best known of recent faith healers was revivalist-television personality Kathryn Kuhlman, who died in 1976. A similar strain appears in the faith-to-riches ministry of the Reverend Frederick J. Eicherenkoetter II—or "Rev. Ike," as he is better known —a black evangelist who promises prosperity in return for faith in God and economic generosity to the preacher's cause. These all follow in the tradition of the controversial faith healer Aimee Semple McPherson, a female Elmer Gantry in the eyes of many, whose public career was plagued by scandal.

Perhaps the most recent and well known of the active self-help preachers demonstrates the persistence of the New Thought-Peale tradition. Peale's mantle has seemingly passed to a younger disciple, Robert H. Schuller, a native of rural Iowa and also a son of the Dutch Reformed Church. Schuller began his controversial ministry atop a drive-in theater refreshment stand in Garden Grove, California, a suburban community near Disneyland. Schuller, too, has written many books on his own modification of Peale's famous credo, "possibility thinking." He is best known, however, for weekly telecasts from his impressive drive-in church. The services and sermons are, in effect, dramatizations of the literary method pioneered by Peale and the strain of thought alive in America for over one hundred years. Its persistence and vitality are amply indicated by Schuller's meteoric success; his weekly program, "The Hour of Power," is now broadcast nationwide. In addition, Schuller's congregation is now constructing on its already well-developed campus a fourteen-million-dollar all-glass "Crystal Cathedrale," designed by world famous architects Philip Johnson and John Burgee.

The tradition of New Thought, Christian Science, and the popularity of "positive thinking" presents, in effect, a second and influential self-help tradition in America that emphasizes the instrumental utility of religious belief. Faith or the acquisition of a new affirmative frame of mind becomes a means of mending one's psychic or physical ills. In the older Puritan-endorsed self-help philosophy, the individual sought justification of the success-getting strategies and goals by assessing the extent to which those methods and ends conformed to Christian principles of fairness, charity, and stewardship. The New Thought tradition inverted this older perspective by making the curative and endowing powers of God the vehicle to success and well-being. Right attitudes or affirmative prayer becomes the means by which the individual acquires the traits and attitudes necessary for becoming a success. Moral questions about the appropriateness of affluence or means of acquisition receive little or no attention. In a kind of mental behavioralism, the individual, through autosuggestion, produces an attitude and expectation of success that will yield the reality. The results validate faith and constitute an empirical test of the truth and efficacy of religion.

REFERENCE WORKS

The inquiry into the theme of self-help and its interaction with American religious thought has not yet progressed sufficiently to yield bibliographies or checklists specifically devoted to cataloging primary or secondary materials. For a listing of primary sources on a given topic, the best scholars can do is to consult the notes and bibliographical essays supplied in a number of secondary books on a particular interest. Fortunately, some very good, but by no means definitive, bibliographies do exist in such works.

In the general history of self-help in America, Irvin G. Wyllie supplies an erratically useful "Note on Sources" at the end of *The Self-Made Man in America: The Myth of Rags to Riches.* Wyllie's bibliographic comment, as in the case of the text itself, is primarily useful for establishing a checklist of significant authors of both primary and secondary sources, rather than for the beginnings of any comprehensive listing of works by those authors. A somewhat better bibliographical article is contained in John G. Cawelti's *Apostles of the Self-Made Man.* It is more complete, analytic, and discerning insofar as Cawelti, an eminent scholar and interpreter of American popular culture, attempts to discuss problems of bibliographical detective work. As in Wyllie's work, the very nature of the broad historical survey that Cawelti undertakes limits the extent to which he can establish or provide exhaustive listings. Much to its credit, it does evaluate existing books on particular figures and subjects.

Still another survey on self-help and success is Richard Weiss's *The American Myth of Success: From Horatio Alger to Norman Vincent Peale,* which contains a very good selective bibliography, especially enumerating the more influential writers of the early New Thought movement as they affected psychological and religious thought. The extensive notes offer a good resource for contemporaneous comment from a wide range of sources. The most complete listing and discussion of primary and secondary sources for self-help appears in the extensive notes to Richard M. Huber's *The American Idea of Success.* The thorough research and comprehensive intent of Huber's work as a whole accounts for its greater usefulness.

Of indispensable value generally to students of American religious history is Nelson Burr's two-volume *A Critical Bibliography of Religion in America.* This lengthy bibliographic discussion offers the most reliable and efficient starting place for any inquiry into religious institutional history as well as into the relations between society and religion. New books in American religious history published since Burr's work are regularly reviewed in the quarterly journal *Church History* and in a newer periodical, *Religious Studies Review.* Pertinent articles and historical essays appearing in periodicals are listed in the quarterly bibliography of recent historical articles in American journals by *The Journal of American History,* formerly known as the *Mississippi Valley Historical Review.* More recent than Burr's work is the selective bibliography that cites some six hundred titles in thirty-two areas of interest, supplied by Sydney E. Ahlstrom in *A Religious History of the American People,* winner of a National Book Award for 1972.

A good introduction to the controversial Weberian thesis—a key focus in almost any discussion on the relation between individualism and religions—appears in Burr's "Religion and Capitalism," in volume II of *A Critical Bibliography of Religion in America.* A discussion of sources for the "Gospel of Wealth," which is for some a latter-day manifestation of the Weberian thesis, is also found in Burr. Of additional usefulness for background and as suggestions for further reading on this topic is Robert W. Green's casebook, *Protestantism and Capitalism: The Weber Thesis and Its Critics.*

An objective and thorough history, much less a satisfactory bibliography, of Christian Science is presently not possible because the directors of the Church of Christ, Scientist, prohibit free access to the archives of the Mother Church in Boston. Scholars of Christian Science suggest that there is in the collection an enormous quantity of unpublished material by and about Mrs. Eddy and subsequent church leaders. Because of the numerous and seeming inevitability of opposing views of Mrs. Eddy and her movement, the objective scholar will be impatient until free access to this archival material is permitted. Modern editions of Mrs. Eddy's writings have been issued by the Christian Science Publishing Society. Early editions of Mrs. Eddy's *Science and Health* (1875), which the author revised significantly, are rare, but Edwin Dakin lists locations for these in the partly annotated bibliography to *Mrs. Eddy: The Biography of a Virginal Mind.* Dakin also mentions libraries that have complete or nearly complete holdings of various Christian Science periodicals. The most complete bibliography of works about Christian Science by members, admirers, and critics is found in Charles S. Braden's *Christian Science Today: Power, Policy, Practice.* The list of some two hundred eighty titles includes everything from historical background materials, biographies, and theological refutations to testimonial confessions, inspirational guides, and some thirteen pro-Scientist novels. The fullest listing of Mrs. Eddy's unpublished writing is in the notes to Robert Peel's three-volume biography, *Mary Baker Eddy: The Years of Discovery, Mary Baker Eddy: The Years of Trial,* and *Mary Baker Eddy: The Years of Triumph.*

For materials on the New Thought movement, Charles Braden is again the most exhaustive bibliographer. His *Spirits in Rebellion: The Rise and Development of New Thought* contains nearly six hundred items of primary material itemized in ten general categories. Included in the listings are approximately one hundred New Thought periodicals, about twenty of which survive into the present. Braden also mentions the locations for access to the original Quimby manuscripts. The original handwritten copies are in the Library of Congress. Photocopies are available at the Bridwell Library of Southern Methodist University and the library of the Pacific School of Religion, Berkeley, California. The greatest part of the Quimby writings is also available in *The Quimby Manuscripts,* edited by Horatio W. Dresser. For materials on the historical and religious context into which both Christian Science and New Thought came, see Paul A. Carter's extensive listing of contemporary religious documents in *The Spiritual Crisis of the Gilded Age.* The selective bibliography and notes to Richard Weiss's *The American Myth of Success* are useful for establishing the specific appeal of New Thought in its historical setting.

Since the primary means of communication of various self-help ideas has been the printed word, in both inspirational and fictional genres, bibliographies detailing such materials and their popularity are especially useful, if only to provide a listing of those authors who had extraordinary influence among the many who wrote. The most accessible of such general guides are: Frank Luther Mott's *Golden Multitudes*; Alice Payne Hackett's *70 Years of Best-Sellers, 1895-1965*; James D. Hart's *The Popular Book: A History of America's Literary Taste*; and Louis Schneider and Sanford M. Dornbusch's *Popular Religion: Inspiration Books in America.*

In addition to larger questions on the relation of literature and religion, the specific best-selling novels featuring the interplay of religion and society throughout American history are discussed in Burr's *A Critical Bibliography*. A more detailed discussion and listing can be found in an (unfortunately) unpublished doctoral dissertation by Ralph Allison Carey, "Best-Selling Religion: A History of Popular Religious Thought in America as Reflected in Religious Best-Sellers, 1850-1960."

Unpublished dissertation studies of fiction in the late nineteenth century —the heyday of religious fiction and a watershed for notions of self-help and religion—are with comprehensive intent. See Elmer F. Suderman's "Religion and the American Novel, 1870-1900" and, for a narrower focus, important for the understanding of the crisis of religious epistemology that struck the Gilded Age, Roy M. Anker's "Doubt and Faith in Late Nineteenth-Century American Fiction." A general survey and discussion of more recent religious self-help literature, most of it nonfiction, appears in Donald Meyer's *The Positive-Thinkers: A Study of the American Quest for Health, Wealth, and Personal Power from Mary Baker Eddy to Norman Vincent Peale.*

A superb and thorough bibliographical discussion of primary and secondary sources on the Pentecostal and charismatic healing movements is found in David Edwin Harrell, Jr.'s *All Things Are Possible: The Healing and Charismatic Revivals in Modern America*. The survey satisfactorily delves into almost all related areas, from history to tongue-speaking and critical estimates.

RESEARCH COLLECTIONS

Research collections of either secular or religious self-help literature are almost nonexistent. Because of its great popularity in its day, much of the literature discussed in this essay can be found in major public or university libraries as well as in book stores that specialize in old and used books. Even though he is located at a rural midwestern college, this author has had little difficulty in obtaining all necessary materials for this study through interlibrary loan services.

Bridwell Library of Southern Methodist University has established a New Thought collection, collecting books, pamphlets, periodicals, personalia, archives, and miscellaneous documents of people and organizations associated with the New Thought movement. More recent materials can be located at the office of the International New Thought Alliance, 7677 Sunset Boulevard, Hollywood, California.

Materials on Christian Science—periodicals and unpublished primary source materials—are located at the Mother Church in Boston. While it is generally believed that the collection of unpublished documents is extensive, there is a sizeable and important portion of the holdings to which the public is not permitted access, as many scholars have complained. In the past, access has been granted in proportion to the scholar's likely fealty to Christian Science.

Since many of the recent declaimers of self-help have been prominent churchmen, full collections of their writings and electronically recorded messages are retained in the archives and libraries of the congregations served. Hence, Norman Vincent Peale's numerous books and a full run of his magazine *Guideposts* can be found at Marble Collegiate Church in New York City. Similarly, the Robert H. Schuller Televangelism Association, which produces Schuller's weekly "The Hour of Power," retains tapes of all broadcasts and regularly prints in pamphlet form Schuller's sermons. Free access is permitted at the association's offices on the campus of Garden Grove Community Church, Garden Grove, California.

Oral Roberts University in Tulsa, Oklahoma, has the only significant collection of Pentacostal material. The problems of research in the area are acute because revivalist traditions usually thrived on the spoken word and evangelists often did not bother to retain notes or printed texts of their work. Often, the best resources for information about revivalist events and traditions are participants or observers of the events and personalities.

HISTORY AND CRITICISM

For its supposed prominence and influence in American culture, few books dealing specifically with helf-help ideologies have been written, and an adequate comprehensive history of self-help in relation to American religion and its environing culture is still to be completed. Needless to say, a plethora of interpretive books on innumerable facets and overall meanings of American religion have appeared in recent decades. While these studies lie outside the purview of this essay, any full view of self-help in American culture must at sometime or another consult them.

The work of two authors in particular bears brief mention, for they are of indispensable importance in dealing with the meaning and significance of self-help within the long dominant religious tone of American life. The earliest of these works is Max Weber's well-known and controversial *The Protestant Ethic and the Spirit of Capitalism,* which argues that the American economic system was the direct and inevitable result of Puritan Calvinism, and that Puritanism was in fact to a considerable extent economic in its incentive.

H. Richard Niebuhr's *The Kingdom of God in America* disputes Weber and others in positing the thesis that any potential unitary vision of American history must deal with the ambivalent Protestant response to the central Calvinistic notion of the transcendent majesty and wisdom of God, which no man could hope to emulate. While this standpoint proved useful in critiquing the established order during the Reformation, this same stance did not translate readily into visions of the means of creating an orderly and godly society. Also useful is Niebuhr's *Christ and Culture,* which details various possible Christian attitudes toward the potential of both secular and religious cultures to fulfill God's kingdom. The practical exemplum of the tension between, and the historical process in, Christian theological and social innovation, and the press of secular culture, is demonstrated in Niebuhr's *The Social Sources of Denominationalism.* The work of these two writers offers an introduction to basic issues and methodology surrounding self-help and success themes in American cultural history.

Given the persistence of self-help literature, the study of this theme as a phenomenon in and as an index to American culture is a recent development, as are most studies of American popular culture. The first published study to appear was Irvin G. Wyllie's *The Self-Made Man in America: The Myth of Rags to Riches.* As first studies tend to be, Wyllie's is useful, but it has largely been superceded by subsequent authors. The book is organized in chapters centered on particular values and motifs of self-help literature, and consequently there is little sense of chronological development or of the distinctions between one writer and another. Further, Wyllie gives only scant attention to the pre-nineteenth-century expressions of self-help aspiration. He concludes that the literature as a whole glorified poverty, rural childhoods, female influences, inward determination, industry, and reliability. Protestant Christianity is seen to be a major proponent of the rightness of success and it raises only incidental objections about greed and selfishness and the dismissal of the stewardship ideal.

In contrast to the other books under discussion here, Wyllie provides a useful chapter on criticism of self-help, arising from new sociological studies of the truth of the rags-to-riches mythology. Wyllie seems to expect the imminent demise of the cruel joke that was the self-help credo. His hopes were foiled; the publication of *The Self-Made Man in America* coincides with a resurgence of self-help in the pastoral encouragements of Norman Vincent Peale and a host of others.

A far better book is John Cawelti's *Apostles of the Self-Made Man,* insofar as it carefully chronicles distinctions and changes in America's understanding of success and the route to it. Cawelti treats Franklin's ideal of economic success as an incentive to virtue and Jefferson's view of self-government as a means to practical and moral self-improvement. Literature throughout the nineteenth century reveals conflict between the ideal of holistic self-improvement and mere economic acquisition, although the moral emphasis becomes a subsidiary strain by the close of the century. The last remnant of the holistic ideal of self-culture appears in the popularized spiritual saga of Abraham Lincoln and in Emerson's belief in the infinite potential of the whole man, which is brought to fulfillment by communion with the Oversoul. Cawelti offers a healthy corrective to present images of Horatio Alger as a mindless proselytizer of the rags-to-riches idea. Rather, the Alger novels stress the importance of luck in success in relation to modest ambitions and a spirit of helplessness.

Materialistic renderings of the self-help ethos appear in the Gilded-Age best-selling novels of Mrs. E. D. E. N. Southworth and minister E. P. Roe, whose fiction is too briefly treated for the kinds of conclusions Cawelti makes about Roe's changing views of American society. Mark Twain, William Dean Howells, and Henry James are examined for their critiques of the corruption, injustice, and barrenness of America's vision of easy wealth. These minority voices of protest were drowned out by an image of success rephrased to meet the needs of a new corporate economic order. The new apologists of success fully dispensed with lingering moral notions about the religious usefulness and meaning of work and embraced competition and the reward of wealth as the sole ends of individual effort. Business acumen and personal power became the new means to wealth. Twentieth-century, positive-thinking, success literature exhibits a confusion of ends between inner tranquility and material wealth and a confusion about which is the means to the other. In the closing pages, Cawelti examines the attitudes toward success of Theodore Dreiser, F. Scott Fitzgerald, Robert Penn Warren, and John Dewey, all of whom would argue for a return to older and more holistic virtues of success.

In *The American Myth of Success: From Horatio Alger to Norman Vincent Peale,* Richard Weiss inevitably retraces some of the ground of Wyllie and Cawelti. To their work he extends two necessary correctives. First, Weiss's survey finds a greater prominence of critical and cautionary advice against greed in self-help books from McGuffey to Horatio Alger, E. P. Roe, and New Thought. Second, Weiss also gives due prominence to the considerable and neglected influence of New Thought, although he over-states its connection with Emersonian transcendentalism. He also correctly stresses the significance of New Thought's pragmatic and utilitarian tests for the truth of religious belief and its connections with the emergence of psychotherapy.

The latest, fullest, and, in some ways, best survey of the interplay between religion and self-help is in *The American Idea of Success* by Richard M. Huber. Like Weiss, Huber extensively details the ambivalence toward material success that has characterized almost all self-help litera-ture. He convincingly disputes Cawelti's assertion of the prominence of Social Darwinist justifications for competition and success. In tracing the secular and religious rationales for self-help, Huber is particularly per-ceptive in dealing with the ambiguities of success in the larger context of America's visions of herself as a special and chosen nation of opportunity. He also exhibits an acute sympathy toward the social and economic com-plexities in which America, from Puritanism to Peale, attempted to work out its own peculiar sense of destiny. More than any other chronicler of our theme, Huber bothers to delve briefly and helpfully into the biogra-phies of the self-help counselors.

Differing markedly from the dispassionate scholarly work of Wyllie, Cawelti, Weiss, and Huber is Donald Meyer's *The Positive Thinkers: A Study of the American Quest of Health, Wealth, and Personal Power from Mary Baker Eddy to Norman Vincent Peale.* The tone of Meyer's work tends toward the judgmental and the glib in his characterization of self-help among the assorted popularizers from New Thought to the pres-ent. The virtue of *The Positive Thinkers* lies in the diagnosis of the social and psychological temper of the Gilded and the Modern ages that made the new theologies and psychologies ready answers to widespread religious and moral malaise. As such, Meyer explores changing sex roles amid new feminine leisure, the anxiety wrought in the business world by an amoral code, the loss of relevance and creativity in mainline Protestantism, and the appeal of psychotherapeutic remedies to problems of guilt.

A straightforward and careful scholarly survey of twentieth-century best-selling religious self-help guides is found in *Popular Religion: Inspira-tional Books in America* by sociologists Louis Schneider and Sanford M. Dornbusch. Through systematic and painstaking content analysis, the authors scrutinize the work of Fox, Fosdick, Peale, Liebman, and others for their attitudes toward traditional religious doctrines of God, man, salvation, guilt, health, and piety, to name a few. Of particular merit is the authors' careful labeling of themes and trends with the precise language and clarity of formal sociological study of religion, an element that is often unfortunately missing in studies of religion and self-help.

A useful general analysis of the origins and theological views of *The Religious Bodies of America* is provided by F. E. Mayer. Good recent introductory surveys of the growth and theological content of the various groups following the general tradition of Phineas Quimby are the sympathetic treatments of J. Stillson Judah in *The History and Philosophy of the Metaphysical Movements in America* and Charles S. Braden's *These Also Believe: A Study of Modern American Religious Cults and Minority Religious Movements*. Both books treat such groups as Theosophy, divine science, and the Unity School of Christianity. A somewhat older volume, *Modern Religious Cults and Movements* by Gaius Glenn Atkins, retains its usefulness for its perceptive summary of contemporary religious problems. Among a number of hostile conservative Protestant critical works, noting the doctrinal aberrations of Christian Science and New Thought, the most theologically mature is Anthony A. Hoekema's *The Four Major Cults: Christian Science, Jehovah's Witnesses, Mormonism, and Seventh-Day Adventism.*

As noted in the historic outline above, almost all the literature on Mary Baker Eddy and Christian Science is marred by partisan attitudes, ranging from hagiolatry to debunkery, with little in between. Needless to say, it is difficult for the disinterested observer to arrive at something close to an objective or balanced view of Mrs. Eddy and her movement. The adulatory strain is evidenced in the official biography by Sybil Wilbur, *The Life of Mary Baker Eddy*, which was first published in 1907 as a revision of articles that appeared in *Human Life* magazine. It is now published by the Christian Science Publishing Society.

An antagonistic biography, *The Life of Mary Baker Eddy and the History of Christian Science* by Georgine Milmine, appeared shortly thereafter, following a first draft in the muckraking *McClure's Magazine*. So hostile was the Christian Science reaction to the book, which pandered to the reader's worst suspicions, that the copyright was later purchased and the plates destroyed by a friend of Christian Science. The book has since been reissued by Baker Book House in Grand Rapids. Such has been the pattern, however, that has surrounded books published about Mrs. Eddy and Christian Science. Whether in press commentary or in books, critical accounts of Mrs. Eddy or Christian Science have been met with resolute resistance by the board of directors and Publishing Society of Christian Science, an intransigence that has prevailed since the death of Mrs. Eddy.

Edwin Dakin's well-documented, convincing, and unnecessarily caustic study, *Mrs. Eddy: The Biography of a Virginal Mind*, sees Mrs. Eddy as beset by hysterical paranoia throughout her life. Before publication of

Dakin's work, the Christian Science leadership sought to prevent publication by intimidating the publisher, Charles Scribner and Son, and after failing there, they mounted a national campaign to obstruct sales of the book. The Christian Science Church has also voiced its official disapproval of the comprehensive biography *Mary Baker Eddy: The Truth and the Tradition* by two eminent and still-respected former Christian Scientists, Ernest Sutherland Bates and John Valentine Dittemore. The same is true for Hugh A. Studdert-Kennedy's appreciative *Mrs. Eddy: Her Life, Her Work, Her Place in History*.

As a whole, these books extend fair and sympathetic treatment to Mrs. Eddy, attempting to do justice to her sincerity, originality, and leadership, while not losing sight of her quite human failings of rigidity, defensiveness, and pride. Books that have won approval by the Church are Lyman Powell's *Mary Baker Eddy: A Life-Size Portrait* and Norman Beaseley's *The Cross and the Crown*. While he is not a Christian Scientist, Beaseley's several books on Christian Science are nonetheless so sentimentally adulatory that they are barely sufferable even for the religiously sympathetic reader.

Surely the best work thus far for its sheer wealth of material, much of it previously unpublished, and for its admirable efforts at objectivity is Robert Peel's three-volume biography: *Mary Baker Eddy: The Years of Discovery, Mary Baker Eddy: The Years of Trial*, and *Mary Baker Eddy: The Years of Triumph*. An open apologist for Christian Science, Peel attempts, perhaps too facilely, to ignore or explain away many of the critiques of Mrs. Eddy. The book would have been better if Peel had directly confronted and dealt with the critics instead of relegating their comments to the notes.

Stephen Gottschalk's *The Emergence of Christian Science in American Religious Life* stands beside Peel's work as an admirable effort to deal fairly and objectively with Mrs. Eddy and her movement. Gottschalk's full and sympathetic treatment contains a perceptive analysis of the several Victorian religious crises that made Protestant America receptive to the particular appeal of Christian Science. Gottschalk argues that in the face of the new scientism, Darwinism especially, and biblical criticism, Christian Science provided in its healing theories the possibility of an empirically verifiable criterion for the truth of religion. Another virtue of Gottschalk's work is his excellent, and probably best available, explication of Mrs. Eddy's sometimes elusive thought. The sometimes controversial history of Christian Science since the death of Mrs. Eddy in 1910 is covered in Charles S. Braden's *Christian Science Today: Power, Policy, Practice*. Braden straightforwardly chronicles the various disputes over orthodox Christian Science that have led to the exclusion of members and the banning of books.

The opening chapters of Robert Peel's *Christian Science: Its Encounter with American Culture* also attempt to convey the tone of pre-Civil War religious experimentation, especially in transcendentalism, that eventually made the nation receptive to Christian Science. The remainder of the book deals with Mrs. Eddy's occasional relationship with transcendentalist Bronson Alcott. Henry Steiger's *Christian Science and Philosophy* does not deal with the intellectual background of Christian Science, but rather it is an after-the-fact attempt at philosophical justification for Christian Science.

The most thorough history that is devoted exclusively to New Thought is Charles S. Braden's *Spirits in Rebellion: The Rise and Development of New Thought*. Braden's work is comprehensive in describing Quimby's work and the intellectual geneologies of his followers. In addition to a systematic survey of New Thought theology, Braden provides a complete treatment of the various New Thought churches and organizations in this country and abroad. Gail Thain Parker's *Mind Cure in New England: From the Civil War to World War I* offers a sympathetic, if somewhat impressionistic, interpretation of various New Thought figures and tendencies. Increased religious doubt, more leisure, and suspicion of orthodox medicine give rise to a quest for psychic fulfillment that is otherwise not available in a listless orthodoxy, a repressed feminism, and a frantic work ethic. A flawed book, *Mind Cure* suffers from a lack of systematic discussion and close textual reading, which makes it elliptical and obscure.

A paucity of secondary materials exists on the Pentecostal and charismatic healing revivals in this century. A useful and sympathetic overview of the healing tradition in the history of Christianity is Morton T. Kelsey's *Healing and Christianity*. A brief history of Pentecostalism and its doctrinal departures from historical creedalism is found in Frederick Dale Bruner's *A Theology of the Holy Spirit: The Pentecostal Experience and the New Testament Witness*.

A useful anthology of divergent views on *The Charismatic Movement* is edited by Michael Hamilton. A scholarly treatment of *Modern Revivalism: From Charles Grandison Finney to Billy Graham* is given by William G. McLoughlin. Dealing specifically with Pentecostal and charismatic healing is David Edwin Harrell, Jr.'s *All Things Are Possible: The Healing and Charismatic Revivals in Modern America*. Harrell treats such popular figures as Aimee Semple McPherson, Oral Roberts, and Kathryn Kuhlman. A less objective, though still informative, study is James Morris's *The Preachers*, which includes studies of the backgrounds and messages of faith healers Oral Roberts, Kathryn Kuhlman, and Reverend Ike, as well as a number of politically reactionary evangelical preachers.

314   *American Popular Culture*

BIBLIOGRAPHY

BOOKS AND ARTICLES

Ahlstrom, Sydney E. *A Religious History of the American People*. New Haven: Yale University Press, 1972.

Anker, Roy M. "Doubt and Faith in Late Nineteenth-Century American Fiction." Ph.D. dissertation, Michigan State University, 1973.

Atkins, Gaius Glenn. *Modern Religious Cults and Movements*. New York: Fleming H. Revell Company, 1923.

Bates, Ernest Sutherland, and John Valentine Dittemore. *Mary Baker Eddy: The Truth and the Tradition*. New York: Alfred A. Knopf, 1932.

Beaseley, Norman. *The Cross and the Crown: The History of Christian Science*. New York: Duell, Sloan, and Pearce, and Little, Brown, 1952.

———. *The Continuing Spirit*. New York: Duell, Sloan, and Pearce, 1958.

———. *Mary Baker Eddy*. New York: Duell, Sloan, and Pearce, 1963.

Bellah, Robert N. *The Broken Covenant: American Civil Religion in a Time of Trial*. New York: Seabury Press, 1975.

Braden, Charles S. *These Also Believe: A Study of Modern American Religious Cults and Minority Religious Movements*. New York: Macmillan, 1949.

———. *Spirits in Rebellion: The Rise and Development of New Thought*. Dallas: Southern Methodist University Press, 1958.

———. *Christian Science Today: Power, Policy, Practice*. Dallas: Southern Methodist University Press, 1963.

Bromberg, Walter. *From Shaman to Psychotherapist: A History of the Treatment of Mental Illness*. Chicago: Henry Regnery, 1975.

Bruner, Frederick Dale. *A Theology of the Holy Spirit: The Pentecostal Experience and the New Testament Witness*. Grand Rapids, Mich.: William B. Eerdmans, 1970.

Burr, Nelson R., in collaboration with James Ward Smith and A. Leland Jamison. *A Critical Bibliography of Religion in America*. 2 vols. Princeton: Princeton University Press, 1971.

Carey, Ralph Allison. "Best-Selling Religion: A History of Popular Religious Thought in America as Reflected in Religious Best Sellers, 1850-1960." Ph.D. dissertation, Michigan State University, 1971.

Carter, Paul A. *The Spiritual Crisis of the Gilded Age*. DeKalb: Northern Illinois University, 1971.

Cawelti, John G. *Apostles of the Self-Made Man*. Chicago: University of Chicago Press, 1965.

Cherry, Conrad. *God's New Israel: Religious Interpretations of American History*. Englewood Cliffs, N.J.: Prentice-Hall, 1971.

Dakin, Edwin Franden. *Mrs. Eddy: The Biography of a Virginal Mind*. New York: Scribner, 1929.

Dresser, Horatio W. *A History of the New Thought Movement*. New York: Thomas Y. Crowell, 1919.

———, ed. *The Quimby Manuscripts*. New York: Thomas Y. Crowell, 1921.

Gottschalk, Stephen. *The Emergence of Christian Science in American Religious Life*. Berkeley: University of California Press, 1973.

Green, Robert W., ed. *Protestantism and Capitalism: The Weber Thesis and Its Critics*. Boston: D. C. Heath, 1959.

Griswold, A. Whitney. "The American Gospel of Success." Ph.D. dissertation, Yale University, 1934.

Hackett, Alice Payne. *70 Years of Best Sellers, 1895-1965*. New York: R. R. Bowker, 1967.

Hamilton, Michael P., ed. *The Charismatic Movement*. Grand Rapids, Mich.: William B. Eerdmans, 1975.

Harrell, David Edwin, Jr. *All Things Are Possible: The Healing and Charismatic Revivals in Modern America*. Bloomington: Indiana University Press, 1975.

Hart, James D. *The Popular Book: A History of America's Literary Taste*. New York: Oxford University Press, 1950.

Herberg, Will. *Protestant, Catholic, Jew: An Essay in American Religious Sociology*. Rev. ed. New York: Anchor Books, 1960.

Hoekema, Anthony A. *The Four Major Cults: Christian Science, Jehovah's Witnesses, Mormonism, Seventh-Day Adventism*. Grand Rapids, Mich.: William B. Eerdmans, 1963.

Huber, Richard M. *The American Idea of Success*. New York: McGraw-Hill, 1971.

Johnson, Paul. *A History of Christianity*. New York: Atheneum, 1977.

Judah, J. Stillson. *The History and Philosophy of the Metaphysical Movements in America*. Philadelphia: Westminster Press, 1967.

Kelsey, Morton T. *Healing and Christianity: In Ancient Thought and Modern Times*. New York: Harper and Row, 1973.

Lynn, Kenneth S. *The Dream of Success: A Study of the Modern American Imagination*. Boston: Little, Brown, 1955.

McConnell, Donald. *Economic Virtues in the United States: A History and Interpretation*. New York: Arno Press, 1973.

McLoughlin, William G., Jr. *Modern Revivalism: From Charles Grandison Finney to Billy Graham*. New York: Ronald Press, 1959.

Mayer, F. E. *The Religious Bodies of America*. St. Louis: Concordia Publishing House, 1961.

Meyer, Donald. *The Positive Thinkers: A Study of the American Quest for Health, Wealth, and Personal Power from Mary Baker Eddy to Norman Vincent Peale*. Garden City, N.Y.: Doubleday, 1965.

Milmine, Georgine. *The Life of Mary Baker Eddy and the History of Christian Science*. 2d ed. Grand Rapids, Mich.: Baker Book House, 1971.

Morris, James. *The Preachers*. New York: St. Martin's Press, 1973.

Mott, Frank Luther. *Golden Multitudes: The Story of Best Sellers in the United States*. New York: Macmillan, 1947.

Niebuhr, H. Richard. *The Kingdom of God in America*. New York: Harper and Row, 1937.

———. *Christ and Culture*. New York: Harper and Row, 1951.

———. *The Social Sources of Denominationalism*. Cleveland: World Publishing, 1957.

Parker, Gail Thain. *Mind Cure in New England: From the Civil War to World War I*. Hanover, N.H.: University Press of New England, 1973.

Peel, Robert. *Christian Science: Its Encounter with American Culture.* New York: Henry Holt, 1958.

———. *Mary Baker Eddy: The Years of Discovery.* New York: Holt, Rinehart, and Winston, 1966.

———. *Mary Baker Eddy: The Years of Trial.* New York: Holt, Rinehart, and Winston, 1971.

———. *Mary Baker Eddy: The Years of Triumph.* New York: Holt, Rinehart, and Winston, 1977.

Powell, Lyman. *Mary Baker Eddy: A Life-Size Portrait.* Boston: Christian Science Publishing Society, 1930.

Rischin, Moses, ed. *The American Gospel of Success: Individualism and Beyond.* Chicago: Quadrangle Books, 1965.

Schneider, Louis, and Sanford M. Dornbusch. *Popular Religion: Inspiration Books in America.* Chicago: University of Chicago Press, 1958.

Smith, James Ward, and A. Leland Jamison, eds. *The Shaping of American Religion.* Princeton: Princeton University Press, 1961.

Steiger, Henry W. *Christian Science and Philosophy.* New York: Philosophical Library, 1948.

Studdert-Kennedy, Hugh A. *Mrs. Eddy: Her Life, Her Work, Her Place in History.* San Francisco: Farallon Press, 1947.

Suderman, Elmer F. "Religion and the American Novel, 1870-1900." Ph.D. dissertation, University of Kansas, 1961.

Weber, Max. *The Protestant Ethic and the Spirit of Capitalism.* Translated by Talcott Parsons. New York: Charles Scribner, 1958.

Weiss, Richard. *The American Myth of Success: From Horatio Alger to Norman Vincent Peale.* New York: Basic Books, 1969.

Whalen, William J. *Faiths for the Few: A Study of Minority Religions.* Milwaukee: Bruce, 1963.

Wilbur, Sybil. *The Life of Mary Baker Eddy.* Boston: Christian Science Publishing Society, 1913.

Wyllie, Irvin G. *The Self-Made Man in America: The Myth of Rags to Riches.* New York: Free Press, 1954.

Zweig, Stefan. *Mental Healers: Franz Anton Mesmer, Mary Baker Eddy, Sigmund Freud.* New York: Frederick Ungar, 1962.

PERIODICALS

Church History. Wallingford, Pa., 1932-.

Journal of American History (formerly *Mississippi Valley Historical Review*). Bloomington, In., 1914-.

Religious Studies Review. Waterloo, Ontario, Canada, 1975-.

CHAPTER 13. Romantic Fiction

Kay J. Mussell

In the literary sense, all popular fiction is romantic. It embodies, in John Cawelti's phrase, a "moral fantasy" that allows its readers, who include most literate Americans, to transcend the bounds of real life and enter a world in which things occur as they are "supposed to," where certain kinds of desired experience can be lived vicariously. Popular fiction is not *realistic*, is not intended to be by its authors, and is not desired to be by its readers. But because the term "romantic," as used by Richard Chase and others to define a type of novel, explains virtually all types of popular fiction, the term is used in the context of this essay to refer to a particular kind of popular fiction.

The romantic novel or romantic story, in popular fiction, is a story about a love relationship, a courtship, and a marriage. It can either take the form that Robert Palfrey Utter and Gwendolyn Bridges Needham described in 1936 as "the typical plot of the English novel," which "has love for the starting-post and marriage for the finish line." Or, the plot can concern the problems of an already-achieved marriage, with difficulties between husband and wife being resolved somehow at the end, in which the wife is rewarded with either a better marriage with her current husband or a new marriage with a new lover. There are some romantic novels of the "anti-romance" type that tend to reinforce the assumptions of the form. These are novels in which the value structure is unchanged, but in which the heroine behaves in such a way that she cannot be rewarded with marriage in the end. These, too, are romantic novels, although the inversion of the plot makes them serve as a cautionary tale rather than as a model to be emulated. Because the tensions and issues inherent in love stories are women's concerns, romantic fiction is almost entirely a female form of reading.

317

HISTORIC OUTLINE

Many novels in literary history revolve around these questions of love, courtship, and marriage from a woman's perspective. The tension for a woman in the process of achieving identity through a lasting marriage is a profound one that has been dramatized in fiction extensively from Samuel Richardson's *Pamela* (1741), to the most recent issue of *Redbook* or *Good Housekeeping*, or to this month's selection of eight full-length Harlequin romances, sent by subscription to women throughout the United States, Canada, and Great Britain. The satisfaction gained by many women through reading such fiction is unquestionable. What is perhaps most significant about the popular romantic novel, however, is how little the basic assumptions of the story have changed from some of the earliest manifestations in American fiction to the most recent.

The story of a romantic novel begins with an assumption—unquestioned and unexamined except in a few books—that the necessary, preordained, and basic goal of any woman is to achieve a satisfying, mature, and all-fulfilling marriage. The primacy of romantic love, in defining a woman's place in the world and her personal and moral worth, is rarely in doubt in these books. The plot is often diffuse, but it never loses sight of that goal. Although other kinds of events and actions by the protagonist may take up much of the novel, they are always related eventually to the woman's marital status and condition of happiness at the end of the book. Thus, although much of the action of *Gone with the Wind* (1936) concerns Scarlett O'Hara's experiences during the Civil War and Reconstruction, the underlying value structure of the book is prescribed by Scarlett's relationships with men and, especially, by the contrast between Scarlett and Melanie Wilkes. Similarly, Maria Susanna Cummins's *The Lamplighter* (1854) traces the childhood and young adulthood of its main character, Gertie, showing how she learned to be a worthy and moral young woman through the influence of various other characters on her life. However, the novel confirms her identity at the end by allowing her to marry the young hero, who has seemed throughout most of the book to be merely a friend to Gertie while attracted to another, and richer, young woman.

Using John Cawelti's approach to popular fiction—that of formulaic analysis—it would be necessary to discuss romantic fiction as a group of formulas, rather than as a single one. Romantic formulas intersect with several other kinds of popular fiction: the gothic, the historical, the juvenile, the sentimental, the domestic, the seduction. But they cannot be entirely identified with any of these other formulas. In addition, the sustained critical work on romantic fiction is just beginning to emerge in scholarship, so there is no general agreement yet on the definitions of different types of romantic fiction. At the moment, perhaps the most useful approach is to cast a wide net, assuming that novels that tell the story of a romance and how it was all-important in the life of a woman, all other factors being in one way or another subordinate to an all-consuming love relationship, are romantic fiction. The fine formulaic definition can develop out of the necessary bibliographical and critical work that remains to be done.

One of the difficulties in dealing with this sort of popular fiction is that it is such an ephemeral form. Some examples are so widely popular and so often reprinted that they come to mind immediately: Susanna Rowson's *Charlotte Temple* (1791) or Margaret Mitchell's *Gone with the Wind*. Others have certainly been lost forever as the last cracked and crumbling copy, published by a local printer as a favor to a neighboring author, has disappeared in the trash after an attic was cleaned. Romantic novels are almost never reviewed, unless they are highly publicized blockbusters. Authors who write them tend to be relatively private persons and are rarely interviewed or written about. Many authors of romantic novels are very prolific writers, publishing several books per year for a grateful and insatiable audience, making large amounts of money from their work, but reaping very little acclaim from the general public.

Romantic novels are the fare of public libraries, which have large circulations for these books but which do not have to rebind or reorder the majority of them when they wear out because the audience usually demands new ones. Such books are also commonplace in drug stores and grocery stores. Romantic fiction is a staple in women's magazines today, as it has been for almost two centuries. It has been common in subscription series of novels sold by "dime novel" publishers in the nineteenth century and as named series (Harlequin Romances, Harlequin Presents, Barbara Cartland's Library of Love) in the twentieth century. It is easy to find current examples of the form; it was probably as easy to find them in 1880 as it is today. But it is difficult today to find 1880 examples or even 1920 or 1930 versions because many of these novels leave very little trace and many of them are impossible to identify as romantic novels from a mere title or author's name.

The first American example of a popular romantic novel was probably Susanna Rowson's *Charlotte Temple,* one of the great best sellers of American literary history. First published in Britain by a woman who almost immediately moved to America to set up a school for young ladies, *Charlotte Temple* went through more than two hundred editions, forty of them before the author's death in the 1820s. The first American edition was published in Philadelphia in 1794. As recently as the early part of the twentieth century, it was still in print; one 1905 edition contained a number of photographs, including one of Charlotte's reputed grave in New York City. *Charlotte Temple* was a classic seduction novel about a young girl who was so foolish as to allow herself to be carried off to America by a young officer; when she became pregnant, he abandoned her, leaving her to die miserably after giving birth to a daughter, whose life was later chronicled by Rowson in *Lucy Temple or Charlotte's Daughter* (1828).

Many other seduction novels were popular in the early nineteenth century. Mrs. Hannah W. Foster's *The Coquette* (1797), Eliza Vicery's *Emily Hamilton* (1803), and several anonymous novels, such as *Fidelity Rewarded* (1796) and *Amelia, or the Faithless Briton* (1798), told the familiar story. Most of these, incidentally, were presented to the public as true stories, thinly disguised by changing names and places. Since seduction stories served so consciously as cautionary tales, the claim for their truth is logical. Although, it might be just as reasonable to conclude that the novels claimed a factual basis to combat the current prejudice against the novels as harmful because they were made up of lies. After the early nineteenth century, a full-blown seduction story was hard to find. The tensions of the precarious position in which a "loose woman" could find herself were still important in later romantic novels, but the explicit warning about men, the specific if somewhat euphemistic story about sexuality, was less significant in romantic fiction.

From the 1820s until after the Civil War, romantic fiction was dominated by a group of women novelists usually referred to as the "domestic sentimentalists." They included writers such as Catharine Maria Sedgwick, Lydia Maria Child, Fanny Fern (Ruth Payton Willis), Mary Jane Holmes, Ann Sophia Stephens, Maria Susanna Cummins, and others. The work of these women has been more thoroughly documented than that of any other romantic novelists, and new critical studies of their work emerge every year with the impetus of the women's studies movement in scholarship.

Although critics disagree, sometimes diametrically, about the meaning of the work of these women, there seems little doubt that the stories they tell are basically stories about relationships between men and women. Almost all the heroines are married, happily, at the end of the books. Between the beginning and the end, males may be less in evidence than females, as the heroines spend their time solving domestic difficulties and improving their character, saving souls, learning to be "true women"; but despite the trials of domestic life, the reconciliation with woman's place in a good marriage is where the plot ends.

These were the novels that prompted Nathaniel Hawthorne's heartfelt cry in a letter to his publisher in 1855, a few years after *The Scarlet Letter*

(1850) has been less than enthusiastically received by the mass reading audience.

America is now wholly given over to a d----d mob of scribbling women, and I should have no chance of success while the public taste is occupied with their trash—and should be ashamed of myself if I did succeed. What is the mystery of these innumerable editions of the "Lamplighter," and other books neither better nor worse?—worse they could not be, and better they need not be, when they sell by the 100,000 . . .

It is ironic to note that the output of these women included a rather large number of historical novels about women in Puritan New England, some of whom ran afoul of the religious and civil authorities of the colony, although for offenses more acceptable to nineteenth-century taste than was adultery. Hawthorne might be forgiven if he found as too contemptible the audience that embraced Sedgwick's *Hope Leslie* (1827) and Eliza B. Lee's *Naomi* (1848) more willingly than they did his novel about Hester Prynne.

After the Civil War, much romantic fiction was found in dime-novel series and story papers, as well as in full-length novels, often serialized in newspapers and magazines prior to book publication. Augusta Jane Evans Wilson and Mrs. E. D. E. N. Southworth were especially popular during this period, although the work of many of the domestic sentimentalists was still in print and widely popular. Since there are few studies of romantic fiction in this period, it is more difficult to identify authors and titles, but the genre flourished. Romantic novels about working girls, written by Laura Jean Libbey, were one example; others were some of the historical novels of Mary Johnston and others. A particularly interesting writer of romantic fiction, who also wrote numerous advice books, popular history and Bible studies, and edited a magazine, was Isabella Alden (known as "Pansy"). Her niece, Grace Livingston Hill, was to become one of the popular romantic novelists of the twentieth century.

Lists of best sellers are available from 1895 onward, so it becomes an easier task to identify romantic novels that did well in the marketplace. Those books that did not sell widely enough to appear in these compilations are still hard to retrieve, but enough information is available to indicate that the love story was in style and relatively unchanged. Kathleen Norris's novels of family and domestic drama were especially popular during the first thirty years of the twentieth century. Mary Roberts Rinehart, better known for detective and gothic novels, also wrote a few straight romances for her wide audience; her books were regularly on the bestseller lists throughout the period, regardless of their type.

Grace Livingston Hill's novels of romance and traditional religion were popular alongside the novels of Fannie Hurst and Faith Baldwin. Emilie Loring's books also sold widely. Only a very few romantic novels, however, were great best sellers until the 1930s. *Gone with the Wind* was a romantic novel that appealed to a much wider audience than most—to men as well as to women. It was, of course, an incredibly popular book immediately after publication; it was awarded the Pulitzer Prize; and it was made into one of the classic films of Hollywood in 1939. The 1977 edition of the best-seller lists, Alice Payne Hackett's *Eighty Years of Best-sellers*, lists it as the number eleven book on the all-time hardbound best-seller list; it is the top fiction book on the list after several cookbooks, Kahlil Gibran's *The Prophet*, and five Dr. Seuss books. With the story of Scarlett O'Hara, romantic fiction made the big time in a way that it had not since Augusta Jane Evans Wilson's *St. Elmo* (1867). Incidentally, the number twelve book on the all-time list is also a work of romantic fiction—Anya Seton's *The Winthrop Woman* (1958), a novel of the Massachusetts Bay Colony, which seems to be an enduring setting in popular romantic fiction.

Following *Gone with the Wind*, the next big romantic book was Daphne duMaurier's *Rebecca* (1938), the work of a British author who has always been very popular in this country. Kathleen Winsor's *Forever Amber* (1944) was also important. Most recently, Rosemary Rogers's *Dark Fires* (1975) has reached the all-time list of books that have sold more than two million copies. It is significant to note that two of these books, *Gone with the Wind* and *Forever Amber*, are inversions of the romantic book in that their heroines are women who do not deserve a happy marriage and who are left alone by the men they love. It may be that this inversion is more likely to appeal to an audience that is partly male than a book that is a more straightforward retelling of the love story.

The post-World War II period has been a very fruitful one for the popular romantic novel in America. Novels by British writers have been readily available in paperback and in libraries and have been widely read. There is little sense in trying to separate the works of British and American authors during this period, except for the record, since both sell widely in both countries and are almost routinely published on both sides of the Atlantic. Particularly popular in the last two decades have been British authors Georgette Heyer, Barbara Cartland, and Dorothy Eden, as well as the Americans Anya Seton, Frances Parkinson Keyes, and Rosemary Rogers. The Harlequin romances, cheap paperback originals from Canada and affiliated with the firm of Mills and Boon in Britain, have also been widely read. These books, like the dime novels of the nineteenth century, are sold on book racks as well as by subscription. Most of them are straightforward romances—love stories set in interesting or exotic places or about people with interesting or exotic careers.

Magazines have also flourished on love stories in their fiction pages, from the most serious and uplifting of the women's magazines— *Godey's Lady's Book*—in the nineteenth century to *Good Housekeeping* in the twentieth. Confession magazines, love comics, and pulps are twentieth-century versions of the nineteenth-century story papers.

The drama of courtship and marriage has had a strong hold on the imaginations of American women readers for two centuries. The specifics of the plot have changed over the years, but the value structure and shape of the books has changed relatively little. Amber, in *Forever Amber*, does not die for her adultery as does Charlotte Temple, but the lesson of the two novels is clearly related. Melanie is allowed a happy and fulfilling marriage that is denied to Scarlett, even though Scarlett may have had the greater love, since Rhett is so much more passionate than Ashley. In domestic sentimental novels, women spend their time in domestic trivia rather than in the social whirl of more recent romantic novels by Georgette Heyer and others, but their behavior and their reward for virtue have not changed.

In the absence of good critical studies and bibliographies, it is difficult to say just how widespread romantic fiction has been in American literary history; but the evidence is clear enough to indicate that it has been both pervasive and persistent. One suspects that there is more of it still submerged than seems possible even now.

REFERENCE WORKS

There is no single reference guide or bibliographical tool that can be used to identify romantic novels or to survey criticism about them. There are, however, some standard references and bibliographies that include such fiction.

Perhaps the major tool that now exists for finding romantic novels is a massive twenty-five-volume guide entitled *Bibliography of English Language Fiction in the Library of Congress Through 1950*, which is subdivided into three separate and complete bibliographies and compiled by R. Glenn Wright. These volumes are composed of reproduced cards from the Library of Congress shelf list. The sets are organized, respectively, by author, title, and chronology. Because the cards themselves are reproduced, there is much information that would not be available in a standard bibliographical format. The Library of Congress, as a copyright depository, has many of the novels published in the United States. The guides are organized within each of the three sets by nationality, and there are additional indexes to translators and translations. Particularly for the early period, when not many novels were being published in America, the chronological bibliography is exceptionally useful. Later, the author bibliography is more helpful, because once a researcher identifies an author as having written romantic fiction, an entire survey of the author's work in the Library of Congress is readily available. Although not all books written in English are represented (since not all are in the Library of Congress collection), and the bibliography cannot be used to make definitive lists of works, the Library of Congress collection of fiction in English is comprehensive enough to make it a good place to start. *The Author Catalog and Title Catalog* of the Microbook Library of American Civilization also offers a guide to certain titles available in microform.

Some general studies of American fiction provide some information about popular novels as well and can be useful in a survey of the field. Notable here is Arthur Hobson Quinn's *American Fiction: An Historical and Critical Survey* for the large number of plot summaries he includes. Henri Petter's *The Early American Novel* is an excellent monograph that has valuable bibliographical sections for materials up to 1820. He includes a number of synopses of novels at the end, which is an extraordinarily useful tool for identifying types of fiction; there are also three bibliographies of novels of the period, sources from the period, and modern criticism. Lyle H. Wright's various definitive lists of American imprints through most of the nineteenth century are notably useful, especially since a serious effort is continuing to make all these available in microform. Another book that provides some limited information on earlier novels is Ernest A. Baker's *A Guide to the Best Fiction in English*.

Surveys of popular culture in America also provide good sources for titles and authors of romantic fiction. The definitive work is Russel B. Nye's *The Unembarrassed Muse*, which has good survey sections on romantic novels. Other sources that focus strictly on books include James D. Hart's *The Popular Book* and Frank Luther Mott's *Golden Multitudes;* both are studies of the best seller in America and are filled with information about popular books of all types. For materials since 1895, the R. R. Bowker Company's periodic updates of best-seller lists by Alice Payne Hackett are the best sources available. These, however, list only books that achieved best-seller status, so that many thousands of popular formula novels do not appear on these lists.

Since there is so little critical work on these novels, there is very little bibliographical aid to critical essays and books. However, two useful bibliographies of materials in women's studies are helpful. Carol Fairbanks Myers's *Women in Literature: Criticism of the Seventies* is a bibliography of materials about women in literature, some feminist criticism, biographies of women writers, interviews and some reviews, covering the period from January 1970 to June 1975. The three volumes of *Women's Work and Women's Studies*, compiled by the Women's Center at Barnard College, provide bibliographical guides to the field of women's studies in a large number of areas, year by year from 1971 to 1974. These volumes also provide reports of work in progress. One specialized bibliography, *They Wrote for a Living: A Bibliography of the Works of Susan Bogert Warner and Anna Bartlett Warner*, by Dorothy Hurlbut Sanderson, was recently published. A 1978 monograph by Nina Baym, *Woman's Fiction: A Guide to Novels by and About Women in America 1820-1870*, also contains some useful bibliographical material. For Susanna Rowson, R. W. G. Vail's *Susanna Haswell Rowson, the Author of Charlotte Temple: A Bibliographical Study* is comprehensive and standard.

RESEARCH COLLECTIONS

There are no research collections devoted strictly to romantic fiction, which makes the researcher's job a difficult one. However, there are collections of popular American novels, as well as some paper and manuscript collections, that should be consulted.

As the United States copyright depository, the Library of Congress collection is excellent, particularly in the Rare Book Room, where there is an (unfortunately) uncataloged collection of more than twenty thousand paperback dime novels. Finding romantic novels in this collection is a hit or miss process since the finders' guide lists the collection only by series title; but some of those are descriptive and will aid in locating book titles and authors' names. The Rare Book Room also has more than a dozen separate editions of Rowson's *Charlotte Temple*, including a dime-novel reprint with an "authentic" portrait of Charlotte in high Victorian dress. The general fiction collection at the Library of Congress also contains a wealth of material. In many cases, fairly complete hardbound collections of particular authors' works exist virtually untouched on the shelves of the PZ3 category. If an author who wrote romantic fiction can be identified, the chances are that the works published in the twentieth century will be readily available.

The New York Public Library has several collections that include popular fiction. The Berg Collection of English and American Literature is excellent; the Rare Book Division offers both the Frank P. O'Brien Collection of Beadle Dime Novels (one thousand four hundred volumes) and a chapbook file. The Arents Collection of books in parts (including serials, "shilling shockers," and "penny dreadfuls") also includes romantic fiction.

Elmira College in Elmira, New York, has a one hundred-volume cataloged collection entitled "Genteel Women's Reading, 1855-1955." Barnard College contains the Bertha Van Riper Overbury Gift, which consists of nearly two thousand books, mostly rare, written by American women, as well as almost one thousand manuscripts. The Cleveland Public Library collection has dime novels and other nineteenth-century romances. In Portland, Maine, the Westbrook College Library has a collection of one thousand two hundred volumes written by Maine women writers. The collection is especially noteworthy for some rare editions of novels by Mme. Wood, one of the earliest American writers of romantic and gothic fiction.

Manuscripts and personal papers for writers of romantic fiction are even more difficult to find, although library collections are beginning to reflect the scholarly interest in popular culture materials. Boston University's Mugar Memorial Library, for example, is collecting the literary and personal papers, correspondence, and published articles by and about more than one thousand modern published authors, including materials on several romantic writers such as Anya Seton, Dorothy Eden, Phyllis Whitney, Margaret Culkin Banning, and Faith Baldwin. A complete list of authors included is available from the curator of the Division of Special Collections.

Some individual authors are represented by their papers and manuscripts in major research collections. Ellen B. Brandt, author of a recent biography of Susanna Rowson, notes that the best collection of Rowson material is at the American Antiquarian Society, although she also found items at the University of Pennsylvania Rare Book Room, the Pennsylvania Historical Society, the Philadelphia Free Library, and the New York Historical Society, among other standard research libraries.

Catharine Maria Sedgwick, who wrote *Hope Leslie* (1827) and *A New England Tale* (1822) among others, lived in Stockbridge, Massachusetts, where her papers, manuscripts, and other memorabilia are to be found in the Stockbridge Library Association's Sedgwick Family Collection. Caroline Lee Hentz has diaries and letters in the Southern Historical Collection at the University of North Carolina, as well as letters in the Chamberlain Collection of the Boston Public Library.

Lydia Francis Maria Child wrote prolifically in many forms other than the romantic novel; her romantic fiction includes *Hobomok* (1824) and *A Romance of the Republic* (1867). Her papers are in the Hofstra University Library, which includes some manuscripts; letters are in the Ellis Gray Loring Collection of the New York Public Library, the F. G. and S. B. Shaw Papers of the Houghton Library at Harvard University, and the Schlesinger Library at Radcliffe College. Elizabeth Oakes Smith, wife of Seba Smith the creator of Jack Downing, wrote *Riches Without Wings* (1838); her papers are in the New York Public Library. Ann Sophia Stephens (1813-1866) wrote several novels of the gothic romantic type, as well as *Malaeska* (1860), the first dime novel. Her letters are in the New York Public Library.

Mrs. E. D. E. N. Southworth, one of the most prolific of the romantic writers, can be studied at the Duke University Library, where there is a collection of 342 items. Susan Warner and her sister Anna, authors of a number of books separately and together, lived on Constitution Island in the Hudson River, near West Point. The Constitution Island Association maintains their home and some memorabilia and papers. Susan (under the name Elizabeth Wetherell) wrote one of the period's most popular novels, *The Wide Wide World* (1850). The memorabilia of Mary Jane Holmes, author of more than forty books between 1854 and 1905, is in the Seymour Library in Brockport, New York.

Helen Hunt Jackson, who wrote *Ramona* (1884), is represented in the collections of the Huntington Library and the Jones Library in Amherst, Massachusetts; the latter collection does not circulate. Amelia E. Barr emigrated to the United States from England and wrote more than sixty novels, some romantic and some historical. Her papers are in the Archives Division of the Texas State Library; the collection is restricted. Papers of Harriet Prescott Spofford are in the Historical Society of Pennsylvania and the Essex Institute in Salem, Massachusetts. The New York Public Library has the letters of Laura Jean Libbey.

Mary Johnston, the Virginia author of historical and romantic fiction, donated her papers to the University of Virginia; the collection contains more than four thousand items. Mary Roberts Rinehart gave more than four hundred cataloged manuscripts, pictures, memorabilia, and biographical items to the University of Pittsburgh Library. Kathleen Norris donated her papers to Stanford University; there is an unpublished guide to the collection in the library. Frances Parkinson Keyes had a long career as a writer; her papers from 1952-1963 are in the University of Virginia Library. Materials on Fannie Hurst can be found at the Olin Library, Washington University, St. Louis, at the Special Collections of the Goldfarb Library at Brandeis University, and at the University of Texas Library. Papers of both Margaret Culkin Banning and Faith Baldwin are in the Boston University Library.

Materials relating to Margaret Mitchell can be found in the Atlanta Public Library (access is restricted), at Agnes Scott College in Georgia, and at Boston University and Harvard University. The manuscripts of Marcia Davenport are in the Manuscript Division of the Library of Congress. There are approximately three thousand five hundred items, including literary manuscripts, galley proofs, press clippings, working drafts, notes, and one hundred items of correspondence with Maxwell Perkins, her editor on her major work of romantic fiction, *The Valley of Decision* (1942). Legal briefs and records of the attempt by the Commonwealth of Massachusetts to ban Kathleen Winsor's *Forever Amber* on grounds of obscenity can be found in the Library of Congress Law Library.

HISTORY AND CRITICISM

In recent years, the impetus of women's studies in scholarship has spurred the study of romantic fiction, both as a part of larger studies of women and as a subject in itself. Until the experience of women in America was subject to this reinterpretation, critical work on romantic fiction, although often excellent, was random. An occasional dissertation or antiquarian work appeared, and many general works on American fiction included at least brief sections on romantic fiction. However, there was never any firm agreement about what the novels should be called or on how they should be evaluated.

Background material for understanding popular romantic fiction comprises an enormous number of works, but only a few need citation. Most of the studies of the medieval romance are far too specialized to be applicable to popular romantic fiction in America; the worlds of the two types of literature are far apart. A notable exception, however, is the small volume by Gillian Beer, *The Romance*, which is a formalistic approach to the genre. It deals almost entirely with European and pre-1800 romances, but its brief analysis of the relation between the romance and its readers is suggestive for further study of all types of romantic fiction. Two monographs on English fiction are more directly applicable to American popular romantic fiction. J. M. S. Tompkins's *The Popular Novel in England, 1770-1800* has a chapter on romantic and historical fiction in the period that is exceptionally good for understanding the English backgrounds of the emerging American novel. Robert Kiely's *The Romantic Novel in England* deals with aesthetic definitions of romantic fiction but does not make invidious comparisons between serious and popular fiction. Kiely does not discuss the popular audience, but that lies outside the bounds of his subject. Although none of these three books refers to American fiction at all, they are each important.

Much more directly relevant is a recently reprinted 1935 monograph by Mary Sumner Benson, *Women in Eighteenth-Century America*. Benson's chapter on "Women in Early American Literature" is a good survey of novels, plays, and magazines as they related to American women, although she consciously ignores "numerous seond-rate novels of romantic adventure."

There are two essential references on American fiction prior to 1830— one very old but still useful, one relatively recent. Lily D. Loshe's *The Early American Novel, 1789-1830* was first published in 1907. The author attempts definitions of the forms of the first fiction in America. More thorough and analytical is Henri Petter's *The Early American Novel*. Petter has a long and excellent section on "the love story," in which he discriminates between types and conventions. The book is extensively annotated and has a number of bibliographical aids.

Three general studies of the American novel in historical context are worth consulting for basic information. Arthur Hobson Quinn's *American Fiction: An Historical and Critical Survey*, although dated, is a large compendium of plot summaries, but it is useful for identifying many forgotten novelists and books. Edward Wagenknecht's *Cavalcade of the American Novel* is somewhat more critical and contains an excellent bibliography. The best of the three is Alexander Cowie's *The Rise of the American Novel*, which includes good individual sections on a number of the relevant novels and authors.

Two other standard works on the American novel are more immediately relevant to the study of popular romantic fiction. Richard Chase's *The American Novel and Its Tradition* is a brilliant and influential work on major American fiction, in which Chase argues that American fiction has been, for historical and cultural reasons, more successful as romance than as realism. Although he is not interested in popular romances, some of his formulations about the world of fiction are significant. Because Leslie Fiedler, in *Love and Death in the American Novel*, writes extensively about woman in fiction, his book is also useful for studying popular romantic fiction. He uses more popular books as evidence than does Chase.

A few of the general studies of popular fiction in America are good sources. Ernest E. Leisy's *The American Historical Novel* refers to a number of books of the type, but it is primarily of bibliographical interest. Frank Luther Mott's *Golden Multitudes* is a study of the best seller in America. It is useful, although out of date and somewhat devoted to trivia. Mott's perspective on the best seller often leads to more problems than it solves. He is interested in numbers of copies sold, so he relies on estimates from date of publication to the present, thus raising certain books to best-seller status that were never popular with a mass audience. Much more analytically and conceptually valid is James D. Hart's *The Popular Book: A History of America's Literary Taste*. As the title indicates, Hart focuses on the issue of taste; his chapters deal with types of literature in certain periods. There are good sections on romantic fiction throughout the book. Carl Bode's *Anatomy of American Popular Culture* analyzes romantic fiction, among other phenomena, during the 1840s. The most recent comprehensive work is also the best: Russel B. Nye's *The Unembarrassed Muse*. His discussion of romantic fiction sets out a number of formulas and definitions and mentions numerous titles and authors as examples of the type. The major theoretical work is John G. Cawelti's *Adventure, Mystery, and Romance*. Cawelti is exceptionally insightful on the definition of the popular romance and particularly suggestive on the relationship between the romance and what he calls the "social melodrama." Scholars will be working with and developing his approaches to popular fictional formulas for some time. This book can be ignored only at one's peril.

A different kind of data can be obtained from studies of book publishing and library policies in America. Although none of these books is analytical in any serious respect, all provide insight and material. H. Lehman-Haupt, L. C. Wroth, and Rollo Silver's study *The Book in America* is an excellent background. John W. Tebbel's *A History of Book Publishing in the United States* offers valuable material on publishers and copyright laws, information that is vital for understanding the close parallels and overlaps between British and American popular romantic fiction.

Several more limited studies also pertain. G. H. Orians's "Censure of Fiction in American Magazines and Romances 1789-1810" delineates the reasons for the outcry against the novel in America, presenting the arguments of those who believed that it was subversive of public values because it was untrue and immoral. William Charvat's brief *Literary Publishing in America 1790-1850* has invaluable information on the economics of book publishing and the distribution of books in that period. Raymond Shove's *Cheap Book Production in the United States 1870-1891* is good on the book industry during the period, but it does not address the issue of romantic fiction directly.

Dee Garrison's essay "Immoral Fiction in the Late Victorian Library" is a study of an 1881 questionnaire by the American Library Association to seventy major public libraries about the fiction they censored. Of the list of "questionable" authors cited by the A.L.A., ten were writers of women's romances. Garrison tries to show why some librarians considered these women subversive of the public morality. A final study is long and basic. *Fiction in Public Libraries 1876-1900* by Esther J. Carrier provides some good discussion of the popularity of Mrs. E. D. E. N. Southworth and Mary Jane Holmes, among others, as well as further discussion of the censorship controversy analyzed by Garrison.

Since much romantic fiction was published in series by the publishers of dime novels in the nineteenth century, two good studies of those publishers are helpful. Albert Johannsen's two-volume work, *The House of Beadle and Adams*, and Quentin Reynolds's *The Fiction Factory*, about Street and Smith, are both good guides to the policies, authors, titles, and popularity of the dime novel in its heyday.

A recent book that provides important basic information about women's magazine fiction—a relatively neglected area—is Mirabel Cecil's *Heroines in Love 1750-1974*. Cecil surveys magazine romantic fiction over more than two centuries, providing in each chapter a breezy overview of a particular era as well as an excerpt or a representative story. She covers both British and American fiction. The work is comprehensive, but it contains no bibliography or analysis. It is more suggestive than useful, but it is essential nonetheless since these stories are not surveyed elsewhere.

Until the recent feminist approaches to nineteenth-century popular romantic fiction, there were a few excellent critical sources that still cannot be overlooked. The best of them is Herbert Ross Brown's *The Sentimental Novel in America 1789-1860*, published in 1940 and only partially superseded in 1978 by Nina Baym's study to be discussed below. Brown used the catalog of a New York circulating library to identify books from the period and wrote a delightful and solid book on the types of fiction that were most popular. Much analysis of romantic fiction is included, and Brown's work is especially interesting on the seduction story. Helen Waite Papashvily's *All the Happy Endings* is a more popularized book; it is a pre-feminist approach to the domestic romance, arguing that the books are actually submerged revolts against the male-dominated culture. Her book has a good unannotated bibliography of secondary material prior to 1954, but no list of primary sources. Her chatty, biographical approach to the material is especially good on Southworth. Alexander Cowie's "The Vogue of the Domestic Novel" is an excerpt from his larger study that was published several years later. F. L. Pattee's *The Feminine Fifties* has a survey chapter on the "scribbling women," but it has no bibliography and is condescending toward the material, and thus is not particularly helpful.

Beatrice Hofstadter's "Popular Culture and the Romantic Heroine" is an analysis of the heroines of six popular novels from the mid-nineteenth century to the mid-twentieth century. It is a good and interesting comparative study. Much more diffuse, although worth noting, is Robert J. Ward's "Europe in American Historical Romances 1890-1910," which is an overview of the characters and settings of 118 novels by Americans. The article is cursory, but it provides much material for further analysis.

Three works on women in fiction before the women's studies movement have valuable information as well. *Pamela's Daughters* by Robert Palfrey Utter and Gwendolyn Bridges Needham is a very long work about images of women in British fiction, with some minimal attention given to American books. It focuses on types of women in novels and is particularly worthy of attention in its excellent analysis of women's economic and domestic roles portrayed in fiction, as well as its argument that that precariousness of those roles made the love plot particularly attractive and significant for women readers. Dorothy Deegan's *The Stereotype of the Single Woman in American Novels* uses lists of significant American books and analyzes them for stereotypes. It suggests that women's roles in fiction are much more limited than in real life and that American women should be prepared for the possibility of living the single life. William

Wasserstrom's *Heiress of All the Ages: Sex and Sentiment in the General Tradition* argues that in genteel fiction from the 1830s to World War I the function of sex is domesticated in marriage, reconciling the figures of the virgin and the mistress into that of the wife. He refers almost entirely to serious literature, but his analysis is also relevant to popular fiction.

Fairly recent work in the emerging field of popular culture has also occasionally dealt with romantic fiction. In a collection of essays written by members of a graduate seminar in popular culture at Michigan State University, *New Dimensions in Popular Culture*, edited by Russel B. Nye, two of the papers relate directly to the subject. Ellen Hoekstra's "The Pedestal Myth Reinforced: Women's Magazine Fiction 1900-1920" is a good general survey of the major magazines. She reports that most of the stories were of the "boy-meets-girl" type. Leslie Smith's essay, "Through Rose-Colored Glasses: Some American Victorian Sentimental Novels," is about Mary Jane Holmes, Mrs. E. D. E. N. Southworth, and Sylvanus Cobb, Jr., and it provides a good basic introductory study. Another former graduate student at Michigan State University, Kathryn Weibel, published her dissertation as *Mirror, Mirror: Images of Women Reflected in Popular Culture*. The first chapter of this excellent study is an analytical history of women in popular fiction and is particularly perceptive on romantic fiction.

One of the major areas of omission in the study of romantic fiction is any direct analysis of the readers themselves. Impressionistic evidence strongly indicates that the audience for love stories is almost entirely female; but the expertise to study that audience is more the province of sociologists than of literary or historical critics. It is noteworthy, then, that sociologist Peter H. Mann in Great Britain has been working on popular romantic fiction and its readers for some time. Mann used the mailing list of subscribers to the Mills and Boon romance series in England, sending them two long questionnaires—one, in 1968; and the other, four or five years later. Mann received a good rate of return for a mail questionnaire, indicating a high level of interest on the part of the respondents. The reports show that the readership is overwhelmingly female, represents a wide range of age levels and occupations as well as housewives, and has a much higher level of education than the surveyors had expected. This material is particularly interesting since the Mills and Boon novels are marketed in the United States and Canada as Harlequin romances. The evidence gathered in Great Britain is, of course, not directly valid in the United States, but it is at least suggestive. Mann's reports are offered and evaluated in *The Romantic Novel: A Survey of Reading Habits* and *A New Survey: The Facts About Romantic Fiction*. Two other books by Mann are also excellent theoretical approaches to popular fiction from the sociological perspective: *Books and Reading* and *Books: Buyers and Borrowers.*

In the last decade, and especially in the past three years, the influence of women's studies in scholarship has become apparent in approaches to romantic fiction. The studies range from the blindly political to the brilliantly innovative, and the number of new essays and monographs seems to increase geometrically. An early anthology of material on women in popular culture contains some good, although uneven, work. *Images of Women in Fiction: Feminist Perspectives*, edited by Susan Koppelman Cornillon, appeared in 1972. Although many of the articles are relevant and worth consulting, the most interesting in this context is a suggestive, if superficial, essay by Joanna Russ, "What Can a Heroine Do? or Why Women Can't Write." Russ argues that the useful myths that inform literary works are male myths and that women exist in them only as reflected entities; thus, the central experience for women in fiction is courtship and marriage. The rest of women's lives cannot be conventionally portrayed in fiction.

Three major works of scholarship in women's studies deal almost entirely with British fiction, but they are exceptionally good models for careful, innovative approaches to women's fiction. The first two, Patricia Meyer Spacks's *The Female Imagination* and Elaine Showalter's *The Female Tradition in the English Novel: From Charlotte Brönte to Doris Lessing*, are good literary criticism from a feminist perspective. The third, Ellen Moers's *Literary Women*, posits an unusual approach to the female author, attempting to define the conventions, concerns, and experiences of women that take shape in literature. Many of these are issues that relate to romantic fiction. The book is especially suggestive in its discussion of what Moers refers to as "female heroineism," her term for the heroic possibilities and limits for the female protagonists of novels written by women. In describing "heroineism," Moers goes a long way toward evaluating the reasons why romance, in the popular sense, is primarily a women's genre.

A growing list of works by women scholars, primarily nineteenth-century historians interested in New England, has added greatly to our knowledge of romantic fiction between 1820 and 1870. Some of these studies are not directly about popular fiction, but they all approach women in American culture in ways that illuminate the fiction; many of them discuss the fiction as an integral part of the work. Barbara Welter was a pioneer in this approach; her 1966 article, "The Cult of True Womanhood," in *American Quarterly*, has been very influential on later scholars. This essay and others are reprinted in her *Dimity Convictions: The American Woman in the Nineteenth Century*, a book that includes essays on adolescence, medical problems, anti-intellectualism, women's religious novels, Anna Katharine Green, and Margaret Fuller. In her introduction to a collection of writings by American women, *The Oven Birds: American Women on Womanhood, 1820-1920*, Gail Thain Parker discusses the problems of women who lacked heroineic models and how this affected their writing. Kathryn Kish Sklar's excellent biography *Catharine Beecher: A Study in American Domesticity* adds much to an understanding of the woman as writer in the period. Although Catharine Beecher did not write novels, and her sister Harriet Beecher Stowe was much more than a romantic writer, the fact that so many of the romantic novelists of the period also wrote advice books for women on etiquette, domestic economy, education, and other issues addressed by Beecher makes this study of the conditions of a single woman's life a valuable one. A more general study, and another excellent one, is Susan P. Conrad's *Perish the Thought: Intellectual Woman in Romantic America 1830-1860*. Conrad argues that the work of the popular novelists, with its emphasis on home and love and marriage, reinforced the problems of female intellectuals in America.

In 1978, two different but exceptionally important works were published. Ann Douglas's *The Feminization of American Culture* has received much more critical attention and controversial commentary than Nina Baym's *Woman's Fiction: A Guide to Novels by and About Women in America 1820-1870*. Baym and Douglas acknowledge each other's work and "agree to disagree." Douglas suggests that the nineteenth century saw a progressive loss of power both for clergymen and for women that led to a debased religious sensibility and a turning to fiction to work out the implications of daily problems, resulting in a pervasive and evasive sentimentality and convention. There is a great deal of excellent background material on women's romantic fiction, especially in its more sentimental forms. Douglas's approach is biographical, rather than based on a reading of the novels as is Baym's. Baym provides long plot descriptions and analyses for a number of important forgotten romantic novels. She uses all the available biographical sources and feminist scholarship, although she is most interested in close readings of the works themselves. Although the book is very important in the field and is exceptionally thorough and useful, Baym sometimes strains her analysis by trying to make too strong a case for "her" authors as opposed to writers of seduction or gothic fiction; thus, she fails to see many of the essential similarities between them. However, the book is the best single volume on the subject to date and it should be influential and significant for some time to come.

Other studies of groups of individual romantic writers are unscholarly and superficial, but even they provide useful data about the writers and their works, and the occasional biography or dissertation is sometimes remarkably useful. A New York editor, Grant Overton, published two separate volumes with the same name in the early part of this century. The two versions of *The Women Who Make Our Novels* are composed mainly of journalistic ballyhoo for the writers, but there is also some solid information about such women as Mary Roberts Rinehart, Kathleen Norris, Mary Johnston, Amelia E. Barr, Temple Bailey, Faith Baldwin, Margaret Culkin Banning, Fannie Hurst, Margaret Widdemer, and other writers who are mostly ignored in a scholarly context. A less useful book, probably written for children, is Winifred and Frances Kirkland's *Girls Who Became Writers*, which deals superficially with Pearl Buck, Mary Roberts Rinehart, Sarah Josepha Hale, and Louisa May Alcott.

On individual novelists, the available information is variable and sketchy. There has been much interest in Susanna Rowson in recent years since she wrote such an important early and popular book in *Charlotte Temple* and since the book inspired so many imitators, even though it was derivative in its turn of the earlier British *Clarissa Harlowe*. The introduction by William S. Kable in *Three Early American Novels* is a basic introduction to Rowson; the volume also anthologizes two works by Charles Brockden Brown. An essay in Susan Koppelman Cornillon's previously cited anthology by Kathleen Conway McGrath, "Popular Literature as Social Reinforcement," is a standard, somewhat simplistic, approach to the popularity of Rowson's novel. A recent biography by Ellen B. Brandt, *Susanna Haswell Rowson: America's First Best-Selling Novelist*, is a serious, heavily researched chronological biography with a critical analysis of Rowson's books and a good bibliography. Three previous studies of Rowson are also significant. Elias Nason's *A Memoir of Mrs. Susanna Rowson* is Victorian hagiography. But *The Romance of the Association; or, One Last Glimpse of Charlotte Temple and Eliza Wharton* by Caroline Wells Dall is a fascinating example of Charlotte-mania in that the author in 1875 was trying to provide historical background to the actual events of both *Charlotte Temple* and Foster's *The Coquette*, popular seduction novels reputedly based on fact. R. W. G. Vail's *Susanna Haswell Rowson, the Author of Charlotte Temple: A Bibliographical Study* is a guide to the various editions of the book and has been the definitive source since its publication in 1933 by the American Antiquarian Society.

A graduate student at Columbia University in the 1920s published the only thoroughly useful materials relating to Elizabeth Oakes Smith; Mary Alice Wyman's two volumes are entitled *Selections from the Autobiography of Elizabeth Oakes Smith* and *Two American Pioneers: Seba Smith and Elizabeth Oakes Smith*. Interest in Catharine Maria Sedgwick has been somewhat higher, although her major works are not in print at this time. In 1871, Mary E. Dewey's *Life and Letters of Catharine M. Sedgwick* was issued. This remained the standard source, supplemented by a Catholic University dissertation in 1937, Sister Mary Michael Welsh's *Catharine Maria Sedgwick: Her Position in the Literature and Thought of Her Time up to 1860*, until Edward Halsey Foster's volume for the Twayne series, *Catharine Maria Sedgwick*. An interesting recent article is Michael's Davitt Bell's "History and Romance Convention in Catharine Sedgwick's *Hope Leslie*."

Another author who has attracted some attention wrote small amounts of romantic fiction herself, but as the editor of *Godey's Lady's Book*, she published romantic stories for a number of years. Ruth E. Finley's *The Lady of Godey's: Sarah Josepha Hale* provides a standard biography with some information about the fiction in the magazine. Isabelle Webb Entrikin's *Sarah Josepha Hale and Godey's Lady's Book* is a dissertation with a good comprehensive bibliography of Hale's published work. Norma R. Fryatt's *Sarah Josepha Hale: The Life and Times of a Nineteenth-Century Career Woman* is a biography for children written in a breathless and gushy style. One major writer of the period about whom a major biographical, critical, and bibliographical study is long overdue is Mrs. E. D. E. N. Southworth; the only full-length study is still Regis Louise Boyle's 1939 dissertation, *Mrs. E. D. E. N. Southworth, Novelist*.

Occasional materials relating to romantic novelists come from local history organizations or local institutions. The Constitution Island Association, which preserves the home of the Warner sisters, compiled a book about the island for a meeting of the Garden Club of America in 1936. A brief essay, "Susan and Anna Warner: 'The Brontë Sisters of America,' " is included. More general, but more revealing of attitudes, is Nathaniel Hall's laudatory *A Sermon. Preached in the First Church, Dorchester, on the Sunday (October 8, 1866) Following upon the Decease of Maria S. Cummins*. He portrays the author of *The Lamplighter* (the book that prompted Hawthorne's imprecations about "d----d scribbling women") as a female paragon. Another author who deserves more critical attention is Constance Fenimore Woolson; existing studies indicate some of her novels are romantic, perhaps even gothic, in their conventions. Notable works are John Dwight Kern's *Constance Fenimore Woolson: Literary Pioneer* and Rayburn S. Moore's Twayne volume *Constance Fenimore Woolson*. Two published dissertations are the only full-length treatment of two other authors: Elizabeth K. Halbeisen's *Harriet Prescott Spofford: A Romantic Survival* and William Perry Fidler's *Augusta Evans Wilson 1835-1909*. Both are basic, if uninspired.

A very few brief works on Mary Roberts Rinehart are available, although none is more than interesting. Robert H. Davis's *Mary Roberts Rinehart: A Sketch of the Woman and Her Work* includes selections by Davis, Grant Overton, and Rinehart herself. The pamphlet is uncritical, but it is better than Overton's gushy *The Woman Behind the Door . . . Mary Roberts Rinehart*, which was published as a glorified ad for one of her novels. Russel B. Nye's seminar at Michigan State University produced a better initial study of Rinehart in Arnold R. Hoffman's "Social History and the Crime Fiction of Mary Roberts Rinehart"; his bibliography is especially useful. Grace Livingston Hill was the subject of a highly flattering memoir by Jean Karr, *Grace Livingston Hill: Her Story and Her Writings*. Margaret Widdemer was superficially discussed in Dorothy Scarborough's *Margaret Widdemer, a Biography* in 1925.

Although no major critical work has as yet been done on Margaret Mitchell and *Gone with the Wind*, there are some useful works. A 1954 thesis by William Carter Pollard, available on microcard, "Gone with the Wind: Story of a Best Seller," is a substantial study of the popularity of the book. The Macmillan Company issued a self-congratulatory volume on the twenty-fifth anniversary of the book's publication, *Gone with the Wind and Its Author Margaret Mitchell*, containing some surprisingly interesting information. Finis Farr's chatty biography, *Margaret Mitchell of Atlanta*, is particularly good on the subject of how the book was published. William Pratt's *Scarlett Fever* is a large-sized picture book about the book as phenomenon, including much valuable material on the making of the film. Richard Harwell edited *Margaret Mitchell's Gone with the Wind Letters 1936-1949*, a collection of letters written to her about the book, which gives valuable insight into the book's audience.

Autobiographical materials by romantic writers are probably even less reliable than the journalistic approaches available, but they are at least sources for basic materials that can be further investigated. Isabella M. Alden's *Memories of Yesterdays* is an autobiography edited by her niece Grace Livingston Hill. Other memoirs include Amelia E. Barr's *All the Days of My Life* and Fannie Hurst's long and fascinating *Anatomy of Me*. More useful than most is the large amount of autobiographical writing done by Frances Parkinson Keyes, beginning with *Letters from a Senator's Wife* in 1924. A more thorough account of her life in Washington is *Capital Kaleidoscope: The Story of a Washington Hostess*. *The Cost of a Best Seller* is her description of the emotional and physical toll on the writer; *Along a Little Way* describes her conversion to Catholicism. The best two volumes on the backgrounds of her writing are *Roses in December* and *All Flags Flying: Reminiscences of Frances Parkinson Keyes*; together they constitute a long autobiography, the latter incomplete on her death. As if to prove that twentieth-century American romantic writers can also write advice and domestic economy books, Keyes published a surprisingly interesting book in 1955, *The Frances Parkinson Keyes Cookbook*. Dividing the sections of the book into geographic areas where she had lived, she gives much personal history along with the recipes.

Kathleen Norris, who married a brother of Frank Norris and whose sister married William Rose Benét, wrote two very interesting autobiographical volumes that incidentally give insight into American letters in the period as well as into her own life. *Noon: An Autobiographical Sketch* describes her life through middle age; *Family Gathering* is a lengthy and comprehensive work. Mary Roberts Rinehart also wrote some autobiographical materials, including the brief *Writing Is Work* and a fuller, and later supplemented, volume entitled *My Story*.

Mrs. Mary Virginia H. Terhune called her reminiscences *Marion Harland's Autobiography*, after her pen name. Margaret Widdemer's *Golden Friends I Had* is not only an autobiography but it is also a fairly thorough set of sketches of most major literary figures of the twentieth century, including a few romantic writers. *Summers at the Colony* is a separately published excerpt about her experiences at the McDowell Colony. One more biography, *Susan Warner*, by Anna B. Warner, is actually more like a joint autobiography since the Warner sisters collaborated on many writings.

Criticism of romantic fiction stands today at a particularly interesting moment. The autobiographical and journalistic sources provide some detail about the writers; the basic literary and historical works to give background are in place or are emerging; and women's studies provides the interest and the climate for further scholarly work in the field. A few years ago, it might not have been worthwhile to write this essay. In a few years, it will undoubtedly have to be revised significantly.

BIBLIOGRAPHY

BOOKS AND ARTICLES

Alden, Isabella M. [Pansy]. *Memories of Yesterdays*. Philadelphia: J. B. Lippincott, 1931.

Baker, Ernest A. *A Guide to the Best Fiction in English*. London: George Routledge, 1913.

Barr, Amelia E. *All the Days of My Life: An Autobiography*. New York: D. Appleton, 1913.

Baym, Nina. *Woman's Fiction: A Guide to Novels by and About Women in America 1820-1870*. Ithaca, N.Y.: Cornell University Press, 1978.

Beer, Gillian. *The Romance*. London: Methuen, 1970.

Bell, Michael Davitt. "History and Romance Convention in Catharine Sedgwick's *Hope Leslie*." *American Quarterly*, 22 (Summer 1970), 213-21.

Benson, Mary Sumner. *Women in Eighteenth-Century America*. New York: Columbia University Press, 1935; AMS Press, 1976.

Bode, Carl. *Anatomy of American Popular Culture*. Berkeley: University of California Press, 1960.

Boyle, Regis Louise. *Mrs. E.D.E.N. Southworth, Novelist*. Washington, D.C.: Catholic University Press, 1939.

Brandt, Ellen B. *Susanna Haswell Rowson: America's First Best-Selling Novelist*. Chicago: Serbra Press, 1975.

Brown, Herbert Ross. *The Sentimental Novel in America 1789-1860*. Durham, N.C.: Duke University Press, 1940; New York: Octagon Books, 1975.

Carrier, Esther J. *Fiction in Public Libraries 1876-1900*. New York: Scarecrow Press, 1965.

Cawelti, John G. *Adventure, Mystery, and Romance:Formula Stories as Art and Popular Culture*. Chicago: University of Chicago Press, 1976.

Cecil, Mirabel. *Heroines in Love 1750-1974*. London: Michael Joseph, 1974.

Charvat, William. *Literary Publishing in America 1790-1850*. Philadelphia: University of Pennsylvania Press, 1959.

Chase, Richard. *The American Novel and Its Tradition*. Garden City, N.Y.: Doubleday (Anchor), 1957.

Conrad, Susan P. *Perish the Thought: Intellectual Women in Romantic America 1830-1860*. New York: Oxford University Press, 1976.

Constitution Island Association. "Susan and Anna Warner: 'The Brönte Sisters of America.'" In *Constitution Island*. New York: compiled for the meeting of the Garden Club of America, 1936.

Cornillon, Susan Koppelman, ed. *Images of Women in Fiction: Feminist Perspectives*. Bowling Green, Ohio: Bowling Green University Popular Press, 1972.

Cowie, Alexander. "The Vogue of the Domestic Novel." *South Atlantic Quarterly*, 41 (October 1942), 416-25.

―――. *The Rise of the American Novel*. New York: American Book, 1948, 1951.

Dall, Caroline Wells. *The Romance of the Association; or, One Last Glimpse of Charlotte Temple and Eliza Wharton: A Curiousity of Literature and Life*. Cambridge: Press of John Wilson and Son, 1875.

Davis, Robert H. *Mary Roberts Rinehart: A Sketch of the Woman and Her Work*. New York: George H. Doran, 1925.

Deegan, Dorothy Yost. *The Stereotype of the Single Woman in American Novels: A Social Study with Implications for the Education of Women*. New York: King's Crown Press, 1951; Octagon Books, 1969.

Dewey, Mary E., ed. *Life and Letters of Catharine M. Sedgwick*. New York: Harper and Brothers, 1871.

Douglas, Ann. *The Feminization of American Culture*. New York: Alfred A. Knopf, 1978.

Entrikin, Isabelle Webb. *Sarah Josepha Hale and "Godey's Lady Book."* Lancaster, Pa.: Lancaster Press, 1946.

Farr, Finis. *Margaret Mitchell of Atlanta*. New York: Morrow, 1965.

Fidler, William Perry. *Augusta Evans Wilson 1835-1909*. University: University of Alabama Press, 1951.

Fiedler, Leslie A. *Love and Death in the American Novel*. New York: Criterion, 1960; Dell, 1966.

Finley, Ruth E. *The Lady of Godey's: Sarah Josepha Hale*. Philadelphia: Lippincott, 1931; New York: Arno, 1974.

Foster, Edward Halsey. *Catharine Maria Sedgwick*. New York: Twayne, 1974.

Fryatt, Norma R. *Sarah Josepha Hale: The Life and Times of a Nineteenth-Century Career Woman*. New York: Hawthorn Books, 1975.

Garrison, Dee. "Immoral Fiction in the Late Victorian Library." *American Quarterly*, 28 (Spring 1976), 71-89.

Hackett, Alice Payne, and James Henry Burke. *Eighty Years of Best Sellers*. New York: R. R. Bowker, 1977.

Halbeisen, Elizabeth K. *Harriet Prescott Spofford: A Romantic Survival*. Philadelphia: University of Pennsylvania Press, 1935.

Hall, Nathaniel. *A Sermon. Preached in the First Church, Dorchester, on the Sunday (October 8, 1866) Following upon the Decease of Maria S. Cummins*. Cambridge: Riverside Press (private distribution), 1866.

Hart, James D. *The Popular Book: A History of America's Literary Taste*. New York: Oxford University Press, 1950; Westport, Conn.: Greenwood Press, 1976.

Harwell, Richard, ed. *Margaret Mitchell's Gone with the Wind Letters 1936-1949*. New York: Macmillan, 1976.

Hoekstra, Ellen. "The Pedestal Myth Reinforced: Women's Magazine Fiction 1900-1920." In *New Dimensions in Popular Culture*. Edited by Russel B. Nye. Bowling Green, Ohio: Bowling Green University Popular Press, 1972.

Hoffman, Arnold R. "Social History and the Crime Fiction of Mary Roberts Rinehart." In *New Dimensions in Popular Culture*. Edited by Russel B. Nye. Bowling Green, Ohio: Bowling Green University Popular Press, 1972.

Hofstadter, Beatrice. "Popular Culture and the Romantic Heroine." *American Scholar* (Winter 1960-1961), 98-116.

Hurst, Fannie. *Anatomy of Me*. Garden City, N.Y.: Doubleday, 1958.

Johannsen, Albert. *The House of Beadle and Adams*. Norman: University of Oklahoma Press, 1950, 1962.

Kable, William S., ed. *Three Early American Novels*. Columbus, Ohio: Charles E. Merrill, 1970.

Karr, Jean. *Grace Livingston Hill: Her Story and Her Writings*. New York: Greenberg, 1948.

Kern, John Dwight. *Constance Fenimore Woolson: Literary Pioneer*. Philadelphia: University of Pennsylvania Press, 1934.

Keyes, Frances Parkinson. *Letters from a Senator's Wife*. New York: D. Appleton, 1924.

———. *Capital Kaleidoscope: The Story of a Washington Hostess*. New York: Harper, 1937.

———. *The Cost of a Best Seller*. New York: Julian Messner, 1950.

———. *The Frances Parkinson Keyes Cookbook*. Garden City, N.Y.: Doubleday, 1955.

———. *Roses in December*. Garden City, N.Y.: Doubleday, 1960.

———. *Along a Little Way*. New York: P. J. Kennedy, 1940; Hawthorn Books, 1962.

———. *All Flags Flying: Reminiscences of Frances Parkinson Keyes*. New York: McGraw-Hill, 1972.

Kiely, Robert. *The Romantic Novel in England*. Cambridge: Harvard University Press, 1972.

Kirkland, Winifred, and Frances Kirkland. *Girls Who Became Writers*. New

York: Harper and Row, 1933; Freeport, N.Y.: Books for Libraries Press, 1971.

Koch, Donald A. "Introduction." In *Tempest and Sunshine* by Mary Jane Holmes and *The Lamplighter* by Maria Susanna Cummins. New York: Odyssey, 1968.

Lehman-Haupt, H., L. C. Wroth, and Rollo Silver. *The Book in America.* New York: Bowker, 1952.

Leisy, Ernest E. *The American Historical Novel.* Norman: University of Oklahoma Press, 1950.

Loshe, Lily D. *The Early American Novel, 1789-1830.* New York: Columbia University Press, 1907; Ungar, 1966.

McGrath, Kathleen Conway. "Popular Literature as Social Reinforcement: The Case of *Charlotte Temple.*" In *Images of Women in Literature: Feminist Perspectives.* Edited by Susan Koppelman Cornillon. Bowling Green, Ohio: Bowling Green University Popular Press, 1972.

Macmillan Co. *Gone with the Wind and Its Author Margaret Mitchell.* New York: Macmillan, 1961.

Mann, Peter H. *Books and Reading.* London: Andre Deutsch, 1969.

——. *The Romantic Novel: A Survey of Reading Habits.* London: Mills and Boon, 1969.

——. *Books: Buyers and Borrowers.* London: Andre Deutsch, 1971.

——. *A New Survey: The Facts About Romantic Fiction.* London: Mills and Boon, 1974.

Microbook Library of American Civilization. *Author Catalog and Title Catalog.* Edited by Herman C. Bernick. Chicago: Library Resources, 1972.

Moers, Ellen. *Literary Women.* Garden City, N.Y.: Doubleday, 1977.

Moore, Rayburn S. *Constance Fenimore Woolson.* New York: Twayne, 1963.

Mott, Frank Luther. *Golden Multitudes.* New York: Macmillan, 1947.

Myers, Carol Fairbanks. *Women in Literature: Criticism of the Seventies.* Metuchen, N.J.: Scarecrow Press, 1976.

Nason, Elias. *A Memoir of Mrs. Susanna Rowson.* Albany, N.Y.: Joel Munsell, 1870.

Norris, Kathleen. *Noon: An Autobiographical Sketch.* Garden City, N.Y.: Doubleday, Page, 1925.

——. *Family Gathering.* Garden City, N.Y.: Doubleday, 1959.

Nye, Russel B. *The Unembarrassed Muse.* New York: Dial Press, 1970.

——, ed. *New Dimensions in Popular Culture.* Bowling Green, Ohio: Bowling Green University Popular Press, 1972.

Orians, G. H. "Censure of Fiction in American Magazines and Romances 1789-1810." *PMLA,* 52 (March 1937), 195-214.

Overton, Grant. *The Women Who Make Our Novels.* New York: Moffet, Yard, 1918.

——. *The Women Who Make Our Novels.* New York: Dodd, Mead, 1928.

——. *The Woman Behind the Door . . . Mary Roberts Rinehart.* New York: Farrar and Rinehart, 1930.

Papashvily, Helen W. *All the Happy Endings.* New York: Harper, 1956; Port Washington, N.Y.: Kennikat, 1972.

Parker, Gail Thain, ed. *The Oven Birds: American Women on Womanhood, 1820-1920.* Garden City, N.Y.: Doubleday (Anchor), 1972.

Pattee, F. L. *The Feminine Fifties.* New York: D. Appleton Century, 1940.

Petter, Henri. *The Early American Novel.* Columbus: Ohio State University Press, 1971.

Pollard, William Carter. "Gone with the Wind: Story of a Best Seller." Microcard thesis, Florida State University, 1954.

Pratt, William. *Scarlett Fever.* New York: Macmillan, 1977.

Quinn, Arthur Hobson. *American Fiction: An Historical and Critical Survey.* New York: Appleton-Century-Crofts, 1936, 1964.

Reynolds, Quentin. *The Fiction Factory.* New York: Random House, 1955.

Rinehart, Mary Roberts. *My Story.* New York: Farrar and Rinehart, 1931; also *My Story: A New Edition and Seventeen New Years.* New York: Rinehart, 1948.

―――. *Writing Is Work.* Boston: The Writer, 1939.

Russ, Joanna. "What Can a Heroine Do? or Why Women Can't Write." In *Images of Women in Literature: Feminist Perspectives.* Edited by Susan Koppelman Cornillon. Bowling Green, Ohio: Bowling Green University Popular Press, 1972.

Sanderson, Dorothy Hurlbut. *They Wrote for a Living: A Bibliography of the Works of Susan Bogert Warner and Anna Bartlett Warner.* West Point, N.Y.: Constitution Island Association, 1976.

Scarborough, Dorothy. *Margaret Widdemer, a Biography.* New York: Harcourt, Brace, 1925.

Shove, Raymond H. *Cheap Book Production in the United States, 1870-1891.* Urbana: University of Illinois Press, 1937.

Showalter, Elaine. *The Female Tradition in the English Novel: From Charlotte Brönte to Doris Lessing.* Princeton: Princeton University Press, 1976.

Sklar, Kathryn Kish. *Catharine Beecher: A Study in American Domesticity.* New Haven: Yale University Press, 1973.

Smith, Leslie. "Through Rose-Colored Glasses: Some American Victorian Sentimental Novels." In *New Dimensions in Popular Culture.* Edited by Russel B. Nye. Bowling Green, Ohio: Bowling Green University Popular Press, 1972.

Spacks, Patricia Meyer. *The Female Imagination.* New York: Alfred Knopf, 1975.

Tebbel, John W. *A History of Book Publishing in the United States.* New York: Bowker, 1972.

Terhune, Mary Virginia H. *Marion Harland's Autobiography.* New York: Harper and Bros, 1910.

Tompkins, J. M. S. *The Popular Novel in England (1770-1800).* London: Methuen, 1932, 1969.

Utter, Robert Palfrey, and Gwendolyn Bridges Needham. *Pamela's Daughters.* New York: Macmillan, 1936; Russell and Russell, 1972.

Vail, R. W. G. *Susanna Haswell Rowson, the Author of Charlotte Temple: A*

Bibliographical Study. Worcester, Mass.: American Antiquarian Society, 1933.

Wagenknecht, Edward. *Cavalcade of the American Novel*. New York: Holt, Rinehart, Winston, 1952.

Ward, Robert J. "Europe in American Historical Romances 1890-1910." *Midcontinent American Studies Journal*, 8 (Spring 1967), 90-97.

Warner, Anna B. *Susan Warner*. New York: G. P. Putnam's Sons, 1909.

Wasserstrom, William. *Heiress of All the Ages: Sex and Sentiment in the Genteel Tradition*. Minneapolis: University of Minnesota Press, 1959.

Weibel, Kathryn. *Mirror, Mirror: Images of Women Reflected in Popular Culture*. Garden City, N.Y.: Doubleday (Anchor), 1977.

Welsh, Sister Mary Michael. *Catharine Maria Sedgwick: Her Position in the Literature and Thought of Her Time up to 1860*. Washington, D.C.: Catholic University Press, 1937.

Welter, Barbara. "The Cult of True Womanhood." *American Quarterly*, 18 (Summer 1966), 151-74.

————. *Dimity Convictions: The American Woman in the Nineteenth Century*. Athens, Ohio: Ohio University Press, 1976.

Widdemer, Margaret. *Golden Friends I Had*. Garden City, N.Y.: Doubleday, 1964.

————. *Summers at the Colony*. Syracuse: Syracuse University Library Associates, 1964.

Women's Center, Barnard College. *Women's Work and Women's Studies*, vol. I and II. Pittsburgh: KNOW, Inc., 1971, 1972; vol. III. Old Westbury, N.Y.: The Feminist Press, 1973-1974.

Wright, Lyle H. *American Fiction 1774-1850*. San Marino, Calif.: Huntington Library, 1939.

————. *Bibliography*. Los Angeles: William Andrews Clark Memorial Library, University of California, 1966.

————. *American Fiction 1774-1900*. Louisville, Ky.: Lost Cause Press, 1970.

Wright, R. Glenn, comp. *Author Bibliography of English Language Fiction in the Library of Congress Through 1950*. Boston: G. K. Hall, 1973.

————. *Chronological Bibliography of English Language Fiction in the Library of Congress Through 1950*. Boston: G. K. Hall, 1974.

————. *Title Bibliography of English Language Fiction in the Library of Congress Through 1950*. Boston: G. K. Hall, 1976.

Wyman, Mary Alice. *Selections from the Autobiography of Elizabeth Oakes Smith*. Lewiston, Me.: Lewiston Journal, 1924.

————. *Two American Pioneers: Seba Smith and Elizabeth Oakes Smith*. New York: Columbia University Press, 1927.

CHAPTER 14. Verse and Popular Poetry

Janice Radway

While virtually every field in popular culture studies is plagued by the problems inherent in defining and identifying a proper object for analysis, these difficulties become particularly acute, in fact almost prohibitive, when the subject under scrutiny is popular poetry and verse. Several individual poets have become extraordinarily "popular" figures during the course of American cultural development, in the sense that they were, or are now, personally familiar to a large portion of the population. However, very few single volumes of actual poetry have ever achieved best-seller status at the time of their publication.

Frank Luther Mott, who conservatively defines the best seller as a work purchased in the decade of publication by 1 percent of the total population of the continental United States, lists only seven individual volumes of poetry by American poets as best sellers in the years from 1662 to 1945. Included in this list, however, is Walt Whitman's *Leaves of Grass* (1855), of which only a few hundred copies were actually sold in the year of publication itself. Mott is able to retain the work on his list only because, through cheap reprints, the requisite number of copies was eventually sold in the course of the entire decade. But there is an obvious and significant difference between Whitman's status as a popular poet and that of Henry Wadsworth Longfellow, whose *Hiawatha* (1855) sold two thousand five hundred copies during the week of publication alone and nearly eighteen thousand more during the next three months.

Although Mott's figures are therefore of little help to the researcher interested in identifying America's popular poets, assistance is not easily found elsewhere. Even if one could decide on an appropriate measure for the popularity of this genre, which has never approached the novel in sales, such publication figures for volumes of poetry are not readily available. Many literary historians of the eighteenth and nineteenth centuries do include poets now unfamiliar to us in their dictionaries and encyclopedias, but there is almost no way of determining whether such figures were truly popular or only minor poets who produced elitist verse of secondary quality.

The problem is further compounded by the fact that nearly every newspaper and popular magazine published in the United States has, at one time or another, included poetry that cannot be termed "elite" or "artistic." On the other hand, many of these same versifiers have neither produced an entire volume of poetry nor reached a national audience transcending regional, economic, and social limits. As a result, one has to question whether such poetry should be included in a study of popular forms, or whether it ought to be excluded as a variant of American folk culture.

These problems are of more than incidental significance because the way this field of study is delineated necessarily affects the character and validity of the conclusions drawn. Any thesis, therefore, about the place, development, or significance of poetry in the popular culture of the United States is, in reality, little more than a highly speculative hypothesis that can only be tested through further research.

The poets mentioned in the following survey have, accordingly, been selected on the basis of a fairly rigorous procedure. All of those occasional versifiers whose extant work is now limited to individual poems found in magazines, newspapers, or anthologies have been excluded. Of the remaining professional poets, only those for whom substantial sales figures or other indications of general popularity are available will be found in this history. In the case of the eighteenth- and nineteenth-century poets, I found it necessary to rely heavily on Rufus Griswold's *The Poets and Poetry of America*, a best-selling literary encyclopedia, which itself went through more than sixteen editions. If Griswold includes a poet, refers to his or her popularity, and I could confirm that popularity in some other source, then that poet has been added as well. Although the resulting list is therefore quite limited, these few figures are the only American poets whose work can be readily identified as poetry read by more than a very small portion of the population.

HISTORIC OUTLINE

In the years immediately following the settlement of the American colonies, two distinct forms of verse emerged as the basis of a popular poetic tradition. While religious and practical considerations tended to diminish interest in the high art of poesy as it was then practiced in England, the early colonist found definite merit in religious poetry of a didactic nature and in informational verse designed for the circulation of news. Accordingly, it is not surprising to discover that the first truly popular

American poems were those of the *Bay Psalm Book* (1640) and the numerous "broadsides" hawked by street peddlers.

While the two kinds of verse appeared vastly different on the surface, they exhibited a common interest in content as well as a very obvious disinterest in matters of aesthetic form. Indeed, the editors of the *Bay Psalm Book* apologized for the rustic quality of their verse with the observation that "if therefore the verses are not always so smooth and elegant as some may desire or expect; let them consider that God's Altar needs no polishing."

Like the broadside verse that told of specific crimes, births, deaths, and holidays, early American religious poetry was thus designed to refer explicitly to the world inhabited by its reader. Language was not something to be manipulated for its own sake, but rather a tool to be used for instruction and information. It is this exclusive emphasis on the referential aspect of language that has continued to differentiate America's popular verse from her more self-conscious, deliberately aesthetic poetry of the elite tradition.

Throughout the late seventeenth and early eighteenth centuries, most of the poetry read by the majority of the populace was amateur verse published outside the three major literary centers of Philadelphia, New York, and Boston. Such verse was highly topical and therefore largely ephemeral. It was published by a local printer in pamphlet form and financed by the author himself. Much of the verse, like the "Massachusetts Liberty Song," centered about the revolutionary war, although religious teaching continued to be the primary subject of American amateur verse for the next one hundred fifty years. A vast quantity of this sort of verse was included in the almanacs that began to appear as early as 1639 and that quickly became an indispensable guide for every colonial home.

Two professional poets, however, did reach a relatively large audience even before growing industrialization began to revolutionize the printing industry. As far as can be determined, Michael Wigglesworth's *Day of Doom* (1662) was the most popular poem in America for well over one hundred years. The first edition of eighteen hundred copies was exhausted in the year of publication, a remarkable achievement considering the sparse population of the colonies at the time. While Wigglesworth's verse was certainly more accomplished than that of his amateur contemporaries, the poem probably achieved popular status because its theological content was remarkably expressive of the people's beliefs.

That this was the case with John Trumbull's "McFingal" (1775) is obvious since none of the poetry he later produced ever excited the interest of readers as did this patently political, Hudribrastic attack on the manners and men of Tory America. The poem went through thirty editions during the next century and, according to one literary historian, furnished many popular proverbs that were quoted long after the war that had sparked it had ended. "McFingal's" patriotic sentiments were quoted by innumerable political orators, and the poem itself was a standard entry in both poetic anthologies and school textbooks for the next hundred years.

Until Lydia Huntley Sigourney's poetry began to dominate the scene, most eighteenth-century Americans read little more verse than that appearing in the almanacs. Occasionally, a poem by a professional poet would strike the popular imagination and it would then be widely circulated and much discussed. It is, however, difficult to determine exactly how well known such figures as William Treat Paine, John Pierpont, or James Gates Percival ever became. Paine's publication of *Adams and Liberty* earned him $750, a very large sum for any book in 1797. Pierpont's "The Airs of Palestine" (1816) seems to have attracted a great deal of attention, as did Percival's sentimental Byronic epic, "The Suicide," which occupied twelve, long, magazine pages. While it is fairly certain that these men were widely known and read outside the small literary community of the period, none ever achieved the general popularity enjoyed by Mrs. Sigourney, the "Sweet Singer of Hartford."

Lydia Huntley Sigourney began writing poetry in 1798, published forty-six volumes of poetry in her lifetime, and, until the appearance of Long-fellow, was America's most popular poet. Her first verse collection, *Moral Pieces in Prose and Verse* (1816), made it abundantly clear that for her, poetry was not a mere ornament to life, but rather a direct vehicle for moral instruction. Although her poems dealt with nearly every subject imaginable, each was designed to instruct the reader in the inestimable value of the chaste and moral Christian life. Her *Letters to Young Ladies* (1833) was especially popular—it eventually went through twenty American editions—and was followed by the equally popular *Letters to Mothers* (1838).

Mrs. Sigourney was one of the first American poets to compose lines upon request for the commemoration of special events. Her "occasional" poems memorialized many of her dedicated readers, whose relatives sought solace for their loss in her highly "poetical" sentiments and "uplifting language." It is important to note that although Mrs. Sigourney's poetry always referred directly to the world, it did so in language that clearly set itself off from the mundane discourse of everyday life. She was extraordinarily adept at striking a balance between the events of this world and the meaning they were thought to have in the more important ethereal realm of the spirit. While it is not completely accurate to think of American popular poetry as a "formula," Mrs. Sigourney's combination of the sublime with the small seems to have set a pattern followed fruitfully thereafter by nearly every popular American bard.

Lydia Sigourney's extraordinary popularity was challenged for a time in the 1830s by that of another occasional poet, Charles Sprague. He first attracted attention in 1829 when he delivered the Phi Beta Kappa poem at Harvard University's commencement. Although the poem was a highly conventional treatment of the forms "Curiosity" could take, it seems to have struck a popular chord, for it was widely circulated during the next ten years. Sprague thereafter wrote many odes for public and private occasions, including one "written on the accidental meeting of all the surviving members of a family."

Although William Cullen Bryant never became as popular a figure as Longfellow, he was able to earn a substantial living on the basis of his poetry publication. By 1842, he could command a fifty-dollar fee for a single magazine poem, while his individual volumes sold at the respectable rate of one thousand seven hundred copies per year. His work seems not to have excited as much general interest as that of some of his contemporaries, for he is included less often in anthologies and textbooks than either Mrs. Sigourney, Sprague, or the remarkable Longfellow. Still, he appears to have been generally known and popularly appreciated.

It was, however, Henry Wadsworth Longfellow who established himself most successfully in the minds of his fellow Americans as the country's unofficial poet laureate. At a time when the poetic vocation was still scorned as a generally ornamental, effeminate occupation, he was able to command respect as a spokesman for the American spirit. His first volume of poetry, *Voices of the Night* (1839), sold nine hundred copies in thirty days, four thousand three hundred in a single year. This seems to have set a precedent, for Longfellow earned more than $7,000 in royalties on *Hiawatha* alone in the next ten years. In fact, every volume he produced after the first was subject to advance sale. *Evangeline* (1847) sold 6,050 copies in the first two years after publication; twenty thousand copies of *Hiawatha* (1855) were purchased in the first three months alone; and in London, ten thousand copies of *The Courtship of Miles Standish* (1858) were sold in a single day.

No doubt many factors contributed to Longfellow's unprecedented popularity, not the least of which was the skill with which he played the part demanded of him by his readers. However, it is also certain that his ability to combine European erudition and a sense of the past with a characteristically American enthusiasm and optimism was also widely appreciated. This variation of Mrs. Sigourney's method, characterized by the combination of the elevated with the ordinary, served Longfellow well. He produced innumerable very learned poems, complete with classical allusions on ordinary topics familiar to his mass of readers. He was generally extolled for his high moral sentiment, for the depth of his feeling, as well as for the breadth of his knowledge. It did not matter to most of his readers that his versification was conservative, or that his poetic treatment occasionally bordered on the sentimental or the melodramatic. What was of primary importance to them was his ability to comment on the higher meaning of their daily lives in an easily comprehensible style. As Russel Nye has suggested in *The Unembarrassed Muse*, it was Longfellow's clarity and ability to unravel apparent complexities that most endeared him to his huge audience.

Longfellow was aided in his task of satisfying the young country's need for poetic interpretation and edification by men such as James Russell Lowell, Oliver Wendell Holmes, Josiah Gilbert Holland, and John Greenleaf Whittier. Although none ever came close to Longfellow's popularity, each was called on again and again to comment publicly on the "meaning" of the American experience.

Holmes was a well-known occasional poet who produced lines on commencements, feasts, town meeting, births, deaths, and special holidays. Lowell also produced topical poetry, but he was best known for his satirical verse in "The Bigelow Papers" as well as for his extravagant historical epic, "The Vision of Sir Launfal" (1848), which sold nearly one hundred seventy-five thousand copies during the decade after publication. Holland began his career as a poet in the magazines but graduated soon thereafter to complete volumes of verse. His two-hundred-page epic, *Bittersweet* (1858), setting forth the thesis that evil is part of the Divine Plan, first made his reputation as a poet of the people. When he composed the *Life of Abraham Lincoln* in 1865, eighty thousand readers snatched up his eulogy. Like his poetic forefathers, Holland's goal was didactic, and his message emphasized the need for religion in American life.

But even though Holmes, Lowell, and Holland were thus well known, their poetry did not touch the hearts of their fellow Americans in the exact way that the verses of John Greenleaf Whittier did. Indeed, Whittier's preoccupation with the pastoral values of rural existence seems to have endeared him all the more to America because it appeared at that precise moment when industry and urbanization were becoming a serious threat to a disappearing way of life. Although his first volume, *Lays of My Home* (1843), was well received, it was "Snowbound" (1866) which solidified Whittier's reputation with the masses. The poem's homely but sincere language, its nostalgic sentimentality, and detailed evocation of the hardship of country life made it especially attractive to a swiftly urbanizing people who were anything but sure that they wished to put the past behind them. Twenty-eight thousand copies of "Snowbound" were sold during the first year, and Whittier eventually realized more than $100,000 in royalties from its sale alone. As Van Wyck Brooks has pointed out, "Snowbound" was the safeguard of America's memory and the touchstone of its past. Whittier, like Longfellow and Sigourney before him, was remarkably good at couching America's highest sentiments about God, country, and the family in language slightly but definitely removed from the vernacular of the people. As a result, he was quoted and deferred to unceasingly throughout the nineteenth century as one of America's most honored sages.

Although Alice and Phoebe Cary never achieved the status of American sages, they did produce more than fifteen volumes between them that reached a specific segment of the American population. Born in Cincinnati, Ohio, the sisters composed verses on motherhood, family, and farm-life that were especially well known among women and in the midwestern United States. While their verse was neither so refined nor so polished as that of their better-known contemporaries, the sentiments they expressed were almost identical to those of Holmes, Holland, or Whittier. In fact, these lines from Alice's poem "Dying Hymn" (1865), while a bit more effusive, are not very different from numerous poems composed by the other three:

> That faith to me a courage gives
> Low as the grave, to go:
> I know that my Redeemer lives:
> That I shall live, I know.

> The palace walls I almost see,
> Where dwells my Lord and King:
> O grave, where is thy Victory!
> O death, where is thy sting!

Although many other poets like the Carys achieved regional popularity during the middle decades of the nineteenth century, none seems to have developed a reputation comparable to that of Bryant, Longfellow, or Whittier. John Godfrey Saxe, "the witty poet," was read for his satirical comments on the follies of social life, but he actually made his reputation by traveling throughout the country giving oral presentations. Nathaniel Parker Willis published nine volumes of verse throughout his lifetime, but he was better known as an editor, literary fop, and travel writer. In addition, many versifiers developed a following during the Civil War, when poetic sentiments were in particular demand. But as the war ended, and the broadsides in which they were published disappeared, so too did the poets.

This situation did not alter drastically in the last half of the century either. Thomas Bailey Aldrich achieved a measure of popularity with his "Ballad of Babie Bell" (1858) and thereafter published numerous poems on love, God, and the ubiquitous family. Still, he was most widely celebrated for his fiction and criticism, produced while he was editor of the

Atlantic Monthly. Bayard Taylor, also an editor, produced a great deal of poetry that sold fairly well. However, his reputation was not strong enough to guarantee the success of any of his verse, for several of his epic poems, including "Lars, a Pastoral of Norway" (1873) and "The Prophet" (1874), were definite failures.

Perhaps the one poet of the late nineteenth century who came closest to rivaling the popular reputations of Longfellow and Whittier was James Whitcomb Riley, whose rustic Hoosier dialect and homespun philosophy struck a responsive chord in the now almost-wholly urban America. His idealizations of farm and country life were enormously popular throughout the country, despite the fact that the peculiar language he employed was nearly incomprehensible to some. Riley produced fourteen volumes of cheerful poetic sentiment, all of which were characterized by regular rhythms and easily memorized rhymes. Like nearly all of America's popular poets, he was obsessed with the family, childhood, and days gone by. His poetry, like Whittier's and Longfellow's, embodied the vision of America in which his fellow Americans most wanted to believe. The fact that the vision existed only in the poetry troubled almost no one, least of all Riley.

During the final decades of the century, three poets developed national reputations similar to Riley's in that they were identified with a unique section of the country. Will Carleton, a Michigan newspaperman, began his poetic career with "Betsy and I Are Out," a ballad about lost love, first published in *The Toledo Blade* in 1871. When newspapers across the country reprinted the poem, it was an immediate success. Three years later, Carleton published *Farm Ballads* (1873), a collection full of lavish sentiment and careful descriptions of the farming Midwest. The combination was perfectly suitable for the popular demand, and, by his death in 1912, more than six hundred thousand copies of the book had been sold.

Madison Cawein of Louisville, Kentucky, was never as popular as either Carleton or Riley, but his thirty-six volumes of verse did make him the most prolific southern writer of the decade. Although most of his lyrics were as sentimental, patriotic, and religious as those of nearly every other poet of the period, his realistic description of the southern landscape tended to set his work apart as something quite unique.

Joaquim Miller was not, like Cawein, known for the precision of his imagery. Indeed, he was extravagantly praised as the one American poet capable of capturing the grandeur of the magnificent West. Something of a showman, Miller exploited his frontier roots, traveling about the country dressed in buckskins to give poetry readings. Except for his evocative portrayal of the desert and the life of the American Indian, Miller's poetry is indistinguishable from the "heartfelt lyrics" of Carleton or Cawein.

This characteristic emphasis on sentimentality continued throughout the first years of the twentieth century. Most of the American popular verse published in 1900 was as closely centered about the home and family as it had been a century earlier. Although the kind of subject matter that could be treated in a poem had been extended and realistic description tended to appear more often, rhyme was still a necessary component, as was a lightly lilting rhythm. No doubt this was, in part, due to the continuing use of poetry for recitations in the schools and for orations at official occasions.

This public and rhetorical function slowly began to disappear, however, in the early years of the new century, when American popular verse gradually turned inward and became more contemplative and personal. There is no easy way to tell whether the change was produced by the difficulties of life in an increasingly impersonal world, or by the ridicule heaped on popular verse by the newly avant-garde elite poets. In any event, the change was generally noticeable, especially in the verse produced by America's newspaper poets, including Eugene Field and Ella Wheeler Wilcox. Field, who was associated with the city of Chicago, was particularly good at producing poetry about the innocence and beauty of childhood and was perhaps best known for "Little Boy Blue" (1887) and "Dutch Lullaby: Wynken, Blyken, and Nod" (1895). Wilcox, like Field, was adept at describing the inner life in subdued but sentimental terms and once remarked that her purpose was "to raise the unhappy and guide those who need it."

Poetry enjoyed something of a renaissance during World War I, when large numbers of people were willing to purchase single volumes of verse in addition to the traditional anthologies that had continued in popularity throughout the early years of the century. This increase in the "demand" for verse that spoke to the people is also evident in both the local newspapers and national magazines of the period. While many of the poems were written by the "mothers," "fathers," and "sisters" of the American soldier, by far the largest segment of verse was produced by the young infantrymen who had gone to Europe to "make the world safe for democracy." Among the most well known were John McCrae ("In Flanders Field" 1919), Alan Seeger ("I Have a Rendezvous with Death" 1917), and Joyce Kilmer ("Trees" 1913), all of whom were killed in the battlefields of France.

None of the soldier-poets, however, could match the popularity of the Michigan newspaper poet, Edgar A. Guest, who extended his early regional reputation by publishing large quantities of verse about the war. Although Guest did not participate in the conflict, it was the implicit subject behind most of his poetry. Indeed, his primary concern during the years 1914-1917 was the war experience as it was lived by those on the "home front." Then, throughout the 1920s, he consolidated his national reputation by continuing to write about home, work, and God. He rightly conceived of his verse as a "mirror" of the values adhered to by his audience, and that audience ratified his conception by purchasing his volumes in increasingly large numbers.

The history of American popular poetry after Guest is largely the history of anthologies, which continued to be successful despite the fact that few people were willing to purchase single volumes of verse. Most of these collections, like Burton Stevenson's *The Home Book of Verse* and Hazel Felleman's *Best Loved Poems of the American People*, were organized by subject matter rather than by poet, testifying to the fact that American popular poetry continued to function referentially for its audience by portraying a familiar world. Longfellow, Whittier, Bryant, and Riley continued as the traditional favorites although the least ambiguous poems by Carl Sandburg and Robert Frost were also given prominent display. It is hard to determine, however, whether Frost's popularity was the result of his posture as the quintessentially American "poetic figure," or of a genuine interest in and demand for his poetry. The former speculation does seem more plausible since he was nearly always represented in the popular anthologies by the same two poems, "Stopping by Woods on a Snowy Evening" (1923) and "The Road Not Taken" (1915).

The only two poets who have managed to sell large numbers of single volumes of poetry during the second half of the twentieth century are Kahlil Gibran and Rod McKuen. Gibran first developed a large audience during the 1920s, when his Oriental mysticism satisfied the American public's interest in the exotic and the bohemian. He wrote eleven volumes before he died in 1931, all of which included a curious mixture of parables, aphorisms, verses, and short narratives. His best-known book, however, was *The Prophet* (1923), which was resurrected in the mid-1960s as a kind of handbook for the counterculture. To date, *The Prophet* has sold more than three million copies.

Also a phenomenon of the mid-1960s, Rod McKuen's poetry was especially popular with the young. His first book of verse, *Stanyan Street and Other Sorrows*, appeared in 1954 to a decidedly indifferent reception. But when *Listen to the Warm* was published in 1963, it immediately made the best-seller list, and McKuen became an instant celebrity. His verse differs somewhat from traditional popular poetry in that it is explicitly erotic, written in a free-verse style, and lacks any kind of end-rhyme. However, the language is as referential and familiar as that of Longfellow, Riley, or Guest, in that it explicitly describes the inner emotional life of the modern adolescent. Although his major themes—loneliness, lost love, and the need for human communication—are slightly different from those of his poetic forebears, the generally hopeful note sounded by his sentimental conclusions is not. In that sense, it is possible to see a direct line of development in American popular poetry extending from Lydia Huntley Sigourney through Henry Wadsworth Longfellow, James Whitcomb Riley, and Edgar Guest, to Rod McKuen.

REFERENCE WORKS

American popular poetry has, until recently, excited very little serious critical attention. As a consequence of this state of neglect, there is no full-length reference work available that is devoted solely to the "poets of the people." However, a good introduction to the field can be found in Russel B. Nye's comprehensive history of the popular arts, *The Unembarrassed Muse.* Nye's chapter on "Rhymes for Everybody" is a historical survey that is both more detailed and complete than the one I have been able to provide here. While Nye does not list all the volumes published by the authors he cites, the essay is a good starting point in any attempt to identify those poets who did achieve a measure of popularity in the United States.

Frank Luther Mott's *Golden Multitudes* and Alice Payne Hackett's *Fifty Years of Best Sellers* are both useful in that they provide specific figures for some of the most popular poets. However, neither volume goes much beyond the two or three poets who could compete with American novelists in overall sales. James Hart's *The Popular Book* includes a few names and details missing from these other general studies and, as a result, it is a useful supplement. His *The Oxford Companion to American Literature* also includes short paragraphs on a small number of popular versifiers, but once again his comments are generally limited to the most obvious and best-documented among them.

Biographical sketches and bibliographical listings are scattered throughout a number of sources. Perhaps the most useful volume for the earliest poets is Rufus Wilmot Griswold's *The Poets and Poetry of America,* initially published in 1842 and revised through 1872. Although Griswold only occasionally identifies his poets as popular, he includes many minor figures whose renown can usually be verified elsewhere. This volume is particularly noteworthy because it includes selections from poets whose work might otherwise be hard to locate.

The Cyclopaedia of American Literature by Evert and George Duyckinck is another good guide to America's early popular poets. The Duyckincks include biographical and critical sketches on many minor figures although, unfortunately, they usually make no reference to the popularity of the poetry. If this volume is supplemented by Frank McAlpine's *Our Album of Authors* and Oscar Adams's *A Dictionary of American Authors,* a fairly good picture can be developed of the major popular poets through the early years of the twentieth century. Additional biographies can then be found in Stanley J. Kunitz and Howard Haycraft's *American Authors, 1600-1900*, which is particularly useful because it lists major works and secondary sources about the figures it includes.

Jacob Blanck's *Bibliography of American Literature* includes complete bibliographic listings for almost all of the more important popular poets. However, a few of the best-known figures such as Guest and Gibran are excluded. In cases such as these, it is necessary to rely on individual studies devoted to these figures. In Guest's case, the relevant source is Royce Howes's biography, *Edgar Guest*, while for Gibran, the volume to check is *Kahlil Gibran: Wings of Thought, the People's Philosopher* by Joseph Ghougassin.

In addition to these general sources, there are several volumes available devoted exclusively to poetry produced in colonial America. While much of the verse that is documented is elite, anonymous, or folk, the listings are complete and thus include those works that achieved a national reputation. The single best source here is Oscar Wegelin's *Early American Poetry*, which has been supplemented by Roger Stoddard's *A Catalogue of Books and Pamphlets Unrecorded in Oscar Wegelin's "Early American Poetry."* Leo Lemay's *A Calendar of American Poetry in the Colonial Newspapers and Magazines* extends the list supplied by Wegelin and Stoddard, while William Scheik and Jo Ella Doggett's *Seventeenth-Century American Poetry: A Reference Guide* provides a comprehensive survey of the criticism devoted to the period.

There are no comprehensive guides available at the moment to reviews of individual poets, secondary sources, or criticism in the general field of American popular poetry.

RESEARCH COLLECTIONS

American popular verse is well represented in several major research collections devoted more generally to American poetry at large. The most comprehensive among these is the Harris Collection of American Poetry housed at Brown University. This extraordinary collection includes more than one hundred thousand volumes of poems and plays, many of which were written by poets forgotten long ago. A complete, twelve-volume catalog to the collection was issued in 1972 by G. K. Hall and Company.

The New York Public Library also possesses a major collection of American poetry, although its holdings are confined largely to the years 1610 to 1820. A catalog to this grouping was compiled and published by J. G. Frank in 1917. The Van Pelt Library at the University of Pennsylvania also houses a large collection relating to American poetry, including many first editions and hard-to-locate volumes of the popular poets. There are two catalogs, neither of which, however, is completely up to date. *The Check-*

list of Poetry by American Authors Published in the English Colonies lists only those works printed before 1865. *Literary Writings in America: A Bibliography* is a photo-offset of the card catalog at Van Pelt Library, prepared as a WPA project from 1938 to 1942. This bibliography, however, does not list anything the library acquired after 1942, nor does it list its extensive holdings of secondary sources relating to America's poets.

In his *Subject Collections* (fourth edition, 1974), Lee Ash lists several other concentrations of books of major interest to any researcher concerned with popular American poetry. The New York State Library in Albany holds a ten thousand-volume collection of American poetry, strong in both the "minor" poets and early broadside ballads. The Florida State University at Tallahassee possesses a Childhood in Poetry Collection, which includes the works of "hundreds of minor poets" relating specifically to childhood. A five-volume catalog of the holdings by John Mackay Shaw was published by the Gale Research Company in 1967. In addition, the Poetry Society of America at the Van Voorhis Library in New York maintains a four thousand-volume collection of poetry, while the Beloit College Library in Wisconsin holds three thousand volumes of contemporary American poetry published by vanity presses.

The manuscripts and papers of America's popular poets, like those of most of her authors, are scattered throughout the country. The Houghton Library at Harvard University, however, possesses at least one or two manuscripts or letters by every important popular poet. Its most significant holdings are the papers of Longfellow, Lowell, and Whittier, although it also has substantial portions of the papers of Thomas B. Aldrich, Eugene Field, Joyce Kilmer, Charles Sprague, Alan Seeger, and Bayard Taylor.

The Huntington Library in San Marino, California, also holds large numbers of manuscripts and letters by America's popular poets. Among its large collections are papers relating to Alice and Phoebe Cary, Eugene Field, Joachin Miller, James Whitcomb Riley, Lydia Huntley Sigourney, Bayard Taylor, Nathaniel Parker Willis, and Ella Wheeler Wilcox. In addition to these collections at Harvard and the Huntington, there is another major concentration of papers at the Alderman Library at the University of Virginia. It numbers among its holdings significant portions of the papers of the Cary sisters, Joyce Kilmer, James Russell Lowell, Joachin Miller, John Godfrey Saxe, Charles Sprague, and Nathaniel Parker Willis.

The New York Public Library holds most of the papers of William Cullen Bryant and Josiah Gilbert Holland, while those of Oliver Wendell Holmes are located at the Library of Congress. All of Will Carleton's papers are held by the Hillsdale College Library in Hillsdale, Michigan, while most of Madison Cawein's papers are split between the Bentley Historical Library at the University of Michigan and Yale University. Yale also possesses most of the papers of James Gates Percival, John Pierpont, and Lydia Huntley Sigourney, as well as some by Holland, Saxe, Miller, Taylor, and Willis. The Rutgers University Library holds four scrapbooks relating to Joyce Kilmer, while the Indiana University Library holds a sixty-two hundred-piece collection pertaining to James Whitcomb Riley. The few extant papers of Michael Wigglesworth can be found at the Massachusetts Historical Society and the Indiana University Library.

While poetry anthologies are also a good source for anyone interested in American popular verse, space limitations preclude their mention here. These are so numerous, however, that one or two can usually be found in even the smallest municipal library. Besides the Stevenson and Felleman volumes mentioned earlier, the most interesting are Slason Thompson's *The Humbler Poets*, George Cheever's *The American Commonplace Book of Poetry*, Henry Coates's *The Fireside Encyclopedia of Poetry*, Brander Matthews's *American Familiar Verse*, and Roy J. Cook's *One Hundred and One Famous Poems*.

HISTORY AND CRITICISM

Although Russel B. Nye's chapter in *The Unembarrassed Muse* is currently the only analysis available that focuses on the entire history of American popular poetry, several more general volumes on American literature treat the poets in question in a more than cursory manner. Most notable among these is perhaps Van Wyck Brooks's four-volume study, *Makers and Finders: A History of the Writer in America, 1800-1915*. Although Brooks's subject is all of American literature, he mentions many of the country's popular writers and is generally sensitive to the qualities in their work that appealed to a large portion of the population.

Equally, if not more, valuable to the student of popular poetry is James Lawrence Onderdonk's *History of American Verse, 1610-1897*. Onderdonk also covers "all" of America's poetry, but his definition of the canon is much broader than that of modern literary historians. As a result, he includes most of the country's nationally popular poets and attempts to discern the peculiar "excellence" he believes they must have had in order to warrant such popularity. His opinions are an excellent guide to the sort of middle-of-the-road taste in the nineteenth century that understood the significance of Whitman and Dickinson but actually preferred the work of Bryant, Longfellow, and Whittier.

Alfred Kreymborg also treats several of America's popular poets in *A History of American Poetry: Our Singing Strength*, but his critical evaluations are all affected by the typical twentieth-century bias toward the avant-garde. As a result, he tends to dismiss as insignificant any poetry that was formally conservative. This sort of bias is not so evident in Fred

Lewis Pattee's *A History of American Literature Since 1870*, which includes sympathetic treatments of Will Carleton, Madison Cawein, James Whitcomb Riley, and Eugene Field, among others. Pattee's long discussion of Joaquim Miller is especially interesting since he considers Miller a major figure in contemporary American letters. His opinion, indeed, often seems to accord with that of the populace at large—a fact that confers a sort of "guide" status on the volume.

Another more specific historical study of use to the student of popular verse is Carlin T. Kindilien's *American Poetry in the 1890's*. Based on the Harris Collection at Brown University, Kindilien's study covers "the general state of poetry during the decade," including, as a consequence, both anthology and newspaper verse, the work of the most familiar popular poets, and that of several "lost" elite poets as well. His initial chapter on "The Literary Scene" treats poetry publication in the decade as part of an overall state of affairs or tradition, and his analysis of the "average" poetry anthology produced from within that tradition is most interesting. Kindilien treats both Joaquim Miller and Madison Cawein at some length, as representative figures of the dominant romantic tendency in the poetry of the period. His evaluations, while not uncritical, are judicious and careful in their attempt to discover those elements that made this poetry appealing to so many. Kindilien is also quite sympathetic to the work of Carleton and Riley since he is willing to accord validity and legitimacy to the tradition of rural humor in which they worked.

Although Howard Cook covers most of America's elite poets in *Our Poets of Today* (1919), he also includes many popular figures as well, such as John McCrae, Joyce Kilmer, Alan Seeger, Edgar Guest, and Ella Wheeler Wilcox. His analysis generally involves a biographical sketch, a selection of verse, and a critical assessment, which once again attempts to determine the reasons for the people's verdict.

Another historical study that covers a limited period of American poetry production is Harold S. Jantz's *The First Century of New England Verse*. This volume includes an historical and critical discussion of many unknown early poets and poems, as well as selections and an extensive bibliography. While most of the material Jantz treats was not "popular" in the sense that it was read by large numbers of people, most of the poets he treats were amateur versifiers writing for their own personal reasons and thus cannot be included in the "high-art" tradition.

Two last historical studies, while not devoted exclusively to popular poetry, can be of some use to the student of the subject. These are William Charvat's *Literary Publishing in America, 1790-1850* and *The Profession of Authorship in America, 1800-1870*. The first volume provides some interesting background material on the rise of an American publishing industry that was always concerned with the desires of its audience. Charvat extends his interest in the relationship between publisher and public in the second volume, where he specifically considers "The Popularization of Poetry" in the early nineteenth century and then attempts to measure the extent and reasons for Longfellow's popularity. Charvat here includes a discussion of Longfellow's earnings as a poet as well as sales figures for nearly all the poetry he produced in his lifetime.

American doctoral dissertations are also a good source of historical, critical, and biographical material on popular poets and poetry. In fact, there are so many that it is impossible to mention even the most significant ones here. However, all those completed before 1965 can be found in Lawrence McNamee's *Dissertations in English and American Literature*, while more recent ones are listed in the Modern Language Association yearly bibliographies. There are biographical and critical dissertations on every popular poet considered here, as well as more general historical treatments of themes, trends, and traditions.

Perhaps one of the most significant of these, because it specifically treats the subject of popular poetry as well as the problems involved in defining it, is Wilma J. Clark's "The Levels of Poetry: An Exploration of the Dichotomy Between Nineteenth-Century American Popular Poetry and Elitest Poetry." Aside from the more general theoretical issues Clark treats, she also includes critical discussions of the work of Lydia Huntley Sigourney, Ella Wheeler Wilcox, Bayard Taylor, Will Carleton, and Henry Wadsworth Longfellow. I might also mention here Delwyn L. Sneller's "Popular and Prophetic Traditions in the Poetry of John Greenleaf Whittier" because, like Clark, Sneller directly confronts the "problem" of a popular poetic tradition and the nature of its relationship to the more widely known and extensively studied elite tradition.

Recent critical analysis of American popular poetry has reflected the pervasive influence of "new criticism" and, as a result, it has been largely limited to studies of individual poets and poems. In numerous articles published in lesser-known literary journals and listed in general bibliographies, America's popular poets are treated as "minor" literary figures whose second-rate verse does not stand up under the rigorous critical procedures of textual exigesis. While such treatment has at least prevented many of these figures from disappearing into oblivion, it has not illuminated the central problem of the relationship between the popular poetic tradition and American culture at large.

In the early years of the twentieth century, however, a substantial amount of serious attention was still devoted to a discussion and analysis of the functions of popular verse. Indeed, many of these essays can still be of use to the student interested in the American popular poetic tradition. Two of the most interesting are A. C. Henderson's "The Folk Poetry of These States" and R. Z. Deats's "Poetry for the Populace," both of which attempt some sort of definition of the aims and purposes of "poetry for the people." Henderson tends to collapse the distinctions between folk and popular poetry and thus considers James Whitcomb Riley, Bret Harte, and James Russell Lowell as indigenously American folk poets. Nevertheless, his article is useful because of its willingness to consider verse appreciated by the masses as a literary tradition related to, but distinct from, the tradition of classical "art" poetry.

Deats's essay is an examination of the poetry printed in America's popular magazines in an attempt to determine the nature of America's "thought-patterns" in 1942. As a result, he focuses on the themes and moods of the poetry rather than on its verse patterns or language. His perspective on the poetry is thus much closer to that of the people who enjoy it, and he is accordingly quite sympathetic to the popular poets' attempt to keep the "spirit and flame of poetry" alive in a "prosy age."

Because so little bibliographic work has been done on American popular poetry, there is no comprehensive guide available to the interested student that lists either these early analyses of the popular verse tradition or the later interpretations of individual poems and poets. The relevant articles are listed, however, in Lewis Leary's *Articles on American Literature 1900-1950 and 1950-1967* as well as in the later MLA bibliographies. Leary is particularly useful for the early, more general articles, while the *MLA Bibliography* yields many interesting essays if one focuses on the individual author listings.

BIBLIOGRAPHY

BOOKS AND ARTICLES

Adams, Oscar F. *A Dictionary of American Authors.* 5th ed. Boston: Houghton Mifflin, 1905.

Ash, Lee. *Subject Collections: A Guide to Special Book Collections and Subject Emphases as Reported by University, College, Public and Special Libraries, and Museums in the United States and Canada.* 4th ed. New York: R. R. Bowker, 1974.

Blanck, Jacob. *Bibliography of American Literature.* New Haven: Yale University Press, 1955-.

Brooks, Van Wyck. *Makers and Finders: A History of the Writer in America, 1800-1915.* 4 vols. New York: E. P. Dutton, 1956.

Brown University Library. *Dictionary Catalogue of the Harris Collection of American Poetry and Plays.* 12 vols. Boston: G. K. Hall, 1972.

Charvat, William. *Literary Publishing in America, 1790-1850.* Philadelphia: University of Pennsylvania Press, 1959.

———. *The Profession of Authorship in America, 1800-1870.* Columbus: Ohio State University Press, 1968.

Checklist of Poetry by American Authors Published in the English Colonies of

North America and the United States Through 1865 in the Possession of the Rare Book Collection at the University of Pennsylvania. Compiled by Albert von Chorba, Jr. Philadelphia: University of Pennsylvania Press, 1951.

Cheever, George B. *The American Commonplace Book of Poetry.* Boston: Carter, Hendee, 1831.

Clark, Wilma J. "The Levels of Poetry: An Exploration of the Dichotomy Between Nineteenth-Century American Popular Poetry and Elitest Poetry." Ph.D. dissertation. Michigan State University, 1972.

Coates, Henry M. *The Fireside Encyclopedia of Poetry.* Philadelphia: Porter and Coates, 1879.

Cook, Howard. *Our Poets of Today.* New York: Moffat, 1919.

Cook, Roy J. *One Hundred and One Famous Poems.* Rev. ed. Chicago: Cable, 1929.

Deats, R. Z. "Poetry for the Populace." *Sewanee Review,* 50 (July 1942), 374-88.

Duyckinck, Evert, and George Duyckinck. *The Cyclopaedia of American Literature.* New York: Charles Scribner's Sons, 1856.

Early American Poetry, 1610-1820, a List of Works in the New York Public Library. Compiled by J. G. Frank. New York: New York Public Library, 1917.

Felleman, Hazel. *The Best Loved Poems of the American People.* New York: Garden City Publishing, 1936.

Ghougassin, Joseph P. *Kahlil Gibran: Wings of Thought, the People's Philosopher.* New York: Philosophical Library, 1973.

Griswold, Rufus Wilmot. *The Poets and Poetry of America.* New York: James Miller Publisher, 1872.

Hackett, Alice Payne. *Fifty Years of Best Sellers, 1895-1945.* New York: R. R. Bowker, 1945.

Hart, James. *The Popular Book.* Berkeley: University of California Press, 1961.

———. *The Oxford Companion to American Literature.* 4th ed. New York: Oxford University Press, 1965.

Henderson, A. C. "The Folk Poetry of These States." *Poetry,* 16 (August 1920), 264-73.

Howes, Royce. *Edgar Guest: A Biography.* Chicago: Reilly and Lee, 1953.

Jantz, Harold. *The First Century of New England Verse.* Worcester, Mass: American Antiquarian Society, 1962.

Kindilien, Carlin T. *American Poetry in the 1890's.* Providence, R.I.: Brown University Press, 1956.

Kreymborg, Alfred. *A History of American Poetry: Our Singing Strength.* New York: Tudor, 1934.

Kunitz, Stanley, and Howard Haycraft. *American Authors, 1600-1900.* New York: H. W. Wilson, 1938.

Leary, Lewis. *Articles on American Literature, 1900-1950,* and *1950-1967.* Durham, N.C.: Duke University Press, 1954, 1970.

Lemay, Leo. *A Calendar of American Poetry in the Colonial Newspapers and Magazines.* Worcester, Mass.: American Antiquarian Society, 1972.

Literary Writings in America: A Bibliography. WPA Project at the University of Pennsylvania. Millwood, N.Y.: Kto Press, 1977.

McAlpine, Frank. *Our Album of Authors: A Cyclopedia of Popular Literary People.* Philadelphia: Elliot and Beezley, 1886.

McNamee, Lawrence. *Dissertations in English and American Literature, 1865-1964.* New York: R. R. Bowker, 1968.

Matthews, Brander. *American Familiar Verse.* New York: Longmans, Green, 1904.

MLA International Bibliography of Books and Articles on the Modern Languages and Literatures. New York: Modern Language Association of America, 1922-.

Mott, Frank Luther. *Golden Multitudes.* New York: Macmillan, 1947.

Nye, Russel B. *The Unembarrassed Muse: The Popular Arts in America.* New York: Dial Press, 1970.

Onderdonk, James Lawrence. *History of American Verse, 1610-1897.* Chicago: A. C. McClurg, 1901.

Pattee, Fred Lewis. *A History of American Literature Since 1870.* New York: Century, 1921.

Scheick, Willam J., and Jo Ella Doggett. *Seventeenth-Century American Poetry: A Reference Guide.* Boston: G. K. Hall, 1977.

Shaw, John Mackay. *Childhood in Poetry: A Catalogue of the Books of English and American Poets in the Library of the Florida State University.* Tallahassee: Robert M. Strozier Library, Florida State University, 1967.

Sneller, Delwyn. "Popular and Prophetic Traditions in the Poetry of John Greenleaf Whittier." Ph.D. dissertation, Michigan State University, 1972.

Stevenson, Burton. *The Home Book of Verse, American and English, 1580-1920.* 6th ed. New York: Henry Holt, 1930.

Stoddard, Roger. *A Catalogue of Books and Pamphlets Unrecorded in Oscar Wegelin's "Early American Poetry."* Providence, R.I.: Friends of the Library of Brown University, 1969.

Thompson, Slason. *The Humbler Poets: A Collection of Newspaper and Periodical Verse.* Chicago: Jansen, McClurg, 1886.

Wegelin, Oscar. *Early American Poetry: A Compilation of the Titles and Volumes of Verse and Broadsides by Writers Born or Residing in North America.* New York: P. Smith, 1930.

CHAPTER 15. Women in Popular Culture

Katherine Fishburn

Because of its emphasis on content or authorship rather than form, the study of women in popular culture presents problems different from the generic-based studies. Choosing an entire sex to research means that there is more material available to examine since all popular culture in some fashion portrays women (even that which omits them lends itself to a discussion of the reasons for their absence). It also means that this material, though plentiful, is less obviously accessible because many authors do not index women's subjects. Although there are currently several resources specifically aimed at the question of women in popular culture, the majority are general studies of period and/or genre which include, as part of a larger focus, the role of women as readers, authors, or characters. In this essay, I have tried to maintain a balance between offering too much material, which would duplicate work already done in the other essays in this series, and offering too little, which would make this essay less than thorough at best. To maintain the balance, I have tried to include those works both primarily and incidentally concerned with women in popular culture, with an emphasis on the former.

HISTORIC OUTLINE

Rather than attempt a working definition of each form documented, it seems more appropriate to describe, in brief, the role of women in popular culture. From the beginning, women have appeared in American popular culture in one way or another. At times, as readers, they seemed to be, in fact, its prime movers. They certainly have been among the major producers and purchasers of some of its most famous and profitable products. Not only did women demand and devour the early sentimental romances, but they also wrote most of them—and appeared in the "starring roles" with discouraging consistency. While these "scribbling women," as Hawthorne bitterly labelled them, were engaged in popular fiction, others were filling private journals with copious observations about colonial and Jacksonian era home life. With the invention of speedier and more efficient printing presses in the late 1800s, the ladies' magazines came into their own as one of the most potent social forces of the nineteenth century. They, in turn, have been replaced by the equally seductive women's magazines of the twentieth century. Nor has the female role been a minor one in the history of the movies. From the silent film to the seventies, the image of women in film—either by her presence or, more recently, by her absence—has been a clue to the American way of life.

Since her appearance on these shores as a "lady," the American woman has been intimately involved with popular culture: as its source, sustenance, and subject. She can be described, without exaggeration, therefore, as the true mother of American popular culture. This is not to say, however, that the only image of women in American popular culture is that of the mother. Nor is it contained in the virgin-whore dichotomy. Rather, the image of the American female is as complex as her culture, appearing in various guises at different times.

In our very earliest popular culture, for example, in the Indian captivity stories, the conflict of good versus evil took center stage, with the grace of God overshadowing any human heroes or heroines. Believing that the Indian was the devil's disciple, the American colonists interpreted capture by the savages from a religious perspective, seeing the captivity itself as an opportunity for God to test their faith. The most popular of these tales was one by Mrs. Mary Rowlandson, which appeared in no fewer than thirty-one editions. It carried the descriptive, but cumbersome, title *The Sovereignty and Goodness of God . . . , Being a Narrative of the Captivity and Restoration of Mrs. Mary Rowlandson* (2d edition, 1682). Although its protagonist is a woman, its subject is religion. In time this would change, as the Indian captivity tales, in conjunction with the British novel of sensibility and the American accounts of witchcraft, were to provide the basis for our heavily formulaic and indisputably female fiction of the next two hundred years.

Perhaps the most stunningly successful of these forms was the sentimental tearjerker, best exemplified in Susanna Haswell Rowson's *Charlotte Temple: A Tale of Truth* (1791). A Britisher by birth, Susanna Haswell visited the colonies with her parents before moving here permanently with her husband William Rowson in 1797. As so frequently occurs in the strange history of women in American popular culture, the very women whose writings encourage mindless passivity in females have themselves been highly businesslike professionals. Not only was Rowson a notable author, but she also founded a girls' school in Boston and participated in numerous business and intellectual ventures.

Her heroine, Charlotte Temple, seems to be Rowson's negative print. Taking her cue from and riding the crest of Samuel Richardson's international popularity, Mrs. Rowson constructed a sentimental tale of seduction that became an archetype in its own right. Calling her novel "A Tale of Truth," she sought to disarm those critics who still considered fiction immoral. (In fact, *Charlotte Temple* is apparently based on events in Rowson's own family.) Through her heavy-handed didacticism, she used her story to convince readers that the wages of sin is death. Charlotte's "sin" is that of losing her virginity—a fall that would provide the plots of many forms of American popular culture in the years to come. Her punishment for her moment of foolish weakness is to die while giving birth to a daughter. Like other writers who followed her, Rowson makes it clear that any marriage at all is to be preferred to this ignominious ending. With this stand, she clearly deviated from Richardson's conclusion to *Clarissa* (1748), in which the death of the unmarried heroine is a kind of existential victory. In *Charlotte Temple*, Rowson also planted the seeds of the feminine mystique, whose influence American women are still struggling to overcome. For Charlotte, unlike her creator, is fate's plaything, the perfect victim who is unable to distinguish between true and false love.

The descendants of Charlotte Temple are alive and well and appearing in the immensely popular gothic and Harlequin romances, which sell in such large numbers that they have their own sections in many bookstores. The image of women in these escape fantasies, as in other popular genres such as detective and science fiction, is less than positive. With the exception of works like Ursula LeGuin's *The Left Hand of Darkness*, which skirts the issue through androgyny, popular fiction continues the tradition of portraying women as helpless, mindless creatures. If they are major characters in the romances, they are but booty to be won, princesses to be rescued, or companions to be tolerated in science fiction. Other roles for women are as monster robots and black widow spiders. Even such "feminist" best sellers as Alix Kates Shulman's *The Memoirs of an Ex-Prom Queen* seem to be nothing more than "sexploitation" told from a woman's point of view rather than from a man's. The contents of today's women's magazines reflect a similar transformation from muted to frank sexuality in their portrayal of women.

As early as 1709, when Richard Steele founded *The Tatler* and included a column intended for women, magazines have been alert to the needs and buying power of their female readers. In 1787, when Noah Webster founded *The American Magazine* in New York, he too had the interest of the ladies at heart, promising in his first issue that his *"fair readers* may be assured that no inconsiderable pains will be taken to furnish them entertainment." Toward this end, he published gothic and sentimental fiction and began the "how-to" columns that would later provide the substance of the specialty magazines of the twentieth century. In 1821, *The Saturday Evening Post* tried to attract women through its department called "The Ladies' Friend," which featured poetry and articles appropriate for the gentle sex. The purpose of these early magazines, as ostensibly was that of early novels, was instruction. Because of their popularity and because there were no public libraries where hungry readers might turn for more substantial fare, the influence of these publications was immense. The opportunity for female "education" contained in these isolated departments of the general magazines was nothing, however, compared to the power generated by the "ladies' magazines" themselves. Their history is at the heart of the development of American advertising: at the core of the mass marketing of mores, tastes, fashion, food, and literature that has transformed the face of America and that of the American woman in the past one hundred fifty years.

The *Ladies' Magazine*, established in 1828 in Boston by Mrs. Sarah Josepha Hale, was to become the foundation for the multibillion-dollar business of selling American housewives a bill of goods. Although the genesis of these ladies' magazines initially gave housewives a certain stature and pride in their work, their ultimate effect has been to glorify what many consider to be second-class citizenship. (One of the most powerful of the early editors, Edward Bok, discouraged women from entering business because there they would "lose their gentleness and womanliness.") Like the motion pictures that were to follow eighty years later, the magazines both recognized and codified the status of women in the United States. One of the most popular of these proselytizers was the brainchild of Louis Antoine Godey. *Godey's Lady's Book* was the hybrid born of the merger between Godey's own *Lady's Book* (founded in Philadelphia in 1830) and Sarah Hale's *Ladies' Magazine* (which he bought out in 1837). Sarah Hale was the editor from 1837 to 1877, during which time she increased circulation, encouraged female contributors to sign their names (rather than using just their initials or the anonymous "A Lady"), and, in general, left her mark on the magazine and on magazine history. Her editorial policy was to promote women's education, but to ignore politics. She featured recipes, health and beauty aids, embroidery patterns, and "embellishments"—the latter were those ornate illustrations and hand-painted fashion plates for which *Godey's* was justifiably famous. In short, Sarah Josepha Hale designed the archetypal magazine for women.

When *Godey's* folded in 1898, it simply left more room for its imitators and competitors, such as Cyris H. K. Curtis's *Ladies' Home Journal*. (It was founded in 1883 as *Ladies' Journal and Practical Housekeeper*, but it appeared, from its ambiguously laid out masthead, to be entitled the *Ladies' Home Journal.*) As Godey's most astute move had been to hire Sarah Hale, so Curtis's was to hire Edward Bok, who took over as editor in 1889. And, in his turn, Edward Bok was to leave his mark permanently on the ladies' magazines. Setting out, in his own words, to "uplift" and "inspire" his readers, he made it a point to establish an intimate relationship with them. To do this, he wrote one advice column as "Ruth Ashmore" called "Side Talk to Girls" and, in a bold new move, another under his own name called "At Home with the Editor." In his zeal to reform America, he supported several causes, some more successfully than others; among them were campaigns against patent medicines, Paris fashions, aigrettes, and venereal disease—this last was a daring stand that cost him thousands of subscribers. Historically, perhaps his most significant contribution to the magazine trade was his decision in 1897 to widen the domestic coverage of the *Journal* by including architectural plans in the magazine; this feature was followed by photographs of the interiors of homes, which were categorized according to whether or not they were in good taste.

Although *Godey's* and the *Journal* were the "big two" of the early ladies' magazines, several others were being published concurrently. The fashion magazines, which had begun primarily as pattern catalogs, were represented by *The Delineator* (1873-1937), *Harper's Bazar* (1867, becoming *Harper's Bazaar* in 1929), and *Vogue* (1892). Other magazines modeled on the *Journal* were *McCall's* (1870), *Woman's Home Companion* (1873) and *Good Housekeeping* (1885). Although each magazine tried to promote its individuality through various gimmicks (the *Journal's* resilient slogan "Never Underestimate the Power of a Woman"; *McCall's* abortive "togetherness" campaign; the influential *Good Housekeeping* seal of approval), all directed their material exclusively to women—in particular, the mother who stayed at home.

Their formulas were magical until World War II. With the increasing availability of other diversionary and "instructive" media (such as television, radio, newspapers with colored supplements, cheap paperbacks, and movies), with a market glutted by virtually indistinguishable journals, and with the need for women to work because their men were at war, women's magazines began to decline. Their recent resurgence, along with such specialized publications as *Seventeen* (1944), is no doubt a result of their willingness to revamp their appearance. By modernizing their formats and raising their level of sexual tolerance, they have managed to hold their own in a competitive market.

Ironically, these current "ladies' magazines" are sometimes nearly indistinguishable not so much from each other as from their male counterparts, such as Hugh Hefner's *Playboy* (1953). Although their photography, fiction, and cartoons are not yet as graphic sexually as that of the men's magazines, they are certainly fully as suggestive. This state inevitably leads one to the conclusion that today's liberated housewife and/or career woman is just as susceptible to sexuality as her ancestors were to sentimentality. Perhaps the most interesting feature of their metamorphosis is that, except for the maverick *Viva* (1973) and the occasional *Cosmopolitan* (1886) centerfold, the fascination in both men's and women's magazines is with the female figure. In this, the modern glossies and their venerable ancestors share a common conviction that it is the images of women that sell magazines.

With the advent of the movies in the twentieth century, a new medium took over the task of determining American femininity. From Mary Pickford to Raquel Welch, and all the transformations in between, the movie actress has both reflected and projected an image of American womanhood: showing women what they are and, more importantly, what they can become. One of the trade secrets of the moneymakers in Hollywood has been an uncanny ability to depict and define the American taste in women: its virgins and viragos, its fantasies and nightmares. If the movies are not responsible for the American male's obsession with the breast, they at least brought the fascination to light, not incidentally making profits in direct proportion to bra size. Even before the days of Marilyn Monroe, the movies made "it"—the original version of "sex appeal"—a household word by promoting Clara Bow's role in *It* (1927). On the other hand, when necessary, the movies could even help the American war effort by portraying women not as sex objects but as Rosie the riveter in such movies as *Swing Shift Maisie* (1943) and *Since You Went Away* (1944).

It is no coincidence that the first big star of the silent era was the childlike Mary Pickford, who, with her innocent curls, epitomized the ideal of virtuous Victorian womanhood. Known to her fans as "The Girl with the Curl," Pickford made this image her hallmark until she was incapable of escaping its obvious limitations. Incredibly, like some sort of female Dorian Grey, as she matured off screen, she seemed to be changeless onscreen: playing a young child in *A Poor Little Rich Girl* in 1917 when she was twenty-four, and a twelve-year-old in *Little Annie Rooney* when she was thirty-two. Ironically, as so often happens with female pop-culture figures, these cinematic images of her as a girlish ragamuffin belied her real-life power and womanliness. Although she clung to her successful formula well into her thirties, she had the grace and good sense to retire at forty, after alienating her fans by trying to change her image to keep up with the Roaring Twenties.

If Mary Pickford was a genius at ruling the hearts of the American people by her ingenuous on-screen antics, David Wark Griffith was the

man behind the throne. Personally enamoured of the girl-children he promoted, he single-handedly brought more of them to the screen than anyone else in this period. Among his other stars were Lillian and Dorothy
Gish (sixteen and fourteen) and Mae Marsh (seventeen). Typical of his
productions and moral proclivities is the infamous *The Birth of a Nation*
(1915), in which Elsie Stoneman (Lillian Gish), white and pure, is
threatened with rape by a black man. Her little sister (Mae Marsh),
similarly threatened, throws herself off a cliff to her death. Griffith's classic
scene, however, is in *Way Down East* (1920), where a young woman
(Lillian Gish), having been deceived and seduced, is sent out mercilessly
by her unforgiving father into a winter storm.

Complementing Griffith's rather unbelievable vestal virgins was Theda
Bara's equally unbelievable voracious vamp. Rather than expressing purity, Bara exuded a crude Victorian sex appeal that was so extreme as to
be rendered harmless. With her exotic makeup and costumes, her arrival
on the screen (*A Fool There Was*, 1915), signaled a period of sexual
freedom in film not to be rivaled again until recently. The cinematic sex
she created was symptomatic of the changing social mores and the increasing freedom of the American woman. Drawn out of the home by
the war, middle-class women began to assume responsibilities unheard of
in their ranks since colonial times. Accompanying their vocational reha-
bilitation and emancipation was a new interest in more sophisticated
movies. At the top of the list were Cecil B. De Mille's creations, such as
the splashily successful and shockingly open (for the times) film about
marital infidelity, *Old Wives for New* (1918).

All this innocent easy sexuality was brought to a grinding halt in the
early 1930s by the implementation of the Production Code—the film industry's self-imposed censorship that severely limited the roles allowed
women. It certainly spelled the doom of one of the screen's greatest originals, the self-sufficient and outrageously funny Mae West, who was unable to survive a climate inimical to her brand of sexuality. After the
complexities and mysteries of the almost-androgynous Greta Garbo and
Marlene Dietrich and the tough sexuality of Jean Harlow—all of whom
were sex stars of pre-Code days—audiences were forced to content themselves with the more wholesome images of Katharine Hepburn, Jean
Arthur, and the young Shirley Temple. The women in the comedies of
the 1930s were no longer sensual; they were clever and witty companions
to their men or feisty competitors engaged in the battle of the sexes.
During this period many of the most successful screenwriters were themselves women; two of the major ones were the recently rediscovered Anita
Loos and Frances Marion.

After the war ended, and the need for women factory workers and
escape fantasies waned, the movies returned once more to the tried and

true formula of women's sexuality in the unmistakable form of Marilyn Monroe and her many mammary imitators, such as Jayne Mansfield and Kim Novak. The reign of these sex goddesses was stormy but brief, confined primarily to the 1950s and early 1960s. Although the Production Code has been gradually circumvented in the industry's double-edged attempt to keep afloat financially and encourage artistic freedom, the latest images of women are less than attractive. The new freedom has brought with it a new fear of women's sexuality, it would seem, as directors such as Sam Peckinpah continue to depict women's sex drives as rape fantasies.

If the movies that included women in their scripts in the 1960s and early 1970s were almost paranoid about female sexuality, they were matched film by film by stories in which women played minor roles at best. These "macho" films, such as *Easy Rider* (1969), *Butch Cassidy and the Sundance Kid* (1970), and *Midnight Cowboy* (1969), seem to suggest a disturbing lack of interest in women that is reflected in television programming of this period. Although several movies have appeared in the last year that would suggest a return of major roles for women (*The Turning Point, An Unmarried Woman, Julia*), it remains to be seen whether this will be a passing fancy or an important shift in cinematic values. The future of women directors is also uncertain as Claudia Weill, Joan Tewkesbury, and Jane Wagner begin to break into the male bastions of the feature film. Whether or not these women will be the Dorothy Arzners of the 1970s and 1980s should become apparent shortly as their works gain public attention.

REFERENCE WORKS

In recent years, a number of bibliographies on women have been compiled. Although collectively they contain a wealth of information, individually each is limited in some fashion. A corollary problem is the fact that many strive for a general and even an international appeal; as a result, researchers in the topic of women in American popular culture must sift through a great deal of data to find appropriate entries.

One of the most comprehensive bibliographies of recent material is Albert Krichmar's *The Women's Movement in the Seventies: An International English-Language Bibliography*. The entries are annotated (with a few exceptions), accurate, and arranged alphabetically according to subject headings—and, quite helpfully, by country. The most pertinent heading is "North America—U.S.: Cultural and Literary Studies" (pp. 271-88), which contains nearly two hundred items; included in this section are books, articles, and dissertations completed in the 1970s on women in literature, film, music, art, education, and other related fields. Several historical periods are also represented.

A more specialized and much briefer bibliography is entitled "Popular Culture," appearing in Barbara Friedman et al., *Women's Work and Women's Studies/1973-1974, A Bibliography*. Again, this work is limited to studies published only very recently. Intended primarily as a working list, it also contains information on work in progress as of 1974. Only occasionally annotated, the seventy entries are helpful mainly because the editors have restricted themselves to the topic of women in popular culture. Other sections of the book of some interest are "History," "Literary Criticism," and "Bibliographies and Resources." The book includes an appendix of bibliographical sources and an index of authors.

Another source that is limited to current work is Carol F. Myers's *Women in Literature: Criticism of the Seventies*, which catalogs material appearing in print from January 1970 to Spring 1976. International in scope, it is alphabetized in part one according to topics; part two is a general bibliography. The critics and editors are indexed.

A more sweeping work is Albert Krichmar's *The Women's Rights Movement in the United States, 1848-1970, A Bibliography and Sourcebook*. The bibliography itself contains 5,170 entries; a separate section on manuscript sources contains 402 entries. These latter sources are arranged by state and indexed by content. Although the bibliography is not annotated, it is organized by subjects and indexed by both author and subject. Relevant headings include: "General," "Economic Status," "Education," "Religion," and "Biography." Included also is a list of women's-liberation serials.

Another resource is Helen Wheeler's *Womanhood Media: Current Resources About Women*, which contains 318 annotated entries with categories and subcategories such as "The Arts," "Literature and Rhetoric," and "Fiction." Wheeler also includes titles of pamphlets, movement periodicals, and special issues on the woman. (For instructors interested in establishing a feminist curriculum, she also includes what she calls "a basic book collection," pp. 105-96, of nonsexist writings.) Three years after the appearance of this work, Wheeler published *Womanhood Media Supplement: Additional Current Resources About Women*, which, as she says in the preface, will be her last attempt to keep up with the burgeoning field of women's studies.

A highly specialized work is *The Black Family and the Black Woman: A Bibliography*, which was prepared by the library staff and the Afro-American Studies Department of Indiana University. The material documented is held by the university; it includes lists of primary material written by black women ("Anthologies with Black Women as Editors,"

"Other Anthologies with Writings by Black Women," "Works by Individual Authors") and a section of "Bio/Criticism." A companion work in this field would be Lenwood G. Davis's *The Black Woman in American Society: A Selected Annotated Bibliography*, which contains 562 annotated entries of books and articles on the American black woman. There is also a helpful list of U.S. libraries with major black history collections. The book is indexed by subject and author.

Ora Williams has also published "A Bibliography of Works Written by American Black Women," which is divided into several useful categories such as "Bibliographies and Guides to Collections," "Novels," "Short Stories," and so on. George P. Rawick's *From Sundown to Sunup: The Making of the Black Community* contains a bibliography of slave narratives, including those written by women; Rawick also lists his secondary sources. Russell C. Brignano's *Black Americans in Autobiography* is an annotated compendium of autobiographies and autobiographical books written since the Civil War, arranged alphabetically by author; the titles are indexed, and the book contains a list of locations and institutions for cross-reference.

Another specialized bibliography is Dawn Lander Gherman's "Frontier and Wilderness: American Women Authors," which is a working, annotated checklist of American prose literature by and about women in the American wilderness. One of its strongest features is the documentation of material on red, black, and white American women. This checklist includes: both primary and secondary sources, a list of bibliographies consulted, and brief discussions on captivity narratives, secondary sources, and fiction, which should be useful for those just beginning to research the field of wilderness literature.

In 1975, Jayne Loader compiled "Women in the Left, 1906-1941, A Bibliography of Primary Sources," which is indexed and prefaced by a table of contents. The entries are annotated and accompanied by a series of commentaries about the problems a bibliographer encounters in this area. In the same year, the Michigan Department of State published a "Bibliography of Sources Relating to Women" as part of its bicentennial observation; this pamphlet contains information about unpublished sources for women's studies that are held in various Michigan institutions.

A recent publication that recognizes the topic of women in popular culture (which the Modern Language Association does not) is *Abstracts of Popular Culture*, whose most relevant index headings are "Women: American" and "Women's: History." The material is abstracted from periodicals. *Women Studies Abstracts* is a quarterly magazine that covers a wide range of periodicals and books; appropriate topics are "History" and "Literature and Art." Each volume is accompanied by a cumulative index. The annotations are thorough, but, so far, each issue only highlights a handful of articles on this subject. *The Standard Periodical Directory* indexes women's periodicals under "Women's Liberation" and "Women's: Fashions." *Ulrich's International Periodicals Directory* indexes "Women's Interests"; especially helpful in an uncertain field is the section on cessations, since it gives the publishing history of defunct periodicals. The Library of Congress *New Serials Titles*, of course, can be useful for tracking down the libraries that have holdings of some of the more obscure journals in women's studies. The subject catalogs of most libraries will list their holdings of women's journals under a heading such as "Women: Periodicals."

The following resources provide information on individual women. *Notable American Women, 1607-1950: A Biographical Dictionary* contains brief biographies of women who were born after 1607 and who died before 1950 (with only five exceptions). This is a mammoth scholarly work of 1,337 articles (twenty-two of which include two or more figures), which also contains a brief historical survey of America and its women written by Janet Wilson James. Frances E. Willard and Mary A. Livermore's *American Women: Fifteen Hundred Biographies with over 1,400 Portraits* is a comprehensive encyclopedia of nineteenth-century women, arranged alphabetically, and indexed by professional contributions. An earlier version of this work, entitled *A Woman of the Century*, is available in a facsimile reprint of the 1893 edition.

Information on living authors appears in the latest edition of *Who's Who of American Women: A Biographical Dictionary of Notable Living American Women, 1977-1978*. Tamar Berkowitz's *Who's Who and Where in Women's Studies* is an educational directory that lists the names of women's-studies instructors and their courses. It is not annotated. In 1973, the Sense and Sensibility Collective published *Women and Literature: An Annotated Bibliography of Women Writers*, a revised and expanded version of one that first appeared in Susan Cornillon's *Images of Women In Fiction*. All the authors included write fiction and most are contemporary. Except for occasional brief biographies, the entries are composed almost exclusively of lists of books these authors have written; each novel is annotated. *Women and Literature* is arranged alphabetically by author and contains a fairly comprehensive subject index. (Other checklists can be found in the discussion of the several popular culture genres that follows.)

Although a start has been made, there is still much work to be done in women's bibliographies, as Patricia K. Ballou observes in her review essay, "Bibliographies for Research on Women." In this article, Ballou surveys a wide variety but, confined by her subject, a small number of checklists. Her topics range from the general to history and literature. She also mentions several bibliographies in the social sciences that she has categorized by specific discipline. A less successful attempt to gather bibliographies is Margrit Eichler's *An Annotated Selected Bibliography of Bibliographies on Women*. It is very brief and covers mostly those lists that would be of interest to students of feminism or politics rather than students of popular culture. The standard resource in this area, the *Bibliographic Index*, catalogs published bibliographies under "Women: Fiction," "Women: History," and "Women: United States."

For lists of periodicals that have dedicated entire issues to women, there are several reasonably complete sources for recent years. In its own way, Susan Cardinale's *Special Issues of Serials About Women, 1965-1975* is quite thorough, but it excludes all women's periodicals per se. It is annotated and arranged alphabetically by serial title. See also: *Womanhood Media* by Helen Wheeler and *Women Studies Abstracts* (discussed above) and the section below on women's periodicals and special issues for more information on this topic.

RESEARCH COLLECTIONS

As women contribute to all forms of popular culture, either as its authors or as its subjects, any major collection of primary resources would certainly include some material relevant to them. But because the serious study of women per se is a fairly recent activity, many of the available collections remain hidden. Exceptions to this situation are the letters and diaries of early American women, which are cataloged by several major research libraries. The New York Public Library and the Houghton Library of Harvard University, for example, house the correspondence of Mary Louise Booth, Lydia Maria Child, and Elizabeth Palmer Peabody. In its extensive archives, the Schlesinger Library of Radcliffe College houses the papers of Antoinette Brown Blackwell, Caroline Wells Healey Dall, and Elizabeth Cady Stanton and the Lydia Maria Child correspondence. It also contains documents on medicine, law, and the women's liberation movement. Founded in 1943, the library holds more than thirteen thousand volumes, in addition to its collection of journals and newsletters. The Sophia Smith Collection in the William Allan Neilson Library of Smith College contains over one million manuscript pieces on the social and intellectual history of women, with an emphasis on Americans. Its subjects include: Lucretia Mott, Lucy Stone, and Sojourner Truth. The 1971 *Catalog of the Sophia Smith Collection*, produced by the Smith College Library, describes the collection's major primary and secondary sources. The Boston Public Library's Galatea Collection, founded by Thomas Wentworth Higginson, features material on women in history and the suffragette movement.

The letters of Mrs. E. D. E. N. Southworth are held by Duke University Library. The Louisa May Alcott manuscripts are in the Harvard University Library. The American Woman's Collection of the Connecticut College Library contains miscellaneous information on such women as Frances Perkins and Lydia H. Sigourney; most of the material remains uncataloged. The University of North Carolina at Greensboro houses a special collection on women from the sixteenth century to the twentieth in its Walter Clinton Jackson Library; included are works on physical education, sociology, and women's suffrage.

Pine Manor Junior College in Chestnut Hill, Massachusetts, lists 298 volumes of first editions of distinguished women writers from 1833 to 1932. The Hamilton Library of Elmira College, in Elmira, New York, holds a one-hundred-volume collection of Genteel Women's Reading from 1855 to 1955. The books and manuscripts of Edna Ferber are held by the University of Wisconsin Library at Madison. The Russel B. Nye Popular Culture Collection of the Michigan State University Library houses about six hundred books in girls' detective fiction, such as Nancy Drew, the Bobbsey Twins, and Cherry Ames. This collection also contains a substantial holding of Harlequin romances (two thousand) and small samples of other romances and gothic novels; related romance and confession magazines number about one thousand. Both the Brooklyn Public Library and the Drexel Institute of Technology library have collections on clothing, dress, and fashions in women's history.

A few collections on black American women have been established. Some of these are the Afro-American Woman's Collection in the Bennett College Library, mentioned above; founded in 1946, this collection contains information from the eighteenth to the twentieth centuries. The Schlesinger Library, also mentioned above, houses the Charlotte Hawkins Brown Papers. The Library of Congress has the Mary Church Terrell Papers and the Booker T. Washington Papers, the latter making references to Mary Margaret Washington. For reference books and articles describing the holdings on black women, see Ora Williams's "A Bibliography of Works Written by American Black Women."

Other topical collections that contain contributions by women are the Ayer Collection at Chicago's Newberry Library, which is one of the most extensive collections of Indian captivity tales in the country. (Others are held by the New York Historical Society and the New York State Library.) New York University's Division of Special Collections houses the one-thousand-volume Edward G. Levy Collection of Dime Novels.

The Alverna College Research Center on Women (Milwaukee, Wisconsin) maintains files on sex stereotyping, images of women, and examples of sexism in the media; also available are bibliographies and seminar reports on the status of women. The Women's History Research Center, Inc. (Berkeley, California) manages the International Women's

History Archive and a Topical Research Library. In cooperation with Bell & Howell, it publishes *Herstory*, a collection of microfilm volumes of contemporary women's journals and newsletters. The center also publishes directories of women's periodicals and films. The Woman's Educational Equity Communications Network (Bethesda, Maryland) is developing a repository of materials devoted to women in education, including papers on women in literature such as those presented at Modern Language Association conferences.

The Library of Congress, of course, contains invaluable resources on and by women. Lee Ash's *Subject Collections* indexes several topics relating to women and can be useful in locating major collections of material on women. Unfortunately, it does not index popular culture as a category. *Research Guide in Women's Studies* by Naomi B. Lynn et al. lists a few collections. In *Women's Movement Media: A Source Guide*, Cynthia Ellen Harrison includes a thoroughly annotated listing of libraries and their holdings on women; she even includes addresses and telephone numbers.

HISTORY AND CRITICISM

GENERAL

Although a number of scholars are currently working on exciting projects in women's popular culture, there is, to date, only one full-length study available on the subject. Kathryn Weibel's *Mirror, Mirror: Images of Women Reflected in Popular Culture* is a well-written historical survey of the standard images of women in various media: fiction, television, film, fashion and women's magazines, and magazine advertising. As a general introduction, this book is particularly helpful because Weibel documents her extensive knowledge of the subject with evaluative bibliographical footnotes. By including full chapters on television and fashion, she makes accessible material heretofore found primarily in specialized journals. That she acknowledges the study of advertising is also significant, since this, too, is an area that needs further attention. *Mirror, Mirror* is thoroughly indexed and is an important contribution to a field of study whose parameters are still being defined.

Other important books that provide historical backgrounds are: Jean E. Friedman and William G. Shade's *Our American Sisters: Women in American Life and Thought*; Barbara Welter's *Dimity Convictions: The American Woman in the Nineteenth Century*; Ann Douglas's *The Feminization of American Culture*; Nancy F. Cott's *The Bonds of Womanhood: "Woman's Sphere" in New England, 1780-1835*; and Susan Phinney Conrad's *Perish the Thought: Intellectual Women in Romantic America, 1830-1860*. Friedman and Shade's book is an interdisciplinary collection of twenty-four essays reprinted from various learned journals. The book is organized into four historical periods (colonial, Victorian, progressive, and modern); each is prefaced by an introductory essay written by the editors and includes suggestions for further reading. The selections represent thoroughly documented historical research both on black and on white women. Barbara Welter's *Dimity Convictions* is also a collection of essays, most of which have appeared elsewhere. Because these essays were intended for separate publication, they are somewhat repetitious in a single book. However, Welter is a good writer and an excellent scholar who has contributed significantly to the rediscovery of women's history. The book's structural weakness, therefore, is more than compensated for by her ideas. Here is a useful sourcebook for sociological, historical, and medical information. Two of her important essays are reprinted there: "The Cult of True Womanhood, 1800-1860" and "Anti-Intellectualism and the American Woman."

Ann Douglas's *The Feminization of American Culture* is a brilliant investigation into the intimate relationship between the contemporaneous disestablishment of the American clergy and the American woman. Carefully argued and painstakingly documented, this fascinating book offers a wealth of bibliographical and biographical detail and is a must for scholars pursuing an understanding of nineteenth- and twentieth-century America.

To Nancy Cott, the phrase "the bonds of womanhood" has a double meaning; her thesis is that the very distinction that separated women from men also brought women together as a powerful political group. In her book, which is based on sermons, magazine articles, secondary sources, and the unpublished letters and diaries of one hundred women, she traces this development in American culture, illustrating the effects of economic progress and religion on its women. In her opinion, the domestic fiction of the late eighteenth century and early nineteenth century was popular because it reassured those women who, for lack of an alternative vision, were forced to believe in the myth of the sanctity of home and hearth. Cott's book is indexed and mentions the locations of the manuscripts she cites. In *Perish the Thought*, Susan Conrad examines the women intellectuals' interpretation of the nineteenth-century feminine ideal and how they tried to transform it as a result of their contact with romanticism. The book is indexed and offers a selected bibliography of primary and secondary sources.

Three other books provide historical information on different subcultures, the American South, and blacks. Anne Firor Scott's *The Southern Lady: From Pedestal to Politics 1830-1930* is useful as a portrait of what the upper-class southern white woman was like and what she became as a result of the Civil War. She, too, quotes from diaries, letters, magazines, and unpublished manuscripts and spends some time on popular literature and its authors. Scott's footnotes are informative, and she includes a supplemental bibliographical essay. Gerda Lerner's impressive collection of papers, *Black Women in White America*, documents the history of black women from the early nineteenth century to the present. Her materials range from diaries to newspaper articles and court transcripts. Two valuable essays supplement the text: a discussion of the location of her primary sources and a series of bibliographical notes containing information on secondary sources. In *Black Rage*, William H. Grier and Price M. Cobbs describe the pernicious effects of slavery on black women (see their chapter, "Achieving Womanhood," in particular).

In various ways, the following books supplement the above information on American women: Janice Delaney, Mary Jane Lupton, and Emily Toth's *The Curse: A Cultural History of Menstruation*; Germaine Greer's *The Female Eunuch*; Ashley Montagu's *The Natural Superiority of Women*; Robert J. Lifton, ed., *The Woman in America* (a symposium that originally appeared as a special issue of *Daedalus*, which contains the well-known essay by Erik H. Erikson, "Inner and Outer Space: Reflections of Womanhood"); Phyllis Chesler's *Women and Madness*; and Adrienne Richs's *Of Woman Born: Motherhood as Experience and Institution*. H. R. Hays's *The Dangerous Sex: The Myth of Feminine Evil* is an historical account of men's negative attitudes toward women, which draws on literary and anthropological examples. Betty Friedan's *The Feminine Mystique* explores the origins and consequences of the American mystification of its women. In her investigation, she discusses the role of the mass media in promulgating the myth of the happy housewife. Vivian Gornick and Barbara K. Moran's *Woman in Sexist Society* is an anthology of twenty-nine articles on social, political, and literary issues. Because of its range, it is often repetitious, but the essays are mostly well documented with informative footnotes. Particularly relevant essays are: Naomi Weisstein's "Psychology Constructs the Female," Lucy Komisar's "The Image of Woman in Advertising," and Wendy Martin's "Seduced and Abandoned in the New World: The Image of Woman in American Fiction."

Two books that are composed primarily of illustrations are: Agnes Rogers's *Women Are Here to Stay: The Durable Sex in Its Infinite Variety Through Half a Century of American Life*, a collection of photographs, paintings, fashion illustrations, and cartoons; and Carol Wald's *Myth America: Picturing Women 1865-1945*, a portfolio of popular art published in the form of prints, advertisements, and postcards. A work that intermixes interviews and commentaries with illustrations is Maxine Nunes and Deanna White's *The Lace Ghetto*; although it emphasizes Canadian popular culture, its contents are not irrelevant to America's history.

POPULAR FICTION

Not only does popular fiction retain in the late twentieth century the appeal it enjoyed in the nineteenth, but it continues to attract scholars who seek to understand its special role in American culture. A truly original approach is that of Helen Waite Papashvily's *All the Happy Endings: A Study of the Domestic Novel in America, the Women Who Wrote It, the Women Who Read It, in the Nineteenth Century.* Papashvily's thesis is that nineteenth-century domestic novels are cryptic political tracts, written and read by women who chaffed under their repressive social conditions. In arguing her unusual case, she musters considerable evidence from the popular books of this period, finding in them a pattern of feminine behavior that she characterizes as ruthless in its attempts to disarm the male enemy. Although readers might discount her interpretations as too facile, she provides substantial biographical, sociological, and political backgrounds that illuminate her discussions of the books themselves. *All the Happy Endings* contains an index and a bibliography; it is not footnoted.

A general history of the development of sentimental fiction is Herbert Ross Brown's *The Sentimental Novel in America 1789-1860*, which traces the influence of Richardson and Sterne on the American novel. The most relevant chapters for women and literature are: "Sex and Sensibility," in which Brown discusses the female novelists and describes the sentimental heroines; "The Sentimental Formula," in which he provides a paradigmatic description of the genre; and "Home, Sweet Home," in which he discusses the imagery and themes of the domestic novelists. Although it is rather repetitious since Brown has organized his work by ideas rather than by authors, the book is carefully and thoroughly documented and it is regarded as an important introduction to sentimental fiction.

Other studies that give attention to women's fiction are three that focus on the phenomenon of best sellers. Frank Luther Mott's *Golden Multitudes: The Story of Best Sellers in the United States* covers the period from colonial times to 1945. In describing these popular books, Mott discusses their publishing history, offers some background material on their authors, and speculates on the reason for their success. The text is indexed and contains three appendixes that list overall best sellers in the United States, better sellers, and annual best sellers in the book stores. Mott also gives a working definition of the term "best sellers."

Working from the foundation that Mott laid, James D. Hart published his more scholarly investigation of the subject in 1950. His study, *The Popular Book: A History of America's Literary Taste*, is an attempt to explain the success of popular books in terms of historical and sociological data; it covers the period from 1561 to 1949. In his book, Hart devotes considerable space to the women novelists (although he is quite critical of their works) and indexes several women's topics. Another helpful feature is his bibliographical checklist, in which he describes the secondary sources he used to write each chapter. Hart's text is illustrated and includes a chronological index of all the books he discusses.

A more recent examination of best sellers is Suzanne Ellery Greene's 1974 study, *Books for Pleasure: Popular Fiction 1914-1945.* Greene's method is to list the best sellers in a given time span at the beginning of a chapter and then discuss their characteristic contents and formulas. Although this approach often verges on simplistic summarization, it is interesting to follow the social patterns they seem to project from decade to decade, and Greene emphasizes the roles of women and the family in her investigation of these books.

A perennial source of information on what books are selling well is Alice Payne Hackett's series, whose latest compendium now bears the title *80 Years of Best Sellers 1895-1975;* this volume brings up to date *70 Years of Best Sellers* and is coauthored by James Henry Burke. Lily Deming Loshe's *The Early American Novel* provides useful plot summaries of difficult-to-locate books. Although her summaries can be trusted, some of her other information is no longer valid since the book was published in 1907 before certain facts were available about early American fiction (she attributes the authorship of *The Power of Sympathy* to Sarah Wentworth Morton, for example, when it has been since determined that its author is William Hill Brown).

Several scholars have taken a thematic look at popular women's fiction. Dorothy Yost Deegan's 1951 book, *The Stereotype of the Single Woman in American Novels,* is one of the first examples of this approach. Obviously a dissertation, this study's methodology is to use a so-called scientific sampling of American fiction in order to establish an unbiased general description of single females. Since the author herself advocates "mothering" as a woman's highest vocation, her conclusions must be taken with some skepticism. She does provide, however, an appendix of single-woman characters that appeared from 1851 to 1935 in 125 American novels. In her 1966 book *The Troublesome Helpmate: A History of Misogyny in Literature,* Katherine Rogers surveys a selected number of works from biblical and classical times to the twentieth century that seem to her to exhibit their authors' misogynistic attitudes. Although it promises much, it mostly describes the male authors Rogers has chosen to indict. A better book on the subject is Mary Ellmann's *Thinking About Women,* which, although often indecipherable, is an entertaining and serious look at misogynous stereotypes in literature that insist, by virtue of their sheer repetitiveness, that women are pious, passive, and unstable. Another fine book is Ernest Earnest's *The American Eve in Fact and Fiction, 1775-1914.* Earnest's thesis is that literature is not an accurate measure of women's accomplishments, interests, intelligence, and activities in this period of American history. His book is a well-documented and persuasive comparison that suggests a discrepancy between how American women really lived, according to their letters and diaries, and how they are portrayed by the imaginative literature of their time. The only problem with this book is that some of its extensive bibliographical information contains errors regarding publishers and dates.

Still other books that are relevant to women and popular literature are: William Wasserstrom's *Heiress of All the Ages: Sex and Sentiment in the Genteel Tradition*, an examination of the relationship between literature and society in America from the 1830s to World War I; Judith Fryer's *The Faces of Eve: Women in the Nineteenth-Century American Novel*, which concentrates, with the lone exception of Kate Chopin, on male novelists; and Kathryn Weibel's *Mirror, Mirror*, which contains a chapter on images of women in fiction. Russel Nye, in his extensive history, *The Unembarrassed Muse: The Popular Arts in America*, surveys women's literature as part of his discussion of the development of popular fiction and poetry. Leslie Fiedler's *Love and Death in the American Novel* explores the peculiarly American sexual milieu that keeps the male's positive sexual relationships with women out of its literature. Annette Kolodny's *The Lay of the Land: Metaphor as Experiment and History in American Life and Letters* documents the overt and covert sexual imagery of American male authors, which she compares to that of rape. A rather uneven collection of essays is Susan Koppelman Cornillon's *Images of Women in Fiction: Feminist Perspectives*; the best essays are those that explore the influence of society on literature, such as Joanna Russ's "The Image of Women in Science Fiction," Kathleen Conway McGrath's "Popular Literature as Social Reinforcement: The Case of *Charlotte Temple*," and Cornillon's own contribution, "The Fiction of Fiction."

MAGAZINES

Of all the women involved in magazine publishing, Sarah Josepha Hale continues to attract the most attention. Two early works on this remarkable woman are Ruth Finley's *The Lady of Godey's: Sarah Josepha Hale* and Isabelle Webb Entrikin's *Sarah Josepha Hale and Godey's Lady's Book.* Both works are well-documented biographies (the latter is a dissertation) and both reflect the esteem in which she is held by these two writers, an admiration that occasionally interferes with their ability to estimate her worth. More recent evaluations of Hale's accomplishments (such as that found in Ann Douglas's *The Feminization of American Culture*) regard her in a less favorable light, finding her apolitical stance reactionary and hardly mitigated by her interest in women's education. No one, however, tries to underestimate her power and her influence on American magazines and mores.

Four histories of magazines contain information about women's periodicals. Helen Woodward's *The Lady Persuaders*, although it contains a wealth of information about such magazines as *Godey's*, *McCall's*, *Ladies' Home Journal*, and *Cosmopolitan*, is virtually undocumented, and her facts are not always to be trusted. It has few footnotes, no bibliography, and is without an index. Much of Woodward's information is "firsthand" since she worked for years at *Cosmopolitan*; much is also taken from others' research. Nor is Woodward without her prejudices, admitting near the end of her book her dislike of women's magazines.

A more scholarly and reliable study is Frank Luther Mott's *A History of American Magazines 1741-1930*. Familiar to students of the genre, this important work is especially valuable in that it is thoroughly indexed. Each of the first four volumes has its own index, and the final volume includes a cumulative index for the entire work. In all five indexes, there are extensive entries on women and women's subjects. Volumes I through IV contain essays on various topics in magazine history, which are followed by a section entitled "Sketches of Important Magazines." Volume V is exclusively sketches. Since women's magazines played a crucial role in the development of the American periodical, they are given careful consideration in Mott's *History*. His essays cover such subjects as female education and the women question. He also quotes liberally from the prospectus of each magazine he highlights, giving its publishing history in the form of publisher, editor, name changes, and important dates. All five volumes are illustrated.

Another, less extensive, general history is James Playsted Wood's *Magazines in the United States*, 3d edition. This single-volume history does not index the topic of women, only the names of the journals and the major figures in the field. It contains a brief general bibliography, however, and the table of contents is fairly descriptive, featuring, among other topics, women's magazines. A final survey is Theodore Peterson's *Magazines in the Twentieth Century*, which is a study of recent periodicals (not all of which have survived into the 1970s). Its most relevant chapters are "Advertising: Its Growth and Effects" and "The Old Leaders That Survived" (*McCall's*, *Ladies' Home Journal*, and others). It, too, is illustrated.

A book that is composed almost entirely of illustrations is Jane Trahey's *Harper's Bazaar: 100 Years of the American Female*. There is no interpretative text, only sixteen literary selections purporting to reveal *Harper's* contributions to American female culture; many of these selections, however, were not even written by an "American female." It is fun to browse through, but it is less than scholarly. Other attempts to illustrate the relationship between American women and their magazines are more substantial: Dominic Ricciotti's "Popular Art in *Godey's Lady's Book:* An Image of the American Woman, 1830-1860" and Phyllis Tortora's "Fashion Magazines Mirror Changing Role of Women" are examples. A fine essay on this subject, "Images of Women in Women's Magazines and Magazine Advertising," appears in Kathryn Weibel's *Mirror, Mirror.* Images of women found in men's magazines is discussed in Richard A. Kallan and Robert D. Brook's "The Playmate of the Month: Naked But Nice" and in Lee D. Rossi's "The Whore vs. The Girl-Next-Door: Stereotypes of Woman in *Playboy, Penthouse,* and *Oui.*" Cornelia Butler Flora's "The Passive Female: Her Comparative Image by Class and Culture in Women's Magazine Fiction" is a study of the image of women in magazine short stories.

FILM

Several different kinds of materials are available for research in the field of women and film. Resources include specialized full-length histories, special issues of journals, theoretical articles, and bibliographies.

Perhaps the most comprehensive and readable study is Marjorie Rosen's *Popcorn Venus: Women, Movies & the American Dream.* Because Rosen's thesis is largely sociopolitical, her history illustrates what she sees as a paradoxical cause-and-effect relationship between film and society. On the one hand, she argues that the movies have hastened women's liberation by changing the way women see the world. On the other, she finds an unspoken male (commercial) conspiracy to use the movies to keep women in their place. Working from this premise, she discusses the films chronologically, isolating them by decade to show their historical transformation. There is a brief epilogue on women directors, a bibliography, and an index. The text is easy to follow, and Rosen's material is well organized. Another full-length historical study is Molly Haskell's *From Reverence to Rape: The Treatment of Women in the Movies,* which appeared the same year as Rosen's (1973). This book, although often provocative in its approach, is strangely unreadable. Part of the problem is that Haskell, film critic of the *Village Voice,* tends to wander, making her ideas hard to follow. Purporting to write a chronological history, Haskell interrupts the flow too often by an almost stream-of-consciousness style. Although her index lists the dates of all the films she discusses, she seldom includes them in her text, making for further confusion. Hers is also a sociopolitical approach that largely condemns the image of women in American film. At the beginning of her book, she provides some interesting theoretical apparatus. Both Rosen's and Haskell's books are illustrated.

Two other books published in 1973 are Joan Mellen's *Women and Their Sexuality in the New Film* and Marsha McCreadie's *The American Movie*

Goddess. Unlike Rosen's and Haskell's books, Mellen's is a series of topical essays on U.S. and continental films. Half of her chapters are devoted to discussions of filmmakers. The best chapters are her theoretical essays on the bourgeois woman, female sexuality, and lesbianism in the film. Although her book focuses on recent works, she has included an essay on Mae West that provides a somewhat uneasy feminist interpretation of West's films. *The American Movie Goddess* is a collection of essays and brief quotations intended to be used as a sourcebook for a college-level introductory writing course.

A more scholarly collection is Karyn Kay and Gerald Peary's *Women and the Cinema: A Critical Anthology.* These essays, some reprinted and some original, fall under no critical umbrella. They range from feminist perspectives and theory to interviews with women in film production. The book is indexed and provides several helpful bibliographies, a specialized one after each chapter and a general one at the end. Currently, it is the only far-ranging illustrated anthology of women in film that is available.

A compendium of very brief filmographies is Ian and Elizabeth Cameron's *Dames,* which includes seventy-four actresses whom the editors consider "female heavies," "tarts," or "singers."

Because most critics discuss primarily the role of women when they discuss sexuality in the films, it is not surprising that at least one book that investigates this topic actually focuses almost exclusively on women's sexuality. Alexander Walker's method in *Sex in the Movies: The Celluloid Sacrifice,* like that of most critics of this topic, is to compare the on-screen images of movie stars with their off screen experiences. As a result, Walker provides biographies of most of the major American sex goddesses from Theda Bara to Elizabeth Taylor. Of particular interest is his essay on the decline of American cinematic censorship, in which he explores the relationship between the Production Code and the Catholic Legion of Decency. One cavil: Walker, a Britisher, is convinced that the United States is a matriarchy and quotes from certain comedies of the 1960s to prove that the American male has been castrated by the likes of Doris Day and other American females.

In *Sex Psyche Etcetera in the Film,* Parker Tyler offers a rather glib assessment of the decline and fall of famous actresses ("The Awful Fate of the Sex Goddess"). Although he strives for ironic disapproval of their treatment, his own essay smacks of misogyny and is, ultimately, superficial. An anthology of more thoughtful essays on the subject is *Sexuality in the Movies,* edited by Thomas R. Atkins, which includes chapters on social backgrounds, sexual theory, and interpretations of individual films. The book is liberally illustrated.

In *Movies: A Psychological Study,* Martha Wolfenstein and Nathan Leites describe the various guises of "the Good-Bad Girl" as she appears in American films. The essay is reprinted in Bernard Rosenberg and David Manning White's *Mass Culture: The Popular Arts in America*. It is disappointingly more descriptive than interpretative. Although it contains no specific topics on women, Lewis Jacobs's *The Rise of the American Film: A Critical History* is useful as a general guide to the contributions of women to American film. Another book that discusses the role of women in a larger framework is Donald Bogle's *Toms, Coons, Mulattoes, Mammies, and Bucks: An Interpretative History of Blacks in American Films*. Since most studies of the film concentrate on white heroines, this book is a necessary corrective to their somewhat narrow perspective. One author who does mention blacks in her general survey "Images of Women in Movies" is Kathryn Weibel (*Mirror, Mirror*).

Sharon Smith's *Women Who Make Movies* is a directory of bibliographical information on U.S. and foreign women filmmakers since 1896 and contains a current listing of U.S. women filmmakers. Jeanne Betancourt's *Women in Focus* is an alphabetical compendium of more than seventy-five films about women—some written and directed by women, others by men, all with a feminist perspective. The films are thoroughly annotated, and the book contains a bibliography of film periodicals and secondary sources about women. The Women's Film Co-Op publishes a catalog describing short and feature films by and/or about women that can be ordered from the Co-Op at 200 Main Street, Northhampton, Massachusetts 01060. The Women's History Research Center, Inc. sells a catalog entitled *Films by and/or About Women*, which lists hundreds of films, filmmakers, and distributors. The catalog itself is annotated and provides complete rental information. It can be ordered from the Research Center at 2325 Oak Street, Berkeley, California 94708.

A specialized journal in the field is *Women and Film*, founded in 1972. Unfortunately, it was discontinued in 1976. It is available in microfilm from University Microfilm International, Ann Arbor. In 1971-1972, the *Film Library Quarterly* ran a special issue on "Women in Film," as did *Take One*. Both issues concentrate on current developments in film, with some emphasis on reconsidering woman's role in the history of film.

JOURNALS

The following journals have devoted special issues to women in the past few years: *Chicago Journalism Review* (July 1971), "Women and the Media" (articles on women in newspaper work); *College English* (May 1971, articles on literature and writing by Florence Howe, Annis Pratt, Elaine Showalter, and others); *Film Library Quarterly* (Winter 1971-1972), "Women in Film" (interview with Madeline Anderson, reviews of films by and about women, and other articles); *Futures* (October 1975), "Women and the Future" (articles on women's roles in world change, women in education, women in science fiction); *Journal of Communication* (Spring 1974, articles on images of women in television); (Spring 1975, "Women in Detective Fiction: Symposium"); *Journal of American Folklore* (January 1975), "Women and Folklore" (symposium on frontier women, rap groups, black women, images of women in folklore); and *Take One* (January 1972), "Women in Film" (articles on women directors, reviews of women's films, interviews with Shirley Clarke and Joyce Wieland). For more information on other journals, see Cardinale's bibliography and *Women Studies Abstracts.*

Because of the recent resurgence of scholarly interest in women's studies, a number of specialized journals have been founded—some still going strong; others lasting only a few issues. The following is a selective list of those that are either easily available or particularly appropriate to women in popular culture. *Feminist Studies,* a journal dedicated to opening "new areas of feminist research and critique"; *Quest: A Feminist Quarterly*—each issue carries a special title; of interest are "Future Visions and Fantasies" (vol. 2, no. 1) and "Race, Class and Culture" (vol. 3, no. 4); *Regionalism and the Female Imagination* (continuation of *The Kate Chopin Newsletter*), short articles on women regionalists; *Signs, Journal of Women in Culture and Society,* an interdisciplinary journal typically containing articles, review essays, letters and "Archives," a list of lost or forgotten documents written before 1950; *University of Michigan Papers in Women's Studies,* an interdisciplinary feminist journal that carries articles, monographs, reviews, annotated bibliographies; *Women and Literature,* a "scholarly journal of women writers and the literary treatment of women up to 1900," containing notes on work in progress and an annual bibliography of women in English and American literature before the twentieth century in addition to articles; and *Women's Studies,* an interdisciplinary journal that has featured a special issue on androgyny (vol. 2, no. 2). For titles of other journals, see the section on bibliography, below.

BIBLIOGRAPHY

BOOKS, ARTICLES, AND SPECIAL ISSUES

Ash, Lee. *Subject Collections: A Guide to Special Book Collections and Subject Emphases as Reported by University, College, Public and Special Libraries, and Museums in the United States and Canada.* 4th ed. New York: R. R. Bowker, 1974.

Atkins, Thomas R., ed. *Sexuality in the Movies.* Bloomington: Indiana University Press, 1975.

Ballou, Patricia K. "Bibliographies for Research on Women" (review essay). *Signs, Journal of Women in Culture and Society,* 3 (Winter 1977), 436-50.

Berkowitz, Tamar, ed. *Who's Who and Where in Women's Studies.* Old Westbury, N.Y.: Feminist Press, 1974.

Betancourt, Jeanne. *Women in Focus.* Dayton, Ohio: Pflaum Publishing, 1974.

Bibliographic Index: A Cumulative Bibliography of Bibliographies. New York: H. W. Wilson, 1978.

Bibliography of Sources Relating to Women. Lansing: Michigan History Division, Michigan Department of State, 1975.

The Black Family and the Black Woman: A Bibliography. Bloomington, Ind.: Prepared by library staff and the Afro-American Studies Department, Indiana University, 1972.

Bogle, Donald. *Toms, Coons, Mulattoes, Mammies, and Bucks: An Interpretative History of Blacks in American Films.* New York: Viking Press, 1973.

Brignano, Russell C. *Black Americans in Autobiography. An Annotated Bibliography of Autobiographies and Autobiographical Books, Written Since the Civil War.* Durham, N.C.: Duke University Press, 1974.

Brown, Herbert Ross. *The Sentimental Novel in America 1789-1860.* Durham, N.C.: Duke University Press, 1940.

Cameron, Ian, and Elizabeth Cameron. *Dames.* New York: Praeger, 1969.

Cardinale, Susan. *Special Issues of Serials About Women, 1965-1975.* Monticello, Ill.: Council of Planning Librarians, 1976.

Chesler, Phyllis. *Women and Madness.* Garden City, N.Y.: Doubleday, 1972.

Chicago Journalism Review. Special issue "Women and the Media," 4, No. 7 (July 1971).

College English. Issue devoted to women, 32, No. 8 (May 1971).

Conrad, Susan Phinney. *Perish the Thought: Intellectual Women in Romantic America, 1830-1860.* New York: Oxford University Press, 1976.

Cornillon, Susan Koppelman. "The Fiction of Fiction." In *Images of Women in Fiction: Feminist Perspectives.* Edited by Susan Koppelman Cornillon. Bowling Green, Ohio: Bowling Green University Popular Press, 1972, pp. 113-30.

————, ed. *Images of Women in Fiction: Feminist Perspectives.* Bowling Green, Ohio: Bowling Green University Popular Press, 1972.

Cott, Nancy F. *The Bonds of Womanhood: "Woman's Sphere" in New England, 1780-1835.* New Haven: Yale University Press, 1977.

Davis, Lenwood G. *The Black Woman in American Society: A Selected Annotated Bibliography.* Boston: G. K. Hall, 1975.

Deegan, Dorothy Yost. *The Stereotype of the Single Woman in American Novels: A Social Study with Implications for the Education of Women.* New York: King's Crown Press, Columbia University, 1951.

Delaney, Janice, Mary Jane Lupton, and Emily Toth. *The Curse: A Cultural History of Menstruation.* New York: Mentor Books, 1976.

Douglas, Ann. *The Feminization of American Culture.* New York: Alfred A. Knopf, 1977.

Earnest, Ernest. *The American Eve in Fact and Fiction, 1775-1914.* Urbana: University of Illinois Press, 1974.

Eichler, Margrit. *An Annotated Selected Bibliography of Bibliographies on Women.* Waterloo, Ottawa: University of Waterloo, Department of Sociology, 1973. Printed by the AUCL Committee on the Status of Women, Ottawa, Canada.

Ellmann, Mary. *Thinking About Women.* New York: Harcourt Brace Jovanovich, 1968.

Entrikin, Isabelle Webb. *Sarah Josepha Hale and Godey's Lady's Book.* Philadelphia: Lancaster Press, 1946.

Fiedler, Leslie. *Love and Death in the American Novel.* New York: Criterion Books, 1960.

Film Library Quarterly. Special issue "Women in Film," 5, No. 1 (Winter 1971-1972).

Finley, Ruth E. *The Lady of Godey's: Sarah Josepha Hale.* Philadelphia: J. B. Lippincott, 1931.

Flora, Cornelia Butler. "The Passive Female: Her Comparative Image by Class and Culture in Women's Magazine Fiction." *Journal of Marriage and the Family,* 33 (August 1971), 435-44.

Friedan, Betty. *The Feminine Mystique.* New York: W. W. Norton, 1963.

Friedman, Barbara, et al., eds. *Women's Work and Women's Studies/1973-1974, A Bibliography.* New York: Barnard College Women's Center, 1975. Distributed by the Feminist Press.

Friedman, Jean E., and William G. Shade, eds. *Our American Sisters: Women in American Life and Thought.* 2d ed. Boston: Allyn and Bacon, 1973.

Fryer, Judith. *The Faces of Eve: Women in the Nineteenth-Century American Novel.* New York: Oxford University Press, 1976.

Futures. Special issue "Women and the Future," 7, No. 5 (October 1975).

Gherman, Dawn Lander. "Frontier and Wilderness: American Women Authors," *University of Michigan Papers in Women's Studies,* 2, No. 2 (1975), 7-38.

Gornick, Vivian, and Barbara K. Moran, eds. *Woman in Sexist Society.* New York: Basic Books, 1971.

Graubard. Stephen R., ed. *The Woman in America.* Special issue of *Daedalus,* 93 (Spring 1964), 577-803. See Robert J. Lifton, ed., *The Woman in America.*

Greene, Suzanne Ellery. *Books for Pleasure: Popular Fiction 1914-1945.* Bowling Green, Ohio: Bowling Green University Popular Press, 1974.

Greer, Germaine. *The Female Eunuch.* New York: McGraw-Hill, 1970.

Grier, William H., and Price M. Cobbs. *Black Rage.* New York: Basic Books, 1968.

Hackett, Alice Payne, and James Henry Burke. *80 Years of Best-Sellers 1895-1975.* New York: R. R. Bowker, 1977.

Harrison, Cynthia Ellen. *Women's Movement Media: A Source Guide.* New York: R. R. Bowker, 1975.

Hart, James D. *The Popular Book: A History of America's Literary Taste.* New York: Oxford University Press, 1950.

Haskell, Molly. *From Reverence to Rape: The Treatment of Women in the Movies.* New York: Holt, Rinehart & Winston, 1973.

Hays, H[offman] R[eynolds]. *The Dangerous Sex: The Myth of Feminine Evil.* New York: G. P. Putnam's Sons, 1964.

Jacobs, Lewis. *The Rise of the American Film: A Critical History.* Rev. ed., with an essay "Experimental Cinema in America 1921-1947." New York: Teachers College Press, 1967.

Journal of American Folklore. Special issue "Women and Folklore," 88, No. 347 (January-March 1975).

Journal of Communication. Special issue on women, 24, No. 2 (Spring 1974).

———. "Women in Detective Fiction" Symposium, 25 (Spring 1975), 98-119.

Kallan, Richard A., and Robert D. Brooks. "The Playmate of the Month: Naked But Nice." *Journal of Popular Culture*, 8 (Fall 1974), 328-36.

Kay, Karyn, and Gerald Peary, eds. *Women and the Cinema: A Critical Anthology*. New York: E. P. Dutton, 1977.

Kolodny, Annette. *The Lay of the Land: Metaphor as Experience and History in American Life and Letters*. Chapel Hill: University of North Carolina Press, 1975.

Krichmar, Albert. *The Women's Rights Movement in the United States, 1848-1970. A Bibliography and Sourcebook*. Metuchen, N.J.: Scarecrow Press, 1972.

———. *The Women's Movement in the Seventies: An International English-Language Bibliography*. Metuchen, N.J.: Scarecrow Press, 1977.

Lerner, Gerda, ed. *Black Women in White America: A Documentary History*. New York: Vintage Books, 1972.

Lifton, Robert Jay, ed. *The Woman in America*. Boston: Houghton Mifflin, 1965. Published first as special issue of *Daedalus*; see Stephen R. Graubard.

Loader, Jayne. "Women in the Left, 1906-1941, A Bibliography of Primary Sources." *University of Michigan Papers in Women's Studies*, 2 (September 1975), 9-82.

Loshe, Lily Deming. *The Early American Novel*. New York: Columbia University Press, 1907.

Lynn, Naomi B., Ann B. Matasar, and Marie Barovic Rosenberg. *Research Guide in Women's Studies*. Morristown, N.J.: General Learning Press, 1974.

McCreadie, Marsha, ed. *The American Movie Goddess*. New York: John Wiley & Sons, 1973.

McGrath, Kathleen Conway. "Popular Literature as Social Reinforcement: The Case of *Charlotte Temple*." In *Images of Women in Fiction: Feminist Perspectives*. Edited by Susan Koppelman Cornillon. Bowling Green, Ohio: Bowling Green University Popular Press, 1972, pp. 21-27.

Mason, Bobbie Ann. *The Girl Sleuth: A Feminist Guide*. Old Westbury, N.Y.: Feminist Press, 1975.

Mellen, Joan. *Women and Their Sexuality in the New Film*. New York: Horizon Press, 1973.

Meyers, Carol Fairbanks. *Women in Literature: Criticism of the Seventies*. Metuchen, N.J.: Scarecrow Press, 1976.

Montagu, Ashley. *The Natural Superiority of Women*. Rev. ed. New York: Collier Books, 1952, 1968.

Mott, Frank Luther. *A History of American Magazines 1741-1930*. 5 vols. Cambridge: Belknap Press of Harvard University Press, 1938-1939, 1957, and 1966.

———. *Golden Multitudes: The Story of Best Sellers in the United States*. New York: R. R. Bowker, 1947 and 1960.

Notable American Women, 1607-1950: A Biographical Dictionary. Cambridge: Belknap Press of Harvard University Press, 1971.

Nunes, Maxine, and Deanna White. *The Lace Ghetto.* Toronto: New Press, 1972.

Nye, Russel B. *The Unembarrassed Muse: The Popular Arts in America.* New York: Dial Press, 1970.

Papashvily, Helen Waite. *All the Happy Endings: A Study of the Domestic Novel in America, the Women Who Wrote It, the Women Who Read It, in the Nineteenth Century.* New York: Harper & Brothers, 1956.

Peterson, Theodore. *Magazines in the Twentieth Century.* 2d ed. Urbana: University of Illinois Press, 1964.

Rawick, George P. *From Sundown to Sunup: The Making of the Black Community.* Westport, Conn.: Greenwood Press, 1972. Part of a series, *The American Slave: A Composite Autobiography.*

Ricciotti, Dominic. "Popular Art in *Godey's Lady's Book*: An Image of the American Woman, 1830-1860." *History of New Hampshire,* 27 (1972), 3-26.

Rich, Adrienne. *Of Woman Born: Motherhood as Experience and Institution.* New York: W. W. Norton, 1976.

Rogers, Agnes. *Women Are Here to Stay: The Durable Sex in Its Infinite Variety Through Half a Century of American Life.* New York: Harper & Brothers, 1949.

Rogers, Katherine. *The Troublesome Helpmate: A History of Misogyny in Literature.* Seattle: University of Washington Press, 1966.

Rosen, Marjorie. *Popcorn Venus: Women, Movies & the American Dream.* New York: Coward, McCann & Geoghegan, 1973.

Rosenberg, Bernard, and David Manning White, eds. *Mass Culture: The Popular Arts in America.* Glencoe, Ill.: The Free Press, 1957, 1963.

Rossi, Lee D. "The Whore vs. The Girl-Next-Door: Stereotypes of Woman in *Playboy, Penthouse,* and *Oui." Journal of Popular Culture,* 9 (Summer 1975), 90-94.

Russ, Joanna. "The Image of Women in Science Fiction." In *Images of Women in Fiction: Feminist Perspectives.* Edited by Susan Koppelman Cornillon. Bowling Green, Ohio: Bowling Green University Popular Press, 1972, pp. 79-94.

Scott, Anne Firor. *The Southern Lady: From Pedestal to Politics 1830-1930.* Chicago: University of Chicago Press, 1970.

Sense and Sensibility Collective. *Women and Literature: An Annotated Bibliography of Women Writers.* 2d ed., revised and expanded. Cambridge, Mass.: Sense and Sensibility Collective, 1973.

Smith, Sharon. *Women Who Make Movies.* New York: Hopkinson and Blake, 1975.

Smith College Library. *Catalog of the Sophia Smith Collection.* Northampton, Mass.: Smith College, 1971, 1976.

The Standard Periodical Directory. 5th ed. New York: Oxbridge Communications, 1977.

Take One. Special issue "Women and Film," 3, No. 2 (January 1972).

Tortora, Phyllis. "Fashion Magazines Mirror Changing Role of Women." *Journal of Home Economics*, 65 (March 1973), 19-23.

Trahey, Jane, ed. *Harper's Bazaar: 100 Years of the American Female*. New York: Random House, 1967.

Tyler, Parker. *Sex Psyche Etcetera in the Film*. New York: Horizon Press, 1969.

Ulrich's International Periodicals Directory. 17th ed., 1977-1978. New York: R. R. Bowker, 1977.

Wald, Carol. *Myth America: Picturing Women 1865-1945*. Text by Judith Papachriston. New York: Pantheon Books, 1975.

Walker, Alexander. *Sex in the Movies: The Celluloid Sacrifice*. Baltimore: Penguin Books, 1968. First published as *The Celluloid Sacrifice*, London: Michael Joseph, 1966.

Wasserstrom, William. *Heiress of All the Ages: Sex and Sentiment in the Genteel Tradition*. Minneapolis: University of Minnesota Press, 1959.

Weibel, Kathryn. *Mirror, Mirror: Images of Women Reflected in Popular Culture*. Garden City, N.Y.: Anchor Books-Doubleday, 1977.

Welter, Barbara. "Anti-Intellectualism and the American Woman, 1800-1860." *Mid-America*, 48 (October 1966), 258-70. Reprinted in Barbara Welter, *Dimity Convictions*.

―――. "The Cult of True Womanhood, 1820-1860." *American Quarterly*, 18 (Summer 1966), 151-75. Reprinted in Barbara Welter, *Dimity Convictions*.

―――. *Dimity Convictions: The American Woman in the Nineteenth Century*. Athens: Ohio University Press, 1976.

Wheeler, Helen. *Womanhood Media: Current Resources About Women*. Metuchen, N.J.: Scarecrow Press, 1972.

Who's Who of American Women: A Biographical Dictionary of Notable Living American Women, 1977-1978. Chicago: A. N. Marquise, 1977-1978.

Willard, Frances E., and Mary A. Livermore. *American Women. Fifteen Hundred Biographies with over 1,400 Portraits*. Rev. ed. 2 vols. New York: Mast, Crowell & Kirkpatrick, 1897.

―――. *A Woman of the Century. Fourteen Hundred-Seventy Biographical Sketches Accompanied by Portraits of Leading American Women in All Walks of Life*. New Introduction by Leslie Shepard. Reprint of 1893 ed. Detroit: Gale Research, 1967.

Williams, Ora. "A Bibliography of Works Written by American Black Women." *CLA Journal*, 15 (March 1972), 354-77.

Wolfenstein, Martha, and Nathan Leites. *Movies: A Psychological Study*. Glencoe, Ill.: Free Press, 1950.

The Women's Film Co-Op. 1972 Catalogue. Northampton, Mass.: The Women's Film Co-Op, 1972.

Women's History Research Center, Inc. *Films by and/or About Women*. Berkeley, Calif.: Women's History Research Center, 1972.

Wood, James Playsted. *Magazines in the United States*. 3d ed. New York: Ronald Press, 1971.

Woodward, Helen. *The Lady Persuaders*. New York: Ivan Obolensky, 1960.

PERIODICALS

Abstracts of Popular Culture: A Quarterly Publication of International Popular Phenomenon. Bowling Green, Ohio, 1976-.

Feminist Studies. College Park, Md., 1972-.

Quest: A Feminist Quarterly. Washington, D.C., 1974-.

Regionalism and the Female Imagination (formerly *Kate Chopin Newsletter*). State College, Pa., 1977-1979.

Signs, Journal of Women in Culture and Society. Chicago, 1975-.

University of Michigan Papers in Women's Studies. Ann Arbor, Mich., 1974-.

Women and Film. Berkeley, Calif., 1972-1976.

Women and Literature. New Brunswick, N.J., 3, 1975-.

Women Studies Abstracts. Rush, N.Y., 1972-.

Women's Studies. Flushing, N.Y., 1972-.

Proper Name Index

About the Contributors

ROY M. ANKER is assistant professor of English and chair of the Department of Language and Literature at Northwestern College, Orange City, Iowa. His teaching and research interests include popular religion, contemporary fiction, and Holocaust studies. He has given numerous professional papers and frequently publishes reviews and articles in periodicals that deal with religion, politics, and culture. His current project is a book-length reevaluation of the fiction of Thornton Wilder.

ROBERT A. ARMOUR is associate professor of English at Virginia Commonwealth University. He is especially interested in interdisciplinary teaching and has been team-teaching a course on death and dying with J. Carol Williams for several years. Their joint research projects have resulted in several articles on the funeral industry. In addition, he has written numerous articles and books on film.

CHARLES CAMP is Maryland State folklorist and occasional adjunct professor of folklore at the University of Maryland and American University. His articles on traditional music, crafts, architecture, and cookery have appeared in *Southern Exposure*, *New York Folklore Quarterly*, and the *Journal of American Folklore*. He is currently at work on a guide to Maryland folk culture and a collection of federal writers' project foodways research.

KATHERINE FISHBURN is assistant professor of English at Michigan State University, where she teaches courses in women's fiction, contemporary literature, and Southern regionalism. She is author of *Richard Wright's Hero: The Faces of a Rebel Victim* and other critical essays. In 1978-79 she was awarded the Academic Administrative Internship for Women, Office of Provost, Michigan State University. She is currently writing a book on Doris Lessing.

ROBERT GALBREATH is coordinator of the Honors Program at the University of Wisconsin-Milwaukee. His training is in European and American intellectual history, with particular emphasis on the occult in modern thought and popular culture. He edited *The Occult: Studies and Evaluations* and has published articles on Rudolf Steiner, Hermann Hesse, A. E. Waite, visionary literature, science fiction, and criticism. He is currently secretary of the Science Fiction Research Association and is preparing studies on Ursula K. Le Guin, modern gnosticism, and historical explanations of occult revivals.

SUZANNE ELLERY GREENE is professor of history at Morgan State University, where she teaches in the graduate program in popular culture. Her recent research and writing have been in the area of urban culture and history. She is author of *Books for Pleasure*, a study of American best-selling novels from 1914 to 1945.

M. THOMAS INGE, editor of this volume, is professor and chairman of the Department of English at Virginia Commonwealth University. He has published books on William Faulkner, American humor, southern literature, and ethnic American writing, and he is a founding editor of two publications: *Resources for American Literary Study* and *American Humor: An Interdisciplinary Newsletter*. In addition to editing several series of reference guides in popular culture for Greenwood Press, he is engaged in research on the history, development, and appreciation of American comic strips and comic books.

R. GORDON KELLY is associate director of the American Studies Program at the University of Maryland. He was previously in the Department of English at Virginia Commonwealth University and the American Civilization Department at the University of Pennsylvania. One of his principal interests is in the relationship between literature and history, and his publications include *Mother Was a Lady*, a study of late nineteenth-century periodical fiction for children.

RICHARD N. MASTELLER is assistant professor of English at Whitman College. Research for his doctorate in American Studies at the University of Minnesota was aided by an internship at the International Museum of Photography at George Eastman House, where he explored the parallel romanticism evident in American literature and in the photography of Alfred Stieglizt and Edward Weston. He has written articles for *Images* and *Prospects: An Annual of American Cultural Studies* and has organized a photographic exhibition, "The Auto As Icon," to explore the effects of photographic presentation on cultural symbols. His teaching interests include American literature, the history and cultural influence of photography, and American Studies methodology.

BERNARD MERGEN is associate professor of American civilization at George Washington University, where he participates in a seminar in material culture offered in cooperation with the Smithsonian Institution. His research interests include the history of labor and leisure, especially the evolution of attitudes toward work and play. He has published articles in *American Quarterly, The South Atlantic Quarterly, Industrial and Labor Relations Review, Play: Anthropological Perspectives*, and other books and journals.

KAY J. MUSSELL is director of the American Studies Program at the American University and was formerly a member of the Department of English at George Mason University. Her research interests are primarily in the area of women in American popular culture, and she is currently completing a study of women's romantic novels in the mid-twentieth century.

NANCY POGEL is an associate professor of American thought and language and assistant director of student affairs, University College, Michigan State University. Her primary research and teaching interests are American humor and American film. She has delivered papers and published articles on film humor, Jewish humor, Mark Twain and other midwestern humorists, and Constance Rourke. She is presently an associate textual editor of *Walt Whitman, The Journalism*, Volume II, and she is completing a book-length manuscript on Woody Allen's films.

JANICE RADWAY is assistant professor and undergraduate chairperson of American Civilization at the University of Pennsylvania. She is a Council Member at Large of the Popular Culture Association and has published articles on a theory of popular culture in the *Journal of Popular Culture* and *Texas Studies in Language and Literature*. She is currently at work on a study of the divergence between popular and elite literature as a historically determined phenomenon.

PAUL SOMERS, JR. is associate professor of American thought and language at Michigan State University. His publications include articles in *The French Review, The South Atlantic Quarterly,* and *Twentieth Century Literature,* as well as a short story in *Harper's.* He has compiled bibliographies of articles on mass culture for *American Quarterly* and is presently a bibliographer for *Midamerica: The Yearbook for the Society for the Study of Midwestern Literature.* With Nancy Pogel, he is co-author of *The Jehovah's Witness Jokebook.*

J. CAROL WILLIAMS is assistant professor of philosophy and religious studies at Virginia Commonwealth University. Her philosophical articles on perception and semantics have appeared in the *Southern Journal of Philosophy* and *Man and World.* In addition to her work in philosophy, she teaches an interdisciplinary course on death and has written several essays on aspects of death ranging from the images of death in popular music to the rhetoric of the funeral industry.

ELIZABETH WILLIAMSON is an instructor of English at Virginia Commonwealth University. She has also worked as a copywriter and public relations researcher. A few of her annotated checklists on American humor have appeared in *American Humor: An Interdisciplinary Newsletter.* She is currently working on a book tracing the influence of Emily Dickinson on Mary Tyler Moore.

DON B. WILMETH is professor of theatre arts and English and chairman of the Department of Theatre Arts at Brown University. He serves on the boards of the American Society of Theatre Research, the Theatre Library Association, and the Society for the Advancement of Education, is theatre columnist for *U.S.A. Today,* an advisory editor for *Nineteenth Century Theatre Research,* book review editor for *The Theatre Journal,* and author of numerous articles in major theatre journals. He is the editor of two reference guides, *The American Stage to World War I* and *American and British Popular Entertainment,* and is author of a biography of the English actor George Frederick Cooke to be published by Greenwood Press in 1980. He is currently completing a glossary of popular entertainment terms, slang, and argot also for Greenwood Press.

RICHARD GUY WILSON is associate professor of architectural history at the University of Virginia. He has published in the areas of historic preservation and American architecture. He is currently completing work on a large museum exhibit and book for the Smithsonian Institution and the Brooklyn Museum entitled *The American Renaissance, 1876-1917,* which is touring the United States in 1979-1980.

DATE DUE

AP 9 '82			
GAYLORD			PRINTED IN U.S.A.